Assessing Intelligence in Children and Adolescents

A Practical Guide for Evidence-based Assessment

Second Edition

JOHN H. KRANZLER
University of Florida

RANDY G. FLOYD
University of Memphis

ROWMAN & LITTLEFIELD
Lanham • Boulder • New York • London

Executive Editor: Mark Kerr
Editorial Assistant: Courtney Packard

Credits and acknowledgments for material borrowed from other sources, and reproduced with permission, appear on the appropriate pages within the text.

Published by Rowman & Littlefield
An imprint of The Rowman & Littlefield Publishing Group, Inc.
4501 Forbes Boulevard, Suite 200, Lanham, Maryland 20706
www.rowman.com

6 Tinworth Street, London SE11 5AL, United Kingdom

Copyright © 2020 by The Rowman & Littlefield Publishing Group, Inc.

All rights reserved. No part of this book may be reproduced in any form or by any electronic or mechanical means, including information storage and retrieval systems, without written permission from the publisher, except by a reviewer who may quote passages in a review.

British Library Cataloguing in Publication Information Available

Library of Congress Cataloging-in-Publication Data

978-1-5381-2714-8 (cloth)
978-1-5381-2715-5 (paperback)
978-1-5381-2716-2 (electronic)

∞™ The paper used in this publication meets the minimum requirements of American National Standard for Information Sciences—Permanence of Paper for Printed Library Materials, ANSI/NISO Z39.48-1992.

Contents

Acknowledgments		v
Preface		vii
1	What Is Intelligence?	1
2	How and Why Do People Differ in Intelligence?	17
3	Ethics in Assessment	33
4	Basic Psychometric Principles That Inform Score Interpretation	43
5	The Assessment Process with Children and Adolescents, with Ryan L. Farmer and Richard J. McNulty	87
6	Evaluation and Use of the Wechsler Intelligence Scale for Children, Fifth Edition, with Emily K. Lewis and Richard J. McNulty	131
7	A Review of Intelligence Tests, with Emily K. Lewis and Ryan L. Farmer	155
8	Interpreting Intelligence Test Scores	191
9	Evidence-Based Practice and Cognitive Interventions	217
10	Sharing the Results from Intelligence Tests	233
11	Assessment of Intellectual Disability	267
12	Assessment of Intellectual Giftedness	283
13	Assessment of Specific Learning Disabilities	303
14	Assessment of Children and Adolescents from Diverse Cultural and Linguistic Backgrounds	325
References		347
Index		383
About the Authors		401

Acknowledgments

We thank the many people who supported us during our writing of this book. In particular, we thank our wives and children, Theresa, Zachary, and Justin (JHK) and Carrie and Sophie (RGF), for their patience with us while we worked on the second edition. We also thank Dr. Ryan Farmer, assistant professor at Oklahoma State University, as well as Emily Lewis and Richard McNulty, who are doctoral students at the University of Memphis, for their contributions to chapters as coauthors. We extend our appreciation to doctoral students in our graduate programs who contributed literature reviews, article retrieval, and formatting and proofing activities. They are Kacey Gilbert and Mary Elizabeth Moody at the University of Florida and Lauren Fennimore, Sequoya Fitzpatrick, and Emily Lewis at the University of Memphis. We are thankful that Patrick McNicholas, a doctoral candidate at the University of Memphis, shared redacted reports that were adapted and incorporated into the chapter focused on report writing. In addition, Dr. Farmer and Dr. Nick Benson, associate professor at Baylor University, provided insightful feedback about other chapters and guided us to new resources and ways of thinking. Last, but not least, we would like to express thanks to our editor, Mark Kerr, for his assistance and oversight, but especially for giving us the freedom to write the book we wanted to write. We believe this edition vastly improves upon the first edition and that is due in large part to Mark. Thank you.

Preface

This book is a practical guide to the intellectual assessment of children and adolescents in schools and related settings. Although primarily intended for students of school psychology and practicing school psychologists, it also should be useful for those involved with making decisions in schools that are based, in part, on the results of intelligence tests, including counselors, teachers, administrators, and other school personnel. In writing it, we placed particular emphasis on evidence-based practices pertaining to the use and interpretation of intelligence tests. The goal of the evidence-based practices movement is to "identify, disseminate, and promote the adoption of practices with demonstrated research support" (Kratochwill, 2007, p. 829). This involves evaluation of the "quality, robustness, or validity of scientific evidence as it is brought to bear on decisions regarding the adoption, implementation, and/or evaluation of services" (Kratochwill, 2007, p. 830). The evidence-based practices movement aims to improve the quality of psychological service delivery. Professional practices that are innovative, including those related to the administration and interpretation of intelligence tests, must be substantiated with scientific evidence before they are broadly implemented (Reddy, Forman, Stoiber, & Gonzalez, 2017).

Statement of Need

The assessment of intelligence has long been mandated by law for eligibility determination for special education and related services (e.g., intellectual disabilities [ID], specific learning disabilities [SLD], and intellectual giftedness). Under the Individuals with Disabilities Education Improvement Act (IDEA, 2004), regulations are explicit for evaluation procedures that delineate the role of intelligence tests for identifying disabilities and for determining eligibility for special education and related services. In the past, intelligence test scores (IQs) primarily had been used in schools as benchmarks against which to compare academic achievement or adaptive functioning. For example, prior to 2004, SLD was widely defined in state regulations as a discrepancy in cognitive functioning. Children and youth were identified with SLD—and still are in a number of states—when their academic performance or rate of skill acquisition fell substantially below what one would expect based on their IQ, when that discrepancy is not attributable to certain exclusionary criteria (e.g., inadequate educational opportunity, mental health issues, sensory impairment, and ID). At the current time, however, there are three different general approaches to SLD identification: IQ-Achievement discrepancy, Response-to-Intervention (RtI), and patterns of strengths and weaknesses (PSW). All three methods share some common features, such as a definition of SLD as "unexpected underachievement" and ruling out exclusionary criteria, but they differ markedly on the need for the administration of intelligence tests and how those tests are interpreted when they are given. To the best of our knowledge, at present, none of the books on intellectual assessment currently available critically reviews the scientific evidence regarding the role played by intelligence tests within each of these approaches. One of the intentions of this book was to fill that gap.

In addition to addressing this need in the literature, many available books on intellectual assessment tend to be theoretically "agnostic" and present a range of theories and models of intelligence (e.g., Sattler, 2018), thereby implying that readers should pick and choose any theory to meet their needs or personal predilections. Researchers in the field of intelligence, however, largely agree on the major substantive conclusions regarding the structure of cognitive abilities, the nature of individual differences, and other major emphases of research. Thus, another intention of this book was to emphasize the predominant theory of intelligence in the field today—the psychometric approach. Although there are a number of other theories of intelligence, the psychometric approach has by far the most empirical support in the literature.

Finally, the available books on intellectual assessment tend to describe approaches for interpreting test scores that, we believe, overstate the utility of intra-individual (ipsative) analysis and the PSW methods for differential diagnosis and intervention planning. Although research on intelligence and its assessment may one day lead to breakthroughs, the empirical data at the present time do not clearly substantiate the validity of disordinal models (aptitude-by-treatment interactions) to inform decision making, although they do provide support for ordinal models (high versus low general cognitive ability). Therefore, this book presents a method for interpreting test scores that emphasizes the interpretation of global composite scores rather than individual subtests, with implications for ordinal models of intervention when applied to conditions of incomplete instruction (Braden & Shaw, 2009). In sum, we have written this book to address the need for an updated, evidence-based, user-friendly resource on intellectual assessment of children and youth.

Description of the Content

This book is a practical guide for school psychologists, school counselors, school social workers, teachers, administrators, and other school personnel working with children, adolescents, and their families. This revised edition differs from the first edition in a number of important ways. First, every chapter has been updated and expanded to incorporate advances in research, theory, and test development made since the first edition. We believe that the revised edition reflects the current state-of-the-art regarding the use and interpretation of intelligence tests with scientific support. Second, we created a new chapter focusing solely on the Wechsler Intelligence Scale for Children, Fifth Edition (WISC-V; Wechsler, 2014a). Over the past 40 years, the WISC-V and its prior editions consistently have been one of the most widely used instruments overall by school psychologists. According to the results of a recent survey on test use and assessment practices of school psychologists, it is *by far* the most widely used instrument and is clearly the "gold standard" for measuring intelligence in school psychology today (Benson et al., 2019). Thus, we provide an in-depth review of the WISC-V to highlight its strengths and also its weaknesses. Third, we replaced a chapter in the first edition devoted to the use of intelligence tests within a problem-solving, RtI model with a chapter on the use of intelligence tests for designing interventions in the schools. When students struggle to reach minimum standards, the educational system must either (a) directly develop the underlying aptitude for learning or (b) design alternative instructional interventions for particular aptitudes. In this chapter, we reviewed research that targets interventions on specific cognitive abilities and also research on aptitude-by-treatment interactions in the cognitive domain.

The book consists of 14 chapters, and they include tables and figures, as well as a number of checklists and assessment forms that professionals can integrate easily into their practices. Throughout our chapters and in our examples, we incorporated gender-neutral personal pronouns (e.g., singular "they" and "ze") and honorifics (e.g., Mx) to both recognize an emerging sea change in writing and also signal our support for people with nonbinary, gender queer, gender fluid, agender, and other identities outside the gender binary.

Chapter 1 describes the definition and nature of intelligence from the psychometric perspective, as well as some of the criticisms of this model. In this edition, we added discussion of the bifactor model of intelligence.

Chapter 2 discusses how and why individuals differ in intelligence. It includes an explanation of research in the differential model, or quantitative behavior genetics, as well as the implications of this model for modifying intelligence. In this edition, we added a section called Where in the Brain Is Intelligence? And we expanded discussion of contemporary training programs designed to increase intelligence.

Chapter 3 highlights ethical principles and standards most relevant to testing children and adolescents. In particular, it reviews the most recent ethical guidelines from the American Psychological Association and the National Association of School Psychologists. In this edition, we also addressed nascent ethical and legal challenges related to technology, record keeping, and data security.

Chapter 4 highlights test standards guiding the selection and use of intelligence tests, and it continues with a review of critical characteristics, including norming and item scaling as well as the reliability and validity of their scores. This information will promote selection of the best intelligence tests by practitioners based, in part, on the age, ability level, and backgrounds of the clients they serve. In this edition, we addressed more fully item-level characteristics, exploratory factor analysis, and classification accuracy.

Chapter 5 addresses the reasons for assessment, typical assessment processes, and potential influences on test performance that can be controlled during standardized testing or acknowledged when interpreting test results. It also provides practical screening tools that will promote the most accurate assessment of cognitive abilities through standardized testing. In this edition, we revised the Screening Tool for Assessment forms to address English language proficiency and acculturation, added sections focused on test accommodations and behavior management during testing, and included recommendations for incorporating emergent assessment technology (e.g., tablet-based test administration).

Chapter 6 is a new chapter that focuses on the WISC-V. In this chapter, we briefly review the history of the WISC, followed by an in-depth description of its organization, materials, and scores, for both the traditional administration format and the new Q-interactive format. We also cover the response processes contributing to the overall score, as well as associated accommodations for these subtests. Last, we review the norming, scaling, and psychometric properties of the WISC-V's key composite scores.

Chapter 7 provides a broad overview of the array of intelligence tests that are available to users. This includes full-length multidimensional intelligence tests, which are the most well-known and commonly used in research and practice, as well as a number of the most widely used nonverbal intelligence tests and brief and abbreviated intelligence tests. In this edition, we updated entries for four tests and added an entry for the Detroit Test of Learning Abilities, Fifth Edition (Hammill, McGhee, & Ehrler, 2018).

Chapter 8 focuses on interpretation of examinee responses and resulting scores. It targets interpreting data from qualitative and quantitative perspectives, using interpretive strategies based on an understanding of the nature of cognitive abilities, and reliance on the scientific research base that illuminates empirically supported practices. We highlight our Keep-It-Simple-Scholar (KISS) evidence-based model of test interpretation. In this edition, we provide examples of common but likely problematic interpretive practices in contrast to the KISS model.

Chapter 9 is a new chapter that reviews the methodology used in research on interventions that target cognitive abilities, and the results of that research, as well as literature on aptitude-by-treatment interactions in the cognitive domain. We offer recommendations that can be included in psychological assessment reports that are consistent with this knowledge base and our KISS model.

Chapter 10 discusses best practices in the sharing of results of intelligence testing through the psychological assessment reports and face-to-face contact with the parents or caregivers. It also addresses the process of sharing assessment results with supervisors during supervision meetings. In this edition, we included new content addressing different styles of reports as well as a summary of new recommendations from the recently published *Publication Manual of the American Psychological Association, Seventh Edition (2019)*.

Chapter 11 describes the clinical condition known as ID and offers practical guidelines for assessing children suspected of having this condition. It addresses varying diagnostic and eligibility criteria for ID, offers recommendations for best practices in assessment, and discusses best practices when interpreting test results.

Chapter 12 discusses the use of intelligence tests in the identification of giftedness. We first review contemporary theories of giftedness. Following this, we address the definition of giftedness and issues in its identification.

Chapter 13 examines the different conceptualizations of SLD and the implications of these definitions in its identification. The use of intelligence tests in the identification of SLD has long been surrounded by controversy—and continues to this day. In this edition, we added a review of the PSW approach to SLD identification. We address best practices in assessment that apply regardless of the SLD criteria used for identification.

Chapter 14 discusses best practices in the use of intelligence tests with children and youth from diverse backgrounds. After briefly reviewing research on test bias, we address the pros and cons of the most widely recommended best practices with this population.

CHAPTER 1

What Is Intelligence?

Many view the measurement of intelligence to be one of psychology's greatest contributions to society (Nisbett et al., 2012). Tests of intelligence are widely used in education, business, government, and the military, mainly because the overall score on these tests ("IQ") is more predictive of many important social outcomes than any other measurable psychological trait independent of IQ. In addition to their use in these contexts to diagnose, admit, and employ, IQ scores also are importantly related to a wide range of important social behaviors, including years of education, socioeconomic status, law-abidingness, and income, among many others. As Gottfredson (2008) stated, "Used with skill and responsibility, intelligence tests yield information of great value and precision not otherwise available to administrators, clinicians, and scientists" (p. 561).

Given their widespread use, it is easy to overlook the fact that the intelligence tests used today originally were created for use in the schools. Alfred Binet (1857–1911) and Théophile Simon (1873–1961) were commissioned by the French Ministry of Education to develop a means of identifying children who were "at risk" for educational failure. Today, intelligence tests are used in school settings in countries all over the world. In the United States, the assessment of intelligence is mandated by current federal special education law—the Individuals with Disabilities Education Improvement Act of 2004 (IDEA, 2004)—for the identification of intellectual disability (ID). In addition, IDEA allows, but does not require, the use of intelligence tests for the identification of specific learning disability (SLD). Finally, although gifted students are not protected under IDEA in its current form, exceptionally high intelligence is a key component used in most states to identify intellectual giftedness (McClain & Pfeiffer, 2012).

In the schools, the overall score on intelligence tests primarily is used as a benchmark against which to compare students' current academic achievement or adaptive behavior (i.e., age-appropriate ability to act independently, interact socially with others, care for oneself, etc.). For example, ID is identified when an individual has significantly below-average IQ and comparable deficits in adaptive functioning, among other criteria. In contrast, SLD traditionally has been identified when a significant discrepancy exists between an individual's level of academic performance and IQ that cannot be explained by certain exclusionary criteria (e.g., inadequate educational opportunities and sensory disorders). Several contemporary approaches, however, are based on the analysis of patterns of strengths and weaknesses in an individual's cognitive profile to identify SLD (e.g., Flanagan, Costa, Palma, Leahy, Alfonso, & Ortiz, 2018). For identification of giftedness, high IQs are seen as necessary but not sufficient for high accomplishment. For example, motivation, creativity, and task commitment also are required (Reis & Renzulli, 2011). Chapters 11–13 provide more detailed information on the use of intelligence tests in schools for the determination of eligibility for special education and related services.

The purpose of this chapter is to define *intelligence* and to describe how people differ in terms of their intellectual abilities. We begin by addressing two common objections to intelligence research and assessment. The first objection asserts that because intelligence is not a real thing, how can we measure something that does not exist? The second objection contends that, because we have no consensus definition of intelligence, how can we measure something we cannot define?

Does Intelligence Exist?

The great American psychologist E. L. Thorndike (1874–1949) stated that "whatever exists at all exists in some amount" (Thorndike, 1918, p. 16, as quoted in Eysenck, 1973). Many laypersons also believe that intelligence exists as a "real thing" that underlies intelligent behavior (Berg & Sternberg, 1992). Treating an abstract concept as a concrete, physical entity, however, is a common mistake in reasoning known as *reification*. Intelligence, like gravity, is nothing more than an idea, or construct, that exists in the minds of scientists. Scientific constructs are hypothetical variables that are not directly observable.

Individuals exist, of course, and their behavior can be observed and measured. Careful examination of these measurements leads to the development of constructs that attempt to explain these factual observations. The appropriateness and usefulness of these constructs depends upon the degree to which they help us understand, describe, and predict behavior. Thorndike, therefore, was wrong: Intelligence is not a "real thing" that exists in some amount. It is a hypothetical construct that scientists have posited to explain certain types of behavior. *Intelligence*, then, exists, but only as a scientific construct.

How Can We Measure Something We Cannot Define?

Despite more than 100 years of theory and research, the field of psychology never has reached a consensus on a definition of *intelligence* (e.g., see Sternberg & Kaufman, 2011). No other psychological phenomenon has proven harder to define than intelligence. In 1921, the *Journal of Educational Psychology* published a symposium titled

"Intelligence and Its Measurement" (Buckingham, 1921). In this symposium the editor asked 14 leading experts to define intelligence, among other questions. He received 14 different replies. Sample responses from selected experts included the following:

- "The power of good responses from the point of view of fact." (Thorndike)
- "The ability to carry on abstract thinking." (Terman)
- "Intelligence involves the capacity to acquire capacity." (Woodrow)
- "The ability of the individual to adapt himself adequately to relatively new situations in life." (Pintner)
- "Intelligence is what the tests test." (Boring)

The only point on which the respondents generally agreed was that intelligence is related to "higher mental processes," such as abstract reasoning or problem solving. The main source of disagreement in this symposium concerned whether intelligence is one single general ability or a number of different abilities.

In 1986, Sternberg and Detterman published a book titled *What Is Intelligence?* They were interested in determining whether consensus was greater among researchers at that time than it had been 65 years earlier. They asked 24 prominent experts in the field of intelligence to respond to the same questions the participants answered in the 1921 symposium. Here are a few sample definitions of intelligence from these experts:

- "Intelligence is a quality of adaptive behavior." (Anastasi)
- "Intelligence is the repertoire of knowledge and skills available to a person at a particular point in time." (Humphreys)
- "Intelligence is defined as the general factor . . . of psychological tests." (Jensen)
- "Intelligence is the reification of an entity that does not exist; it is a number of somewhat independent broad abilities." (Horn)

As Sternberg and Detterman (1986) noted, "striking diversity" was apparent among the respondents' definitions, despite more than half a century of research on the nature and measurement of intelligence since the 1921 symposium. Nonetheless, consistent with the earlier findings, most of the participants mentioned that intelligence is related to higher-order cognitive functions. Differences among experts also were prevalent on the "one versus many" question of the generality of intelligence.

CONCEPTIONS OF INTELLIGENCE

One reason for this lack of consensus stems from the fact that one can view intelligence from different perspectives (see Eysenck, 1998). Figure 1.1 shows the relationship among three different conceptions of intelligence. The first concerns the biological substrate that underlies all intelligent thought and action. *Biological intelligence* sets the limits of intellectual development. Intelligence is influenced by genetics, because genes determine the neurological structures and the physiological and biochemical functioning of the brain. As shown within the circle for biologi-

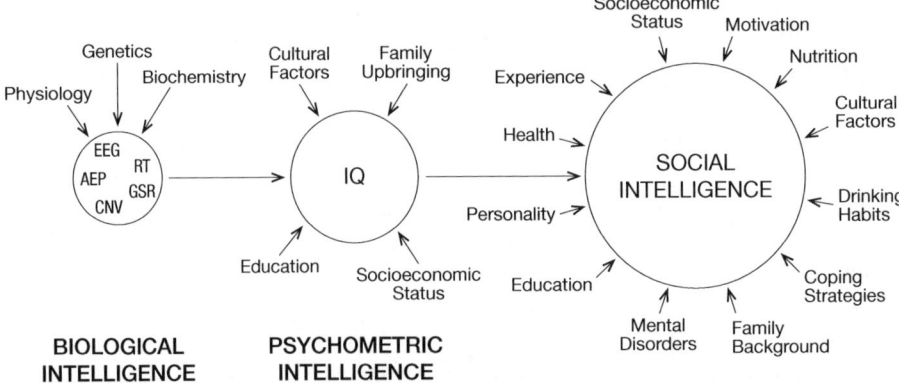

Figure 1.1. Relations among biological, psychometric, and social (or practical) intelligence. Source: Eysenck (1988, p. 62). EEG = electroencephalograph, RT = reaction time, GSR = galvanic skin response, CNV = central nerve conduction velocity, and AEP = averaged evoked potentials.

cal intelligence, brain functioning can be measured in a number of different ways, including the electroencephalograph (EEG), averaged evoked potentials (AEP), galvanic skin response (GSR), central nerve conduction velocity (CNV), and reaction time (RT) on elementary cognitive tasks, among other methods such as functional magnetic imagining (fMRI; e.g., see Haier, 2017).

The second conception of intelligence is psychometric intelligence. *Psychometric intelligence* refers to the "intelligent" behavior that is sampled on intelligence tests. Individual differences in biological intelligence can be measured only indirectly by psychometric intelligence tests. The behaviors measured on these tests are related to biological functioning, but they also are influenced by one's background and experience. Cultural factors, family upbringing, level and quality of education, and socioeconomic status are all importantly related to intelligence test performance (e.g., Jensen, 1998a).

The third and final conception of intelligence is social (or practical) intelligence. *Social intelligence* refers to the overt behavior that is considered "intelligent" in specific contexts, cultures, or both. Examples include academic achievement in school and performance at work. What is considered intelligent behavior may differ to some degree across contexts and cultures, even though the basic cognitive and biological processes underlying such behavior may be the same (e.g., Sternberg, 2018). Intelligent behavior in the "real world" is determined in part by biological intelligence and in part by background and experience, but also by a host of other noncognitive factors (e.g., personality, healthy lifestyle, and mental health).

Thus, although these three meanings of the term *intelligence* overlap to a considerable degree, they differ in their breadth, or inclusiveness. Given that intelligence can be viewed in different ways, perhaps it is not surprising that a consensus definition has eluded the field. It is important to note that this lack of consensus worries scientists much less than it appears to worry journalists, the mass media, and other laypersons. This is because scientists are more aware that consensus definitions come at the end of a line of investigation, not near the beginning when inquiry still is in the formative stages. In fact, some leading scholars do not believe that "intelligence" is a useful scientific concept at all. As Gottfredson (2018) stated, this is "in part because scholars have applied the word to ever more numerous and varied forms of aptness. No longer informative either are the long-standing debates over how best 'to define' intelligence, as if a natural phenomenon could be formed or banished by expert consensus" (pp. 131–132).

In any case, the key point to keep in mind is not whether tests of intelligence measure something that we all can agree upon, but whether we have discovered something that is worth measuring. As we shall see in chapter 2, despite the absence of an expert consensus definition of intelligence, the vast amount of research that has been conducted over the past century clearly supports its meaningfulness as a scientific construct that can be assessed with considerable accuracy. The bottom line is this: We use intelligence tests because they predict many important social outcomes better than anything else that we currently can measure independently of IQ (e.g., Gottfredson, 2011).

Theories of Intelligence

Scientific knowledge consists of the gradual accumulation of information by different researchers, from different types of research, and in different domains. Scientific theories essentially are "bold conjectures" that attempt to explain the known evidence in a field of study. According to philosopher of science Karl Popper (1968), "good" scientific theories make important and useful predictions that can be subjected to empirical tests. Theories that are not potentially falsifiable are known as *pseudoscientific* theories (e.g., astrology and psychoanalysis). Theories of *intelligence* are scientific theories that attempt to explain differences among individuals in their ability to solve the myriad problems people confront almost daily, to learn from those experiences, and to adapt to a changing environment (e.g., Deary, 2012). Theories of intelligence, however, vary greatly in the degree to which they have been substantiated and, as a result, the extent to which they are accepted in the scientific community.

THE PSYCHOMETRIC PARADIGM

At present, the scientific theory that has by far the most empirical support is the psychometric approach to the study of intelligence. Although various competing theories of intelligence are in the literature (e.g., Chen & Gardner, 2018; Naglieri & Otero, 2018; Sternberg, 2018), the psychometric paradigm "has not only inspired the most research and attracted the most attention (up to this time) but is by far the most widely used in practical settings" (Neisser et al., 1996, p. 77).

Psychometrics is the scientific field of inquiry concerned with the measurement of psychological constructs. Although psychometricians study other psychological phenomena (e.g., personality, attitudes, and beliefs), the definition and measurement of intelligence has been a primary focus. According to the psychometric paradigm, intelligence involves the ability to reason abstractly, solve complex problems, and acquire new knowledge. Gottfredson (2018) defined the psychometric conception of intelligence in lay terms as

> a very general capacity that, among other things, involves the ability to reason, plan, solve problems, think abstractly, comprehend complex ideas, learn quickly and learn from experience. It is not merely book learning, a narrow academic skill, or test-taking smarts. Rather it reflects a broader and deeper capability for comprehending our surroundings—"catching on," "making sense" of things, or "figuring out what to do." (p. 133)

Contrary to the view of expert opinion often reported by the mass media, most contemporary scholars with expertise in the field of intelligence agree with this working definition of intelligence (Deary, 2012; Snyderman & Rothman, 1987).

PSYCHOMETRIC *G*

Two facts of nature must be explained by any viable theory of intelligence—and both are addressed adequately in the psychometric paradigm. The first is known as the *positive manifold* (Spearman, 1904). The positive manifold refers to the fact that all tests of cognitive ability (i.e., objectively scored tests on which individual differences are not due to sensory acuity or motor deftness) are positively intercorrelated. This means that, on average, individuals who score high on one kind of cognitive test tend to score high on *every* other kind of cognitive test, and vice versa. The existence of the positive manifold indicates that all tests of cognitive ability share something in common that is related to differences in performance (i.e., an underlying source of individual differences, or variance).

The second fact of nature that must be explained by any theory of intelligence pertains to the description of the underlying structure of these positive intercorrelations. Specifically, the central question here is whether these correlations are related to a single cognitive ability or to a number of different cognitive abilities. Spearman (1904) hypothesized that the positive manifold results from a single underlying general ability that is shared by all tests. In other words, he asserted that all cognitive tests correlate positively because they measure the same thing to some degree. He invented factor analysis to estimate this underlying source of variance, which he called the *general factor*, or simply psychometric *g*. The purpose of factor analysis is to determine whether the correlations among a number of cognitive tests can be explained by some smaller number of inferred hypothetical constructs (i.e., factors; Carroll, 1993). Specifically, Spearman hypothesized that every test measures *g* and one other ability that is unique to that specific test (or highly similar tests).

Figure 1.2 depicts Spearman's original two-factor theory. This figure shows the relationship among seven intelligence tests and psychometric *g*. As can be seen here, each of these tests overlaps to some degree with *g* (as expected, given the positive manifold), but not with each other. Also note that some subtests are more closely related to *g* than others. T1, T3, and T5, for example, overlap to a considerable extent with psychometric *g*, whereas T2 and T6 are related to *g* to a much lesser degree. The portions of each

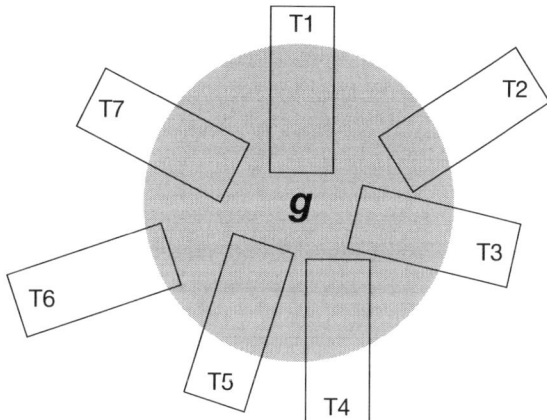

Figure 1.2. Spearman's two-factor theory of intelligence.

subtest that do not overlap with psychometric g reflect the portion of individual differences that are specific to each respective test (including random influences on its scores).

What is psychometric g? Perhaps the most undisputed fact about g is that it is related to information-processing complexity (e.g., see Gottfredson, 2018; Jensen, 1998a). Spearman discovered that the tests correlating most highly with g—or the most g-loaded tests—are those that involve what he called *abstractness* and the *eduction of relations and correlates* (Spearman & Jones, 1950). Abstractness refers to ideas and concepts that cannot be perceived directly by the senses. The eduction of relations and correlates pertains to the perception of relations through inductive or deductive reasoning, as opposed to the simple reproduction of known rules. For example, take tests of cognitive ability that involve mathematics. Tests that correlate the most highly with psychometric g are those that involve solving problems, such as word problems in which the requisite arithmetic operations are not made explicit. To answer correctly, one must deduce from the description of the problem which arithmetic operations are required and then apply them. In contrast, tests that involve the routine application of explicit arithmetic operations, such as simple addition and subtraction worksheets, tend to be much less g-loaded. That is, the relative g-loadedness of these kinds of tests is not related to the fact that they concern mathematics, but to the complexity of information processing required.

In addition to tasks that require inferring relations about abstract concepts, tests that correlate highly with psychometric g are those that require more conscious mental manipulation. A straightforward illustration of this phenomenon can be found by comparing the g-loadings of measures such as the Forward and Backward sections of the Digit Span subtest from the Wechsler Intelligence Scale for Children, Fifth Edition (WISC-V; Wechsler, 2014a). On both, one must repeat a string of digits presented once at a rate of one digit per second. In Digit Span Forward the digits are repeated in the same order as presented, and in Digit Span Backward in the opposite order as presented. Thus, on Digit Span Backward, one must retain the string of digits that has been presented in short-term memory and then repeat them, just as in Digit Span

Forward, but with the added requirement of reversing the digits before repeating them. Because reversing the digits involves more conscious mental manipulation, Digit Span Backward is more highly correlated with g than is Digit Span Forward.

Another noteworthy characteristic of g is that it cannot be described in terms of the surface characteristics of the different cognitive ability tests that were used in factor analysis to derive it. Spearman referred to this phenomenon as the *indifference of the indicator* (Spearman & Jones, 1950). For example, take the Block Design and Vocabulary subtests of the WISC-V. On Block Design one must arrange colored blocks to match a pattern, and on Vocabulary one must define the meaning of different words. With their entirely different information content and response requirements, these two subtests clearly call for quite different thought processes, yet they are two of the most highly g-loaded subtests on the WISC-V. A test's correlation with g, therefore, is related to the complexity of information processing required, rather than to its requisite specific skills or knowledge content.

Although it is now well established that psychometric g is related to processing complexity on cognitive tasks and not their surface characteristics, it is important to note that this is merely a description of g. Like all factors, g is not, strictly speaking, an explanatory construct. Factor analysis can be used to explain how various cognitive ability tests are related to each other, but it does not provide a causal explanation of the abilities or how they are organized. Therefore, the construct of g itself calls for an explanation. As Eysenck (1998) stated, "It is one thing to postulate a general factor of intelligence as the central conception in the theoretical framework which explains the observed phenomena in the field of mental testing; it is a different thing to postulate the nature of this factor" (p. 10).

The underlying causal mechanism of g still is largely unknown. The hypothesis that Spearman (1904) used most often to "explain" psychometric g was "mental energy." However, he remained agnostic with regard to its physical cause, primarily because research on the brain at the time was too primitive to shed any light on the physiological nature of g. Over the past 30 years, however, contemporary brain imaging research has found that individual differences in intelligence are integrally related to the connections among specific areas of the brain and their structural and functional characteristics (e.g., Haier, 2018). In chapter 2, we further discuss how and why individuals differ in intelligence.

GROUP FACTORS

Not long after Spearman (1927) introduced the two-factor theory, he and other pioneers in factor analysis discovered group factors in addition to g. Unlike g, which enters into all cognitive tests, group factors are common only to certain groups of tests that require the same kinds of item content (e.g., verbal, numerical, or spatial) or cognitive processes (e.g., oral fluency, short-term memory, perceptual speed).

Thurstone's (1938) theory of *primary mental abilities* (PMAs) was the first theory of intelligence that did not include a general factor. His theory was based on the results of a new statistical technique that he developed, called *multiple factor analysis*. Multiple factor analysis initially allowed for the identification of a number of cognitive abilities but no general factor. Thurstone's methodology also allowed for the identification of different kinds of cognitive abilities that were related to the factors that he discovered. Like Spearman's approach, his methodology was a product of his assumptions. Whereas Spearman's method of factor analysis was based on the assumption that only one factor is present in the correlation matrix, Thurstone's method was predicated on the notion of multiple abilities and no general ability.

Thurstone originally believed that the positive manifold is not the result of a general factor that underlies all tests of cognitive abilities but stems from a number of fundamental abilities or PMAs. He identified the following seven PMAs: Verbal Comprehension, Perceptual Speed, Space Visualization, Inductive Reasoning, Deductive Reasoning, Rote Memory, and Number Facility. These factors were seen to be related to a variety of tests that shared common features. He believed that performance on any particular test, however, did not involve all of the PMAs. Thurstone developed a special set of tests, called the PMA tests, to measure each of these factors.

For Thurstone's theory to be correct, each of the PMA tests had to correlate with only one factor. Further, there would be no general factor with which every test correlated (representing psychometric *g*). This pattern of results in factor analysis is known as *simple structure*. Table 1.1 presents an idealized version of the results of a factor analysis showing simple structure. As can be seen here, it includes six tests of cognitive ability and three factors. Each of the tests correlates perfectly with one factor and not at all with the other factors. In this case, each test represents a single group factor, uncontaminated by any other PMA. The factors are interpreted in terms of the characteristics of the tests on which they load. Thurstone's goal was to develop a battery of "factor-pure" tests such as these to measure each of the PMAs.

Results of factor analyses of Thurstone's PMA tests, however, did not contradict the existence of a general factor (e.g., see Cattell, 1971). Because all tests correlate with psychometric *g* to some extent, it is only possible to approximate simple structure by allowing the factors themselves to be correlated. However, when this is done, the resulting correlations between factors can be factor-analyzed. When these correlations are factor-analyzed, psychometric *g* emerges as a second-order factor. When factor analyses are conducted at different levels, this is known as *higher-order factor analysis*. Thus, the finding that there is a psychometric *g* as well as group factors among the PMA tests indicates that Spearman and Thurstone were both correct in what they initially believed but incorrect about what they disbelieved.

Table 1.1. Idealized version of simple structure

Test	Factor I	Factor II	Factor III
A	1.00	—	—
B	1.00	—	—
C	—	1.00	—
D	—	1.00	—
E	—	—	1.00
F	—	—	1.00

Agreement finally was reached on a general psychometric paradigm that has lasted to this day (see Carroll, 1993). According to this paradigm, individuals have a number of different abilities for solving intellectual problems and for adapting to the environment. Among these abilities, psychometric g is particularly important. In addition to g, specific abilities deal with various types of problems under specific circumstances, such as those involving visual-spatial or numerical reasoning, or memory. During this early period of research, a number of theories postulated by such factor-analytic luminaries as Vernon, Cattell, and Guilford attempted to describe the structure of human cognitive abilities (see Carroll, 1982). Nonetheless, because opinions differed about the most appropriate method of factor analysis, consensus as to the best model of the structure of cognitive ability was not reached.

THE STRUCTURE OF INTELLIGENCE

One of the main reasons for this lack of consensus with regard to the structure of intelligence had to do with the fact that the early theorists were limited to a type of factor analysis called *exploratory factor analysis* (EFA). EFA is most useful in the early stages of research, when initial hypotheses about the underlying factors are generated. EFA does not test the fit between competing theories and the data within a statistical modeling framework. In the 1980s, however, use of a new statistical procedure known as *confirmatory factor analysis* (CFA) provided a way out of this theoretical dead end. CFA is a general model of factor analysis that contains all earlier models as special cases. CFA is a "sharper" factor-analytic tool than earlier models and can be used both to estimate and to test alternative factor models. In CFA, specific theories are used to construct models of the underlying structure of a battery of tests to determine how well they "fit" or explain the data. Further, the "goodness-of-fit" provided by the models based on competing theories can be examined to determine which one provides the best description of the data. The results of initial analyses using this new approach showed that a hierarchical model of cognitive ability provided a good fit to the data (e.g., Keith & Reynolds, 2012; Gustafsson, 1984). In these models, both g and a number of group factors are represented as independent dimensions of cognitive ability (e.g., Johnson, te Nijenhuis, & Bouchard, 2008). Because a second-order psychometric g represents what is shared by all of the first-order group factors, in higher-order models its effect on the cognitive tasks in the test battery used to derive the factors is indirect—that is, mediated by the first-order factors.

At the current time, the most widely accepted theory of the structure of human cognitive abilities is Carroll's (1993) three-stratum theory (e.g., Brody, 1994; Eysenck, 1994; Sternberg, 1994). Carroll's theory is based on the re-analysis of 467 data sets. It is largely an extension and expansion of the earlier theories of cognitive abilities, such as the Horn-Cattell theory of fluid and crystallized abilities (Gf-Gc; Horn, 1994; Horn & Noll, 1997). According to Carroll, "There is abundant evidence for a factor of general intelligence" (1993, p. 624) and also for a number of group factors. As shown in Figure 1.3, in the three-stratum theory psychometric g and group factors are arranged in a hierarchy based on their generality. *Generality* refers to the number

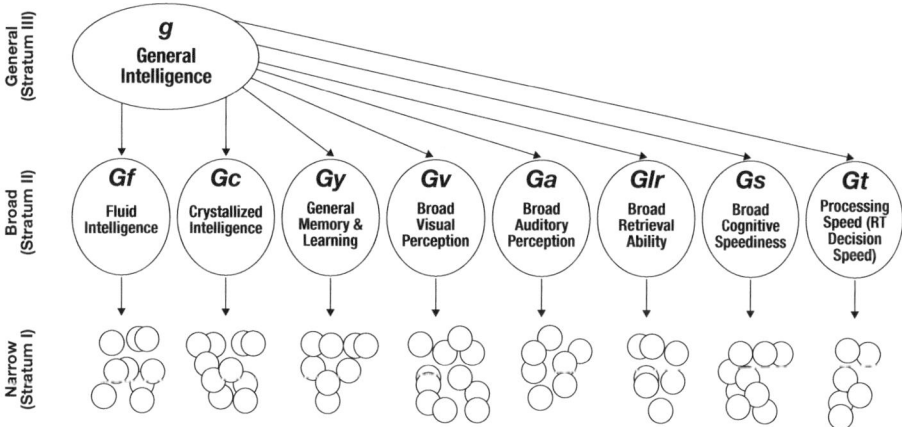

Figure 1.3. Carroll's three-stratum theory of the structure of human cognitive abilities. Based on Carroll (1993).

of other factors with which a particular factor is correlated. The most general factor, psychometric g, is located at the apex of this hierarchical structure at stratum III. Every test of cognitive ability measures g to some extent. Eight broad cognitive abilities (e.g., Fluid Intelligence and Crystallized Intelligence) that are similar to Thurstone's PMAs constitute stratum II; and stratum I consists of many narrow cognitive abilities (e.g., Visual Memory, Spelling, and Word Fluency). In the three-stratum theory, therefore, intelligence is multidimensional and consists of many different cognitive abilities at different levels of generality.

During the late 1990s and early 2000s, Carroll's (1993) three-stratum theory and Horn and Cattell's Gf-Gc theory were integrated into what is referred to as the Cattell-Horn-Carroll (CHC) theory of cognitive abilities. This model has the same factor structure as the three-stratum theory, with a prominent psychometric g, but with differences among the broad abilities posited at stratum II (e.g., Schneider & McGrew, 2018). Originally consisting of 10 broad abilities at stratum II, the CHC theory has expanded over time and now postulates 18 broad abilities. Over the past two decades, the CHC theory increasingly has been used by test developers to create theoretically driven tests that measure general and broad factors of human intelligence (cf. Canivez & Youngstrom, 2019; McGill & Dombrowski, 2019).

CHC THEORY AND IQ TESTING

Due to the practical limitations of psychological assessment, the number of cognitive abilities measured on standardized tests of intelligence tends to be fairly small. In addition to psychometric g, virtually all intelligence tests measure no more than three to five broad abilities at stratum II of CHC theory (e.g., see Flanagan et al., 2013, p. 85). For example, the WISC-V is the most widely used intelligence test with children and youth (Benson et al., 2019). A recent study by Reynolds and Keith (2017) found that the WISC-V measures g and the following five broad abilities: Fluid Reasoning, Verbal

Comprehension, Visual Spatial Ability, Working Memory, and Processing Speed (cf. Canivez, Watkins, & Dombrowski, 2015; Dombrowski, Canivez, & Watkins, 2018).

What do intelligence tests measure? All intelligence tests primarily measure the same thing—namely, general cognitive ability, or psychometric g (Jensen, 1998a). The global composite score on virtually every intelligence test for children and adolescents is an excellent measure of g (e.g., Dombrowski, Canivez, & Watkins, 2018; Floyd, Reynolds, Farmer, & Kranzler, 2013; Reynolds & Keith, 2017; Reynolds, Floyd, & Niileksela, 2013). Psychometric g is the largest factor underlying individual differences on intelligence tests, usually explaining more variance than all of the group factors combined, even when intelligence tests are not developed within the framework of CHC theory (e.g., see Kranzler & Keith, 1999). On the WISC-V, for example, Canivez and Watkins (2016) found that psychometric g accounted for more than 80% of the total true score variance. They also found that, of the five broad ability composite scores on the WISC-V, only one (Processing Speed) accounted for a sufficient amount of variance to warrant clinical interpretation.

Further, the predictive validity of intelligence tests is largely a function of psychometric g. On most educational and occupational external criteria, the general factor typically explains 70% to 90% of the variance that is predictable from psychological tests, depending on the criterion (e.g., Kaufman, Reynolds, Kaufman, Liu, & McGrew, 2012; Roth et al., 2015; Thorndike, 1985, 1986). Zaboski, Kranzler, and Gage (2019) recently conducted a meta-analysis of the relations between the broad abilities in CHC theory and academic achievement to determine the effect size for these relations across age groups. Results of their analyses show that, although psychometric g and one or more broad cognitive abilities were substantially related to each area of academic achievement, g had by far the strongest relations across all domains of academic achievement. On average, g explained more than 50% of the variance in achievement, which was more than all of the broad cognitive abilities taken as a whole. The only broad cognitive ability found to have an important relation to academic achievement, in addition to general ability, was Crystallized Intelligence—and only with achievement outcomes in reading for older age groups.

Moreover, because g is related to the complexity of information processing, Zaboski et al.'s results indicated that educational outcomes that involve perceiving abstract or conceptual relationships were predicted best by it, such as those required by reading comprehension and mathematics reasoning; those that primarily involve rote learning or associative memory, such as reading decoding and basic mathematics, were predicted less well. In addition to the prediction of educational criteria, psychometric g is predictive of many important social outcomes beyond tests, such as years of education and socioeconomic status (Gottfredson, 2018). The general factor also is related (negatively) to such problem behavior as dropping out of high school, living in poverty, and incarceration (e.g., Herrnstein & Murray, 1994).

Despite the predictiveness of psychometric g, the predictiveness of intelligence tests is far from perfect. Roth et al. (2015) recently conducted a meta-analysis of the correlation between tests of intelligence tests and school grades. Results of their analyses, which involved 240 independent studies with a total sample of more than 100,000 participants, revealed a true population correlation of .54, after correction for range restriction and sampling and measurement error. On standardized tests, the correlation between the overall score on intelligence tests and reading comprehension is approximately .70. Thus, the IQ score—at best—explains about 50% of the differences between children in their ability to comprehend text. This means that up to 50% of the remaining variance must be explained by other cognitive and noncognitive variables beyond *g*, such as conscientiousness and ambition. Predictive validity coefficients between *g* and outcomes in the workplace typically are lower. As Gottfredson (1997) stated, this implies that "the effects of intelligence—like other psychological traits—are probabilistic, not deterministic. Higher intelligence improves the *odds* of success in school and work. It is an advantage, not a guarantee. Many other things matter" (p. 116; emphasis in original).

Jensen (1998a) hypothesized that a number of personality traits interact with psychometric *g* to produce individual differences in real-world outcomes. According to him, exceptional accomplishment requires a high level of *g*, but also conscientiousness, ambition, and typical intellectual engagement, or TIE, which refers to the likelihood that a person will perform near their maximum level in everyday life. Ackerman's (2018) *intelligence-as-process, personality, interests, and intelligence-as-knowledge* (PPIK) framework, for example, is an ambitious attempt to explain individual differences in domain knowledge in adulthood as a function of the complex interaction between an individual's cognitive abilities, TIE, and affective (personality) and conative (interests, motivation) traits. Thus, although the predictive validity of cognitive ability tests in real-world settings is largely a function of *g*, it is far from perfect, and other cognitive and noncognitive variables are importantly involved.

Beyond CHC Theory

CRITICISM OF THE PSYCHOMETRIC PARADIGM

The main criticism of the psychometric paradigm is not that it is incorrect, as it has substantial empirical support, but that it is incomplete. According to Sternberg (2018), this approach focuses on only one or, at most, two of the essential aspects of intelligence, and thus cannot lead to a complete understanding of intelligence. Others, such as Ceci (1990), have argued that the syllogism implied in this line of investigation (*g* = IQ = real-world success) obscures the complex link between micro-level processing and intelligent behavior. Ceci also has contended that alternative interpretations of the data are possible.

In addition, although higher-order models are now widely accepted theories of the structure of intelligence, it is also important to note that "the consensus is by no means unanimous, and in any case, scientific truth is not decided by plurality (or even majority) vote" (Sternberg, 1996, p. 11). Although many researchers within the psychometric paradigm today agree that the structure of human cognitive abilities is multidimensional, at least some question the appropriateness of an overarching psychometric *g* at stratum III of the factor hierarchy. In fact, several theories of intelligence outside the psychometric approach do not include a general ability at all, such as the triarchic theory of successful intelligence (Sternberg, 2018), the theory of multiple intelligences (Chen & Gardner, 2018), the Planning, Attention, Simultaneous, and Successive (PASS) processes theory (e.g., Naglieri & Otero, 2018), and the bio-ecological framework (e.g., Ceci, 1990). Nevertheless, despite the postulation of these competing theories, the psychometric paradigm—with its vast empirical support—is clearly the predominant theory of intelligence at the current time.

BIFACTOR MODEL OF INTELLIGENCE

During the past decade, a number of researchers have advocated for the bifactor model as a viable alternative to higher-order models, such as CHC theory (e.g., Beaujean, Parkin, & Parker, 2014; Gignac, 2008; Gignac & Watkins, 2013; Kranzler, Benson, & Floyd, 2015; Reise, 2012; Watkins & Beaujean, 2014). Figure 1.4 displays a higher-order model and a bifactor model for WISC-V (Wechsler, 2014a), which we feature in chapter 7. The bifactor model differs from the higher-order model in a number of important ways:

1. In the bifactor model psychometric g is specified as a first-order "breadth" factor that directly affects scores on all tests. In the higher-order model, in comparison, g directly affects lower-order factors and indirectly affects test scores. As a result, interpretation of the general factor in bifactor models is more straightforward than

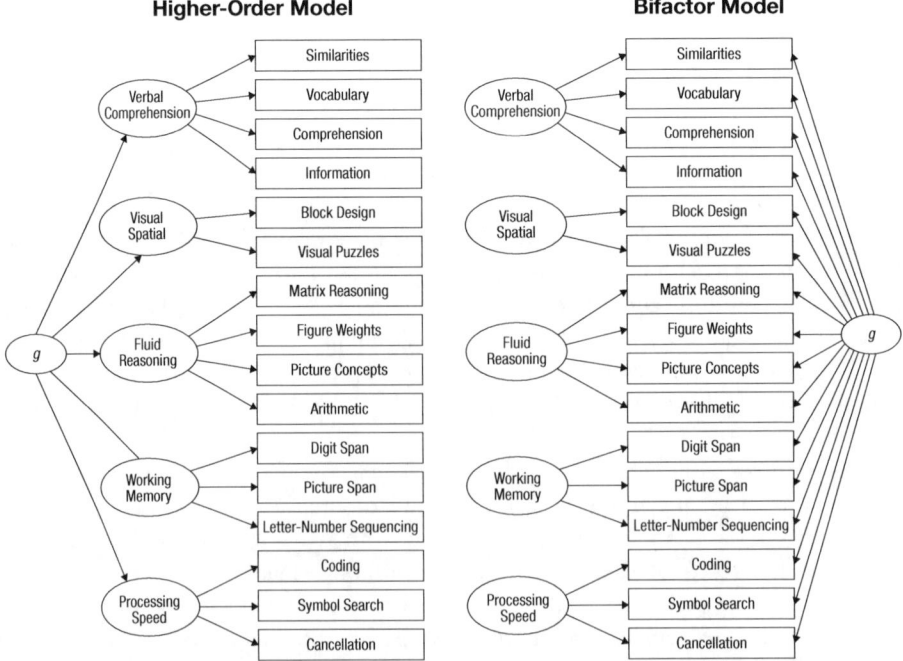

Figure 1.4. Higher-order and bifactor models for the Wechsler Intelligence Scale for Children, Fifth Edition.

it is in the higher-order models. In higher-order models, lower-order factors are defined by certain test scores, and the higher-order general factor is defined by these lower-order factors and not by test scores (Beaujean et al., 2014). These higher-order factors are thus "abstractions of abstraction even more removed from the measured variables" (Thompson, 2004, pp. 73–74). In contrast, the general factor in a bifactor model reflects the direct effects of the construct of psychometric g on all test scores. Consequently, the bifactor model "can be particularly useful in testing whether a subset of the domain specific factors predict external variables, over and above the general factor, as the domain specific factors are directly represented as independent factors" (p. 197).
2. In the bifactor model, the more specific cognitive ability factors (often called group factors in bifactor models) reflect the variance shared in test scores after accounting for the effects of psychometric g. Like the general factor in the bifactor model, they are also first-order factors, but they affect only subsets of test scores. They represent specific cognitive abilities that are uncorrelated with psychometric g and the other group factors. As a result, each factor represents only one cognitive ability—regardless of its stratum.
3. Finally, a number of studies using CFA have found that bifactor models provide superior fit to intelligence test norming data than do higher-order models (e.g., Gignac, 2008; Gignac & Watkins, 2013; Watkins & Beaujean, 2014).

In sum, based on its potential benefits and recent research results, it is clear that the bifactor model is a viable alternative to higher-order models, such as CHC theory. In addition, some recently have argued that Carroll's three-stratum theory, upon which CHC theory is based in large part, is more consistent with a bifactor model, not a higher-order model such as CHC theory (e.g., Beaujean, 2015b).

Summary

What, then, is intelligence? Most experts agree that intelligence involves the ability to reason and think abstractly, acquire new knowledge, and solve complex problems (Gottfredson, 2018). The vast literature on the structure of human cognitive abilities indicates that it is multidimensional, although current debate concerns whether it is best described by a higher-order or bifactor model. In any case, what this means for the practical use of intelligence tests is that any single score on intelligence tests will not explain the full range of these dimensions. Nevertheless, of the various cognitive abilities, g plays a particularly important role. All of the most widely used tests of intelligence primarily measure the same thing—psychometric g. Not only is g the largest factor in batteries of cognitive tests, but it is also the "active ingredient" in cognitive tests' predictiveness. Psychometric g is not merely linked to the surface characteristics of cognitive ability tests; rather, g is *directly* related to the complexity of information processing. Finally, psychometric g is measured quite well by most, if not all, of the most widely used intelligence tests. Certain group factors also are measured on most of these tests, but typically no more than a few are measured on any one test.

CHAPTER 2

How and Why Do People Differ in Intelligence?

It is a truism that no two people are exactly the same. Indeed, individuals differ on virtually every biological and psychological attribute that can be measured. Individual differences are observed on physical characteristics, such as height, weight, blood type and pressure, visual acuity, and eye coloration, but they also are observed on psychological characteristics, such as personality, values, interests, and academic achievement, among others. Individuals also differ in intelligence (IQ)—that is, in their general, broad, and narrow cognitive abilities (e.g., see Schneider & McGrew, 2018).

The scientific study of how and why people differ in terms of their psychological characteristics is known as *differential psychology* (e.g., Revelle, Wilt, & Condon, 2011). In contrast to *experimental psychology*, where differences among people are seen as a source of error to be controlled, differential psychology considers those differences as the focus of research. For school psychologists and other professionals who work with children and youth with learning problems, understanding individual differences in intelligence is particularly important—not only for the identification of school-related difficulties, but also for the effective planning and implementation of school-based interventions (e.g., Floyd & Kranzler, 2019).

The purpose of this chapter is to explain how and why individuals differ in intelligence. We begin by discussing how individuals of the same age differ in intelligence. We then discuss developmental differences. Finally, we address why individuals differ in intelligence, considering the effects of genes, the environment, and their interplay on intelligence as well as the malleability of intelligence.

The Distribution of Intelligence

Around 1870, the Belgium astronomer Adolphe Quetelet (1796–1874) made a discovery about individual differences that impressed him greatly. His method was to select a physical characteristic, such as height, obtain measurements on a large number of individuals, and then arrange the results in a frequency distribution. He found the same pattern of results over and over, for all sorts of different things. Quetelet discovered that the distribution of these characteristics closely approximated a bell-shaped curve. The symmetrical, bell-shaped curve that results from plotting human characteristics on frequency polygons is known as the *normal (or Gaussian) distribution*. The normal curve is bell-shaped, perfectly symmetrical, and has a certain degree of "peakedness."

Sir Francis Galton (1822–1911) was the first to discover that individual differences in intelligence closely approximate the normal distribution. Figure 2.1 shows an idealized normal distribution of intelligence test scores (IQs). As can be seen here, the average (or mean) of the distribution is 100. Most individuals have scores that are near the average, with increasingly fewer scores near the extremes of each tail. The figure also displays the percentage of cases in the distribution that can be found in the different areas of all normal curves when standard scores are used (e.g., z scores, T scores, or IQ scores). This is very important from a practical standpoint, because it allows us to determine the percentage of cases in the distribution that fall below or above any particular score, or the percentage of cases falling between any two scores.

Given that the percentage of scores always equals 100%, a person's IQ can be understood in terms of its *percentile rank*. Percentile ranks frequently are used to describe standardized test scores, and for good reason: They are the easiest kind of score to understand. The percentile rank of a score is simply the percentage of the whole distribution falling below that score on the test. An individual whose score is at the 75th percentile scored higher than about 75% of the persons in the norm group,

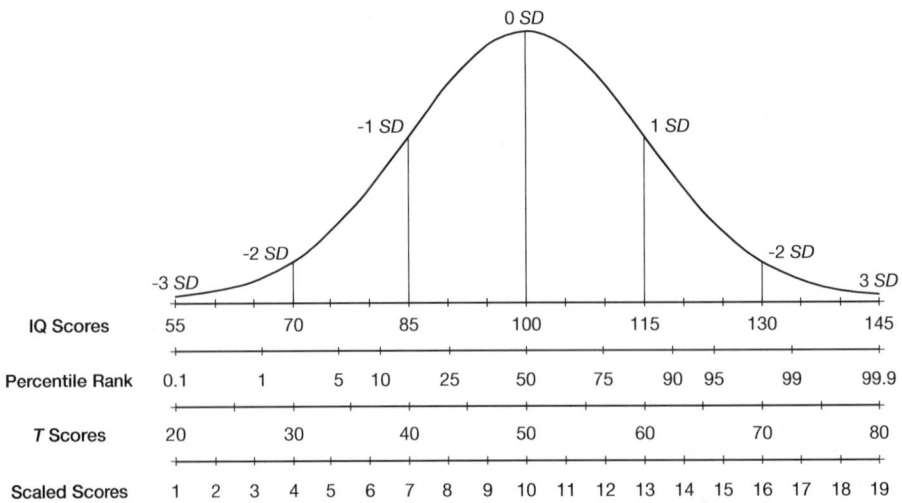

Figure 2.1. A theoretical normal distribution with associated standardized scores.

someone whose score is at the 50th percentile scored higher than about 50%, and so on. Most intelligence tests are developed to have a mean standard score of 100 and standard deviation of 15. Therefore, an IQ of 115, for example, has a percentile rank of 84, meaning that it surpasses 84% of all scores in the normative sample. Roughly 68% of the population has IQs that fall between 85 and 115, which is considered the "average" range of intelligence.

The normal distribution serves as a reasonably accurate model of the frequency distribution of intelligence test scores. For individuals with IQs falling between 70 and 130, which accounts for approximately 95% of the population, the normal curve is a very good model of the distribution of scores. Nevertheless, when the 5% of scores at the extreme tails of the distribution are included, the normal distribution is not perfectly accurate. Much of the deviation from the normal curve for intelligence is due to the fact that a greater proportion of individuals with IQs at the very low end of the distribution (i.e., below 50 or so) than predicted by the normal curve.

Intellectual disability (ID) typically is defined by IQ scores below 70 or 75 (among other criteria; see Chapter 10). Individuals with IQs between 50 and 70 represent the lower tail of normal variability in intelligence. IQ scores below 50, however, do not tend to result from normal variability (e.g., Percy, 2007) but either from accidents of nature (i.e., single gene defects or chromosomal abnormalities) or brain damage (e.g., birth complications, extreme nutritional deficiency, and head injury). These anomalous conditions tend to have such dramatic effects that they completely outweigh the usual genetic and environmental factors that determine a person's intelligence. Nevertheless, for most practical purposes, the normal curve provides a reasonable approximation to the distribution of intelligence—particularly when dealing with individuals within two standard deviations of the mean of the distribution.

Developmental Differences in Intelligence

Alfred Binet (1857–1911) is widely regarded as the father of modern intelligence tests. The French Ministry of Education commissioned Binet and Théophile Simon (1873–1961) to find a way to identify children and youth who were at risk for educational failure. Binet and Simon began with the assumption that children become more intelligent with age, because older children are capable of doing things that younger children cannot. They developed a set of short questions and simple tasks that most children were capable of answering at different ages. They then administered these items to representative samples of children at 1-year intervals from age 3 to 15 years. Binet and Simon grouped items based on the percentage of children in each age group who got each item correct. For example, if a particular test item could be solved by the average child at the age of 6 years, then the age-level of that item was 6 years. Any child who passed this item was said to have a *mental age* (MA) of 6 years. They identified five items at each age level so that they could measure MA in months as well as years. By comparing MA to *chronological age* (CA), Binet and Simon were able to determine whether a child was above or below average in relation to their same-age peers. They found that, any each age level, the distribution of scores on their intelligence test was approximately normal.

Wilhelm Stern (1871–1938) was the first to describe intelligence by the ratio of MA to CA to derive a *mental quotient*, which later was changed to the *intelligence quotient*, or IQ. IQ was obtained by multiplying by 100 to remove the decimal point; that is, IQ = MA/CA x 100. Thus, an 8-year-old child with an MA equivalent to the average 10-year-old would have an IQ of 125 (10/8 X 100); an 8-year-old child with an MA equivalent to the average 8-year-old would have an IQ of 100 (10/8 X 100); and an 8-year-old with an MA equivalent to the average 6-year-old would have an IQ of 75 (6/8 X 100). Despite its appeal, it quickly became apparent that the IQ scale is not useful after about 16 years of age, given that intellectual skills do not continue to develop steadily after that age. For adults this method is clearly inappropriate, because their MA would remain relatively constant, while their CA constantly would increase with time. Although many teenagers perhaps would believe in the veracity of the consistently decreasing IQ of their parents, this is clearly inappropriate. For this reason, all current intelligence tests use a point scale in which an individual's score is compared to a normative sample of same-age peers.

Regarding the growth of intelligence, between the ages of 4 and 12 years or so, the rate of cognitive growth is fairly linear. After that age, the rate of gain begins to decrease gradually as the individual reaches maturity between 16 and 20 years of age, where cognitive development begins to plateau. The development of intelligence, therefore, is similar to that of height. Although scores on intelligence tests are relatively unstable during infancy and the preschool years, they stabilize rather quickly during the early school years and remain that way throughout adulthood (e.g., Humphreys, 1989). This means that the rank order of intelligence test scores will tend to remain relatively the same as individuals develop from childhood to adulthood. Prior to age 4 or 5, however, the long-term stability and predictive power of intelligence tests are of less value. In addition, the stability of test scores decreases as the time interval between initial testing and follow-up testing occurs. More recent test results will be a better indicator of one's current cognitive ability than tests administered in the distant past.

Figure 2.2 shows the growth curves for psychometric *g* for two hypothetical individuals. Although the cognitive ability of each of them increases over time, plateauing around the age of 15 years, their relative ranking remains the same. Because children's IQ scores are derived from comparison to same-age peers, this means that children's scores on intelligence tests will remain relatively the same, despite the fact that their cognitive ability is developing steadily. An 8-year-old and a 16-year-old with IQs of 100 are not the same in terms of their general reasoning abilities. On the contrary, it simply means that they are average for their respective age groups. Those who obtain the same IQ score from one age to another simply have maintained their relative standing in relation to same-age peers, while their cognitive abilities may have developed considerably. In addition, the development of cognitive ability begins to plateau at roughly the same time regardless of one's level of psychometric *g*. It is also important to note that, despite the fact that intelligence test scores generally are quite stable over time, the consistency of scores is not perfect. Just like height, many individuals' level of intelligence may remain roughly constant in relation to same-age

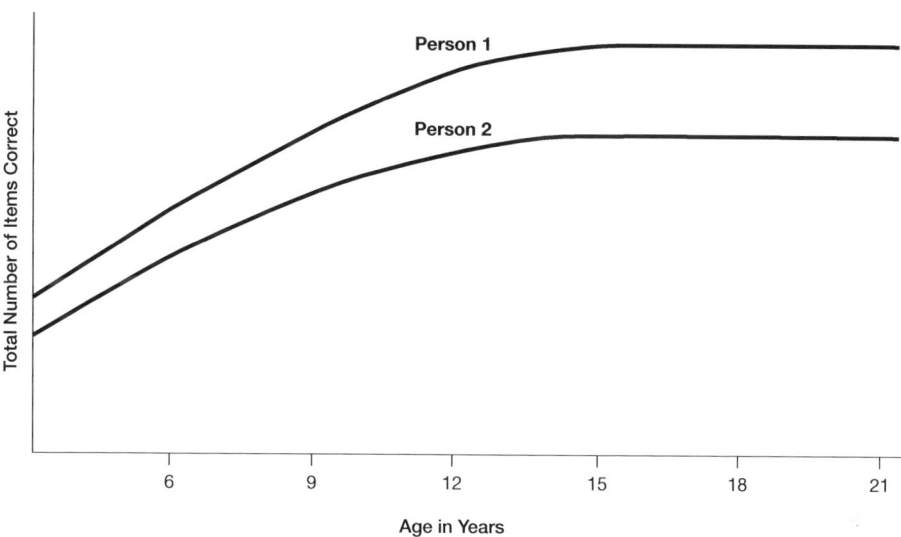

Figure 2.2. Growth curve of psychometric g with age for two individuals.

peers over time, but others' may not. The average change in IQ scores for individuals between 12 and 17 years of age, for example, is about 7 points, and for some people as much as 18 points (e.g., Neisser et al., 1996).

Although much is known about the development of intelligence through childhood, research on change in cognitive abilities in adulthood and old age is less clear—largely due to methodological issues surrounding the use of cross-sectional research designs, cohort effects, and differences in the cognitive abilities that are measured and how they are measured across studies (e.g., see Salthouse, 2010). Nevertheless, examination of the age-norms for widely used intelligence tests for adults, such as the Wechsler Adult Intelligence Scales—Fourth Edition (WAIS-IV; Wechsler, 2008), suggests that developmental trends across age are fairly clear (e.g., Deary, 2001). For some tests on the WAIS-IV, there is little change across age among adults, whereas for other tests, age-related decrements in ability are apparent. The tests on which older and younger people tend to compare well are vocabulary, general information, and verbal reasoning. These tests draw upon one's knowledge base that has been accumulated through experience over time (i.e., Comprehension-Knowledge, or Gc). The cognitive subtests on which marked differences between older and younger people are observed are those that tend to be speeded or involve abstract or spatial reasoning. These tests measure current cognitive functioning, because they involve solving problems here and now, often with novel content and under speeded conditions (i.e., Fluid Intelligence, or Gf).

In a recent large-scale study, Salthouse (2019) examined age trends for adults in four cognitive domains (i.e., Memory, Speed, Reasoning, and Vocabulary) with cross-sectional data for more than 5,000 participants and longitudinal data for approximately 1,600 participants. Results of his study were similar, indicating that memory and reasoning abilities decline modestly until about age 65, after which their rate of decline increases. Processing speed begins to decline when people are in their 30s, and decreases thereafter at a linear rate. Vocabulary knowledge, however, tends to increase until people are in their 60s and then declines only modestly after that time. As Salthouse stated, "These patterns, and particularly the early declines in cognitive functioning in presumably healthy adults, should be recognized when attempting to distinguish abnormal or pathological cognitive declines from normal cognitive aging" (p. 22). Further research on the study of cognitive aging is needed, however, particularly given the fact that life expectancy is increasing dramatically, and thus the proportion of older people in the population is growing.

Why Do People Differ in Intelligence?

Given the controversy that has surrounded research on the so-called nature-nurture issue in intelligence over the years, it may come as a surprise to learn that the main focus of research in this area no longer involves the question of whether individual differences in intelligence are related to genes or the environment (Nisbett et al., 2012). Most, if not all, psychologists now believe that *both* genetic and environmental factors are at least partly related to variability in intelligence (Snyderman & Rothman, 1987). As Ceci (1990) stated, "There are so many reports in the behavior-genetics literature of substantial heritability coefficients, calculated from an enormous variety of sources, that it is unlikely they could all be wrong" (p. 130). Rather, the focus of much contemporary research has moved beyond whether intelligence is related to heredity or environment. The emphasis of much contemporary research is on the identification of specific genes responsible for the heritability of intelligence and determining pathways between genes and behavior (e.g., Plomin & Deary, 2015). Before discussing research on the heritability of intelligence, it is important briefly to overview the research methodology used to examine why individuals differ in behavioral traits such as intelligence.

QUANTITATIVE BEHAVIORAL GENETICS OF INTELLIGENCE

Quantitative behavioral genetics, or the *differential model*, is used to examine the contributions of genetics and the environment to individual differences in behavioral traits. Research in behavioral genetics is best understood as an attempt to partition *variance*. Variance is the average of the squared deviations of every score from the mean of the distribution:

$$S = \frac{\Sigma (X - \bar{X})^2}{N}$$

where: Σ means "the sum of," X refers to each obtained score, $\bar{X}$ is the mean of X, and N refers to the total number of scores. The variance is interpreted as the "amount of information" in a distribution (Cronbach, 1990).

In quantitative behavior genetics, variance in an observable, measurable characteristic of an individual—the phenotypic (VP)—is partitioned into components of variance related to genes—the genotype (VG)—and the environment (VE). Thus, VP = VG + VE. The proportion of variance in the phenotype that is attributable to variance in the genotype is known as the *heritability* (h^2) of a particular trait (h^2 = VG / VP). *Environmentality* reflects differences in the phenotype that are associated with the environment and with measurement error (i.e., 1 - h^2). The environmental component of variance can be further partitioned into two subcomponents, *shared* and *non-shared*. Shared environmental influences reflect common experiences that make individuals in the same family similar to each other and different from those in other families (e.g., socioeconomic status, parenting style). Non-shared environmental influences reflect unique life experiences that make members of the same family different from one another (i.e., peer groups). It is important to note that these sources of environmental influences refer to *effects* and not *events*, because children in the same family may experience the same event differently (e.g., parental divorce).

Another important source of variance concerns gene-environment interplay, which refers to gene-environment interactions and correlations. Gene-environment interaction occurs when there are nonlinear combinations of genetic and environmental effects on behavior. This interaction occurs when the impact of the environment upon a particular characteristic depends upon an individual's genotype. In contrast, gene-environment correlation refers to relation between the environments to which individuals are exposed and their genetic propensities. Gene-environment correlations can be passive, reactive, or active. A passive gene-environment correlation exists when individuals passively inherit environments that are correlated with their genetic predispositions. A reactive gene-environment correlation refers to environments selected or created by others in reaction to an individual's genetic predisposition. Last, an active gene-environment correlation occurs when individuals select or create environments correlated with their genotypes.

All procedures for estimating the relative contributions of heredity and environment in quantitative behavior genetics involve correlating measurements taken from groups of people who are and are not biologically related and then comparing these correlations with those expected from a purely genetic hypothesis. The genetic correlation for identical, or *monozygotic* (MZ), twins is 1.00, because they share 100% of their genetic makeup. Because non-twin offspring (i.e., full siblings) receive 50% of their genes from each parent, the parent-child genetic correlation is .50. The genetic correlation for fraternal, or *dizygotic* (DZ), twins is also .50, because they also share 50% of their genes. Persons who are not biologically related have no genes in common, so the genetic correlation between these individuals is .00. When the correlations for a particular kinship (e.g., MZ twins) differ substantially from the predicted genetic correlation, results do not substantiate a purely genetic hypothesis. If family members bear no resemblance, then the genetic hypothesis is disconfirmed for that particular trait.

Family, twin, and adoption studies are the three basic research designs used in the differential model. These designs essentially exploit different combinations of genotypes and environments that occur naturally in the population. In family studies, estimates of h^2 are based on comparisons of parents with their offspring and of siblings with each other. Because members of the same family share both common genes and environment, evidence of familial similarity is consistent with the genetic hypothesis but cannot confirm it. Twin and adoption studies must be used to separate the relative contributions of genetics and the environment to phenotypic variance because they essentially control for the effects of genes or the environment.

Twins studies are one of the most powerful designs in the differential model. If a particular trait is influenced by genetics, then the correlation between MZ twins should be greater than the correlation between DZ twins, because MZ twins share 100% of their genes and DZ twins share only 50%. Correlations for MZ and DZ twins reared together reflect the phenotypic variance accounted for by the combined effects of genes and common environment. Adoption studies are another invaluable source of information on the relative contributions of genetics and the environment to phenotypic variance, because they too separate the effects of common genes and common environment. In adoption studies, adoptive parents are compared to their adopted children, to whom they are completely genetically dissimilar, and biological parents are compared to their adopted-away children, with whom they have no environmental experiences in common. Any resemblance between adopted children and their adoptive parents, therefore, can be attributed to the effects of shared environment; conversely, any resemblance between adopted-away children and their biological parents can be attributed to genetics. Pairs of adopted and biologically related children reared together also can be compared in adoption studies to estimate the effects of common environment. Particularly noteworthy are studies in which the adoption and twin methods are combined. In these studies, of which there are relatively few, MZ and DZ twins who have been separated at birth and reared apart are compared.

Several important points must be kept in mind when interpreting h^2 estimates. First, h^2 is a statistic that describes the ratio of genotypic variance to phenotypic variance in a population. Although it does indicate that physiological functioning is related to individual differences in the trait, it provides no information on the specific areas of the brain responsible for that variation or how they operate. Second, estimates of h^2 refer to populations, not to individuals. An h^2 of .50 does not indicate that half of an individual's measured trait is attributable to genes and half to the environment. Third, estimates of h^2 that are greater than zero do not imply biological determinism. Genotypes do not directly cause phenotypic expression. As Rushton (1995) stated, "They code for enzymes, which, under the influence of the environment, lay down tracts in the brains and nervous systems of individuals, thus differentially affecting people's minds and the choices they make about behavioral alternatives" (p. 61).

HERITABILITY OF INTELLIGENCE ACROSS THE LIFE SPAN

Bouchard and McGue (1981) reviewed the literature of familial studies of the heritability of intelligence. They examined the results of more than 100 independent studies, summarizing more than 500 correlations between more than 100,000 family members. Taken as a whole, results of these studies were consistent with a genetic hypothesis but

Table 2.1. Average IQ Correlations among Family Members

Relationship	Average r	Number of Pairs
Reared-Together Biological Relatives		
MZ Twins	.86	4,671
DZ Twins	.60	5,533
Siblings	.47	26,473
Parent-Offspring	.42	8,433
Half-Siblings	.35	200
Cousins	.15	1,176
Reared-Apart Biological Relatives		
MZ Twins	.72	65
Siblings	.24	203
Parent-Offspring	.24	720
Reared-Together Non-biological Relatives		
Siblings	.32	714
Parent-Offspring	.24	720

Note: MZ = Monozygotic; DZ = Dizygotic. Adapted from McGue, Bouchard, Iacono, & Lykken (1993).

also provided support for the influence of the environment on individual differences in intelligence (see Table 2.1). Not only were the correlations between MZ twins greater than those between family members with less genetic overlap, even when MZ twins are reared apart, but the obtained correlations across kinships do not deviate substantially from the expected genetic correlations. Evidence for the role of environment can be seen in the fact that correlations between biological relatives reared together are greater than those between individuals of the same degree of kinship reared apart; and correlations between nonbiological relatives reared together are substantially greater than zero. Neither of these findings can be explained by genetics alone. For these data, h^2 for general intelligence was estimated to be .51 (Chipeur, Rovine, & Plomin, 1990), indicating that slightly more than half of the phenotypic variance is accounted for by genetic factors. Shared environmental influences accounted for 11% to 35% of the variance, depending on kinship data used in the estimation. Non-shared environmental variance was found to explain 14% to 38% of the variance. Therefore, results of this review indicated that environment and genetics contribute roughly equally to variability in intelligence.

More recent reviews of the genetic studies of intelligence, however, have reached a somewhat different conclusion regarding the relative contributions of heritability and environmentality to individual differences in general intelligence across the life span (e.g., Plomin & Deary, 2015). Results of more recent research has shown that the correlation between the IQs of MZ twins increases across the life span. The correlation between DZ twins, in contrast, although fairly stable between 4 to 20 years of age, decreases dramatically after late adolescence. Interestingly, shared environmental influences tend to account for between 30% to 40% of the variance in IQ until the age of about 20 years, after which the amount of variance explained by shared environment drops to zero (Loehlin, 2007). Non-shared environmental effects, in comparison, remain fairly constant across the life span, explaining somewhere between 10% to 20% of the variance from 4–6 years of age into adulthood. Current estimates indicate that the heritability of intelligence increases substantially from about 20% in infancy to about 40% to 50% in childhood and adolescence and about 80% in adulthood, but declines somewhat to about 60% after 80 years of age, with the same genes affecting intelligence throughout the life span (Plomin & Deary, 2015).

Although shared environmental effects are widely held to be responsible for the similarity in intelligence between children raised in the same family (e.g., socioeconomic status), according to behavioral genetic research much of this resemblance results from shared genes. In contrast, shared environmental effects contribute relatively little, if at all, to individual differences in intelligence across the life span. Instead, behavioral genetics research has shown that "most of the effective environmental influence on personality and psychopathology and on cognitive development after childhood is not shared by two children growing up in the same family" (Haworth & Plomin, 2012, p. 535). Thus, in addition to substantial genetic influences, the environmental effects that are most important for understanding individual differences in intelligence are non-shared, which means that these effects are related to an individual's perception or experience of those environments or to environmental experiences that are unique to them (Haworth & Plomin, 2012).

Why does the heritability of intelligence increase from childhood to adulthood? The most likely explanation is genotype-environment correlation. Children do not select the environments into which they are born. Environments that are favorable or unfavorable to the development of particular traits are imposed upon them. An example of a passive genotype-environment correlation related to intelligence is when children with superior mathematical genotypes are born to and raised by parents who provide a mathematically stimulating environment. A common example of a reactive genotype-environment correlation in the schools is when children who are academically precocious are identified and placed in special classes for the intellectually gifted (see Chapter 12). Last, an active genotype-environment correlation occurs when children with superior scientific genotypes spend more time thinking and learning about science than other children, regardless of whether anyone wants them to. The result of genotype-environment correlations is to amplify the effect of genes on intelligence, thereby increasing heritability coefficients with age.

In addition to these findings, behavior genetics research has revealed that sometimes the same genes are related to more than one observed behavior. This is known as pleiotropy. Research has shown that genetic effects are highly pleiotropic for intelligence (e.g., Plomin & Kovas, 2005). Although the average correlation among the different broad cognitive abilities in Carroll's (1993) three-stratum model is about .30, on average, genetic correlations among these abilities are typically greater than .60. In other words, *generalist genes* influence the heritability of all cognitive abilities rather than specific genetic effects at different strata. Moreover, these general genetic effects also influence academic achievement. In a study of more than 5,000 pairs of early adolescent twins, for example, Davis, Haworth, and Plomin (2009) found that genetic correlations between intelligence and reading, mathematics, and language were quite high, ranging from .86 to .91. As Plomin and Deary (2015) stated, "This finding of strong genome-wide pleiotropy across diverse cognitive and learning abilities, indexed by general intelligence, is a major finding about the origins of individual differences in intelligence" (p. 102). Despite the fact that the heritability of intelligence is well established, variations in specific genes have yet to be identified that are related to intelligence (e.g., Payton, 2009). In other words, there is no intelligence gene. Rather, it appears that the heritability of intelligence is caused by many genes with very small effects.

WHERE IN THE BRAIN IS INTELLIGENCE?

The substantial heritability of intelligence clearly indicates that it is related to the brain. As Gottfredson (2016) stated, "Virtually all differences in brain structure and function correlate to some extent with general cognitive ability" (p. 134). For example, overall brain size is related to intelligence. McDaniel (2005) conducted a meta-analysis of 37 studies with 1,530 healthy children and adults to examine the relationship between *in vivo* brain volume and intelligence. He found that the best estimate of the true population correlation between brain size and intelligence was .33, with slightly higher correlations for females than males and for adults than children. In a review of the relation between whole brain size and general cognitive ability in studies using brain imagery techniques, Rushton and Ankeny (2009) found a mean correlation of .40 in 28 samples with a total sample size of 1,359. They also found a mean correlation between external head size measures and general cognitive ability of .20 in 59 samples with a total sample size of 63,405. Thus, as these reviews indicate, the preponderance of evidence demonstrates that brain size is moderately positively correlated with intelligence.

In 2007, Jung and Haier published a review of 37 studies examining the relations between intelligence and brain function (e.g., regional cerebral glucose metabolism rate) and structure (e.g., gray and white matter volumes). They concluded that certain regions of the brain and the pathways between them are associated with individual differences in intelligence, with the most salient areas located in the parietal and frontal lobes. Known as the *parieto-frontal integration theory* (P-FIT), Jung and Haier postulated that the relevant areas related to the intelligence are distributed throughout the brain and correspond to different stages of information processing.

Figure 2.3 shows the stages of information processing in the P-FIT theory proposed by Colom, Karama, Jung, and Haier (2010). The first stage involves the processing of sensory information in the occipital and temporal areas of the brain (BAs 18, 19, 21, and 37). These BAs are involved in processing of visual and auditory information (e.g., recognition, analysis, and elaboration of inputs). The integration and abstraction of the inputted sensory information occurs in the second stage, which involves in the parietal areas of the brain (i.e., BAs 7, 39, and 40). In the third stage of processing, the parietal areas interact with the frontal lobes (especially BAs 6, 9, 10, 45, 46, and 47), where complex information processing occurs, such as problem solving, evaluation, and hypothesis testing. Another area of the frontal lobes (BA 32) is involved during this stage in the selection of a best response and the inhibition of alternative responses. In addition, throughout these stages, "white matter . . . is thought to play a

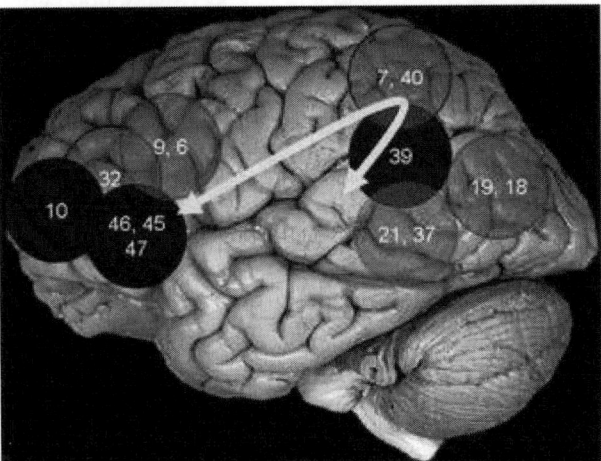

Figure 2.3. Brain regions by Brodmann area (BA) associated with better performance on measures of intelligence and reasoning that define the parieto-frontal integration theory (PFIT). Numbers denote specific BAs; dark circles show left-hemisphere findings, and light circles show bilateral findings. The arrow indicates the arcuate fasciculus white matter pathway. Reproduced from Haier (2017, p. 93).

critical role in reliable and efficient communication of information across these brain processing networks" (as cited in Haier, 2018, p. 221). Results of research on brain networks that have been published more recently are generally consistent with the P-FIT theory, with some modifications (see Haier, 2017). Nonetheless, despite recent theoretical advances, the prediction of intelligence test performance from the results of brain imaging has proven elusive (Haier, 2018).

MALLEABILITY OF INTELLIGENCE

The effects that genes have on individual differences in intelligence are better described as genetic influence than as genetic determinism. Being born with a particular set of genes does *not* predetermine behavioral traits, including intelligence. Particular genotypes do not correlate perfectly with expressed phenotypes. This is seen clearly in the correlations for identical twins reared together that are less than perfect. Despite the fact that identical twins share the same genotype, their expressed level of intelligence is highly correlated but not exactly the same. These differences can only be explained by the environment. "Gene action always involves an environment—at least a biochemical environment, and often an ecological one" (Neisser et al., 1996, p. 84). Thus, traits with heritable components, such as intelligence, are susceptible to environmental intervention.

Behavior geneticists use the concept of *reaction range* (RR) to explain variability in phenotypes for a particular genotype. Figure 2.4 shows the hypothetical effects of three different environments (viz., restricted, natural, and enriched) upon four

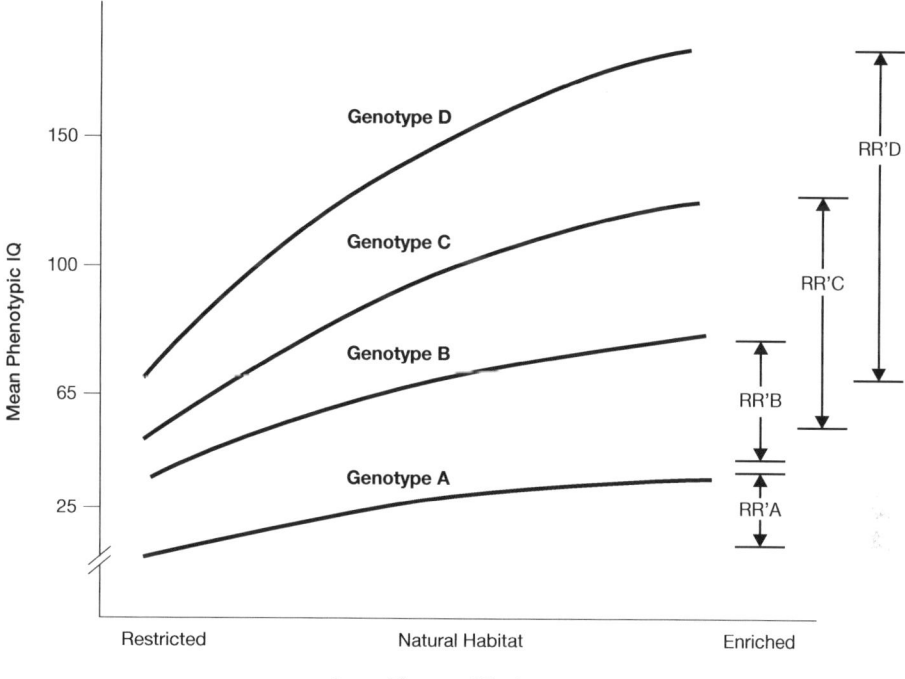

Figure 2.4. Hypothetical reaction range (RR) for four genotypes. Adapted from Platt and Sanislow (1988, p. 255).

different genotypes for the expression of intelligence. For all genotypes, the level of intelligence expressed is lower when individuals are raised in a deprived environment and higher when they are brought up in an enriched environment. The RR for any genotype is limited, however, as reflected in the vertical lines on the right of the figure. As can be seen here, within any particular environment individuals will have differences, depending upon their genotypes. Also, the RR is larger for some genotypes than for others. More specifically, the RR is wider for those with more advantaged genotypes. Genes, therefore, do not determine behavior; instead, they determine a range of responses to the environment. Over the course of development, therefore, environmental effects can give rise to considerable variation in the phenotypic expression of any single genotype. Nevertheless, as Jensen (1981) asserted, "There are probabilistic limits to the reaction range, and one of the tasks of genetic analysis is to explore the extent of those limits in the natural environment and to discover the environmental agents that affect them" (p. 485).

Given that intelligence is significantly related to a wide range of important life outcomes, even small increases could have profound ramifications in society, especially for individuals at the extremes of the distribution. How malleable is intelligence? As stated in *Intelligence: Knowns and Unknowns*, the report of a task force established by the Board of Scientific Affairs of the American Psychological Association on intelligence, "No one doubts that normal child development requires a certain minimum level of responsible care. Severely deprived, neglectful, or abusive environments must have negative effects on a great many aspects—including intellectual—of development" (Neisser et al., 1996, p. 88). Beyond that minimum level, however, how and how much can intelligence be raised?

Early Research on Malleability

Early research on increasing intelligence indicated that malleability of IQ has limits (e.g., Jensen, 1998; Spitz, 1999). Results of early intervention programs for preschoolers, such as Project Head Start, consistently showed a "fade out" of any gains in IQ points within 3 years of program termination (for reviews, see Clarke & Clarke, 1989; Locurto, 1991; Spitz, 1986). In addition, those few intervention programs that resulted in substantial and durable gains in IQs often failed to evince comparable improvement on tasks that are highly correlated with IQ. On the Milwaukee Project (e.g., Garber, 1988), for example, large differences of about 30 IQ points were observed between the experimental and control groups, but no significant differences were observed on measures of academic achievement closely related to intelligence, such as reading comprehension. These results suggest that these gains in IQ resulted from "teaching to the test" and did not reflect real increases in IQ (e.g., Jensen, 1989a). Last, although early research revealed that certain cognitive skills can be taught "at least to some of the people, some of the time" (Sternberg, 1996, p. 13), such learning typically was found to be quite domain specific and had limited general transfer to other cognitive domains (e.g., Detterman & Sternberg, 1993).

Contemporary Research on Malleability

Over the past two decades, a considerable amount of research has been conducted on cognitive-training programs for enhancing general cognitive ability, especially for ameliorating its decline among the elderly (e.g., Sala & Gobet, 2018). Underlying much of this research is the theory of *neural plasticity* (e.g., Karbach & Schubert, 2013). Neural plasticity refers to the ability of the nervous system to modify itself in response to experience or injury. The aim of many of these cognitive-training programs is to provide experiences that produce functional and anatomical changes in the neural system that result in improvements in cognitive function. The assumption underlying these programs is that increases in general cognitive ability—or at least certain broad abilities (e.g., fluid intelligence, memory, and processing speed)—are a by-product of domain-specific training.

Of the domain-specific cognitive-training programs studied in recent years, those involving working memory have attracted the most attention. One of the most basic principles of cognitive psychology is the limited capacity of short-term memory. This refers to the restriction of information from the perceptual system and of information retrieved from long-term memory that can be simultaneously processed. Although working memory often is used interchangeably with short-term memory, most cognitive scientists consider them distinct. Whereas short-term memory refers to a limited capacity store of information that is subject to rapid decay, working memory is defined as "a brain system that provides temporary storage and manipulation of the information necessary for . . . complex cognitive tasks" (Baddeley, 1992, p. 556). Because working memory is involved with the processing of complex information, which is directly related to psychometric g, research has focused on examining whether intensive training to increase the capacity of working memory has beneficial effects on other cognitive abilities that depend on it. As Melby-Lervåg and Hulme (2013) stated, it is important to note that these programs do not appear to rest on any detailed task analysis or theoretical account of the mechanisms by which such adaptive training regimes would be expected to improve working memory capacity. Rather, these programs seem to be based on what might be seen as a fairly naive "physical-energetic" model such that repeatedly "loading" a limited cognitive resource will lead to it increasing in capacity, perhaps somewhat analogously to strengthening a muscle by repeated use (p. 272).

According to the results of recent meta-analyses, working memory training programs have negligible effects on general cognitive ability and other cognitive abilities that involve working memory (Melby-Lervåg & Hulme, 2013; Melby-Lervåg, Redick, & Hulme, 2016)). Although reliable short-term improvements in verbal and nonverbal working memory typically are observed, these gains are not maintained several months after the end of training. More important theoretically and practically, however, are results of research on *near-* and *far-transfer* effects of working memory training programs. Near-transfer effects are effects on tasks that are highly similar to those trained and far-transfer effects are effects that are different from those trained. Melby-Lervåg and colleagues found no evidence of far-transfer effects on measures of verbal ability, word decoding, or arithmetic, even immediately after the end of working memory training. In another meta-analysis, Sala and Gobet (2018) also found that videogame training, music and chess instruction, and so-called brain-training programs (e.g., Lumosity) all had minimal effects on domain-general cognitive abilities, such as psychometric g. We address the practical implications of these findings in Chapter 9.

Summary on Malleability

Taken as a whole, research indicates that IQ is *imperfectly malleable*. With the exception of instances of extreme social isolation, neglect, and malnutrition, most environments are functionally equivalent for the development of intelligence. Indeed, in the absence of significant change to prevailing social and educational conditions, these findings imply that even substantial alteration of known environments will have a very limited effect on IQ. Of course, the failure of most intervention programs over the past 50 years to dramatically increase IQ does not preclude novel interventions from doing so in the future. Nonetheless, "if environmental interventions are to succeed, they must be truly novel ones, representing kinds of treatments that will be new to most populations" (Rowe, 1994, p. 223). Thus, early and contemporary research has shown that the malleability of intelligence is very limited.

Summary and Conclusion

Much of the research and theory on individual differences in intelligence can be summed up as follows:

- the distribution of general intelligence is approximately normal among people of the same age;
- intelligence develops from childhood to maturity, plateauing around 16 years of age;
- changes in cognitive abilities occur across the life span, with cognitive abilities related to Gc being the least affected and those related to Gf being the most affected;
- both genetic and environmental factors are importantly related to individual differences in intelligence, but the relative contribution of each changes over the life span;
- intelligence is related to brain size, as well as to brain structure and function; and
- the malleability of IQ is very limited.

CHAPTER 3

Ethics in Assessment

It is important that students in training and professionals engaged in the practice of psychology read and frequently review the most recent ethical guidelines from the American Psychological Association (APA; www.apa.org/ethics/code/index.aspx). For those engaged in the practice of school psychology (especially in school settings), we also recommend referencing similar guidelines from the National Association of School Psychologists (NASP; www.nasponline.org/standards/2010standards.aspx). This chapter highlights the ethical principles and standards from these two professional groups that are most relevant to testing children and adolescents, and it deals with nascent challenges related to technology, record keeping, and data security.

In many ways, this chapter forms one segment of the foundation for the remainder of the chapters in this book that focus on professional practices. For broader coverage of ethical standards and principles, as well as coverage of laws and court decisions relevant to testing children and adolescents, consider all of the rich content in Jacob, Decker, and Timmerman Lugg (2016), the ethical framework described by Belitz (2018), and case studies included in Armistead, Williams, and Jacob (2011) and Koocher and Keith-Spiegel (2016). Content from the *Standards for Educational and Psychological Testing* (American Educational Research Association [AERA], APA, & National Council on Measurement in Education [NCME], 2016) is discussed in Chapter 4.

The American Psychological Association

In its Ethical Principles of Psychologists and Code of Conduct, including the 2010 and 2016 Amendments, the APA (2002, 2010a, 2016) addresses five general principles that should serve as aspirations for professional practice: beneficence and nonmaleficence, fidelity and responsibility, integrity, justice, and respect for people's rights and dignity.[1] Table 3.1 presents descriptions of these general principles. The APA's

---

1. Standard 1.02 (Conflicts between Ethics and Law, Regulations, or Other Governing Legal Authority) and Standard 1.03 (Conflicts between Ethics and Organizational Demands) were revised in 2010, and Standard 3.04 (Avoiding Harm) was revised in 2016. Otherwise, at the time of publication of this book, the 2010 and 2016 Amendments mark APA's most recent ethical principles and code of conduct.

Table 3.1. General Ethical Principles from the American Psychological Association's Ethical Principles of Psychologists and Code of Conduct and Their Descriptions

Beneficence and Nonmaleficence
Psychologists strive to benefit those with whom they work and take care to do no harm.

Fidelity and Responsibility
Psychologists . . . uphold professional standards of conduct, clarify their professional roles and obligations, accept appropriate responsibility for their behavior, and seek to manage conflicts of interest that could lead to exploitation or harm.

Integrity
Psychologists seek to promote accuracy, honesty, and truthfulness in the science, teaching, and practice of psychology.

Justice
Psychologists . . . take precautions to ensure that their potential biases, the boundaries of their competence, and the limitations of their expertise do not lead to or condone unjust practices.

Respect for People's Rights and Dignity
Psychologists respect the dignity and worth of all people, and the rights of individuals to privacy, confidentiality, and self-determination. . . . Psychologists are aware of and respect cultural, individual, and role differences, including those based on age, gender, gender identity, race, ethnicity, culture, national origin, religion, sexual orientation, disability, language, and socioeconomic status and consider these factors when working with members of such groups. Psychologists try to eliminate the effect on their work of biases based on those factors.

Note: The official citations that should be used in referencing this material are as follows:

American Psychological Association. (2002). Ethical principles of psychologists and code of conduct. *American Psychologist, 57,* 1060–1073.
American Psychological Association. (2010a). Amendments to the 2002 ethical principles of psychologists and code of conduct. *American Psychologist, 65,* 493.
American Psychological Association. (2016). Revision of ethical standard 3.04 of the "Ethical Principles of Psychologists and Code of Conduct" (2002, as amended 2010). *American Psychologist, 71,* 900

Ethical Principles of Psychologists and Code of Conduct also includes 10 specific ethical standards. Table 3.2 lists each of these standards and highlights some that are most relevant to the practice of intelligence testing. In particular, Standard 9 comprises 11 standards related to assessment. They address four themes: *high-quality assessments, control of information, interpretation of assessment results,* and *competence.*

High-quality assessments are supported by three standards of Standard 9. Standard 9.01 states that psychologists should base their conclusions and recommendations offered in oral and written reports on evidence from the most appropriate methods of assessment. Opinions about a person's psychosocial functioning should be based on the results of a formal assessment, not on hearsay, rumors, or other sources of unverifiable information. In the same vein, Standard 9.02 conveys that psychologists should rely on sound evidence when selecting assessment techniques to use, modify, and interpret. More specifically, they should consider reliability and validity evidence (see

Table 3.2. Ethical Standards from the American Psychological Association's Ethical Principles of Psychologists and Code of Conduct (Including the 2010 and 2016 Amendments)

Standard 1: Resolving Ethical Issues

Standard 2: Competence
2.01 Boundaries of Competence
(b) Where scientific or professional knowledge in the discipline of psychology establishes that an understanding of factors associated with age, gender, gender identity, race, ethnicity, culture, national origin, religion, sexual orientation, disability, language, or socioeconomic status is essential for effective implementation of their services or research, psychologists have or obtain the training, experience, consultation, or supervision necessary to ensure the competence of their services, or they make appropriate referrals.

2.03 Maintaining Competence
Psychologists undertake ongoing efforts to develop and maintain their competence.

2.04 Bases for Scientific and Professional Judgments
Psychologists' work is based upon established scientific and professional knowledge of the discipline.

Standard 3: Human Relations
3.09 Cooperation with Other Professionals
When indicated and professionally appropriate, psychologists cooperate with other professionals in order to serve their clients/patients effectively and appropriately.

3.10 Informed Consent
(a) When psychologists conduct research or provide assessment, they obtain the informed consent of the individual or individuals using language that is reasonably understandable to that person or persons [in most circumstances].
(b) For persons who are legally incapable of giving informed consent, psychologists nevertheless (1) provide an appropriate explanation, (2) seek the individual's assent, (3) consider such persons' preferences and best interests, and (4) obtain appropriate permission from a legally authorized person, if such substitute consent is permitted or required by law.

Standard 4: Privacy and Confidentiality
4.01 Maintaining Confidentiality
Psychologists have a primary obligation and take reasonable precautions to protect confidential information obtained through or stored in any medium.

4.02 Discussing the Limits of Confidentiality
(a) Psychologists discuss with persons and organizations with whom they establish a scientific or professional relationship (1) the relevant limits of confidentiality and (2) the foreseeable uses of the information generated through their psychological activities.

(continued)

Table 3.2. *Continued*

Standard 5: Advertising and Other Public Statements

Standard 6: Record Keeping and Fees
6.01 Documentation of Professional and Scientific Work and Maintenance of Records
Psychologists create, and to the extent the records are under their control, maintain, disseminate, store, retain, and dispose of records and data relating to their professional and scientific work.

Standard 7: Education and Training

Standard 8: Research and Publication

Standard 9: Assessment

Standard 10: Therapy

Note: Copyright © 2010 by the American Psychological Association. Adapted with permission. The official citations that should be used in referencing this material are as follows:

American Psychological Association. (2002). Ethical principles of psychologists and code of conduct. *American Psychologist, 57,* 1060–1073.
American Psychological Association. (2010a). Amendments to the 2002 ethical principles of psychologists and code of conduct. *American Psychologist, 65,* 493.
American Psychological Association. (2016). Revision of ethical standard 3.04 of the "Ethical Principles of Psychologists and Code of Conduct" (2002, as amended 2010). *American Psychologist, 71,* 900.
No further reproduction or distribution is permitted without written permission from the American Psychological Association.

Chapter 4) relevant to their assessment techniques and the clients they serve; and when this evidence is not strong or plentiful, they should articulate the limitations of their assessment results. Thus, psychologists should work diligently in selecting, administering, scoring, and interpreting the results of their assessment instruments to ensure that they produce the most accurate results and yield the best outcomes for their clients. Finally, in Standard 9.08, psychologists are implored to avoid old and obsolete tests as a basis for current assessments, decisions about interventions, or recommendations. In reference to intelligence testing, tests normed more than 15 years ago should be avoided (see Chapter 4). Psychologists have about a 2-year window in which they should make the transition from an older version of a test to a more recently published version of that test, and we encourage careful consideration of the psychometric merits and practical constraints of adopting the newer test during the period leading up to the transition (see Beaujean, 2015a; Lichtenstein, 2010). Psychologists must stay up to date in their knowledge of contemporary tests and assessment practices.

Control of information is addressed in three standards. Two focus on informed consent and confidentiality. Standard 9.03 states that psychologists should ensure (1) that their clients are informed about the nature and purpose of the assessment, what other parties (if any) are privy to the information yielded by the assessment, and confidentiality and its limits as well as (2) that they (or, in the case of minors, their parents) consent to the assessment. Psychologists always inform clients about the kind of assessment they are about to conduct and tell them in a language they can understand why they are assessing them. Psychologists also obtain informed consent before conducting assessments, except when (1) the assessment is required by law or government regulations; (2) informed consent is implied as part of a customary educational, institutional, or organizational activity; or (3) one purpose of the testing is to evaluate a client's ability to make decisions independently of a guardian. Individuals with questionable capacity include children and people with cognitive impairments, developmental delays, or forms of dementia.

Standard 9.04 targets release of assessment results and conveys that psychologists release these results only to their clients, others to whom their clients have released the results, and others as required by law or court order. Assessment results include the following: a test taker's raw and standardized scores; the test taker's actual responses to test questions and stimuli; and the psychologist's notations and records about the test taker's statements and behavior during the assessment. In addition, in Standard 9.11, psychologists are implored to maintain *test security* by avoiding release of test manuals, test items, test pages, other testing materials, and test protocols, consistent with law and contractual obligations. Because well-developed assessment instruments are the products of years of effort to develop and refine them, it is important for test users to honor these efforts. More specifically, users are prohibited not only from duplicating these resources in hard copy and digital forms without permission but also from sharing specific test content—and even response strategies—that might inflate test scores due to invalidity in assessment (see Chapter 5). Essentially, revealing such information spoils the test's ability to differentiate those who possess the underlying knowledge, skills, or abilities from those who do not; in other words, validity is undermined. Consistent with this theme, in practice administrations during training, answers to items should not be provided upon a test taker's request, and at no point should others not in training be allowed to peruse the testing materials or be advised regarding how to improve performance on such tests.

It is important to note that completed test protocols are "educational records" in school settings. So, despite psychologists' being held to high standards for maintaining privacy and confidentiality of records as well as intellectual property rights, copyright interests, and test security standards, parents' rights to examine their offspring's records may supersede them. Thus, they may examine test protocols, including specific items, but this review typically is conducted with guidance by a competent professional. Parents, however, do not have a legal right to review a psychologist's personal notes.

Interpretation of results is addressed in three standards. Standard 9.06 implores psychologists to consider any attribute of the person being assessed that might undermine the accuracy of test interpretations. These attributes include external and internal influences not relevant to the knowledge, skills, or abilities targeted by the assessment, such as the client's test-taking approach as well as situational, personal, linguistic, and cultural differences (see Chapters 5 and 14). Standard 9.09 reminds psychologists that they are responsible for drawing valid conclusions from the assessment instruments that they employ as part of their assessments, regardless of who administers and scores these instruments and in cases of electronic administration and scoring. In addition, Standard 9.10 implores psychologists to convey assessment results clearly to clients.

Finally, *competence* is addressed not only by Standard 2 in general (see Table 3.2) but also by Standard 9.07 of Standard 9. In it, psychologists are encouraged to ensure that psychological techniques are employed only by qualified individuals or, in the case of training, under the supervision of those who are qualified.

The National Association of School Psychologists

In its Principles for Professional Ethics, the NASP (2010a) addresses many of the same themes, principles, and specific ethical standards as addressed in the APA's (2002, 2010a, 2016) Ethical Principles of Psychologists and Code of Conduct, but the NASP uses slightly different terms to describe them. In this section of the chapter, the NASP's broad ethical themes I, III, and IV are discussed first, then emphasis is placed on the broad ethical theme II because of its focus on assessment. Again, full access to the NASP's Principles for Professional Ethics (2010a) is available at www.nasponline.org/standards/2010standards.aspx.

GENERAL PRINCIPLES

Theme I addresses three principles related to respecting the dignity and rights of all individuals to whom school psychologists provide services. These principles are most similar to the five general ones offered by the APA (see Table 3.1). They implore school psychologists to honor the rights of others to participate (or to decline participation) in the services they provide. For example, school psychologists should ensure that parents provide informed consent (typically, written consent) for the provision of extensive or ongoing psychological or special education services (including assessment) for their children before these services begin. Although administration of all tests requires consent, because they could be seen as intrusions on privacy beyond what might be expected in the course of ordinary school activities, other assessment practices (such as review of records, classroom observations, academic screening, and progress monitoring) typically do not require parental consent, if those conducting them are employees of the district in which they practice. School psychologists also should consider seeking and obtaining children's assent (i.e., their affirmative agreement) to participate in assessment or intervention activities; such assent is not required legally or ethically, but it is best practice (Jacob et al., 2016). Further, these principles guarantee the rights to privacy and confidentiality to those who participate in school psychology services while promoting information about the limits of confidentiality. Finally, school psychologists should promote fairness and justice for all.

Theme III addresses honesty and integrity in interactions with parents, students, and other professionals. Its principles urge school psychologists to present their competencies accurately and to convey the nature and scope of their services clearly. School psychologists should collaborate and engage in respectful interactions with other professionals to promote the well-being of students and families with whom they work. In addition, they should strive to avoid relationships in which they may lose objectivity and diminish their effectiveness because of prior and ongoing personal relationships or their service in multiple professional roles (as evidenced through financial or other conflicts of interest).

Theme IV addresses responsibilities to society as a whole and to more specific institutions within it. Its five principles encourage school psychologists to apply their knowledge and skills to promote healthy environments for students. School psychologists should be aware of federal, state, and local laws governing educational and psychological practices. They should contribute to the instruction, mentoring, and supervision of those joining the field or desiring to expand their skills as well as conducting and disseminating research. Finally, they should be self-aware of ethical conflicts they may experience and act accordingly as well as provide peer monitoring to promote public trust in school psychology services.

COMPETENCE IN ASSESSMENT

Of all of the general ethical themes the NASP highlighted, Theme II most directly addresses competence and responsibilities in assessment practices. Its first principle addresses competence. School psychologists should reflect on their training experiences and engage in only those practices stemming from these experiences. They also are encouraged to enhance their skills in providing services to students and families from diverse backgrounds as well as to engage in other professional development activities (e.g., attending professional conferences and engaging in self-study) to remain current in their knowledge and practices. In the same vein, the second principle encourages conscientious professional behavior and acceptance of the responsibilities that come with being a school psychologist. Specific reference is made to ensuring the accuracy of written reports, communicating assessment results and other information clearly, and monitoring the effects of recommendations and interventions. (See Chapter 10 for more information about preparing psychological reports and presenting information to parents and other caregivers.)

The third principle directly addresses assessment and intervention practices; we highlight specific recommendations addressing assessment practices. One series of recommendations addresses measurement integrity and the fidelity of interpretations. For instance, school psychologists should rely on scientific evidence to select optimal assessment instruments. In particular, they should select those with the strongest body of reliability and validity evidence supporting their use for the intended purposes (see Chapter 4). They should not violate the rules for uniform administration of standardized assessment instruments (see Chapter 5); if they do so, by error or by design through the use of test accommodations, they should report this in their oral and written descriptions of assessment results (see Chapter 10). Further, they should use the most recently published and up-to-date normative data available (see Chapter 4) and exercise sound professional judgment in evaluating the results of computer-generated summaries of results and interpretive narratives.

Theme II also includes recommendations addressing general ideals of assessment practices. These ideals include conducting broad and comprehensive assessments. They should stem from multiple sources of information, including informants (e.g., teachers, parents, and students) and assessment instruments, and represent all areas of suspected disability, such as health, vision, hearing, social-emotional functioning, motor abilities, and communicative status. When these comprehensive assessments are complete, results should be presented to others in a clear and meaningful way (see Chapter 10). In addition, several recommendations are provided for assessing children from culturally and linguistically diverse backgrounds. For example, school psychologists should conduct assessments that are valid for all of those assessed. Thus, the process of selecting assessment instruments should include consideration of the test taker's disabilities and other limitations, as well as the test taker's cultural, linguistic, and experiential background (see Chapters 5 and 14). Further, administration of assessment instruments and interpretation of their results also should take into account these characteristics of the test taker to ensure that the results accurately represent the targeted constructs being measured. For example, school psychologists should promote quality control in the training and use of interpreters during testing practices (see Chapter 14).

Theme II also addresses record keeping. In particular, school psychologists are implored to include in their records only documented and relevant information from reliable sources, which include psychological reports (see Chapter 10). Consideration of this standard should ensure that school psychologists report only information that is directly relevant to the referral concerns or eligibility decisions. For example, they should reflect on whether personal information about a student's immediate and extended family (e.g., histories of substance use or mental health problems) is relevant to the referral for assessment. In addition, they should ensure that they report the source of such information to support its truth value.

The final principle under Theme II addresses intellectual property and copyright law, as well as record keeping, test security, and parents' and guardians' access to testing material (as previously discussed). It is particularly important to make sure that access to assessment results on computers and computer networks is restricted to authorized professionals. If this is not possible, then it is best to avoid the use of networked computers altogether and to use the best personal computer security available. Psychologists also should assume that e-mail is permanent and potentially public.

Technology, Record Keeping, and Data Security

Technology has altered the realm of administration and scoring of intelligence test during the past decade, and we feel increasing pressure as graduate educators to expand our use of technologies that go well beyond the physical test kit and paper-and-pencil-based administration formats. For example, in a survey by Benson et al. (2019) conducted in 2017, more than 85% of school psychologists reported that they scored intelligence tests online or used computer software, and about 32% said they did so exclusively. Further, almost half reported that they administered these tests online. Pearson's Q-Interactive and PAR iConnect facilitate online administration and scoring of several intelligence tests (see, e.g., Chapter 6). Although we are not fully comfortable as graduate educators with the full-scale adoption of tests administered in this manner without empirical evidence supporting their equivalence with the standard test administration format, we embrace administration and scoring technologies that reduce clerical errors in scoring (see Styck & Walsch, 2016). Further, we understand the potential for online administrations to reduce related errors during testing and produce more exacting scores across a wider variety of constructs than that currently measured (e.g., reaction time). These findings of widespread use of these technologies by Benson et al. indicate the importance of understanding how ethical standards apply to how these technologies should be employed.

It is important to evaluate new assessment technologies, such as administration of tests via tablet computers (e.g., iPads), to determine whether they measure the same knowledge, skills, and abilities as well as or better than their tangible counterparts. Sometimes, *comparability* and *equivalence* are used to refer to this desired property. This question of alternate versions of tests is addressed further in Chapter 4 when discussing reliability and validity, as ethical test users should ensure that new instruments meet the standards of practice before employing them with their clients.

Although we feel confident that the question of the comparability or equivalence of the reliability and validity evidence supporting online testing can be evaluated to a degree that is consistent with both APA and NASP ethics codes, it is not as clear which standards we should follow to maintain the privacy of those with whom we work when we employ digital and cloud-based storage. As evident in Table 3.1, APA's (2002, 2010a, 2016) Ethical Principles of Psychologists and Code of Conduct addresses privacy and confidentiality in Section 4. In particular, standard 4.01 compels us to "take reasonable precautions to protect confidential information obtained through or stored in any medium" (p. 7). Along the same line, standard 4.02, in addressing the limits of confidentiality, conveys that those "who offer services, products, or information via electronic transmission inform clients/patients of the risks to privacy and limits of confidentiality" (p. 7). In addition, Section 6 deals with record keeping and addresses how psychologists should maintain the security of the information they collect and record. Standard 6.01 conveys they should "maintain, disseminate, store, retain, and dispose of records and data relating to their professional and scientific work" (p. 9). Likewise, Standard 6.02 implores them to "maintain confidentiality in creating, storing, accessing, transferring, and disposing of records under their control, whether these are written, automated, or in any other medium" and offers a caveat related to situations in which "confidential information concerning recipients of psychological services is entered into databases or systems of records available to persons whose access has not been consented to by the recipient" (p. 9). These points are amplified in the APA (2007) record-keeping guidelines (APA, 2007; https://www.apa.org/pubs/journals/features/record-keeping.pdf)—especially guidelines 3, 6, and 9.

NASP's (2010a) Principles for Professional Ethics discuss these topics when addressing privacy and confidentiality (Principle I.2) and school-based record keeping (Principle II.4). Most notably, Standard I.2.2 states that school psychologists "do not seek or store private information about clients that is not needed in the provision of services" (p. 5). Further, Standard II.4.1 states that

> school psychologists discuss with parents and adult students their rights regarding creation, modification, storage, and disposal of psychological and educational records that result from the provision of services. Parents and adult students are notified of the electronic storage and transmission of personally identifiable school psychological records and the associated risks to privacy. (p. 8)

Standard II.4.7 conveys that "school psychologists protect electronic files from unauthorized release or modification (e.g., by using passwords and encryption)" (pp. 8–9).

Users of this technology should strive to keep these ethical principles and standards in mind as they apply them to their current practices. Still, they should be prepared to answer some difficult questions (Clark, Gulin, Heller, & Vrana, 2017; Devereaux & Gottlieb, 2012). For example, what information should be shared with parents when obtaining informed consent for assessment? Should they be told that both personal information and test results will be stored by a test publishing company, perhaps ad infinitum? To protect the privacy of information that will be saved on a server, test users should include as little personal identifying information as possible (beyond date of birth, which is used for determining norms) when entering information about the test takers they assess. Rather than employing full names, they should use initials; school names and other identifying information should be omitted. More broadly, Lustgarten (2015) offered practical strategies to promote privacy of information that all educators, practitioners, and administrators should review. These strategies include employing firewalls and passwords on all devices (including iPads), ensuring that data are transferred following encryption, using devoted hardware (iPads for only administration and scoring and not e-mailing), and employing stand-alone (air-gapped) computers for storage of information.

Summary

Intelligence testing should be grounded in the ethics of psychology. We find that with each additional reading of the APA's (2002, 2010a, 2016) Ethical Principles of Psychologists and Code of Conduct and the NASP's (2010a) Principles for Professional Ethics, we are inspired to do more than is commonplace and to be stronger advocates for students, families, and schools. We also are reminded of general and specific standards that we meet only partially or inconsistently.

On the one hand, we should aspire to ideals such as beneficence, justice, and integrity; strive for excellence in all aspects of our practices; and engage in lifelong learning to achieve and maintain expertise in professional ethics. On the other hand, we should be practical in applying day-to-day ethical practices involving assessment. We should remember that our clients have the right to know the services we provide and the right to privacy; that assessment results are privileged and sensitive information; that our test content should remain secure to ensure its validity in assessment; and that we should strive to use the best assessment instruments and promote optimal testing environments to produce the most meaningful test results. We hope that the following chapters provide the information that will allow you, our readers, to reach these goals most effectively.

CHAPTER 4
Basic Psychometric Principles That Inform Score Interpretation

Before interpreting the scores yielded by intelligence tests, it is important to fully understand the calculations and characteristics of these scores as well as the evidence supporting their use. This chapter begins with a description of test scores, and it continues with a review of the most critical characteristics of tests and related measures—including norming, item scaling, and the reliability and validity of scores. With this information, you will be better able to select the most appropriate intelligence tests for your needs, based in part on the age, ability level, and backgrounds of those you serve.

Test Scores

As we begin this chapter, we want to draw attention to some of the common features evident across intelligence tests. First, check out Figure 4.1. It contains a variety of items such as those seen in individually and group-administered intelligence tests. They are clustered into three item sets to feature their similarities and differences. Item Set 1 focuses on the different ways that knowledge of a word can be assessed; Item Set 2 highlights an array of items targeting reasoning skills; and Item Set 3 demonstrates how items focusing on short-term memory (or working memory) may increase in complexity. Try to complete each item, and while doing so, think about what steps must be followed to produce a correct response. Look at the stimuli—words, numbers, images, and shapes. Consider what basic skills and prior knowledge are needed to complete the items correctly. Consider the different actions you must engage in to complete the items.

Figure 4.1. Example Test Items in Three Sets

EXAMPLE TEST ITEMS IN THREE SETS

Item Set 1

1. "What does what the word amble mean?"
2. Circle the word that means the same as amble: Large   Walk   Plenty   Hop
3. "Point to the person who is ambling."

4. "Show me how to amble."
5. Write a word that completes this analogy: Jump is to leap as amble is to what?

_____

Item Set 2

1. Turtle is to slow as cheetah is to which of the following?   Lazy   Excited   Fast   Soft
2. In a race, the cat runs faster than the dog, the horse runs slower than the dog, and the zebra runs faster than the cat. Who wins the race?   Cat   Dog   Horse   Zebra
3. By following the number pattern, tell me what number comes next in the series: 5, 10, 15, and then what?
4. Complete this series by writing in the final number: 2, 4, 16, ___
5. Write in the number in the parenthesis that would complete the fourth pair: (7, 5) (8, 6) (9, 7) (10, __)
6.

Circle the picture below that goes in the empty box above.

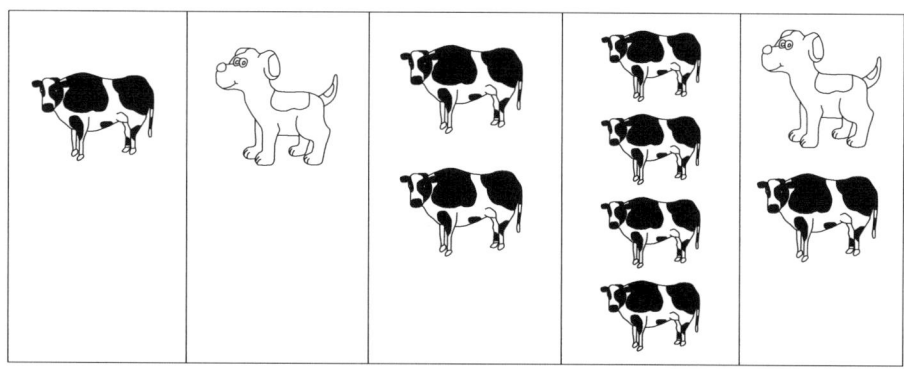

7. Tell me what number goes in the empty cell below:

8	40	35
5	25	20
3		10

8. The two dogs go together a certain way. Which cow here (point to the array of four on the right) follows the same pattern with this cow (point to the cow on the left) as the dogs follow?

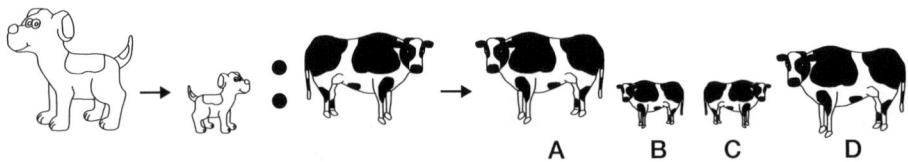

9. Which shape in the array (A, B, C, or D) completes the analogy?

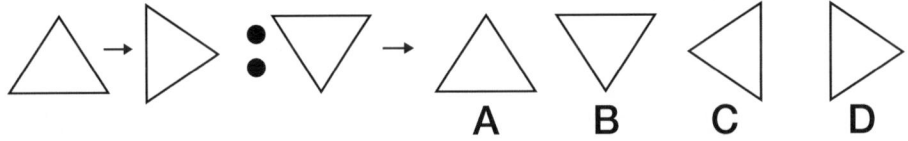

BASIC PSYCHOMETRIC PRINCIPLES   47

Item Set 3

1. Repeat these numbers to me: 49283 (presented at 1-second intervals).
2. Listen to these numbers and repeat them in reverse order: 49283.
3. Listen to these numbers and repeat them in decending order, from highest to lowest: 49283.
4. Listen to these numbers and tap on the corresponding circles below when I say "Go.": 49283
5. Watch me tap these circles, and then tap them in ascending order, from lowest to highest, according to the numbers within the circles when I say "Go." (Then, tap the numbers 49283—without vocalizing them—at 1-second intervals and then say "Go.")

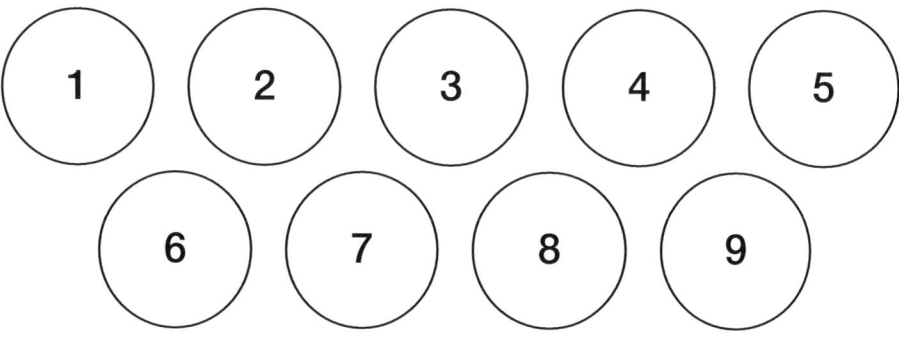

Across every intelligence test, the most important scores they yield will be based on an examinee's performance across items—perhaps 50 to 100 items—just like those in Figure 4.1. Most items on intelligence tests are scored 0 (if incorrect) or 1 (if correct), but some items are scored on a multi-point scale (0, 1, and 2), and others are scored considering bonus points for speed (0 for an incorrect response and 6, 5, or 4 based on the length of completion time in seconds). Item-level scores are the foundation for all of the other scores intelligence tests yield, but interpreting them has substantial limitations. Most notably, item-level scores are highly unreliable. Items are one-time experiences and reflect only a small slice of knowledge, skills, or abilities in an area. As a result, unintentional and unexpected events during testing, certain test-taking strategies, or other idiosyncratic behaviors of the test taker may lead to scores that do not well reflect the intended goal of the item. For example, an opportunistic test taker may guess correctly on an item that seems to be well beyond their skill level, leading to an overestimate of their skills in an area. On the other hand, an anxious test taker may be unable to recall information they typically know well, leading to a deflated score associated with their knowledge in a domain. Good luck and bad luck, in terms of influences undermining measurement accuracy, are real phenomena that should be minimized during testing situations.

Everyone who has taken a quiz knows that item scores are used to determine scores such as *percentage correct*. If a test taker answered 15 of the 20 items on the quiz correctly, their "grade" on a 100-point scale would be 75 out of 100 or 75%. More precisely, the percentage correct score was 75%. Despite common experience in completing quizzes and calculating this type of score, percentage correct rarely is reported from intelligence tests. Their subtests include items that tend to increase in difficulty, so each item cannot be treated as equal, as is implicit in this formula. Percentage correct scores should not be confused with percentile rank values, which are discussed later in this chapter.

Table 4.1 includes facsimile score tables such as those appearing on the covers of test records and in scoring output from software and Web-based interfaces. Scan the tables. The top one alone has at least 30 numerical values. What information is most important to review? What is the difference between subtests addressed in the top table and composites addressed in the bottom table? What are raw scores, and how are they different from scaled scores, age equivalents, percentile ranks, and all of the other scores reported? Are any of these scores on the same scale? It seems like higher scores generally are associated with other high scores, so are some of the scales like temperature measured in Celsius and Fahrenheit or distance measured in meters and feet? What are confidence intervals, and is something noteworthy about being 95% confident? Most of the scores appear to be average. That's good, right? But what about the low score on Subtest 1? Is that really bad? Stay engaged, as this section of the chapter will address these questions.

RAW SCORES

As evident in Table 4.1, one of the first scores that will be apparent is the *raw score*. In this case, the adjective *raw* refers to the fact that the score has not been changed

Table 4.1. Sample Score Tables from an Intelligence Test

Subtest Raw Score to Scaled Score Conversion Table

Subtest Name	Raw Score	Age Equivalent	Scaled Score	Percentile Rank	95% Confidence Interval	Score Label
Subtest 1	14	6-2	5	5	3-7	Low
Subtest 2	22	8-10	9	37	7-11	Average
Subtest 3	17	8-10	9	37	15-19	Average
Subtest 4	16	8-2	8	25	6-10	Average
Subtest 5	26	9-10	10	50	8-12	Average
Subtest 6	13	8-10	9	37	7-11	Average

Sum of Scaled Scores to Composite Score Conversion Table

Composite Name	Sum of Scaled Scores	Composite Score	Percentile Rank	95% Confidence Interval	Score Label
Composite 1	26	84	14	78-93	Low Average
Composite 2	33	91	27	84-99	Average
Composite 3	39	97	42	90-105	Average
Total Composite	98	87	19	82-93	Low Average

beyond a basic form. The raw scores most typically mentioned in test manuals and research represent the number of correct responses and the number of points earned, but occasionally they are the number of errors made during a subtest. Most typically, the raw score is the sum of item scores across items of the same type (grouped into what commonly are called *subtests*). It is this summing of numerous item scores across reasonably correlated items that builds the explanatory and predictive power evidenced by intelligence tests (Jensen, 1981).

Although raw scores are the foundation for all other scores, interpreting them in their basic form has substantial limitations. In particular, they lack meaningfulness in determining whether performance can be considered "normal" or exceptionally high or low. For instance, a raw score of 10 on a subtest targeting vocabulary knowledge may be well above average for a 5-year-old in comparison to same-age peers but well below average for an 18-year-old. When interpreting someone's test score, we need to know, at a minimum, something about the group of persons with whom they are being compared (the norm group) and how they performed in comparison with that group. A test's usefulness will be strongly influenced by the group(s) on which it was normed. Fortunately, the norm group of most intelligence tests is a large, representative sample of people. The process of norm referencing, discussed later in this chapter, addresses this limitation.

AGE EQUIVALENTS

Age equivalents are reported by some intelligence tests. In Table 4.1, they range from 6-2 to 9-10, as they typically are expressed in years and months with a hyphen between the numbers, such as 7-1, 8-11, and 10-10. (Sometimes, the years and months are separated by a colon.) Age equivalents represent the age level (in years and months) that maps onto the examinee's raw score in a confusing way. For example, the age equivalent of 6-2 for the raw score of 14 for Subtest 1 (evident in Table 4.1) means that, when the performance of those in the norming sample was considered by the test developers across narrow age groupings, children in their second month of their sixth year (hence 6-2) earned, on average, a raw score of 14 on this subtest. Although many children at this age level had a higher raw score, and many others had a lower raw score, the age equivalent to which the examinee's raw score is anchored is the score we would expect that most children of a certain age would earn.

But what does this score convey? Is 6-2 a high or low score—better than expected or not so much? It depends on the age of the examinee. Of course, for an adult, this probably would be an exceptionally low score. However, based on these score tables and review of raw scores and age equivalents, we do not know and cannot infer the age of the test taker in question.

Traditionally (but erroneously), age equivalents have been interpreted as reflecting "mental age," and inferences indicating that a test taker has the "mind of a 2-year-old" and the like have been drawn from them. They are gross representations of an individual's level of development inferred from cross-sectional patterns of scores from a norming sample. The comparisons across age levels are statistical and not necessarily related to particular developmental milestones; age equivalents do not reference criteria that should be met at a certain age (e.g., being able to speak in three-word sentences by age 2, or being able to identify all of the continents by age 9). Because the reference point at every age level is the mean raw score for that small group, age equivalents also do not reference the range of individual differences in abilities at every age level. In the same vein, they do not indicate that about half of test takers at every age level (e.g., at 6 years, 2 months) obtain a higher raw score and that about half of test takers at that age level obtain a lower raw score. Perhaps most important, they do not reveal how deviant a test taker is from same-age peers. Finally, like the raw scores on which they are based, age equivalents are prone to variation due to error in measurement. As a result, on poorly constructed tests, age equivalents may appear to jump around a lot due to unequal units along their scales. As an extreme example, a 1-point increase in a raw score of 14 (to 15) may mean a 2-year increase in age equivalents (from 6-2 to 8-2), whereas the same change in raw scores at one point higher (from 15 to 16) may lead to only a 1-month increase in age equivalents (from 8-2 to 8-3). Although well-scaled items (due to improved scaling technology) have lessened problems with unequal units along age equivalent scales, these scores are particularly prone to misinterpretation.

GRADE EQUIVALENTS

Like age equivalents, grade equivalents typically are expressed in grade levels and months of the school year (10 months at most are considered; 0 is September), with a decimal point in between the numbers, such as 7.1, 8.9, and 10.5. (If the value on the right side of the point exceeds 9, the score probably is an age equivalent.) As grade equivalents are obtained using the same basic method as age equivalents, they reflect the particular point during the school year at which the average raw score earned by a narrow grade-based group equals the raw score an individual earned. Grade equivalents are interpreted more frequently when yielded by achievement tests than when yielded by intelligence tests. For example, a parent might conclude (albeit erroneously) from a grade equivalent of 5.0 that "their first grader is reading on a fifth-grade level."

Like age equivalents, the comparisons across grade levels and months of the school year are statistical and not content related; grade equivalents do not reference criteria that should be met in a certain grade or school curriculum. They also do not indicate that about half of children at the grade level associated with the score in question would obtain a higher raw score and that about half of children at that grade level would obtain a lower raw score. Nor do they indicate how deviant a child is from expectations based on comparison to same-grade peers. They also have unequal units along their scale. Further, their use assumes that growth is consistent across the academic year and across school years, which clearly is not the case in the achievement areas (Nese et al., 2012; Skibbe, Grimm, Bowles, & Morrison, 2012). Grade equivalents are not produced by most intelligence tests; based on our review, none of the intelligence tests described in this book except the Woodcock-Johnson IV Tests of Cognitive Abilities (Schrank, McGrew, & Mather, 2014b) produces grade equivalents.

NORM-BASED SCORES

The most commonly used and meaningful scores from intelligence tests represent individual differences in abilities inferred from the deviation of the individual's performance from the average performance of a group to which they belong. They are scaled scores, composites scores, and percentile ranks evident in Table 4.1. In order to interpret these scores accurately, it is important to understand their foundation in data from norm groups.

As discussed in Chapter 1, the foundation for the scientific study of intelligence is the natural phenomenon of individual differences in cognitive abilities; individuals of all ages differ in their level and speed of performance on cognitive tasks. In the practice of psychology, an understanding of these individual differences is derived from consideration of where an individual's test performance falls when compared to expectations established via a norm sample. A norm sample ideally is a large sample of persons whose characteristics are similar to those of the individual being tested (e.g., age); this sample produces results (i.e., norms) to which the individual's results can be compared. These norms allow for a better understanding of typical levels of performance (and variation around it) at different levels of development. Ideally, norm samples would include every individual in a population, but doing so is unfeasible. Instead, norm samples should be as large and as representative of the targeted population as possible.

Sometimes the term *standardization sample* is used to refer to the norm sample. For the most part, these terms are used interchangeably, but standardization refers to the use of the same directions, sample items, practice trials, feedback, and scoring guidelines for everyone completing a test. Standardization is a necessity for accurate and comparable results to be obtained across administration of tests, and without it, accurate norms would be impossible. We suppose that criterion-referenced tests, which typically make no reference to the performance of comparable others, could stem from standardization samples and not norm samples; for most tests, however, standardization samples and norm samples are the same.

Norm samples are the products of extensive efforts to develop test items, standardize them across those administering and scoring the items, evaluate the reactions of examiners and examinees in real-world settings, and then have a multitude of examinees complete them under those standardized conditions. The database that results from the extensive administration of those items across a test is the norm sample, and it enhances understanding of the typical levels of performance and variation around it at different levels of development. Age-based norms are the most common type of norms used with intelligence tests. Some intelligence tests cover an extremely broad age range (from toddlerhood to late adulthood), whereas others cover a narrower age range (e.g., 6 to 16 years).

In traditional norming procedures, a sizable sample of volunteers at every age level completes the intelligence tests under standardized conditions. From their performance, descriptive statistics (e.g., *means*, the average score, and *standard deviations*, a measure of variation of scores) are obtained; each raw score is then transformed into a standardized score (sometimes through an intermediate score based on a sophisticated multivariate analysis called item response theory); and norm tables are constructed to link those raw scores to the norm-referenced scores for test users. First, we discuss the general class of norm-referenced scores called standardized scores, then we discuss the associated percentile ranks. Later, we discuss norm tables as they relate to scoring intelligence tests and determining whether sufficiently easy items, sufficiently difficult items, and a steady progression of increasingly difficult items are present.

Standardized scores. Standardized scores stem from the comparison of raw scores (or sums of any type of scores) to a mean score from a group with reference to the standard deviation of that group. Most graduate students and professionals with undergraduate training in statistics are familiar with the formula for calculating z scores. For any distribution, z scores have a mean of 0 and a standard deviation of 1, and they typically range from -3.0 to $+3.0$. Positive z scores indicate that the raw score in question is higher in magnitude than the mean for the sample, and negative z scores indicate that the raw score in question is lower in magnitude than the mean for the sample.

A z score for an individual can be calculated as a difference between an obtained score (X) and a sample mean divided by the standard deviation from the sample. For example, if the raw score mean across 100 third graders who completed a vocabulary subtest was 20 and the standard deviation for this group was 4, the following z scores could be produced for test takers with raw scores of 20, 28, and 14.

- A test taker with a raw score of 20 receives a z score of 0.
- A test taker with a raw score of 28 receives a z score of 2.0.
- A test taker with a raw score of 14 receives a z score of -1.5.

All standardized scores are calculated in essentially the same manner, but the means and standard deviations of these standardized scores are set subjectively. (These set points may be very different from the original raw score distribution, but that should not matter very much when administering and scoring intelligence tests.) As a result of the standardization of raw scores, each standardized score represents its proximity to the mean of the referenced norm group. As a result, individual differences in the targeted ability are represented in these standardized scores. Standardizing the raw score allows for comparisons to be made between scores from the same intelligence test or across scores from different tests. In contrast to age equivalents and grade equivalents, standardized scores have more equal units along the scale.

The most common type of standardized scores yielded by intelligence tests are deviation IQ scores; they often are called standard scores. They have a mean of 100 and a standard deviation of 15. Most IQs and closely associated composite scores across intelligence tests are scaled by using these deviation IQ scores; these scores are listed as Composite Scores in the bottom half of Table 4.1. Intelligence tests typically are limited to a range of deviation IQ scores from four standard deviations below the mean (40) to four standard deviations above the mean (160). Score range labels often indicate that deviation IQ scores from approximately 10 points above and below 100 are in the Average range, and additional score range labels are applied to scores approximately 10 points above and below the Average range (e.g., 81 to 89 = Low Average and 110 to 119 = High Average). More information on these score labels is provided in Chapter 10.

In order to differentiate subtest scores from IQ and other composite scores, intelligence test authors often have them yield other types of standardized scores. Some intelligence test subtests yield scaled scores, which have a mean of 10 and a standard deviation of 3. Those reported in Table 4.1 for subtests use this metric. Score range labels often indicate that scaled scores from approximately 8 to 12 are in the Average range, and additional score range labels are applied to scores approximately 2 points above and below the Average range (e.g., 13 to 14 = High Average and 6 to 7 = Low Average). However, other tests use T scores, which have a mean of 50 and a standard deviation of 10. As is evident in Figure 2.1 (in Chapter 2), these standardized scores generally are interchangeable with the deviation IQ scores.

Although these three types of standardized scores typically are interchangeable, the ranges of these scores and their scaling make a difference. For example, as evident in Figure 2.1, scaled scores are limited to a lower end range of 3 and 1/3 standard deviations (i.e., a scaled score of 1), whereas deviation IQ scores and T scores can go many standard deviations lower before reaching a score of 1, the end point on the scale. In addition, scores with smaller standard deviations (e.g., scaled scores) rather than larger standard deviations (e.g., deviation IQ scores) lead to more abrupt score "jumps" between one area of the normal curve and another area with one score point difference. Because standardized scores tend to be limited to whole numbers, each scaled score spans 1/3 of a standard deviation, each T score 1/10 of a standard deviation, and each deviation IQ score 1/15 of a standard deviation. That is, gaps are far wider in the normal curve between scores for scaled scores than for deviation IQ scores. For example, as evident in Figure 2.1, the amount of area under the curve between a scaled score of 10 and a scaled score of 13 is almost 35%; in contrast, the difference between a deviation IQ score of 100 and a deviation IQ score of 103 is only about 3%. We considered these limitations in subtest scaling (versus IQ and composite scores that tend to use deviation IQ scores) when recommending that subtest scores not typically be interpreted in Chapter 8.

Percentile ranks. Like standardized scores, percentile ranks provide a representation of an examinee's relative position (following rank order) within the norm group. In particular, they indicate the percentage of the norm group that scored the same as or lower than the examinee. Values tend to range from 0.1 to 99.9. Percentile ranks sometimes are expressed as percentages that reflect the area under the normal curve (see Figure 2.1). Like standardized scores, they allow comparisons to be made between scores within and across intelligence tests. For example, referencing Table 4.1, the percentile rank for Subtest 1 indicates that the test taker's raw score was as high or higher than only about 5% of those in the comparison norm group (likely based on age norms), whereas the percentile rank for Subtest 5 indicates that the test taker's raw score was as high or higher than about half of those in the comparison norm group. The same comparisons can be made for the composite scores, despite the fact that the composite scores are associated with different standardized scores (i.e., deviation IQ scores versus scaled scores). The test taker's score was as high or higher than about 14% of those in the comparison norm group on Composite 1 but as high or higher than about 42% on Composite 3.

Percentile ranks share some limitations with standardized scores, and they have some limitations of their own. Like some standardized scores, their range is somewhat limited. When percentile ranks as whole numbers are considered, they reach a ceiling at the 99th percentile and a floor at the 1st percentile. Scores higher or lower than these points will yield percentile rank differences of a fraction of a point (e.g., 99.53, 99.62, 99.69, 99.74, etc.), and at another point (approximately 3 2/3 standard deviations above or below the mean), the percentile ranks are differentiated by thousandths of a point. These decimal fractions are challenging to explain clearly, and we discuss them further in Chapter 10. In contrast to standardized scores, percentile ranks have unequal units along their scale. As evident in Figure 2.1, a 10-point difference between percentile ranks near the mean (e.g., between percentile ranks of 40 and 50) indicates small differences in standardized scores (i.e., deviation IQ scores of about 96 and 100) and would thus be of little importance, whereas in the tails of the normal curve, a 10-point difference between percentile ranks indicates substantial and perhaps important differences.

CONFIDENCE INTERVALS

Table 4.1 presents confidence intervals expressed as a range of scores (from low to high), and they are always on the same scale as their associated standardized score (e.g., scaled scores, T scores, or deviation IQ scores). In fact, the table presents confidence intervals ranges based on scale scores (for subtests) and deviation IQ scores (for composites). These confidence intervals drive home the point that no test and no score is error free. They all are tainted by random measurement error.

Just as we commonly hear the results of political polls and opinion surveys followed by mention of the margin for error (e.g., "plus or minus 5 percentage points"), many norm-referenced scores can be surrounded by bands of error. The width of the bands of error tell us how much to expect a test taker's obtained score (the single norm-referenced score yielded by the test) to vary from their "true score" if the test taker were administered the same test repeatedly.

Picture two archers of varying skill levels shooting at a target on a calm day. Both archers aim at the target's center, the bull's-eye, and both shoot 10 arrows. Because neither archer is perfectly accurate and because environmental influences, such as wind and humidity, affect the trajectory of each arrow, we would expect arrows to be scattered about the target in a predictable pattern—with a higher density in the middle of the target and a lower density toward the borders of the target. However, these patterns will be likely to differ for the two archers. The more skilled archer will hit the bull's-eye occasionally and will have a greater number of arrows near it and relatively few arrows near the border. In contrast, the less skilled archer may hit near the bull's-eye with a couple of arrows but will scatter others around the target, with a greater number of arrows near the border and perhaps some arrows missing the target altogether.

The archers' skill level is equivalent to *reliability*. Less skilled archers scatter their arrows across a wider range of segments of the target than more skilled archers, and less reliable tests produce scores that are more likely to vary more across the range of hypothetical administrations of the test than the scores of more reliable tests. In addition, to continue with this metaphor, it is possible (although highly improbable) that the more skilled archer will miss the target altogether with one arrow, while hitting the bull's-eye with another and coming very close to it with the vast majority of their other arrows. In such a case, we could hypothesize that the one errant shot is due to "bad luck" or some extraneous, distracting influence, but we would understand that although it is not likely to happen again, such a bad shot is not outside the hypothetical range of possible shots. However, the shot does not appear to be representative of the archer's true skill level. Similarly, the less skilled archer may hit the bull's-eye while missing the target altogether across all other shots; this perfect shot could be considered a random, improbable occurrence (i.e., really good luck) within the hypothetical range of possible shots and not representative of the archer's true skill level. The most accurate estimates of an archer's skill level would stem from shooting multiple arrows across multiple trials. Similarly, the most reliable scores tend to stem from multiple items from multiple subtests considered together in a composite score.

In order to better understand confidence intervals, it is necessary to understand the standard error of measurement (*SEM*). The *SEM* is based in part on the reliability coefficient (most commonly, the internal consistency reliability coefficient, discussed in the next section); the other key variable is the standard deviation of the score in question. Confidence intervals are most commonly reported for standardized scores (and specifically for deviation IQ scores), so we focus on them here. The formula for the *SEM* requires that an estimate of error be obtained by subtracting the reliability coefficient from 1.0. The square root of this difference is then obtained, and it is multiplied by the standard deviation of the score (in the case of a deviation IQ score, that would be 15).

If the reliability of a score is .97, and its standard deviation is 15, the formula can be applied in this manner:

$SEM = 15 (SQRT(1 - .97))$
$SEM = 15 (SQRT(.03))$
$SEM = 15 (.1732)$
$SEM = 2.60$

Notice what happens to the *SEM* when the reliability of the score is far lower (.80):

$SEM = 15 (SQRT(1 - .80))$
$SEM = 15 (SQRT(.20))$
$SEM = 15 (.4472)$
$SEM = 6.71$

As a result of the lower reliability of the second score, the *SEM* value has increased about 2½ times, and that is concerning.

This *SEM* is the standard deviation of the distribution of *true scores* around, most basically, the actual score obtained by a test taker. True scores are hypothetical entities that represent—with perfect accuracy—the targeted knowledge, skill, or ability. If we consider the normal curve discussed earlier in this chapter and presented in Figure 2.1, the same rules for area under the normal curve apply to the distribution of error around the obtained score. For example, because the *SEM* is the standard deviation of the distribution of hypothetical true scores, we know that the chance is about 68% that an individual's true score would fall between 1 *SEM* above the obtained score (the "plus") and 1 *SEM* below the obtained score (the "minus"). For instance, considering a test taker's obtained IQ of 100 and a *SEM* of 2.6, we can anticipate that a test taker's true IQ would fall within the range of 97.4 and 102.6 about two out of three times (i.e., 68% of the time).

It is rare that *SEM* values themselves are reported in the practice of psychology. From our experience, they occasionally are reported for subtests, but usually, they are transformed into confidence intervals. Thus, knowing the area under the curve, we can use *SEM* values to calculate confidence intervals that represent the range of true scores around the obtained score beyond 1 *SEM*. A confidence interval is calculated by multiplying the *SEM* by standard deviation units expressed as *z* scores. For example, we would multiply the *SEM* by 1.65 to obtain the 90% confidence interval, by 1.96 to obtain the 95% confidence interval, and by 2.58 to obtain the 99% confidence interval.

For reference, the *SEM* of 2.6 (based on a score with a reliability of .97) produces these confidence intervals:

90% confidence interval: ±4.29
95% confidence interval: ±5.10
99% confidence interval: ±6.71

In comparison, for our score with a reliability of .80, considering the *SEM* of 6.71, these are the confidence intervals:

90% confidence interval: ±11.07
95% confidence interval: ±13.15
99% confidence interval: ±17.31

Notice how much wider these intervals are than those for a score with a reliability of .97, and consider the range of scores included in a confidence interval when the full range is unpacked (by doubling the interval value to form a full confidence interval band). Seeing these contrast due to differences in reliability, it is clear that the reason the confidence interval is wider for Composites 1, 2, and 3 (with a confidence interval spread of 15 points, roughly ±7.5) in Table 4.1 than for the Total Composite (with a spread of 11 points, roughly ±5.5) is because the three numbered composites are less reliable than the total composite.

Our review of intelligence tests indicated that most test authors center confidence intervals around an *estimated true score* versus the actual score earned by the test taker (aka the obtained score). This practice is apparent when the confidence interval values above and below the obtained score are not symmetrical. See how, for example, the confidence intervals for the composite scores in the bottom half of Table 4.1 do not have the actual composite score at the center of their range. For Composite 1, the bands of error seem very lopsided, considering that the composite score is 84 and the confidence interval is 78 to 93 (15 points but minus 6, plus 9), whereas the other two composite scores have the same range of 15 points but the division is minus 7, plus 8). Estimated true scores (also called *regressed true scores*) always are closer to the mean of the population distribution than obtained scores unless the score is at the mean. Obtained scores are more deviant from the mean in part because of error (i.e., chance deviations) due to guessing, bad luck, or the like. Estimated true scores are derived by (1) multiplying the difference between the obtained score and the mean by the same reliability coefficient used to calculate the *SEM* and (2) adding this product to the mean. Because no measurement has perfect reliability, the difference from the population score mean (e.g., 100) for the estimated true score is always smaller in magnitude than the difference from the population score mean of the obtained score; it is a product of multiplying this difference by a value less than 1 (e.g., .95). This formula explains, in part, why Composite 1, which is more deviant from the mean than the other two composites, would have an estimated true score that is more deviant from its obtained score. In addition, almost every prominent intelligence test produces confidence intervals based on adjustments to the *SEM* by multiplying it by the same reliability coefficient to produce the *standard error of the estimated true score* (*SEE*). The *SEE* values always are smaller than the *SEM* values, for the same reason explicated for the estimated true score: We are multiplying it by a number that is less than 1.0.

In many ways, confidence intervals produce a paradoxical effect. In using them, we seem to sacrifice precision (as represented by a single obtained score) for confidence in estimating the test taker's true score. The more confident we are that the true score falls within the *SEM* or *SEE* interval (e.g., 95% confident), the less precise we are;

conversely, the less confident we are (e.g., 68% confident), the more precise we are. Confidence intervals show us that we may, in fact, better represent the abilities we have targeted by expressing performance as a range of scores. Confidence intervals should be employed when reporting results (see Chapter 10).

OTHER SCORES

Advances in psychometrics, particularly item response theory (see Embretson & Reise, 2000), have permitted the transformation of raw scores into more refined scores that have equal units along their scales. Examples include *ability scores* from the Differential Ability Scales, Second Edition (Elliott, 2007); *change-sensitive scores* from the Stanford-Binet Intelligence Scales, Fifth Edition (Roid, 2003); and *W scores* from the Woodcock-Johnson IV Tests of Cognitive Abilities (Schrank et al., 2014b; see Chapter 7 for more details about these tests). These scores are absolute in measuring the targeted ability (unlike norm-referenced scores) and may be useful in examining change in the abilities underlying test performance across time. However, most test users do not interpret these scores. Although such scores offer promise in evaluating change over time, intelligence tests are not typically used in this manner.

Evaluating the Evidence Supporting Score Interpretation

Now that you have a sense of which score types are the most important to interpret, it is time to consider which scores of each type should attract your attention. In particular we want to point out a key resource. In addition to the American Psychological Association's (APA's) Ethical Principles of Psychologists and Code of Conduct and the National Association of School Psychologists' (NASP's) Principles for Professional Ethics (APA, 2002, 2010a; NASP, 2010a; see Chapter 3), you should be familiar with the *Standards for Educational and Psychological Testing* (American Educational Research Association [AERA], APA, & National Council on Measurement in Education [NCME], 2014). Using the general standards and guidelines for test use from the *Standards* document, we present criteria for evaluating the quality of norming, item scaling, and reliability and validity of scores yielded by intelligence tests.

EVALUATING NORM SAMPLES

As norms affect the accuracy and meaningfulness of the most important data derived from intelligence tests—their norm-referenced scores—it is important to scrutinize these tests' norm samples. Typically, norm samples are evaluated according to their recency, their representativeness, and their size. This information typically is provided in a general description in technical manuals accompanying tests, but it is also important to review the age ranges associated with specific norm groups—those forming the norms and presented in norm tables—to evaluate the appropriateness of norm samples.

Recency. The recency of norms can be evaluated based on how near in time the data were collected relative to when the test is used. As described in the ethical standards discussed in Chapter 3, it is best to avoid tests that are old and outdated. This recommendation is in place because outdated norms may no longer match the experiences and ability levels of those being tested. For one thing, older tests might include item content that no longer is valid for modern-day test takers, which could produce biased scores. Further, the evidence indicates rising ability levels across time in populations (called the *Flynn effect*; Flynn, 1984, 1987, 1999, 2007), with older norms producing inflated scores compared to more recent norms. The Flynn effect refers to the increase in intelligence test scores that has been observed in the United States and elsewhere over the past century. In an analysis of 73 studies, involving more than 7,500 participants, Flynn (1987) found that every successive intelligence test standardization sample performed better than its predecessor. Flynn estimated that IQ scores increase an average of 3 points per decade, or 0.3 points per year. The increase in IQ implies that scores on older tests are likely to be inflated in comparison to those on newer tests with contemporary norms. The secular increase in IQ implies that scores on older tests are likely to be inflated in comparison to scores on tests with contemporary norms. Therefore, it is essential to use the most recently normed tests.

To evaluate the recency of norms, examine not only the date of a test's publication but also, and more important, the period during which its norming data were collected. Ideally, use only intelligence tests that have been normed within the past 10 years. Tests with norming data collected earlier should be used sparingly and probably should be avoided.

Representativeness. The representativeness of norms is equally important. It can be evaluated according to the extensiveness of sampling (1) across data collection sites and regions (e.g., U.S. states) and (2) across demographic characteristics (i.e., gender, race, ethnicity, socioeconomic status, and community size). Of course, norming samples consisting only of participants from a single region would not meet the requirement of national norming and almost certainly would fail to represent the targeted population. Some norms for intelligence tests stem from statistical weighting of contributions by specified subgroups to enhance the representativeness, but if such weighting is not used, a simple way to determine representativeness of the sample is to examine the match between the specific characteristics of the norm sample and those from the referenced census report used as a benchmark for norming. For example, comparisons could be made according to geographic characteristics (e.g., region of the country, population size, and urban versus rural settings) and demographic characteristics (e.g., race, ethnicity, gender, and socioeconomic status). Discrepancies between specific characteristics of the norm sample and those from the respective census that are greater than 5 percentage points have been reported as indicating oversampling or undersampling (Floyd & Bose, 2003). As discussed in Chapter 14, the absence of a particular test taker's demographic group from the norming sample is not ipso facto evidence that a test is biased. The test may produce biased scores, but it may not. Evidence of bias can be determined only by scientific research.

It has been claimed that individuals with disabilities and those who receive extremely high and extremely low scores should be included in the norming samples—and some intelligence test samples make a point to ensure that such cases are included—but it is becoming increasingly common for *extrapolated norms* to be used. Extrapolated norms are derived from statistical manipulations of the distributions of test scores to ensure that they fully represent the population as a whole; they compensate for the fact that the norming data may not, in fact, represent the population well. For example, extrapolated norms can produce an IQ of 185 for children age 5 years old, although no one on the normative sample actually obtained an IQ that high. Fully representative norms based on expansive ability sampling are extremely difficult to obtain, because it is (a) so hard to find sufficient numbers of people with extremely high IQs and (b) so hard to test those with extremely low IQs due to potentially confounding factors.

Developmental sensitivity. The age range covered by each segment of the norms must be considered to ensure that they are sensitive to developmental differences, especially during the periods when cognitive growth is most rapid (i.e., up to about 16 to 20 years of age; see Chapter 2). That is, divisions of the norms should help to disentangle the effects of maturation and experience associated with age (as confounds) from individual differences in the display of the targeted abilities (as targeted by norm-referenced scores). Without an effort to eliminate these confounds, the norms would underestimate the abilities of the youngest children at the targeted age level (producing lower scores) and overestimate the abilities of the oldest children in the targeted age level (producing higher scores; Flanagan, Ortiz, Alfonso, & Mascolo, 2006).

Although parents, teachers, and other professionals tend to ground their developmental expectations in a child or adolescent's whole age in years or whole grade levels in school, norm divisions representing narrower periods of time (e.g., a half year, a quarter, or a few months) often are necessary to produce the most accurate norm-referenced scores. Many tests (especially those targeting very young children) include norm sample blocks representing rather narrow periods of time (e.g., 2 months and 3 months). In contrast, when developmental differences across age groups would not be anticipated (e.g., during the decade of the 30s), norm sample blocks often are much broader (e.g., 5 to 10 years; Flanagan et al., 2006). According to Bracken (2000), in addition to considering the breadth of these blocks, it is important to evaluate the actual norm tables to judge their adequacy—especially when a test taker is "on the very upper cusp of one age level and who is about to 'graduate' to the next age level" (p. 42). Bracken has shared that one way to evaluate this developmental sensitivity (not to be confused with diagnostic sensitivity and the like) of the norms is to review the norm tables and "examine the difference in standard scores associated with a given raw score as you progress from one table to the next. If the standard score increases by large amounts (e.g., +1 1/3 standard deviations), the test may provide too gross an estimate of ability to instill much confidence in the resultant score" (p. 42). To address this issue, standard score values should be compared at levels near the mean, about one standard deviation above the mean, and about one standard deviation below the mean, beginning with the block associated with the age of the prospective examinee.

In recent decades, many test authors have addressed the developmental sensitivity of norms by using procedures associated with *continuous norming* (also called *inferential norming*; Lenhard, Lenhard, Suggate, & Segerer, 2018; Zachary & Gorsuch, 1985). Using traditional norming techniques, descriptive statistics (mainly the mean and standard deviation) are obtained for test takers at specified age levels (e.g., 6-year-olds, 7-year-olds, and the like), and these statistics are used to calculate norm-referenced scores, as previously described. As age is a continuous variable and not a discrete one, continuous norming, instead, involves considering test scores from a wide age range of test takers (including perhaps some younger and older than those targeted by the test) and applying sophisticated statistical methods (e.g., polynomial regression analysis) to mathematically model these descriptive statistics for test takers at each developmental level. Then, these results can be integrated across ages (and adjusted by "smoothing" procedures), so that a picture of the developmental expectations of test takers is better represented and the norms are more sensitive to them. Test norms developed using these methods are noteworthy and superior to those developed via more conventional methods—especially if the analytic sample is large enough (Zhu & Chen, 2011). Most tests mention their use of continuous norming, but details rarely are provided.

Norm sample size and size of norm blocks. In general, larger norm samples indicate higher-quality norming and more trustworthy norm-referenced scores; even with application of continuous norming procedures, smaller samples can produce results that are not representative of the population (Zhu & Chen, 2011). Thus, it is important to consider the size of each age-based interval of the norms. According to common standards (e.g., Emmons & Alfonso, 2005; Flanagan & Alfonso, 1995; cf. Hammill, Brown, & Bryant, 1992), each 1-year age-based interval of the norms can be judged to be acceptable if it includes at least 100 individuals. This standard seems reasonable to us. However, evaluating this characteristic sometimes is tricky, because some tests present norm sample sizes across wide age ranges (e.g., 1-year increments) in the body of the technical manuals but rely on norm sample blocks representing narrower time segments (e.g., 3- to 6-month intervals), as previously discussed. In such cases, the mean number of participants per norm block can be estimated by dividing the number of participants reported across the wider age range by the number of norm-related segments by which it is divided. For instance, if 120 children age 4 were reported to compose a 1-year norm block, but norms were calculated in three 4-month blocks (4:0–4:3, 4:4–4:7, and 4:8–4:11), an average of 40 children per norm block would be assumed. This value would be unacceptable based on the goal of including at least 100 children in this group, and we believe that an absolute low-end standard should be 30 children per norm block. Later in this book (Chapters 6 and 7), we (a) reproduce some of the results from Norfolk et al. (2015), who applied this method to the norms from 17 intelligence tests, and (b) extend those results for tests not included. We employed the four-level classification of norm block sizes from Norfolk et al. in our evaluations:

> Tests with norm blocks consistently containing 30 or more participants were classified as meeting the *minimum* standard. Tests with norm blocks consistently containing 50 or more participants were classified as meeting

the *medium* standard. Tests with norm blocks consistently containing 100 or more participants were classified as meeting the *highest* standard. If a test contained less than 30 participants at any age level of the norm blocks, it was classified as *insufficient* for meeting proposed standards. (p. 8)

In some cases, the material supporting test kits (e.g., manuals and software) do not allow for this evaluation to be completed. For example, tests that have no printed norm tables (such as the Woodcock-Johnson IV Tests of Cognitive Abilities; Schrank et al., 2014b, and the Detroit Tests of Learning Abilities, Fifth Edition; Hammill, McGhee, & Ehrler, 2018) cannot be evaluated in this manner. Further, some tests—notably several recently published ones, including the Kaufman Assessment Battery for Children, Second Edition Normative Update (KABC-2 NU; A. Kaufman & N. Kaufman, 2018) and the Universal Nonverbal Intelligence Test, Second Edition (Bracken & McCallum, 2016)—do not convey the exact number of participants per narrow age range. In such cases, estimates of the sample size associated with each norm block are even more coarsely calculated. The most straightforward method involves taking the total sample size and dividing it by the number of norm blocks. For example, the KABC-2 NU included 700 participants in its norming sample. Across its 16-year age span (3–18), it includes 47 norm blocks: for ages 3–5, in 3-month blocks (12); for ages 6–14, in 4-month blocks (27); and for ages 15–18, in 6-month blocks (8). Following through on the division of 700 participants by 47 norm blocks, the quotient is a measly 14.9. Using Norfolk et al.'s (2015) evaluative labels, this is insufficient.

Scaling

RANGE OF NORM-REFERENCED SCORES

When assessing children or adolescents suspected of having intellectual disability (see Chapter 11) or intellectual giftedness (see Chapter 12), it is important to know the range of scores yielded by the intelligence tests that will be used. In addition, in order to differentiate between ability levels at every point across this range, item gradients for intelligence test subtests should be evaluated.

Item scaling techniques. Test authors typically devote much time and effort to developing, selecting, and scaling items for their instruments. As noted previously, items are usually scaled from easiest to most difficult. Test takers begin with items that most individuals of the same age would successfully complete, progress through items that are neither too easy nor too difficult for them, and reach items on the threshold of their current knowledge and skills. In order to evaluate the quality of an intelligence test, you must consider the methods used to scale these test items.

Traditional techniques used for item scaling include item difficulty analysis, in which items are evaluated according to the percentage of examinees passing those items. After administering the preliminary set of items to large groups of individuals, test authors using these techniques can identify patterns of scores across items and place the items in order from those passed by the greatest number of individuals to those passed by the least number of individuals. During recent decades, techniques based on item response theory (often referred to only as IRT, although we continue to use the full term) have replaced more traditional techniques such as item difficulty analysis. Item response theory analysis considers not only item difficulty but also the relation between passing the item and effectively the summation of all of the items considered in the analysis (often called item discrimination) and random error (often called guessing). One common type of item response theory analysis is referred to as Rasch modeling (Rasch, 1960). This analysis, focused on accurately measuring the latent trait (or ability) underlying performance on an item, produces a purer method of evaluating item difficulty than any other single traditional technique, and for most intelligence test subtests, it is the optimal method for scaling items. When reviewing technical information about an intelligence test, it is fair to expect the test developer to have used item response theory to scale items.

Adequacy of scale floors. A *scale floor* refers to the lowest norm-referenced score that can be obtained. When these floors are too high, the full range of ability at its lowest levels cannot be assessed, because, at the subtest level, items are too difficult for test takers with low ability; too few easy items for them are included. Thus, it is not surprising that problems with scale floors are most frequently apparent at the youngest age levels targeted by intelligence tests, as it is challenging for test developers to generate a sufficient number of very easy items to represent the full range of ability during the earliest developmental stages. Here is the problem with inadequate floors: even when a test taker has performed poorly (say, answering only one item correctly), they will earn a score that is relatively close to what is considered average based on the norms. Subtest scores with insufficient floors will overestimate the abilities of those who are near the lowest end of the ability range, and this overestimation will be transferred to all of the composite scores to which that subtest contributes.

Floors for subtests can be evaluated by examining norm tables and using scoring programs. An example norm table focusing on converting subtest raw scores to scaled scores is included in Table 4.2. To identify an inadequate subtest floor (aka a *floor violation*), a raw score of 1 on a subtest does not yield a norm-referenced score equal to or exceeding two standard deviations below the normative mean (a deviation IQ score of 70 or lower, a *T* score of 30 or lower, or a scaled score of 4 or lower (Bracken, 1987; Bracken, Keith, & Walker, 1998; Bradley-Johnson & Durmusoglu, 2005). For composite scores that stem from summing norm-referenced scores from subtests, floor violations are apparent if the lowest basic score (e.g., the sum of scaled scores) is associated with a norm-referenced score less than two standard deviations below the mean.

Table 4.2 includes the full range of raw scores for four subtests, and the total number of items on each is different (from 17 items to 21 items). In order to determine the scaled score obtained for each raw score, find the appropriate cell with the subtest raw score column and identify the scaled score associated with it. For example, a raw score of 10 on Subtest 1 yields a scaled score of 8, but the same raw score on Subtest 2 yields a scaled score of 11. Do not worry about this difference in scaling, as it does not necessary matter in evaluating floors.

To identify floor violations, the first step is to identify the scaled score threshold associated with an adequate scale floor. Recall that a floor violation is evident for scaled

Table 4.2. Sample Subtest Raw Score to Scaled Score Conversion Table

Scaled Score	Subtest 1	Subtest 2	Subtest 3	Subtest 4	Scaled Score
1	0–1	—	—	0–1	1
2	2	—	—	2–3	2
3	3	—	—	4–5	3
4	4–5	—	0–1	6–7	4
5	6–7	0	2	8–9	5
6	8	1–2	3–4	10	6
7	9	3	5	11–12	7
8	10	4	6–7	12–13	8
9	11–12	5–6	8–9	14	9
10	13	7–8	10	15–16	10
11	14	9–10	10–11	—	11
12	15	11–12	12	17	12
13	16–17	13	13–14	18	13
14	18	14	15	—	14
15	19–20	15	16	—	15
16	—	16	17	19	16
17	—	17	—	20	17
18	—	18	—	—	18
19	—	19	—	21	19

scores when a raw score of 1 does not yield a scaled score of 4 or lower. Thus, the row including raw scores associated with the scaled score of 4 should attract our attention. Next find the cells that include raw scores of 1 for each subtest. For Subtest 1 and Subtest 4, raw scores of 1 are associated with a scaled score of 1, which clearly indicates an adequate floor, as a scaled score of 1 is well more than 2 standard deviation below the mean. In contrast, the floors are not as low for Subtests 2 and 3. Notice that no subtest raw scores for these subtests are associated with scaled scores of 1, 2, and 3. Often, dashes at the top of a norm table (with lower raw scores and lower norm-referenced scores at the top) give some indication that the test floors are inadequate. For Subtest 2, a raw score of 1 (or 2) is associated with a scaled score of 6. As that scaled score is not 4 or lower, Subtest 2 demonstrates a floor violation at this age level. This is a serious problem, and the subtest scaled score and any composite score to which this subtest contributes is likely inflated for test takers in this age range who have the lowest ability. For Subtest 3, the floor clearly is not an extremely low one, but it is not apparent that a floor violation is present. In fact, as the raw score of 1 is associated with a scaled score of 4, this subtest has met the criterion for an adequate floor (just barely) and is not deemed problematic.

Adequacy of scale ceilings. A *scale ceiling* refers to the highest norm-referenced score that can be obtained. When ceilings are too low, the full range of ability at its highest levels cannot be assessed. This scenario is the opposite of the one occurring when test takers with low ability are assessed. As a result of such problems with ceilings, those with high ability are likely to have their abilities underestimated. Even when test takers perform extremely well on a subtest, answering every item correctly, they will earn a score relatively close to what is considered average. Too few difficult items are on the subtest to sufficiently challenge such test takers at this level. For this reason, ceiling violations are most frequently identified at the oldest age levels targeted by intelligence tests designed for children and adolescents. (This would not be the case for tests that include norms for adults in late adulthood.)

Ceilings for subtests also can be evaluated by examining norm tables and using scoring programs. If the highest possible raw score does not yield a norm-referenced score equal to or exceeding two standard deviations above the normative mean (i.e., a deviation IQ score of 130 or higher, a T score of 70 or higher, or a scaled score of 16 or higher), a *ceiling violation* is evident (Bracken, 1987; Bracken et al., 1998; Bradley-Johnson & Durmusoglu, 2005). For composite scores, ceiling violations can be identified if the highest basic score (e.g., the sum of scaled scores) is associated with a norm-referenced score less than two standard deviations above the mean.

Like the process for identifying floor violations, the first step to identify potential ceiling violations is to determine the scaled score threshold associated with an adequate scale ceiling. Recall that a ceiling violation is evident for scaled scores when the highest possible raw score does not yield a scaled score of 16 or higher. Thus, the row including raw scores associated with the scaled score of 16 in Table 4.2 should attract our attention. As the highest raw score values for each subtest ranged from 17 items to 21 items, you cannot look for a single number, but it is easy to identify the highest raw score for each subtest by conducting a visual scan. In cases such as Table 4.2, this is the raw score value that is at the bottom of each relevant column: 20, 19, 17, and 21 for Subtests 1–4.

As it is readily apparent from reviewing Table 4.2 that Subtests 2 and 4 include items associated with the highest possible scaled scores (19), neither demonstrates a ceiling violation, as 19 well exceeds the criterion scaled score of 16. Dashes at the bottom of a norm table (with higher raw scores and higher norm-referenced scores at the bottom) give some indication that the ceiling is not adequate, so we can see potential problems with Subtests 1 and 3. For Subtest 1, its highest raw score (20) is associated with a scaled score of 15, which reveals a ceiling violation. A perfect score on this subtest would yield a score less than two standard deviations above the mean, and the subtest score and any related composite to which it contributes would underestimate the ability of the highest ability test taker at this age level. For Subtest 3, its highest raw score (17) meets this criterion of being at least two standard deviations above the mean (the scaled score of 16), and it (again, just barely) is not deemed problematic.

Adequacy of item gradients. Appropriately scaled items should not only proceed from easy to difficult but also do so without rapidly progressing from easy to difficult items. An example of inappropriate item scaling for an achievement test would be a math subtest that includes easy single-digit multiplication items, advanced trigonometry items, and no items of intermediate difficulty. Such inappropriate scaling, as revealed through *item-gradient violations*, also can be identified by a careful review of norm tables.

Ideally, the relation between item scores and norm-referenced scores should be consistent as they both increase; this relation is referred to as the *item gradient*. According to Krasa (2007),

> When the item gradient ... is too steep, it does not sufficiently absorb "noise"—that is, errors irrelevant to the construct being tested (such as carelessness or distractibility) can lead to an abrupt change in standard score that does not reflect a true difference in the ability being tested. (p. 4)

When this standard is not met, huge "jumps" in ability estimates (as evidenced by the norm-referenced scores) might be the product of guessing correctly on a single item. For example, with woefully inadequate item gradients, a test taker could go from having a slightly-above-average scaled score of 11 to a well-above-average norm-referenced score of 15 because they guessed correctly on one item. Massive gaps in abilities estimates might stem from the converse; failing one item might cause the norm-referenced score to drop precipitously.

Item-gradient violations for subtests, which are most closely linked to item-level performance, can be identified. Such a violation is present if there is not at least one raw score point associated with each one-third of a standard deviation unit in the norms (Bracken, 1987). For example, deviation IQ scores should not change more than 5 points per 1 raw score point change; T scores should not change more than 3 points per 1 raw score point change; and scaled scores should not change more than 1 point per 1 raw score point change. The key to finding these item-gradient violations when reviewing test norms is to examine the density of raw scores between the scale floor and the scale ceiling—the space between the lowest raw score and the highest raw score. As evident in Table 4.2, Subtests 1, 2, and 3 include at least one raw score point per scaled score. There are no gaps (marked by dashes across the item gradient); in fact, in numerous instances a pair of raw scores yields the same scaled score. However, Subtest 4 demonstrates an uneven item gradient for the age level in question. Notice that there is one item-gradient violation between raw scores of 16 and 17, another between raw scores of 20 and 21, and a particularly large one between raw scores of 18 and 19. In this last case, a test taker who guessed correctly on an item they typically would not have answered correctly would earn a scaled score one full standard deviation higher as a result (as a raw score of 18 equals a scaled score of 13 and a raw score of 19 yields a scaled score of 16).

As evident later in this book, we do not recommend routine interpretation of subtest scores. Item-gradient violations for subtests, however, should not be ignored because subtest scores contribute to the composite scores we are more confident in interpreting. Due to composite scores pooling variability across subtests (and each subtest pooling across items), they should absorb most of the "noise" associated with item-gradient violations and other sources of error in measurement.

Reliability

DEFINITION

Assessment results should be as precise and consistent as possible. Certainly, none of us would want scoring errors to affect test scores, and we would look askance if we learned that someone obtained an IQ in the Superior range one day and an IQ in the Low Average range the following day after taking the same test. The term *reliability* is used to represent this valued score characteristic—consistency across measurements. Quantitative values targeting reliability represent the extent to which unexplained and apparently random inconsistency across replications, called *measurement error* or *random error*, affects test scores. These unpredictable fluctuations are unavoidable; no test produces a perfect, 100% replicable measurement of any phenomenon. Even in the natural sciences, tools targeting physical measurements are affected by error. For example, rulers and tape measures expand and contract as the temperature fluctuates; even quantum clocks, which probably are the most accurate measures of time, vary slightly (e.g., by 1 second in a billion years) under some conditions.

In testing, we most frequently attribute measurement error to the person taking the test, and particularly to the person's variation in determination, anxiety, and alertness from item to item or from day to day. Further, guessing correctly (producing spuriously high scores) comes into play, as do memory retrieval problems (leading to incorrect responses and producing spuriously low scores). In the same vein, those taking the test may respond in different ways to items because of prior experiences. For instance, they may fail items that typically are easier for others (e.g., early presidents of the United States) because they are uninterested in the item content but may answer items that typically are more difficult for others (e.g., earth science) because they have a special interest in that area. In addition to fluctuation due to the person, external factors may produce these fluctuations. Examples include the time of day in which the test is taken, distractions in the testing environment, and examiners' deviations in administration and scoring.

Reliability is an important precondition for the validity of test results and their interpretations. According to the immediately previous edition of *Standards* (AERA et al., 1999), "To the extent that scores reflect random errors of measurement, their potential for accurate prediction of criteria, for beneficial examinee diagnosis, and for wise decision making is limited" (p. 31). This relationship between reliability and validity is important. In fact, it is this relation that leads us and many other scholars to discourage interpretation of less reliable intelligence test subtest scores and encourage interpretation of more reliable composite scores, such as IQs.

EVALUATING RELIABILITY AND DETERMINING EFFECTS OF ERROR

Although we expect variability stemming from the characteristics of examinees and the circumstances external to them, we assume consistency in scores across replications. This consistency in intelligence test scores typically is evaluated using three methods producing reliability coefficients: *internal consistency*, *test–retest reliability*, and *scorer consistency*. Coefficients close to 1.00 indicate high levels of reliability and acceptable levels of measurement error, whereas coefficients below .70 indicate low reliability and unacceptably high levels of measurement error (Hunsley & Mash, 2018). For scores from intelligence tests and high-stakes diagnosis and eligibility decisions, minimal standards for reliability should be far higher than .70.

Internal consistency. The type of reliability coefficient most often reported focuses on item-level consistency evident from a single testing session. These internal consistency coefficients tend to be the highest of all reliability coefficients, and they most frequently are used to calculate confidence interval values. They often are reported as Cronbach's coefficient alpha (α), which represents the average item-to-item relation across the entire scale in question. Alternately, split-half reliability analysis, which examines the relations between odd and even items or between items from the first half and second half of a scale, may be employed. If we assume that all intelligence test subtest items are positively correlated, the greater number of items a subtest includes, the higher its internal consistency reliability coefficient will be. This phenomenon is predicted by the Spearman-Brown prophecy formula (Brown, 1910; Spearman, 1910). Although these reliability analyses commonly are used to determine the internal consistency of intelligence test subtests, the internal consistency of resulting composites, such as IQs, often are determined by using subtest internal consistency coefficients and subtest intercorrelations (Nunnally & Bernstein, 1994).

In general, the closer the analysis of reliability is to the item level, the lower the internal consistency reliability coefficient will be. Items are most strongly affected by measurement error, but these effects are diminished as more and more items are considered in concert—from subtest scores, to composite scores formed from only a few subtests, and to composite scores stemming from numerous subtests. Thus, the most global composites tend to be the most reliable. When high-stakes decisions are to be made, we suggest using a lower-end standard of .90 for internal consistency reliability coefficients (Bracken, 1987; McGrew & Flanagan, 1998); scores with values below .90 should not be interpreted. Higher reliability values almost always are better, but a particular sweet spot—and perhaps a de facto ceiling—appears to be within the range of .90 to .95 (Streiner, 2003).

Test–retest reliability. Evaluation of consistency across replications is most apparent when the same instrument is administered twice across a brief period (typically a month or less). When the relations between scores stemming from these two administrations are quantified using a statistical technique called the Pearson product–moment correlation, an understanding about reliability across time is yielded. The resultant correlation value, the Pearson coefficient, typically is represented by the letter r, and it represents the relations between two variables. In principle, these values range from -1.0 (representing a perfect negative correlation) to 1.0 (representing a perfect positive correlation). A Pearson r value at or near 0 indicates the absence of a relation, and larger absolute values indicate increasingly strong relations. These relations are relative ones and do not consider the absolute score differences (as revealed by differences in means for the two variables entered into the analysis). As a result, Pearson correlations are insensitive to differences in the magnitude of scores from the initial testing to the follow-up testing. This insensitivity is a good thing, because performance on intelligence tests often is better upon retesting (due to practice effects; Calamia, Markon, & Tranel, 2012; Matarazzo, Carmody, & Jacobs, 1980). We discuss Pearson coefficients more as we address inter-rater reliability and validity evidence based on external relations in sections that follow.

Test–retest reliability coefficients commonly are reported for intelligence test subtests and composites, and they may be the only type of reliability coefficient reported for speeded subtests, because traditional internal consistency reliability coefficients cannot be calculated for speeded subtests (unless advanced item response theory techniques are used). Test–retest reliability coefficients are degraded by multiple influences; both the length of the interval between test and retest and the nature of the ability being targeted should be considered in evaluating them. Typically, the longer the interval between initial and follow-up testing (e.g., 1 month vs. 6 months), the lower the reliability coefficient will be. Further, if the ability being targeted tends to vary because of influences associated with the examinee and the effects of testing environment (e.g., Processing Speed), test–retest reliability coefficients will tend to be lower than those for abilities that tend to be more resistant to these influences (e.g., psychometric g). Generally, test–retest reliability coefficients in the form of Pearson's r are lower than internal consistency reliability coefficients, and when high-stakes decisions are to be made, we suggest using a lower-end standard of .90 across a 1-month span or less (Bracken, 1987; McGrew & Flanagan, 1998).

Scorer consistency. Those persons scoring intelligence tests also produce measurement error in scores—especially when scores are based on subjective judgments about the quality of responses (Styck & Walsch, 2016). This type of measurement error most frequently is quantified by *interrater agreement* indexes and *interrater reliability* coefficients. Interrater agreement indexes stem from analysis of individual items across a subtest, and they typically are reported as a percentage (representing *percentage agreement*) and not as a coefficient. For example, if two raters agree that 5 of 10 responses should earn a point and that 3 of the remaining 5 responses should not earn a point, then their percentage agreement in scoring is 80%. *Kappa* is sometimes reported rather than percentage agreement. It controls for chance agreement, and its values (usually in coefficient form) usually are lower in magnitude than corresponding percentage agreement values.

In contrast, interrater reliability coefficients typically stem from analysis of summed item scores across items obtained from independent scoring of responses across two examiners; they typically are the result of Pearson product–moment correlations. To compare and contrast these two indexes of scorer consistency, review Table 4.3. Across the 15 items scored on a 3-point scale by two raters, the scores were almost identical: 17 for Rater 1 and 18 for Rater 2. Further, the average item score for Rater 1 was 1.13, whereas it was 1.20 for Rater 2. When the item-by-item agreement in scoring was considered (see "Agreement" column in Table 4.3), the interrater agreement index (reported as percentage agreement) was 67%, because only 10 of the 15 items were scored exactly the same way. When the correspondence of the rank ordering of item-level scores above and below their respective rater-specific means was considered and reported as a Pearson coefficient, the interrater reliability coefficient of .76 was somewhat modest but higher in magnitude than the interrater agreement index.

Table 4.3. An Item-Scoring Example Yielding Interrater Agreement and Interrater Reliability Coefficients

			Agreement analysis		Pearson product-moment correlation analysis				
Item number	Rater 1 score	Rater 2 score	Agreement	Agreement score	Rater 1 deviation from M	Rater 2 deviation from M	Product of deviations from M	Squared Rater 1 deviation from M	Squared Rater 2 deviation from M
1	2	2	Yes	1	0.87	0.80	0.69	0.75	0.64
2	2	2	Yes	1	0.87	0.80	0.69	0.75	0.64
3	2	2	Yes	1	0.87	0.80	0.69	0.75	0.64
4	2	2	Yes	1	0.87	0.80	0.69	0.75	0.64
5	1	2	No	0	-0.13	0.80	-0.11	0.02	0.64
6	2	1	No	0	0.87	-0.20	-0.17	0.75	0.04
7	2	2	Yes	1	0.87	0.80	0.69	0.75	0.64
8	1	1	Yes	1	-0.13	-0.20	0.03	0.02	0.04
9	1	2	No	0	-0.13	0.80	-0.11	0.02	0.64
10	1	1	Yes	1	-0.13	-0.20	0.03	0.02	0.04
11	0	0	Yes	1	-1.13	-1.20	1.36	1.28	1.44
12	1	0	No	0	-0.13	-1.20	0.16	0.02	1.44
13	0	1	No	0	-1.13	-0.20	0.23	1.28	0.04
14	0	0	Yes	1	-1.13	-1.20	1.36	1.28	1.44
15	0	0	Yes	1	-1.13	-1.20	1.36	1.28	1.44
Sum	17	18		10			7.60	9.73	10.40
Average	1.13	1.20							

Percentage agreement

Agreements = 10
Total items = 15   = **.67, or 67%**

Pearson correlation

r = Sum of products of deviations for raters = 7.60 = .76
Square root of (squared Rater 1   Square root of (9.73 × 10.40)
Deviation from M times squared Rater 2
deviation from M)

Based on standards for interrater reliability and interrater agreement for assessment instruments targeting child and adolescent behavioral and emotional problems (e.g., Achenbach, McConaughy, & Howell, 1987; Floyd & Bose, 2003; Hunsley & Mash, 2018), interrater reliability of .60 or higher and interrater agreement of 60% or higher are desirable. Because the range of responses is much narrower, and scoring tends to be clearer with intelligence tests subtests than many other assessment instruments, reasonable lower-end standards for scorer consistency should be .80 for interrater reliability and 80% for interrater agreement.

Validity

DEFINITION

Whereas *reliability* refers to consistency across measurements (e.g., across items, across multiple administration of the same tests, or across scorers), *validity* refers to representing the concept or characteristic being targeted by the assessment instrument in a complete and meaningful way. According to the *Standards* (AERA et al., 2014),

> Validity refers to the degree to which evidence and theory support the interpretations of test scores by proposed uses of tests. Validity is, therefore, the most fundamental consideration in developing and evaluating tests. The process of validation involves accumulating evidence to provide a sound scientific basis for the proposed score interpretations.... When test scores are used or interpreted in more than one way, each intended interpretation must be validated. (p. 11)

As apparent in this definition, tests do not possess validity; it is a misnomer to refer to a "valid test." Instead, you should refer, generally, to a score supported by substantial validity evidence and, as validity is conditional (based on the intended uses of a test's scores), to a test supported by validity evidence that instills confidence in accomplishing a goal. For example, an IQ from a test targeting high-ability preschool students might be valid for identifying intellectual giftedness (see Chapter 12), but if several of its subtests contributing to the IQ demonstrated floor violations, it would not be valid for identifying students with intellectual disability (see Chapter 11). Thus, details and conditions should be specified when discussing validity. You should ask, "Do I have solid evidence supporting my use of these scores to reach my goals?"

When considering validity evidence supporting uses and interpretations of intelligence tests scores, *construct validity* offers an overarching conceptual framework. The term *construct* refers to the concept or characteristic that the assessment instrument is intended to measure, and in the case of intelligence tests, the construct typically is a cognitive ability. For example, measures of psychometric g represent the ability to thinking abstractly, the capacity to acquire knowledge, and problem-solving skills (Neisser et al., 1996). From this perspective, both test authors and test users should consider and articulate what construct is being targeted by all scores. In doing so, they must consider both (1) how fine-grained or global the intended interpretation is and (2) what evidence has supported their favored interpretation. For example, does an intelligence test subtest requiring children to provide definitions to English words measure psychometric *g*, Crystallized Intelligence, word knowledge, the ability to articulate word definitions, listening ability, an enriched language environment, expressive language skills, long-term memory, concept formation, or executive system functioning? Of course, it is extremely rare that interpretations of scores are limited to only one meaning, but the wide array of constructs presented in this sample seems to represent what Kelley (1927) called the *jingle-jangle fallacy*. The *jingle fallacy* refers to using the same label to describe different constructs, and the *jangle fallacy*, which is more relevant to this example, refers to using different labels to describe similar constructs. Because of such problems in selecting the targeted construct, it is important to rely on theory and prior research (as described in Chapters 1 and 2; see also Beaujean & Benson, 2019b) to develop an explicit statement of the proposed interpretation of scores and score patterns. This validity argument then can be evaluated on the basis of existing evidence.

EVALUATING VALIDITY EVIDENCE

Although the classic tripartite model of validity (focusing on apparently distinct types of validity—*content*, *criterion-related*, and *construct*) is still employed in some test technical manuals and in some of the psychology literature, this model is outdated. Modern conceptions of validity represent validity as a unitary concept; evidence of all types inform the construct validity of the inferences drawn from assessment results and subsequent decisions. Consistent with the *Standards* (AERA et al., 2014), this validity evidence can be compartmentalized into five validity strands, with evidence based on

1. test content,
2. response processes,
3. internal structure,
4. relations with other variables, and
5. the consequences of testing.

A body of validity evidence should be evaluated by considering potential confounds in measurement that may undermine valid interpretations. The *Standards* document refers to these potential confounds as rival hypotheses and encourages consideration of both *construct underrepresentation* and *construct-irrelevant variance*. According to the *Standards* (AERA et al., 2014),

> Construct underrepresentation refers to the degree to which a test fails to capture important aspects of the construct. It implies a narrowed meaning of test scores because the test does not adequately sample some types of content, engage some psychological processes, or elicit some ways of responding that are encompassed by the intended construct. Take, for example, a test intended as a comprehensive measure of anxiety. A particular test might underrepresent the intended construct because it measures only

physiological reactions and not emotional, cognitive, or situational components. As another example, a test of reading comprehension intended to measure children's ability to read and interpret stories with understanding might not contain a sufficient variety of reading passages or might ignore a common type of reading material. (p. 12)

Construct-irrelevant variance reflects "the degree to which test scores are affected by processes that are extraneous to the test's intended purpose. The test scores may be systematically influenced to some extent by processes that are not part of the construct" (AERA et al., p. 12). On an intelligence test, for example, construct-irrelevant components might include the language of the test or its culture loading, because most intelligence tests are developed and validated for English-speaking test takers born and raised in the United States (see Chapter 14 for further discussion). When the test performance of those from diverse backgrounds primarily reflects their level of acculturation and English-language proficiency rather than the cognitive ability constructs the test was intended to measure, the interpretation of scores is invalid.

Using the concept of construct validity espoused in the *Standards* and considering both construct underrepresentation and construct irrelevance as contributors to rival hypotheses, you should evaluate evidence for its contribution to interpretations and to revealing potential sources of invalidity. In the sections that follow, we discuss each type of validity evidence and address its contribution to identifying construct underrepresentation and construct irrelevance in the sections that follow. In doing so, we highlight a few key pieces of evidence most relevant to intelligence test interpretation that are associated with each type of validity evidence.

Content. Evidence based on *test content* refers to substantiation that an instrument's items accurately represent the targeted construct or constructs in a complete, accurate, and unadulterated manner. According to the *Standards* (AERA et al., 2014), "Test content refers to the themes, wording, and format of the items, tasks, or questions on a test. Administration and scoring may also be relevant to content-based evidence" (p. 14). As apparent in Table 4.4, item development begins based on theory and prior literature, and items are evaluated by content experts and piloted in the field to obtain feedback from test users and to generate data for analysis. Although validity evidence based on content often is based on human judgment, statistical methods also may be used to test validity arguments. For intelligence tests, item content should introduce cognitive complexity and primarily include information (e.g., item presentations and response formats) that does not introduce construct irrelevance for most test takers.

Cognitive complexity. In the case of academic achievement tests (reading, mathematics, and writing tests) and tests of specific knowledge (e.g., a language proficiency test), it is important to ensure that the item content reflects the same words, phrases, symbols, problems, and concepts that the domain of study does in the real world. However, for intelligence tests, the content does not matter very much for most test takers, per se, as long as the content is heterogeneous. According to Jensen (1980),

> Any given item cannot, of course, be without content, but the content is a mere vehicle for the essential elements of intelligence test items. The essential elements involved expression of relationships. According to this view,

Table 4.4. Definitions of and Methods to Demonstrate the Five Strands of Validity Evidence

Evidence based on test content—substantiation that an instrument's items accurately represent the targeted constructs in a complete, accurate, and unbiased manner.

- Development of items based on strong theory, literature review, established educational or psychiatric diagnostic classifications, and review of case histories
- Expert analysis of gender, racial, cultural, or age bias in items
- Review and item tryouts by test users in applied settings
- Statistical analyses of items (e.g., differential item functioning, point–biserial correlations, and item characteristic curve analyses)

Evidence based on response processes—substantiation of the real or presumed behaviors that test takers exhibit when completing subtest items.

- Evaluation of instrument instructions and response formats
- Observations of test takers' behaviors (e.g., eye movements) during completion of items
- Interviews with test takers about thought processes during completion of subtest items
- "Think-aloud" protocols with test takers during completion of subtest items
- Task decomposition analyses of subtest items

Evidence based on internal structure—substantiation that an instrument's item level or summative scores are related to other measures from the instrument in the manner expected.

- Correlations between items within a subtest
- Correlations between subtest scores
- Exploratory factor analysis (EFA)
- Confirmatory factor analysis (CFA)

Evidence based on relations with other variables—substantiation that item-level or summative scores from an instrument relate in a systematic way with other measures, such as scores from other instruments, demographic variables (e.g., age and gender), and educational or diagnostic classifications.

- Correlations with measures of the same or similar constructs
- Correlations with measures of distinct or dissimilar constructs
- Correlations with scores from well-validated instruments
- Prediction of current or future phenomena
- Group difference analyses (aka clinical group comparisons)

Evidence based on the consequences of testing—substantiation that scores and decisions based on them produce intended and not unintended consequences for those completing the test.

- Evaluation of treatment utility of assessment
- Evaluation of classification rates of racial and ethnic groups as labeled disabled versus not disabled

Note: Content is based in part on Table 2 from Floyd and Bose (2003).

> there is no limit to the number of specific kinds of items that can measure intelligence. The number and variety of items that can be invented for intelligence test is limited only by the imagination of the task constructor. But, if the items are to measure intelligence, they must all possess certain abstract properties, described by Spearman as presenting the possibility for the *eduction of relations and correlates* (emphasis in original). This has much the same meaning as inductive ("relations") and deductive ("correlates") reasoning. *Eduction of relations* (emphasis in original) means inferring the general rule from specific instances (i.e., induction). *Eduction of correlates* (emphasis in original) means making up or recognizing a specific instance when given one other specific instance and the general rule (i.e., deduction). (p. 127)

It is popular among some scholars to review items and hypothesize what specific factors may be measured by them; often, factor analysis supports these hypotheses. For example, items requiring test takers to name pictures that become increasingly obscure are seen to measure the broad ability Crystallized Intelligence, and items that require rotation of geometric shapes are seen to measure the broad ability of Visual Processing. Across the items in Item Set 2 in Figure 4.1, it is easy to see the features associated with reasoning, such as inferring and applying rules when exposed to patterns of words, pictures, and symbol across items. As a result, reasoning tests are some of the most well-studied and commonplace across intelligence tests.

What cannot easily be captured from review of item content is how well items measure the central features of intelligence. Tests of knowledge are common across intelligence tests, but it is less obvious how they measure the central features of intelligence. To make this point clear, Jensen (1980) highlighted vocabulary tests, as they

> are among the best measures of intelligence, because the acquisition of word meanings is highly dependent on the *education* of meaning from the contexts in which the words are encountered. Vocabulary for the most part is not acquired by rote memorization or through formal instruction. The meaning of a word most usually is acquired by encountering the word in some context that permits at least some partial inference as to its meaning. . . . Thus the acquisition of vocabulary is not as much a pattern of learning and memory as it is of generalization, discrimination, eduction, and inference. (p. 146)

A deeper analysis considering eduction of relations and correlates—as they relate to cognitive complexity—often is needed. According to Gottfredson (2016), complexity is "an attribute of cognitive tasks and refers to differences in the cognitive load they impose for successful performance" (p. 216). Gottfredson and Saklofske (2009) asserted that

> task complexity increases . . . with greater amount and abstractness of information to integrate; more irrelevant information to ignore; a need to draw inferences or select appropriate procedures; and greater uncertainty, unpredictability, and fluidity of task, information, and circumstance. (p. 188)

The complexity of items including the exact same content—five numbers presented orally—is evident in Item Set 3 in Figure 4.1. Item 1 begins fairly simply, asking the test taker to repeat the numbers. Item 2 increases the complexity by asking that the number be repeated in reverse order. Clearly, this is more challenging, as the numbers must be "held in mind" and then repeated from those heard last to those heard first. Item 3 seems to up the ante of complexity by requiring the numbers to be retained temporarily, evaluated for their properties (rank order), and then repeated. Item 4 alters the modality of response by asking the test taker to retain the numbers while scanning the array of circles, identifying those numbers, and pointing to them. Finally, Item 5 requires even more complexity—perhaps recoding the numbers that are tapped into words, retaining those words for the numbers in mind, reordering those words in ascending order, retaining those reordered words, scanning the array of circles, and tapping them out. Clearly, items with cognitive complexity seem to better measure what commonly is referred to as intelligence than those that may be difficult but not complex (e.g., memorizing 20 telephone numbers in 5 minutes; Gottfredson, 2016).

Differences in presentation and response format. The structure of the test item can make a big difference in what construct is measured, and it should not be detrimental to the measurement of that construct. Some structural features can be observed directly or otherwise easily inferred from items. For example, the item presentation—be it oral, visual, or written—can affect the test taker's access to the content. In addition, the way in which the examinee responds to the item—be it orally or through some motor response—also may be detrimental. Ideally, these influences should not unduly affect performance and prevent access to the test items.

Across Item Set 1 (from a vocabulary test) in Figure 4.1, all items were designed to measure knowledge about the same word. Consider both the test stimuli used as input—that must be heard, viewed, or read—and the output mechanisms—the test taker's response requirements. Some items were intended to be read by an examiner (1, 3, and 4), so the content is oral, and other items were intended to be read by the examinee, so the content is written. Item 2 presents multiple-choice options in terms of written words, and Item 3 contains pictorial content among the response options. Circling (likely with a pencil) is required for Item 2, and pointing is required for Item 3. In contrast, Items 1, 4, and 5 require generation—verses identification—of the answers. An extended oral response is required for Item 1, a full-body motor response is required for Item 4, and a single-word oral response is required for Item 5.

Test developers are acutely aware of how response processes may undermine the validity of test scores. Using the examples from Item Set 1 in Figure 4.1, we can judge that the validity of an inference about the vocabulary knowledge of a test taker who is deaf would be erroneous if they were unable to hear the items presented orally by an examiner. Similarly, a test taker who could not read would be unable to access the test content on items requiring them to read the test item, and test takers who are unable to move their arms would be unable to respond via circling items with a pencil, pointing, or acting out responses. In these cases, the construct-irrelevant influences of hearing acuity, reading skill, and motor skills may be detrimental to the measurement of vocabulary knowledge. Chapter 5 will address test accommodations that address these influences.

Careful design of test items can obviate problems with access to test items for some test takers. For example, according to Jensen (1980), nonverbal tests minimize language requirements on the test taker and

> require no reading but are based on figural materials, pictures of objects, geometric patterns, symbols, and the like. The directions are usually verbal, but a good nonverbal test begins with items of a particular type that are so simple that virtually all the subjects can catch on to the requirements of the task without verbal instructions, or with pantomimed instructions by the tester.... Nonverbal items are answered by making marks of some kind on the test or on a specially prepared answer sheet. (p. 132)

Further, in order to address test takers who have not fully acculturated, culture-reduced items

> do not involve content that is peculiar to a particular period, locality, or culture, or skills that are specifically taught in school. Items involving pictures of cultural artifacts such as vehicles, furniture, musical instruments, or household appliances, for example, are culture, loaded as compared to culture-reduced items involving lines, circles, triangles, and rectangles. (Jensen, 1980, p. 133)

Chapter 14 will address how English language proficiency and acculturation affect access to test items and provide examples of prominent nonverbal intelligence tests and culture-reduced items.

Response processes. Evidence based on *response processes* refers to substantiation of the real or hypothesized steps that test takers follow when completing items. Typically, inferences made about psychological processes or cognitive operations must be drawn from responses to test stimuli. As evident in Table 4.4, these responses can be inferred from review of test stimuli, as previously discussed. For example, cognitive tasks can be dissected into their component operations (see Carroll, 1993); reviewers can evaluate test items to determine their match with the targeted response processes; and text can be analyzed by using readability and cohesion metrics (e.g., Flesch, 1949; Graesser, McNamara, Louwerse, & Cai, 2004). Individuals taking the test can inform us about the accuracy of our validity arguments. For example, test takers may be asked to "think aloud" during test completion or to respond to questions about strategies they used (see Ericsson & Simon, 1993), and their responses can be evaluated to identify themes consistent with the targeted constructs. More sophisticated methods, such as eye-tracking technology and recording of response times, also provide validity evidence based on response processes. Despite the promise of these methods to generate evidence based on response processes, they rarely are applied to intelligence tests and almost never addressed in test technical manuals.

Internal structure. Messick (1995) stated that "the internal structure of the assessment (i.e., interrelations among the scored aspects of tasks and subtask performance) should be consistent with what is known about the internal structure of the domain.... This... is called structural fidelity" (p. 746). In other words, evidence based on internal structure refers to substantiation that a test's items or resultant scores are related to other variables from the test itself in the expected manner. (If the relations are with some other variables external to the test, another type of validity evidence is considered, as we discuss in the next section.) As discussed earlier in the chapter, correlations between item scores and subtest or composite scores, between subtest scores, and between composite scores provide such evidence. These correlations typically are Pearson correlations or variants of them. In some instances, correlations between item scores, as also evaluated in internal consistency analysis (described previously), contribute such validity evidence.

Some of the most sophisticated methods for examining internal structure of tests are exploratory factor analysis (EFA) and confirmatory factor analysis (CFA), as described in Chapter 1. These analyses may use item scores to study the latent variables underlying patterns of correlations, but most of the research with intelligence tests (especially the research presented in test technical manuals) focuses on relations between subtest scores. As made evident in Chapter 1, factor analysis has provided strong evidence for the structure of human cognitive abilities. It helped to form the foundation for psychometric theories of intelligence, and it continues to offer insights today (Beaujean & Benson, 2019a; Keith & M. Reynolds, 2010, 2012).

Tables 4.5 and 4.6 highlight examples of some of the most common and important findings from factor-analytic research with intelligence tests. Table 4.5 presents some of the results from an EFA of six subtests from an intelligence test. In it, the factor analyst elected to specify that only the relations common across all of these subtests be considered. On tests of intelligence, the general factor, a latent variable that is a distillate of what is common across these subtests, typically accounts for more than 50% of the shared variance (Jensen, 1998a). After this general factor is specified, its relations with its six component subtests can be examined in the form of standardized factor loadings. These factor loadings are essentially Pearson r correlations between a subtest score variable and the general factor. They range from -1.0 to 1.0, but intelligence test subtest loadings on the general factor should never be negative (see Chapter 1). As evident in Table 4.5, all subtests have positive factor loadings, and they range from .43 to .77. When we square the factor loading values, we obtain an estimate of the percentage of variance in each subtest that can be attributable to that factor, called communality estimates. Commonality estimates, as decimal fractions, often are converted to percentages for ease of communication. These values are always smaller than the factor loadings, as evident in the values in the table that range from 18% to 60%. In such cases, communality estimates represent the total percentage of variance accounted for in a subtest across all of the factors that were specified, and in this particular case, they represent the variance attributable to the general factor.

Table 4.5. Factor Loadings and Communalities for a One-Factor Model

Subtest	Factor loading	Communality (h^2)
Subtest 1	.77	.60
Subtest 2	.69	.48
Subtest 3	.64	.41
Subtest 4	.73	.54
Subtest 5	.49	.24
Subtest 6	.43	.18

Table 4.6. Pattern Coefficients from a Three-Factor Model with an Oblique Rotation

Subtest	Factor 1	Factor 2	Factor 3
Subtest 1	**.74**	.11	.04
Subtest 2	**.88**	−.04	−.01
Subtest 3	.09	**.67**	−.05
Subtest 4	−.05	**.88**	.04
Subtest 5	−.04	.01	**.76**
Subtest 6	.07	−.03	**.54**
Factor correlations			
Factor 1	—	.63	.48
Factor 2	.63	—	.57
Factor 3	.48	.57	—

As the evidence in Table 4.5 points to the fact that the six subtests included in this analysis are varied in the extent to which they are related to this general factor, we can infer that the general factor adequately represents the construct of psychometric *g*. This model is essentially Spearman's two-factor model, as described in Chapter 1, as all of the variance associated with what is not the general factor is considered unique to subtests. In this case, we can interpret these factor loadings as *g loadings*. For example, Subtests 1 and 4 have values above .70, which we would consider high *g* loadings. Subtests 2 and 3 have values between .50 and .69, which are considered medium *g* loadings. The final two subtests have values less than .50, and we would consider them low *g* loadings. These results convey to us that all of the subtests measure the same thing, perhaps psychometric *g*, but they do so with varying levels of accuracy.

Table 4.6 presents results from the same six subtests (and the same data set). In this case, the factor analyst elected to specify that three factors underlie the patterns of relations between and among these subtests. Further, the analyst evaluated the relations between these factors using a statistical method called an oblique rotation (examples include promax and direct oblimin), which assumes that the factors are correlated and produces estimates of these relations for each pair of factors. These rotation methods can produce several types of factor loadings, but we presented pattern coefficients in Table 4.6.

Notice in Table 4.6 that all subtests have at least one positive factor loading that is > .50. When values of that are lower than about .10 in magnitude (whether positive or negative) are ignored (as they represent negligible relations), each subtest is associated with only one of the factors, a feature called *simple structure* (Thurstone, 1954). It is apparent that whatever Factor 1 represents, subtests 1 and 2 correlate highly with it, and the same conclusions can be drawn about Factor 2 (with subtests 3 and 4) and Factor 3 (with subtests 5 and 6). Conversely, we can infer that these subtests are indicators (or measures) of that factor. For example, we may conclude based on these patterns of results and reviewing the content and response processes associated with each subtest that Factor 1 represents the cognitive ability of Crystallized Intelligence, Factor 2 represents Fluid Reasoning, and Factor 3 represents Processing Speed. In many cases, these conclusions and labeling of factors are subjective, and that is why models such as the CHC theory are important for both test design and interpretation of factor-analytic results.

The factor loadings presented in the top half of Table 4.6 seem to convey to us that these six subtests measure three different latent abilities (and not one) and that they do so quite well. However, the correlations between the factors (.48 to .63, presented in the bottom half of Table 4.6) are noteworthy, as they reveal that the factors are not independent and that a higher-order ability, perhaps psychometric g, accounts for their shared relations. The information included in this table can be used to alter the results in a way that evaluates the effects of a general factor (likely psychometric g) on subtests from the effects of more specific factors on those subtests. The analysis that produces these results is the Schmid-Leiman transformation, which famously was used by Carroll (1993) in his 460+ analyses described in his magnum opus. In many ways, the results from the Schmid-Leiman transformation look similar to those from a bifactor model (see Chapter 2), as all subtests tend to demonstrate salient loadings on the general factor, and only some subtests demonstrate salient loadings on more specific factors.

As evident in Table 4.7, all subtests yielded salient loadings on the general factor (.38 to .75). These results are relatively similar to the g loadings presented in Table 4.5, with only Subtests 1 and 2 being notably lower (by .11 and .09, respectively). Subtests 1 and 3 have the highest loadings, and Subtests 5 and 6 have the lowest loadings. Notice that the subtests demonstrate similar patterns in relations with three specific factors as they did with the correlated three factors presented in Table 4.6. In all cases, the loadings, however, are notably lower, as these factor loadings are based on all of the variance in scores that remains once the general factor variance has been accounted for. Thus, these factors are based on *residual* reliable variance.

Factor analysis also can produce a statistic that has a very specific purpose. If the targeted construct is psychometric g, that statistic, omega hierarchical, gets to the heart of the validity question about whether stratum III composites, such as IQs, measure psychometric g with fidelity. According to Watkins (2017), omega hierarchical (ω_h)

> reflects variance attributable to a common factor and is therefore a measure of the precision with which a score assesses a single construct. When applied to the general factor, ω_h is the ratio of the variance of the general factor compared to the total test variance. . . . A high ω_h coefficient indicates that the

Table 4.7. Factor Loadings from Schmid-Leiman Transformed Factor Solution with a General Factor and Three Specific Factors

		Specific factors		
Subtest	General factor	Factor 1	Factor 2	Factor 3
Subtest 1	**.66**	**.50**	.05	.03
Subtest 2	**.60**	**.60**	−.02	−.01
Subtest 3	**.61**	.06	**.34**	−.04
Subtest 4	**.75**	−.03	**.44**	.03
Subtest 5	**.48**	−.03	.01	**.57**
Subtest 6	**.38**	.05	−.01	**.41**

general factor is the dominant source of systematic variance in the test score. Conversely, a low ω_h coefficient indicates that group factors and/or uniqueness account for the majority of reliable variance in the test score. (p. 1115)

Essentially, omega hierarchical represents the *g* saturation of an IQ, and as you will see in later chapters, results across numerous studies using this metric indicate that most IQ scores represent psychometric *g* very accurately. In contrast, related statistics such *omega hierarchical subscale* indicate that specific ability factors (independent of psychometric *g*) uniformly demonstrate substantially weaker validity evidence based on internal structure than psychometric *g* (McGill, Dombrowski, & Canivez, 2018).

External relations. To establish the meaning of test scores, they must be related to external criteria. The main goal when investigating the *external relations* of a test is to examine the pattern of relations between its scores and other measures and variables, such as scores from other instruments, demographic variables (e.g., age and gender), and educational or diagnostic classifications. Construct validity is supported when the pattern of relations between test scores and the external criteria is both rational and consistent with hypotheses based on theory. Conversely, construct validity is not supported when the pattern of relations cannot be explained by hypotheses based on theory. This type of validity evidence seems to be most prevalent in test technical manuals and in the research literature; it often composes more than half of the validity evidence presented in these manuals.

Evidence of external relations includes correlations between measures of the same or similar constructs, often called *convergent relations*, as well as correlations between measures of dissimilar constructs, often called *discriminant relations*. Analysis of convergent and discriminant relations tends to be theoretically focused, whereas analysis of *criterion-related validity* tends to be more practical. For example, it makes sense that scores from a new intelligence test would correlate highly with those from an older, classic intelligence test if both were administered to the same children over a brief period. Such evidence would yield *concurrent validity* evidence for the new test when compared to the "gold standard" criteria yielded by the older, classic intelligence test. Further, when examining criterion-related validity, important social and educational outcomes measured later in time may serve as criteria for comparison. For example, as described in Chapter 1, IQs demonstrate strong *predictive validity* evidence by yielding sizable positive correlations with long-term academic outcomes. Again, correlations reflecting convergent and discriminant relations and concurrent and predictive validity evidence are typically Pearson correlations. Finally, validity evidence from external relations also can surface from comparisons of known groups (often clinical groups, such as children with intellectual disability, known to differ on the construct being measured). Such results produce what some researchers (e.g., Floyd, Shaver, & McGrew, 2003; Haynes, Smith, & Hunsley, 2018) call *discriminative validity* (not discriminant validity) evidence.

Although classification accuracy studies (sometimes also called *diagnostic accuracy or diagnostic utility* studies) rarely are undertaken in the evaluation of intelligence tests and their scores, we should conduct (and demand) more of them. They are particularly useful in determining whether any score meets our expectations in terms of assisting in the identification of an established condition, such as a psychiatric diagnosis (e.g., intellectual disability) or a special education eligibility area (e.g., intellectual giftedness). Basically, the relation between a score in question (typically a continuous variable) and a dichotomous outcome (presence or absence of the condition) is examined. However, the meaningfulness of the score in practice can be mirrored by examining varying points along its scale—cut points, if you will—and how they can maximize identification of individuals with the condition (true positives), in the form of "hits," and minimize identification of those without the condition (true negatives), in the form of "false alarms." Some of the key technical terms (unfortunately, remarkably similar ones) are sensitivity and specificity. *Sensitivity* reflects the proportion of participants with the condition who have been identified by the cut score in question; *specificity* reflects the proportion of participants without the condition who have not been identified by the cut score in question.

Take for example using a cut score of an IQ of 70 in identifying intellectual disability (as is the focus of Chapter 11). Criteria for the condition (American Psychiatric Association, 2013; Schalock et al., 2010) tend to specify an IQ of about 70, but many state eligibility criteria for special education in recent years still adhere to a rigid cut score of 70 (McNicholas et al., 2018). If we review hypothetical intelligence test data from 100 children with intellectual disability and 100 children without intellectual disability, all identified using formal procedures before the study in question began, we could determine sensitivity and specificity of the score of 70 in identifying these students. As evident in Table 4.8, in this example, the IQ of 70 correctly identified 85 of the 100 students with intellectual disability and correctly identified 98 of the 100 children without intellectual disability. However, it also missed a full 15 students with intellectual disability; they are considered false negatives. Sensitivity was 85% and specificity was 98%, with a false alarm rate of only 2%. That's not terrible, but can we adjust the cut score to maximize both sensitivity and specificity?

Table 4.8 presents results after the cut score was raised to an IQ of 75 based on statements from professional organizations (e.g., Schalock et al., 2010) indicating that the IQ should be about 70 or below, considering confidence intervals that span 5 points above the score of 70, which means 75. Results indicate a major increase in sensitivity—with the higher IQ correctly identifying 94 of the 100 students. Although there was some decrement in specificity, the difference was not stark (96% versus 98%). The false alarm rate doubled from 2% to 4%, but that is not necessarily problematic. With this adjustment, sensitivity and specificity have been maximized. As both false negatives and false alarms have been reduced, we would argue that a flexible cutoff of 70 plus or minus 5 has greater clinical utility than a cut score of 70. Consistent with the literature on improving efficiency of psychological assessment (e.g., Canivez, 2019; Haynes et al., 2018), we encourage more frequent use of classification accuracy studies in intelligence test research.

Consequences. Evidence based on the consequences of testing refers to substantiation that scores and decisions based on them produce intended and not unintended consequences for those taking the tests, depending on the purpose of the assessment. In terms of intended consequences, some assert that treatment utility of assessment (Hayes, Nelson, & Jarrett, 1987; Nelson-Gray, 2003)—evidence that measurable benefits stem from test interpretation—provides positive evidence supporting intended consequences. We address evidence of this type in more detail in Chapter 9, as we discuss developing

Table 4.8. Example Contingency Tables and Calculation of Classification Agreement

		Intellectual Disability Classification	
		Present	*Absent*
Intelligence Test Score of 70	At or Below Cut	A = 85 (True Positives)	B = 2 (False Positives)
	Above Cut	C = 15 (False Negatives)	D = 98 (True Negatives)
	Total	A + C = 100	B + D = 100

Sensitivity = A/(A + C) = 85/100 = .85 or 85%
Specificity = D/(B + D) = 98/100 = .98 or 98%
False alarm rate = 1 − Specificity = 1 − .98 = .02 or 2%

		Intellectual Disability Classification	
		Present	*Absent*
Intelligence Test Score of 75	At or Below Cut	A = 94 (True Positives)	B = 4 (False Positives)
	Above Cut	C = 6 (False Negatives)	D = 96 (True Negatives)
	Total	A + C = 100	B + D = 100

Sensitivity = A/(A + C) = 94/100 = .94 or 94%
Specificity = D/(B + D) = 96/100 = .96 or 96%
False alarm rate = 1 − Specificity = 1 − .96 = .04 or 4%

recommendations and interventions based on results from intelligence tests. Others have argued that overrepresentation and underrepresentation of racial and ethnic minority groups in the United States in special education constitute evidence of invalidity in assessment, and as a result, intelligence tests have been the target of criticism.

Evidence based on the consequences, however, is understudied and poorly understood (see Braden & Kratochwill, 1997; Cizek, Bowen, & Church, 2010). Many researchers are uncertain about the inclusion of this type of validity evidence along with the other four, because it does not appear to be a relevant criterion for evaluating the validity of certain instruments. For example, do yardsticks provide invalid measures of height because basketball players are taller on average than the general population? Obviously, they do not. On the one hand, we appreciate a focus on promoting efforts to enhance the body of support for the positive outcomes of test results—especially as it relates to development of evidence-based interventions to address learning and behavioral problems. We also recognize that this type of validity evidence challenges us to consider how sources of invalidity in testing (i.e., construct underrepresentation or construct-irrelevant variance) might impact individuals and groups and produce adverse consequences (see Messick, 1995). On the other hand, we fear that excessive emphasis on what appears to be adverse consequences—without carefully designed scientific research studies and consideration of ecological influences outside of the testing context—will lead to unfounded animosity directed toward testing in schools and related settings, due to presumed invalidity and bias. (See Chapter 14 for further discussion of test bias.)

MAKING SENSE OF VALIDITY EVIDENCE

As we have stated previously, when validity evidence is being considered, details and conditions should be specified. Asking "Do I have solid evidence supporting my use of these scores to reach my goal?" ensures consideration of these details and conditions. According to the *Standards* (AERA et al., 2014), "A sound validity argument integrates various strands of evidence into a coherent account of the degree to which existing evidence and theory support the intended interpretation of test scores for specific uses" (p. 21). Many argue that the validation of any instrument and its scores is an ongoing process, stemming from a process of testing rival hypotheses (especially related to evaluation of construct-irrelevant influences). However, there probably is a point at which a "good enough" body of validity evidence is available for the provisional application of test score interpretation.

Selecting the Best Tests for Your Needs

Following the *Standards*, you should be able to (1) consider both the context of the assessment and the personal characteristics and background of each child or adolescent you are slated to assess and (2) select tests that most accurately measure their cognitive abilities. However, doing so is no easy feat. First, consider the stakes involved in the assessment. Most decisions involving intelligence tests are high-stakes decisions, such as diagnosis or eligibility determination. These decisions require higher standards of evidence, and this requirement should lead to employing a more conservative approach to score interpretation. Then, consider the quality of the norms, the reliability of resultant scores, and validity evidence for the intelligence tests that are available. In general, these steps can be completed easily, but also consider carefully the individual's characteristics, including age, presenting problems, sensory acuity, motor development, language proficiency, background characteristics, and so on, when selecting intelligence tests to administer to him or her.

In order to address these goals, seek out published test reviews of intelligence tests. Perhaps the best source for such reviews is the Buros Center for Testing (www.buros.org), which publishes a series of *Mental Measurement Yearbooks*. Further, several peer-reviewed journals—including *Assessment for Effective Intervention*, the *Canadian Journal of School Psychology*, and the *Journal of Psychoeducational Assessment*—publish test reviews. Although such narrative reviews do not provide systematic, objective evaluations of the tests they target, they can pave the way for your careful review of tests.

The benefit of reading a test's technical manual from cover to cover, however, cannot be understated. It is important to note that the validity evidence often provided by publishers in test manuals typically is not guided by theory (Beaujean & Benson, 2019b). In Cronbach's (1989) words: "The good news is that today's manuals rarely flood users with jawboning speculative defenses. The bad news is that they rarely report incisive checks into rival hypotheses, followed by an integrative argument. Rather they rake together miscellaneous correlations" (p. 155). In addition, examiners should pay particular attention to the norming process, review the norm table for scaling problems, and evaluate the reliability estimates and the body of validity evidence for the scores that will be interpreted. Further, they should consider these test properties and score properties for the specific test takers they will assess. They should, for example, compare the test takers' characteristics to those of the norm sample and consider scaling issues subtest by subtest, reliability estimates score by score, and validity evidence appropriate for their age and for the referral concern. To assist in this process, we have reviewed, evaluated, and described characteristics of the most prominent full-length intelligence tests, nonverbal intelligence tests, and brief and abbreviated intelligence tests in chapters 6 and 7. Further, Form 4.1 includes a checklist designed to aid in evaluating and selecting the best intelligence test for your needs. This checklist addresses basic demographic characteristics, the referral concern, screening results (see Chapter 5), test norming, and measurement properties associated with varying score types.

Summary

This chapter highlighted standards guiding the selection and use of tests, and it has reviewed their most critical characteristics. We encourage you to promote measurement integrity through careful test reviews and test selection before you begin testing, rather than calling on this information after you have noticed an oddball score that does not fit with the remainder of the information from your assessment. The intelligence tests available to you are stronger than ever before. Your efforts to select the best tests for your needs should yield dividends in producing more accurate and meaningful results for those you test.

CHAPTER 5

The Assessment Process with Children and Adolescents

with Ryan L. Farmer and Richard J. McNulty[1]

It is important to have a strong knowledge of the reasons for assessment, the typical steps taken during the assessment process, and the potential influences on test performance that can be assessed, controlled during standardized testing, or acknowledged when interpreting test results. This chapter addresses these issues and provides practical tools that will promote the most accurate assessment of cognitive abilities through standardized testing.

The Comprehensive Assessment Process— and How Intelligence Tests Fit In

Assessment is a broad term that refers to the process of collecting data to make informed decisions. Psychological and educational assessments typically are conducted for one of five reasons (and sometimes for multiple reasons):

1. First, they are conducted for *screening* purposes—to rapidly identify those with specified characteristics, so that more in-depth assessment may be conducted. Screening children for hearing or vision deficiencies, for reading problems (via oral reading fluency probes), and for internalizing problems such as depressive disorders (via self-report rating scales) is relatively common. Intelligence tests (including brief or abbreviated intelligence tests; see Chapters 6 and 7) often are used to screen for intellectual disability (ID) and intellectual giftedness.
2. Second, assessments may be conducted for *diagnosis* or *eligibility determination*. Assessment data may be used to determine whether a child or adolescent meets one of the criteria for a mental disorder as outlined in the *Diagnostic and Statistical Manual*

---

[1]. Dr. Ryan L. Farmer is an assistant professor at Oklahoma State University. His research interests include evidence-based approaches to assessment in school psychology. Richard J. McNulty is a doctoral candidate in school psychology at the University of Memphis. His research interests include intelligence assessment, treatment utility of assessment, and emotional regulation.

of Mental Disorders (American Psychiatric Association, 2013), or such assessment may be prescribed by legislation (currently the Individuals with Disabilities Education Improvement Act of 2004 [IDEA, 2004]) to determine eligibility for special education services.

3. Third, assessment may be conducted for *problem solving*—to identify problems, validate them, and develop interventions to address a concern.
4. Fourth, assessments may be completed for *evaluation* purposes. These assessments inform judgments about a person's level of competence, whether standards have been met, or if change in the desired direction has been achieved. For example, evaluation of a reading intervention program may be achieved through repeated assessments of oral reading fluency skills (via progress monitoring).
5. Finally, assessments may be completed as *indirect interventions*—because of their direct effects on the person being assessed—so that the process of completing the assessment leads to changes in the person and their behavior.

It is important to understand that *testing* is a more specific term than *assessment*, and that testing typically is only one component of an assessment. *Testing* refers to the process of collecting data via standardized procedures for obtaining samples of behavior and drawing conclusions about the constructs underlying these behaviors. A *construct* is an "attribute of people, assumed to be reflected in test performance" (Cronbach & Meehl, 1955, p. 283). In the case of intelligence tests, these constructs are cognitive abilities. When considering testing, most psychologists think of individualized standardized testing (i.e., tests administered by an examiner on a one-to-one basis with the test taker for screening, diagnostic, or eligibility purposes), and this book focuses on such tests. In contrast, many people think about group-administered tests—those administered to a class or to all students in a school (as in end-of-the-year, high-stakes tests) for evaluation purposes.

Just as tests are only one component of the assessment process, it includes many other components: reviews of records (e.g., report cards, prior reports and test scores, and incident reports); reviews of permanent products (e.g., completed class assignments); interviews conducted with parents, teachers, and other caregivers; systematic direct observations in classroom, home, or clinic settings; behavior rating scales completed by parents, teachers, and other caregivers; and interviews with and self-report rating scales completed by children and adolescents. Given the high degree of comorbidity (i.e., overlap) of academic and behavior problems displayed by children and adolescents, comprehensive assessments often are necessary to ensure that all relevant problems are evaluated. Best practice in assessment is to complete a multi-method, multi-source, and multi-setting assessment of children and adolescents' learning as well as their behavioral and emotional functioning (American Educational Research Association [AERA], American Psychological Association [APA], & National Council on Measurement in Education [NCME], 2014; Whitcomb, 2017). Such assessments largely are mandated for determining eligibility for special education. Thus, the best assessments draw data from (a) many different assessment techniques, (b) from the test taker being assessed as well as multiple knowledgeable persons who observe the test taker, and (c) from behaviors displayed across more than one setting (e.g., the testing session alone).

Intelligence tests are only one component—and sometimes an unessential component—of comprehensive assessments. Because intelligence tests produce measures of one of the most explanatory variables in all of the social sciences, psychometric g, we believe that they should be considered in seeking answers to children's academic problems. We do not claim, however, (1) that they should always be included in a comprehensive assessment or (2) that hours and hours of intelligence testing and days of poring over its results are necessary in most cases. In fact, we recommend the following texts that address a variety of academic and behavioral problems, related assessment practices, and evidence-based interventions: Briesch, Volpe, and Floyd (2018); Mash & Barkley, 2014; Prinstein, Youngstrom, Mash, and Barkley (2019); Steege, Pratt, Wickerd, Guare, and Watson (2019); and Whitcomb (2017).

Preliminary Assessment

GATHERING BACKGROUND INFORMATION

A thorough description of the personal history of the test taker being assessed should be obtained prior to administering intelligence tests. By doing so, case conceptualization is furthered, preparation for testing is enhanced, and professional relationships are facilitated. Background information often is needed to determine age of onset of the presenting problem (i.e., during which developmental period the problem surfaced); the presumed causes of the problem (e.g., whether the problem runs in the family); the course or prognosis of the problem (i.e., whether the presenting problem may resolve itself or become worse over time); and the results of previous assessments or interventions. In particular, the following types of information should be obtained: referral information; demographic information (including age, grade, race, and ethnicity); family structure and history; and the test taker's medical history (including prenatal and perinatal history, genetic conditions, ear infections, head injuries, surgeries, and hospitalizations), developmental history (including speech–language milestones and motor milestones), social history (including major life stressors and traumatic events); and educational history (including grades, prior test scores, academic problems, behavior problems, and prior interventions).

Although this information could be obtained by using a response form (aka paper-and-pencil format—e.g., the Behavior Assessment System for Children, Third Edition [BASC-3] Structured Developmental History Form; C. Reynolds & Kamphaus, 2015a), this information should be obtained in an interview if possible. Interviews provide the opportunity to follow up on issues raised by informants, and they also facilitate building rapport. (The working relationship between an assessment professional and the test taker during assessment often is called *rapport*.) Your rapport with informants will promote their engagement in the assessment process and facilitate your clear communication of results after the assessment is complete.

SCREENING FOR ACCESS SKILLS

A thorough screening for possible barriers to testing should be conducted prior to completing intelligence tests. Throughout this chapter, we consistently address methods to identify and prevent or minimize construct-irrelevant influences on test scores (AERA et al., 2014). These confounds, as they apply to validity evidence, are described in more detail in Chapter 4, but in this chapter, we address them as relevant to individual testing cases. According to Bracken (2000),

> An assumption made about the psychoeducational assessment process is that examiners have made every effort to eliminate all identifiable construct-irrelevant influences on the child or adolescent's performance and the resultant test scores. That is, the goal in assessment is to limit assessment to only construct-relevant attributes (e.g., intelligence), while limiting the influence of construct-irrelevant sources of variation (e.g., fatigue, lack of cooperation, emotional lability). Before important decisions can be made with confidence about a child or adolescent's future educational plans, possible treatments, or medications, examiners must be comfortable with the validity of assessment results. Only when all construct-irrelevant sources of variation have been eliminated or optimally controlled can examiners attest to the validity of the assessment results. (p. 33)

Another way to discuss construct-relevance and irrelevance is by considering alternate terms that are at least a bit more transparent: *target skills* and *access skills* (Braden & Elliott, 2003; Phillips, 1994). Target skills refer to the intended focus of the test— what it was designed to measure. As discussed in Chapter 4, intelligence test items usually involve the ability to think abstractly, the capacity to acquire knowledge, and complex problem-solving skills in their assessment of general intelligence. Access skills, in contrast, refer to relatively basic behavioral and cognitive capabilities that assist the test taker in completing items. Without these access skills, the target skills cannot be measured accurately. Access skills may include the following (if they are not otherwise targeted by the test):

> attending, listening to and understanding language, seeing, sitting still for an extended period of time, reading, writing, following directions, manipulating materials, tracking examiner's movements and related materials, processing information in a timely manner, working for a sustained period of time, communicating personal needs, [and] asking questions when they do not understand. (Braden & Elliott, 2003, p. 4)

Relating back to our earlier terms, the absence of access skills and errors in employing them likely contribute to construct-irrelevant variance in measurement. During testing, sensory and motor deficits and limited language proficiency often cause problems with test taker's access to test items and produce serious confounds in resulting scores. For example, a test taker with amblyopia, also known as lazy eye, may not be able to review visual patterns in matrices and apply their reasoning skills in answering items. A test taker with motor impairment associated with spastic cerebral palsy may be unable to hold a pencil and quickly and accurately draw small shapes when measuring processing speed or draw a path through a maze when examining visual-spatial and planning skills. A test taker with ID may have such deficits with functional communication skills so they may be unable to follow verbal directions or answer verbally administered questions in order to demonstrate the necessary target skills (American Speech-Language-Hearing Association [ASHA], 2018). As more than 20% of the United States population speaks a language in their homes other than English (United States Census Bureau, 2018), many test takers who are English-language learners may be bridled with problems related to access to English language-based content in tests. Although some assert that identifying problems such as these is one goal of intelligence testing, we view doing so as a preliminary goal of the assessment process and not as a goal of intelligence testing per se, where measurement accuracy is vital.

Examiners engaged in intelligence testing should be aware of these potential problems and strive to reduce their effects so that scores best represent the target skills, which are cognitive ability constructs. Whenever possible, testing should not commence until formal screening for sensory impairments that may limit access to test content have been conducted. These screenings should be completed by optometrists, audiologists, medical staff, and other qualified professionals. However, access to these formal screenings prior to testing may be a luxury for many engaged in intelligence testing (e.g., psychologists in private practice). Even in those settings where vision and hearing screenings are conducted routinely, the examiner may not have access to this information prior to testing, and it is unlikely that there is corresponding screening of motor skill deficits, articulation errors, and language skills prior to testing. Rather than occurring in sequence (with screenings occurring prior to testing), in most multidisciplinary settings, all of these assessment activities are completed independently and shared at the end of that process. In this section, we feature two methods for identifying potential problems with access skills prior to testing and follow with an introduction to test accommodations.

Screening Tool for Assessment Rating Forms. Informal methods can be used to screen for problems with sensory acuity, speech and language, motor control, and behavior as potential confounds. Based on our review of the literature and consultation with professionals in such fields as optometry, audiology, speech–language pathology, and physical therapy, we identified items that parents, teachers, or both should complete as part of the initial stage of assessment (American Speech–Language–Hearing Association, n.d.; Centers for Disease Control and Prevention, n.d.; Gordon-Brannan, 1994; Colour Blind Awareness, n.d.; Teller, McDonald, Preston, Sebris, & Dobson, 2008; Mathers, Keyes, & Wright, 2010; Suttle, 2001). In this book, we offer several assessment tools that are collectively called the Screening Tool for Assessment (STA).

Form 5.1 is the STA Parent and Caregiver Screening Form, and Form 5.2 is the STA Teacher Screening Form. These forms include items addressing visual acuity problems (items 1–6), color blindness (items 7–10), auditory acuity problems (items 11–16), speech and articulation problems (items 17–22), fine motor problems (items 23–29), noncompliance (items 30–32), and language and cultural differences (items 33–37). All items marked "Yes" indicate a potential problem except items 21 and 22, which include percentages, and items 28 and 29, which indicate potential problems with marked "No." If the patterns of item-level responses indicate serious concerns (e.g., if more than half of the items in a section are marked as indicating a problem), delay testing and inquire about access skills, discuss whether prior screenings have indicated concerns in these areas, and consider whether more thorough screening should be conducted before engaging in intelligence testing.

Screening Tool for Assessment Direct Screening. In addition to the Screening Tool for Assessment Rating Forms, we offer assessment tools that home in on access skills and related confounds prior to beginning testing. The STA Direct Screening Form (see Forms 5.3 and 5.4) begins with general questions targeting emotional states and preparedness for testing. The first section covers global impressions of health and mental state, the prior night's sleep, feelings of confidence, and motivation. The next section includes items devoted to screening for sensory deficits and fine motor control problems. A final item addresses language proficiency. These questions are not intended to be administered in a rigid fashion; instead, they should guide your brief screening interview. Be sure to follow up responses with appropriate extenders, paraphrasing, more specific questions ("What else happened this morning?"), and "soft" commands (e.g., "Tell me more about it"). There is no reason to complete additional screening if all evidence converges on the absence of sensory deficits and fine motor control problems, but direct assessment of these issues may be useful. The remainder of the STA Direct Screening Form includes items targeting sensory deficits, fine motor control problems, as well as articulation problems and intelligibility.

First, the STA Direct Screening Form includes items targeting visual acuity. Children and adolescents are asked to name letters printed on a page to screen for potential vision problems that may interfere with the test administration (see Form 5.3 for instructions and Form 5.4 for items). The letters printed on the top line should be large and distinct enough for every test taker to see, and corrective feedback can be used to train young or low-functioning test takers. It is essentially a teaching trial. After the completion of this trial, ask test takers to read the rows below it. Because no intelligence test uses type smaller than the second row of letters (from the top) in Form 5.4 (i.e., 12-point type), we initially considered the vision screening to be passed if the test taker accurately reads seven of the nine items in any row below the top row. A carefully designed study of third-, fourth-, and fifth-grade students by Hawkins (2016) revealed that a score of 34 or lower (missing at least two items) best differentiated between students in an experimental condition that simulated vison problems and students who read without simulated impairment. Do not administer the vision screening items to those (especially young children) who have not yet mastered the names of all letters of the alphabet. An alternate version of the letter-based STA vision screening is described later in this section.

Second, direct assessment items target color blindness. Test takers are asked to identify the colors of six squares. They should be able to identify all six colors, and errors in identifying the red and green squares will be especially indicative of color blindness in those old enough and high-functioning enough to know color names. Hawkins (2016) indicated that missing any item indicates potential color blindness among students in third grade and older. Do not administer the color-blindness items to those who have not yet mastered the names of the basic colors. The color-blindness screener is not included in this book, but the entire STA Direct Screening Test, which includes this screener with color images, can be downloaded at https://textbooks.rowman.com/STA_DST

Third, direct assessment items target fine motor skills (see Form 5.3 for instructions and Form 5.4 for items). Test takers are asked to trace a horizontal line, a star, and a circle, and to write a simple sentence. Do not administer the item requiring writing to those (especially young children) who have not yet mastered letter printing. Consider deviations from the lines and malformed letters, as well as unsteady pencil grips, hand tremors and jerky movements, impulsive and messy responding, and signs of frustration when a test taker is completing these items, as these may be associated with fine motor control problems. In general, responses are judged qualitatively. The screening is passed if (a) the test taker responds with reasonable accuracy in tracing or (b) their writing would be legible to a stranger who would not know what the sentence in the last item should say. In evaluating the three tracing items (the line, star, and circle), Hawkins (2016) awarded 1 point for each segment of the line or shape that was marked. Considering a total of 176 segments (with the line having 25 segments, the star having 86 segments, and the circle having 65 segments), a score of 135 or lower most accurately classified students who were in a condition that simulated motor problems.

The remaining direct assessment items from the STA Direct Screening Form do not require visual stimuli (as those included in Form 5.4 do). The next items target auditory acuity (see Form 5.3). These screening items require the test taker to play a listening game, where you give brief commands and the test taker points to parts of their face and body (Howard, 1992). During Part A, administer all of the items in a slightly louder voice than typical to establish a baseline understanding of the commands. For test takers who struggle with this part (perhaps due to vocabulary knowledge), provide additional instruction and model where to point; repeat until they are able to complete all items correctly. In cases where mastery cannot be demonstrated, omit the failed item or items when administering the next set of items. During Part B, ask the test taker to close their eyes while you re-administer the items in a whisper. During Part B, observe behavioral signs of hearing problems, such as turning the head to favor one ear and delayed or vague responding (e.g., hovering of the hand near their head). The screening is passed if the test taker responds accurately to at least five of the seven items in Part B. Results from Hawkins, Farmer, and Floyd (2014) indicate that, despite the careful design of Part A (to ensure test taker understanding), some preschool-age children may struggle in identifying their hair, shoulders, and chins. More information is needed before offering a cut score associated with passing this item.

Finally, direct assessment items target articulation and intelligibility (see Form 5.3). The test taker is asked to close their eyes and to repeat words you have stated at a normal volume. These items were developed for the STA on the basis of Shriberg's (1993) findings regarding the development of more challenging phonemes in children. Phonemes included in each word represent the so-called Late 8 sounds (i.e., the last eight sounds that children are expected to acquire in speech). Phonemes are represented in three positions (initial, medial, and final) across the words (when possible), because these phonemes present different levels of difficulty at each position. For our purposes, we have used the International Phonetic Alphabet when sounds match the English alphabet letters (e.g., /l/). However, when appropriate phonetic symbols would not be commonly recognized, a representation of that phoneme appears in quotation marks. When you are considering patterns of responses, keep in mind that 75% of children should acquire the phonemes /l/, /z/, /s/, *sh*, and *zh* by age 5. The phoneme *th* (voiced, as in the word *although*, and voiceless, as in the word *think*) and /r/ should be acquired by age 6 (Shriberg, 1993). We previously reasoned that the screening was passed if the test taker provides at least 20 of the 23 correct phonemes, but Hawkins (2016) revealed that a score of 16 and lower best differentiated between third- through fifth-grade students with simulated articulation problems and students without simulated problems. Hawkins et al. (2014) also revealed that dialect differences among African American, Black, and Hispanic preschool students should be considered carefully when scoring items involving the phoneme *th*. (See Charity, Scarborough, & Griffin, 2004 for more information.)

In addition, a brief rating of intelligibility is available that coincides with items on the STA Parent/Caregiver and Teacher Screening Forms (Forms 5.1 and 5.2). *Intelligibility* is best defined by Bowen (1998) as the percentage of an individual's spoken language that can be readily understood by an unfamiliar listener. Flipsen's (2006) intelligibility formula is as follows:

$$\frac{\text{Age in years}}{4} * 100 = \% \text{ understood by an unfamiliar listener}$$

As such, a child's intelligibility should increase by 25% for each year after birth. A 1-year-old is expected to be 25% intelligible to strangers, whereas a 3-year-old is expected to be 75% intelligible to strangers. Taking comparable ratings from familiar listeners (e.g., parents) and unfamiliar listeners (e.g., you as the examiner) results in a clinical, albeit subjective, accounting of intelligibility in children. For the purposes of assessment, low intelligibility can affect a child's ability to respond verbally to items. As such, low intelligibility ratings should be considered potentially invalidating when your examiner rating is below 75%. In these cases, it may be wise to consider using language-reduced composite scores or multidimensional nonverbal intelligence tests.

As noted previously, even knowledge of letter names may be associated with access to target skills. This fact is certainly true for the STA vision screening. As most young children and some test takers with developmental disabilities may not have mastered the ability to name letters, they may be unable to complete its practice items correctly. To begin to address this problem, we offer a version of the STA vision screening that uses only pictographic images; it is available on the Open Science Framework (https://osf.io/pjceb/). It is an adaptation of the LEA symbols test (Hyvärinen, Nasanen, & Laurinen, 1980), which included four symbols in the form of line drawings. The apple and circle (or "ring") images and the pentagon (or "house") and square images were of similar size and shape so that those with poor vision might mislabel them as they decrease in size. Our adaptation of the STA vision screening based on the LEA symbols includes six line drawings: a heart and a circle, a pentagon and a square, and a star and a triangle. During initial trials, all of the images are introduced by the examiner in large form and labeled verbally. After the test taker correctly labels each one, 29 items are presented—with three-to-six images per page—and the test taker is prompted to expressively label each shape. The final item set includes images that are each 0.25 inch by 0.25 inch. Hawkins et al. (2014) demonstrated that despite the careful design of Part A (to ensure test taker understanding), preschool-age students in Head Start settings may have particular trouble in consistently labeling the square and the triangle, so alternate labels may need to be employed with similar students.

Considering Access and Developing Test Accommodations

If problems associated with access skills cannot be corrected before an assessment (e.g., vision problems corrected with glasses), review intelligence test items to determine if they require the access skills. Here, review what you can see and read (i.e., item content) as well as what you imagine the test taker doing to answer the items correctly (i.e., response processes). As most intelligence tests are designed to include a variety of stimuli, tap into numerous cognitive processes, and require a number of different response processes—in part to minimize the effects of any facilitating or interfering factors associated with any of these elements—identifying problems with access will be challenging. To promote both accuracy and fairness in testing (AERA et al., 2014; see also Chapter 13), we recommend the following: Select tests that exclude content or requirements that prevent full access. Consider alternative scores when students may be unable to access all content on a test. Adapt the test's features to remove or reduce the problems with access.

NONVERBAL TESTS AND LANGUAGE-REDUCED COMPOSITES

If a test taker's access is limited due to functional communication deficits or limited English language proficiency, a class of instruments often called *nonverbal intelligence tests* probably should be employed. They have been constructed to minimize or eliminate (a) the use of written and oral instruction and (b) written and oral responses. Such tests favor symbols, images, and pantomime for the delivery of instructions while providing nonvocal response options, such as pointing and the use of tangible stimuli.

One of the key arguments supporting this perspective is that these tests have been designed for the very specific purpose they are used—to reduce problems with access. Thus, they do not require the examiner to develop accommodations that have not been properly evaluated in research. We highlight three of these tests in Chapter 7. In addition to nonverbal intelligence tests, several comprehensive intelligence tests produce scores from a subset of their subtests that were deemed as the least affected by access to language- and English-based content. These scores often are referred to as "nonverbal composites," but they probably are better conceived as "language-reduced." We also review some of them in Chapters 6 and 7.

OTHER ALTERNATIVE SCORES AND SUBSTITUTIONS

Some intelligence tests produce alternative scores that should be comparable to more comprehensive ones but stem from a fewer number of subtests. In doing so, they provide examiners opportunities to reduce problems with access and obtain norm-referenced scores while not requiring novel accommodations. For example, we discuss the General Ability Index and Nonverbal Index from the Wechsler Intelligence Scale for Children, Fifth Edition (WISC-V; Wechsler, 2014a) as alternatives to the test's Full Scale IQ in Chapter 6. This test also allows for one subtest to be substituted for another in calculating its Full Scale IQ, but some evidence shows that subtest substitution increases error in measurement (Zhu, Cayton, & Chen, 2016). We suggest employing these alternative scores based on careful consideration of access prior to testing. In some rare cases, after unexpected problems with access surface during testing, they also may be employed.

ACCOMMODATIONS BASED ON PRESENTATION, REQUIREMENTS, AND RESPONSE FORMATS

Test accommodations refer to changes in the way test information is presented to the test taker and alterations in the manner they may respond. Technically, these are violations in test standardization, as discussed later in this chapter. However, accommodations are developed to remove or reduce accessibility problems while maintaining integrity of measurement of target skills. For example, on an intelligence test subtest intended to measure the specific ability to rotate line drawings mentally, identify those that match a pattern, and point to the correct drawings, a test taker with motor impairment could be allowed more time to point to the drawing than typically allowed or to state which drawings are their answers by uttering a number associated with the drawings. In this case, the targeted skill (or ability) would be maintained. In contrast, a subtest targeting visual scanning speed (aka processing speed) includes in its targeted skills the speed component. If a test taker were given extended time to complete this subtest, the targeted skills (or construct) would not be measured accurately, and the results would be upwardly biased of that test taker.

With the greatest of caution and consultation with other experienced professionals, accommodations should be implemented to remove or reduce potential confounds. Examples include enlarging test stimuli, using American Sign Language, and employing augmentative and alternative communication methods (Beukelman & Mirenda, 2013). The American Speech-Language-Hearing Association (2019) has conveyed that these augmentative and alternative communication methods include

> a variety of techniques and tools, including picture communication boards, line drawings, speech-generating devices (SGDs), tangible objects, manual signs, gestures, and finger spelling, to help the individual express thoughts, wants and needs, feelings, and ideas. (para. 2)

Braden and Elliott (2003) provided rich and instructive examples of appropriate and inappropriate accommodations for subtests from the Stanford-Binet, Fifth Edition (Roid, 2003), and Thompson et al. (2018) addressed accommodations for students with severe disabilities.

The Testing Process

In this section, we address how to prepare yourself and the testing environment for testing, how to establish rules and expectations for the testing session, how to build rapport and interact with children and adolescents during test administration, how to observe test session behaviors, and how to judge the "validity" of the test results.

PREPARING FOR TESTING

As you prepare for the testing session, be physically and mentally ready to test; appropriately arrange the testing materials and adjust the testing environment to maximize efficiency and eliminate potential confounds; and have a thorough grasp of the test's administration procedures (e.g., rules for subtest stopping points and querying).

Dress, accessories, and equipment. Because most testing sessions last approximately 2 hours, dress comfortably yet professionally. Although most sessions will be completed at a table with you sitting in a chair, you may need to sit on and crawl about on the floor when you are testing young children. Dressing in comfortable slacks and loose-fitting clothes is important (see Bracken, 2000, for more information about testing young children). In addition, be mindful of how your accessories may interfere with testing. For example, decorative rings and bracelets should be avoided, and discretion should be used in selecting ties, necklaces, and earrings. These personal items should not become distractions during testing.

In the same vein, we discourage use of cell phones during testing. Although we know psychologists who use their cell phones for timing during testing, the risk is too great for cell phones to cause distractions by vibrating, ringing, beeping, or otherwise providing audible notifications. If you do use a cell phone, it is best to turn on the "Do Not Disturb" feature if it has one. In addition, it is common for children to use their parents' cell phones for games and other activities, so they may see your phone as a game console rather than a part of the testing equipment. Further, without numerous adjustments to settings, smartphones are likely to auto-lock for security purposes, time out to save power, and without warning, lock up or restart. Notifications may block access to timers, and alarms may disrupt the testing session. Occasionally, we have seen psychologists using wrist watches for timing. Unless such a watch is removed from the wrist, using it will be cumbersome; further, wrist watches often are somewhat difficult to manipulate because of their small buttons and small touch screens. We recommend using reliable, old-school athletic digital stopwatches or digital kitchen timers. These devices should fit in the palm of the hand, count up (and not only down, as some timers do), and have beepers removed or turned off so that they operate silently.

It is becoming increasingly common for intelligence and achievement tests to require devices that play audio files during administration. In general, (1) select the highest-quality equipment (i.e., a device with high-fidelity speakers) and (2) test this equipment before initiating assessment. As a matter of general convenience, invest in a protective screen to cover the device and make sure that the screen is clean and free of potentially distracting fingerprints prior to the assessment (Dries, Dumont, & Viezel, 2017). Confirm that batteries are sufficiently charged and all other applications are closed prior to testing. You also should consider the test taker's characteristics, including whether the use of a laptop computer to present items will introduce a distraction during testing. Because computer system updates can effectively block your use of your device, you should ensure that your audio player is functioning properly.

Computer-assisted assessments (such as Q-Interactive, discussed in Chapter 6, which employs two iPads) require planning that is different from traditional paper-and-pencil tests. For example, the examiner must ensure that both devices are configured, synced, and ready for use. Generally, device configuration can be done once, but review it prior to each assessment to ensure smooth and timely testing. To prepare the iPads for assessment, change a number of their default settings under the Settings menu. They include disabling gestures on the test taker's iPad (to prevent them from exiting the app during testing), disabling auto correction and auto capitalization, and disabling the auto brightness option. You should consider disabling the home button on the test taker's device through the "Guided Access" feature (so that the test taker does not exit the application). Ideally, you also should disable notifications so that calendar and other alerts do not disrupt testing.

After changing some default settings, the examiner also will need to configure the device to optimal settings. For example, set the auto lock settings to 15 minutes on both devices so that they do not go into sleep mode when the test taker's device is not used for display and adjust the display settings on the test taker's iPad to maximize its brightness. Final considerations in the configuration process include syncing the iPads to ready them for testing, activating Wi-Fi, and enabling Bluetooth. In order to complete the syncing process, you will be required to download the Assess app from the App store and log into your account. Within this application's setting menu, select "Application Mode" in order to set one iPad to "practitioner" and another to "client." A helpful user's guide currently is available in the Support tab of the Q-interactive website, and it should be consulted before the first testing session. Having the devices configured and synced, the examiner must create a client profile on the Q-Interactive Central platform. Importantly, this platform is accessible through an iPad or a computer, so the examiner need not wait for the assessment session to initiate a profile. Once in Q-Interactive Central, create the profile by entering the client's standard personal data. Once a test is selected, you can tailor the assessment battery under the "Batteries" tab by selecting the subtests you wish to administer.

Finally, you should have other materials at your disposal. Of course, numerous pencils are usually needed, and you will need to consider variations in the types of pencils required across tests. For example, erasers are prohibited during administration of some tests; they should be removed before testing. In addition, often #2 lead pencils are called for, but sometimes red pencils are required. You also should maintain a collection of tangible incentives. For example, small stickers may be useful to reinforce attentive and compliant behaviors during testing. For young children, small food items (e.g., M&Ms and raisins) may be helpful for the same purpose. Issues pertaining to the use of reinforcers are addressed later in the chapter.

Selecting and arranging the testing environment. You should select a testing environment that has minimal distractions and otherwise is ideal for testing (Bracken, 2000). The room should be well lighted, kept at a comfortable temperature, and have adequate ventilation. It should contain furniture that is appropriately sized for the test taker. Chairs should be short enough so that a child's feet can touch the floor, and if they cannot, consider placing a box or large books under the test taker's feet (Kamphaus, 2001). Tabletops should have smooth surfaces, and children should be able to reach them without straining. If these ideals cannot be met, do not panic; follow the teacher's maxim of *modify and adjust* to prevent or minimize construct-irrelevant influences.

You should consider where you and the test taker should sit. The pattern of seating (e.g., sitting across from test takers or beside them) almost always is dictated by the test's standardized procedures. In general, strive to seat yourself at the long end of a rectangular table (if possible) in order to arrange your materials more easily and to allow for more writing space. Circular tables are not ideal for testing when (a) they are so wide that you cannot comfortably reach across the table or (b) it is difficult to distance testing material appropriately from the table's edge and to judge the correctness of some responses when the table has no straight edge. Be sure to seat the test taker so that they are not facing distractions (e.g., a window with a view of the playground).

You should consider the time of day for testing. For example, in high school settings, adolescents may be groggy in the morning, so testing in the early afternoon may be ideal. In clinic settings, you must weigh the costs and benefits of testing at the end of the school day and in the early evening versus having the test taker miss school to complete testing. It is wise to discuss the best times of the day for testing with parents, teachers, and with sufficient age and self-awareness, the test takers themselves.

Finally, for two reasons, you should reserve enough time to complete each test in its entirety. First, most tests were normed that way. Second, completing a test in one session prevents you from having to use different norms to score subtests if the delay is extremely lengthy. (In general, if the delay between sessions is no more than 2 weeks, use the test taker's age at the time of the first session unless other recommendations appear in the test's scoring guidelines.)

Working with parents during testing. What should you do if parents request that they be able to observe your testing session by sitting in the testing room with you? It is not a good idea to allow parents to do so if the test taker is age 4 or older (see Bracken, 2000). We have found that most parents understand and respond appropriately when it is explained that the tests were not developed to be completed with a parent in the room and that their being in the room may be disruptive to the test taker and lead to lower scores. Kamphaus (2001) suggested that parents also should be told to consider how stressful it may be (for them) to observe the assessment: "Parents want their child to do well, and when they do not, it can be extremely punishing to a parent, especially when they know that their child is taking an intelligence test" (p. 98). If a parent insists on being in the room, or if the test taker will not separate from the parent despite coaxing, the parent can sit in the testing room outside the test taker's line of vision (i.e., behind the test taker). The parent should be instructed (1) to stay silent during testing and (2) not to reveal the content of test items after the session is complete (in order to maintain test security).

Knowing the test and preparing testing materials. We cannot stress enough the importance of being prepared for testing. It is vital not only (a) to prepare yourself for testing, bring the right support materials, and select and arrange the testing environment but also (b) to know the administration and scoring procedures well and (c) to prepare the testing materials for an efficient administration. Sattler (2008) conveyed the importance of preparation for testing—especially for psychologists in training:

> Your goal is to know your tasks well enough that the test administration flows nicely, leaving you time to observe and record the test taker's behavior. To do this you will need to have learned how to apply the administration and scoring rules, how to find test materials quickly, and how to introduce and remove the test materials without breaking the interaction and flow between you and the test taker. Do not study a test manual as you give the test, because doing so will prolong the testing, may increase the test taker's anxiety, and may lead to mistakes in administration. However, in most cases you must refer to the directions and scoring guidelines in the test manual as you administer the test. Most individually administered tests do not require you to memorize test directions. Use highlighters, adhesive flags, index tabs, and other aids to facilitate swift and efficient use of the test manual. (p. 201)

When you are first learning to administer a test, it can be daunting to remember all of the rules for a standardized administration while maintaining rapport, administering and scoring items, and observing test behavior. To help you reach these goals, mark up your test records in advance of testing. Start points can be circled; varied rules for discontinuing can be highlighted; and unique queries, pronunciations of items, and reminders to prevent common errors can be written on sticky notes or in blank spaces on test records. These markings will lessen the amount of information you need to juggle in your mind during testing.

In addition to knowing the intricacies of the tests and their administration, it is useful to prepare your test materials (opening manuals to the correct page, setting up easels, laying out pencils, organizing manipulatives for presentation, etc.) before initiating the testing session. Of course, if you are pressed for time, these activities can be completed while building rapport. However, this dual tasking is not ideal, because it does not allow you to exert optimal attending skills during the early stage of building rapport.

BEGINNING TESTING

First contact and initial rapport building. Because most intelligence tests require one-on-one administration, you will often need to retrieve the test taker from a classroom or other school setting (for a school-based assessment) or from a waiting room (for a clinic-based assessment) to initiate testing. It is important to begin developing rapport from the initial contact and to maintain rapport throughout the testing sessions. This rapport is likely to be relatively short term—across fewer than four sessions and perhaps an additional meeting to describe the results. Your goal in fostering rapport is to obtain information about the test taker versus facilitating discussion, reflection, and initiation of therapeutic techniques and strategies for addressing psychological problems (as in counseling and psychotherapy). Thus, the goal of building and maintaining rapport during testing is to ensure enough of a bond with the test taker to decrease negative emotions (e.g., fear or worry) that might undermine the assessment and increase motivation to respond to test items and questions. In doing so, you want to consider the test taker's age and find the appropriate balance between being approachable (fun, interesting, and humorous) and being more formal and businesslike (Bracken, 2000).

Before you meet the test taker for the first time, consider information you possess that may aid you in generating conversations with them. For example, you already may have gathered information from parents (via their completion of initial interviews or developmental history forms), from teachers during prior meetings, and from direct observations of the test taker. In addition, you may have viewed materials posted outside their classroom and learned something about them and the recent classroom projects they completed. File this information and retrieve it when developing questions and conversation points.

When you first meet the test taker, smile, greet the test taker in a friendly manner, and use their name. We suggest offering your hand to shake, and, with young children, squatting to be roughly at their eye level when you first meet them. Also, keep the greeting brief; you will have more time to chat and explain your goals soon afterward. You might say, "Hi, Erica. My name is Ms. Barker. I am here to work with you today and talk about school. Please walk with me to my room." We admit to falling prey to a strategy that, on occasion, backfires. Consistent with guidelines for securing a child or adolescent's assent during research projects, we often ask, "Would you like to come with me?" at the end of our greetings. The occasional problem is that children or adolescents may respond negatively, saying that they would rather not do so. When such a response occurs, it lengthens the greeting process, but it may also allow the test taker to express reasons for hesitations that you can address.

As you begin to converse with the test taker while you walk toward the testing room, continue building rapport by asking open-ended questions about "easy" topics (hobbies, how the day is going, any fun activities the test taker has completed recently, etc.). We find discussion of favorite colors or favorite letters (for young children), pets, and sports to be particularly easy for many children. Remember what you learned about the test taker from your prior information gathering. As you facilitate conversation, strive to be engaging and enthusiastic about the test taker's responses and experiences. Use extenders (e.g., "Oh" and "Umm") and brief positive feedback (e.g., "That's cool" and "I like that, too") in response to the test taker's statements, so that you do not monopolize the conversation. Most children and adolescents appreciate this focused attention from an adult.

Addressing the purpose of assessment and confidentiality. Once the test taker is in the testing room and you have silenced your cell phone and placed a "Do Not Disturb" sign on the door, you can provide more details about your goals for the testing session. Although excellent scripts are offered in Sattler (2018) and Kamphaus (2001), use a script such as this one that is appropriately modified to address important issues related to the assessment. You might begin by saying the following: "I met your mother/father and your teacher, and now I want to get to know you. They tell me that you have been having a hard time at school. I want to know more about what you already have learned at school and how you go about learning new things, and I want to talk about what we can do to make school better for you. Our work today should last about 2 hours. Is this a good plan to you?" Most children and adolescents will nod their heads. Then you might ask the test taker to repeat to you what you have said. Say, "So tell me what we're going to do today," and accept any reasonable summary.

Consistent with the legal and ethical guidelines discussed in Chapter 3, it is important to explain confidentiality and its limits. Although we do not believe that these issues commonly are addressed with children or adolescents before testing sessions, it is best practice to do so. You might say, "We need to follow certain rules when we work together today. I want you to feel that you can talk to me, so I'll keep what you tell me between you and me [or private]. That means that I won't go telling your friends, anyone outside of school, or anyone else besides your parents and teacher[s] about our work together. What I share with your parents and teacher[s] will be things to make school better for you. How does that sound?"

Then you can explain confidentiality and its limits as follows by saying: "Again, I will keep our work together private unless several things happen: (1) You tell me that someone (like an adult) has hurt you or someone you know; (2) you tell me that you are going to hurt someone; (3) you tell me that you are going to hurt yourself; or (4) a court judge requires me to share the information. When these things happen, you and I would need to talk more about them and share them with your parents, teacher[s], and other adults who care about you. What do you think about this part?"

You can close the introduction to the testing session by summarizing, adding other rules (see the section focused on Behavior Excesses and Deficits later in this chapter), encouraging communication with you, and perhaps inserting humor as a bridge to introducing the test. You might say, "Other than these things, what we talk about stays between you and me, because I want to help make school better for you. It is very important that you try your best and that you are honest with me so that we can figure out things together."

You may want to add other rules, depending on the test taker's age. For example, for young children, you may add rules about staying in the room and asking your permission before touching objects in the room. For others, you also may want to encourage them to communicate their discomfort at any point during the testing session. Finally, you can consider lightening the mood by telling a joke or by saying something obviously incorrect. For example, some of our favorite strategies are calling a child by the wrong name (e.g., "OK, are you ready to move on, Allie-Sammy-Billy?" and "So I've forgotten. Your name is LeBron Jones, right?") and indicating that the test taker is much older than their actual age (e.g., "I have it written here that you are 10 years old. Is that right?" and "So is it correct that you are in the ninth grade?"). Almost all children will correct your errors. If these questions are asked with a wry smile, we have found that children tend to find them a bit silly; when you say, "Oh, that's right!" and shake your head, throw up your arms, and look exasperated by your error, this technique aids in building rapport. You should develop your own strategies like these to lighten the mood.

Introduction to testing. Most intelligence tests have incorporated introductions to testing in their standardized procedures, but we encourage you to review them carefully and enhance them with some additional content to promote clear expectations. Essentially, you want to ensure that test takers understand at least four different components of the testing:

1. that they will complete various tasks,
2. that some of these tasks' items will be easy and others difficult,
3. that they should exert effort and persistence to do their best, and
4. that is it acceptable to report that they do not know answers.

We tend to read introductory directions for most intelligence tests and supplement these with "It's OK to ask questions, guess, or say, 'I don't know.'"

INTERACTING WITH TEST TAKERS DURING TESTING

If you are reasonably confident that the test taker has no sensory acuity, fine motor, speech, or other personal problems or language and cultural differences that will undermine testing, introduce the first test items. In general, begin testing when the test taker appears ready—and sooner rather than later. If you need to develop accommodations or otherwise alter the testing, take a break and re-center.

We cannot stress enough the importance of following standardized procedures with almost rigid adherence. Psychologists in training should think about their own experience of taking group-based standardized tests, such as the ACT, the SAT, and the GRE (Kamphaus, 2001). You should consider all of the rules and decorum (the proctors, the reading of scripts, and the strict time limits) that are central to the standardized testing enterprise, and strive to replicate such strict adherence. You should read instructions, item introductions, and feedback after errors exactly as they are written—even if you are motivated to improve the test taker's understanding. For example, Sattler (2018) implored examiners to "never ad lib, add extraneous words, leave out words from instructions or the test questions, or change any test directions because you think that the altered wording would improve the child's performance (unless the test manual permits changes)" (p. 209).

Audio presentations. When you are using an audio player to present items, it is important to look away from the test taker (e.g., at your test record) when the item is being played and then look expectantly at the test taker once the item has been completed. In addition, it is important to stop the presentation of items (when allowed) to allow test takers who are slow to respond more time to formulate a response. For items that play continuously, we recommend (1) being conscious that the next item may be presented before a response can been offered and (2) stopping or pausing the presentation of items before such incidents occur.

Timing. Accurate timing of items on intelligence tests is vital to measuring individual differences in cognitive abilities, and we have five points to offer about timing:

First, there is no good reason to hide your stopwatch or otherwise be surreptitious in timing. We agree with Kamphaus (2001) that you should be natural about timing and use of the stopwatch. Now, perhaps more than ever, children and adolescents are accustomed to completing timed (and fluency-based) tests; it is unlikely that they will be unnerved by your using it.

Second, timing should begin once you have completed the instructions. Once timing for an item or subtest has been initiated, do not stop timing until the item is complete or the time limit has ended. Do not stop timing when children or adolescents ask questions, when they make errors in response to individual items, or when you must prompt to maintain standardization.

Third, discontinue the items or subtests when the time limit has expired, or record the exact completion time (typically rounding down to the nearest second versus recording minutes, seconds, and milliseconds).

Fourth, score the last response provided within the time limit. Most subtests have you award no credit for items completed after the time limit, although in a few exceptions partial credit is given for incomplete performance.

Finally, do not share the time limit or the time remaining with the test taker, even if asked. If you are asked a question during a timed trial, you might make eye contact, calmly say, "Just keep working," and then break eye contact so as to not engage in conversation.

Some tests have an explicit description of "soft time limits" targeting items—especially items requiring expression of knowledge and oral expression. In general, present the next test item after allowing a test taker an appropriate amount of time to respond to a difficult question. However, some tests require that a response to an item be given in about 20 or 30 seconds, to enhance the efficiency of testing. Other tests, as noted previously, apply an absolute time limit to item-level responses. You should find the right balance between (a) allowing test takers to continue working on responses after the time limit has expired and (b) stopping them in development of a response and ushering them to the next item. It is important, however, to score the response that was available before the time limit expired.

Reversal and discontinue rules. Some of the most important decisions you make during testing are associated with the first items administered on each subtest. If you have taken the ACT, SAT, GRE, or other group-based tests, you might expect that intelligence tests would include, in their subtests, a large number of items and that the test taker is given the opportunity to complete as many of them as possible. However, as noted previously, the items included in the most widely used intelligence test subtests are ordered from least difficult to most difficult. Thus, some items may be far too difficult for very young children (e.g., "What does *onomatopoeia* mean?") and far too easy for adolescents and adults ("Point to the wheel").

Most intelligence test subtests are designed so that you need not administer all of the test items, with the administration generally beginning with the least challenging items and ending with the most challenging items. The level of easiness and difficulty of the items differs across test takers, however. Typically, the first item you administer is associated with an age-related start point. Perhaps 6- and 7-year-olds begin with the first item, but 8- and 9-year-olds begin with item 6, and so on. When we can reason that the earliest items on the subtest are so easy that most every test taker who is 8 and 9 years old would answer them correctly, it is not informative to administer those items. However, when the start point is not the first item, it is important that all children in the older age groups are able to demonstrate a solid level of performance, sometimes called a *basal*, by answering at least a few initial items correctly. When they do, we tend to say that a basal has been established, and when they do not, the examiner must administer additional easier items. Most often, this means reversing administration, item by item (or set of items, for some tests), until a basal is established or the first item has been administered.

As items become more difficult across a subtest, at some point items are too difficult for most test takers. When a test taker has little to no chance of being able to answer items correctly, it is not sensible to administer those items. In fact, doing so might lead to frustration, disappointment, and a deluge of tears in the test taker and also extend your testing time substantially (to the point of tears from your eyes). When the test taker appears to have "topped out" in answering items correctly to a point, we can state that a *ceiling* has been established. (This term is consistent with its use when referring to ceilings in Chapter 4.)

In order to establish a ceiling, it is common for many subtests to require that a certain number of items be failed. Thus, examiners must enforce discontinue rules (e.g., stopping after the test taker fails four consecutive items) to be confident that a ceiling has been established. Although some intelligence test subtests employ decision rules related to cumulative numbers of items answered correctly (e.g., discontinue if 14 or fewer items are answered correctly), most employ a discontinue rule associated with the number of consecutive failed items.

Overall, it is very important to have followed the reversal and discontinue rules and established basals and ceilings during the test session. If errors are made in doing so, the resulting raw score (and subsequent norm-referenced scores) will be incorrect, and the resulting norm-referenced score will be invalid. As modeled in Figure 5.1, examiners should clearly mark their basals and ceilings with brackets on their protocols to confirm that they have established them, to demonstrate to others who may review the protocol that standardized procedures were followed, and, most important, to prevent costly errors that may affect the lives of test takers.

Adhering to correct starting points, as well as reversal and discontinue rules, is more automated on digital assessment platforms, such as Q-Interactive. Although administration rules are posted under the information icon for tests such as the WISC-V, the system is preset to follow them by default. For example, the Q-Interactive platform will establish age-appropriate starting points based on a test taker's date of birth. However, at the beginning of a subtest, the examiner is offered the opportunity to accept or override this option. Similarly, Q-Interactive triggers a reversal or discontinue alert

106 CHAPTER 5

Figure 5.1. Example markup for basal set establishment and counting items below the basal set.

message when such criteria are not met. The examiner is offered the opportunity to override this prompt for ceilings and continue testing if they wish to administer additional items to further "test the limits" or if they are uncertain about scoring some prior items that may have been included in the ceiling.

Extending and clarifying responses. During testing, you may need to encourage the test taker to extend or clarify an initial response. Typically, offer *queries*, such as "What do you mean?" and "Tell me more about it." Although these queries are very similar across intelligence tests, always use the queries prescribed by each test. We recommend using sticky notes or the like in the test record to remind you of these queries when you are administering several different tests as part of an assessment. For most intelligence tests, the administration manual provides sample responses that must be queried, but you also should query vague responses, regionalisms, or slang responses that are not clearly incorrect. However, be careful not to query any clear-cut responses that contain enough information to score without a query. Further, record on your protocol and in "Contextual Event" notations in Q-Interactive when you queried (using Q to represent a query).

In general, when scoring a verbal response consider all parts of a response—those parts that are offered before the query is issued, and those offered after the query is issued. In other words, score the whole of the response. For example, when asked about the meaning of the word *colander*, the test taker offers "You use it in the kitchen with water," and after you query the response, they offer, "It keeps you from pouring hot pasta down the drain," you would consider both parts of the response, and the test taker would earn as many points as if they had combined both parts into one sentence. It gets tricky, however, when the response after the query is mediocre or outright flawed. If you issue a query, and the test taker offers a weak response or otherwise fails to improve the initial response (e.g., "Colanders are plastic and white"), score the quality of the initial

ASSESSMENT PROCESS WITH CHILDREN AND ADOLESCENTS

response. If the query reveals a fundamental misconception—a totally flawed understanding—about the content of the item (e.g., "Colanders chop up food into pieces"), the initial response, regardless of its quality, is spoiled, and the item is scored 0. Spoiled responses are rare, and it is important not to waste time over thinking whether poor responses reflect a fundamental misconception.

Recording and scoring responses. You should record verbatim responses to the degree possible. Record them in the lines on the test record or beside the item. Use abbreviations, such as those that follow to speed up the recording process:

DK = don't know
NR = no response
P = prompt issued
PC = points correctly
R = item repeated
TF = time failure

Further, Flanagan and Alfonso (2017) provide more than 20 other abbreviations, such as @ for "at," "B" for "both," and "ST" for "something." You can make up your own as long as you know what the abbreviation is supposed to represent. One of the most common administration and recording procedures that an examiner will use is querying and the subsequent scoring of test taker responses. As modeled in Figure 5.2, the examiner can use (Q) to indicate where an administrative query occurred within the test taker's response. Further, we find it helpful to annotate the point value and administrative directions (e.g., 1-point query) associated with a response below segments of a test taker's response. These procedures may facilitate scoring after the test administration is complete.

Figure 5.2. Example markup for documenting query and response annotation of test taker response.

Exercise discretion in selecting only the core of the responses to record. For instance, you need not record the initial stem of a response (e.g., "I think that an encyclopedia is a . . ."), interjections (e.g., "Darn!"), or idiosyncratic responses (e.g., "I think we learned that in third grade" or "That is a tough one!") that are not clinically meaningful. Thus, extraneous content need not be recorded. It also is important to be able to use abbreviations when appropriate, but never place them in the item-scoring column. For digitally administered assessments in Q-Interactive, familiarize yourself with how to make observational notes in the specific assessment program you are using. For example, in WISC-V digital assessment, the examiner would press the Pencil icon to access notes and may further specify the category of note to general, subtest, or item specific dimensions. Contextual event buttons often are located at the side of a screen for quick abbreviated observational notes.

You should strive for a brisk administration while also taking your time to score responses concurrently with the administration. If you cannot decide on a score for an item, leave it blank, mark it with a question mark, continue to the next item, and meet the discontinue rule without including the item in question. At a later time, score the item in question, and adjust your raw score accordingly. When you are scoring, both example responses and general scoring criteria should be consulted, but keep in mind that the examples listed in the test manuals are guides to scoring and that some professional judgment (aka "real thinking" on your part) may be required. If you are a beginning tester or are learning a new test, we strongly encourage you to have a second party review your item scoring and raw score calculation. We also are strong advocates of using scoring software to prevent errors that often surface when consulting norm tables presented in test manuals.

It is important to score all items according to the examples, general criteria, and scoring guides provided in test manuals and to avoid applying subjective judgments that "bend the rules" for test takers. However, as just noted, professional judgment is needed—especially in cases where the test taker responds in a manner that is more sophisticated than the sample responses. For example, an adolescent may respond to a picture vocabulary item by reporting the genus and species of a beetle, rather than referring to it as an "insect" in general or a "beetle" more specifically. Some children may calculate the exact number of weeks in a year (yielding a decimal fraction), versus telling you that 52 full weeks are in the year. In such cases, it is incumbent on you to search books or the Internet, or to do the calculations yourself, to determine whether the response is correct or incorrect. In addition, do not penalize the test taker for mispronunciations due to articulation problems or to regional or dialect differences.

It is difficult to know how to score initial responses that include both correct and incorrect components. Although you always should consult the test manuals for specific guidelines, here are two commonalities across them. First, if several responses to an item are given, ask which one the test taker wants you to score. You can say, "You said X, and you said Y. Which one is it?" or the like. (Note that some intelligence test manuals encourage you to score the last response given.) Second, for many tests, if the test taker provides numerous correct responses of varying quality and the item is scored on a scale, score the best response.

Breaks, check-ins, and encouragement. It is important to monitor the test taker's motivation and persistence during testing and to encourage full responses to all items. Throughout the testing session, "read" the test taker's behavior, including facial expressions, posture, and verbalizations, to determine their level of motivation and fatigue (Kamphaus, 2001). Although you typically want to keep small talk to a minimum during subtests, we recommend "checking in" between subtests with questions such as "How are you feeling?" and "Ready for the next one?" to gauge motivation and fatigue. We encourage energetic, brisk administrations of the tests, but for some children and adolescents, you may call for breaks every 30 minutes or so. You must consider, though, that (1) some children and adolescents have a difficult time readjusting to the testing session after a break and (2) in a school setting, breaks lengthen the assessment session and potentially prevent exposure to valuable instructional content in the classroom setting.

Engaging in strategies to encourage full expression of knowledge and skills during testing is vital. Although you are able to provide encouraging feedback after correct responses to sample items—and some tests do, in fact, allow for such feedback after responses to test items— generally you should strive to give no indication of whether responses to test items are correct or incorrect. In particular, do not indicate the quality of the test taker's responses through your facial expressions or your verbalizations. We encourage our graduate students in training to practice their "stone face with a smile" expressions throughout testing, and to develop nonevaluative verbalizations that can be used consistently. For example, we believe that saying "OK" or "That's fine," and nodding after responses, are both acceptable behaviors—as long as examiners are diligent about using them for both correct and incorrect responses. Others may assert that presenting the next item signals clearly that the last response has been accepted, but we find that, with preschool- and elementary-school-age students, some other way of accepting their response seems warmer and more responsive.

We recommend two types of feedback designed to praise a test taker's effort during testing:

First, use various comments to recognize effort. Examples include "Thanks for your hard work," "I like how you thought through that one," "Excellent effort! Keep it up!" and "Keep giving it your all." We also encourage well-timed general comments, such as "You are doing a great job," and "Good work," that cannot be linked to correct responses and that are intermingled with comments about effort. (More information about verbal reinforcement is included in the following section.)

Second, we encourage physical gestures and brief physical contact, such as fist bumps. We admit to engaging in some seemingly hokey behaviors, such as prompting test takers to give us "high fives" and offering "thumbs-up" gestures paired with phrases such as "Good job" and a smile. Of course, these behaviors must be moderated in keeping with the test taker's age. For example, preschoolers tend to enjoy silliness from adults, but the same cannot be said for many adolescents. In particular, adolescents may be particularly sensitive to insinuation of false praise or to repetition of platitudes.

You should strive to monitor the motivation and persistence of test takers in responding, and you may need to encourage them to attempt the most difficult test items you present. Although you already may have shared with them that they can report that they do not know some answers (and that no one is expected to be able to answer all items), encourage them to guess by reminding them with "It's OK to guess" or "It's OK to answer even if you are not sure," and encouraging them to "Give it a try" or "Go ahead. Try it." After using these techniques (and driving home the point that guessing is not a problem) and reading their behaviors as the testing progresses, you may also ask, "Want to give it a try or move to the next one?" or "Want to pass on this one?" Further, be sensitive to their perceptions of failures and remind them that effort is more important to you than correct responses. Some benefit seems to come from reminding children and adolescents that some items were developed for older adults. You may say, "Remember I told you that some of these items would be hard; they must made for grownups, huh?" or "That was a tough one, wasn't it? Still, I like how diligently you worked on it."

Responding to questions. Some anxious or inquisitive test takers may barrage you with questions. Others, due to some of their limitations, may require you to respond to pleas for assistance. For example, some may ask you for feedback on items, asking "Was I right?" or "How am I doing?"; others may ask you for the answers to questions that they could not produce. Your standard responses to these issues should be to say, kindly, that you cannot tell them how well they are doing or what the correct answers are. Comments such as "You're doing fine, and I appreciate your hard work," and "Your answer sounds good to me" work well. We often refer to our testing rules to justify our inability to share the correct answers. We say, "I'm sorry that I can't tell you; it's one of the rules I must follow in doing my job."

Unless the test item targets an ability that would be enhanced by repeating the item (e.g., subtests targeting Short-Term Memory or Listening Ability), you can repeat questions or items upon request, but when you do so, it is important that you repeat it in its entirety so that you do not parse its components for them. For example, on a subtest targeting quantitative reasoning that requires children to calculate the difference in miles between two cities, a child might ask, "Did you say in miles?" Rather than replying in the affirmative, repeat the whole item to require the test taker to parse the important information from it. You also may repeat items when a response suggests that the test taker misheard or misunderstood words used in the item.

Performance Validity and Problem Behaviors

The testing process requires the test taker to participate actively in the process, so two of your goals during this process should be to (a) evaluate the extent of that engagement and (b) use strategies during testing to facilitate it. In this section, we address how to screen for intentional efforts to perform poorly on tests. Further, we outline strategies that may be useful in preventing and responding to behavior excesses (e.g., defiance, physical aggression, and self-injurious behavior) and behavioral deficits (e.g., passive noncompliance and withdrawal) during testing.

PERFORMANCE VALIDITY

The typical goal of test takers in completing an intelligence test is to perform as well as possible, as correctly answered items increase resulting scores. In rare cases, test takers may see long-term benefits for performing poorly on intelligence tests. This is particularly true in cases when additional services are provided and supports (sometimes financial) are offered, such as when ID and specific learning disabilities are identified. According to Floyd, Farmer, Schneider, and McGrew (in press),

> During testing, the clinician should be conscious of the test taker's motivation to respond and employ methods to enhance completion of practice trials, attempts at problem-solving, and guessing when in doubt. Most intelligence tests include such practice trials, employ very basic test items

before proceeding to more challenging ones, and incorporate standardized prompts to encourage responding. Furthermore, as most intelligence tests are individually administered and include multiple subtests requiring varied inputs and response processes, boredom tends to be reduced, fatigue can be monitored, and engagement is facilitated. However, examiners . . . should also be aware of the potential for feigned intellectual impairment, sometimes called malingering. (para. 70)

Malingering has been defined as "the intentional production of false or grossly exaggerated physical or psychological symptoms, motivated by external incentives" (APA, 2013, p. 726).

As noted in the previous quote and elsewhere in this chapter, test examiners should observe test session behaviors carefully to determine whether malingering occurred, poor effort led to lower scores, or some other construct-irrelevant influences weakened measurement accuracy. Considering a lack of good evidence to support the ability of test examiners to consistently identify malingering, poor effort, and the like based on such test-session data (Emhoff, Lynch, & McCaffrey, 2018), performance validity measures appear to be needed. Performance validity refers to a determination that the test taker displayed sufficient effort and engagement during testing to warrant interpretation of the resultant scores.

We do not believe that most professionals who employ intelligence tests integrate performance validity measures into their assessments. Perhaps it is based on the assumption that children and adolescents do not have the motivation or self-control to malinger effectively. However, increasing numbers of performance validity measures on the market are supported by ample validity evidence. In fact, they are increasingly popular among some practitioners who are heavily involved in assessment (e.g., clinical neuropsychology; Tonks, Whitfield, Williams, Slater, & Frampton, 2018). The most studied performance validity measure is the Test of Memory Malingering (TOMM; Tombaugh, 1996). The TOMM involves test takers in a learning trial in which they must identify pictures to which they were previously exposed. When they perform worse than chance in identifying them, malingering is indicated. The TOMM was designed for test takers ages 17 to 73, but evidence from sensitivity and specificity studies is that it may be viable as a screener for some children and adolescents. For example, in a simulation study, Rambo, Callahan, Hogan, Hullmann, and Wrape (2015) demonstrated the potential of the TOMM to identify children as young as age 6 who were instructed to malinger. Thus, its sensitivity to malingering appears to be high even for young children, but false positives likely are common at this age. In particular, Ploetz, Mazur-Mosiewicz, Kirkwood, Sherman, and Brooks (2016) found that children with neurological diagnoses were able to perform consistently better than chance on the TOMM during a clinical assessment when they were ages 8 and older. Their low failure rate relative to children ages 5 to 7 indicates the potential of this measure with older children.

The central problem with employing performance validity measures with children and test takers with disabilities is that they will perform similarly to those who are malingering for reasons other than purposeful exaggeration of symptoms. This pattern indicates that these individuals are at high risk of false positives, which would unnecessarily complicate the interpretation process. Based on their comprehensive review of the literature, Mazur-Mosiewicz, Ford, Chapman, and Farabough (2018) concluded that the evidence supporting the TOMM was too tenuous to recommend at present. As they stated,

> Without relevant, quality validation and normative studies, the TOMM should not be used clinically with young children or children suspected of having significant cognitive issues. Failing performance on the TOMM does not necessarily indicate poor effort or invalidate the neuropsychological profile. Instead, it may be reflective of other factors, particularly in children below age 6, children with lower intellectual abilities (especially FSIQ ≤ 75), children with multiple diagnoses, or children with more severe neurological diagnoses. (p. 113)

We anticipate that revised TOMM cut scores for children and adolescents (with and without disabilities) will be propagated and used in practice in the near future.

In contrast to the TOMM, the Memory Validity Profile (MVP; Sherman & Brooks, 2015) is designed for children and adolescents. It includes both verbal memory and visual memory facets and produces a total score. With the goal of addressing the false positives among young children and adolescents in mind, it includes stringent cut scores (for malingering) for different age levels based on a norming sample of more than 1,200 youth. Thus, across ages, these cut scores identify only 5% or less of those from the norming sample as malingering. Further analysis of children with neurological diagnoses by Brooks, Fay-McClymont, MacAllister, Vasserman, and Sherman (2019) confirmed that these cut scores produced similar results with children and adolescents with a variety of diagnoses across age groups. Further, to address performance by those who are lowest functioning, they demonstrated that the MVP Visual score had the lowest false positive rate of all scores (only 6%) with students with extremely low IQs (< 70). We hope to see accumulating evidence supporting use of the MVP across settings.

Following their comprehensive review of the literature, Emhoff et al. (2018) encouraged test examiners routinely to include performance validity measures across their assessments. We agree that they increasingly should be employed—especially in cases where malingering or otherwise poor performance might be suspected. It is doubtful that they would be useful for gifted assessments, but we see their potential most when assessing ID. We agree with Emhoff et al. that cut scores offered by the authors of the performance validity test or peer-reviewed publications cannot be applied rigidly without considering (a) limitations of the measures, (b) the context of cases, and (c) other sources of information from a comprehensive assessment. Intelligence test examiners almost certainly will see more performance validity measures embedded in their tests in the near future.

BEHAVIOR EXCESSES AND DEFICITS

As much as 65% of children in the general population present with some type of challenging behavior (Kalb & Loeber, 2003), and examiners have reported that these behaviors are especially difficult to overcome during testing (Gilmore & Campbell, 2019). The impact of challenging behavior during testing should not be dismissed, as these behaviors likely function as construct-irrelevant influences. Consider a situation in which an examiner is attempting to administer a working memory subtest requiring repetition of digits to a child who is running around the examination room, grabbing at items from the table or test kit, and providing no response or nonsensical responses (e.g., "1, 2, buckle my shoe!") when an item is presented. Although it certainly is *possible* to obtain a subtest raw score in such an occasion, that score probably is a reflection of both working memory and the test taker's challenging behavior rather than working memory alone. Further, the score most likely is a low estimate of the test taker's working memory ability. The concern in situations such as this one is that challenging behaviors likely result in invalid scores, which may mislead you and others involved in the test taker's life in your subsequent decision making. Examiners should anticipate challenging behavior from some children. As a result, the prepared examiner is familiar with and ready to apply effective strategies from the applied behavior analysis literature. Herschell, Greco, Filcheck, and McNeil (2002) and Floyd et al. (in press) have offered a number of recommendations for examiners prior to testing, during the testing session, and in response to challenging behavior, and we extend them here.

Prior to testing. Before testing, examiners may not know that a particular child is likely to engage in challenging behavior. However, basic strategies can be employed regardless of this knowledge that can facilitate testing for all test takers:

First, examiners should prepare the examination room to minimize distractions. This can be accomplished by having only necessary furniture, stationary chairs (i.e., chairs that do not spin or tilt), minimal decoration, and only items necessary for testing. For example, it may be appealing to conduct testing in the same room where one conducts therapy, but the presence of toys, games, and other stimuli increase the likelihood of challenging behavior. When examiners do not have the autonomy to remove or modify the testing environment, other strategies may be helpful. For instance, the examiner may arrange the room to reduce the number of distractors within sight or reach of the test taker, place themselves between the test taker and distractors, or place themselves between the test taker and the door. In addition, generally it is good advice to set up as much of the testing stimuli (e.g., having one's stimulus books within reach) prior to the test taker's arrival, as this minimizes down time. Finally, when tangible or edible reinforcement is to be used, having the test taker's preferred items available—within reach but out of sight and reach of the test taker.

Examiners also are encouraged to pay close attention to their rapport with the test taker as well as the rules established during the testing session. For instance, engaging in play activities with the test taker, using and repeating phrases spoken by the test taker, and pairing oneself with preferred reinforcement all prior to initiating testing may function to establish rapport (see Lugo, King, Lamphere, & McArdle, 2017). The examiner should establish clear rules to minimize the likelihood of inappropriate behavior. Technically speaking, "rules are explicit statements that define behavior expectations and help to establish a predictable teaching and learning environment" (Gable, Hester, Rock, & Hughes, 2009, p. 196). In the case of the testing environment, a small number of simple, positively worded, specific rules related to your expectations for the test taker (e.g., "sit in your seat" and "follow instructions") should be introduced at the beginning of the testing session (Alter & Haydon, 2017) and repeated during appropriate times (e.g., prior to returning to testing from a break). Rules should be given one at a time and tied to consequences (i.e., reinforcement) when appropriate. Finally, when reinforcers are to be used during the testing session, the contingencies under which they are to be used should be clarified at the beginning of the session in the same fashion as other rules. We do not recommend the use of punishment-based strategies, as indirect effects of punishment include an increase in (a) emotional reactions, (b) escape-maintained behaviors (e.g., elopement), (c) aggression (Lerman & Vorndran, 2002), and (d) potential harm to rapport—all of which may function as construct-irrelevant influences in their own right.

Reactive strategies. As noted in the previous section, examiners frequently are encouraged to provide praise for effort and participation during the test session. Phrases such as "I love the way you're working!" are fairly common fare. Behavior-specific praise (BSP) has been shown to increase on-task behavior, task completion, and compliance (Brophy, 1981; Chalk & Bizo, 2004; Kirby & Shields, 1972). In addition to increasing appropriate behavior, BSP that focuses on sitting, attending, and hard work is *not* focused on the accuracy of the test taker's responses, which would violate standardization and has the potential to shape responses selectively. To be clear, praising correct answers and ignoring incorrect answers is a serious problem. One strategy to avoid inadvertently reinforcing answers is to preemptively decide when BSP for appropriate behavior (e.g., sitting) will occur.

Depending upon the developmental level and needs of the test taker, the examiner may wish to provide very dense reinforcement (i.e., occurring very frequently) or lean reinforcement (i.e., occurring sparingly) throughout the session. The optimal density of reinforcement can be determined based on knowledge of reinforcement schedules (see Cooper, Heron, & Heward, 2020). For instance, knowing that a test taker is likely to present with challenging behavior may warrant a denser schedule, such as a continuous reinforcement schedule (i.e., providing reinforcement following every item during which the test taker engaged in appropriate behavior), whereas test takers less likely to present with challenging behavior may function well with a lean intermittent reinforcement schedule (e.g., providing reinforcement following randomly selected items).

Deciding upon the type of reinforcement to use is an idiographic process. That is, some children may not like the attention provided by an examiner using BSP, whereas others may seek it out. Reinforcement is a very personal concept, and the types of reinforcement selected for an individual test taker will need to be determined through conversation with stakeholders as well as observations and interactions with the test taker. Nothing is wrong with asking a test taker, "What do you want to work for today?" and integrating that reward into your behavior management. Some test takers may not be able to provide answers; thus, more systematic procedures may be warranted to determine reinforcers (i.e., preference assessment; Hagopian, Long, & Rush, 2004). Test takers, for instance, simply may want to escape or avoid the challenging nature of the test itself. In such cases, effective use of negative reinforcement in the form of breaks may be warranted. When using breaks, it is important to be strategic and to (a) limit the amount of time taken, (b) space breaks to minimize disruption to the testing procedure, and (c) ensure that breaks do not follow inappropriate behavior.

In addition to BSP and strategic breaks, examiners may consider the use of tangible or edible reinforcers, though this practice has been debated frequently (see Fish, 1988). We agree with Sattler (2008) that such incentives should not be used under normal circumstances; they may introduce unnecessary complexity and potential hazards into the testing situation (e.g., activating food allergies and choking, in the case of food items). However, we have seen benefits of the use of incentives with preschool-age children, children with ID, and children with attention-deficit/hyperactivity disorder when they are used to reinforce compliance and responding to items. We offer three recommendations:

1. First, food items often interfere with testing because they have the potential to make a mess (e.g., Goldfish crumbs on the testing table or chocolaty saliva running down a child's mouth). Reserve food items for preschoolers and children with severe developmental disabilities who have a history with use of these food items in assessment and therapy sessions.
2. Second, for older children and adolescents, use a token economy or point system so that they earn points or tokens that can be traded at the end of the testing session for valued items (e.g., trading cards, stickers, and colorful pencils). If you decide to use food items, obtain the permission of parents to do so and have them supply the items. Some food items, such as fruit candies and marshmallows, may be prohibited by the family (as they may contain prohibited ingredients, such as gelatin), and food allergies are increasingly common.
3. Finally, use food items to reinforce compliance (e.g., sitting quietly) and responding to each item.

If challenging behavior occurs, repetition of rules may be helpful. For instance, reminding test takers of the consequences associated with appropriate behavior (e.g., "When you follow directions, we get to color for a minute.") may be useful. Further, using if-then and when-then statements may help to redirect test takers to the test. Importantly, it is absolutely critical that examiners are consistent throughout the testing session with rules they have established and their use of contingencies. Finally, examiners should refrain from making statements that they cannot or are unwilling to enforce.

OBSERVING BEHAVIORS DURING THE TEST SESSION

As we noted earlier in this chapter, you should observe test session behaviors to judge how these behaviors might undermine the validity of your results. Even if you have gone through all of the efforts to eliminate or to control optimally for construct-irrelevant sources of variation in test scores, it is possible that some of the test taker's characteristics may exert their influences and produce biased results. In particular, behaviors that produce downwardly biased results, such as those associated with anxiety, fatigue, inattention, extreme disappointment, and noncompliance, should be monitored closely.

Commonplace practices. Two practices for recording and summarizing test session behaviors have become commonplace:

The first practice is writing descriptions of behaviors of interest in the margins of the test record. These narrative "behavior observations" may be used to enhance memory when examiners are summarizing test results and writing reports, as well as to contribute to a better understanding of low norm-referenced scores yielded after testing has been completed. These behavior observations often are written concisely. Examples include such notes as "Seems anxious: fidgety, picks at skin around fingernails," "Says hates math," or "Is a live wire: bouncing in chair, grabbing testing materials, out of seat." Although some of these behaviors may be a reaction to test content (e.g., math), these behaviors sometimes represent our failures to eliminate or optimally control for construct-irrelevant influences. Because behavior in one-on-one testing environment does not accurately represent behaviors in other environments, you should be more concerned about producing valid test scores than about observing the test taker's reaction to the testing session. Do not sit passively and record behaviors that confound your results; you should intervene. For example, with an adolescent who appears to lack motivation, you could ask, "Is everything OK? You seem tired"; problem-solve based on the response and terminate the testing session if needed (Kamphaus, 2001).

The second practice is summarizing (after testing is complete) noteworthy behaviors displayed during the testing session. Almost every intelligence test record includes a brief checklist or prompts addressing language usage, attention, activity level, attitude, cooperativeness, mood, and self-confidence. Both methods may assist you in describing the testing environment in your report after detailed memories of the session have decayed.

Innovative practices. Two innovative practices cast light on our understanding of test session behaviors and their potential influences on the validity of assessment:

First, A. S. Kaufman, N. L. Kaufman, and their collaborators (see A. Kaufman & N. Kaufman, 2004a) developed a brilliant way to monitor and record potential construct-irrelevant influences on item-level performance: having the examiner review and complete a brief checklist of common influences associated with each subtest. Their *qualitative indicators* include *disrupting indicators*, such as not monitoring accuracy, failing to sustain attention, impulsively responding incorrectly, perseverating despite feedback, refusing to engage in a task, being reluctant to commit to a response or to respond when uncertain, and worrying about time limits. Conversely, they include *enhancing indicators*, such as closing eyes to concentrate, asking for repetition of items, persevering after initial struggles, trying out options, being unusually focused, verbalizing related knowledge or a strategy for recall, and working quickly but carefully. Reviewing a checklist of such items during or after the administration of each subtest allows examiners to identify and document potentially confounding influences.

Second, rating scales have been developed to assess behavioral excesses that may interfere with test performance. Two of the most well-developed and psychometrically sound instruments of this kind are the Guide to Assessment of Test Session Behavior (Glutting & Oakland, 1993) and the Achenbach System for Empirically

Based Assessment Test Observation Form (TOF; McConaughy & Achenbach, 2004). The completion of post-assessment rating scales such as the TOF may be especially useful for students in training, because it sensitizes them to unusual and perhaps meaningful behaviors during the testing session. For discussion of these methods, see McConaughy (2005).

Accuracy of recording behavior observations. Examiners' narrative descriptions and ratings of observations completed after the testing session are likely to be negatively affected by errors in memory (Lilienfeld, Ammirati, & David, 2012; Watkins, 2009), so we encourage recording behaviors of interest immediately after they occur during testing. The most accurate summaries of behaviors during the test session probably would stem from review of such notes recorded in the protocol. These varying types of behavior observations can be completed in concert, but we encourage relying first on direct observation and immediate recording of them. We should conclude, perhaps, that upon reflection, specific behaviors were not undermining test scores unless notes indicated such throughout protocol.

POSTTESTING CONSIDERATIONS

Debriefing. We admit to making the mistake of not conducting some sort of debriefing after completing a test session (and not teaching our graduate students to do so). After a full testing session, it is tempting to say, "We're done today. Thanks for working so hard with me. Let's go back to your classroom," or the like, but it is an ideal practice to spend a bit more time debriefing.

First, it may help to maintain rapport with the test taker—especially if multiple testing sessions will be completed. Kamphaus (2001) has suggested honestly acknowledging challenges the test taker faced during testing. Statements such as "I realize that you were a little unhappy about being here today, but you tried hard to do what I asked, and I really appreciate that" (Kamphaus, 2001, p. 111) may go a long way in building and maintaining rapport with the test taker. In addition, it may allow you to answer questions or allay fears the test taker may have.

Second, if you inquire about the test taker's experience of the test, as well as what they liked and did not like, you may identify construct-irrelevant influences on test results.

Third, debriefing is consistent with the goal of keeping the test taker informed about the outcomes of the testing. Sattler (2008) suggested repeating some of your introductory statements regarding these outcomes, such as your sharing that you will summarize the results in a report and meet with parents and teachers to discuss the results so that the test taker's experience at school will be improved. We strongly encourage taking additional time at the end of each testing session to debrief the test taker.

Validity of results. After testing is complete, you must determine whether the administration produced results that appear to be "valid." Validity was discussed previously when considering whether the test taker malingered or otherwise failed to exert sufficient effort, but the validity of results, broadly speaking, is substantially more nebulous. Essentially, you need to determine whether the intelligence test subtests were administered in a way—and the test taker reacted to them in a way—that permits you to say with confidence that the resulting scores well represent the ability or abilities you targeted. In other words, you must judge whether the inferences made about the test taker's cognitive abilities are reasonably accurate, based on their test behavior.

Although statements about the validity of testing results often are made at a global level when printed in reports (see Chapter 10 for examples), we encourage consideration of the validity of subtest scores, which are the foundation of all other scores for intelligence tests. It is possible that the results from one subtest are invalid and all other results are valid. We encourage you to specify which scores are likely invalid and describe what led to this conclusion.

Perhaps a continuum of validity of assessment exists. On one end is an ideal testing environment and a perfect standardized administration. No interruptions occurred; the test taker was optimally motivated to respond and displayed no behavior problems; and the performance was consistent across items, with no apparent guessing or failure to answer the easiest items. Such sessions are not uncommon. On the other end is a testing session that goes awry. You are testing in a broom closet near a noisy hallway and a train track; you are not at your best due to caffeine withdrawal; you fumble through the testing materials; and the test taker is unruly and unmotivated. In cases such as the latter, you may conclude that all of the data collected as part of the testing that day are meaningless in representing the test taker's cognitive abilities. If you suspect that the testing conditions resulted in scores with inadequate validity, do not report the scores in your report or discuss them as they may mislead, misinform, or bias the decision-making process (Galanter & Patel, 2005; Youngstrom, Choukas-Bradley, Calhoun, & Jensen-Doss, 2015). You should schedule another testing session promptly and develop a plan for improving it. Further, briefly summarize this event in your report, justify your decision not to report your initial results, and describe your rationale for administrating a second intelligence test.

The most difficult validity decisions are those between the extremes on the continuum—those cases in which some interference in measurement during testing probably occurred. We have found that these instances rarely are addressed by examiners and included in reports, but we urge giving more attention to them and their influence on test scores. They may stem from influences generally associated with the testing environment. For example, some children and adolescents may be less engaged in testing late in the session, and their lessened engagement may lead to lower scores on the last few subtests administered. Others may struggle in completing items from one subtest and seem to be dejected afterward. Still others will react in an unexpected way to standard test directions, test items, and prompts and queries. For example, some simply will not understand the requirements of the task as a whole, despite completing practice items satisfactorily. Others may adopt the strategy of providing you more information than you required—going on and on when defining words or providing the correct answer and also five variants of it. Still others will offer a new response—effectively changing their answer—when queried for more information. These external influences and idiosyncratic reactions almost certainly have an impact on test scores, but admittedly, it is difficult to determine when they reflect true ability deficits versus construct-irrelevant influences.

Testing of limits and follow-up assessment. At least two methods address potential construct-irrelevant influences and the validity of test results: (1) testing of limits and (2) follow-up testing using similar measures. *Testing of limits* refers to re-administration of subtest items after completion of a test, during which additional cues are given, modeling of correct responses is completed, items are presented in a different fashion, responses are allowed in another modality (e.g., spoken versus written), time limits are eliminated, and probing questions are asked. The goal is to test hypotheses about why a test taker missed an item or series of items. For example, in cases in which the test taker quickly missed all items on a subtest requiring them to repeat orally presented numbers backward, you could use concrete objects (e.g., tiles or blocks with numbers on them) to demonstrate how to reverse numbers presented orally to ensure that the test taker understands what is required. Alternately, you could request that they teach you how to complete an easy item. Afterward, you could administer the items again to determine whether the intervention has yielded dividends. Regardless of the outcome, never change raw scores obtained from a standardized test administration, but consider explaining the reason for a low score and, in rare cases, eliminating the affected score from your report.

In addition, when we develop hypotheses regarding construct-irrelevant influences on test scores, we often engage in some additional testing employing related measures. If we believe that some distraction during testing, some misunderstanding on the test taker's part, or some other influence unduly affected test scores, we sometimes turn to resources offered as part of the cross-battery approach (Flanagan, Ortiz, & Alfonso, 2013) to find an alternative subtest purported to measure the same specific ability to test our hypothesis. For example, if a test taker scored poorly on a subtest that requires repeating orally presented numbers in reverse, we might follow up with a related subtest that requires them to order orally presented numbers and letters in ascending order. Alternately, we might follow up with a subtest that more closely matches the content and response processes of the one in question. Although we are not certain that the extra effort to examine all of our hypotheses in this vein always is warranted, judicious use of this technique may allow you to distinguish more clearly between low scores indicating ability deficits and low scores due to construct-irrelevant influences.

Summary

It is important to have a strong knowledge of the reasons for assessment, typical assessment processes, and potential influences on test performance that can be controlled during testing or acknowledged when interpreting test results. In this chapter, we offered detailed descriptions of these processes and equipped you with tools and resources to facilitate and evaluate the validity of test scores for each child or adolescent you assess.

FORM 5.1

Screening Tool for Assessment (STA)—
Parent and Caregiver Screening Form, Second Edition

Child's name: _____

Glasses/contact lenses: Y / N

Parent or caregiver's name: _____

Hearing aid/cochlear implant: Y / N

Please read each item carefully and circle Yes or No.

1	My child closes or covers one eye when looking at some things.	Yes	No
2	My child frequently squints.	Yes	No
3	My child complains that some images are blurry or hard to see.	Yes	No
4	My child holds objects unusually close when looking at them.	Yes	No
5	My child seems to blink a lot.	Yes	No
6	My child becomes frustrated or upset when doing close-up work such as reading, math, and puzzles.	Yes	No
7	My child uses the wrong color names for objects, such as saying that there are purple leaves on trees.	Yes	No
8	My child has a short attention span when coloring or drawing with colors or colored markers.	Yes	No
9	My child has difficulty identifying red or green.	Yes	No
10	My child has difficulty reading when the words are on colored pages.	Yes	No
11	My child does not respond to loud noises sometimes.	Yes	No
12	My child's listening skills are behind what I expect.	Yes	No
13	My child turns up the volume too loud on electronic equipment.	Yes	No
14	My child does not follow spoken directions well.	Yes	No
15	My child often says, "Huh?" or asks you to repeat something you have said.	Yes	No
16	My child does not respond when called.	Yes	No
17	My child's speech is behind what I expect.	Yes	No
18	My child has difficulty pronouncing some words.	Yes	No
19	My child substitutes sounds in words (e.g., wed for red).	Yes	No

20	My child leaves sounds out of words (e.g., root for fruit).	Yes	No
21	How much of your child's speech do you understand? 25% 50% 75% 100%		
22	How much of your child's speech would a stranger understand? 25% 50% 75% 100%		
23	My child has difficulty stacking blocks.	Yes	No
24	My child has difficulty fitting puzzle pieces together.	Yes	No
25	My child has difficulty drawing a straight line.	Yes	No
26	My child has difficulty drawing a circle.	Yes	No
27	My child has difficulty printing words.	Yes	No
28	I can usually read my child's handwriting.	Yes	No
29	A stranger would usually be able to read my child's handwriting.	Yes	No
30	My child is often defiant.	Yes	No
31	My child often refuses to do what I ask.	Yes	No
32	My child breaks a lot of rules at home.	Yes	No
33	My child speaks a language other than English when talking to friends.	Yes	No
34	My child speaks a language other than English when talking to me and my family.	Yes	No
35	My child has attended schools in which a language other than English was spoken by teachers and students.	Yes	No
36	My child listens to music, reads, and watches TV, movies, and videos in a language other than English.	Yes	No
37	My child frequently participates in holidays and cultural events associated with our family's history outside the United States.	Yes	No

Are there any other issues that might affect how well your child performs during the upcoming testing sessions? Please describe them below.

FORM 5.2

Screening Tool for Assessment (STA)—Teacher Screening Form

Student's name: _____

Glasses/contact lenses: Y / N

Teacher's name: _____

Hearing aid/cochlear implant: Y / N

Please read each item carefully and circle Yes or No.

1	The student closes or covers one eye when looking at some things.	Yes	No
2	The student frequently squints.	Yes	No
3	The student complains that some images are blurry or hard to see.	Yes	No
4	The student holds objects unusually close when looking at them.	Yes	No
5	The student seems to blink a lot.	Yes	No
6	The student becomes frustrated or upset when doing close-up work such as reading, math, and puzzles.	Yes	No
7	The student uses the wrong color names for objects, such as saying that there are purple leaves on trees.	Yes	No
8	The student has a short attention span when coloring or drawing with colors or colored markers.	Yes	No
9	The student has difficulty identifying red or green.	Yes	No
10	The student has difficulty reading when the words are on colored pages.	Yes	No
11	The student does not respond to loud noises sometimes.	Yes	No
12	The student's listening skills are behind what I expect.	Yes	No
13	The student turns up the volume too loud on electronic equipment.	Yes	No
14	The student does not follow spoken directions well.	Yes	No
15	The student often says, "Huh?" or asks you to repeat something you have said.	Yes	No
16	The student does not respond when called.	Yes	No
17	The student's speech is behind what I expect.	Yes	No
18	The student has difficulty pronouncing some words.	Yes	No
19	The student substitutes sounds in words (e.g., wed for red).	Yes	No

20	The student leaves sounds out of words (e.g., root for fruit).	Yes No
21	How much of the student's speech do you understand?	25% 50% 75% 100%
22	How much of the student's speech would a stranger understand?	25% 50% 75% 100%
23	The student has difficulty stacking blocks.	Yes No
24	The student has difficulty fitting puzzle pieces together.	Yes No
25	The student has difficulty drawing a straight line.	Yes No
26	The student has difficulty drawing a circle.	Yes No
27	The student has difficulty printing words.	Yes No
28	I can usually read the student's handwriting.	Yes No
29	A stranger would usually be able to read the student's handwriting.	Yes No
30	The student is often defiant.	Yes No
31	The student often refuses to do what I ask.	Yes No
32	The student breaks a lot of rules at school.	Yes No
33	The student speaks a language other than English when talking to friends.	Yes No
34	The student speaks a language other than English when talking to members of their family.	Yes No
35	The student has attended schools in which a language other than English was spoken by teachers and students.	Yes No
36	The student listens to music, reads, and watches TV, movies, and videos in a language other than English.	Yes No
37	The student frequently participates in holidays and cultural events associated with their family's history outside the United States.	Yes No

Are there any other issues that might affect how well the student performs during the upcoming testing sessions? Please describe them below.

FORM 5.3

Screening Tool for Assessment (STA)—Direct Screening Test Record

Student's name: _____

Glasses/contact lenses: Y / N

Date: _____

Hearing aid/cochlear implant: Y / N

GENERAL SCREENING QUESTIONS

I want to ask you a few questions before we start today.

How are you feeling today?

Did you sleep well last night?

How confident (or nervous) are you feeling about our work together today?

How ready are you to do your best on every task today? or How motivated are you to do well on these tasks today?

Do you wear glasses or contacts or have trouble seeing?

Do you have any trouble telling colors apart? or Are you color-blind?

Do you wear a hearing aid or have trouble hearing?

Do you have any trouble writing with a pencil? or How neat is your handwriting?

Do you have any trouble picking up and moving items such as coins?

What language or languages do you speak or understand?

Note: Paraphrase and follow up with more specific questions if needed. Use the child or adolescent's oral language during interview to estimate intelligibility of speech.

VISION SCREENING

Present Vision Screening items from the STA Direct Screening Response Form.

Look at these letters on this sheet of paper. Please tell me the letters in the top row.

Stimuli	Number incorrect	Total correct
E O P Z T L C D F		/9

Correct errors if necessary, and repeat until all items are correct in sequence.

Without picking up the sheet, tell me the letters in the other rows. There is no reason to go fast. Slow and careful reading is best.

Mark those items missed.

Stimuli	Number incorrect	Total correct
T D P C F Z O E L		/9
D Z E L C F O T P		/9
F E P C T L O Z D		/9

COLOR-BLIND SCREENING

Present Color items from the STA Direct Screening Response Form.

See these squares. Name these colors for me. (Alternatively, **What is this color?**)

Stimuli	Correct response	
Black	Yes	No
Blue	Yes	No
Red	Yes	No
Green	Yes	No
Yellow	Yes	No
Purple	Yes	No

Total correct: /6

FINE MOTOR SCREENING

Present items from the Fine Motor page of the STA Direct Screening Response Form. Administer items in sequence as age and developmental level dictates.

If the examinee attempts to rotate the paper, say, **Don't move the paper; keep it in one place.**

1. **Take this pencil and trace this dotted line. Follow on the line, and make one smooth line.**
2. **Now trace this star. Follow on the lines.**
3. **Now trace this circle. Follow on the line.**
4. **Write this sentence, "The dog ran," on this line.**

Stimuli	Successful		Stimuli	Successful			
Line	Yes	No	Circle	Yes	No	Total Yes:	/4
Star	Yes	No	Sentence	Yes	No		

HEARING SCREENING

Part A: **Let's play a game about listening. I want you to point to parts of your body. Ready? Listen carefully. I will tell you where to point.**

Administer the initial items slightly louder than normal, and correct errors immediately. In correcting errors, model the correct response, and repeat the item (**Touch your hair.** Model touching your hair. **Now do you do it. Touch your hair.**). Following initial errors and correction, repeat all of the items in sequence until mastery of all items is demonstrated. In cases where mastery cannot be demonstrated, omit the failed item or items when administering Part B.

Item	Initial Response		Final Response
Point to your nose.	Yes	No	Yes
Point to your hair.	Yes	No	Yes
Point to your face.	Yes	No	Yes
Point to your ear.	Yes	No	Yes
Point to your chin.	Yes	No	Yes
Point to your shoulder.	Yes	No	Yes
Point to your mouth.	Yes	No	Yes

Part B: **Now I want you to point to the same parts of your body, but this time I want you to close your eyes while I tell you where to point. Ready? Listen carefully.**

Administer items at a low volume that is above that of a whisper but still able to be heard by the examinee. Put your hand a few inches in front of your mouth when presenting items.

Item	Correct response	
Point to your face.	Yes	No
Point to your nose.	Yes	No
Point to your ear.	Yes	No
Point to your hair.	Yes	No
Point to your shoulder.	Yes	No
Point to your mouth.	Yes	No
Point to your chin.	Yes	No

Total correct Part B:

ARTICULATION SCREENING

Please close your eyes, listen carefully, and say what I say.

Carefully articulate each word at a normal volume. Carefully watch the lips of the child or adolescent while he or she is responding.

If you cannot determine how to score a response, say "Please, say (item) again" as often as needed.

Circle the phonemes in the Sounds column that were incorrectly pronounced. Subtract the number of incorrect phonemes from 23 to determine the percentage correct, using the table provided.

Item	Sounds		#Correct	%Correct	#Correct	%Correct
Lizard	/l/	/z/	0	0%	19	83%
This	th	/s/	1	4%	20	87%
Wreath	/r/	th	2	9%	21	91%
Shoes	sh	/z/	3	13%	22	96%
Seal	/s/	/l/	4	17%	23	100%
Think	th	—	5	22%		
Mouthwash	th	sh	6	26%		
Garage	/r/	zh	7	30%		
Feather	th	/r/	8	35%		
Pillow	/l/		9	39%		
Zebra	/z/		10	43%		
Soothe	th		11	48%		
Television	zh		12	52%		
Listen	/s/		13	57%		
Washer	sh		14	61%		
			15	65%		
Total sounds:		23	16	70%		
Number of incorrect sounds: ___			17	74%		
Number of correct sounds: ____			18	78%		

INTELLIGIBILITY

After completing the STA Direct Screening Test, rate the proportion of the child or adolescent's speech you were able to understand.

How much of the child or adolescent's speech did you understand?	Some	Most	Almost all	All
	25%	50%	75%	100%

FORM 5.4

Screening Tool for Assessment (STA)—Direct Screening Response Form

Examinee's name: _____ Date: _____

E O P Z T L C D F

T D P C F Z O E L

D Z E L C F O T P

F E P C T L O Z D

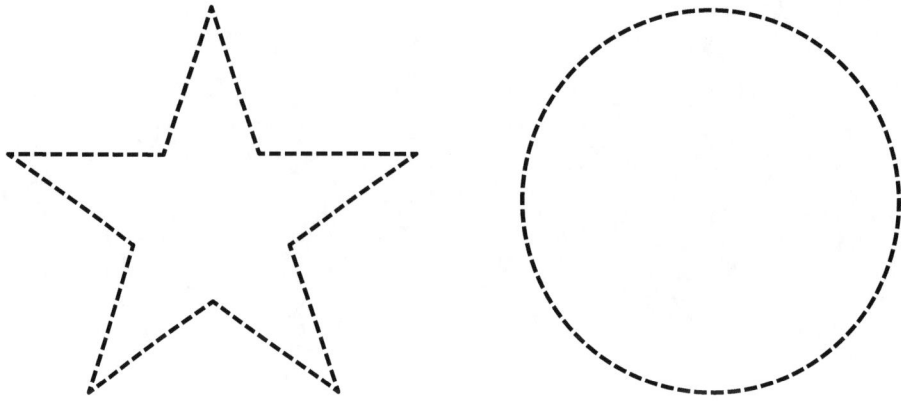

The dog ran.

CHAPTER 6

Evaluation and Use of the Wechsler Intelligence Scale for Children, Fifth Edition

with Emily K. Lewis and Richard J. McNulty[1]

In this edition, we offer a new chapter focused solely on the Wechsler Intelligence Scale for Children, Fifth Edition (WISC-V; Wechsler, 2014a). We do so for three reasons:

First, the WISC-V, like many of the intelligence tests we highlight in this book, is a superbly constructed instrument with a large, representative norming sample and some crucial scores supported by strong reliability and validity evidence. In fact, the WISC-V is accompanied by a substantial amount of information (in its ancillary materials and in peer-reviewed publications) that enables users to critically evaluate key elements and employ an evidence-based approach to test interpretation across a variety of test takers with and without disabilities. We highlight these characteristics in more detail later in this chapter.

Second, the WISC-V and its predecessors routinely have been some of the most commonly administered intelligence tests among school psychologists and clinical psychologists (e.g., Hutton, Dubes, & Muir, 1992; Wilson & Reschly, 1996). In particular, Benson et al.'s (2019) recent survey of school psychologists revealed that the WISC-V is not only the most commonly used intelligence test—used more frequently, on average, than the next five most commonly used intelligence tests *combined*—but also the second most commonly administered assessment instrument period. Almost 80% of school psychologists reported employing the WISC-V at least once during their past year. Their reports of frequency of use revealed that they administered the WISC-V, on average, about 3½ times per month.

Third, the WISC-V has all of the features of the prototypical intelligence test from the 2010s (such as test records, stimulus books, and response booklets) plus some new features that are likely to become commonplace in the 2020s. In particular, it includes options for advanced support technologies (called Q-Interactive) that promote both accuracy and ease in both administration and scoring.

---

1. Emily K. Lewis is a doctoral student in school psychology at the University of Memphis. Her research interests include learning disabilities, academic and behavioral interventions, cross-cultural research, and psychological testing. Richard J. McNulty is a doctoral candidate in school psychology at the University of Memphis. His research interests include intelligence assessment, treatment utility of assessment, and emotional regulation.

In this chapter, we briefly address the WISC-V's history, followed by an in-depth description of WISC-V's organization, materials, and scores, beginning with its subtests and moving to a focus on its composites. We also discuss the response processes of WISC-V subtests contributing to FSIQ as well as associated accommodations for these subtests. We highlight the norming, reliability, scaling, and other psychometric information about the tests' key composites based on the criteria we established as being important in Chapter 5.

Evolution of the WISC-V

The WISC-V has its origins in the Wechsler-Bellevue I, Wechsler's first individually administered intelligence test designed for adults and published in the 1930s (Wechsler, 1939). The first Wechsler Intelligence Scale for Children (Wechsler, 1949) was not published until a decade later, near the beginning of the baby boom in the United States. The test targeted children and adolescents from ages 5 to 15 years and included 11 of the same subtests included in the Wechsler-Bellevue I. A twelfth subtest, Mazes, was added. Like the Wechsler-Bellevue I, it produced norm-referenced scores for each subtest as well as three composites scores: Verbal IQ, Performance IQ, and Full Scale IQ. The Full Scale IQ stemmed from the first 10 subtests administered, and the Verbal IQ and Performance IQ each stemmed from half of these subtests, depending on simple classifications of the subtests into those that required verbal responses or fine motor responses. The two additional subtests not contributing to these scores, Digit Span and Coding, were included to allow examiners to replace subtest scores with more accurate ones if errors in administration or invalidating idiosyncratic responses were identified. It is notable that the original WISC included five of the seven subtests contributing to the WISC-V's Full Scale IQ as well as eight of the WISC-V's total subtests. Of course, all test items included in the WISC-V are different from prior editions, but it is remarkable to see this continuity in test construction across more than 80 years since Wechsler's original design of the test.

A total of 25 years passed after publication of the WISC before the second edition of the test was published: the Wechsler Intelligence Scale for Children, Revised (Wechsler, 1974). Its targeted age range was 6 to 16 years, which remains the same to this day; no new subtests or new composite scores were added. In 1991, the Wechsler Intelligence Scale for Children, Third Edition (WISC-III; Wechsler, 1991) was published, and it included several new features, such as a new subtest (Symbol Search) as well as four composites scores designed to represent patterns of specific abilities evident across subtests. These composites often are called index scores or factor indexes. Both the Symbol Search subtest and two of these index scores, Verbal Comprehension and Processing Speed, remain in the WISC-V. The other index scores, Perceptual Organization and Freedom from Distractibility, have been revised, in part based on accumulating research evidence.

The Wechsler Intelligence Scale for Children, Fourth Edition (WISC-IV; Wechsler, 2003) was published during the early 2000s, and this revision was a fairly substantial one. It was the first edition of the WISC (and first Wechsler scale across the family of related tests) not to produce Verbal and Performance IQ scores. Three of the original WISC subtests were eliminated, in part, to reduce the amount of manipulative materials, such as cards and puzzle pieces. Plus, five new subtests were added, including four subtests that remain in the WISC-V: Matrix Reasoning, which contributes to the FSIQ and a factor index, and three subtests that do not and that can be considered supplemental—Picture Concepts, Letter-Number Sequencing, and Cancellation. The Verbal Comprehension and Processing Speed index scores were retained, and Perceptual Organization and Freedom from Distractibility were redesigned and labeled Perceptual Reasoning and Working Memory.

The WISC-V continues the pattern of substantial revisions evident in the WISC-IV. In particular, all of the item content was altered, so not a single question or stimulus item is the same as prior editions of the test. It was expanded from 15 subtests to 21, omitting 2 WISC-IV subtests and adding 8 new ones. It is the first WISC (and first Wechsler scale) to produce a Full Scale IQ from fewer than 10 subtests (7 actually) and the first to produce five index scores. These index scores include three of the same index scores from the prior version, namely, the Verbal Comprehension Index, the Processing Speed Index, and the Working Memory Index. In addition, the index formerly known as the WISC-III's Perceptual Organization Index and the WISC-IV's Perceptual Reasoning Index is now represented by two index scores more closely aligned with Cattell-Horn-Carroll (CHC) theory: the Fluid Reasoning Index and the Visual Spatial Index. The WISC-V also includes subtests contributing to composites focused more closely on cognitive processes associated with memory storage and retrieval.

Composition of the WISC-V

DESCRIPTIONS OF SUBTESTS

As noted previously, the WISC-V includes 21 subtests. Their items typically are administered orally, via stimulus books and response booklets, and manipulatives are limited to only cubes. Alternatively, all subtests may be administered and scored primarily in digital format via Q-Interactive. Some subtests administered by Q-Interactive still require the test taker to employ manipulatives and response booklets when responding, as all subtests are not yet completely digitized.

In this section, we describe the central features of these subtests. This information lays the groundwork for our later discussion of their content and response processes as well as how these subtests essentially are employed as indicators of latent constructs, such as psychometric g and more specific abilities, rather than as more direct measures of the cognitive processes they appear to target. We have highlighted variations in the administration format for the first 10 subtests when they differed across standard paper-and-pencil and digital formats via Q-Interactive.

Block Design requires the test taker to replicate a set of modeled or printed two-dimensional geometric patterns during a timed administration. The standard administration requires manipulation of red and white colored cubes. Administration via Q-Interactive involves limited variation from standard practices for the test taker but notable changes for the examiner. The geometrical pattern is presented to the test taker through their iPad display rather than a booklet, and they are asked to construct their design using the standard tangible cubes found in "briefcase kits." Significant differences in presentation and recording format are involved for the examiner. Rather than flipping stimuli pages to present items, the examiner touches a "Show Picture" button to prompt the stimuli page to display on the test taker's device. A built-in timer is included on the examiner's display in order to record timing, with an "adjust timer" feature that permits modification to the time in the event the timer is stopped erroneously. The examiner documents the test taker's constructed response design by tapping the on-screen graphic. Rotation errors are notated by placing two fingers on the touchscreen over the design model and twisting. Points are awarded by tapping on the screen over the corresponding button (e.g., 2 points, 1 point, and 0 points). Dimension errors can be tagged by touching the corresponding on-screen button, but for qualitative information, the other errors should be recorded through the use of a note.

Similarities require the test taker to listen to the examiner present two words sharing common features and articulate what those features are. For example, the examiner might ask how a bird and an airplane are alike. This format largely is equivalent between standard and digital administrations. The Q-Interactive platform enables the examiner to highlight one or multiple standard responses out of a "pick list" of possible responses that correspond to different point values. Moreover, a response box (called the "verbatim response field") at the bottom of the screen enables the examiner to document verbatim test taker responses if they are not adequately found in the "pick list." Standard notations (e.g., "don't know" and queries) may be highlighted by touching the contextual event buttons on the screen. For teaching items found early in the test administration, a button may be touched to reveal the necessary prompts to be administered by the examiner. An audio recording option is available to capture the test taker's responses. Points are awarded by tapping on the screen over the corresponding button.

Matrix Reasoning requires the test taker to review a series of images in an incomplete grid and identify the correct answer that completes the grid from five different options. Using Q-Interactive, rather than turning a stimulus book page, the examiner displays the images on the test taker's device. A view of the test taker's window is displayed on the examiner's screen, and the correct response is indicated by a green outline. After the test taker touches their response, the response selection will be indicated in an examiner's window with gray shading. Points are automatically awarded based on test taker response.

Digit Span requires the test taker to repeat sequentially or in a reversed order a series of orally presented number sequences. The WISC-V Digit Span subtest includes three sections: Forward, Backward, and Sequencing. The test taker requirement is identical across standard and digital formats, whereas examiner administration includes minor differences. For example, the test taker's response is scored by touching the appropriate point button. If no points were awarded, you should capture the test taker's response by writing it (via stylus) in the "Response" box at the bottom of the screen. An audio recording option is available to capture the test taker's audible responses on test items. Interfaces are similar across all three components of the Digit Span subtest, including Forward, Backward, and Sequencing.

Coding requires the test taker to draw symbols that are paired with a series of shapes or numbers according to a key. The test taker is required to perform this task as quickly as possible during a timed administration. The standard administration requires the test taker to reproduce symbols on a page using an eraserless pencil. The Q-Interactive assessment affords two possible formats. Examiners may continue to use the standard administration methods and then enter raw scores into Q-Interactive to derive scaled scores. Alternatively, as of April 2016, the examiner can administer Coding completely via the digital medium. Importantly, this medium includes substantial alterations to the administration format, including a multiple-choice response design in which the test taker is required to indicate their response through touching the screen. Doing so eliminates the test taker's writing requirements as well as the potential for rotation errors and the option of self-correction. Thus, the digital format removes many of the graphomotor demands inherent in the standard administration. A built-in timer that counts down is included.

Vocabulary requires the test taker orally to define a series of words presented orally. Some test takers may be asked to label pictures. The digital administration format is similar to that of Similarities. Interaction between the test taker and the digital device is limited to items 1 through 4, which include visual stimuli. For those items, the examiner touches the "Show Picture Button" when they are ready to display the visual stimulus, which will appear on the test taker's device. They remove the device from the test taker after Item 4. Teaching prompts are included for certain items. There are given answers to choose from, or responses can be recorded verbatim. The point value needs to be assigned by the examiner, however.

Figure Weights requires the test taker to view images of scales with missing weights and select the response option that keeps the scales balanced. Using Q-Interactive, rather than turning a stimulus book page, the examiner displays the images on the test taker's device; the test taker responds by selecting response options on the screen. The administration and scoring of Figure Weights using Q-Interactive is consistent with that for Matrix Reasoning.

Visual Puzzles requires the test taker to view a completed puzzle and select three response options that, when combined, reconstruct the puzzle. When using Q-Interactive, the examiner presents the images and response options on the test taker's device, and they respond by touching the screen.

Picture Span requires the test taker to view a stimulus display containing one or more pictures for a specified period (typically 5 seconds) and then select the picture or pictures (in sequential order) from options on another page. From the examiner's perspective, a number of important administration differences between the standard and Q-Interactive format should be noted. In general, the administration of each item includes two consecutive examiner screens (called "cards"). The first screen manages the administration of the stimulus page on the test taker's device. The examiner will work their way from top to bottom down this screen. A countdown associated with the length of item exposure is displayed within the "Show Picture" button itself. Upon completion of the automated countdown, the display on the test taker's device changes from stimulus to response screen. (Essentially, this is the automated equivalent to flipping the stimulus page in the standard format.) If an interruption occurs during stimulus exposure, a "Hide picture" is present on the examiner's screen and may be used to suspend stimulus exposure. The examiner "swipes" to a second, scoring-related screen upon delivering the second prompt (e.g., "Touch the pictures in the order I showed you"). On the scoring screen, the examiner may view the response menu displayed on the test taker's device. As the test taker sequentially touches picture options, the selected picture response is highlighted on the examiner screen. All correctly identified pictures are highlighted in green; incorrect responses are highlighted in red. The test taker's response sequence (e.g., A-C-E-D) is captured by Q-Interactive and displayed on the examiner's device directly above the "Client View" window. The examiner must score the item by comparing the response sequence and correct picture identification (i.e., green or red highlights) to point criteria.

Symbol Search requires the test taker to scan a series of paired groups of symbols (with each pair consisting of a target group and a search group) and indicate whether a target symbol appears in a search group. The test taker is required to perform this task as quickly as possible under a timed administration. As for Coding, the standard format employs a response booklet, and the test taker must make marks with an eraserless pencil. The Q-Interactive format for Symbol Search requires test takers to select their response by touching the appropriate symbol in a search group. Importantly, a limited number of rows are simultaneously visible on the digital device, and only one center row is active at a time for test taker selection. Because peripheral rows are not active, no self-correction is possible on the digital format of this test. During the timed test itself, a timer on the examiner's device tracks elapsed time. As the test taker completes a touch response for each row, the selected symbol is highlighted on the examiner's device in green or red, representing correct or incorrect responses, respectively. When the timer reaches the designated time limit, the subtest ends, and items are no longer displayed on either device.

Information requires the test taker to answer a series of orally presented questions that tap knowledge about common events, objects, places, and people.

Picture Concepts requires the test taker to review a series of images presented in rows and to identify images across two or three rows that form a common class. For example, the puppy in the first row, the cat in the second row, and the parrot in the third row would be identified following the class of pets or, more broadly, animals.

Letter-Number Sequencing requires the test taker to listen a series of letters and numbers presented orally in a mixed-up order and then say the complete series with the numbers first in ascending order and the letters in alphabetical order.

Cancellation requires the test taker to scan an arrangement of shapes and indicate whether or not target shapes appear in the arrangement. The test taker is required to perform this task as quickly as possible under a timed administration.

Comprehension requires the test taker to respond to orally presented questions that focus on everyday problems or understanding of social rules and concepts.

Arithmetic requires the test taker mentally to solve a series of orally presented arithmetic problems and respond orally. Initial items include visual stimuli.

In addition to the subtests that have appeared on prior editions of the Wechsler scales, five new subtests are offered within the WISC-V. It is notable that, despite their being included on an intelligence test labeled as such, users are warned that these subtests were "not designed as . . . measure[s] of intelligence but to enable clinicians to identify difficulties in cognitive processes associated with academic learning" (Wechsler, 2014a, p. 13). These subtests primarily focus on memory storage and retrieval:

- Naming Speed Literacy requires the test taker to label stimuli rapidly according to their color as well as their names (in terms of objects, numbers, and letters).
- Naming Speed Quantity requires the test taker to count rapidly and report the number of squares within a box.
- Immediate Symbol Translation requires the test taker to learn the verbal labels associated with symbols presented on the page and apply this learning when the symbols are sequenced to form phrases and sentences.
- Delayed Symbol Translation requires the test taker to recall the same verbal labels associated with symbols presented on the stimulus page during Immediate Symbol Translation, without reteaching.
- Recognition Symbol Translation requires the test taker to apply their memories of the verbal labels and symbols learned during Immediate Symbol Translation by pointing to the symbols on the stimulus book page as the verbal labels for the symbols are provided by the examiner.

Comparability of Subtest Scores across Standard and Digital Administration Formats

The computer-based administration format of WISC-V subtests via Q-Interactive raises important questions pertaining to administration errors and format equivalence. Given the widely documented prevalence of significant administration errors evident in student and practitioner intelligence testing (e.g., Styck & Walsh, 2016), optimism is widely expressed that a more automated process would reduce the element of human error. Although such hopes for digital administration appear to be well-founded, especially in the case of reducing errors related to score calculation and administration (Noland, 2017), it is important to remember that the bulk of administration errors occur during verbal subtests such as Similarities, Vocabulary, and Comprehension (Cormier et al., 2019; Mrazik, Janzen, Dombrowski, Barford, & Krawchuk, 2012). Given the strong overlap between standard and digital format on these subtests, it is not evident how the digital administration medium would significantly contribute to incremental accuracy. For example, the failure to query is pervasive in administration (Kaufman, Raiford, & Coalson, 2016) and is not likely to be remedied by replicating the page display of standard administrations on an iPad screen. Continued examiner training, practice, and vigilance will be required—even in a digital world—to ensure accurate scores.

In general, do test takers' scores differ in ways that are due to the format of the test administration? Results from non-peer-reviewed equivalence studies conducted by Pearson Inc. suggest that score differences between administration formats generally are small and that the two forms are clinically equivalent. Although these studies found statistically significant format effects on the Block Design, Arithmetic, and Comprehension subtests, with test takers tending to score higher on digital assessment administrations on the latter two subtests, the test taker and device had weak statistical interaction, and the effect sizes for these differences were small to medium in magnitude. In fact, they reached but did not exceed the threshold criterion for equivalence of 0.20 set by Pearson (Daniel, Wahlstrom, & Zhang, 2014). Similarly, digital-based administration resulted in higher scaled scores on the Coding subtest. Standardized differences between formats was 0.23, slightly exceeding the effect size threshold set by Pearson. Practically speaking, this difference is more than one-half of a scaled score point (Raiford et al., 2016). It is important to note, however, that no research has been published on the equivalence of the administration format using all 10 core subtests of the WISC-V. The study by Daniel et al. (2014) examined all but the Processing Speed Index subtests, and the Raiford et al. (2016) study, using a different sample, only examined the Processing Speed Index subtests. In addition, independent research has yet to be published on the equivalence of administration formats on the WISC-V.

Reliability and Validity of Subtests Scores

Reliability. The WISC-V produces scaled scores for all 21 subtests as well as 10 scaled or standard "process scores" based on variations of the Block Design, Cancellation, Digit Span, and Naming Speed Literacy subtests.[1] As we discussed in Chapter 4, one of the key assumptions in the administration of assessment instruments is that they produce results that are reliable—across items, across time, and across raters. There must be sufficient evidence of reliability before proceeding with score interpretation; oral or written descriptions provided to parents, teachers, and other professionals; and the development of interventions.

Turn to Table 6.1 to review a summary of the reliability information for the WISC-V subtests, and recall that our standards for reliability should be high—ideally .95 or higher for internal consistency reliability estimates.[2] We know that we can settle for reliability estimates as low as .90, that we should be highly skeptical of values less than that, and that we probably should ignore scores altogether that have values of less than .70. The WISC-V subtests' reliability coefficients summarized in Table 6.1 are most frequently split-half reliability coefficients stemming from the correlations between the sum of the scores from half the items and the sum of the scores from the other half of items on the subtest. (Historically, the sum of the odd-numbered items

---

[1]. Process scores are based on an approach that "emphasizes the qualitative evaluation of test performance (e.g., performing error analysis, recording behavior observations, and testing the limits)" (Wechsler, 2014c, p. 17), but we do not highlight them in this chapter. See Chapter 8 for more information about qualitative analysis of test score performance.

[2]. We are impressed that the WISC-V support materials also include reliability estimates for samples of children and adolescents with identified special education and clinical conditions, but we have not summarized them here.

Table 6.1. Reliability Coefficients for WISC-V Subtests across 1-Year Age Groups (Ages 6–16)

Subtest	Average reliability	Lowest reliability (age group)	Highest reliability (age group)
Block Design	.84	.80 (14)	.88 (8)
Similarities	.87	.81 (11)	.89 (6, 13)
Matrix Reasoning	.87	.82 (11)	.90 (12)
Digit Span	.91	.89 (9)	.93 (12)
Coding	.83	.78 (6–7)	.89 (14–16)
Vocabulary	.87	.83 (6, 8)	.91 (12)
Figure Weights	.94	.91 (6)	.96 (10)
Visual Puzzles	.89	.87 (8)	.92 (15)
Picture Span	.85	.82 (7)	.87 (8, 9)
Symbol Search	.81	.67 (12, 13)	.87 (14–16)
Information	.86	.81 (8, 11)	.90 (16)
Picture Concepts	.83	.78 (16)	.85 (10, 11)
Letter-Number Sequencing	.86	.80 (10)	.93 (6)
Cancellation	.82	.80 (6, 7)	.84 (10, 11)
Comprehension	.83	.76 (6)	.88 (14)
Arithmetic	.90	.88 (6, 8)	.92 (10, 14, 16)
Naming Speed Literacy	.86	.79 (8–9)	.92 (14–16)
Naming Speed Quantity	.83	.79 (6–7)	.86 (11)
Immediate Symbol Translation	.88	.85 (8–9)	.93 (10)
Delayed Symbol Translation	.87	.85 (8–9)	.89 (12–13)
Recognition Symbol Translation	.82	.78 (12–13)	.88 (6–7)

Note: All values are based on results reported in Wechsler (2016c).

was correlated with the sum of the even-numbered items, but that is not specified in the WISC-V materials. Plus, the halves could be selected at random.)

The problem with the split-half reliability method alone is that it focuses on two halves of each subtest and not on all of the items across the subtest. To address this problem, a statistical correction—the Spearman-Brown formula—can be applied to produce a reliability estimate that represents the full-length subtest. For a portion of the WISC-V subtests (the speeded ones: Coding, Symbol Search, Cancellation, Naming Speed Literacy, Naming Speed Quantity, Immediate Symbol Translation, Delayed Symbol Translation, and Recognition Symbol Translation), the reliability estimates presented in Table 6.1 are test–retest reliability coefficients stemming from two administrations of the WISC-V across 9 to 82 days ($M = 26$; Wechsler, 2014c). Based on what is known about the results stemming from these two methods, the test–retest reliability coefficients almost always are lower in magnitude (even when corrected for range restriction) than the corrected split-half reliability estimates. This pattern is evident in Table 6.1, too.

Values presented in Table 6.1 reveal that, on average across ages 6 to 16, only three WISC-V subtests have reliability values at or above .90: Figure Weights, Arithmetic, and Digit Span. In fact, the average value for Figure Weights of .94—and its individual values ranging from .91 to .96 across the WISC-V's 11 one-year age groups (6–16)—are stellar. The remainder of the 13 WISC-V subtests, however, have average reliability values from .81 to .89, and for some age groups, these values are less than .80. Some are even less than .70 (i.e., Symbol Search). These reliability coefficients alone should give test users who hold themselves to high professional standards pause. This pattern of results is one reason why we do not encourage interpretation of subtests. Subtests typically—with a few exceptions—do not have sufficient reliability for routine interpretation. Further, this inadequate reliability means that when these subtests are interpreted in comparison to each other—in a subtest score profile—illusions of meaning surface (McGill, Dombrowski, & Canivez, 2018; Watkins, 2009). Although confidence intervals could be plotted around subtest scores to recognize their lower reliability, confidence intervals are not typically produced for the WISC-V subtests. In contrast to subtest scores, composites scores, which stem from aggregating those subtest scores, typically are far more reliable. Thus, we recommend that you attend to them rather than subtest scores.

Validity evidence. We also draw your attention to the percentages presented in Table 6.2. These are squared g loadings, which represent the percentage of variance associated with the latent factor, psychometric g. They stem from seven studies published in peer-reviewed journals and analyses of the WISC-V norming data (Canivez, Dombrowski, & Watkins, 2018; Canivez, Watkins, & Dombrowski, 2016; Canivez, Watkins, & Dombrowski, 2017; Chen, Zhang, Raiford, Zhu, & Weiss, 2015; Dombrowski, Canivez, & Watkins, 2018; Dombrowski, Canivez, Watkins, & Beaujean, 2015; Reynolds & Keith, 2017) and one independent sample (Canivez et al., 2018). However, they are produced from a variety of exploratory and confirmatory factor analytic methods and modeled features, and, in some cases, they stem from different age groups.

As described in Chapter 4, g loadings are effectively validity estimates indicating the degree to which each subtest measures psychometric g. When they are squared, they reveal the g saturation of the score—the percentage of variance attributable to psychometric g that reasonably accounts for individual differences across people. When considering subtests, g saturation values of 49% or higher are considered high, values within the span of 25% and 48% are considered medium, and values less than 25% are considered low. In Table 6.1, subtest g saturation at high, medium, and low levels is marked in terms of strength—with high values in the darkest shading and low values without shading.

It is apparent that the long-term storage and retrieval subtests have not received the scrutiny by researchers that other, more traditional WISC-V subtests have. In reviewing Table 6.2, note that no studies have reported the g saturation of the five new long-term storage and retrieval subtests; we found a paucity of research that has examined their validity. Next, notice the range of values across subtests in each column. For example, Chen et al. (2015) reported g saturation values that ranged from a high of 52% for Arithmetic to 4% for Cancellation. If the goal of a subtest, at least in part, is to measure psychometric g with accuracy, Vocabulary does reasonably well but not stellar (as 48% of its variance could be attributed to specific abilities, random error, and something unique to the subtest). Cancellation clearly is not, in any sense, a strong correlate of psychometric g based on these results. Median values across studies, methods, and samples are presented on the right side of the table. Four subtests have

Table 6.2. Percentage of Variance in WISC-V Subtests Attributable to Psychometric g across Studies, Models, and Data Sets

Subtest	Chen et al. (2015) CFA, HO, 5 Factors, Full Norm	Dombrowski et al. (2015) EB-FA, 5 Factors, Full Norm	Canivez et al. (2016) EFA, First Factor, 4 Factors, Full Norm	Canivez et al. (2016) EFA, S-L Transformation, 4 Factors, Full Norm	Reynolds & Keith (2017) CFA, HO, 5 Factors, Full Norm	Reynolds & Keith (2017) CFA, Bifactor, 5 Factors, Full Norm	Canivez et al. (2017) CFA, Bifactor, 4 Factors, Full Norm	Canivez et al. (2017) CFA, Bifactor, 4 Factors, Full Norm	Canivez et al. (2017) CFA, HO, 5 Factors, Full Norm	Dombrowski et al. (2018) EFA, S-L Transformation, 4 Factors, 6-8 Norm	Dombrowski et al. (2018) EFA, S-L Transformation, 4 Factors, 9-11 Norm	Dombrowski et al. (2018) EFA, S-L Transformation, 4 Factors, 12-14 Norm	Dombrowski et al. (2018) EFA, S-L Transformation, 5 Factors, 15-16 Norm	Canivez et al. (2018) EFA, First Factor, 4 Factors, Clinical	Canivez et al. (2018) EFA, EB-FA, 4 Factors, Clinical	Canivez et al. (2018) EFA, S-L Transformation, 5 Factors, Clinical	Canivez et al. (2018) CFA, Bifactor, 4 Factors, Clinical	Median	Standard Deviation
Block Design	45%	41%	45%	41%	40%	41%	41%	45%	46%	48%	46%	46%	56%	58%	45%	42%	41%	45%	5%
Similarities	48%	61%	56%	48%	50%	52%	52%	48%	49%	49%	46%	53%	52%	56%	50%	52%	50%	51%	4%
Matrix Reasoning	45%	36%	40%	37%	41%	41%	41%	45%	45%	38%	26%	40%	30%	52%	44%	41%	46%	41%	6%
Digit Span	44%	38%	49%	46%	45%	44%	44%	44%	42%	29%	28%	44%	14%	45%	46%	46%	58%	44%	10%
Coding	16%	20%	18%	15%	14%	44%	14%	13%	13%	35%	24%	16%	33%	33%	29%	28%	27%	18%	8%
Vocabulary	52%	64%	59%	50%	55%	53%	53%	49%	49%	44%	46%	56%	52%	56%	50%	52%	55%	52%	5%
Figure Weights	45%	36%	41%	37%	42%	41%	42%	44%	45%	24%	36%	48%	30%	50%	41%	38%	48%	41%	8%
Visual Puzzles	48%	41%	46%	43%	44%	44%	42%	46%	49%	41%	40%	50%	52%	64%	49%	48%	50%	46%	6%
Picture Span	26%	27%	33%	30%	27%	30%	30%	30%	29%	7%	22%	35%	19%	37%	37%	38%	40%	30%	8%

(continued)

Table 6.2. Continued

Subtest	Chen et al. (2015) CFA, HO, 5 Factors, Full Norm	Dombrowski et al. (2015) EB-FA, 5 Factors, Full Norm	Canivez et al. (2016) EFA, First Factor, 4 Factors, Full Norm	Canivez et al. (2016) EFA, S-L Transformation, 4 Factors, Full Norm	Reynolds & Keith (2017) CFA, HO, 5 Factors, Full Norm	Reynolds & Keith (2017) CFA, Bifactor, 5 Factors, Full Norm	Canivez et al. (2017) CFA, Bifactor, 4 Factors, Full Norm	Canivez et al. (2017) CFA, Bifactor, 4 Factors, Full Norm	Canivez et al. (2017) CFA, HO, 5 Factors, Full Norm	Dombrowski et al. (2018) EFA, S-L Transformation, 4 Factors, 6-8 Norm	Dombrowski et al. (2018) EFA, S-L Transformation, 4 Factors, 9-11 Norm	Dombrowski et al. (2018) EFA, S-L Transformation, 4 Factors, 12-14 Norm	Dombrowski et al. (2018) EFA, S-L Transformation, 5 Factors, 15-16 Norm	Canivez et al. (2018) EFA, First Factor, 4 Factors, Clinical	Canivez et al. (2018) EFA, EB-FA, 4 Factors, Clinical	Canivez et al. (2018) EFA, S-L Transformation, 5 Factors, Clinical	Canivez et al. (2018) CFA, Bifactor, 4 Factors, Clinical	Median	Standard Deviation
Symbol Search	16%	25%	23%	19%	18%	19%	19%	18%	18%	38%	25%	19%	49%	38%	33%	33%	30%	23%	10%
Information	49%	61%	56%	48%	52%	52%	52%	—	—	—	—	—	—	—	—	—	—	52%	5%
Picture Concepts	29%	27%	27%	24%	27%	29%	28%	—	—	—	—	—	—	—	—	—	—	27%	2%
Letter-Number Sequencing	41%	38%	48%	44%	44%	42%	42%	—	—	—	—	—	—	—	—	—	—	42%	3%
Cancellation	4%	7%	5%	4%	4%	4%	4%	—	—	—	—	—	—	—	—	—	—	4%	1%
Comprehension	36%	48%	44%	36%	38%	39%	39%	—	—	—	—	—	—	—	—	—	—	39%	4%
Arithmetic	50%	48%	52%	48%	55%	55%	55%	—	—	—	—	—	—	—	—	—	—	52%	3%

Note: All values are squared *g* loadings, rounded to two decimal places, and reported as a percentage. The darker shading indicates high *g* saturation and the lighter shading indicates medium *g* saturation. To our knowledge, the subtests Naming Speed Literacy, Naming Speed Quantity, Immediate Symbol Translation, Delayed Symbol Translation, and Recognition Symbol Translation have not been included in any factor-analytic studies. CFA = confirmatory factor analysis, HO = higher-order model, Full Norm = full norming sample, EB-FA = exploratory bifactor analysis, EFA = exploratory factor analysis, S-L = Schmid-Leiman, Norm = portion of full norming sample, Clinical = clinical sample.

median values that are in the high range: Similarities, Vocabulary, Information, and Arithmetic. Two subtests have median values that are in the low range: Coding and Cancellation. The third subtest in the processing speed domain is just barely in the medium range (Symbol Search, with a median value of 23%).

Finally, look at the variation across the studies, methods, and samples. For the most part, the *g* saturation values are remarkably consistent, with a median standard deviation across subtests of only 5%. Many of the differences seen in labeling of the *g* saturation values (indicated by shading) are those on the borderline (around 49% in many cases). Later, as we discuss the subtests that contribute to composite scores, we will return to this table and examine the subtests that contribute to the most prominent WISC-V scores (e.g., the FSIQ). The Coding subtest is clearly the outlier among these seven subtests.

For the remainder of this chapter, we focus on the more reliable (and uniformly more *g*-saturated) composite scores, rather than subtests. Still, we deem it important to consider the content as well as response requirements of the items included in subtests, as this information will aid in (a) the selection of subtests to measure the general construct of psychometric *g* and more specific abilities through these composites as well as (b) the determination of what content might interfere with test takers' access to subtest items.

Evaluation of the WISC-V Norming and Score Composites

NORMING

As evident in Table 6.3, the WISC-V's norming data were collected from 2013 to 2014 across 49 of the United States. The test developers followed a norming plan based on the 2012 U.S. Census and used continuous norming procedures. There are at least approximately 66 individuals per norm table block across age levels. Using Norfolk et al.'s (2015) evaluative labels, the WISC-V's norm blocks are of medium size.

WISC-V COMPOSITES

The WISC-V's subtests can be used in varying combinations to form 16 composite scores: a full-scale IQ; what are called by the test's developers *primary* indexes, *ancillary* indexes, and *complementary* indexes; and two "expanded" composite scores offered post-publication (Raiford, Drozdick, Zhang, & Zhou, 2015; Wechsler, 2014a). See Table 6.3. We have organized our presentation of information about these composite scores not according to the terms employed primarily by WISC-V developers (i.e., primary, ancillary, and complementary), but according to their level of generality, as either broad or general cognitive ability composites.

Table 6.3. Psychometric Evaluation of the Wechsler Intelligence Scale for Children, Fifth Edition

Publisher: Pearson
Publication date: 2014
Age range: 16:0–90:11

Norming Information

Norm sample N: 2,200
Dates collected: 2013–2014
Census data: 2012
Number U.S. states sampled: 49
Characteristics considered: Age, sex, race/ethnicity, parent education level, and geographic region
Continuous norming: Yes
Norm blocks: Elementary: Medium; Middle and High: Medium

Scores Provided

Stratum III Composite

Full Scale IQ
- 7 subtests with no floor or ceiling violations
- Yields standard score, PR, and CIs
- Standard score range: 50–150
- Mean internal consistency reliability = .96

General Ability Index
- 5 subtests with no floor or ceiling violations
- Yields standard score, PR, and CIs
- Standard score range: 40–160
- Mean internal consistency reliability = .96

Nonverbal Index
- 6 subtests with no floor or ceiling violations
- Yields standard score, PR, and CIs
- Standard score range: 40–160
- Mean internal consistency reliability = .95

Auditory Working Memory Index
- 2 subtests
- Yields standard score, PR, and CIs
- Standard score range: 45–155
- Mean internal consistency reliability = .93

Verbal (Expanded Crystallized) Index
- 3 subtests
- Yields standard score, PR, and CIs
- Standard score range: 45–155
- Mean internal consistency reliability = .95

Expanded Fluid Index
- 3 subtests
- Yields standard score, PR, and CIs
- Standard score range: 45–155
- Mean internal consistency reliability = .95

Subtests
- 21 subtests yielding scaled scores

Stratum II Composites

Verbal Comprehension Index
- 2 subtests
- Yields standard score, PR, and CIs
- Standard score range: 50–150
- Mean internal consistency reliability = .92

Visual Spatial Index
- 2 subtests
- Yields standard score, PR, and CIs
- Standard score range: 45–155
- Mean internal consistency reliability = .92

Fluid Reasoning Index
- 2 subtests
- Yields standard score, PR, and CIs
- Standard score range: 45–155
- Mean internal consistency reliability = .93

Working Memory Index
- 2 subtests
- Yields standard score, PR, and CIs
- Standard score range: 45–155
- Mean internal consistency reliability = .92

Processing Speed Index
- 2 subtests
- Yields standard score, PR, and CIs
- Standard score range: 45–155
- Mean internal consistency reliability = .88

Quantitative Reasoning Index
- 2 subtests
- Yields standard score, PR, and CIs
- Standard score range: 45–155
- Mean internal consistency reliability = .95

Other Information

Item scaling: Traditional
Bias evaluation: Bias review panel and statistical analysis of item bias
Spanish edition: Yes (Argentina, Chile, Mexico, Spain)
Confidence interval method: Standard error of the estimated true score (*SEE*) centered around the estimated true score
Electronic scoring and report writing system: Yes

Stratum III composites. The WISC-V produces a stratum III composite called the Full Scale IQ (FSIQ). "Full scale" in its title is a misnomer, because the FSIQ stems from only 7 of the WISC-V's 10 core subtests and only 7 of its 21 total subtests. Using the test record as a guide, the first seven subtests (Block Design through Figure Weights) contribute to this score. Upon analysis, these subtests have no floor or ceiling violations. The average internal consistency reliability value for the FSIQ was .96 across ages, and these values never fell below .96 at any age level. One study yielded omega hierarchical values indicating that the Full Scale IQ is highly *g* saturated.[3] Employing the WISC-V norming sample data, Reynolds and Keith (2017) reported a value of .80, so we can conclude that the FSIQ's *g* saturation is 80%, which is much higher than any subtest (see Table 6.1).

The WISC-V also produces a stratum III composite called the General Ability Index (GAI). This score is formed from five subtests. Digit Span and Coding from the FSIQ are omitted, and the remaining subtests demonstrate no floor or ceiling violations (see Table 6.3). The average internal consistency reliability value of the GAI was .96 across ages, and these values never fell below .95 at any age level. Reynolds and Keith (2017) reported an omega hierarchical value for the GAI of .77, so we can conclude that the FSIQ's *g* saturation is slightly lower than the FSIQ and at 77%. The GAI, therefore, is a viable alternative to the FSIQ in testing those who have fine motor impairments or who are hard of hearing (as addressed later in this chapter).

Furthermore, the WISC-V also includes a Nonverbal Index, which was designed to represent psychometric *g* without requiring oral responses; it is the modern equivalent of Wechsler's Performance IQ (Wechsler, 1939, 1949, 1974, 1991). It includes six subtests that span three or four domains: Block Design, Matrix Reasoning, Coding, Figure Weights, Visual Puzzles, and Picture Span. Thus, this composite shares four of the seven subtests with the FSIQ and includes two additional subtests. The average internal consistency reliability value for the Nonverbal Index was .95 across ages, and these values never fell below .95 at any age level. The language-reduced Nonverbal Index may be a viable alternative to the FSIQ and particularly useful in testing those who have hearing impairments, limited English proficiency, and expressive language deficits. However, other intelligence tests reviewed in Chapter 7 are more completely language reduced, and the orally presented directions introducing these subtests contributing to the Nonverbal Index remain somewhat lengthy.

Stratum II composites. As noted earlier in this chapter, the WISC-V produces five composite scores representing the broad abilities associated with CHC theory. Each composite stems from two subtests: Verbal Comprehension, Visual Spatial, Fluid Reasoning, Working Memory, and Processing Speed (see Table 6.3). The average reliability values for these indexes were above .90 for all but the Processing Speed Index ($M = .88$). Although the inferior reliability values of the Processing Speed Index are noteworthy, it is clear that they are, in part, a product of the method by which they

---

3. Other studies beyond Reynolds and Keith (2017) have produced omega hierarchical values based on the WISC-V subtests, but these other studies have not focused primarily on the 7 subtests that contribute to the FSIQ. For example, Dombrowski, Canivez, and Watkins (2017) suggested that a composite stemming from the first 10 WISC-V subtests (Block Design through Symbol Search) would produce omega hierarchical values ranging from .78 to .84 across age groups and models.

were obtained for its constituent subtests, test–retest reliability studies, versus internal consistency analysis used to obtain reliability values for all other subtests.

Some composites have been added to the WISC-V to address a more narrow range of content, and others have been added to promote broader construct coverage. For example, the Quantitative Reasoning Index is a more narrowly focused composite than the Fluid Reasoning Index as it involves primarily numerical content and requires operations involving numerical quantities; it stems from the Figure Weights and Arithmetic subtests. Auditory Working Memory is also a more narrowly focused composite than the Working Memory Index as it involves only auditory stimuli; it stems from Digit Span and Letter Number Sequencing. This composite is composed of the same subtests as the WISC-IV's Working Memory Index (Wechsler, 2003).

Moving to broader content coverage, two composites are offered to enhance the measurement of the abilities targeted by the Verbal Comprehensive Index and the Fluid Reasoning Index; they are the Verbal (Expanded Crystallized) Index and the Expanded Fluid Index (sometimes called the Expanded Fluid-3 Index; Raiford et al., 2015). The Verbal (Expanded Crystallized) Index includes the Information and Comprehension subtests (in addition to the Similarities and Vocabulary subtests that contribute to the Verbal Comprehension Index). The Expanded Fluid Index includes the Picture Concepts and Arithmetic subtests (in addition to Matrix Reasoning and Figure Weights that contribute to the Fluid Reasoning Index).

None of the new subtests—Naming Speed Literacy, Naming Speed Quantity, Immediate Symbol Translation, Delayed Symbol Translation, and Recognition Symbol Translation—contribute to any of the stratum III composites. However, their inclusion means that, for the first time in its history, the WISC-V produces composites focused on memory storage and retrieval. They include two narrowly focused composites, Naming Speed and Symbol Translation, which both are formed from two subtests, as well as Storage and Retrieval, which is formed from all four subtests. The specific composition of these composites is featured in Table 6.4, but we do not feature them in Table 6.3, as there does not appear to be sufficient validity evidence, at present, to support their interpretation as measures of stratum II abilities. Additional validity evidence is needed to support their use and interpretation.

Questions about the Validity of the Stratum II Composite Scores

When we consider the body of research examining the validity evidence supporting the use and interpretation of these stratum II composites, some conflicting findings from factor-analytic research are evident, and there is an absence of evidence in other cases. For example, Chen et al. (2015) and M. Reynolds and Keith (2017) provide evidence from confirmatory factor analysis of the viability of five first-order (and second-stratum) abilities associated with the WISC-V's primary indexes: Verbal Comprehension, Visual Spatial, Fluid Reasoning, Working Memory, and Processing Speed. However,

Table 6.4. Composite Score Composition for the 16 WISC-V Subtests

Subtest	Full Scale IQ	General Ability Index	Nonverbal Index	Verbal Comprehension	Verbal (Expanded Crystallized) Index	Visual Spatial	Fluid Reasoning	Quantitative Reasoning	**Expanded Fluid Index**	Working Memory	Auditory Working Memory	Processing Speed	Cognitive Proficiency	Storage and Retrieval	Naming Speed	Symbol Translation
Block Design	ü	✓	✓			✓										
Similarities	✓	✓		✓	✓											
Matrix Reasoning	✓	✓	✓				✓		✓							
Digit Span	✓									✓	✓		✓			
Coding	✓											✓	✓			
Vocabulary		✓		✓	✓											
Figure Weights		✓					✓	✓	✓							
Visual Puzzles			✓			✓										
Picture Span			✓							✓						
Symbol Search			✓									✓				
Information					✓											
Picture Concepts									✓							
Letter-Number Sequencing											✓					
Cancellation												✓				
Comprehension					✓											
Arithmetic								✓	✓							
Naming Speed Literacy														✓	✓	
Naming Speed Quantity														✓	✓	
Immediate Symbol Translation														✓		✓
Delayed Symbol Translation														✓		✓
Recognition Symbol Translation														✓		✓

Note: The bolded composites were not offered in the original release of the WISC-V but can be obtained using post-publication supporting documentation (Raiford, Drozdick, Zhang, & Zhou, 2015).

a number of other studies (Canivez et al., 2018; Canivez, 2016; Canivez et al., 2017; Chen et al., 2015; Dombrowski et al., 2018; Dombrowski et al., 2015), including those employing (1) exploratory factor analysis (including exploratory bifactor analysis and transformations of results from correlated factors models into higher-order factor models) and (2) confirmatory factor analysis (using bifactor and higher-order models), found that the Fluid Reasoning factor is redundant with psychometric g and that several of the first-order factors are not sufficiently replicable to warrant interpretation. Canivez and Watkins (2016), for example, found that psychometric g accounted for more than 80% of the total true score variance across the WISC-V subtests. They also found that, of the five broad ability factors on the WISC-V, only Processing Speed accounted for a sufficient amount of true score variance to warrant interpretation. Despite such disagreement on the true factor structure of the WISC-V, we feel confident that the instrument as a whole measures general intelligence quite well. Nonetheless, we are uneasy about (a) the validity of the subtests contributing to the Processing Speed Index as indicators of general intelligence, (b) the distinction between the Visual Spatial and Fluid Reasoning subtests, and (c) the construct validity of the Fluid Reasoning Index (in measuring something different than the FSIQ).

Adapting the WISC-V

In Chapter 5, we stressed the importance of considering access skills prior to testing and discussed test accommodations. As we asserted, to promote accuracy in measurement and fairness in testing: (a) tests that exclude item content or requirements that prevent full access should be selected, (b) alternate compositions of tests and alternate scores from them should be considered, and (c) test features should be adapted in a way to ensure that the targeted construct is assessed accurately. Across the intelligence tests reviewed in this book, the WISC-V provides some of the most well-developed methods for addressing problems with access. Yet, it has limitations in design that may be better addressed by other tests (as evident in Chapter 7).

Table 6.5 presents five types of item content and test features that may be barriers to access: orally, delivered directions, verbal content (as defined in Chapter 4), visual content, use of pencils, and use of manipulative materials. These barriers may be particularly salient for test takers who are deaf or hard of hearing, those who are blind or have vision impairments, and those who have fine motor impairments. In addition, they are likely to affect English language learners. For each WISC-V subtest, we have identified those barriers, and this analysis of WISC-V subtests will guide the discussion of accommodations and other testing alternatives in sections that follow. We repeat our caveat from Chapter 5: These alternative practices, including accommodations, should not be undertaken in a haphazard manner. In many cases, consultation with other experienced professionals may be required, and alterations to the standardized administration of any test should be documented in psychological reports and conveyed when reporting results orally to those in the life of the test taker.

Table 6.5. WISC-V Subtest Design Elements That May Introduce Access Problems

Subtest	Orally Delivered Instructions	Verbal Item Content	Visual Item Content	Pencil Use Required	Test Manipulatives Employed
Block Design	✓		✓		✓
Similarities	✓	✓			
Matrix Reasoning	✓		✓		
Digit Span	✓	✓			
Coding	✓		✓	✓[2]	
Vocabulary	✓	✓	✓[1]		
Figure Weights	✓		✓		
Visual Puzzles	✓		✓		
Picture Span	✓		✓		
Symbol Search	✓		✓	✓[2]	
Information	✓	✓			
Picture Concepts	✓		✓		
Letter-Number Sequencing	✓	✓			
Cancellation	✓		✓	✓	
Comprehension	✓	✓			
Arithmetic	✓	✓	✓[1]		
Naming Speed Literacy	✓		✓		
Naming Speed Quantity	✓		✓		
Immediate Symbol Translation	✓	✓	✓		
Delayed Symbol Translation	✓	✓	✓		
Recognition Symbol Translation	✓	✓	✓		

Note: [1] = Some of the earliest items on the scales for these subtests are pictorial. For Vocabulary, later items are presented both orally and in print. [2] = The standard administration requires pencil use; however, administration via Q-Interactive includes a multiple-choice response design in which the test taker is required to indicate their response through touching the tablet's screen.

GENERAL FLEXIBILITY IN ADMINISTRATION WITH THE WISC-V

Historically, the WISC-V and its prior editions have been some of the most flexible of all major intelligence tests in that a test examiner was able to (a) substitute some subtests for others before obtaining composite scores and (b) prorate composite scores when only a subset of subtests was scored. We assume that these steps were more likely to be conducted after testing, following examiner errors or idiosyncratic responses from test takers, than proactively for students with sensory or physical disabilities. However, we have no data to support this assumption.[4] We do know that, for many other tests, one of these unexpected events (an error or idiosyncratic response) can lead the examiner to abandon the whole test administration—especially when an IQ is required as part of the assessment—so we always have appreciated this flexibility in design.

The WISC-V continues to allow substitution of one subtest for another in calculating its seven-subtest FSIQ. The test's accompanying manual provides prescriptions that guide substitutions, as it is desirable that the substituted subtest be associated with the same index area as the subtest to be replaced. For example, Visual Puzzles can replace Block Design, and Symbol Search can replace Coding. Looking at Table 6.5, and considering only the first seven subtests contributing to the FSIQ, only Block Design stands alone in any category. It requires manipulation of cubes, which could be a barrier to access for test takers with fine motor problems. However, the same types of deficits that are likely to affect manipulation of cubes during that subtest also are likely to affect Coding, which requires use of a pencil when administered via the standard format. Despite research indicating that substitution is likely to increase error in measurement (Zhu, Cayton, & Chen, 2016), we view the option of using substitution in calculating the FSIQ as a valuable feature. We cannot, however, see a way that substitution could be used proactively to address potential problems with access, as most barriers to access affect more than a single WISC-V subtest.

The WISC-V also continues to allow for proration in obtaining the FSIQ, but six of the seven subtests contributing to the FSIQ are required. Thus, the same limitations evident in substitution are evident with proration, and substitution and proration cannot be employed in combination. However, cross-referencing Table 6.5 with Table 6.4 may shed light on viable composites that approximate the FSIQ without including subtests that introduce problems with access. We address some of them in sections that follow.

TEST TAKERS WHO ARE DEAF OR HARD OF HEARING

The WISC-V is supported by an exceptional resource written by Day, Adams Costa, and Raiford (2015). This report guides test examiners to develop accommodations for test takers who are deaf or hard of hearing. Doing so is a challenge, because, as can be seen from review of Table 6.5, every one of the WISC-V subtests includes instructions delivered orally—and sometimes quite a lot of them. Although some subtests do not include verbal item content or require an oral response, these subtests are at best labeled "language-reduced." Day et al. meticulously reviewed the technical and practical issues associated with testing children and adolescents who are deaf or hearing impaired. In particularly, they described how the WISC-V norming data did not include participants with uncorrected hearing loss and how there is currently no reliability and

---

4. Of course, it would be unethical to substitute a higher subtest score for a lower one simply to increase the FSIQ and without evidence that the score to be replaced was invalid. Similarly, a higher subtest score would not be substituted to obtain a lower IQ. Substitutions should be principled and always reported as constituting a deviation from standardized procedures.

limited validity data (cf. Adams Costa, Day, & Raiford, 2016) to support use of the WISC-V with this population. We await further research in this area.

Day et al. (2015) further described potential accommodations in using of American Sign Language, assistive learning devices, auditory modalities, and cued speech, among others, during testing, and rigorously evaluated the viability of each across the WISC-V subtests. As is apparent in Table 6.5, the six subtests contributing to the Nonverbal Index (Block Design, Matrix Reasoning, Coding, Figure Weights, Visual Puzzles, and Picture Span) seem most viable for assessing test takers who are deaf or hard of hearing. Seeing the strengths of these subtests and the psychometric properties associated with the index, the WISC-V seems to be a viable alternative to the FSIQ for some test takers who are deaf or hearing impaired.

TEST TAKERS WITH MOTOR IMPAIRMENTS

Fine motor impairments, such as those experienced by persons with cerebral palsy (Yin Foo, Guppy, & Johnston, 2013), may prevent access to test content and impair the performance of test takers who otherwise would score higher were these confounds to be removed. Table 6.5 indicates which WISC-V subtests require use of a pencil or manipulatives. Across revisions of the test, these motor requirements have been greatly reduced; for example, only two subtests (Block Design and Coding) contributing to the FSIQ require motoric responses. In contrast, the WISC-III required motoric responses during Coding, Picture Arrangement (involving cards), Block Design, and Object Assembly (involving puzzle pieces).

Although we found some references to substituting the WISC-V Visual Puzzles subtest for Block Design, this intervention only helps so much, as Coding has no viable replacement for persons with motor impairments. In fact, this subtest and its alternatives (Symbol Search and Cancellation) also require rapid and repeated motor response during a timed administration. Based on review of Tables 6.4 and 6.5, it is possible that the Verbal Comprehension Index, the Fluid Reasoning Index, and to a lesser extent, the Working Memory Index, could be viewed as highly limited proxies for the FSIQ for students with motor impairments. However, no unique composite is yielded from only the six subtests that contribute to these three composites. The three subtest composites, Verbal (Expanded Crystallized) Index, and Fluid Index-Expanded, might also be viable for this population, but additional research is needed to substantiate this claim.

As an alternative, Piovesana, Harrison, and Ducat (2017) offered a short form of the WISC-V that comprises six subtests with no motor requirements. This short form produces a Motor-Free Intelligence Quotient (MFIQ) and three more specific composites. Its subtests include Similarities, Digit Span, Vocabulary, Figure Weights, Visual Puzzles, and Letter-Number Sequencing. Piovesana et al. reported the MFSIQ's internal consistency reliability to be .97. Using descriptive statistics and reliability statistics for each subtest as well as subtest intercorrelations from the manual supporting the WISC-V, Piovesana et al. also provided norm-referenced data to support applied use of this short form. At the time of publication of this book, these adapted scores had not been evaluated with students having motor impairments or otherwise, so additional research is needed to support use of the MFIQ in practice.

TEST TAKERS WHO ARE BLIND, VISUALLY IMPAIRED, OR COLOR-BLIND

The WISC-V's support materials do not provide guidance to test examiners when working with children and adolescents who are blind or visually impaired. Review of Table 6.5 reveals that five of the subtests that contribute to the FSIQ include visual content, and the earliest items on Vocabulary do as well. The high concentration of visual content is a benefit when working with test takers who are deaf or hearing impaired, but it is not so when working with those who are blind or have a visual impairment. The general information we presented about testing those who are blind or visually impaired in Chapter 5 can be reviewed.

It is noteworthy that the WISC-V's supporting documentation, including this online FAQ (https://www.pearsonassessments.com/store/usassessments/en/Store/Professional-Assessments/Cognition-%26-Neuro/Gifted-%26-Talented/Wechsler-Intelligence-Scale-for-Children-%7C-Fifth-Edition-/p/100000771.html?tab=faqs), addresses how the WISC-V was designed to be free of items that may interfere with the performance of those who are color-blind. In referencing the WISC-V's development, the FAQ conveyed that

> items were reviewed by color-perception differences experts, as well as individuals with color-perception differences, during the early stages of the test development process. In addition, acetate overlays have been utilized so that the test developers can understand the appearance of the stimuli to individuals with various color-perception differences. Items are also copied in black and white to check appearance to those with monochromatic color perception. All items are also subjected to an electronic "color-blindness" simulator to check item appearance with every type of color-perception difference and ensure that the intensity and saturation of colors are not confused or result in different responses. For the WISC–V, the colors are yellow, blue, and red; green is not included.

The FAQ further indicated that the nature of color naming time on the Naming Speed Literacy subtest may introduce error with test takers who have extreme problems with color differentiation. We applaud these efforts and encourage test users to evaluate other tests based on such a standard for excellence.

TEST TAKERS WHO ARE ENGLISH LANGUAGE LEARNERS

As described in Chapter 14, students in United States schools are becoming increasingly diverse in terms of variation in culture and languages spoken in their homes, communities, and schools (National Center for Education Statistics, 2019). As Spanish is the most commonly spoken language in the United States after English, most intelligence tests have a version that has been translated into Spanish (see also Chapter 7). The WISC-V is one of those tests.

The Wechsler Intelligence Scale for Children. Fifth Edition, Spanish (WISC–V Spanish) includes 14 of the 21 WISC-V subtests (with Picture Concepts, Cancellation, and the new memory tests omitted) and covers the same age range as the WISC-V. All of its supporting materials, directions to test takers, test records, stimulus books, and response booklets are printed in Spanish, so the test is administered completely in Spanish. Norm-referenced scores stem from an equating sample ($N = 220$) that included children and adolescents in the United States (including Puerto Rico) who speak Spanish, have attended United States schools for less than 5 consecutive years, and whose countries of origin primarily were Mexico and the Caribbean.

For six subtests (Block Design, Matrix Reasoning, Coding, Figure Weights, Visual Puzzles, and Symbol Search), instructions were translated while testing materials were retained. Because of this translation into Spanish and the items being viewed as reasonably similarly experienced across groups (regardless of English proficiency), the WISC-V norms for these six subtests, are applied to the WISC-V Spanish. For the eight remaining subtests, extensive revisions to the WISC-V subtests were undertaken—including not only translation into Spanish but also changes in item content and scoring rules. In these cases, the WISC-V norms were not applied, but a series of sophisticated statistical methods, including equating of subtest items across the WISC-V Spanish equating sample and the WISC-V norming sample as well as evaluation of the equated results across smaller samples, were employed. In addition, adjusted scores for the WISC-V Spanish Verbal Comprehension Index and scores from its four associated subtests may be obtained. Considering information obtained about a test taker's background, the adjusted scores may account for personal and environmental influences that may have unduly affected performance in this domain.

Other Forms of the WISC-V

The Wechsler Intelligence Scale for Children truly is a multinational test, which is one of its strengths. For example, the WISC-V has been published in a Canadian edition (Wechsler 2014b). In addition, other versions of the WISC-V have been adapted for use across the globe, including in the following languages and dialects: Arabic, Chinese, Croatian, Czech, Danish, Dutch, English (Australian), Finnish, French (Canada), French (France), German, Greek, Hebrew, Hungarian, Iceland, Italian, Japanese, Korean, Lithuanian, Norwegian, Polish, Portuguese (Brazil), Portuguese (Portugal), Romanian, Slovak, Slovenian, Spanish (Argentina), Spanish (Chile), Spanish (Mexico), Spanish (Spain), and Swedish.

In addition to the international editions of the WISC-V, another member of its family of tests addresses the expectations of neuropsychologists trained to attend to "processing deficits" underlying test performance. In this vein, the Wechsler Intelligence Scale for Children, Fifth Edition Integrated (WISC-V Integrated; Wechsler & Kaplan, 2014) contains 14 "process tests" that reflect changes in the task requirements of the WISC-V subtests through adaptations to their stimuli, response requirements, and the nature of the subtests themselves. Some adaptations to subtests are minor, such as removing time limits, whereas others change the nature of the subtest, such as a version of the Arithmetic subtest that allows for use of paper and pencil rather than requiring calculations to be completed mentally. The most common adaptation is the provision of response options in a multi-choice format. In addition, a new subtest called Sentence Recall requires test takers to listen to a series of questions, answer them, and recall the last words across the series of questions in the correct order. Another new subtest called Spatial Span requires test takers to tap cubes in the same order as (and in the reverse order compared to) the examiner. Most of these process tests yield norm-based scores that can be compared to those stemming from the original standardized administration of subtests from the Wechsler scales. Higher scores on the process tests than on the original subtests are thought to indicate that the process targeted by the adaptation must have interfered with performance on the original subtest. Although we appreciate the creativity evident in developing these alternate versions of the WISC-V subtests, it is not clear to us what practical benefits the WISC-V Integrated might provide its users. Perhaps future research will reveal such benefits as they relate to diagnosis or eligibility or to intervention planning.

Summary and Resources

Given its widespread use and the fact that the WISC-V has some noteworthy features, we highlighted this test in a stand-alone chapter. As we noted at the beginning of this chapter, the WISC-V has a long history of excellence in measurement that has generated a strong evidence base over time. As a result, it has long been the most commonly used intelligence test with children and adolescents across time. Although few of its subtests meet the mark in terms of reliability and strong *g* saturation, its FSIQ does and clearly reflects a pinnacle of applied measurement of psychometric *g*. The WISC-V's alternative IQs also are viable measures of this construct and can be applied in efforts to reduce problems with access to test items for students with sensory and motor impairment. We look forward to additional research examining the WISC-V and its scores well into the next decade.

More information about the WISC-V can be found in these books and chapters:

Flanagan, D. P., & Alfonso, V. C. (2017). *Essentials of WISC-V assessment*. Hoboken, NJ: Wiley.

Kaufman, A. S., Raiford, S. E., & Coalson, D. L. (2016). *Intelligent testing with the WISC-V*. Hoboken, NJ: Wiley.

Raiford, S. E. (2017). *Essentials of WISC-V integrated assessment*. Hoboken, NJ: Wiley.

Raiford, S. E. (2018). The Wechsler Intelligence Scale for Children—Fifth Edition Integrated. In D. P. Flanagan & E. M. McDonough (Eds.), *Contemporary intellectual assessment: Theories, tests, and issues* (4th ed., pp. 302–332). New York, NY: Guilford Press.

Wahlstrom, D., Raiford, S. E., Breaux, K. C., Zhu, J., & Weiss, L. G. (2018). The Wechsler Preschool and Primary Scale of Intelligence—Fourth Edition, Wechsler Intelligence Scale for Children—Fifth Edition, and Wechsler Individual Achievement Test—Third Edition. In D. P. Flanagan & E. M. McDonough (Eds.), *Contemporary intellectual assessment: Theories, tests, and issues* (4th ed., pp. 245–282). New York, NY: Guilford Press.

CHAPTER 7

A Review of Intelligence Tests

with Emily K. Lewis and Ryan L. Farmer[1]

In this chapter, we provide an overview of the array of intelligence tests that are available on the market. First, we target other full-length, multidimensional, individually administered intelligence tests like the Wechsler Intelligence Scale for Children, Fifth Edition (WISC-V, 2014a, covered in Chapter 6) that are the most well-known and commonly used in research and practice. (They are *multidimensional* in that they sample from more than a single stratum II ability domain and numerous stratum I ability domains across their component subtests.) These tests are the ones most likely to be employed in the practice of psychology and education (Benson et al., 2019).

We describe full-length, multidimensional, individually administered nonverbal tests of intelligence that were designed to reduce the effects of English-language skills on test performance. By *nonverbal*, we refer to the process by which an examiner uses the test's items to collect data about a test taker's intelligence. According to McCallum, Bracken, and Wasserman (2001), *nonverbal* in this sense indicates "a test administration process in which no receptive language or expressive language demands are placed on *either* [emphasis in original] the examinee or the examiner. . . . There should be no spoken test directions and there should be no spoken responses required [from] the examinee" (p. 8). Although not all of the tests we reviewed met these strict criteria, all three were developed to promote such nonverbal assessment of ability. We have omitted unidimensional nonverbal intelligence tests that use primarily one method (i.e., matrix reasoning tasks) to measure intelligence. In the same vein, we highlight nonverbal and language-reduced stratum III composite scores embedded in full length, multidimensional intelligence tests.

We also summarize information about two brief intelligence tests. Whether an intelligence test is considered *brief* or *abbreviated* depends on the amount of time required to administer it as well as the breadth of abilities targeted by it (Homack & Reynolds, 2007). A *brief* intelligence test is a stand-alone test composed of only a few

---

1. Emily K. Lewis is a doctoral student in school psychology at the University of Memphis. Her research interests include learning disabilities, academic and behavioral interventions, cross-cultural research, and psychological testing. Dr. Ryan L. Farmer is an assistant professor at Oklahoma State University. His research interests include evidence-based approaches to assessment in school psychology.

subtests administered in standard order and scored in reference to the test's independent norm sample. An *abbreviated* intelligence test, on the other hand, is a short form of a full-length, multidimensional intelligence test.

As we did for the WISC-V in Chapter 6, we provide a narrative description of the central features of each test and offer a summary of norming, score, and other measurement features. Most of this information was obtained from the manuals accompanying each test unless otherwise noted. We do not review inter-scorer consistency evidence or item gradient violations, because they typically are specific to subtests (and, for item gradient violations, to specific age groups) and not composites scores. We also do not review (1) test–retest reliability evidence, because variability in the time intervals between initial and follow-up assessment, as well as sampling error, making evaluation of the typical results presented by test authors challenging to interpret (see Hunsley & Mash, 2018), or (2) bodies of validity evidence because such evidence should be considered in light of specific validity questions. We do, however, highlight some of the most central questions related to the construct validity of tests as a measure of intelligence, including how well scores relate to the construct of psychometric g. Knowing this information before you begin testing, you should be able to evaluate these tests and their scores while considering the characteristics of the test takers you serve.

We place particular emphasis on the measurement characteristics supporting the use and interpretation of stratum III composites (i.e., IQs). In doing so, when the test produces stratum III composites designed to focus on nonverbal content and response processes, we highlight them. Further, we make note of composites that are alternatives to the most commonly employed stratum III composites and that might be classified as abbreviated stratum III composites. These may be important to consider (1) before completing a full-length intelligence test—when subtests from these full-length tests are inappropriate for the test taker in question (e.g., due to motor impairment)—and (2) after testing with full-length intelligence tests—when subtests from these full-length tests have been invalidated (e.g., due to examiner error or other problems in the testing session).

When considering all of these stratum III composites, we pay particular attention to their reliability, their g saturation (often as measured by the omega hierarchical statistic), the number of subtests contributing to them, their subtests' verbal content and response processes involving speeded motor tasks, and psychometric sampling of lower-stratum abilities. For example, we are skeptical of the adequacy of stratum III composites formed from a small number of subtests. As stated by Farmer, Floyd, M. Reynolds, and Berlin (2019),

> When too few subtests are employed, there are at least three risks: (1) there is inadequate content sampling of the universe of cognitive abilities (i.e., psychometric sampling error; Jensen, 1998a); (2) idiosyncratic characteristics of the test taker (e.g., exposure and interest in the content or activities employed by the subtest) may lead to an extremely high or low subtest score that has a disproportional effect on the resulting composite score (e.g., 33% influence with 3 subtests, 14% with 7 subtests, and 10% influence with 10 subtests), and (3) composites that stem from fewer subtests cannot measure

very high and low levels of psychometric *g* as accurately as their longer counterparts (based on what is known about the composite score extremity effect; Schneider, 2016). (n.p.)

Finally, we also address some stratum II composites that may be useful to consider in cases where sufficient validity evidence supports their interpretation.

Full-Length Multidimensional Intelligence Tests

COGNITIVE ASSESSMENT SYSTEM, SECOND EDITION

The Cognitive Assessment System, Second Edition (CAS2; Naglieri, Das, & Goldstein, 2014) is a full-length intelligence test designed for children ages 5 through 18 (see Table 7.1). It includes 12 subtests that are administered orally and via use of stimulus books and response booklets. The original CAS was developed to operationalize the central components of Planning, Attention, Simultaneous, and Successive (PASS) theory, which is based on Luria's neuropsychological model (Naglieri & Otero, 2018), and the CAS2 is its current incarnation. Norming data supporting the CAS2 were collected from 2008 to 2011 across 19 of the United States; the test developers followed a norming plan based on the 2011 U.S. Census. Continuous norming procedures were not reported. For preschool-age students (age 5), the norm block exceeded 50 participants and was deemed to be of medium size (Norfolk et al., 2015). Although the average norm block for elementary-school students included about 50 children, at some age level, it was below 30, which is considered inadequate. All norm blocks for middle- and high-school students included at least 30 participants.

The CAS2 produces two stratum III composites called the Full Scale; 12 subtests form the Full Scale Extended Battery, and 8 subtests form the Full Scale Core Battery. Floor violations at age 5 and ceiling violations at ages 14:6 and older are evident in subtests contributing to the Full Scale Extended Battery, but only ceiling violations at the same age levels are evident in subtests contributing to the Full Scale Core Battery. The average internal consistency reliability value for across ages the Full Scale was .97 for the Extended Battery and .95 for the Core Battery. The PASS composites are formed from 3 subtests in the Extended Battery and 2 subtests in the Core Battery. The average internal consistency reliability values for the composites fell from .90 to .94 for the Extended Battery composites and from .86 to .93 for the Core Battery composites. Average reliability values fell below .90 for only the Attention and Successive composites from the Core Battery.

Based on factor analysis of the original CAS (Naglieri & Das, 1997), these composites can be interpreted from the perspective of the three-stratum theory and the Cattell-Horn-Carroll (CHC) theory (Canivez, 2011; Keith, Kranzler, & Flanagan, 2001; Kranzler & Keith, 1999). For example, the Planning and Attention composites and their subtests appear to measure Processing Speed; the Simultaneous composite and its subtests seem to measure Visual Processing; and the Successive composite and its subtests seem to measure Short-Term Memory (Keith, Kranzler, & Flanagan,

Table 7.1. Psychometric Evaluation of the Cognitive Assessment System, Second Edition (CAS2)

Publisher: PRO-ED
Publication date: 2014
Age range: 5:0–18:11

Norming Information

Norm sample N: 1,342
Dates collected: 2008–2011
Census data: 2011
Number U.S. states sampled: 19
Characteristics considered:
Geographic region, gender, race, ethnicity, family income, educational level of parents, and exceptionality status
Continuous norming: Not specified
Norm block size: Preschool: Medium; Elementary: Insufficient; Middle and High: Minimum

Scores Provided

Stratum III Composites

Full Scale (Extended Battery)
- 12 subtests with floor violations at ages 5:8 and younger, and ceiling violations at ages 14:6 and older
- Yields standard score, PR, and CIs
- Standard score range: 40–160
- Mean internal consistency reliability = .97

Full Scale (Core Battery)
- 8 subtests with no floor violations and ceiling violations at ages 14:6 and older
- Yields standard score, PR, and CIs
- Standard score range: 40–160
- Mean internal consistency reliability = .95

Stratum II Composites

Planning
- 3 (Extended Battery) or 2 subtests (Core Battery)
- Yields standard score, PR, and CIs
- Standard score range: 50–152 (Extended Battery), 52–150 (Core Battery)
- Mean internal consistency reliability = .92 (Extended Battery), .90 (Core Battery)

Attention
- 3 (Extended Battery) or 2 subtests (Core Battery)
- Yields standard score, PR, and CIs
- Standard score range: 50–155 (Extended Battery), 48–154 (Core Battery)
- Mean internal consistency reliability = .90 (Extended Battery), .86 (Core Battery)

Simultaneous
- 3 (Extended Battery) or 2 subtests (Core Battery)
- Yields standard score, PR, and CIs
- Standard score range: 50–152 (Extended Battery), 50–155 (Core Battery)
- Mean internal consistency reliability = .94 (Extended Battery), .93 (Core Battery)

Successive
- 3 (Extended Battery) or 2 subtests (Core Battery)
- Yields standard score, PR, and CIs
- Standard score range: 46–160 (Extended Battery), 45–160 (Core Battery)
- Mean internal consistency reliability = .92 (Extended Battery), .89 (Core Battery)

Subtests
- 12 subtests yielding scaled scores and age equivalents

Other Information

Item scaling: Traditional
Bias evaluation: Statistical analysis of item bias and group comparisons based on Hispanic status
Spanish edition: Yes
Confidence interval method: Standard error of the estimated true score (*SEE*) centered around the estimated true score
Electronic scoring and report-writing system: Yes

Note: In all tables in this chapter, PR = percentile rank and CIs = confidence intervals.

2001; Kranzler & Keith, 1999a). We believe that similar findings would be evident if the same analysis was completed using the CAS2 subtests, but we await independent analysis of the CAS2 norming data.

Although the CAS2 was designed to measure abilities associated with PASS processes, we suspect the CAS2 measures the abilities Visual Processing, Short-Term Memory, and (to a large extent) Processing Speed across its subtests. One of the composite scores measuring Processing Speed (i.e., Attention from the Core Battery) does not meet the minimum standard for reliability we have outlined, but others do. Although the CAS2 was not designed to measure psychometric g, because there is no general cognitive ability in PASS theory, it is clear that it does. Based on (a) the high percentage of subtests apparently measuring Processing Speed that contribute to the Full Scale composites and (b) evidence of their both diminishing the accuracy of IQs measuring psychometric g and increasing the construct-irrelevant influences of Processing Speed on the IQs (Farmer et al., 2019; Keith et al., 2001), it is likely that the CAS2 Full Scale composites are inferior measures of psychometric g when compared to many of the other IQs featured in this book.

We applaud the CAS2 authors' use of theory to guide test construction, and we see the CAS2 as a substantial improvement over its earlier edition. Its updated norms and generally more reliable composite scores overcome some of the limitations of the original CAS. In addition, an electronic scoring and report writing system is available for the CAS2. We note that the CAS2 produces five new supplemental composites. Some composites focus on constructs peripheral to both PASS theory and CHC theory (e.g., executive function), whereas other composites focus on verbal and nonverbal content. We also appreciate the ingenuity in the design of intervention programs linked to the CAS2 (i.e., the PASS Reading Enhancement Program, Das, 1999, and the Cognition Enhancement Training, Das, 2004); see Chapter 9 for more discussion about interventions based on intelligence tests.

Further, Naglieri and colleagues also offer the following three assessment instruments targeting students ages 4 to 18. First, the CAS2: Brief (Naglieri, Das, & Goldstein, 2014b) includes four subtests drawn from or adapted from CAS2 subtests, with each targeting one of the PASS processes; it also yields a Total Score. Second, the CAS2: Española (sometimes marketed as the CAS2: Spanish Supplement Package; Naglieri, Moreno, & Otero, 2017) is a Spanish translation of the CAS2 test materials. It draws on English norms and requires the CAS2 test kit as a base. Finally, the CAS2: Rating Scale (Naglieri, Das, & Goldstein, 2014c) includes 40 items completed by teachers to provide a norm-referenced perspective on behaviors associated with the PASS domains. More information about the CAS2 can be found here:

McGill, R. J. (2015). Test review. [Review of the test *Cognitive Assessment System—Second Edition*]. *Journal of Psychoeducational Assessment, 33*, 375–380.

Naglieri, J. A. (2017). *Essentials of CAS2 assessment*. New York, NY: Wiley.

Naglieri, J. A., & Otero, T. M. (2018). The Cognitive Assessment System—Second Edition. In D. P. Flanagan & E. M. McDonough (Eds.), *Contemporary intellectual assessment: Theories, tests, and issues* (4th ed., pp. 452–485). New York, NY: Guilford Press.

DETROIT TEST OF LEARNING ABILITIES, FIFTH EDITION

The Detroit Test of Learning Abilities, Fifth Edition (DTLA-5; Hammill, McGhee, & Ehrler, 2018) is a full-length intelligence test for those ages 6 to 17 (see Table 7.2). It includes 12 subtests that are administered orally and via stimulus books and response booklets. A total of 7 subtests are new to this edition, and three from the prior edition were not included; thus, the DTLA-5 is a substantially different test than its predecessors. The DTLA-5 norming data were collected from 2011 to 2015 across 30 of the United States. The test developers followed a norming plan based on the 2016 U.S. Census, so at the time of publication of this book, the DTLA-5 is the most recently normed test we have featured. Further, continuous norming procedures were employed. The numbers of individuals per norm block cannot be evaluated in the same manner as with other tests as it has not been reported what the age ranges were for each block. Per 1-year intervals, samples ranged from 104 to 135. If the largest 1-year sample was divided into 3-month blocks or 4-month blocks, the norm block size would meet the minimum standard of 30. However, the smallest 1-year sample would not meet this standard with 3-month blocks. Based on our rough estimations, we view the sample sizes to be adequate across the full range of the test.

The DTLA-5 produces a stratum III composite called General Cognitive Ability. It stems from all 12 subtests. Its average internal consistency reliability value was .98 across ages. Floor violations for its contributing subtests are evident at ages 7:5 and younger, but it has no ceiling violations. The DTLA-5 also produces six stratum II composite scores stemming from two subtests: Acquired Knowledge, Verbal Comprehension, Nonverbal Problem Solving, Verbal Memory, Nonverbal Memory, and Processing Speed. The average internal consistency reliability values ranged from .87 to .95 across age groups. Only Processing Speed fell below the standard of .90. The test also produces two higher-order composites called Reasoning Ability and Processing Ability.

A recent exploratory factor analysis (McNulty & Floyd, 2019) has revealed support for the test's multidimensional structure but casts doubt on the construct validity of two of the DTLA-5's composite scores. Evidence for a higher-order general factor (consistent with the test's General Cognitive Ability composite) as well as five stratum II factors was apparent. Four of these stratum II factors corresponded to the Nonverbal Problem Solving, Verbal Memory, Nonverbal Memory, and Processing Speed composites. However, there was no evidence of differentiation between the subtests forming the Acquired Knowledge and Verbal Comprehension composites; thus, it appears that both of these composites measure the same stratum II ability, which is most likely Crystallized Intelligence. As a result, the General Cognitive Ability composite is weighted more heavily toward this ability than others, as 4 of its 12 contributing subtests measure the same stratum II ability. Based on this study and anomalies evident in the confirmatory factor analysis published by Hammill et al. (2018), we have not reported information about the two other composites yielded by the test. From our perspective, neither the Reasoning Ability composite nor the Processing Ability composite, which are called *domains scores* and formed from six subtests, are supported by sufficient validity evidence (in the form of evidence based on content, response processes, and internal structure) to warrant interpretation.

Table 7.2. Psychometric Evaluation of the Detroit Tests of Learning Abilities, Fifth Edition (DTLA-5)

Publisher: PRO-ED
Publication date: 2018
Age range: 6:0–17:11

Norming Information

Norm sample size: 1,383
Date collected: 2011–2015
Census data: 2016
U.S. states sampled: 30
Characteristics considered:
Geographic area, gender, race, Hispanic status, exceptionality status, household income, educational attainment of parents
Continuous norming: Yes
Norm block size: Cannot be determined

Scores Provided

Stratum III Composite

General Cognitive Ability
- 12 subtests with floor violations at ages 7:5 and younger and no ceiling violations
- Yields standard score, PR, CIs, and age equivalents
- Standard score range: 40–160
- Mean internal consistency reliability = .98

Stratum II Composites

Acquired Knowledge
- 2 subtests
- Yields standard score, PR, CIs, and age equivalents
- Standard score range: 40–160
- Mean internal consistency reliability = .93

Verbal Comprehension
- 2 subtests
- Yields standard score, PR, CIs, and age equivalents
- Standard score range: 40–160
- Mean internal consistency reliability = .95

Nonverbal Problem Solving
- 2 subtests
- Yields standard score, PR, CIs, and age equivalents
- Standard score range: 40–160
- Mean internal consistency reliability = .94

Verbal Memory
- 2 subtests
- Yields standard score, PR, CIs, and age equivalents
- Standard score range: 40–160
- Mean internal consistency reliability = .93

Nonverbal Memory
- 2 subtests
- Yields standard score, PR, CIs, and age equivalents
- Standard score range: 40–160
- Mean internal consistency reliability = .90

Processing Speed
- 2 subtests
- Yields standard score, PR, CIs, and age equivalents
- Standard score range: 40–160
- Mean internal consistency reliability = .87

Subtests
- 12 subtests yielding scaled scores

Other Information

Item scaling: Traditional
Bias evaluation: Statistical analysis of item bias and group comparisons based on gender binary, race, and Hispanic status
Spanish edition: No
Confidence interval method: Standard error of the estimated true score (*SEE*) centered around the estimated true score
Electronic scoring and report-writing system: Yes

The DTLA-5 has some noteworthy features, including its substantial redesign, very recent norms, and an IQ that stems from more than 10 subtests. The DTLA-5 is supported by an electronic scoring and report-writing system. We value both the various methods of test bias that were employed as well as preliminary evaluation of the diagnostic accuracy of the DTLA-5 scores in identifying intellectual disability and intellectual giftedness. More information about the DTLA-5 can be found here:

Rigney, A. M. (2018). Test review. [Review of the test *Detroit Tests of Learning Abilities-Fifth Edition*]. *Journal of Psychoeducational Assessment*, 1–5. https://doi.org/10.1177/0734282918793291

DIFFERENTIAL ABILITY SCALES, SECOND EDITION

The Differential Ability Scales, Second Edition (DAS-II; Elliott, 2007) is a full-length intelligence test comprising three age-specific batteries: one for those ages 2 and 3, another for those ages 3 through 6, and another for those ages 7 through 17 (see Table 7.3). Across batteries, it includes 21 subtests administered orally and via stimulus books and response booklets. Manipulatives include wooden pieces, cubes, plates, plastic animal figures, among others. Norming data were collected from 2002 to 2005 across 49 of the United States; the test developer followed a norming plan based on the 2002 U.S. Census and used continuous norming procedures. These dates of data collection indicate that the DAS-II scores will be inflated (on an absolute scale and relative to other, more recently normed intelligence tests) due to the Flynn effect (Flynn, 1984, 1987, 1999, 2007). There are at least approximately 50 children per norm block across age levels, and at least approximately 100 children per block beginning at age 9:0. Thus, the DAS-II's norm blocks exceeded standards for size.

The DAS-II produces a stratum III composite called General Conceptual Ability; for all batteries but that for the youngest children, this score is formed from six subtests. No floor or ceiling violations for any subtest contribute to the General Conceptual Ability at any age level. Average internal consistency reliability values for the General Conceptual Ability were .93 or higher across batteries, and the General Conceptual Ability composite has demonstrated substantial saturation by psychometric g. For example, M. Reynolds, Floyd, and Niileksela (2013) reported an omega hierarchical value of .82 across age groups, and Canivez and McGill (2016) offered values ranging from .70 to .82 age-differentiated analyses. Both studies drew data from the test's norming sample. Further, analysis of a smaller validity study using an alternate method yielded a corrected g loading value of .92 for the General Conceptual Ability composite, which can be associated with an omega hierarchical value of .85 (Farmer, Floyd, M. Reynolds, & Kranzler, 2014). Based on these findings, at least 70% and up to 85% of the variance in the General Conceptual Ability score can be attributed to the factor it targets, psychometric g.

The DAS-II produces stratum II composite scores labeled Verbal and Nonverbal for all age groups, and for the Upper-Level Early Years Battery and the School-Age Battery, it also produces stratum II composites labeled Spatial, Processing Speed, and Working

Table 7.3. Psychometric Evaluation of the Differential Ability Scales, Second Edition (DAS-II)

Publisher: Harcourt Assessments (on release) and Pearson (current)
Publication date: 2007
Age range: 2:6–17:11

Norming Information

Norm sample N: 3,480
Date collected: 2002–2005
Census data: October 2002
U.S. states sampled: 49, excluding Hawaii
Characteristics considered: Age, sex, race, parental education level, and geographic region
Continuous norming: Yes
Norm block size: Preschool: Medium; Elementary: Medium; Middle and High: Highest

Scores Provided

Lower-Level Early Years Battery (Ages 2:6–3:5)

Stratum III Composite

General Conceptual Ability
- 4 subtests with no floor or ceiling violations
- Yields standard score, PR, and CIs
- Standard score range: 45–165
- Mean internal consistency reliability = .93

Stratum II Composites

Verbal
- 2 subtests
- Yields standard score, PR, and CIs
- Standard score range: 30–170
- Mean internal consistency reliability = .92

Nonverbal
- 2 subtests
- Yields standard score, PR, and CIs
- Standard score range: 32–170
- Mean internal consistency reliability = .87

Subtests
- 8 subtests yielding T scores, PRs, and Ability scores

Upper-Level Early Years Battery (Ages 3:6–6:11)

Stratum III Composite

General Conceptual Ability
- 6 subtests with no floor or ceiling violations
- Yields standard score, PR, and CIs
- Standard score range: 45–165
- Mean internal consistency reliability = .95

Stratum II Composites

Verbal
- 2 subtests
- Yields standard score, PR, and CIs
- Standard score range: 30–170
- Mean internal consistency reliability = .89

Nonverbal
- 2 subtests
- Yields standard score, PR, and CIs
- Standard score range: 32–170
- Mean internal consistency reliability = .86

Spatial
- 2 subtests
- Yields standard score, PR, and CIs
- Standard score range: 34–170
- Mean internal consistency reliability = .95

Processing Speed (not available until age 5:0)
- 2 subtests
- Yields standard score, PR, and CIs
- Standard score range: 30–170
- Mean internal consistency reliability = .89

Working Memory (not available until age 5:0)
- 2 subtests
- Yields standard score, PR, and CIs
- Standard score range: 33–169
- Mean internal consistency reliability = .93

Subtests
- 10 subtests yielding T scores, PRs, and Ability scores

(continued)

Table 7.3. *Continued*

- Mean internal consistency reliability = .95

Differential Ability Scales, Second Edition

School-Age Battery (Ages 7:0–17:11)

Stratum III Composite

General Conceptual Ability
- 6 subtests with no floor or ceiling violations
- Yields standard score, PR, and CIs
- Standard score range: 45–165
- Mean internal consistency reliability = .96

Spatial
- 2 subtests
- Yields standard score, PR, and CIs
- Standard score range: 32–170

Processing Speed
- 2 subtests
- Yields standard score, PR, and CIs
- Standard score range: 30–170
- Mean internal consistency reliability = .90

Working Memory
- 2 subtests
- Yields standard score, PR, and CIs
- Standard score range: 33–169
- Mean internal consistency reliability = .95

Stratum II Composites

Verbal
- 2 subtests
- Yields standard score, PR, and CIs
- Standard score range: 31–169
- Mean internal consistency reliability = .89

Nonverbal
- 2 subtests
- Yields standard score, PR, and CIs
- Standard score range: 31–166
- Mean internal consistency reliability = .93

Subtests
- 14 subtests yielding T scores, PRs, and Ability scores

Other Information

Item scaling: Item response theory
Bias evaluation: Bias review panel, statistical analysis of item bias, and predictive bias evaluation
Spanish edition: Yes
Confidence interval method: Standard error of the estimated true score (*SEE*) centered around the estimated true score
Electronic scoring and report-writing system: Yes, but scoring only

Memory. Average internal consistency reliability values for only the Nonverbal (in both Early Years batteries), Processing Speed (in the Upper-Level Early Years battery), and Verbal composites (in the Upper-Level Early Years and School-Age Batteries) fell below .90. In the batteries for older children, the DAS-II stratum III composites seem to represent Crystallized Intelligence, Fluid Reasoning, Visual Processing, Processing Speed, and Short-Term Memory well (Keith, Low, M. Reynolds, Patel, & Ridley, 2010), and the DAS-II Verbal, Nonverbal, Spatial, and Working Memory composites possess both strong *g* loadings and sizable specific-ability effects at most age levels. Only Processing Speed seems to measure proportionally more specific variance than general-factor variance (Maynard, Floyd, Acklie, & Houston, 2011; Reynolds, 2013).

The DAS-II has some noteworthy features, including scores formed from different subtests at varying ages, allowing for more developmentally sensitive assessment; inclusion of child-friendly manipulatives; and a highly *g*-saturated stratum III composite derived from only six subtests. It produces a language-reduced composite called the Special Nonverbal Composite, and support materials have been provided to administer some subtests in Spanish and American Sign Language. However, at the time of publication of this book, the DAS-II norming sample is too dated. **We recommend that the DAS-II not be used during high-stakes assessments due to the high likelihood of it producing inflated scores**, and we look forward to learning more about a normative update of this test that is projected to begin during 2020. More information about the DAS-II can be found here:

Beran, T. N. (2007). Test review. [Review of the test *Differential Ability Scales, Second Edition*]. *Canadian Journal of School Psychology, 22*, 128–132.

Dumont, R., Willis, J. O., & Elliott, C. D. (2008). *Essentials of DAS-II assessment*. Hoboken, NJ: Wiley.

Elliott, C. D., Salerno, J. D., Dumont, R., & Willis, J. O. (2018). The Differential Ability Scales—Second Edition. In D. P. Flanagan & E. M. McDonough (Eds.), *Contemporary intellectual assessment: Theories, tests, and issues* (4th ed., pp. 360–382). New York, NY: Guilford Press.

Marshal, S. M., McGoey, K. E., & Moschos, S. (2011). Test review. [Review of the test *Differential Ability Scales—Second Edition*]. *Journal of Psychoeducational Assessment, 29*, 89–93.

KAUFMAN ASSESSMENT BATTERY FOR CHILDREN, SECOND EDITION NORMATIVE UPDATE

The Kaufman Assessment Battery for Children, Second Edition Normative Update (KABC-II NU; A. Kaufman & N. Kaufman, 2018) is a full-length intelligence test for those ages 3 through 18 (see Table 7.4). It includes the same 18 subtests that were first published as part of the Kaufman Assessment Battery for Children, Second Edition (A. Kaufman & N. Kaufman, 2004). Subtests vary widely in administration format and testing materials. Items are administered orally and via response books, and manipulatives include cards, cubes, plates, and a plastic animal figure. Only the norming data have been updated in the current edition. As a result, some of the test's measurement properties (e.g., reliability estimates) are slightly different than those reported for the earlier edition.

The KABC-II was developed by using dual theoretical models: the Luria neuropsychological model, which parallels the PASS model used to develop the CAS2 and the more mainstream CHC theory. Norming data for the Normative Update were collected in 2017, and the test developers followed a norming plan based on the 2015 U.S. Census. Continuous norming procedures were not employed, but inferential norming procedures were (see Chapter 4). The KABC-II NU included 700 participants in its norming sample. Across its 16-year age span (3–18), it includes 47 norm blocks: for ages 3–5, in 3-month blocks (12); for ages 6–14, in 4-month blocks (27); and for ages 15–18, in 6-month blocks (8). Following through on the division of 700 participants by 47 norm blocks, the quotient is a measly 14.9. Using Norfolk et al.'s (2015) evaluative labels, the KABC-II NU's average norm block size is of insufficient size.

The KABC-II NU produces a stratum III composite called the Fluid–Crystallized Index. For ages 6 and older, it stems from 10 subtests, but fewer subtests

Table 7.4. Psychometric Evaluation of the Kaufman Assessment Battery for Children, Second Edition, Normative Update (KABC-2 NU)

Publisher: Pearson
Publication date: 2018
Age range: 3:00–18:00

Norming Information

Norm sample N: 700
Date collected: Between January and July 2017
Census data: 2015
U.S. states sampled: Not reported
Characteristics considered: Age, gender, race/ethnicity, parent education level, and geographic region
Continuous norming: No
Norm block size: Preschool: Inadequate; Elementary: Inadequate; Middle and High: Inadequate

Scores Provided

Stratum III Composites

Fluid–Crystallized Index
- 7 (age 3), 9 (ages 4–5), or 10 subtests (ages 6–18) with floor violations at ages 5:2 and younger and ceiling violations at ages 14:8 and older
- Yields standard score, PR, and CIs
- Standard score range: 40–160 (ages 3:0–5:11, 10:00–12:11), 49–160 (ages 6:0–6:11), 45–160 (ages 7:0–9:11), and 47–160 (ages 13:00–18:11)
- Mean internal consistency reliability = .97 (ages 3:0–6:11) and .98 (ages 7:0–18:11)

Mental Processing Index
- 5 (age 3), 7 (ages 4–5), or 8 subtests (ages 6–18) with floor violations at 5:2 and younger and ceiling violations at 14:8 and older
- Yields standard score, PR, and CIs
- Standard score range: 40–160 (ages 3:0–3:11, 5:0–5:11); 41–160 (ages 4:0–4:11); 48–160 (ages 6:0–6:11); 44–160 (ages 7:0–9:11); 43–160 (ages 10:00–12:11); and 48–160 (ages 13:00–18:11)
- Mean internal consistency reliability = .96 (ages 3:0–6:11) and .97 (ages 7:0–18:11)

Nonverbal Index
- 4 subtests with floor violations at ages 4:8 and younger and no ceiling violations
- Yields standard score, PR, and CIs
- Standard score range: 40–160 (ages 3:0–5:11, 7:0–9:11), 46–159 (ages 6:0–6:11), and 47–160 (ages 10:0–12:11, 13:0–18:11)
- Mean internal consistency reliability = .94 (ages 3:0–6:11) and .95 (ages 7:0–18:11)

Stratum II Composites

Crystallized Ability
- 2 subtests
- Yields standard score, PR, and CIs
- Standard score range: 50–154 (ages 4:0–4:11) 48–160 (10:0–18:11); 50–154 (ages 5:0–6:11); 44–160 (ages 7:0–9:11)
- Mean internal consistency reliability = .94 (ages 3:0–6:11) and .96 (ages 7:0–18:11)

Fluid Reasoning
- 2 subtests
- Yields standard score, PR, and CIs
- Standard score range: 51–160 (ages 7:0–18:11)
- Mean internal consistency reliability = .91 (7:0–18:11)

Long-Term Storage and Retrieval
- 2 subtests
- Yields standard score, PR, and CIs
- Standard score range: 48–160 (ages 4:0–18:11)
- Mean internal consistency reliability = .98 (3:0–6:11) and .97 (7:0–18:11)

Short-Term Memory
- 2 subtests
- Yields standard score, PR, and CIs
- Standard score range: 49–158 (ages 4:0–18:11)
- Mean internal consistency reliability = .91 (3:0–6:11) and .91 (7:0–18:11)

Visual-Spatial Processing
- 2 subtests
- Yields standard score, PR, and CIs
- Standard score range: 40–160 (ages 4:0–5:11); 52–158 (ages 6:0–6:11); 48–157 (ages 7:0–9:11); 43–160 (ages 10:0–12:11); 50–160 (ages 13:0–18:11)
- Mean internal consistency reliability = .95 (3:0–6:11) and .95 (7:0–18:11)

Subtests
- 18 subtests yielding scaled scores

Other Information

Item scaling: Traditional
Bias evaluation: Statistical analysis of item bias reported for the same items in KABC-2
Spanish edition: Yes (Spain)
Confidence interval method: Standard error of the estimated true score (*SEE*) centered around the estimated true score
Electronic scoring and report-writing system: Yes

contribute the Fluid–Crystallized Index for 3-year-olds (7 subtests) and 4- and 5-year-olds (9 subtests). The average internal consistency reliability value for the Fluid–Crystallized Index was at least .97 across ages. M. Reynolds et al. (2013) reported an omega hierarchical value of .87 across ages, so more than 85% of the variance in the Fluid–Crystallized Index score can be attributed to psychometric *g*. An alternative to the Fluid–Crystallized Index that omits the two subtests targeting Crystallized Intelligence, called the Mental Processing Composite, has some psychometric properties similar to those of the Fluid–Crystallized Index. For subtests contributing to the Fluid–Crystallized Index and the Mental Processing Composite, floor violations are evident at ages 5:2 and younger, and ceiling violations are evident for ages 14:8 and older. The KABC-II NU's Nonverbal Index includes 4 subtests that contain minimal verbal content and minimize oral responses requirements; subtest floor violations are evident at ages 4:8 and younger. The Nonverbal Index has demonstrated reliability that is only slightly lower than that for the Fluid–Crystallized Index and the Mental Processing Composite.

The KABC-II NU also produces five stratum II composites, and all demonstrate average internal consistency reliability values of .91 or higher. Based on data from the same KABC-II tests and the earlier norming data supporting the prior edition, some evidence supports the validity of these subtests in representing similarly labeled CHC broad abilities (e.g., M. Reynolds, Keith, Fine, Fisher, & Low, 2007), whereas other evidence did not support the viability of the Fluid Reasoning factor (e.g., Benson, Kranzler, & Floyd, 2016; McGill & Dombrowski, 2018). The most recent study employing the KABC-II NU norming data (McGill, 2019) also calls into question the viability of the Fluid Reasoning factor and corresponding KABC-II NU composite.

The KABC-II NU has some noteworthy features, including a dual theoretical interpretive framework; scores formed from different subtests at varying ages, allowing for more developmentally sensitive assessment; and inclusion of unique and engaging subtest activities. The KABC-II NU is supported by a scoring and report-writing system. The *g* saturation of the Fluid-Crystallized Index of its prior edition is impressive, and we assume that similar findings would be evident based on the Normative Update data. The KABC-II NU seems to assess a wider breadth of stratum II abilities than many other tests (with its inclusion of measures targeting Long-Term Retrieval), and it omits subtests measuring Processing Speed, which usually are affected by motor and visual acuity problems and weakly *g* saturated. Test records also address qualitative indicators for each subtest, and the test is linked to a co-normed and comprehensive achievement test. At the time of publication, we found no published reviews of the KABC-II NU, and we are most concerned about the apparently small size of its norming sample. Considering its wide age range (3 to 18), its total norming sample size of 700 seems too small—even with application of inferential norming methods. The following recent chapter and other publications addressing the prior edition discuss many key features apparent in the current edition:

Drozdick, L. W., Singer, J. K., Lichtenberger, E. O., Kaufman, J. C., Kaufman, A. S., & Kaufman, N. L. (2018). The Kaufman Assessment Battery for Children— Second Edition and KABC-II Normative Update. In D. P. Flanagan & E. M.

McDonough (Eds.), *Contemporary intellectual assessment: Theories, tests, and issues* (4th ed., pp. 333–359). New York, NY: Guilford Press.

Kaufman, A. S., Lichtenberger, E. O., Fletcher-Janzen, E., & Kaufman, N. L. (2005). *Essentials of KABC-II assessment.* Hoboken, NJ: Wiley.

Bain, S. K., & Gray, R. (2008). Test review. [Review of the test *Kaufman Assessment Battery for Children—Second Edition*]. *Journal of Psychoeducational Assessment, 26,* 92–101.

REYNOLDS INTELLECTUAL ASSESSMENT SCALES, SECOND EDITION

The Reynolds Intellectual Assessment Scales (RIAS-2; C. Reynolds & Kamphaus, 2015b) is a full-length intelligence test for ages 3 through 94 (see Table 7.5). It includes eight subtests—two beyond its first edition—administered orally and via stimulus book and response booklets. Norming data were collected from January 2013 to August 2014 across 32 of the United States; the test developers followed a norming plan based on the 2012 U.S. Census and used continuous norming procedures. For both the preschool-age level and middle- and high-school levels, the norm block sizes are sufficiently large, but for the elementary-school level (ages 8 to 12), they are slightly below the minimum standard of 30 (with a low sample size of 29 at age 10). These norm block sizes are consistently somewhat larger than those for its predecessor (Norfolk et al., 2015) and reflect a notable improvement in the norming of the RIAS-2.

The RIAS-2 produces a stratum III composite called the Composite Intelligence Index; for all ages, this score is formed from four subtests. The average internal consistency reliability value for the Composite Intelligence Index was .94 across ages. Floor violations for subtests are evident at ages 3:11 and younger, but subtests have no ceiling violations. No estimates of the g saturation of the Composite Intelligence Index have been produced. The RIAS-2 also produces four composite scores: the Verbal Intelligence Index, the Nonverbal Intelligence Index, the Composite Memory Index, and the Speeded Processing Index. Average internal consistency reliability values for these composites were .93 across ages. These composites seem to be somewhat coarse from the perspective of three-stratum theory and CHC theory, and questions surfaced regarding the extent to which the original RIAS Verbal Intelligence Index and Nonverbal Intelligence Index measured specific abilities beyond psychometric g (Nelson & Canivez, 2012; Nelson, Canivez, Lindstrom, & Hatt, 2007).

The RIAS-2 has noteworthy features, including focused measurement of psychometric g across a very broad age range. It omits manipulatives and paper-and-pencil tasks altogether, so its scores are not likely to be confounded by motor impairment. The RIAS-2 is supported by an electronic scoring and report-writing system. It also includes an abbreviated IQ called the Reynolds Intellectual Screening Test, Second Edition Index (see Table 7.5); this two-subtest abbreviated intelligence test can be given alone, like the two other brief intelligence tests described later in this chapter. The RIAS-2 includes some new subtests that do not contribute to its stratum III composites that appear to have little relation to general intelligence. Although we appreciate both the distinction between general and specific abilities in

Table 7.5. Psychometric Evaluation of the Reynolds Intellectual Assessment Scales, Second Edition (RIAS-2)

Publisher: Psychological Assessment Resources
Publication date: 2015
Age range: 3–94

Norming Information

Norm sample N: 2,154
Date collected: January 2013–August 2014
Census data: 2012
Number U.S. states sampled: 32
Characteristics considered: Gender, ethnicity, education level, and region
Continuous norming: Yes
Norm block size: Preschool: Minimum; Elementary: Insufficient; Middle and High: Medium

Scores Provided

Stratum III Composite

Composite Intelligence Index
- 4 subtests with floor violations at ages 3:11 and younger and no ceiling violations
- Yields standard score, PR, T score, z score, normal curve equivalent, stanine, and CIs
- Standard score range: 40–160
- Mean internal consistency reliability = .94

Reynolds Intellectual Screening Test, Second Edition Index
- 2 subtests with floor violations at ages 3:3 and younger and no ceiling violations
- Yields standard score, T score, z score, normal curve equivalent, stanine, PR, and CIs
- Standard score range: 40–160
- Mean internal consistency reliability = .91

Stratum II Composites

Verbal Intelligence Index
- 2 subtests
- Yields standard score, PR, T score, z score, normal curve equivalent, stanine, and CIs
- Standard score range: 40–160
- Mean internal consistency reliability = .92

Nonverbal Intelligence Index
- 2 subtests
- Yields standard score, PR, T score, z score, normal curve equivalent, stanine, and CIs
- Standard score range: 40–160
- Mean internal consistency reliability = .91

Composite Memory Index
- 2 subtests
- Yields standard score, PR, T score, z score, normal curve equivalent, stanine, and CIs
- Standard score range: 40–160
- Mean internal consistency reliability = .90

Speeded Processing Index
- 2 subtests
- Yields standard score, PR, T score, z score, normal curve equivalent, stanine, and CIs
- Standard score range: 40–160
- Mean internal consistency reliability = .99

Subtests
- 8 subtests yielding scaled scores

Other Information

Item scaling: Traditional and item response theory
Bias evaluation: Bias review panel, statistical analysis of item bias, and comparison of reliability coefficients, correlations between age and raw scores, and factor structure across gender binary categories and race/ethnicity
Spanish edition: Yes (record form with Spanish responses)
Confidence interval method: Standard error of the estimated true score (*SEE*) centered around the estimated true score
Electronic scoring and report-writing system: Yes

theory and in measurement, it is not clear to us what will be the benefit of the low g-loading subtests and the related Speeded Processing Index.

The RIAS-2 (like its predecessor) includes fewer subtests contributing to its stratum III composite than most other tests; in fact, it includes only as many as some brief intelligence tests (e.g., the Wechsler Abbreviated Scale of Intelligence, Second Edition; Wechsler, 2011). It is logical that, due to limited sampling of more specific cognitive abilities (mainly those associated with Crystallized Intelligence and Fluid Reasoning) across only four subtests, the RIAS-2's Composite Intelligence Index is an inferior measure of psychometric g compared to many other stratum III composites reviewed in this chapter. We are hopeful that additional research focused on the g saturation of the Composite Intelligence Index sheds light on the veracity of this concern. At present, it is safe to assume that high-stakes assessment decisions probably should be based on broader ability sampling across a greater number of subtests. More information about the RIAS-2 can be found here:

McNicholas, P. J., & Floyd, R. G. (2017). Test review. [Review of the test *Reynolds Intellectual Assessment Scales, Second Edition and Reynolds Intellectual Screening Test, Second Edition*]. *Canadian Journal of School Psychology, 32*, 176–180.

Raines, T. C., Reynolds, C. R., & Kamphaus, R. W. (2018). The Reynolds Intellectual Screening Test, Second Edition, and the Reynolds Intellectual Screening Test, Second Edition. In D. P. Flanagan & E. M. McDonough (Eds.), *Contemporary intellectual assessment: Theories, tests, and issues* (4th ed., pp. 533–552). New York, NY: Guilford Press.

STANFORD-BINET INTELLIGENCE SCALES, FIFTH EDITION

The Stanford-Binet Intelligence Scales, Fifth Edition (SB5; Roid, 2003) is a full-length intelligence test for ages 2 to 89 (see Table 7.6). It includes 10 subtests administered orally, via stimulus books and response booklets, and subtests require a wide variety of manipulatives and other testing materials (e.g., cups, cubes, plates, and small plastic animal figures) during administration. The SB5 was developed on the basis of CHC theory. Norming data were collected from 2001 to 2002 across 40 of the United States; the test developer followed a norming plan based on the 2001 U.S. Census and used continuous norming procedures. As a result of the extended period since norming data were collected, SB5 scores will be inflated substantially due to the Flynn effect. There are at least approximately 40 individuals per norm table block across age levels, and there are more than approximately 50 children per norm table block for ages 5 through 17.

The SB5 produces a stratum III composite called the Full Scale IQ; it is formed from 10 subtests. The average internal consistency reliability value for the Full Scale IQ was .98 across ages. There are floor violations at ages 4:3 and younger but no ceiling violations. From these same subtests, the SB5 produces Verbal IQ and Nonverbal IQ composite scores, each of which is formed from five subtests. Average internal consistency reliability values for these composites were .96 and .95, respectively, across

Table 7.6. Psychometric Evaluation of the Stanford-Binet Intelligence Scales, Fifth Edition (SB5)

Publisher: Riverside
Publication date: 2003
Age range: 2:0–89:11

Norming Information

Norm sample N: 4,800
Dates collected: 2001 and 2002
Census data: 2001
Number U.S. states sampled: 40
Characteristics considered: Age, sex, race, parental or individual education level, and geographic region
Continuous norming: Yes
Norm block size: Preschool: Medium; Elementary: Medium; Middle and High: Medium

Scores Provided

Stratum III Composites

Full Scale IQ
- 10 subtests with floor violations at age 4:3 and younger, and no ceiling violations
- Yields standard score, PR, age equivalency, change-sensitive scores, and CIs
- Standard score range: 40–160
- Mean internal consistency reliability = .98

Verbal IQ
- 5 subtests
- Yields standard score, PR, age equivalency, change sensitive scores, and CIs
- Standard score range: 43–156
- Mean internal consistency reliability = .96

Nonverbal IQ
- 5 subtests
- Yields standard score, PR, age equivalency, change-sensitive scores, and CIs
- Standard score range: 42–158
- Mean internal consistency reliability = .95

Abbreviated IQ
- 2 subtests with no floor or ceiling violations
- Yields standard score, PR, and CIs
- Standard score range: 47–153
- Mean internal consistency reliability = .91

Stratum II Composites

Fluid Reasoning
- 2 subtests
- Yields standard score, PR, age equivalency, change-sensitive scores, and CIs Standard score range: 47–153
- Mean internal consistency reliability = .90

Knowledge
- 2 subtests
- Yields standard score, PR, age equivalency, change-sensitive scores, and CIs
- Standard score range: 49–151
- Mean internal consistency reliability = .92

Quantitative Reasoning
- 2 subtests
- Yields standard score, PR, age equivalency, change-sensitive scores, and CIs
- Standard score range: 50–149
- Mean internal consistency reliability = .92

Visual-Spatial Processing
- 2 subtests
- Yields standard score, PR, age equivalency, change-sensitive scores, and CIs
- Standard score range: 48–152
- Mean internal consistency reliability = .92

Working Memory
- 2 subtests
- Yields standard score, PR, age equivalency, change-sensitive scores, and CIs
- Standard score range: 48–152
- Mean internal consistency reliability = .91

Subtests
- 10 subtests yielding scaled scores

Other Information

Item scaling: Item response theory
Bias evaluation: Statistical analysis of item bias
Spanish edition: No
Confidence interval method: Standard error of the estimated true score (*SEE*) centered around the estimated true score
Electronic scoring and report-writing system: Yes

age levels. These are rather coarse indicators of CHC abilities, but their breadth of psychometric sampling indicates that they probably are stratum III composites. The SB5 produces an abbreviated stratum III composite from the two routing subtests called the Abbreviated IQ; its average internal consistency reliability value is .91. The SB5 also yields five stratum II composite scores; the average internal consistency reliability value for each was .90 or higher across ages. These composites seem to represent similarly labeled CHC broad abilities well; however, several studies have indicated that the SB5 measures little in terms of specific abilities beyond psychometric g (Canivez, 2008; DiStefano & Dombrowski, 2006).

The SB5 has some noteworthy features, including broad age coverage; scores formed from different subtests items at varying ages, allowing for more developmentally sensitive assessment; and inclusion of child-friendly manipulatives. It includes routing subtests to estimate ability-based start points for later subtests and promote expedited administration. The SB5 is supported by an electronic scoring and report-writing system.

Like the DAS-II, the SB5 norming data are now dated. **We recommend that the SB5 not be used during high-stakes assessments due to the high likelihood of it producing inflated scores.** A revision of the SB5 is underway at the time of publication, but we obtained no projected completion date when we contacted its current publisher, PRO-ED, Inc. More information about the SB5 can be found here:

Bain, S. K., & Allin, J. D. (2005). Test review. [Review of the test *Stanford-Binet Intelligence Scales, Fifth Edition*]. *Journal of Psychoeducational Assessment, 23*, 87–95.
Janzen, H. L., Obrzut, J. E., & Marusiak, C. W. (2004). Test review. [Review of the test *Stanford-Binet Intelligence Scales, Fifth Edition*]. *Canadian Journal of School Psychology, 19*, 235–244.
Roid, G. H., & Barram, A. (2004). *Essentials of Stanford-Binet Intelligence Scales (SB5) assessment*. Hoboken, NJ: Wiley.

WECHSLER ADULT INTELLIGENCE SCALE—FOURTH EDITION

The Wechsler Adult Intelligence Scale, Fourth Edition (WAIS-IV; Wechsler, 2008) is a full-length intelligence test for ages 16 to 90. The WAIS-IV includes 15 subtests (see Table 7.7). Items are administered orally, via stimulus books and response booklets, and manipulatives are limited to only cubes. Norming data were collected from March 2007 to April 2008 across 49 of the United States; the test developers followed a norming plan based on the 2005 U.S. Census and used continuous norming procedures. There are 200 individuals per norm table block for ages 16 through 70, and 100 at ages 70 and older.

The WAIS-IV produces a stratum III composite called the Full Scale IQ; for all ages, this is formed from 10 subtests. There are no floor or ceiling violations across the contributing subtests. The average internal consistency reliability value for the Full Scale IQ was .98 across ages, and two studies have yielded omega hierarchical values indicating that the Full Scale IQ is highly g saturated. Watkins (2017) reported a value

Table 7.7. Psychometric Evaluation of the Wechsler Adult Intelligence Scale—Fourth Edition (WAIS-IV)

Publisher: Pearson
Publication date: 2008
Age range: 16:0–90:11

Norming Information

Norm sample N: 2,200
Dates collected: March 2007–April 2008
Census data: 2005
U.S. states sampled: 49
Characteristics considered: Age, sex, race, individual or parental education level, and geographic region
Continuous norming: Yes
Norm block size: Middle and High: Highest

Scores Provided

Stratum III Composite

Full Scale IQ
- 10 subtests with no floor or ceiling violations
- Yields standard score, PR, and CIs
- Standard score range: 50–150
- Mean internal consistency reliability = .98

General Ability Index
- 6 subtests with no floor or ceiling violations
- Yields standard score, PR, and CIs
- Standard score range: 40–160
- Mean internal consistency reliability = .97

Stratum II Composites

Verbal Comprehension Index
- 3 subtests
- Yields standard score, PR, and CIs
- Standard score range: 50–150
- Mean internal consistency reliability = .96

Perceptual Reasoning Index
- 3 subtests
- Yields standard score, PR, and CIs
- Standard score range: 50–150
- Mean internal consistency reliability = .95

Working Memory Index
- 2 subtests
- Yields standard score, PR, and CIs
- Standard score range: 50–150
- Mean internal consistency reliability = .94

Processing Speed Index
- 2 subtests
- Yields standard score, PR, and CIs
- Standard score range: 50–150
- Mean internal consistency reliability = .90

Subtests
- 15 subtests yielding scaled scores

Other Information

Item scaling: Traditional
Bias evaluation: Bias review panel and statistical analysis of item bias
Spanish edition: Yes (Argentina, Chile, Mexico, Spain)
Confidence interval method: Standard error of the estimated true score (*SEE*) centered around the estimated true score
Electronic scoring and report-writing system: Yes

---

of .84 for the full WAIS-IV norming sample data, and Gignac and Watkins (2013) reported values ranging from .84 to .88 across that sample's age groups. Nelson, Canivez, and Watkins (2013) reported values that were somewhat lower, .74, when they employed data from a smaller clinical sample. Across these results, we can conclude that the *g* saturation of the WAIS-IV Full Scale IQ ranges from 74% to 88%.

Like the WISC-V, the WAIS-IV produces a stratum III composite called the General Ability Index. This score is formed from six subtests that demonstrate no floor or ceiling violations (see Table 7.6). These subtests also form also the Verbal Comprehension Index and the Perceptual Reasoning Index from the WAIS-IV. The average internal consistency reliability value of the WAIS-IV General Ability Index was .97 (Lichtenberger & Kaufman, 2009).

The WAIS-IV produces four stratum II composite scores that generally are supported by independent research (e.g., Canivez & Watkins, 2010a, 2010b). The Verbal Comprehension Index and Processing Speed Index seem to represent the abilities of Crystallized Intelligence and Processing Speed well, but questions remain about the validity of the Perceptual Reasoning Index and the Working Memory Index (e.g., Benson, Hulac, & Kranzler, 2010). Average internal consistency reliability values for these composites were .90 or higher across ages.

The WAIS-IV has some noteworthy features, including a one-year overlap with the WISC-V and co-norming with the Wechsler Memory Scale—Fourth Edition. It is supported by an electronic scoring and report-writing system. Its norming data are somewhat dated at the time of publication, but we understand that it is being revised and normed, with a projected publication date in 2021. More information about the WAIS-IV can be found here:

Climie, E. A., & Rostad, K. (2011). Test review. [Review of the test *Wechsler Adult Intelligence Scale, Fourth Edition*]. *Journal of Psychoeducational Assessment, 29*, 581–586.

Drozdick, L. W., Raiford, S. E., Wahlstrom, D., & Weiss, L. G. (2018). The Wechsler Adult Intelligence Scale—Fourth Edition and the Wechsler Memory Scale—Fourth Edition. In D. P. Flanagan & E. M. McDonough (Eds.), *Contemporary intellectual assessment: Theories, tests, and issues* (4th ed., pp. 486–511). New York, NY: Guilford Press.

Hartman, D. E. (2009). Test review. [Review of the test *Wechsler Adult Intelligence Scale, Fourth Edition*]. Return of the gold standard. *Applied Neuropsychology, 16*, 85–87.

Holdnack, J. A., Dozdick, L. W., Weiss, L. G., & Iverson, G. (2013). *WAIS-IV/WMS-IV advanced clinical solutions*. San Diego, CA: Academic Press.

Lichtenberger, E. O., & Kaufman, A. S. (2012). *Essentials of WAIS-IV assessment* (2nd ed.). Hoboken, NJ: Wiley.

Weiss, L. G., Saklofske, D. H., Coalson, D., & Raiford, S. E. (2010). *WAIS-IV clinical use and interpretation: Scientist-practitioner perspectives*. London: Academic Press.

WECHSLER PRESCHOOL AND PRIMARY SCALE OF INTELLIGENCE—FOURTH EDITION

The Wechsler Preschool and Primary Scale of Intelligence—Fourth Edition (WPPSI-IV; Wechsler, 2012) is a full-length intelligence test for children ages 2:6 through 7:7 that includes 7 subtests at ages 2:6 to 3:11 and 15 primary subtests at ages 4:0 to 7:7 (see Table 7.8). Items are administered orally, via stimulus books and response booklets, and several different manipulatives (e.g., cubes and cards) are included. Norming data were collected from 2010 to 2012 across approximately 48 of the United States; the test developers followed a norming plan based on the 2010 U.S. Census and used continuous norming procedures. There are at least ap-

Table 7.8. Psychometric Evaluation of the Wechsler Preschool and Primary Scale of Intelligence, Fourth Edition (WPPSI-IV)

Publisher: Psychological Corporation (on release) and Pearson (current)
Publication date: 2012
Age range: 2:6–7:7

Norming Information

Norm sample N: 1,700
Dates collected: 2010–2012
Census data: 2010
Number U.S. states sampled: Not specified; ~47
Characteristics considered: Age, sex, race, parental education level, and geographic region
Continuous norming: Yes
Norm block size: Preschool: Highest; Elementary: Medium

Scores Provided

Ages 2:6–3:11

Stratum III Composites

Full Scale IQ
- 5 subtests with floor violations at ages 2:11 and younger and no ceiling violations
- Yields standard score, PR, and CIs
- Standard score range: 40–160
- Mean internal consistency reliability = .96

General Ability Index
- 4 subtests with floor violations at ages 2:11 and younger and no ceiling violations
- Yields standard score, PR, and CIs
- Standard score range: 40–160
- Mean internal consistency reliability = .95

Nonverbal
- 4 subtests with floor violations at ages 2:11 and younger and no ceiling violations (ages 2:6–3:11) and 5 subtests with no floor or ceiling violations (ages 4:0–7:7)
- Yields standard score, PR, and CIs
- Standard score range: 40–160 (ages 2:6–3:11), 40–160 (ages 4:0–7:7)

- Mean internal consistency reliability = .95 (ages 2:6–3:11), .95 (ages 4:0–7:7)

Stratum II Composites

Verbal Comprehension
- 2 subtests
- Yields standard score, PR, and CIs
- Standard score range: 45–155
- Mean internal consistency reliability = .94

Visual Spatial
- 2 subtests
- Yields standard score, PR, and CIs
- Standard score range: 45–155
- Mean internal consistency reliability = .89

Working Memory
- 2 subtests
- Yields standard score, PR, and CIs
- Standard score range: 45–155
- Mean internal consistency reliability = .93

Subtests
- 8 subtests yielding scaled scores

Ages 4:0–7:7

Stratum III Composite

Full Scale IQ
- 6 subtests with no floor or ceiling violations
- Yields standard score, PR, and CIs
- Standard score range: 40–160
- Mean internal consistency reliability = .96

Nonverbal
- 5 subtests with no floor or ceiling violations (ages 4:0–7:7)
- Yields standard score, PR, and CIs
- Standard score range: 40–160
- Mean internal consistency reliability = .95

General Ability Index
- 4 subtests with floor violations with no floor or ceiling violations
- Yields standard score, PR, and CIs
- Standard score range: 40–160

(*continued*)

Table 7.8. Continued

- Mean internal consistency reliability =. 95

Stratum II Composites

Verbal Comprehension
- 2 subtests
- Yields standard score, PR, and CIs
- Standard score range: 45–155
- Mean internal consistency reliability = .94

Visual Spatial
- 2 subtests
- Yields standard score, PR, and CIs
- Standard score range: 45–155
- Mean internal consistency reliability = .89

Fluid Reasoning
- 2 subtests
- Yields standard score, PR, and CIs
- Standard score range: 45–155
- Mean internal consistency reliability = .93

Working Memory
- 2 subtests
- Yields standard score, PR, and CIs
- Standard score range: 45–155
- Mean internal consistency reliability = .91

Processing Speed
- 2 subtests
- Yields standard score, PR, and CIs
- Standard score range: 45–150
- Mean internal consistency reliability = .86

Subtests
- 13 subtests yielding scaled scores

Other Information

Item scaling: Traditional
Bias evaluation: Bias review panel and statistical analysis of item bias
Spanish edition: Yes (Argentina, Mexico, Spain)
Confidence interval method: Standard error of the estimated true score (*SEE*) centered around the estimated true score
Electronic scoring and report-writing system: Yes

---

proximately 100 children per norm table block for most age levels, and in the others, approximately 67 per block.

The WPPSI-IV produces a stratum III composite called the Full Scale IQ; for ages 3:11 and younger, this score is formed from five subtests, and for ages 4 years and older, this score is formed from six subtests. For the battery targeting younger children, subtest floor violations are evident for ages 2:11 and younger; for the battery targeting older children, no floor violations are evident. No subtest ceiling violations are evident. The average internal consistency reliability value for the Full Scale IQ was .96 for the two batteries. The WPPSI-IV's General Ability Index, like that from the WISC-V and WAIS-IV, is formed from a subset of the subtests contributing to the Full Scale IQ: two subtests contributing to the Verbal Comprehension Index, one subtest contributing to the Visual Spatial Index (for both the younger and older age groups), and one subtest contributing to the Fluid Reasoning Index (for the older age group). For the youngest age group (2:6–3:11), there are floor violations, but there are none for ages 4 and older. Neither group demonstrated ceiling violations. The WPPSI-IV's Nonverbal Index includes some of the same subtests as the General Ability Index and the Full Scale IQ, but it omits the two subtests from the Verbal Comprehension Index. For the younger age group, it includes four subtests and incorporates those that contribute to the Fluid Reasoning Index and the Working Memory Index. For the older age group, it includes five subtests and incorporates both of those contributing to the Fluid Reasoning Index and one subtest from each of the other indexes. Its psychometric properties are comparable to those from the other stratum III composites.

The WPPSI-IV battery targeting younger children produces three stratum II composite scores: the Verbal Comprehension Index, the Visual Spatial Index, and the Working Memory Index; the battery targeting older children produces two additional composites: the Fluid Reasoning Index and the Processing Speed Index. Average internal consistency reliability values for the Verbal Comprehension Index, the Fluid Reasoning Index, and the Working Memory Index were above the .90 criterion. The Visual Spatial Index, however, did not meet this criterion in either battery, and the Processing Speed Index did not meet this criterion in the battery for older children.

The WPPSI-IV offers some noteworthy features. In general, the WPPSI-IV offers five new subtests, a wider sampling of abilities across domains, and a greater number of stratum II composites than its predecessor. Some of the new subtests and composites focus on working memory measure visual–spatial memory ability rather than auditory immediate memory abilities (aka Short-Term Memory), as most other working memory tasks do. They are likely to measure the same stratum II ability (Visual Processing) as subtests contributing to the Visual Spatial Index. The WPPSI-IV is supported by an electronic scoring and report-writing system. More information can be found here:

Raiford, S. E. & Coalson, D. L. (2014). *Essentials of WPPSI-IV assessment.* Hoboken, NJ: Wiley.

Syeda, M. M. & Climie, E. A. (2014). Test review. [Review of the test *Wechsler Preschool and Primary Scale of Intelligence, Fourth Edition*]. *Journal of Psychoeducational Assessment, 32,* 265–272.

Wahlstrom, D., Raiford, S. E., Breaux, K. C., Zhu, J., & Weiss, L. G. (2018). The Wechsler Preschool and Primary Scale of Intelligence—Fourth Edition, Wechsler Intelligence Scale for Children—Fifth Edition, and Wechsler Individual Achievement Test—Third Edition. In D. P. Flanagan & E. M. McDonough (Eds.), *Contemporary intellectual assessment: Theories, tests, and issues* (4th ed., pp. 245–282). New York, NY: Guilford Press.

WOODCOCK-JOHNSON IV TESTS OF COGNITIVE ABILITIES

The Woodcock-Johnson IV (WJ IV) Tests of Cognitive Abilities (COG; Schrank, McGrew, & Mather, 2014) is a full-length intelligence test for ages 2 through 90 and older (see Table 7.9). It includes 20 subtests administered orally or by audio recording and via stimulus books and response booklets; it incorporates no manipulatives. The WJ IV COG is a revision of the first intelligence test developed on the basis of CHC theory, and it provides the widest array of stratum II composites available in one test.

The WJIV COG norming data were collected from 2009 to 2012 across 46 states: the test developers followed a norming plan based on the projected 2010 U.S. Census and used continuous norming procedures. Citing the limitations of norming all of the WJ IV subtests (including those from the COG and Tests of Achievement), such as

Table 7.9. Psychometric Evaluation of the Woodcock-Johnson IV Tests of Cognitive Abilities (WJ IV COG)

Publisher: Riverside Publishing
Publication date: 2014
Age range: 2:00-90+

Norming Information

Norm sample N: 7,416 (age) and 4,666 (grade)
Dates collected: December 2009–January 2012
Census data: 2010
Number U.S. states sampled: 46
Characteristics considered: Census region, community type, sex, race, ethnicity, type of school/college/, educational attainment of adults, employment status of adults, occupational level of adults in the labor force, parent education of preschool and K–12 students, and country of birth
Continuous norming: Yes
Norm block size: Cannot be determined

Scores Provided

Stratum III Composites

General Intellectual Ability
- 7 subtests with floor violations at age 6:1 and younger and no ceiling violations
- Yields standard score, PR, CIs, W Score, and age- and grade-equivalent scores
- Mean internal consistency reliability = .97

Gf-Gc Composite
- 4 subtests with floor violations at age 5:7 and younger and ceiling violations ages 16:11 and older
- Yields standard score, PR, CIs, W Score, and age- and grade-equivalent scores
- Mean internal consistency reliability = .96

Brief Intellectual Ability
- 3 subtests with floor violations at age 6:1 and younger and no ceiling violations
- Yields standard score, PR, CIs, W Score, and age- and grade-equivalents scores
- Mean internal consistency reliability = .94

Stratum II Composites

Comprehension-Knowledge
- 2 subtests
- Yields standard score, PR, CIs, W Score, and age- and grade-equivalent scores
- Mean internal consistency reliability = .93

Long-Term Retrieval
- 2 subtests
- Yields standard score, PR, CIs, W Score, and age- and grade-equivalent scores
- Mean internal consistency reliability = .97

Visual Processing
- 2 subtests
- Yields standard score, PR, CIs, W Score, and age- and grade-equivalent scores
- interval, W Score age- and grade-equivalent scores
- Mean internal consistency reliability = .85

Auditory Processing
- 2 subtests
- Yields standard score, PR, CIs, W Score, and age- and grade-equivalent scores
- Mean internal consistency reliability = .92

Fluid Reasoning
- 2 subtests
- Yields standard score, PR, CIs, W Score, and age- and grade-equivalent scores
- Mean internal consistency reliability = .94

Short-Term Working Memory
- 2 subtests
- Yields standard score, PR, CIs, W Score, and age- and grade-equivalent scores
- Mean internal consistency reliability = .91

Cognitive Processing Speed
- 2 subtests
- Yields standard score, PR, CIs, W Score, and age- and grade-equivalent scores
- Mean internal consistency reliability = .94

Subtests
- 20 subtests yielding standard scores, PRs, CIs, W scores, and age- and grade-equivalent scores

Other Information

Item scaling: Item response theory
Bias evaluation: Expert content review of items, statistical analysis of item bias
Spanish edition: Yes
Confidence interval method: Standard error of measurement (*SEM*) centered around estimated true score
Electronic scoring and report-writing system: Yes

examinee fatigue and boredom as well as loss of participants over time, McGrew, La-Forte, and Schrank (2014) reported that "a planned incomplete data collection design was used in the WJ IV norming study. Planned incomplete (missing) data collection methods . . . have been developed as a statistically sound method for gathering data given these design constraints" (p. 68). Using multiple matrix sampling techniques, all participants completed a common subset of subtests (18 unnamed ones) as well as subtests unique to their assigned group; the expectation was that participants would be able to complete all of the subtests in a 3-hour period. Following data collection, all missing data were estimated using a statistical analysis generally referred to as multiple imputation; 10 data sets were produced based on this analysis, and one was randomly selected to be the foundation of the norming sample. In pursuit of a representative norming sample, weighting procedures were employed to match data to Census projections across a variety of participant demographic characteristics. As far as we know, the WJ IV is the only individually administered intelligence test we feature in this book that employed these procedures. Because norm-referenced scores from the WJ IV COG can be obtained only by entering the raw scores into its Web interface, norm tables were unavailable for review. As a result, the size of the age unit per block of the norms cannot be reported (Norfolk et al., 2015); however, floor and ceiling violations can be calculated based on information entered into the Web interface (Floyd, Woods, Singh, & Hawkins, 2016).

The WJ IV COG produces three stratum III composites: General Intellectual Ability, Brief Intellectual Ability, and the Gf-Gc composite. The General Intellectual Ability is formed from seven subtests with floor violations at age 6:1 and younger and no ceiling violations. It is notable that this score is derived from weighting of subtest scores according to their g loadings in an effort to increase the quality of measurement of psychometric g. All other intelligence tests included in this chapter's review use equal weighting procedures to yield stratum III composites; in this way, the General Intellectual Ability composite is unique. The average internal consistency reliability value for General Intellectual Ability was .97.

The Brief Intellectual Ability composite is formed from three subtests with floor violations at age 6:1 and younger and no ceiling violations. The average internal consistency reliability value for General Intellectual Ability was .94. New to the WJ IV COG, the Gf-Gc composite is formed from four subtests with floor violations at age 5:7 and younger and ceiling violations at age 16:11 and older. The average internal consistency reliability value for the Gf-Gc composite was .96.

The WJ IV COG produces the widest range of composites designed to measure stratum II composites of any intelligence test reviewed in this book. It includes seven such composites, each stemming from two subtests. As evident in Table 7.9, the average internal consistency reliability values for six of these composites were .90 or higher across ages, but Visual Processing did not meet this standard. It is notable that a pattern of findings from factor-analytic research has surfaced that casts doubts on the validity of these composites. McGrew et al. (2014) provided evidence from confirmatory factor analysis that seemed to support the formation of the test's stratum II composites, but a number of peer-reviewed studies from other researchers (Dombrowski,

McGill, & Canivez, 2016, 2018a, 2018b) employing a range of factor-analytic methods found that most of the factors that correspond to these stratum II composites are not sufficiently replicable to warrant interpretation. Despite such disagreement on the true factor structure for the WJ IV, we feel confident that the instrument as a whole measures general intelligence quite well. However, we are uneasy about its ability to measure distinct stratum II ability via its two-subtest composites.

The WJ IV COG has several notable features. For example, it targets a very broad age range. It omits manipulatives altogether; all items are presented orally or via audio files, test easel pages, or response booklets. It includes subtests designed to measure Auditory Processing, which is unique to the intelligence tests reviewed here, but the subtests targeting this ability make it particularly susceptible to the effects of hearing problems. It is also part of a family of related tests. It was co-normed with a popular achievement test, the WJ IV Tests of Achievement (Shrank, Mather, & McGrew, 2014a).

There is a Spanish version of the WJ IV COG called the Batería IV Woodcock-Muñoz (Woodcock et al., 2019); the WJ IV Tests of Early Cognitive and Academic Development (ECAD) designed for toddler, preschool-age, and early elementary school-age children; and a test addressing language development, the WJ IV Tests of Oral Language (Shrank, Mather, & McGrew, 2014b). The Batería IV Woodcock-Muñoz includes a cognitive battery and 14 subtests that produce some of the same stratum III and stratum II scores as the WJ IV COG. More information is provided in Chapter 14. The ECAD's 10 subtests yield a General Intellectual Ability composite like that from the WJ IV COG as well as scores representing early academic and language-based skills. As its early items were designed to be more age-appropriate for young and intellectually disabled children, it appears to be a viable alternative to the WJ IV COG in some instances. The WJ IV Tests of Oral Language includes 12 subtests—9 administered in English and 3 administered in Spanish—and was designed for assessment of listening comprehension, oral expression, and more specific abilities associated with the development of early literacy skills. Those familiar with the WJ III Tests of Cognitive Abilities will recognize a number of subtests that were updated for the WJ IV Tests of Oral Language. The WJ IV COG and its related tests are supported by an online system supporting scoring and report writing. More information about the WJ IV COG can be found here:

Flanagan, D. P., & Alfonso, V. C. (Eds.). (2016). *WJ IV clinical use and interpretation: Scientist-practitioner perspectives.* New York, NY: Academic Press.

Reynolds, M. R., & Niileksela, C. R. (2015). Test review. [Review of the test *Woodcock-Johnson IV Tests of Cognitive Abilities*]. *Journal of Psychoeducational Assessment, 33,* 299–311.

Schrank, F. A., Decker, S. L., & Garruto, J. M. (2016). *Essentials of WJ IV Cognitive Abilities assessment.* Hoboken, NJ: Wiley.

Schrank, F. A., & Wendling, B. J. (2018). The Woodcock-Johnson IV: Tests of Cognitive Abilities, Tests of Oral Language, and Tests of Achievement. In D. P. Flanagan & E. M. McDonough (Eds.), *Contemporary intellectual assessment: Theories, tests, and issues* (4th ed., pp. 383–451). New York, NY: Guilford Press.

Full-Length Multidimensional Nonverbal Intelligence Tests

LEITER INTERNATIONAL PERFORMANCE SCALE—THIRD EDITION

The Leiter-3 (Roid, Miller, Pomplun, & Koch, 2013) covers a much broader age range (ages 3 through 75) but includes half of the subtests of the Leiter-R (see Table 7.10). The Leiter-3 is administered primarily in pantomime via gestures, and examinees respond by moving cubes and foam shapes, making marks with a purple marker, and pointing. Norming data for the Leiter-3 were collected in 2011 using continuous norming procedures. The number of children per norm table block is small for many age groups. In fact, for ages 6 through 20 and ages 13 through 15, these values were less than 30.

The Leiter-3 produces a stratum III composite called the Nonverbal IQ; it is formed from scores from four subtests. None of these subtests had floor or ceiling

Table 7.10. Psychometric Evaluation of the Leiter International Performance Scale—Third Edition (Leiter-3)

Publisher: Stoelting
Publication date: 2013
Age range: 3:0–75:0+

Norming Information

Norm sample N: 1,603 (typical), 548 (atypical)
Date collected: 2011
Number of U.S. states sampled: 36
Characteristics considered: Age, sex, race, ethnicity, socioeconomic status, community size, geographic region, special education or gifted/ESL status
Continuous norming: Yes
Norm block size: Preschool: Insufficient; Elementary: Insufficient; Middle and High: Insufficient

Scores Provided

Stratum III Composite

Nonverbal IQ
- 4 core subtests with no floor or ceiling violations
- Standard score, growth score, PR, normal curve equivalent, CIs, and age equivalent
- Standard score range: 30–170
- Median internal consistency reliability = .96

Stratum II Composites

Nonverbal Memory:
- 2 subtests
- Standard score, growth score, PR, normal curve equivalent, CIs, and age equivalent
- Standard score range: 48–153
- Median internal consistency reliability = .95

Processing Speed:
- 2 subtests
- Standard score, Growth Score, PR, normal curve equivalent, CIs, and age equivalent
- Standard score range: 48–156
- Median internal consistency reliability = .86

Subtests
- 5 subtests yielding scaled scores

Other Information

Item scaling: Item response theory
Bias evaluation: Statistical analysis of item bias
Confidence interval method: Standard error of measurement (*SEE*) centered around the observed score
Electronic scoring and report-writing system: Yes, but scoring only

violations. The average internal consistency reliability value for the Nonverbal IQ was .96 across ages. The Leiter-3 also produces two stratum II composites: Nonverbal Memory and Processing Speed. The average internal consistency reliability value for the Processing Speed composite did not exceed .90, whereas the Nonverbal Memory composites met this standard.

The Leiter-3 has some noteworthy features, including an accompanying battery designed to assess attention and memory and a rating scale for examiners targeting test session behaviors. The Leiter-3 does not include a self-report rating scale and rating scales for parents and teachers targeting social, cognitive, and emotional domains like its predecessor. A scoring program is available. Here is a recent detailed description of the test:

Roid, G. H., & Koch, C. (2017). Leiter-3: Nonverbal cognitive and neuropsychological assessment. In R. A. McCallum (Ed.), *Handbook of nonverbal assessment* (2nd ed., pp. 127–150). New York, NY: Springer.

UNIVERSAL NONVERBAL INTELLIGENCE TEST, SECOND EDITION

The Universal Nonverbal Intelligence Test, Second Edition (UNIT2; Bracken & McCallum, 2016) is a full-length nonverbal intelligence test for ages 5 through 21 that includes six subtests distributed across four batteries (see Table 7.11). The UNIT2 is administered entirely in pantomime via gestures, and examinees respond by moving chips and cubes, drawing lines with a pencil, and pointing. Norming data were collected from 2010 through 2015 across 33 of the United States; the test developers followed a norming plan based primarily on the 2014 U.S. Census. Continuous norming procedures were not noted.

The UNIT2 included 1603 participants in its norming sample. Across its 14-year age span (5–18), it includes 34 norm blocks: for ages 5 to 9, in 3-month blocks (20); for ages 10 to 14, in 6-month blocks (10); and for ages 15 to 18, in 1-year blocks (4). Following through on the division of 1,603 participants by 34 norm blocks, the quotient is 47.14. Using Norfolk et al.'s (2015) evaluative labels, norm blocks appear to meet the minimum standard and can be consider medium in size.

The UNIT2 produces a stratum III composite called the Full Scale. This composite is formed from six subtests with floor violations at ages 6:5 and younger and ceiling violations at ages 13:0 and older. The average internal consistency reliability value for the Full Scale was .98, and its omega hierarchical value was reported to be .81, so 81% of its variance is attributable to psychometric *g* (Benson, Kranzler, & Floyd, 2018).

The UNIT2 also produces additional stratum III composites, including the Standard Battery with Memory, the Standard Battery without Memory, and the Abbreviated Battery. The Standard Battery scores stem from 4 subtests with floor violations at ages 6:5. The Standard Battery with Memory has no ceiling violations, but the Standard Battery without Memory has ceiling violations at ages 13:0 and older. The average internal consistency reliability values for the Standard Batteries with and without Memory were .96 and .98, respectively. Both include two of the same subtests,

Table 7.11. Psychometric Evaluation of the Universal Nonverbal Intelligence Test, Second Edition (UNIT2)

Publisher: PRO-ED
Publication date: 2016
Age range: 5:0–21:11

Norming Information

Norm sample N: 1,603
Date collected: 2010–2015
Census data: 2014
Number U.S. states sampled: 33 states
Characteristics considered: Geographic region, age, gender, race, Hispanic status, exceptionality status, household income, educational attainment of parents.
Continuous norming: Not specified
Norm block size: Preschool: Insufficient; Elementary: Minimum; Middle and High: Medium

Scores Provided

Stratum III Composite

Full Scale Battery
- 6 subtests with floor violations at ages 6:5 and younger and ceiling violations at 13:0 and older
- Yields standard score, PR, and CIs
- Standard score range: 40–164
- Mean internal consistency reliability = .98

Standard Battery w/ Memory
- 4 subtests with floor violations at ages 6:5 and younger and no ceiling violations
- Yields standard score, PR, and CIs
- Standard score range: 40–165
- Mean internal consistency reliability = .96

Standard Battery without Memory
- 4 subtests with floor violations at ages 6:5 and younger and ceiling violations at 13:0 and older
- Yields standard score, PR, and CIs
- Standard score range: 42–164
- Mean internal consistency reliability = .98

Abbreviated Battery
- 2 subtests with floor violations at ages 5:5 and younger and no ceiling violations
- Yields standard score, PR, and CIs
- Standard score range: 45–160
- Mean internal consistency reliability = .97

Stratum II Composites

Memory
- 2 subtests
- Yields standard score, PR, and CIs
- Standard score range: 45–160
- Mean internal consistency reliability = .93

Reasoning
- 2 subtests
- Yields standard score, PR, and CIs
- Standard score range: 48–158
- Mean internal consistency reliability = .96

Quantitative
- 2 subtests
- Yields standard score, PR, and CIs
- Standard score range: 48–158
- Mean internal consistency reliability = .97

Subtests
- 6 subtests yielding scaled score and age equivalents

Other Information

Item scaling: Traditional
Bias evaluation: Bias review panel; statistical analysis of item bias; and comparisons of reliability of scores, factor structure, and mean levels of performance across gender binary, race, and Hispanic status
Confidence interval method: Standard error of the estimated true score (*SEE*) centered around the estimated true score
Electronic scoring and report-writing system: Yes

but the Battery with Memory includes the Symbolic Memory and Spatial Memory subtests (which form the Memory Index), and the Battery without Memory includes the Number Series and Nonsymbolic Quantity subtests (which form the Quantitative Index). The Standard Battery with Memory has demonstrated a slightly lower omega hierarchical value (.73) than the Standard Battery without Memory (.79)—likely due, in part, to the requirement of complex reasoning on the subtests unique to the Battery without Memory (Benson et al., 2018). However, it is unclear to us what test taker characteristics (e.g., mathematics deficits) might lead examiners to select one of these two composites over the Full Scale Battery, which has superior measurement properties.

The Abbreviated Battery is the final stratum III composite. This score is formed from two subtests with floor violations at ages 5:5 and younger and no ceiling violations. The Abbreviated Battery's average internal consistency reliability value was .97. Despite its high reliability, its omega hierarchical value was shown to be .62 (Benson et al., 2018). The UNIT2 also produces three stratum II composite scores targeting memory, reasoning, and quantitative abilities. Average internal consistency reliability values were above .90 for each composite.

The UNIT2 appears to have overcome many limitations of its predecessor and offers, at the time of this book's publication, the most recently normed nonverbal intelligence test. Its Full Scale Battery includes six subtests (two more than the Lieter-3 and Wechsler Nonverbal Scale of Ability), and its stratum III composite from this battery has demonstrated very high reliability and strong g saturation. An electronic scoring and report writing system is available for the UNIT2. It appears to be the preeminent nonverbal intelligence test on the market today. More information about the UNIT2 can be found here:

McCallum, R. S., & Bracken, B. A. (2018). The Universal Nonverbal Intelligence Test—Second Edition: A multidimensional nonverbal alternative for cognitive assessment. In D. P. Flanagan & E. M. McDonough (Eds.), *Contemporary intellectual assessment: Theories, tests, and issues* (4th ed., pp. 567–586). New York, NY: Guilford Press.

Moore, A. F., McCallum, R. S., & Bracken, B. A. (2017). The Universal Nonverbal Intelligence Test: Second Edition. In R. A. McCallum (Ed.), *Handbook of nonverbal assessment* (2nd ed., pp. 105–126). New York, NY: Springer.

WECHSLER NONVERBAL SCALE OF ABILITY

The Wechsler Nonverbal Scale of Ability (WNV; Wechsler & Naglieri, 2006) is a full-length nonverbal intelligence test for ages 4 through 21 that includes six subtests (see Table 7.12). The WNV is administered primarily by using gestures and pictorial directions (although some orally administered instructions are included). Examinees respond by moving cards and puzzle pieces, pointing to cubes, drawing symbols with a pencil, and pointing. The WNV has two age-specific batteries, one for ages 4:0 to 7:11 and another for ages 8:0 to 21:11. Norming data were collected during the early

Table 7.12. Psychometric Evaluation of the Wechsler Nonverbal Scale of Ability (WNV)

Publisher: Psychological Corporation (on release) and Pearson (current)
Publication date: 2006
Age range: 4:0–21:11
Norm blocks: Preschool: Minimum; Elementary: Minimum; Middle and High: Insufficient

Norming Information

Norm sample N: 1,323 (U.S.) and 875 (Canada)
Date collected: Not specified
Census data: 2003 (U.S.)/2001 (Canada)
Number U.S. states sampled: 50, as well as Puerto Rico; standardization occurred simultaneously in Canada
Characteristics considered: Age, sex, race, parental or individual education level, and geographic region
Continuous norming: Not specified
Norm block size: Preschool: Minimum; Elementary: Minimum; Middle and High: Insufficient

Scores Provided

Stratum III Composite

Full Scale Score-4
- 4 subtests (ages 4:0–7:11 and 8:0–21:11); floor violations at ages 4:11 and younger and no ceiling violations
- Yields standard score, PR, and CIs
- Standard score range: 30–160 (ages 4:0–7:11 and 8:0–21:11);
- Mean internal consistency reliability = .91 (ages 4:0–7:11); .91 (ages 8:0–21:11)

Full Scale Score-2
- 2 subtests
- Yields standard score, PR, and CIs
- Standard score range: 40–160
- Mean internal consistency reliability = .91

Subtests
- 6 subtests yielding T scores

Other Information

Item scaling: Traditional
Bias evaluation: Bias review panel
Spanish edition: Yes (Spain)
Confidence interval method: Standard error of the estimated true score (*SEE*) centered around the estimated true score
Electronic scoring and report-writing system: No

---

to mid-2000s across all 50 of the United States, plus Puerto Rico and Canada; the test developers followed a norming plan based on the 2003 U.S. Census and 2001 data collected by Statistics Canada. As noted for other tests, these norms are likely too dated to employ in high-stakes assessment. For most age levels, there are approximately 50 children per norm table block, and at the oldest age levels, they exceed 100. Only at age 16 does this number fall below 30.

The WNV produces a stratum III composite, the Full Scale Score-4; it is formed from scores from four subtests. Only two subtests (i.e., Matrices and Coding) are shared across subtests that form the FSIQ-4 across the younger and older age levels. No subtest floor or ceiling violations are evident. The average internal consistency reliability value across both batteries for the Full Scale Score-4 was .91, which is notably lower than comparable stratum III composites from the Leiter-3 and UNIT2. A two-subtest Full Scale Score-2 is also produced. The WNV does not produce stratum II composite scores. No scoring or report writing system is available. **We recommend that the WNV**

not be used during high-stakes assessments due to the high likelihood of it producing inflated scores. More information about the WNV can be found here:

Brunnert, K. A., Naglieri, J. A., & Hardy-Braz, S. T. (2008). *Essentials of WNV assessment*. Hoboken, NJ: Wiley.

Jaquett, C. M., & Kirkpatrick, B. A. (2017). Wechsler Nonverbal Scale of Ability. In R. A. McCallum (Ed.), *Handbook of nonverbal assessment* (2nd ed., pp. 151–166). New York, NY: Springer.

Naglieri, J. A., & Otero, T. M. (2018). The Wechsler Nonverbal Scale of Ability: Assessment of culturally and linguistically diverse populations. In D. P. Flanagan & E. M. McDonough (Eds.), *Contemporary intellectual assessment: Theories, tests, and issues* (4th ed., pp. 512–532). New York, NY: Guilford Press.

Massa, I., & Rivera, V. (2009). Test review. [Review of the test *Wechsler Nonverbal Scale of Ability*]. *Journal of Psychoeducational Assessment, 27*, 426–432.

Brief Intelligence Tests

KAUFMAN BRIEF INTELLIGENCE TEST, SECOND EDITION

The Kaufman Brief Intelligence Test, Second Edition (KBIT-2; Kaufman & Kaufman, 2004b) is a brief intelligence test for ages 4 through 90 (see Table 7.13). It includes three subtests. Norming data were collected in 2002 and 2003 across approximately 34 of the United States; the test developers followed a norming plan based on the 2001 U.S. Census. These norms are quite dated at the time of publication of this book. Continuous norming procedures were not noted. The numbers of individuals per norm table block across age levels are smaller than those seen for most tests included in this review. For example, there is an average of only approximately 42 children per block across ages 5 through 10 and only approximately 34 across ages 12 to 15. For some age groups, such as 4-year-olds, these values fall below 30.

The KBIT-2 produces a stratum III composite called the IQ Composite; it is formed from three subtests. These subtests have no floor or ceiling violations. The average internal consistency reliability value for the IQ Composite was .93. The KBIT-2 also produces stratum II composites labeled Verbal and Nonverbal, but it is notable that the Nonverbal composite stems from performance on only one subtest. As a consequence, only the Verbal composite demonstrated an average internal consistency reliability coefficient across age groups that was above .90. The KBIT-2 was normed alongside the Kaufman Brief Achievement Test. No electronic scoring and report-writing system is available. Due to the dated norming data (and some limited evidence of it producing inflated scores relative to other brief intelligence tests; Irby & Floyd, 2017), we cannot recommend its routine use. More information about the KBIT-2 can be found here:

Bain, S. K., & Jaspers, K. E. (2010). Test review. [Review of the test *Kaufman Brief Intelligence Test, Second Edition*]. *Journal of Psychoeducational Assessment, 28*, 167–174.

Table 7.13. Psychometric Evaluation of the Kaufman Brief Intelligence Test, Second Edition (KBIT-2)

Publisher: AGS (on release) and Pearson (current)
Publication date: 2004
Age range: 4:0–90:11

Norming Information

Norm sample N: 2,120
Dates collected: May 2002–May 2003
Census data: March 2001
Number U.S. states sampled: 34
Characteristics considered: Age, sex, parental or individual education level, race/ethnicity, and geographic region
Continuous norming: Not specified
Norm block size: Preschool: Insufficient; Elementary: Minimum; Middle and High: Minimum

Scores Provided

Stratum III Composite

IQ Composite
- 3 subtests with no floor or ceiling violations
- Yields standard score, PR, and CIs
- Standard score range: 40–160
- Mean internal consistency reliability = .93

Stratum II Composites

Verbal
- 2 subtests
- Yields standard score, PR, and CIs
- Standard score range: 40–160
- Mean internal consistency reliability = .91

Nonverbal
- 1 subtest
- Yields standard score, PR, and CIs
- Standard score range: 40–160
- Mean internal consistency reliability = .88

Subtests
- 3 subtests yielding T scores

Other Information

Item scaling: Not specified
Bias evaluation: Items were evaluated, but method not specified
Spanish edition: Yes (Spain)
Confidence interval method: Standard error of measurement (*SEM*) centered around estimated true score
Electronic scoring and report-writing system: No

WECHSLER ABBREVIATED SCALE OF INTELLIGENCE—SECOND EDITION

The Wechsler Abbreviated Scale of Intelligence, Second Edition (WASI-II; Wechsler, 2011) is a brief intelligence test for individuals ages 6 through 90. It includes four subtests that parallel those included in other Wechsler intelligence tests, such as the WISC-IV and the WAIS-IV (see Table 7.14). Norming data were collected from 2010 to 2011 across approximately 45 of the United States; the test developers followed a norming plan based on the 2008 U.S. Census and used continuous norming procedures. There are at least 67 individuals per norm table block across age levels; beginning at age 16, there are at least 100 individuals per block.

The WASI-II produces a stratum III composite called the Full Scale–4; this composite is formed from all four subtests. These subtests have no floor or ceiling violations. The average internal consistency reliability value for the Full Scale–4 was .96. The WASI-II also produces a second stratum III composite called the Full Scale–2; it is

Table 7.14. Psychometric Evaluation of the Wechsler Abbreviated Scale of Intelligence—Second Edition (WASI-II)

Publisher: Pearson
Publication date: 2011
Age range: 6:0–90:0

Norming Information

Norm sample N: 2,300
Dates collected: January 2010–May 2011
Census data: March 2008
Number U.S. states sampled: ~45
Characteristics considered: Age, sex, race, parental or individual education level, and geographic region
Continuous norming: Yes
Norm block size: Elementary: Medium; Middle and High: Medium

Scores Provided

Full Scale-4
- 4 subtests with no floor or ceiling violations
- Yields standard score, PR, and CIs
- Standard score range: 40–160
- Mean internal consistency reliability = .96

Full Scale-2
- 2 subtests with no floor or ceiling violations
- Yields standard score, PR, and CIs
- Standard score range: 45–160
- Mean internal consistency reliability = .93

Stratum II Composites

Verbal Comprehension
- 2 subtests
- Yields standard score, PR, and CIs
- Standard score range: 45–160
- Mean internal consistency reliability = .94

Perceptual Reasoning
- 2 subtests
- Yields standard score, PR, and CIs
- Standard score range: 45–160
- Mean internal consistency reliability = .93

Subtests
- 4 subtests yielding T scores

Other Information

Item scaling: Traditional
Bias evaluation: Statistical analysis of item bias
Spanish edition: No
Confidence interval method: Standard error of the estimated true score (*SEE*) centered around the estimated true score
Electronic scoring and report-writing system: No

---

formed by two of the four subtests contributing to the Full Scale-4. The average internal consistency reliability value for the Full Scale-2 (.93) was slightly lower than that for the Full Scale-4, but it was still above the .90 standard. The WASI-II produces two stratum II composites; average internal consistency reliabilities were .93 or higher across ages.

The WASI-II is the most recently updated brief intelligence test, and its stratum III composites demonstrate excellent psychometric properties. No scoring or report writing system is available. More information about the WASI-II can be found here:

Irby, S. M., & Floyd, R. G. (2013). Test review. [Review of the test *Wechsler Abbreviated Scales of Intelligence, Second Edition*]. *Canadian Journal of School Psychology, 28*, 295–299.

McCrimmon, A. W., & Smith, A. D. (2013). Test review. [Review of the test *Wechsler Abbreviated Scale of Intelligence, Second Edition*]. *Journal of Psychoeducational Assessment, 31*, 337–341.

Summary

We developed and revised this book because we believe that advancements in applied measurement of cognitive abilities have produced numerous sophisticated intelligence tests that produce scores that are useful in the practice of psychology and education. The information presented in this chapter supports our contention. For example, most of the tests we have reviewed demonstrate few measurement flaws. Most draw on up-to-date norms that stem from advanced norming procedures and a deep understanding of measurement of cognitive abilities and include an array of subtests that demonstrate few subtest floor and ceiling violations. Their stratum III composites (i.e., IQs), in particular, demonstrate substantial reliability and construct validity evidence, whereas more narrowly focused composite scores tend to demonstrate less evidence of both psychometric properties. There is no doubt that test users today have an array of tests at their disposal to measure the central features of intelligence.

CHAPTER 8

Interpreting Intelligence Test Scores

This chapter focuses on interpretation of a test taker's responses during completion of intelligence tests and the resulting scores. According to the *Merriam-Webster Dictionary*, the verb *interpret* means "to explain or tell the meaning of" and "to present in understandable terms," and the noun *interpretation* means "the act or the result of explanation." The chapter targets interpreting data from qualitative and quantitative perspectives, using interpretive strategies based on an understanding of the nature of and relations between cognitive abilities and relying on the scientific research base. We begin with discussion of general interpretation frameworks. For instructional purposes, we present an array of examples of interpretation strategies in widespread use (including many problematic ones). Finally, we conclude with a model of score interpretation consistent with both prominent theories of cognitive abilities and standards for evidence-based practice.

Foundations for Interpretation

Interpretive frameworks for understanding performance on intelligence tests generally fall along two dimensions. One dimension reflects the contrast between interpretation of *quantitative* and *qualitative* data. Quantitative approaches draw meaning from the numbers derived from assessment. IQs and frequency counts are examples of quantitative data. In contrast, qualitative approaches draw meaning from differences in the kinds of behaviors exhibited by those being tested. Narrative descriptions of odd test behaviors, recordings of vocalizations, and patterns of errors across items are examples of qualitative data.

The second dimension reflects the contrast between *idiographic* and *nomothetic* interpretations (Allport, 1937). Idiographic interpretations are based on understanding the attributes of an individual—all other things being equal. For example, reviewing a child's developmental history and considering the types of errors made during completion of an intelligence test subtest are consistent with the idiographic approach. Further, idiographic interpretations may reflect the comparison of some of an individual's attributes to their other attributes. These interpretations are *intra*-individual in nature (aka person-relative). Nomothetic interpretations are based on comparison of attributes of an individual to a larger group (e.g., a *norm group*). These interpretations are *inter*-individual in nature and reflect the relative standing of the individual on some measurement; they are norm-based. In this section of the chapter, we consider these two dimensions in concert as we organize discussion of interpretive methods and specific score types.

QUANTITATIVE IDIOGRAPHIC APPROACHES

Quantitative and idiographic methods to interpretation are relatively common in the intelligence-testing literature. We offer four examples:

First, scores can be compared in a pairwise fashion. For instance, two subtests contributing to a composite (e.g., the Wechsler Intelligence Scale for Children, Fifth Edition [WISC-V] Similarities and Vocabulary subtests; Wechsler, 2014a) can be compared to determine if differences between them are so large that one might not trust that both converged in measuring the same ability.

Second, composite scores (e.g., the WISC-V's Verbal Comprehension Index and Fluid Reasoning Index) can be compared in the same matter as subtests. With composite scores, usually more interpretive infrastructure is in place to determine whether these differences are not likely to have occurred by chance (e.g., being statistically significant at an alpha rate of .01) and whether these differences are uncommonly large (e.g., occurring at a low base rate of < 10% in the norming sample). Table 8.1 presents an application of this pairwise comparison using five composite scores that range from a standard score of 88 to a standard score of 126. Notice how the two highest composite scores, Composite 2 and Composite 5 (both of which have the same standard score), are significantly higher (despite some differences being negative values) than Composite 1 (by 23 points) and Composite 4 (by 38 points). Composite 1 and Composite 4 also are significantly lower than Composite 3 (by 18 and 33 points, respectively). All of these statistically significant differences occur at a base rate of < 10%.

Third, *profile analysis* refers to an intra-individual or person-relative comparison of scores. When applied to a multifactorial scale (including intelligence test composites and subtests), it may be called *ipsative analysis* or *scatter analysis* (Sattler, 2018). Profile analysis typically has involved calculation of the average across scores under consideration and subsequent comparison of each score to that average. Table 8.2 presents a profile analysis using the same five composite scores included in Table 8.1. You can see how all five composite scores are compared to the average of 11.8 across them. When the difference between a single score and the average of others is substantial, and the score in question is considerably higher than the person's own average score, then it may be interpreted as indicating a *relative strength*. In contrast, when the difference between a score and the average of other scores is substantial and the score in question is markedly lower than average, the subtest score is interpreted as indicating a *relative weakness*. Composite 4 reflects a weakness relative to the others. In some interpretive

Table 8.1. Example Pairwise Composite-Level Comparison Table

Pairwise composite comparisons	Composite standard score 1	Composite standard score 2	Difference between composite scores	Critical value indicating statistical significance of difference (p < .01)	Significant difference	Base rate of difference
C1—C2	103	126	-23	16.4	Y	4.6%
C1—C3	103	121	-18	15.5	Y	9.0%
C1—C4	103	88	15	16.4	N	16.1%
C1—C5	103	126	-23	19.0	Y	9.5%
C2—C3	126	121	5	14.5	N	35.6%
C2—C4	126	88	38	15.5	Y	0.9%
C2—C5	126	126	0	18.1	N	—
C3—C4	121	88	33	14.5	Y	1.4%
C3—C5	121	126	-5	17.3	N	39.2%
C4—C5	88	126	-38	18.1	Y	1.8%

Note: C = Composite.

Table 8.2. Example Composite-Level Profile Analysis Table

Composite name	Composite standard score	Average across composite scores	Difference between composite score and average	Critical value indicating statistical significance of difference (p < .01)	Base rate of difference	Relative strength or weakness
Composite 1	103	112.8	-9.8	13.0	≤ 15%	—
Composite 2	126	112.8	13.2	11.9	≤ 10%	Strength
Composite 3	121	112.8	8.2	10.8	≤ 25%	—
Composite 4	88	112.8	-24.8	11.9	≤ 2%	Weakness
Composite 5	126	112.8	13.2	14.8	≤ 15%	—

schemes, these labels can be applied only if the difference between the average across scores and the score in question is statistically significant (e.g., at $p < .01$) and if such a difference occurs at a low base rate. In the cases of both Composite 2 and Composite 4, these criteria have been met.

Finally, testing-of-limits (also addressed in Chapter 5) refers to administration techniques conducted after completion of a test's standardized administration. For example, if a test taker seems to misunderstand a lengthy question during administration of a subtest targeting cultural knowledge, the examiner could reword that question—clarifying the points of confusion—and determine whether the rewording evokes the response that was targeted. Typically, performance after this testing-of-limits "intervention" is compared informally to that of the original performance—in a qualitative manner. Such methods have been standardized for some tests, such as the WISC-V and the Wechsler Intelligence Scale for Children, Fifth Edition Integrated (WISC-V Integrated; Wechsler & Kaplan, 2014) described in Chapter 6. Recall that follow-up testing with the WISC-V Integrated often includes adaptations to the original WISC-V subtests, such as providing response options in a multi-choice format. Based on the follow-up assessment, WISC-V Integrated scores can be compared to those from the original standardized administration of subtests from the Wechsler scales. Higher WISC-V Integrated scores than those from the original subtests are thought to indicate that the process targeted by the WISC-V Integrated adaptations must have interfered with performance on the original subtest.

QUALITATIVE IDIOGRAPHIC APPROACHES

There is a tradition of applying qualitative idiographic approaches to interpretation of intelligence tests and related assessment instruments. These approaches make use of the extremely rich data that stem from testing sessions. In essence, every purposeful behavior and involuntary response by the person being tested produces qualitative and idiographic data that can be interpreted as meaningful and relevant to the presenting problem. An examinee's trembling voice, shaking hands, and sweat on the brow may indicate excessive anxiety and perhaps fear. Vocalized self-derision (e.g., "I am so stupid; I just can't remember anything") and statements indicating hopelessness (e.g., "I'll never be smart enough") may indicate a depressive disorder. Asking for orally presented items to be repeated may indicate a hearing problem, just as an examinee's moving their face closer to or farther away from words printed on a page may indicate a vision problem. On the other hand, an examinee's behaviors may indicate adaptive strategies. For example, examinees may benefit from counting on their fingers or "writing" a math problem with a finger on the table. Others may benefit from closing their eyes to screen out distractions or using rehearsal strategies when asked to repeat information presented orally.

This interpretive approach is particularly common among clinical neuropsychologists when they are administering and interpreting intelligence tests (Semrud-Clikeman, Wilkinson, & Wellington, 2005). Drawing on Luria's (1973) clinical approach and the methods associated with the Boston Process Approach (Kaplan,

1998), interpretation is based on careful attention to the input and output mechanisms associated with each test item (as discussed in Chapter 5) as well as on the steps that test takers follow and the errors they make when completing items. Kaplan et al. (1999) argued for the potential benefit of these qualitative idiographic interpretations by stating that "finer analysis of problem-solving behaviors and the parsing of component factors contributing to performance provide the examiner with a deeper understanding of the child's level of processing as well for generating tailored, individual interventions" (p. 2).

It is important to consider at least some types of qualitative idiographic data during a comprehensive assessment. Such data aid in understanding the whole test taker and in generating ideas for intervention strategies that might otherwise be overlooked if only quantitative data are considered. The one-on-one interactions between examiner and test taker during testing sessions provide opportunities—perhaps unique ones—for carefully studying behaviors that may be meaningful and relevant to the presenting problem. For example, an adolescent's facial tics or petit mal seizures previously may have been overlooked by teachers, parents, and other adults in their life, and keen observations of the adolescent during testing may lead to identification of associated disorders. The potential of these data for generating hypotheses to be evaluated via more objective and ecologically valid methods makes this approach highly appealing and potentially useful but also fraught with error (as noted later in this chapter).

QUANTITATIVE NOMOTHETIC APPROACHES

Intelligence test interpretation has strong quantitative and nomothetic foundations. As described in detail in Chapter 2, the foundation for understanding and measuring intelligence in the practice of psychology is the normal curve (see Figure 2.1). The normal curve serves as a reasonably accurate model of the frequency distribution of intelligence test scores, particularly for individuals with IQs falling between 70 and 130, which is the vast majority of test takers. Individual differences in cognitive abilities are inferred from the deviation of the individual's performance from the average performance determined from testing large groups of individuals with similar characteristics (e.g., age). For example, we may compare an 8-year-old child's score against the average score of all 8-year-old children on the same test. For intelligence tests, the expectation is that this group—the *norm group*—is large and representative of the population as a whole (see Chapter 5). As a result of this analysis, standardized scores (including deviation IQ scores, scaled scores, T scores, and the like) as well as percentile ranks are interpreted as revealing statistical deviations above and below the average of the norm group and more abstractly, reflecting highly developed or weakly developed cognitive abilities.

QUALITATIVE NOMOTHETIC APPROACHES

Interpretive methods that focus on the kinds of behaviors—not numerical counts of them—exhibited during testing, and that compare these behaviors to some group-based standard, are extremely uncommon. In fact, by definition, all nomothetic approaches are necessarily quantitative; however, a few interpretive approaches come close to representing this category. For example, some tests, such as the WISC-V (Wechsler, 2014a), allow examiners to (1) observe and record test taker's idiosyncratic behaviors, such as requesting item repetition and offering no active response to items; and (2) determine how rare such behaviors are when compared to those observed in the normative group. Interpretive approaches involving base-rate data have the potential to enhance the meaningfulness of more basic qualitative observations.

Advanced Quantitative Interpretive Methods

So far, we have addressed general interpretive frameworks and the most basic score-based interpretations. This section is devoted to the most prominent methods for understanding patterns of quantitative nomothetic data yielded by tests. With the increasing sophistication of intelligence tests—which now yield a greater number of composite scores than ever before (Frazier & Youngstrom, 2007) and target abilities at various levels of the three-stratum theory (Carroll, 1993)—test users may be overwhelmed with the wealth of information yielded by a single test. In order to make sense of all of this information, we offer guidelines consistent with our prior model of intelligence testing and interpretation (Kranzler & Floyd, 2013).

THE SUCCESSIVE-LEVEL APPROACH

A common integrative approach to interpreting scores from an intelligence test has been the *successive-level approach* (Kranzler et al., 2020a). It is a hierarchical interpretive framework in which dissection of patterns of scores begins with the most global score produced by the test and proceeds to the most specific scores and qualitative interpretations of behavior during testing. In one model, Sattler (2018) offered six stages of test interpretation:

1. The norm-based scores representing the full-scale IQ are interpreted from a normative perspective; these scores usually include the deviation IQ score (with its associated confidence interval) and the percentile rank.
2. The norm-based scores from lower-order composites are interpreted in isolation from a normative perspective; these composites might be based on factor-analytic models (and be classified as stratum II abilities, such as the WISC-V's Fluid Reasoning and Processing Speed composites), but they also may be based on divisions of subtests offered by the test's authors that are based on presumed shared features of the subtests and not factor analysis (e.g., the WISC-V's Quantitative Reasoning). In addition, profile analysis of these composites is conducted to determine the presence of relative strengths and weaknesses.

3. Scores from subtests contributing to each lower-order composite are interpreted in isolation from a normative perspective and using profile analysis at the subtest level to evaluate relative strengths and weaknesses.
4. Scores from subtests are compared across the entirety of the test (including in meaningful pairs, such as comparing a measure of acquired knowledge to a measure of the ability to store and retrieve information).
5. Patterns of item-level scores are evaluated within each subtest. As items are typically ordered from easiest to most difficult based on results from large samples of test takers and sophisticated analysis, a pattern of alternating correct and incorrect responses across the items might signal a problem during the testing.
6. A qualitative idiographic analysis of item-level responses and other behaviors during testing (as described previously) during the test sessions is conducted.

Three surveys from the field of school psychology published across the past 20 years have shed some light on the use of the successive-level approach across services provided to children and adolescents. Pfeiffer, Reddy, Kletzel, Schmelzer, and Boyer (2000) showed that school psychologists were uniform in conveying that interpretation of the full-scale IQ, lower-order composite profile analysis, and subtest profile analysis were all useful and relatively equally so. Mean values (on a 5-point scale from 1, *least useful*, to 5, *most useful*) ranged from 3.6 to 4.0 across the levels of analysis, and median values were 4.0. Almost 70% of respondents viewed profile analysis as one of the most useful methods of score interpretation.

More than a decade later, Sotelo-Dynega and Dixon (2014) demonstrated that approximately four-fifths of school psychologists employ multiple interpretive frameworks. In particular, more than two-thirds reported that they used the interpretive frameworks described in test manuals (which are often consistent with the successive-level approach), and about half reported that they specifically followed the successive-level approach. When asked about interpretation of IQs, only 1% stated that they never interpreted them, almost 40% stated that they always interpreted them, and 45% stated that they interpret them only if there was no significant variation in the score profile of contributing scores (which we discuss in more detail later). When asked about interpretation of composite scores, more than half reported that they always interpreted them, and almost 40% said that they reported them only when there was no significant variation among the contributing subtest scores.

In a recent survey, Kranzler et al. (2020a) found that four-fifths of their sample of school psychology practitioners reported that they interpret IQ scores, two-thirds reported that they interpret lower-order composites, and nearly 70% stated that they interpret subtest profiles. However, fewer than a third reported using a model of score interpretation consistent with the successive-level approach, but it is possible that some respondents use most features of the approach but do not embrace the full approach. Across these studies, a wide array of interpretive methods is being recommended, and there is clear continuity across time in application of these interpretive methods. All of this is despite the absence of evidence and the counterevidence associated with the methods, which we address in the second half of this chapter.

EXAMPLES OF TEST-SPECIFIC INTERPRETIVE APPROACHES

Considering these findings across surveys, for instructional purposes (and not as a matter of endorsement), we summarize the interpretive frameworks recommended in the manuals accompanying the three most recently published tests featured in this book. All employ some variant of the successive-level approach.

Example 1

Recall from Chapter 7 that the Detroit Test of Learning Abilities, Fifth Edition (DTLA-5; Hammill et al., 2018) produces a stratum III composite called General Cognitive Ability stemming from 12 subtests. Half of these subtests contribute to each of two "domain" composites: Reasoning Ability and Processing Ability. In addition, the DTLA-5 also produces six "subdomain" composites: Acquired Knowledge, Verbal Comprehension, Nonverbal Problem Solving, Verbal Memory, Nonverbal Memory, and Processing Speed. It includes 12 subtests, which all must be administered to obtain the General Cognitive Ability composites. Hammill et al. (2018) began their focus on interpretation with the following:

> In most cases, the General Cognitive Ability index is the best estimate of an examinee's cognitive ability. Occasionally, however, it can mask important strengths and weaknesses at the domain, subdomain, or subtest level. For example, notable discrepancies between the Reasoning Ability and Processing Ability indexes or among the subdomains can occur. For this reason, we recommend four steps for interpreting the DTLA-5:
>
> Step 1—Interpret the General Cognitive Ability index.
> Step 2—Interpret the domain composite indexes.
> Step 3—Interpret the subdomain composite indexes.
> Step 4—Interpret subtest performance. (p. 35)

This is a classic successive-level interpretive approach with a quantitative, nomothetic focus, as each step requires the test users to consider their norm-referenced scores, confidence intervals, and percentile ranks.

Later, Hammill et al. (2018) described Step 2 in more detail by encouraging test users to conduct an intra-individual pairwise analysis to determine whether the difference between the test's two domain composites is so great (based on statistical significance and base rate information) as to undermine the "representativeness" of the General Cognitive Ability Index and have this index "mask cognitive problems" evident when reviewing other scores. This section ended with a description of the methods required to evaluate pairwise comparisons between subdomain composites scores and complete a profile analysis across subdomains in order to compare each to the test taker's overall cognitive performance. Hammill et al. refined the traditional definition of relative strengths and weaknesses described previously to include concurrent reference to bona fide normative information. They stated:

> The primary purpose of these analyses is to identify relative strengths (scores that are significantly greater than the student's mean score *and* [emphasis in original] all above the normative average) or weaknesses (scores that are significantly lower than the student's mean score *and* [emphasis in original] fall below the normative average). (p. 39)

The final step, focusing on subtest scores, primarily guides test users to complete a profile analysis. Although there are several references to the superiority of the earlier steps of interpretation and their associated scores, details are provided about how to conduct this analysis and determine the statistical significance and base rate of such differences. Hammill et al. (2018) stated that "these variations should also be interpreted within the context of the theory, consideration of strategy use, and other relevant variables" (p. 40), and subsequently, they capitulated in stating that "important decisions about diagnosis and placement should rest primarily on the interpretation of the composite indexes" (p. 41).

Example 2

As a second example, there is the interpretive framework from the Kaufman Assessment Battery for Children, Second Edition Normative Update (KABC-II NU; A. Kaufman & N. Kaufman, 2018). Its stratum III composite scores include the Fluid–Crystallized Index, Mental Processing Composite, and the Nonverbal Index. It produces five stratum II composites aligned with CHC theory—Crystallized Ability, Fluid Reasoning, Long-Term Storage and Retrieval, Short-Term Memory, and Visual-Spatial Processing—but the Luria-based interpretation can also be applied to the same composites. The test includes 18 subtests, but we suspect that most examiners employ only the 10 that produce the Fluid–Crystallized Index.

Test users must piece together segments of the guidelines for interpretation from the Kaufman Assessment Battery for Children, Second Edition (A. Kaufman & N. Kaufman, 2004) with those from the very brief discussion of interpretation included in the KABC-II NU manual supplement (A. Kaufman & N. Kaufman, 2018). The test's interpretive guidelines (A. Kaufman & N. Kaufman, 2004) began with general rules for conducting pairwise comparisons and profile analysis:

> 1. Interpret a scale index only if the child performed consistently on the subtests that compose the scale. Apply the base rate rule of "< 10%" to define "uncommon variability."
> 2. When determining Personal (relative) Strengths and Weaknesses in the child's profile, use the .05 level of statistical significance.
> 3. Each time a significant difference is found, apply the "< 10%" base rate criterion to determine whether the difference is not only statistically significant but also uncommonly large in its magnitude.
> 4. In order for a difference to be considered potentially valuable for diagnostic and educational purposes, it must be both statistically significant and uncommonly large. (pp. 46–47)

As is evident, intra-individual comparisons are front and center from the beginning of this interpretive approach.

Moving to a more standard model of a successive-level approach to interpretation, A. Kaufman and N. Kaufman (2004) encouraged the test user to first consider the norm-referenced scores from the test's Fluid–Crystallized Index, the Mental Processing Composite, or the Nonverbal Index, depending on the design of the test battery, in order to most validly measure general ability. In the newest version of the manual, A. Kaufman and N. Kaufman (2018) offered clear endorsement of these scores while also showing willingness to adapt their guidelines to address recent research (e.g., McGill, 2016). They stated:

> In the KABC-II manual, it was recommended that a global score not be interpreted if the difference between the child's highest scale index and lowest scale index occur to the base rate of less than 10%. . . . It is important to note that interpretability of scores is different from the question of the validity of scores for decision-making purposes. . . . When a global score is described as uninterpretable, it means that the score does not sufficiently describe the child's overall abilities. . . . Uninterpretable does not mean unusable or invalid. . . . A global score is the most valid score to use whenever a single indicator of overall ability is required . . . regardless of its interpretability. The only situation where a person should use a score other than a global score is if there is a clinical reason to suggest that the global score is invalid because of some factors such as a perceptual handicap or a disruption of the testing session. (p. 66)

The second step of their approach involves interpreting the test taker's profile of stratum II composites—both from a normative and a relative perspective. A. Kaufman and N. Kaufman (2004) described this step as proceeding from

1. Determining whether the composites are interpretable, based on consideration of the differences between their contributing subtests,
2. Evaluating the norm-referenced scores for interpretable composites and identifying normative strengths and normative weaknesses (defined as scores at least one standard deviation above and below the population mean, respectively) across composites,
3. Determining relative strengths and weaknesses based on profile analysis and consideration of base rate information. This step also involves pairwise composite comparisons, and
4. Completing supplemental pairwise subtest-to-composite analysis.

As one of the pioneers of the application of profile analysis (A. Kaufman) is the lead author on the KABC-2 batteries, it is no surprise to see all of the complexity in this test's interpretive approach as well as some of the vacillation in recommendations (e.g., for interpreting the KABC-II's global score) across editions of the test.

Example 3

The third example is the interpretive framework suggested for use with the Universal Nonverbal Intelligence Test, Second Edition (UNIT2; Bracken & McCallum, 2016). Recall that the UNIT2 produces its stratum III composite, the Full Scale; two alternate stratum III composites (the Standard Battery with Memory and Standard Battery without Memory composites); and three stratum II composites, Memory, Reasoning, and Quantitative. The UNIT2 includes six subtests. According to its interpretive guidelines, the first step in interpretation is to interpret the Full Scale, the second step is to interpret the Memory, Reasoning, and Quantitative composites, and the third step is to interpret subtest performance. These steps appear to emphasize a norm-based interpretation. However, there are also numerous references to relative comparisons and profile analysis and provision of resources to evaluate the statistical significance and base rate criteria for score differences. For example, Bracken and McCallum (2016) asserted the following:

> We recommend interpretation at the most global level possible. However, if there is significant and clinically meaningful variability within the global scores, individual subtest variability must be addressed. (p. 76)

Further, the manual includes content that offers interpretive hypotheses based on statistically significant and rare differences between the Memory, Reasoning, and Quantitative composite scores as well as a table offering descriptions of primary and secondary abilities measured by subtests.

General Guidelines for Interpretation of Intelligence Test Scores

In order to evaluate the viability of the successive-level approach and promote evidence-based practices, we encourage test users to attend to three psychometric considerations: reliability, generality, and predictive and incremental validity.

Reliability. Following the principles discussed in Chapter 5, we should only interpret scores that have demonstrated high levels of reliability (.90 or higher). We also know that scores closest to the item level (item-level scores and subtest scores) should not attract our attention to the extent that scores stemming from aggregation across numerous items and several subtests should. Composite scores that exceed minimal standards for internal consistency and test–retest reliability should be the focus of our attention.

As apparent for every intelligence test evaluated in Chapters 6 and 7, stratum III composites (i.e., IQs) yield the highest reliability coefficients, followed by stratum II composites. Because reliability constrains validity, the most reliable scores from intelligence tests will yield the most dividends for predicting educational, occupational, and other life outcomes and addressing the most pressing referral concerns. Examiners should be particular about which scores they interpret, and they should feel comfortable ignoring scores if they do not meet the highest standards of reliability. Further, problems with the reliability of each score make profiles of the same scores particularly prone to misinterpretation—especially considering that the patterns evident in these profiles tend not to be reliable across time (Borsuk, Watkins, & Canivez, 2006; Styck, Beaujean, & Watkins, 2019; Watkins & Smith, 2013). Just because the test or its scoring system produces a score (and score profiles), examiners need not interpret these results or communicate these findings in their oral or written reports.

Generality. In a manner similar to reliability, we know that when scores from numerous items and multiple subtests are aggregated, the influences of specific item content and specific mental processes largely cancel out one another. As a result, more general abilities are measured. In contrast, based on our perceptions and what appears to be common sense, intelligence test subtests appear to measure abilities in very specific ways. For example, a subtest requiring test takers to respond to words presented orally by providing definitions of these words orally seems to measure vocabulary knowledge versus a more general ability associated with thinking abstractly and problem solving. Other subtests also may appear to measure the vocabulary knowledge via different methods, such as having the test taker (1) hear a word presented orally and point to a picture that represents the word or (2) view pictures and name what they depict. These related subtests may share a common element—regardless of the assessment method used—that produces higher or lower scores across individuals. For example, that common element may, in fact, be vocabulary knowledge, which is a stratum I (or narrow) ability. These subtest scores also tend to be highly correlated with subtests measuring knowledge of cultural phenomena and the ability to reason using words. The vocabulary knowledge subtests and other related subtests measuring breadth of knowledge seem to tap into a more general ability that could be called Crystallized Intelligence at stratum II. In this case, the individual subtest characteristics—and even vocabulary knowledge more generally—reflect only pieces of the larger puzzle, because they are more specific than this stratum II (or broad) ability that produces higher and lower scores across similar subtests.

As described in Chapter 1, it is a known fact that almost every measure of cognitive abilities tends to be positively related to most every other measure of cognitive abilities, which suggests that they are measuring the same thing to some degree. How can this be? We can see how vocabulary knowledge subtests measure the same thing and how, on a broader level, Crystallized Intelligence subtests measure the same thing, but how is it possible that vocabulary knowledge subtests measure the same thing as subtests requiring the construction of designs with blocks or the identification of abstract patterns across images on a page? It's *uncommon sense*: Believing the evidence produced through more than 100 years of scientific research (without necessarily experiencing it; see Lilienfeld, Ammirati, & David, 2012) allows us to conclude that there is an extremely general superfactor, psychometric *g*, that underlies score variation across all such subtests. As is apparent in Chapter 6's presentation of the *g* saturation of the WISC-V subtests, intelligence test subtests that look vastly different apparently are measuring the same things to a surprising degree.

Predictive and incremental validity. The ability at the highest level of generality frequently is the largest and most powerful influence on intelligence test scores, and as described in Chapter 2, scores best representing this ability (stratum III composites) tend to produce the strongest relations with important societal outcomes. As we focus on more and more specific abilities or on differences between and among scores rather than this general ability, the explanatory and predictive power afforded to these interpretations decreases dramatically. In fact, for most quantitative idiographic approaches to interpretation, such as comparison of lower-order composites, there is no validity evidence at all—let alone predictive validity evidence—informing their meaning.

From the vantage point of the CHC theory, Zaboski, Kranzler, and Gage's (2018) meta-analysis focused on the relations between cognitive ability scores and concurrent academic achievement scores in the areas of reading and mathematics revealed that predictive relations often attributed to lower-order cognitive abilities actually were misattributions. Their predictive power often comes from their g saturation, and sophisticated analyses are needed to see this pattern. Zaboski et al. (2018) wrote,

> For the overall sample, g had by far the strongest relations across all domains of academic achievement. On average, g explained more than 50% of the variance in achievement, which was more than all of the broad cognitive abilities taken as a whole. . . . The relations between psychometric g and academic achievement can be described as large. Although the vast majority of relations between the broad abilities and achievement had CIs [confidence intervals] that did not contain zero, their effect sizes were generally small. For the total sample, only one or two broad abilities had what can be classified as medium effects per achievement domain. (p. 50)

Based on these and decades of other results, test users should be attuned to the fact that psychometric g most likely is driving the explanatory and predictive power of the IQs as well as most all other intelligence test scores that are substantially g saturated.

Another crucial issue regarding the usefulness of intelligence tests concerns incremental predictive validity. Incremental predictive validity addresses the question of whether scores on a test increase the prediction of important external criteria over other scores on the same test or scores on other established measures. In the typical incremental validity study, scores are entered in a predetermined order in hierarchical (sequential) multiple regression. Evidence of incremental validity is found if the scores entered later in the model explain a significant amount of variance beyond that already accounted for by the scores entered first, as reflected in a statistically significant semi-partial correlation or change in R-squared (ΔR^2). If the scores entered later in the regression analysis (a) do not result in a statistically significant improvement in the prediction of a criterion over and above that explained by the initially entered score or (b) explain a statistically significant but trivial amount of additional unique variance, then the scores entered later are deemed to lack incremental validity based on their redundancy with other scores.

Over the years, a number of studies have been conducted on the incremental validity of different intelligence tests in the prediction of academic achievement, which arguably is the most important predictive outcome for intelligence tests (e.g., Canivez,

2013; Freberg, Vandiver, Watkins, & Canivez, 2008; Glutting, Watkins, Konold, & McDermott, 2006; Kranzler, Benson, & Floyd, 2015). For example, Canivez (2013) found that composite scores on the Wechsler Adult Intelligence Scale-Fourth Edition (WAIS-IV; Wechsler, 2008) rarely accounted for more than 2% of the variance in academic achievement beyond that explained by the overall score and often less than 1%. Kranzler et al. (2015), in contrast, used orthogonal factor scores derived from a bifactor model to examine the predictiveness of latent constructs measured by the WAIS-IV. They found that, in addition to the ubiquitous effect of g, Crystallized Intelligence was the only ability to explain more than 15% of the variance and only for achievement in reading, spelling, and oral communication skills. Results of their study, therefore, are consistent with Zaboski et al.'s meta-analysis insofar as only g and Crystallized Intelligence importantly are related to academic achievement, and for Crystallized Intelligence only in some areas of achievement.

Interpretation of Scores in Isolation

Keeping reliability, generality, and predictive and incremental validity in mind, we now consider scores at each level of interpretation.

STRATUM III COMPOSITES

The successive-level approach begins the right way, as consideration of reliability, generality, and predictive and incremental validity lead us to conclude that the stratum III composites (IQs) should be the first and primary focus of interpretation. Wasserman (2019) asserted:

> Now more than a century after its derivation, Spearman's (1904) g appears to represent near consensus thinking in intelligence . . . Multiple meta-analyses have shown g predicts academic and occupational performance better than any other psychological variable. . . . Prominent scholars have described g as "one of the most replicated results in psychology" (Deary, 2012a, p. 146), as "one of the most central phenomena in all of behavioral science, with broad explanatory powers" (Jensen, 1998a, p. xii), as saturating "almost all human performance (work competence) dispositions" (Meehl, 1990, p. 124), and as sitting at "the heart of the prediction of real-life performances that is possible from tests" (R. L. Thorndike, 1994, p. 150). (p. 215)

It is easy for test users (and other consumers of test results) to equate the scores yielded by the tests with the latent variables they represent. IQs as measures of psychometric g are no different. Of course, they are not perfect representations of g, as random error sullies every applied measurement in psychology and education. However, there is accumulating evidence from both validity evidence based on internal relations, in the form of hierarchical omega estimates, and validity evidence based on relations with other variables, in the form of *g* loadings from joint confirmatory factor analytic studies, that IQs represent the latent variable, psychometric *g*, superbly well (Canivez & McGill, 2016; Farmer, Floyd, M. Reynolds, & Kranzler, 2014; Gignac & Watkins, 2013; M. Reynolds, Floyd, & Niileksela, 2013; M. Reynolds & Keith, 2017; Watkins, 2017). Thus, you typically are standing on solid ground when considering an individual's normative level of performance on IQs.

STRATUM II COMPOSITES

Intelligence tests produce a greater number of lower-order composite scores than ever before. In fact, they grew increasingly popular during the 2000s, due in part to efforts to overcome the limitations of subtest-level interpretation (e.g., McDermott & Glutting, 1997; Watkins & Canivez, 2004). Now, it is impossible to ignore stratum II composites, as they dominate the tables we developed for Chapters 6 and 7. In some cases, intelligence tests produce composite scores that are greater in number than the subtests they include. To many, it may seem harmless to apply nomothetic quantitative interpretive strategies to these scores as they appear to paint a fuller picture of test performance than would focusing on only the IQ. We, however, see at least four practical and psychometric problems that give us pause about doing so.

First, most of these composites are formed from limited sampling of the ability domain they are intended to measure. Most are formed from two subtests, some are formed from three subtests, and it is exceptionally rare to see four subtests contributing to a stratum composite. This is in stark contrast to most stratum III composites (see tables in Chapter 6 and 7) that by design require heterogeneous sampling across numerous ability indicators.

Second, the reliability of stratum II composites tends to be lower than those of their stratum III counterparts, in part due to their stemming from fewer subtests. The internal consistency reliability of many stratum II composites stemming from two subtests are at or above the lower-end standard of .90 but usually below the standard of .95. In general, their reliability has improved across the past couple of decades, but even today, some such composites do not meet the reliability standard.

Third, as noted previously, it is easy to tie the label applied to a score to the latent ability it was designed to measure, or even better, what it seems to measure. Surely the WISC-V (2014a) Vocabulary subtest measures vocabulary knowledge, right? In a sense, this is a "call it like I see it" decision based on content validity evidence. In the case of stratum II composites, doing so seems particularly problematic. In the minds of many, when they refer to specific abilities, they are considering influences on test scores that are independent of psychometric *g* (see Chapter 1). Bifactor models are consistent with this perspective. In fact, when interpretation targets specific abilities, the influence of psychometric *g* on test scores is construct-irrelevant (Gustafsson, 2002; Schneider, 2013). According to Canivez and Youngstrom (2019),

> Replicated research has consistently shown that portions of CHC broad ability variance are substantially smaller than *g* contributions; thus, attributions

of such CHC-based scores representing broad abilities are misappropriated. If CHC is correct, one might expect that substantially larger portions of broad factor scores (Stratum II) ought to be based on that factor and not *g*. It may be that our present tests poorly measure anything supplemental to *g*, so it is difficult to determine exactly what their unique contributions are. (p. 240)

In general, specific-ability variance estimates for stratum II composites tend to be relatively low when compared to total variance and general factor variance; those measures that tend to be strongly influenced by the *g* factor tend to have weaker specific-ability estimates. Basically, very few subtests and only some composite scores measure a sufficient amount of specific-ability variance to warrant their interpretation as indicators of those more specific abilities. Consider Figure 8.1, which extends our discussion of Spearman's two-factor model in Chapter 1. Based largely on Schneider's (2013) results and informed by others (Floyd, McGrew, Barry, Rafael, & Rogers, 2009; Maynard, Floyd, Acklie, & Houston, 2011), this figure demonstrates how five composite scores (such as those from the WISC-V) are influenced by the general factor (*g*), specific abilities, as well as error. We see that the composites display varying yet substantial degrees of *g* saturation. Assuming that Composite 2 was designed to measure Fluid Reasoning, per se, we are not surprised that it is 65% *g* saturated, and assuming that Composite 4 was designed to measure Processing Speed, per se, its low *g* saturation is also expected. Other composites are reasonably equally *g* saturated (at or around 50%). In most cases, this ever-present general-ability variance is magnified for students most likely to struggle in school settings (M. Reynolds, 2013). When we consider that unique features of each composite (uniqueness, u) and random error (e) influence each composite (in a way that theoretically cannot be disentangled), we can assume that the remaining reliable variance associated with each composite (outside the shaded circle and between its border and the straight line breaking up the rectangle) is what was

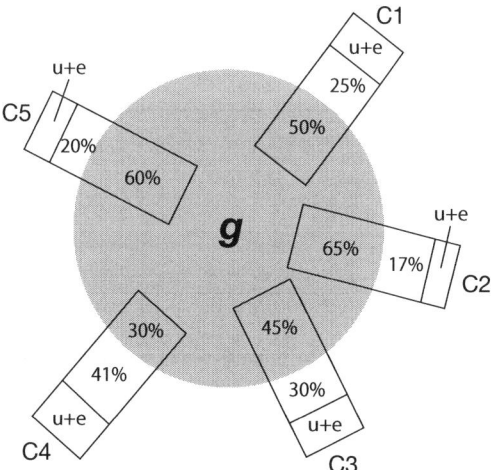

Figure 8.1. Shared, reliable specific, and other variance influencing five composite scores (based, in part on Schneider, 2013). All values represent the percentage of total variance. g = general intelligence, C = composite, u = uniqueness, and e = error.

targeted by the composite, the stratum II ability. Across the composites, these range from 17% to 41% and are smaller in every case than the *g* saturation in every case except for Composite 4.

Finally, increasing evidence is that many of the stratum II composites offered by the most prominent intelligence tests are not supported by sufficient validity evidence based on internal structure. These structural challenges indicate that the factors that these composites are designed to represent do not always hold up across independent analyses, clinical samples, and methods (see, e.g., Benson, Beaujean, McGill, & Dombrowski, 2018). Based on these findings, Canivez and Youngstrom (2019) asserted that

> clinicians are very likely providing interpretations of scores and making inferences about individuals' performances that are not empirically supported and may well lead to erroneous clinical decisions. Interpreting extra scores increase the chances of false positive (Type I) errors. . . . Interpreting scores with inadequate specification or reliable variance at best attenuates the power to detect differences (increasing the Type II error rate); perhaps more problematic, however, is that the numerals provided for scores related to these factors do not actually represent measurement of any attribute—they are only indicative of some statistical chimera that is irrevocably tied to a specific intelligence test. (p. 238)

Wasserman (2019) recently highlighted these finding and noted that the field of ability testing has not yet found its footing in measuring these stratum II abilities, due in part to an overreliance on factor-analytic methods.

We know that interpretation is on shaky ground when our focus is on stratum II abilities, due to these practical and psychometric issues. What at least partially drives our continued reference to and interpretation of these composites is that they seem to paint a more detailed picture of an individual's profile of cognitive abilities than by focusing on only the IQ. We see only three options for interpreting scores as representing specific abilities, and all three have serious limitations:

1. *Follow the current practice of interpreting sufficiently reliable composite scores stemming from two or more subtest scores as representing specific abilities.* This practice fails to consider that general factor variance in these composite scores is construct-irrelevant when the composite targets specific abilities. This approach also relies on trust that the targeted stratum II abilities (modeled here as reliable specific variance) are replicable. In sum, this method is a very crude way to examine individual differences in specific cognitive abilities; it works primarily if the general factor is ignored during interpretation of these composites.
2. *Interpret scores from sufficiently reliable composites (stemming from two or more subtest scores) in a profile of related scores using a profile analysis. When composite scores differ significantly from the profile mean, it indicates that strengths or weaknesses in specific cognitive abilities are at play, as they are presumed to be operating independent of psychometric g. If they are strengths or weaknesses, place more emphasis on them during interpretation.* This practice is far less common than the first, and it has some potential for carefully formulated profile analysis. However, it is limited in several

ways (as addressed more fully later in this chapter). Because such composites tend to vary in the influence of the general factor on them and in their reliability, the amount of variance associated with specific abilities in each composite also varies substantially. One composite score may appear to be significantly different from the others, indicating a specific-ability strength or weakness, but this may be due in large part to its weaker reliability than the others. Further, (1) these composite strengths and weaknesses are likely to be unstable across time (as seen with subtests) and (2) we have no scientific evidence of benefits garnered by using this interpretive practice.

3. *Create specific ability factor scores (removing the construct-irrelevant influences of the g factor on them) and interpret them after they are norm-referenced.* We support the creation of such composite scores that represent separate abilities from varying strata of cognitive abilities (e.g., stratum III, stratum II, etc.) and are excited about recent advances in actualizing this promise (Benson, Kranzler, & Floyd, 2016; Kranzler et al., 2015; Schneider, 2013). At present, however, no intelligence tests produce composites representing specific abilities in this manner. We also suspect that the reliability of these scores will tend to be inadequate because they stem from such small slices of test score variance, but confidence interval values could be applied to them (Schneider, 2013). We remain open-minded about the potential of this method but await the development of a strong body of validity evidence before recommending that it be applied during high-stakes testing.

INTERPRETATION OF SUBTESTS

The successive-level approach and others like it commonly recommend interpreting intelligence test subtests. As noted previously in this chapter and made manifest clearly in Chapter 6, subtests almost always demonstrate reliability that is far inferior to those of IQs and stratum II composites.

Further, subtests have two additional weaknesses: First, as mentioned in Chapter 4, most subtests are scaled (with scaled scores or T scores), so that the measurement of ability is less precise than deviation IQ scores. Second, despite their inferior reliability, confidence interval values are applied to subtests extremely rarely; such values would allow for some control over the influences of error on their scores.

For all of these reasons, subtest scores should not be the focus of interpretation. Norm-referenced subtest scores should be interpreted as indicators of broader and more general abilities—as contributors to IQs and stratum II composites—and not as representations of specific skills or narrow abilities per se.

INTERPRETATION OF ITEM-LEVEL RESPONSES AS INDICATING PROCESSES

The successive-level approach may require the examiner to interpret patterns of item-level responses that are consistent with the qualitative idiographic approaches.

As we have asserted elsewhere (Floyd & Kranzler, 2012), these interpretations, when applied to intelligence tests, are not supported by enough evidence to recommend their routine use for high-stakes decisions. In fact, ideographic interpretation methods designed to identify problems associated with cognitive processes leave clinicians at great risk for errors in interpretation. Many of the inferences about cognitive processes drawn from task-level performance of test takers, like those described by Kaplan et al. (1999) earlier in this chapter, are intuitive and idiosyncratic to those developing them and without a strong theoretical or empirical base. Such associations are worrisome considering the evidence of heuristics, biases, and decision-making errors known to affect qualitative interpretations. There is also ample evidence to expect (a) that there is within-person variability in problem-solving (i.e., individual test takers use a variety of problem-solving strategies) across items within a subtest and (b) there is between-person variability in item-level problem-solving strategies based, in part, on ability level (i.e., individual test takers with higher ability use different strategies to answer the same items than those with lower ability; see Lohman, 2000). Finally, we know (from Chapter 4) that individual items have well-known problems with reliability. As a result, intelligence tests have not been designed to support such item-level interpretation, so there is a veritable absence of validity evidence supporting these practices. Interpreting patterns of item-level responses from intelligence tests seems rife with error and hardly worth the effort.

Engaging in Score Comparisons

A central feature of the successive-level approach and others like it is the comparison of scores. This includes comparisons of composites scores to other composite scores and subtests to other subtests in a pairwise fashion. Sometimes this comparison is guided by the theoretical relations between the constructs they target. For example, the WISC-V (2014a) Digit Span subtest could be compared to the Picture Span subtest ostensibly to compare verbal working memory to visual working memory; and the KABC-II NU (A. Kaufman & N. Kaufman, 2018) Crystallized Ability composite and the Long-Term Retrieval composite logically could be compared to contrast a test taker's prior storage of knowledge and their ability to store new information. Other times, these comparisons appear to be completed primarily in hopes that they generate useful conclusions of some sort. For example, all three stratum III composites from the WISC-V (Full Scale IQ, General Ability Index, and Nonverbal Index), and all three KABC-II NU stratum III composites (Fluid–Crystallized Index, Mental Processing Composite, and the Nonverbal Index) can be compared statistically. When numerous pairwise comparisons are made across scores from a test, the likelihood of identifying a meaningless difference (a false positive) greatly increases; false positives are likely to attract our attention but provide no meaningful information. For this reason, some (e.g., Sattler, 2018) advocate for profile analysis as an alternative to the serial pairwise comparisons—although they effectively are variants of the same method.

Profile analysis of subtests designed to identify strengths and weaknesses relative to the test taker's own average performance has received substantial research attention over the years. Despite the intuitive appeal of conducting a profile analysis of scores, accumulated evidence reveals that this practice is fraught with error and offers no practical benefits (for a review, see McGill, Dombrowski, & Canivez, 2018; and Watkins, Glutting, & Youngstrom, 2005). Unlike stratum III composites, patterns of relative strengths and relative weaknesses for individuals tend to have poor stability across time (Borsuk et al., 2006; Styck et al., 2019; Watkins & Smith, 2013), and relative strengths and relative weaknesses are quite common and almost certainly not indications of learning problems (McGill, 2019; McGill, Styck, Palomares, & Hass, 2016). Plus, the results of profile analysis do not improve diagnostic accuracy and do not help with treatment planning. Not only are patterns of subtests ineffective for group differentiation (e.g., those with and without specific learning disability), but the average profile within any diagnostic category does not characterize the profiles of every member of that group. Specific profiles of a particular diagnostic group also may be characteristic of members in other groups. The most salient criticisms of subtest-level profile analysis also apply to composite score profiles. Composite-level profile analysis methods have been evaluated far less frequently than those at the subtest level, but at present, very little evidence suggests that the subtest or composite score differences on intelligence tests can be used to improve decisions about individuals.

As noted earlier in this chapter, pairwise comparisons of lower-order composite scores and profile analysis of composite and subtests scores also have been conducted to determine the "validity" or "interpretability" of stratum III composites. When statistically significant score differences between constituent composites are found or substantial profile variation (aka "scatter") is evident, one longstanding practice has been to discount the stratum III composite and focus instead on interpreting the individual's profile of composite or subtest scores. In fact, Hale and Fiorello (2001) argued that one should "never interpret the global IQ score if there is significant scatter or score variability" (p. 132). Research, however, has failed to support this contention that the IQ is any less predictive of academic achievement or otherwise less construct valid when significant variability occurs among its constituent composite or subtest scores (Daniel, 2007; Freberg, Vandiver, Watkins, & Canivez, 2008; Kotz, Watkins, & McDermott, 2008; McGill, 2016; Watkins, Glutting, & Lei, 2007). Thus, research supports the interpretation of the IQ even when the scores contributing to it are not consistent. Considering it "invalid" or "uninterpretable" appears to be an antiquated and unfounded practice. The same patterns also appear to be emerging when considering the "validity" or "interpretability" of stratum II composites (Schneider & Roman, 2018).

Waves of Interpretation

So, what can be done, seeing these limitations made manifest across a sizable body of evidence? These results, in a way, seem to contradict our claim that measurement and understanding of cognitive abilities in applied psychology never have been stronger. Still, we see progress.

Across a series of chapters, Kamphaus, Winsor, Rowe, and Kim's (2018) described four waves of test interpretation:

The first wave reflected the quantification of the general level of intelligence. During this wave of interpretation, a focus on psychometric *g* as measured by IQs was predominant, and individuals were placed in rank order primarily on a single scale measuring this ability.

With advancing technology in the form of intelligence test subtests that each yielded norm-referenced scores, the second wave of interpretation emerged. It was characterized by clinical analysis of patterns of subtest scores in addition to the IQ, and idiographic and qualitative interpretations were highlighted. More specifically, subjective and idiosyncratic analysis of subtest profiles guided by psychoanalytic theory and clinical lore typified this approach.

The third wave highlighted advances in psychometrics that guided (1) the application of factor analysis to test interpretation and (2) profile analysis employing subtest scores. In particular, this wave was reflected in greater consideration of the shared measurement properties of subtests (used to form specific-ability composites) and their unique components, as well as the evidence supporting the interpretation of profiles of IQ, composite, and subtest scores.

The fourth wave reflected the application of research-based models of cognitive abilities to the development of tests and score interpretation. The most prominent models guiding the fourth wave have stemmed from the theoretical models of Carroll (1993) and Horn (1991). Despite their differences, these two models have been integrated in the Cattell-Horn-Carroll (CHC) theory (as described in Chapter 1), and it has been promoted as the most well-supported and sophisticated psychometric model of intelligence (Newton & McGrew, 2010; Schneider & McGrew, 2018). Further, authors of prominent intelligence tests developed tests and produced scores representing a number of the broad abilities described in the CHC theory.

We agree with Kamphaus et al. (2018) and others that this fourth wave, and the convergence of research and professional opinion on models such as the CHC theory, afford the test user at least three benefits:

First, it is possible that scores from all intelligence tests can be interpreted using these models. Ideally, test users would not rely primarily on test-specific models that vary substantially from one test to another.

Second, seeing that these different intelligence tests are likely to measure at least some of the same abilities, especially psychometric *g*, test users select those tests that best meet their needs based on the age level and limitations of their typical clients, the clients' referral concerns, and other individual preferences.

Third, they may benefit from education focused on general theoretical model of cognitive abilities and from a subset of books that promote its application to test score interpretation.

The KISS Model in a Fifth Wave

We believe that a fifth wave of interpretation builds on the strengths of the fourth wave and that it will rely on evidence-based and empirically supported interpretations that go beyond primarily factor-analytic research, which have left the field wanting (Canivez & Youngstrom, 2019). Interpretation in this wave will promote more selective and focused intelligence testing. Consistent with the standards for validity evidence cited in Chapter 4, this wave may require test users to apply only those interpretations that are based on highly focused scientific evidence. This wave probably will lead to a vastly restrictive successive-level approach that includes, at most, two levels of interpretation.

The primary level is that of stratum III scores (aka IQs). When lower-order (e.g., stratum II) composite scores are sufficiently reliable, supported by high-quality scientific research indicating their validity (including incremental validity), and address specific questions targeted during the assessment (e.g., a specific knowledge deficit due to deprivation and a talent in the visual-spatial ability domain), they also may be employed. Lower levels of interpretation will be cast aside in favor of (1) instruments designed to measure some of the constructs targeted in high-inference interpretation of subtest profiles and item-level responses and (2) interpretation of only scores supported by a large body of reliability and validity evidence. Item-level scores and scores from intelligence test subtests will not be interpreted. Consistent with the sea change that has led to disregard of idiographic qualitative interpretations of projective tests, the fifth wave may bring about the end of the wide-ranging qualitative idiographic "clinical interpretations" of intelligence test scores that have lingered since their heyday in the second wave (Beaujean & Benson, 2019a).

In contrast to the common interpretive strategies we reviewed in this chapter, we offer the KISS model to guide interpretation in a fifth wave. The acronym KISS, in this case, stands for "Keep it simple, scholar." We think that it represents empirically supported best practices in the field. In particular, it aids in focusing interpretation on scores that are supported by the strongest body of reliability and validity evidence and that stem from test administrations that eliminated (or greatly reduced the influence of) confounds undermining the validity of the results for individual test takers. In doing so, it helps to eliminate features of the test results that may, in fact, lead to patterns of decision-making errors. According to Canivez (2019),

> When including unreliable or irrelevant information in the assessment process, predictions or classifications will suffer from a "dilution effect" whereby predictions are less accurate (Nisbett, Zukier, & Lemley, 1981). Thus, test scores and comparisons that are unsatisfactory in reliability or validity estimates ought not to be considered and this has implications for test selection and test score reporting (i.e., reporting only scores and comparisons that are psychometrically sound). (p. 196)

The KISS model involves 8 steps:

1. **The examiner considers if an intelligence test should be employed during the assessment.** Although an intelligence test may be required as part of regulations and guidelines that examiners must follow, they should ask, Why include an intelligence test in the assessment at all? Is it to eliminate the hypothesis that the test taker has exceptionally low or exceptionally high general intelligence in the absence of other indicators of such? Is it to determine whether a test taker demonstrates the

features of someone with a mental health disorder or a student in need of special education services—including intellectual disability—or intellectual giftedness? Answers to these questions can guide decision making later during this process, and they may lead examiners to determine that other assessment methods (e.g., academic achievement tests and behavior ratings scales reflecting behavior excesses and adaptive deficits) should be the heart of the assessment.

2. **The examiner completes preliminary screening to identify potential confounds prior to administering an intelligence test.** The examiner should complete interviews with parents, caregivers, and teachers; review records of prior formal screenings (e.g., vision, hearing, and speech screenings) and other services provided to the test taker (occupational and physical therapy and articulation therapy); complete the Screening Tool for Assessment (STA) rating forms and the STA Direct Screening Form (see Chapter 5); and engage in any other method of information gathering—prior to testing—to determine whether intelligence testing is likely to be undermined by interfering factors.

3. Using information from steps 1 and 2, **the examiner selects the most appropriate intelligence test.** They should sort through the reliability and validity evidence most relevant to the referral concern (based on the test taker's age and suspected ability level; see Chapter 4), and they should review the content and response processes involved in completing and scoring each subtest contributing to the IQ to identify potential confounds. They select the most evidence-based test and resultant score (or scores) that should produce the least biased outcomes for the individual to be tested. They develop relevant accommodations to eliminate problems with test access and do not hesitate to select alternative scores to represent general intelligence when the test's primary measure of general intelligence is inferior in some way for the individual to be tested.

4. **The examiner completes the testing.** They strive to prevent potential construct-irrelevant influences on test performance during testing, and they recognize and note when such problems surface.

5. **The examiner determines whether invalidity, in the form of construct-irrelevant influences, undermined test results.** They focus on problems with access at the level of the subtest. In the case of invalidity, the examiner employs alternate scores from the same test that remove the subtest or subtests that are invalid or completes follow-up testing with another test.

6. **When the examiner is confident in the accuracy of the results, they interpret the most reliable stratum III composite**, considering its confidence intervals, that is supported by validity evidence for the purposes it was used.

7. With caution, **the examiner reviews norm-referenced stratum II composite scores that meet reliability and validity standards to identify normative strengths and normative weaknesses.** (What is a normative strength or weakness is arbitrary, and we propose that it be defined by scores at or beyond the 90th percentile and at or below the 10th percentile, respectively, considering confidence interval bands.) The purpose is to determine whether these results somehow might be relevant to the goals of the assessment or to the development of interventions to follow. Normative strengths may reveal intense practice associated with an ability

area or a talent through which general intelligence has been channeled. Normative weaknesses (in the absence of construct-irrelevant influences) may reveal types of situations (e.g., involving complex language or visual-spatial stimuli) in which the test taker does not perform at a level commensurate with peers that may be due to lack of exposure to similar situations or personal deficits. Due to the limitations of these stratum II composites scores, their interpretation should (a) occur after centering the interpretive focus on the stratum III composite; (b) be supported by a body of evidence stemming from reports of others, self-reports, permanent products, other test results (included additional testing if necessary), and observational data; and (c) be acted on cautiously, as the results may not be stable over time.

8. **The examiner prepares a psychological report and descriptions of results** for stakeholders that primarily focuses on the results from the stratum III composite. See Chapter 10.

Summary

We understand the motives of those trying to obtain the most information possible from intelligence tests; these tests yield a wealth of information. We recognize that qualitative information from intelligence tests (a) can seem to accurately reflect the patterns of strengths and weaknesses displayed by test takers in their everyday lives and (b) may be seen as important to inform effective interventions. We recognize the rationale for reviewing subtest task requirements and inferring what cognitive processes and abilities they measure; we see value in labeling subtests according to these inferences; and we feel that sufficiently reliable composite scores may be useful to interpret. All of this information, however, cannot be treated equally during interpretation, and we must evaluate it with a discerning eye.

Research does not support the successive-level approach to the interpretation of intelligence tests. In general, the KISS model does not recommend routine interpretation of stratum II composites and suggests little utility and substantial risk in examining relative differences between and among composite and subtests scores or interpreting norm-referenced subtest scores. Based on their history, education, employment, or avocation, some test users may prefer the more descriptive approach to test interpretation that these methods embody, but they should not overstate these results or base high-stakes decisions on them.

Rather, interpretation of intelligence tests should focus primarily on stratum III composites (i.e., IQs). Not only are these scores the best estimates of psychometric *g*, but they also are the most reliable, construct valid, and predictive scores yielded by intelligence tests. The KISS model guides test users to focus their efforts on these scores and to reference broad confidence interval bands surrounding them. It also instructs test users to consider the purpose of their assessment and to tailor their testing toward that purpose and the individual being tested as well as to refer to the evidence base that illuminates empirically supported practices. Focusing interpretation on the stratum III composite also promotes the development of instructional interventions that are likely more effective than those based on more specific ability estimates (see Chapter 9).

CHAPTER 9

Evidence-Based Practice and Cognitive Interventions

Intelligence tests originally were developed to exploit individual differences in cognitive ability to improve school efficiency by helping to identify students at risk for educational failure (Chapman, 1988). The initial use of intelligence tests was to classify students on the basis of general intelligence to fixed educational structures, where students would either adapt to the existing instructional program or drop out. However, passage of the Education for All Children Act in 1975, the precursor to the Individuals with Disabilities Education Act (IDEA, 2004), mandated that a free and appropriate public education be provided to all students, including those with disabilities who had been excluded from the education system.

Since then, society's commitment to equal educational opportunity for all individuals has necessitated that accommodations be made for the diversity of human aptitudes. Because individuals differ in their aptitude for learning prior to instruction, in order to reach common instructional goals for all (e.g., the ability to read and write), the educational system must either (a) directly develop the required aptitudes themselves or (b) adopt alternative instructional treatments for particular aptitudes. The latter alternative implies that different treatments should be selected to maximize their interaction with different student aptitudes. Aptitude-by-treatment interactions (ATIs) occur when the effectiveness of instructional treatments varies as a function of the aptitudes of individuals. Given that research on the malleability of intelligence, or psychometric g, has shown that it is very limited, the search for ATIs in the cognitive domain is essentially the Holy Grail of educational and school psychology.

The purpose of this chapter is threefold:

First, we provide an overview of the research methods that underlie evidence-based practice and guide the selection and implementation of interventions targeting cognitive abilities.

Second, we discuss basic concepts and terms associated with cognitive interventions and extend our review of research evaluating them (see also Chapter 2).

Third, we address the ATIs in the cognitive ability domain, particularly as they relate to our KISS model of interpretation (see Chapter 8) and as they pertain to contemporary practices for the treatment of learning difficulties.

Evidence-Based Practice

Our discussions in prior chapters have highlighted the need for those engaged in intelligence testing to review the scientific evidence supporting the use of these tests and interpretation of their scores. As highlighted in Chapters 4 and 8, those engaged in assessment should be particularly attuned to reliability and validity evidence. In addition, it is incumbent on those engaged in this process to produce results that are meaningful and that lead to both better understanding and improved outcomes for those involved in the assessment. Thus, typically it is expected that the interpretation of assessment results be accompanied by recommendations that someone implement interventions to address the key findings from the assessment. For example, our literature review revealed an array of recommendations like these that follow to address low scores targeting the abilities in Crystallized Intelligence (typically related to English-language vocabulary and culturally bound world knowledge) and low scores targeting Visual Processing (typically related to working with stimuli involving shapes, angles, dimensions, and their relationships). These recommendations include those targeting both instruction (i.e., skills taught and practiced) as well as alterations of instructional, practice, and evaluative activities (also called *accommodations*).

For example, for a test taker with low scores associated with Crystallized Intelligence, recommendations might include the following:

- Include content related to the test taker's specific interests (e.g., hobbies) to promote engagement.
- Provide relevant background information before beginning a reading assignment.
- Study English language prefixes and suffixes to better understand new vocabulary words.
- Encourage the test taker to read magazines, books, and websites (or listen to them, when possible) to enhance their exposure to new words and concepts.
- Simplify words and sentences spoken during oral instruction.
- Offer access to a dictionary or thesaurus.

And for a test taker with low scores associated with Visual Processing, recommendations might include the following:

- Practice tracing copying designs and letters.
- Complete puzzles with themes that relate to the test taker's interest.
- Employ tangible objects to support instruction when discussing more abstract concepts.
- Alter assignments to include highlighting and arrows guiding the test taker through the necessary steps.
- Remove extraneous visual stimuli from assignments and the test taker's desk.
- Do not penalize the test taker for messy handwriting when grading written assignments.

These recommendations are largely intuitive. As evident in these examples, one assumption is that exposure to instruction in a cognitive ability area and practicing

Table 9.1. Foundational Principles Promoting Growth in Academic Achievement Domains

- Every learner can grow across time, as knowledge and skills are malleable.
- Learners develop knowledge and skills at different rates—even when exposed to the same experiences and instruction. Some learners learn more rapidly than others due to aptitude and interest.
- Learners differ somewhat in the knowledge and skills they learn most easily. Some learners develop some competencies more rapidly and easily than other competencies, whereas other learners may struggle to develop competencies in the same areas.
- Intrinsic motivation to learn new knowledge and skills varies across learners, and motivation to learn can be enhanced through reinforcing learning environments.
- Even when provided the opportunity to learn and incentives to learn are present, some learners will not master basic concepts, and very few learners will achieve mastery of the most complex concepts.
- The optimal learning environment provides opportunities for all learners (a) to advance knowledge and skills at an appropriate rate based on their aptitudes for learning and (b) to learn new knowledge and skills in areas that most interest them.

Note: Adapted from Hattie (2008) and Jensen (1998b).

related skills not only enhances the targeted cognitive ability domain but also advances other skills related to it. Alternately, when a test taker has a weakness in a particular cognitive ability, the recommendation may be to work around that weakness (i.e., make an accommodation) rather than intervening directly to improve it. Although learners vary greatly across numerous features, and interventions that appears to work for some may not work for others, a strong evidentiary base reveals central principles of learning that apply to all learners (Hattie, 2008; Jensen, 1998b; see Table 9.1).

In order to link assessment results to interventions, empirical evidence that goes well beyond reliability and validity is needed. Further, to intervene effectively, there must be a commitment to *evidence-based practice*. Evidence-based practice refers to "the integration of the best available research with clinical expertise in the context of patient characteristics, culture, and preferences" (American Psychological Association Presidential Task Force on Evidence-Based Practice, 2006, p. 273).

It is beyond the scope of this chapter (and this book) to outline all of the requisite knowledge necessary to embody the ideals of evidence-based practice, but we want to highlight a few critical areas:

First, evidence-based practitioners must have a firm understanding of research designs underlying intervention studies and the ability to evaluate them and identify unintended and uncontrolled influences. They should be able to identify *independent variables* (i.e., the features of the intervention) and *dependent variables* (i.e., the outcomes thought to reflect intervention effects). They should be aware of problems associated with *sampling bias* (e.g., uncontrolled preexisting differences between groups), how the researchers might subtly influence the study outcomes if they are aware of key features of the study (e.g., who receives what intervention), and how the passage of time and expectancy effects (e.g., placebo effects) seem to lead to changes in outcomes that are as powerful as the effects of the independent variables. Methods to control for these effects include random assignment, blinding, and inclusion of active comparison groups. Indeed, as Melby-Lervåg, Redick, and Hulme (2016) noted in their recent meta-analysis, much of the research on the effectiveness of cognitive training programs can be criticized on methodological grounds (e.g., small sample sizes, the absence of active control groups, and no examination of far-transfer effects). For more information about relevant research designs, we encourage readers to consult Norcross, Hogan, Koocher, and Maggio (2017) and Kettler (2019).

We want to draw attention to two types of studies that often have been considered the preeminent sources of research evidence designed to guide evidence-based practice: randomized controlled trials and meta-analyses. *Randomized controlled trials* are "studies that randomly assign individuals to an intervention group or to a control group, in order to measure the effects of the intervention" (Whitehurst, 2003, p. 1). Two features are important to understand in this type of investigation. First, to control for sampling bias, the initial participants are assigned randomly—placed into groups based on nothing more than chance. With large enough numbers of participants in each group, their differences (as individuals) are expected to cancel out. Second, there is an active control group. That is, participants are randomly assigned to a group that receives the intervention under study, and the others are assigned to a group that completes some activity during the intervention period. In this way, the only difference between the two groups is the experiences of intervention under investigation. For example, participating in the research study and the passage of time between the beginning of the study and the end of the intervention—regardless of the intervention's effects—should not lead to the conclusion that the intervention produced those outcomes. It is important that the treatment and control groups be as comparable as possible with regard to the actual intervention (e.g., requiring the same amount of time during interventions or setting up expectations for positive outcomes, such as with a sugar pill in a medication trial). Whitehurst's (2003) *Identifying and Implementing Educational Practices Supported By Rigorous Evidence: A User Friendly Guide*, offered by the United States Department of Education Institute of Education Sciences National Center for Education Evaluation and Regional Assistance, provides an excellent description of the key elements of randomized controlled trials and discusses practical methods to evaluate interventions based on evidence of their effectiveness.

If you are to trust any single study to guide your recommendations and development of interventions, it should be a well-designed randomized controlled trial. However, it is clear that randomized controlled trials can produce divergent findings. These differences may be due to design features, participant sampling, subtle influences of the researchers, the setting in which an intervention occurs, and so on. In order to address variation in findings across studies, you can call on the other type of study that is at the heart of evidence-based practice: the *meta-analysis*. A meta-analysis typically stems from a comprehensive, systematic search of the literature, identification of studies that meet rigorous requirements, and pooling of results (converted to a common metric called an *effect size estimate*) across studies to produce a quantitative summary of findings across numerous studies. An effect size is a descriptive statistic referring to the magnitude and direction of the difference between two groups or the relationship between two variables. Most commonly, effect size estimates are derived from comparing the average level of performance of an intervention group to the average level of performance of some viable comparison group across the dependent variable. For example, the effect size Cohen's is calculated by subtracting one group's mean from the other group's mean and dividing the difference by what basically is the average of each group's standard deviation. Higher *d* values indicate a larger effect. Meta-analyses also may be able to examine, with sufficient numbers of studies to analyze, whether features of the samples, different types of measures, or specific methods of delivering an intervention may produce different outcomes. These potential influences on the effect sizes are called *moderators*.

The Evidence Base Surrounding Cognitive Interventions

With the standards of evidence-based practice in mind, we turn to interventions targeting cognitive abilities. If cognitive abilities are in any way malleable, as discussed in Chapter 2, it makes sense that efforts should be made to increase them in the hopes that these enhanced abilities improve the quality of life of those involved. For the purpose of this chapter, a cognitive intervention is a manipulation of experience that involves practicing correlates of targeted cognitive abilities. In many ways, these cognitive interventions are thought (perhaps incorrectly) to operate in the same way as learning any new skill or in strengthening our bodies (Melby-Lervåg & Hulme, 2013). For instance, many cognitive interventions are described as equivalent to weight lifting or aerobic training—with the idea that those completing the intervention will (a) become stronger as they stress their muscles and their cardiovascular system with physical training and (b) build more capacity to engage in more rigorous activities in the future. Cognitive interventions, based on our definition, are not identified based on target or outcomes of the intervention. For example, it is well known that nutritional interventions (involving iron and iodine) can improve cognitive functioning in those who are deficient in key nutrients (Protzko, 2017). However welcome these results, they would not be cognitive interventions because no manipulation of experience involves activation of targeted cognitive abilities.

Before summarizing the results of research in this area, we need to make two key distinctions. First, there are differences in the breadth of focus of cognitive interventions (Sala & Gobet, 2019). *Domain-specific interventions* address performance during narrowly focused tasks involving a limited array of stimulus content, cognitive operations, and response requirements. For example, in a well-known study, Chase and Ericsson (1982) recruited two undergraduate students at Carnegie Mellon, with the goal of increasing their ability to remember random strings of digits presented to them orally (as on the Wechsler Intelligence Scale for Children, Fifth Edition [WISC-V], 2014a, Digit Span subtest discussed in Chapter 6). After multiple training sessions per week across 2 years of deliberate practice, one of these students could correctly recall a string of 82 digits; after 5 years, the other could recall 113 digits. These outcomes stemmed from a domain-specific cognitive intervention. Other domain-specific cognitive interventions that have focused on enhanced expertise include music instruction and practice playing chess (Sala & Gobet, 2016). In contrast, *domain-general interventions* focus on cognitive abilities that are thought to operate on multiple cognitive systems and would likely affect performance across tasks. Examples of more domain-general interventions are "brain training programs" such as CogMed and Lumosity. These Web-based interventions include activities designed to address domains such as working memory, reasoning, and processing speed with the expectation of affecting the general cognitive ability system, which might be represented in a measure of general intelligence (see Chapter 2).

Second, we must highlight the distinction between the outcomes of the cognitive interventions by referring to the generalization of results, often called *transfer*. Sala and Gobet (2017) described the differences between *near transfer* and *far transfer* as follows:

> Transfer of learning is something all of us experience in our daily life. Knowledge of Samsung smartphones transfers to iPhones. Driving one's car generalizes to other models of cars. Knowing how to cook spaghetti Bolognese is useful for cooking chicken pasta. All of these are examples of near transfer; that is, the generalization of a set of skills across two (or more) domains tightly related to each other. However, another type of transfer has attracted the attention of researchers for over a century: far transfer. Far transfer occurs when a set of skills generalizes across two (or more) domains that are only loosely related to each other (e.g., mathematics and Latin). (p. 515)

As noted in Chapter 2, one of the key findings from the most well-designed studies and summarized in meta-analytic research is that when domain-specific interventions are implemented, near-transfer effects are demonstrated, but there are no reliable far-transfer effects—especially in academic achievement domains. When more domain-general interventions are employed, the transfer to more general domains does not occur. Here are excerpts from two abstracts to drive home these consistent trends across meta-analyses. Melby-Lervåg and Hulme (2013) summarized their results this way:

> This article presents a meta-analysis of working memory training studies (with a pretest-posttest design and a control group) that have examined transfer to other measures . . . Immediately following training there were reliable improvements on measures of intermediate transfer (verbal and visuospatial working memory). For measures of far transfer (nonverbal ability, verbal ability, word decoding, reading comprehension, arithmetic) there was no convincing evidence of any reliable improvements when working memory training was compared with a treated control condition. . . . The authors conclude that working memory training programs appear to produce short-term, specific training effects that do not generalize to measures of "real-world" cognitive skills. These results seriously question the practical and theoretical importance of current computerized working memory programs as methods of training working memory skills. (p. 270)

Kassai, Futo, Demetrovics, and Takacs (2019) conveyed the following:

> In the present meta-analysis we examined the near- and far-transfer effects of training components of children's executive functions skills: working memory, inhibitory control, and cognitive flexibility. We found a significant near-transfer effect . . . showing that the interventions in the primary studies were successful in training the targeted components. However, we found no convincing evidence of far-transfer. . . . That is, training a component did not have a significant effect on the untrained components. By showing the absence of benefits that generalize beyond the trained components, we question the practical relevance of training specific executive function skills in isolation. (p. 165)

These results are not only theoretically important and thought-provoking, but they also shed light on common assumptions made when developing recommendations and designing interventions following intelligence testing. They indicate that one can learn to perform better on an intelligence test subtest (e.g., WISC-V Digit Span) with deliberate practice (and perhaps lots of it), but that this learning will not result in significant far-transfer effects, such as improving performance in the key areas of academic achievement in school settings—let alone affect anything meaningful in their everyday life. Considering individual differences in learning and the foundational principles listed in Table 9.1, more targeted and practical interventions might prove more worthwhile than those predicated on a narrow cognitive focus and expectations of far transfer. It is clear that intervening directly on the academic knowledge and skills underlying academic achievement is an evidenced-based strategy (Burns et al., 2016; Burns, VanDerHeyden, & Zaslofsky, 2014).

ATIs and Intelligence Tests

So far in this chapter, we have focused largely on cognitive interventions and *main effects* (e.g., the effects of an intervention, per se, on dependent variables). We have highlighted these main effects from analysis of randomized controlled trials and featured in the primary meta-analytic analysis. However, it is possible (yet not broadly apparent from the current research literature) that salient *interaction effects* exist, so that cognitive interventions are more effective for some learners than others. Substantial emphasis has been on these interactions, in the form of ATIs, across the past 60 years, as it is assumed that what intelligence tests measure is an aptitude for learning and that these aptitudes interact with typical educational interventions in schools and related settings. This sections focuses on these interactions.

In his famous presidential address to the American Psychological Association titled "The Two Disciplines of Scientific Psychology," Cronbach (1957) asserted that "the job of applied psychology is to improve decisions about people. The greatest social benefit will come from applied psychology if we can find for each individual the treatment to which he can most easily adapt" (p. 679). Because both personal characteristics and instructional treatments are very diverse, Cronbach contended that "ultimately we should *design* treatments, not to fit the average person, but to fit groups of student with particular aptitude patterns. Conversely, we should seek out the aptitudes which correspond to (interact with) modifiable aspects of the treatment" (p. 681, emphasis in the original). This address helped spark much research in the 1960s and 1970s on the nature of cognitive aptitudes for learning from instruction and the identification of ATIs.

In ATI research, the variables of interest are instructional treatments and learner aptitudes, such as cognitive abilities. These learner aptitudes can be seen as moderators of treatment outcomes (Kraemer, Wilson, Fairburn, & Agras, 2002), and tests that produce scores representing these aptitudes that are subject to ATIs can be said to demonstrate evidence of *treatment utility* (i.e., evidence that measurable benefits stem from test interpretation; Hayes, Nelson, & Jarrett, 1987; Nelson-Gray, 2003), as discussed in Chapter 4. Figure 9.1 shows six possible effects of instructional treatments (T) on outcome averages and outcome-on-aptitude regressions. Although ATIs sometimes are presented within figures in which mean values are plotted pretest to posttest following a treatment (e.g., to examine learning gains) or for alternating treatments (e.g., a treatment matched to an aptitude and a treatment not matched to an aptitude) for two or more groups (see Braden & Shaw, 2009), these figures reflect the relation between the aptitude and the outcome for one treatment (Figure 9.1a) or these relations for two treatments (Figure 9.1b–f). For each figure, the horizontal axis represents the aptitude variable (with lower values on the left and higher values on the right), and the vertical axis represents the outcome variable (with lower values near the bottom of the figure and higher values near the top). The solid lines are lines of best fit to the data; they sometimes are called regression lines.

In Figure 9.1a, the solid line represents the relation of aptitude on outcome for "conventional teaching" using a correlation between aptitude and outcome of .50. In this case, the relation is an expected correlation between (a) IQs measured at the start of instruction and (b) academic achievement measured at the end of instruction (Snow & Yalow, 1984). The two dotted lines represent correlations of approximately .30 and .70 for comparable instructional environments. X and Y represent students with high and low aptitude scores, and the heavy dots in the center of the regression lines represent the average predicted outcome from the average aptitude score (across persons). As can be seen in Figure 9.1a, given the positive correlation between aptitude and outcome, Student X always is predicted to obtain a higher score than Student Y, but the size of the difference in predicted scores varies as a result of the slope of the respective regression lines. Also, Students X and Y both are predicted to perform better in certain instructional environments than others.

The goal of ATI research is to find alternative instructional treatments to conventional teaching, as targeted in Figure 9.1a. For example, Treatment 2 (T2) in Figure 9.1b improves the mean instructional outcome for individuals across all levels of aptitude, and Treatment 3 (T3) in Figure 9.1c improves the performance of those with low aptitude for learning. Figure 9.1d shows the opposite effect to that evident in Figure 9.1c; Treatment 4 (T4) improves the performance of those with high aptitude for learning. Figures 9.1c and 9.1d reflect what is known as an *ordinal interaction*, where the effectiveness of an instructional treatment has more of an effect at one level of

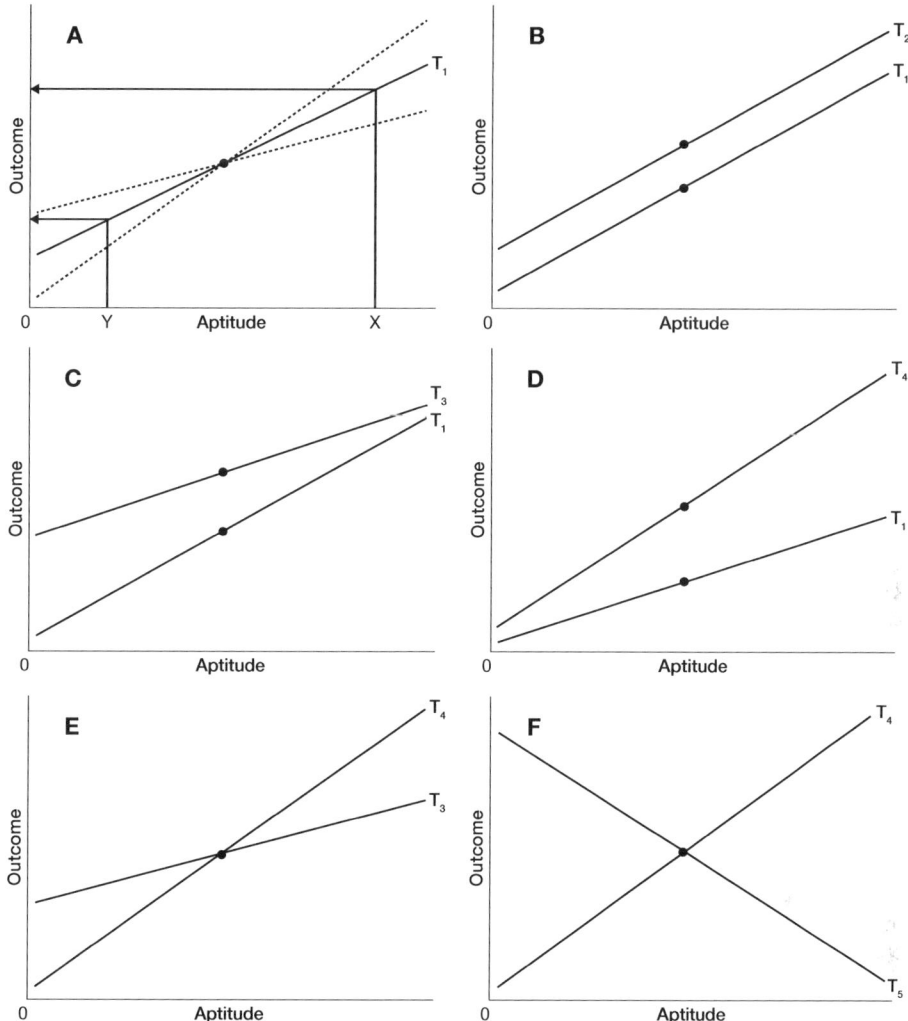

Figure 9.1. Six possible effects of alternative instructional treatments (T) on outcome averages and outcome-on-aptitude regressions. Adapted from Snow and Yalow (1984, p. 528)

aptitude than another. The difference between the heavy dots represents the difference in the average effect size of one instructional treatment over the other, and the degree that the slopes of the regression lines differ from one another represents the extent to which the treatment effect size differs for those with different aptitude scores. Figures 9.1e and 9.1f show the effect of a *disordinal interaction*. In a disordinal interaction, the lines cross, indicating that the instructional treatment has one kind of an effect at one level of aptitude in one condition and a different kind of effect in another condition. These latter ATIs are the kind presumed to be prevalent by those asserting that learning difficulties can be prevented or remediated by matching instructional treatments and specific patterns of cognitive abilities.

In education, the list of instructional treatments that have major beneficial effects on all learners is quite short. As Snow (1998) stated, research indicates that different instructional treatments

> may or may not show main effects favoring one or the other, but such evaluations almost always show vast individual differences in learning among students within any one treatment. They usually show that a particular treatment is effective only for a subgroup of students, if any. They sometimes even show that each treatment is effective for different subgroups of students. In turn, aptitude differences assessed prior to instruction always predict individual differences in learning in general, usually predict individual differences within any treatment, and sometimes also predict which treatment is best for which individual. (pp. 96–97)

When Cronbach (1957) and his colleagues began conducting ATI research, their goal was to discover the most effective instructional treatments to use and the best way to allocate groups of persons with particular aptitudes to these treatments. Cronbach hypothesized that "a general intelligence test is probably the wrong thing to use. This test, being general, predicts success in all subjects, therefore tends to have little interaction with treatment, and so is not the best guide to differential treatment" (p. 681). Instead, in his view, the focus of research should be on identifying those specific aptitudes (including broad and narrow cognitive abilities) that demonstrate interaction effects with modifiable aspects of instructional treatments.

Contrary to the expectations of Cronbach and his colleagues, no specific (broad or narrow) cognitive ability has been identified that reliably demonstrates an ATI in improving the reading, writing, and math problems of children. As Preacher and Sterba (2019) stated, "substantiated claims of ATIs in practice were rare by the mid-1970s (Cronbach & Snow, 1977). They are still rare" (p. 254). Over the past 40 years, research has failed to identify consistent interaction effects between broad and narrow cognitive abilities and instructional treatments (for reviews and meta-analyses, see Braden & Shaw, 2009; Burns et al., 2016; Cronbach & Snow, 1977; Elliott & Resing, 2015; Kearns & Fuchs, 2013; Melby-Lervåg & Hulme, 2013; Stuebing et al., 2014).[1] Indeed, in addressing Fluid Reasoning (Gf), Crystallized Intelligence (Gc), and Visual Processing (Gv), Snow and Lohman (1984) concluded that "ATI research on instruction has not been successful thus far in providing convincing demonstration of the worth of the Gf/Gc/Gv distinction for the purposes of treatment design" (p. 360). As discussed in Chapter 8, underlying all approaches to the intra-individual interpretation of intelligence test scores (e.g., profile analysis and analysis of patterns of cognitive strengths and weaknesses) is the assumption that ATIs in the cognitive ability domain

---

1. Although no systematic and critical evaluation of the research has focused on ATIs stemming from results from the Cognitive Assessment System (CAS; Das & Naglieri, 1997), some evidence published in peer-reviewed journals seems to suggest an ATI between some cognitive abilities (e.g., Planning) in the mathematics domain (Iseman & Naglieri, 2011; Kroesbergen, Van Luit, & Naglieri, 2003) and the reading domain (Parrila, Kendrick, Papapoulos, & Kirby, 1999). However, this linkage is not well replicated across the most well-designed studies. No meta-analysis of these studies has emerged. We remain skeptical of these effects and await independent replications of these findings and a meta-analysis that controls for methodological rigor and assesses publication bias.

can be used to maximize the effectiveness of instructional treatments by pairing them with particular constellations of cognitive ability scores (e.g., Flanagan et al., 2018).

Because no reliable ATIs between specific cognitive abilities and academic achievement exist, those who administer and score intelligence tests must ponder how to address this fact. We have made the case earlier in this book that individual differences in psychometric *g*—a general and relatively stable trait after children reach school age (see Chapter 2)—can be measured reliably and validly with intelligence tests. Thus, psychometric *g* is a *person variable*. According to Bandura's (1978) triadic model of reciprocal determinism, person variables interact with behaviors and the environment (producing mutual effects) throughout development to explain some aspects of both academic accomplishments and academic problems.

In addition to measures of psychometric *g* meeting some of the highest measurement standards and the support for psychometric *g*'s place in developmental theories, individual differences in *g* appear to produce the only well-replicated ATIs in the cognitive ability domain. Psychometric *g* clearly interacts with instruction that differs in structure, directness, and completeness (Braden & Shaw, 2009; Snow, 1998). Here's how:

As we reported in Chapter 1, individual differences in psychometric *g* are related to information-processing complexity (e.g., see Gottfredson, 2018; Jensen, 1998a). Recall from Chapter 4 that cognitive complexity refers to "an attribute of cognitive tasks and refers to differences in the cognitive load they impose for successful performance" (Gottfredson, 2016, p. 216). When we refer to cognitive load of a task, we are referring to the "amount and abstractness of information to integrate; more irrelevant information to ignore; a need to draw inferences or select appropriate procedures; and greater uncertainty, unpredictability, and fluidity of task, information, and circumstance" (Gottfredson & Saklofske, 2009, p. 188). Clearly, some test takers are better able to handle this cognitive complexity than others. As a result, when they complete intelligence tests that contain diverse cognitive tasks that vary in complexity, those who are better able to handle cognitive complexity score higher on intelligence tests than their peers, and those who struggle in handling such cognitive complexity score lower.

It is true across all learners that activities involving multiple interacting elements that tax their memory system (especially their working memory system, as described in Chapter 2) are more challenging than those activities that do not. This is the central premise of cognitive load theory and its application to instruction (De Jong, 2010; Hattie, 2008; Sweller, 1994, 2010). Cognitive load may be conceptualized as intrinsic or extraneous. *Intrinsic cognitive load* refers to the pressures evoked by prior knowledge during learning. *Extraneous cognitive load* refers to pressures within learning environments that effectively are distractions from the center of the learning experience. Cognitive load theory typically is applied to academic interventions with the goal of reducing the cognitive load for novice learners. For example, if academic difficulties identified are due at least partially to general normative weaknesses in the ability to reason abstractly, solve problems, and learn new information, expectations can be altered to acknowledge that (a) interventions designed to address the academic problems are likely to be less effective in producing academic achievement consistent with grade-level expectations and (b) many academic skills are likely to be acquired at a slower rate than expected across school years.

When considering students who learn at a slower rate and who experience or who are at risk for experiencing academic difficulties, an excellent resource is the What Works Clearinghouse (WWC; https://ies.ed.gov/ncee/wwc/FWW). The WWC was created in 2002 by the U.S. Department of Education's Institute of Education Sciences (IES) to provide professionals with a central source of information on the scientific evidence base for interventions in education. In addition to providing critical reviews of the literature, WWC produces practice guides with recommendations that are rated based on strength of the research evidence. For example, in the *IES Practice Guide for Assisting Students Struggling with Reading: Response to Intervention (RtI) and Multi-Tier Intervention in the Primary Grades* (2009), strong evidence supports interventions that are gradual and explicit. As the panel of experts who wrote this practice guide stated:

> Reading instruction should be systematic—building skills gradually and introducing skills first in isolation and then by integrating them with other skills to provide students practice and to build generalization. Students should be given clear, corrective feedback, and cumulative review to ensure understanding and mastery. . . . Reading instruction should also be explicit. Explicit instruction involves a high level of teacher-student interaction that includes frequent opportunities for students to practice the skill and clear, specific corrective feedback. It begins with overt and unambiguous explanations and models. (p. 22)

These instructional practices likely are effective because they reduce the information-processing complexity required for learning to read, which is consistent with research on the ATI between g and academic interventions. Although not all struggling readers are children and youth with below average general cognitive ability, many will be (e.g., Kranzler, Yaraghchi, Matthews, & Otero-Valles, 2020b), so these recommendations should be heeded closely when considering alternative interventions.

However, as some learners can handle heavier cognitive loads than others, and measures of psychometric g represent these individual differences, those with low IQs (many of whom have intellectual disability, see Chapter 11) and those with high IQs (many of whom have intellectual giftedness, see Chapter 12) will benefit from different interventions. These ATIs are ordinal interactions, such as those shown in Figures 9.1c and 9.1d. Thus, some interventions produce improvements in performance of students with high g more than students with low g (see Figure 9.1c), and other interventions produce differential effects (improving performance more for some students and less for others), depending on the level of g (see Figure 9.1d). Table 9.2 shows a summary of research relating psychometric g to various instructional treatments. The largest interaction effects are observed when instructional treatments demand the most complex cognitive processing on the part of learners. As Snow and Lohman (1984) summarized,

> The instructional treatments that most often show this result are characterized as including complex, heavily verbal and abstract material present at

Table 9.2. Summary of Hypotheses Relating Psychometric *g* to Instructional Strategies

Description of Instructional Strategies	Expected Results	
	Student with Low *g*	Student with High *g*
Placing burdens of information processing on learners	Poor	Good
Using elaborate or unusual explanations	Poor	Good
Including discovery or inquiry methods	Poor	Good
Encouraging learner self-direction	Poor	Good
Being relatively unstructured or permissive	Poor	Good
Relying heavily on verbiage	Poor	Good
Rapid pacing of presentation of new information	Poor	Good
Giving minimal essentials for learners to elaborate	Poor	Good
Giving advance organizers on difficult material	Poor	Good
Relieving learners of information-processing burdens	Good	Unclear
Giving all essentials by programmed instruction	Good	Unclear
Simplifying or breaking down the task	Good	Unclear
Providing redundant text	Good	Unclear
Substituting other media for verbiage	Good	Unclear
Using simplified demonstrations, models, or simulations	Good	Poor
Varying the format of programmed instruction	Inconsistent	Inconsistent
Including inserted questions	Inconsistent	Inconsistent
Using diagrammatic or pictorial presentation	Inconsistent	Inconsistent

Note: Adapted from Snow and Yalow (1984), p. 531.

> a relatively rapid pace under conditions in which instruction is incomplete and learners must induce for themselves significant aspects of the instructional message.... As instructional conditions are redesigned to relieve some of this information processing burden, the relation of G aptitude to learning outcome is reduced. The instructional treatments that most often show this result are characterized as including simplifying elaborations and concrete demonstrations, substituting other media for complex verbiage, [and] having a slower, more individualize pace under conditions in which learners' minute-to-minute attention and activities are directed explicitly by instructor control. (p. 355)

Research also suggests that such treatments designed to improve the performance of low-*g* learners actually may impair the performance of high-*g* learners. The most effective instructional treatments for students with low psychometric *g* are those that minimize the complexity of demands on learners. In contrast, for students with high psychometric *g*, the most effective instructional methods are those that increase the complexity of demands on learners (Snow, 1977; Snow & Yalow, 1984). With this in mind, we provide recommendations tailored to those test takers with low and high IQs in Tables 9.3 and 9.4, respectively.

Table 9.3. Instructional Recommendations for Students with Low IQs

- When developing her teaching plans, Valentina's teacher should reduce the amount of information that Valentina should hold "in mind" or retrieve from memory when completing assignments.
- Aaron's teacher should employ visual prompts and other reminders to assist him in completing all of the necessary steps during tasks that require integration of previously learned skills.
- Wei's parents should use clear, simple, and concise explanations when presenting new information.
- Aaliyah's teacher should build a learning environment that helps keep her focused and on task. Aaliyah would benefit from more directed assignments rather than inquiry methods.
- Jan's teacher should provide them with a step-by-step, structured plan on the direction and goals of their work rather than expect self-direction. This would support on-task engagement and task completion.
- Zoey's teacher should provide a structured environment that includes visual and oral prompts from adults and visual aids to support learning.
- Reyansh's teacher should use simple, concise statements to ensure Reyansh understands what is expected.
- Emma's teacher should provide more time for her to process information and practice new skills before providing additional instruction.
- Darnell's teacher should provide him with additional supports (e.g., information and monitoring) to facilitate learning rather than expecting self-direction in learning.
- Saburo's teacher should avoid providing unnecessary materials or information prior to discussing new content so that they are not distracting.
- Claire's parents should present tasks that do not rely on Claire remembering several steps or numerous pieces of information. To support completion of more complex tasks, they should employ interactive charts that contain visual prompts or other reminders.
- When introducing new knowledge or skills, Lucas's teachers should present all of the essential steps and provide the basic resources he needs to demonstrate new learning in those areas.
- Aria's teachers should present activities by breaking down what needs to be done in small, easy steps. These steps might be presented one at a time.
- In providing important information, Ang's teachers should repeat this information multiple times. For example, his teachers may provide him with instructions to complete a worksheet verbally and demonstrate an item or two on the whiteboard.
- Martina's teachers should provide videos or pictures to further explain material instead of using lengthy or wordy instructions.
- Liam's teachers should use simple demonstrations and concrete models to help explain concepts.

Table 9.4. Instructional Recommendations for Students with High IQs

- Camila's teacher should place higher expectations on Camila memorization and problem-solving skills. Camila is a very adaptive learner, and providing them with more challenges would help them grow.
- DeAndre's parents should incorporate more global or abstract styles of explanations to encourage him to investigate areas where he has an incomplete understanding.
- Chole's teacher should provide her hands-on experiences that encourage her to explore, ask questions, and develop alternative scenarios. Discovery and inquiry methods can help develop her problem-solving skills.
- Ebony's teacher should encourage her to make her own decisions about which learning opportunities she should take on. This would build her confidence in guiding her educational experiences.
- Francisco's teachers can use a less structured and more lenient environment for him as it would give him the opportunity to explore beyond the boundaries of an assignment.
- Jess's teacher should use more technical terms associated with the relevant material and provide more detailed explanations of concepts. This would promote a more comprehensive understanding of the material.
- Taran's teacher should consider moving through material at a relatively fast pace, presenting new information frequently. This would keep Taran engaged more consistently and promote growth.
- Shanice's teacher should refrain from providing every piece of information and instead allow her to make connections regarding the material on her own. The need for the added material will present a challenge for Shanice, allowing her to develop self-direction in learning and promoting applications of complex information-processing skills.
- Luis's teacher should provide worksheets that contain an outline or framework for difficult material. This would promote his ability to organize challenging information on his own and bolster his approach to learning cognitively demanding material.
- Asha's teacher should avoid providing demonstrations that reiterate information that was explained previously. Instead, demonstrations should only be used to present novel information.

Summary

Although certain cognitive skills can be enhanced, such learning typically is quite context-bound and shows limited transfer to other domains. We featured ATIs in the cognitive ability domain, particularly as they pertain to contemporary practices for the identification and treatment of learning difficulties. Despite decades of research, no specific cognitive ability has been identified that reliably demonstrates an ATI in improving reading, writing, and math problems. The only ATI that has been found is between psychometric g and methods of instruction that differ in structure, directness, and completeness. As a result, interventions addressing the general intelligence of test takers typically increase or decrease the complexity of tasks and instruction. Such interventions generally are taken for granted by those targeting the development of basic reading, writing, and math skills. Those engaged in intelligence testing should consider the viability of recommendations addressing such interventions with test takers with low IQs and high IQs.

CHAPTER 10

Sharing the Results from Intelligence Tests

Sharing the results from testing is an important and challenging activity. It usually is accomplished through (1) psychological assessment reports and (2) face-to-face contact with the parents or caregivers of the children or adolescents completing the assessment—what we call an *informing session*. We have focused this chapter on these two pathways by which assessment results are shared, and in doing so, largely have limited our discussion to specific test contexts and results from intelligence tests. As report writing and informing sessions require substantial integration of assessment results from a variety of methods and sources, we encourage readers to turn to these excellent texts for broader coverage of these topics and a multitude of examples of assessment reports: Hass and Carriere (2014); Lichtenstein and Ecker (2019); Mather and Jaffe (2016); and Schneider, Lichtenberger, Mather, and N. Kaufman (2018). In order to address the needs of graduate students and early career professionals in training, we also describe the process of sharing assessment results with supervisors during supervision meetings—what we call *staffings*.

Psychological Assessment Reports

PURPOSE

Psychological assessment reports provide a permanent record of the results of the assessment. They address the referral questions and summarize the test taker's history and current functioning based on multiple assessment methods, which may include intelligence tests. They also list recommendations for interventions based on the results (with the knowledge that others probably will be tasked with selecting, implementing, and monitoring these interventions).

STRUCTURE

There is some variation in how these reports are structured. We occasionally see lengthy reports (sometimes 20+ pages in length) that contain paragraphs about every test and every subtest, a detailed summary, and list of recommendations. On the other hand, we occasionally see reports that are filled primarily with tables presenting test results, each preceded by a sentence introducing the test and followed by a brief (two- to three-sentence) presentation of the most meaningful aspects of the results. Across styles, typical reports follow a format like that presented in Box 10.1. We discuss each section of these reports in the paragraphs that follow.

Box 10.1. Sample Psychological Assessment Report

Anywhere Psychological Center
Psychological Assessment
Confidential

Name: Kimberly Hughes	Parents: Nancy and Thomas Hughes
Date of Initial Assessment: 03/20/2019	School: Armstrong Elementary
Date of Birth: 02/14/2012	Grade: Second
Chronological Age: 7 years, 1 months	Examiner: Sophia Livingston, MA

REASON FOR REFERRAL

Kimberly Hughes was referred to the Anywhere Psychological Center by Kimberly's teacher, Mrs. Susan Benton. Kimberly's mother reported that Kimberly is a very bright girl, but sometimes her grades do not reflect this fact. This year, she reported seeing a drop in Kimberly's reading and mathematics scores on classroom assignments. Ms. Hughes reported that Kimberly sometimes is lost in thought and that she frequently brings home incomplete classwork. She has seen these problems worsen since Kimberly enrolled in elementary school.

BACKGROUND INFORMATION

Kimberly is a 7-year-old African American girl who is in the second grade at Armstrong Elementary School. She resides in Any City, Anystate, with her parents and sibling. Kimberly's mother is a social worker, and her father is a tax lawyer. Kimberly has a younger sister, Emily, who is 4 and attends a local Montessori program 5 days a week.

According to Ms. Hughes, her pregnancy with Kimberly was full-term. Ms. Hughes stated that Kimberly was born naturally, was of average weight, and experienced no serious medical conditions. Ms. Hughes reported that Kimberly met all developmental milestones within normal limits and has had no illnesses or injuries beyond those typical in childhood.

According to Ms. Hughes, Kimberly began attending the MidSouth Academy Preschool at the age of 3 and continued at the school through her kindergarten year. Her teachers noted no problems. Kimberly began attending Armstrong Elementary School in first grade. Review of Kimberly's most recent report card shows that she achieved M's (Meets Standards) or E's (Exceeds Standards) in all areas. However, Kimberly's teacher, Mrs. Benton, noted on her report card that Kimberly needs to use her class time more productively. Ms. Hughes reported that Kimberly scored in the 99th percentile for reading on the Standardized Test for Assessment of Reading (STAR) diagnostic test in February of 2019. Ms. Hughes stated that even though this STAR diagnostic test score is extremely high, she has noticed Kimberly's weekly reading scores varying dramatically. Ms. Hughes added that Kimberly frequently loses points on her classwork because items are incomplete.

Ms. Hughes reported that Kimberly is, and has always been, a very bright child. She stated that Kimberly generally is happy and that she loves to read books (especially the Harry Potter series). She shared that Kimberly recently has complained that school is no fun and added that she whines about and protests going to school about twice a week.

Kimberly had not been tested previously, and her hearing and vision screenings are from October 2018 and are reasonably up to date. She passed both screening exams, and there are no indications of hearing or vision problems.

ASSESSMENT TECHNIQUES

Interview with Kimberly's mother, Ms. Hughes
Wechsler Intelligence Scale for Children, Fifth Edition
Woodcock-Johnson III Tests of Achievement
Behavior Assessment System for Children, Third Edition (BASC-3)
    Parent Rating Scales (completed by Mr. Hughes)
    Teacher Rating Scales (completed by Ms. Benton)
Behavioral observations in the classroom
Behavioral observations during testing
Review of records
Review of class assignments

BEHAVIORAL OBSERVATIONS DURING TESTING AND VALIDITY OF ASSESSMENT

Kimberly completed three sessions during the course of the assessment following an interview with her mother, Ms. Hughes. Kimberly's conversational proficiency seemed advanced for her age level; she used several advanced vocabulary words when describing her hobbies and her pet dog. Although Kimberly appeared confident and self-assured throughout the examination, she sometimes was distracted. She was very inquisitive and often asked the examiner questions about herself and the clinic setting. Her completion of the Screening Tool for Assessment Direct Screening form indicated no potential problems associated with her language usage and fine motor skills. During testing, she sometimes stated that she did not know an answer to an item (especially on the Wechsler Intelligence Scale for Children, Fifth Edition), but after being encouraged, she often answered correctly. Across the BASC-3 rating scales, all validity indexes were within the Acceptable range. Overall, it is believed that the results of this assessment are valid estimates of Kimberly's overall intellectual, academic, and psychosocial functioning.

ASSESSMENT RESULTS

Cognitive Abilities

Kimberly completed the Wechsler Intelligence Scale for Children, Fifth Edition. Kimberly's Full Scale IQ score places her in the Extremely High range when compared to other children her age (standard score [SS] = 152). The chances are 9 out of 10 that Kimberly's true score falls within the range from 145 to 155. This score indicates that fewer than 1 in 1,000 children her age would be expected to obtain a score higher than hers (percentile rank [PR] = 99.9).

(continued)

Box 10.1. *Continued*

SUMMARY

Cognitive difficulties were ruled out as the cause of Kimberly's struggles at school by the measure of general intelligence from the Wechsler Intelligence Scale for Children, Fifth Edition. In fact, Kimberly's scores indicate that she has extremely high general intelligence when compared to others her age. (Additional assessment results are not summarized due to space limitations.)

RECOMMENDATIONS

1. The information in this report should be shared with an Individualized Education Program (IEP) team at Armstrong Elementary School to determine whether Kimberly's current level of services is consistent with her educational needs.
2. Kimberly's eligibility for the Gifted and Talented program at Armstrong Elementary should be considered.
3. Ms. Hughes and Kimberly's current teacher, Ms. Benton, should work together to enhance Kimberly's intellectual, emotional, and personality strengths.
4. Ms. Hughes should consider finding Kimberly a mentor in the area of her interest. This mentor might help conceptualize career fields and expertise. A great program that could provide mentors is Mensa International *(www.mensa.org)*.
5. Ms. Hughes should continue to encourage Kimberly to read as a hobby.
6. Kimberly's parents should continue to expose her to a variety of cultural stimuli in order to enrich her life and to help her gain knowledge from new and different experiences.
7. Kimberly's parents should incorporate specific rewards tailored to Kimberly's personality when she brings home schoolwork that is the product of much effort and ingenuity.

Sophia Livingston, MA
Sophia Livingston, MA
Intern

James R. Rhodes, Ph.D.
James R. Rhodes, PhD
License # FL3825347
Health Services Provider

Score Tables
Reynolds Intellectual Assessment Scales (RIAS) Age-Based Scores

Composite Scores	Standard Score	Percentile Rank	Range Based on Age
Composite Intelligence Index	152	99.97	Extremely High
Verbal Intelligence Index	157	99.99	Extremely High
Nonverbal Intelligence Index	128	97	High
Subtest	*T* Score		
Guess What	73		Very High
Verbal Reasoning	91		Extremely High
Odd-Item Out	67		High
What's Missing	62		High Average

(Additional score tables are not included due to space limitations.)

Headings. Most reports begin with a heading labeling the report and a heading labeling the results as confidential. These headings sometimes are placed under the letterhead of the clinic, hospital, or school district through which the assessment was conducted. These introductory headings are followed by a table presenting demographic information about the test taker, and typically the test taker's name is listed as well.

Reason for referral. The first narrative section of the report is the Reason for Referral, which explains why the test taker was referred for a psychological evaluation. This section typically includes the referral source (e.g., classroom teachers) and the specific questions the referral source has about examinee. It also usually includes a summary of the specific behaviors or symptoms displayed by the test taker that led to their referral, briefly documents interventions that have been tried, and lists possible ways assessment results may be used (e.g., determination of eligibility for special education). This section typically is relatively brief.

Background information. The second section often is lengthy, because it addresses the test taker's history. The information gathered for this section typically comes from interviews with parents, teachers, and the test taker and from examination of educational files. It typically includes four general categories of content. First, demographic information is presented in narrative form and extended. Often, the first sentence provides the test taker's age, gender, grade, and school. It is followed by a description of the family unit, listing the names of parents or other caregivers and siblings. Second, the test taker's developmental history and medical history are addressed. Developmental delays, injuries, surgeries, previous mental health diagnoses, and prescription medications are summarized. Third, the test taker's educational history is described. Noteworthy information in this section may include the child's attendance, academic achievement (e.g., test scores, grades, and benchmark assessment results), as well as any prior-grade retention and interventions (e.g., tutoring and counseling). Finally, the results of prior medical, psychological, or psychiatric reports are summarized. Recent problems are detailed; content should increase understanding of the reason for referral. In this section, a description of the test taker's areas of strength and interests sometimes is provided, to underscore the importance of protective factors.

Assessment techniques. Most reports have a section that lists the tests and other assessment techniques (e.g., interviews, review of records, and classroom observations) used to yield results during the assessment. As evident in Box 10.1, these techniques are listed and not written in complete sentences. Published instruments are capitalized (but not italicized), whereas unpublished and informal techniques are not marked with special formatting (such as capitalization of each word).

Behaviors during testing session and validity of assessment. Many reports include a section called "Observations" or "Behavior Observations" preceding the test results. Typical content in this section includes descriptions of behaviors during the testing session, and frequently this section ends with a validity statement. This validity statement is the "stamp of approval" for the testing results. Often, it reads like this: "The results of the standardized testing appear to be valid estimates of Serena's cognitive abilities and achievement." The labels "Observations" and "Behavior Observations" are not descriptive or accurate enough to represent the content of this section, however. For one thing, these section labels are too general; systematic direct observations of behavior may have been completed in settings other than the testing room (e.g., the general education classroom). Second, the typical section label fails to address the key components of this section: (1) the description of the behaviors that may have influenced the meaningfulness of the scores produced by the tests and interactions between the examiner and the test taker and (2) the results of screening conducted before testing (see Chapter 5). We prefer the more descriptive title "Behaviors during Testing Session and Validity of Assessment."

Assessment results. The foundation of the report typically is the section presenting the results of the formal assessment (in contrast to more informal methods, such as loosely structured interviews). In this section, many report writers include descriptions of all tests administered, the scores they produced, and their meaning. Typically, this section begins with the results of intelligence testing; continues to focus on the results of achievement testing; and ends with a focus on behaviors and emotions, assessed via techniques such as caregiver rating scales, direct observations, and self-report rating scales. Each subsection is marked by a heading describing either the construct targeted (e.g., Intelligence or Reading) or the test administered (e.g., Wechsler Intelligence Scale for Children, Fifth Edition, WISC-V, Wechsler, 2014a). Occasionally, score tables will be inserted within each section.

Summary. Many reports conclude with a Summary section. In it, the most important results from the prior sections are grouped. Most often, this section will include one sentence representing each subsection of the Assessment Results section. It is rare that it will contain a synthesis of results, but sometimes it will conclude with sentences addressing diagnosis or eligibility for special education.

Recommendations. The last section containing connected text in most reports usually is devoted to recommendations for parents, other caregivers, and teachers. These recommendations may address special education eligibility processes, additional assessment, home-based and classroom interventions, therapeutic services in clinic settings, and medical interventions. Typically, these recommendations are bulleted or numbered. We addressed recommendations most relevant to intelligence test results in Chapter 9.

Signatures and score tables. The final two sections of a standard psychological assessment report include the signature of the report's author (and perhaps that of their supervisor) as well as tables providing scores from the assessment. It is standard practice for these signatures to follow the body of the report, and they signal that its content has been approved by its author (and the author's supervisor). Many reports conclude with score tables following the signatures. These score tables tend to contain the norm-referenced scores for all relevant subtests and for composites on which interpretations are based, but there is no requirement to report a full range of scores—especially for those scores that do not meet measurement standards and are not interpreted in the body of the report.

Considerations in Writing a Psychological Report

THE IMPORTANCE OF TEMPLATES

Report writing can be mentally taxing and time-consuming. In fact, writing it may require substantially more time than the assessment process itself. Benson et al.'s

(2019) recent survey of practicing school psychologists revealed that they spend, on average, almost 30% of their work week writing and formatting reports. Due to these challenges, it is necessary to use templates (often carefully formatted Word documents) when developing reports. It also is important to consider the viability of text and score tables from test scoring and interpretive software and Web interfaces. More published and online resources are available today than ever before to support report writing (see Chapter 7).

STYLES OF REPORTING TEST RESULTS

Writers use at least three styles to present test results in the body of reports. Our example report in Box 10.1 and description of subsections of this report are most consistent with what has been called a *test-based report*. This style of report includes a series of results from each test and other instruments. Following this style, the results from an intelligence test might be reported first and followed by results from an achievement test, a parent rating scale, a teacher rating scale, and a self-report scale. When more than one instrument associated with each assessment method has been employed, results from like instruments are presented in back-to-back sections (e.g., the results from the WISC-V followed by results from the Woodcock-Johnson IV Tests of Cognitive Abilities). An example of this style of report appears at the top of Table 10.1, and variants of this report sometimes include only a brief description of each assessment instrument and a table of score embedded in text.

Another style of report focuses on integrating information based on the constructs and behaviors targeted during the assessment. Hass and Carriere (2014) have referred to them as *domain-based reports*. Broad domains might include general intellectual functioning, reading, mathematics, writing, externalizing behaviors, and internalizing behaviors; more narrow domains might include working memory, executive functioning, reading comprehension, spelling, hyperactivity, and depression. Following this style, the results from various intelligence tests, achievement tests, and rating scales are merged in one paragraph or lengthier section to address a single domain. For example, qualitative information from interactions during the testing session, results from measures requiring oral production (e.g., such as the WISC-V Similarities and Vocabulary subtests), and parent and teacher ratings of functional communication skills would be described to address the expressive language domain. An example of this style of report appears in the second section of Table 10.1.

A third style of report is one that is focused and meaning-based, guided, in part, by the referral concerns. It may be called a *hypothesis-oriented report* (Ownby, 1997), *referral-based report* (Hass & Carriere, 2014), *major findings report* (Kranzler & Floyd, 2013), and *question-and-answer format report* (Wiener, 1985, 1987; Wiener & Kohler, 1986). Following this style, the body of the report has no uniform structure; each assessment might produce a different structure. Within this section, information from various sources is integrated to address the primary concerns and answer the most pressing questions that precipitated the assessment. Wiener and Costaris (2012) suggested that seven questions guide the organization of the assessment results:

Table 10.1. Examples of Various Styles of Reports

TEST-BASED REPORT EXAMPLE

Sam completed the Wechsler Intelligence Scale for Children, Fifth Edition (WISC-V) to measure hir general and specific cognitive abilities. Hir Full-Scale IQ (FSIQ) is Average and was equal to or higher than 61% of hir same-age peers. Sam's Verbal Comprehension Index score fell in the Very High range, suggesting hir ability to processing verbal information is above most peers hir same age. Hir Visual Spatial Index, Fluid Reasoning Index, Working Memory Index, and Processing Speed Index scores all fell in the Average range, indicating that hir ability to organize visual information, attend to visual detail, integrate visual and motor functions, engage in reasoning, manipulate information in immediate memory, and process simple or routine information quickly are typical of hir same-age peers.

Sam completed the Wechsler Individual Achievement Test, Third Edition (WIAT-III) to measure hir reading, mathematics, and written language skills. Sam's Total Reading skills fell in the Low Average range. Within this domain, ze evidenced skills in the Average range with regard to comprehending and answering questions about written passages (Reading Comprehension) and basic decoding skills (Word Reading and Pseudoword Decoding), yet evidenced skills in the Low Average range in the area of reading fluency (Oral Reading Fluency). Sam's overall Mathematics skills were in the upper limits of the Average range. Hir skills in solving word problems and applying quantitative reasoning skills (Math Problem Solving) were in the Average range. Hir mathematical computation skills involving addition, subtraction, multiplication, and division (Numerical Operations) were in the lower limits of the Above Average range.

Sam completed the Comprehensive Test of Phonological Processing, Second Edition, to measure hir auditory phonological processing skills in the areas of phonological awareness, phonological memory, and rapid naming. Sam's overall Phonological Awareness, as measured by hir ability to manipulate real words, was in the lower limits of the Average range compared to same-age peers. Hir scores varied between tasks. Ze scored in the Low Average range on a task requiring him to isolate individual sounds within real words (Elision). Ze scored in the Average range on a task that required him to blend separated parts of real words (Blending Words). On a task that required him to isolate sounds within words (Phoneme Isolation), ze scored in the Average range.

Using the Behavior Assessment System for Children, Third Edition, Parent Rating Scale, Mrs. Raymond's ratings on the Internalizing Problems Index, Externalizing Problems Index, Behavioral Symptoms Index, and Adaptive Skills Index yielded scores that fell in the Average range. These results suggest that Sam's overall behavioral problems and level of adaptive functioning are similar to others hir age. However, based on her ratings on the Activities of Daily Living scale, Sam lacks skills associated with performing everyday tasks in an acceptable manner.

Based on Sam's ratings on the Behavior Assessment System for Children Self-Report of Personality, hir scores on the School Problems Index, Internalizing Problems Index, Inattention/Hyperactivity Index, Personal Adjustment Index, and Emotional Symptoms Index were all in the Average range. Thus, ze reported that they display behavioral problems and levels of adaptive functioning that are similar to others hir age. The only subscale that was in the Clinically Significant range was Sense of Inadequacy. Ze conveyed that ze feels unsuccessful in school and generally inferior when compared to hir peers.

DOMAIN-BASED REPORT EXAMPLE

(adapted from a report by L. K. Chalukian and R. Lichtenstein presented in Schneider et al., 2018, p. 268)

Attention and Executive Functions

Alexa did not appear to have difficulty maintaining or shifting attention when responding to the structured tasks of the WISC-V. *In fact, she maintained attention well when completing items that required high levels of focus.* However, the BASC-3 ratings completed by her mother and teacher (Ms. Hudson) indicated some concerns in this area, with Attention Problems scale scores falling in the At-Risk range when compared to other students her age. There ratings also placed her in the at-risk range on the Executive Functioning scale, which involves planning, organizing, and self-monitoring to carry out a novel, multipart task or solve a complex problem. Low ratings on items concerning task completion, concentration, and distractibility accounted for the At-Risk Executive Functioning scores. Consistent with this, her teacher rated Alexa as Clinically Significant on Study skills.

QUESTION-AND-ANSWER FORMAT REPORT EXAMPLE

(adapted from Hass & Carriere, 2014, p. 132)

How do Max's cognitive strengths and weaknesses impact his academic achievement?

Max's cognitive abilities were assessed through observations, teacher interviews, parent interviews, and standardized assessment. His overall general cognitive ability is estimated to be in the average range. Based on standardized assessment, classroom observations, and teacher reports, Max demonstrates significant weaknesses in the area of phonological awareness. Max's weaknesses in phonological awareness impact his overall literacy skills.

MAJOR FINDINGS REPORT EXAMPLE

(adapted from Kranzler & Floyd, 2013, p. 156)

Major Finding #1

Consistent with Colin's previous diagnosis of intellectual disability, this assessment indicated that Colin's functioning is notably lower than that of his same-age peers in the intellectual and adaptive domains. Previous assessments had yielded IQ scores in the Extremely Low range for his age. In 2015, his Differential Ability Scales, Second Edition, General Conceptual Ability score was revealed to be 53, and his Leiter International Performance Scale, Third Edition, Full IQ was 47. The current assessment results are congruent with the previous results, as well as with the intellectual functioning criterion for intellectual disability. His Wechsler Intelligence Scale for Children, Fifth Edition, Full Scale IQ (standard score [SS] = 56) in the Extremely Low range compared to others his age.

The previous adaptive behavior assessment in 2015 revealed that Colin's general display of adaptive behaviors was well below average for his age. Based on his mother's report in 2015, his Adaptive Behavior Composite score from the Vineland Adaptive Behavior Scale, Second Edition, Survey Interview was 61. Again, the current assessment results are congruent with the previous findings, as well as with the criteria for mental retardation/intellectual disability. Based on his mother's reports on the Vineland-3 Comprehensive Interview, his Adaptive Behavior Composite was 66, which is in the Very Low range when compared to others his age. The results of this assessment indicate that Colin continues to meet eligibility criteria for intellectual disability and should receive intensive intervention services in the school setting.

1. What is Client's [capitalized in original] name's overall level of ability?
2. At what level is Client's name functioning in reading, written language and mathematics?
3. What factors are interfering with Client's name's progress in school?
4. How is Client's name functioning socially and emotionally?
5. What is an appropriate educational placement and program for Client's name?
6. How can Client's name's parent(s) help Client's name at home?
7. What additional assessment(s)/treatment(s) are required for Client's name? (p. 124)

This style of report also may address questions related to diagnosis or eligibility, such as "Does Ronald have a learning disability in reading?" or "Does Makala display significantly subaverage intellectual ability and functional deficits in adaptive behavior that is consistent with a diagnosis of intellectual disability?" Although these questions may not be included in the reports themselves, such questions guide the development of text within this style of report. Two examples of this style of report appear in the final sections of Table 10.1.

WRITING FOR MULTIPLE AUDIENCES

Different audiences may require different reports (Kamphaus, 2001; Ownby, 1997), and writers should tailor their reports to their probable readers and the settings in which they are working. In this way, Lichtenstein and Ecker (2019) referred to their reports as being "consumer responsive," and they offered keen insights into achieving this goal. For example, parents and other caregivers typically require that the report be written in an accessible manner, and they need guidance about what they can do to improve the test taker's learning and everyday functioning. In addition, they appreciate the report highlighting some of the test taker's positive characteristics and capacity for growth. Consistent with this perspective, Schneider et al. (2018) discussed the importance during the writing process of a writer feeling empathy with those participating in the assessment.

In contrast to parents, teachers and special educators desire information about the test taker's relative levels of performance compared to peers, the match of the results to special education eligibility criteria, and recommendations for evidence-based interventions. Reports also may be written for supervisors, therapists, physicians, and judges (see Tallent, 1993). For these audiences, a shorter report and more technical terms and abbreviations may be acceptable. For example, a report written within a residential facility might focus on an adolescent's suicidal ideation and probability of relapse, whereas a report written as part of a forensic evaluation might emphasize whether a child is prepared to stand trial. We advocate a flexible style of report writing that can be tailored to multiple audiences—a "happy-medium report."

Regardless of the intended audience, reports should be clear and accessible to most readers (Ownby, 1997). For instance, avoid technical terms that many readers may not understand. In particular, avoid using only acronyms; spell out the terms with each use or define each acronym and use the acronym afterward. Harvey (1997) asserted that the key marker of an accessible report is a low readability score. Readability of text is most often measured via the Flesch–Kincaid Grade Level formula. This formula produces a score ranging roughly from 1 to 16 and reflecting the U.S. grade level of reading skill necessary in order to comprehend the analyzed text. Lower scores indicate greater reading ease, and readability values should be kept as low as possible (almost certainly < 12 when the report targets parents). Key variables to understanding readability are the average number of syllables per word and the average number of words per sentence (Flesch, 1948, 1949); accessible reports will exclude multisyllabic words and include relatively brief sentences.

Writers should include the test taker's name and the names of all involved in the assessment (e.g., parents and teachers) in the report, in order to make the sources of the information clear and to contextualize the results. In our reports, we usually refer to the test taker by first name and refer to adults by their last names, preceded by honorifics such as *Ms.*, *Mr.*, *Mrs.*, *Mx*, and *Dr*. Finally, the writer should focus on the meaning of the results and not so much on the assessment instruments and the numbers they produce. Kamphaus (2001) shared that "one way to think of the scores is a means to an end, the end being better understanding of the child" (p. 502). We concur with this wise statement.

GENERAL RULES OF WRITING

The *Publication Manual of the American Psychological Association, Seventh Edition* (American Psychological Association [APA], 2019) is an excellent source for modeling of grammar and style. When most students and some professionals think about APA style, they think narrowly about correctly formatting citations and references. They fail to consider all of the other issues addressed in the publication manual: general writing style; using the correct terms for gender, age, race, and ethnicity; appropriate use of punctuation, numbers, and abbreviations; and grammar and word selection. Table 10.1 summarizes some of the most important recommendations from the publication manual (APA, 2019) that are relevant to writing psychological reports (plus some recommendations of our own).

AVOIDING FOOLISH MISTAKES

Your report may be the only way that many consumers of the information you provide "see you." To ensure that consumers of your reports are not left with a negative impression of your work—or, worse, that the test taker you assessed is incorrectly described or misdiagnosed in your report—engage in multiple proofing strategies to prevent costly errors. Based on our review of the literature (e.g., Pagel, 2011), we recommend that you enter the proofing and editing phase of report generation with the belief that your draft report contains at least one costly error, which you must identify.

First, check and double-check the scores and the labels applied to them in your report. Review your scores in text and scores in the score tables against those from test protocols or scoring software output. You also should compare every score to the label you provide for it (e.g., a standard score of 125 is in the High range). Your heightened neuroticism during this stage will prevent embarrassment later on.

Second, take advantage of electronic text analysis functions in your word processing program. For example, first use the Spelling and Grammar functions in Microsoft Word or other word-processing programs. In particular, make sure that you select the box "Use contextual spelling" to identify potential errors associated with homophone use (e.g., using *there* versus *their*) in Microsoft Word in Word Options. However, if you do not uncheck the boxes in Word Options to "Ignore words in UPPERCASE" and "Ignore words that contain numbers" when checking for spelling errors, you may overlook a spelling error involving an acronym or test abbreviation. You definitely should uncheck them. In addition, based on excellent research by Harvey (1997), obtain readability statistics for your report document. In Word Options in Microsoft Word, make sure that you check the box "Show readability statistics." If the value is too high (> 12), reduce sentence length and reduce the frequency of lengthy words as much as possible.

Third, carefully read through your report from beginning to end while it is on your computer screen (i.e., in the word-processing program). Proofread both for content errors and for mechanical errors (moving your cursor below each word and reading text aloud as you do so). After you make edits to the text, read the sentence before each edit, the sentence containing the edit, and the sentence that follows to ensure that you have not introduced errors.

Finally, print and proofread at least one hard copy; some research indicates that proofreading is more accurate when conducted in the print medium (e.g., Wharton-Michael, 2008). Further, monitor your attention to detail (and, conversely, fatigue) when proofreading; accuracy in identifying errors wanes during the reading of lengthy documents. Knowing this fact may lead you to proofread from beginning to end on the computer screen, and to proofread from the end (section by section) to the beginning in hard-copy form. While you are proofreading the hard copy, you also should review page breaks to ensure that headings are not dissociated from the text that follows and that lists and tables are not split across pages.

Reporting Content in Specific Sections

We now address four sections of the report that typically contain the most information and that require the most time and effort to complete. Before moving forward, we want to express this: There are practically no prohibitions against using text from this book or from other prominent texts focusing on report writing (cited previously) in your reports. In fact, we urge you to use the scripts and more specific text included in this book. To include the most descriptive and clear wording in your reports appropriately, you must overcome the feeling that you are plagiarizing.

BACKGROUND INFORMATION

In addressing the test taker's history, summarize and highlight information that may affect the test taker's functioning in school, home, or community settings. Doing so means that you must select the most pertinent information from a variety of sources, but a careful report writer must follow certain rules. First, clearly indicate the source of the information you are reporting. Two methods address this goal: (1) include a general statement at the beginning of this section and (2) refer to the sources when specificity is needed. In many reports, we begin the Background Information section with a statement such as this one: "Background information was obtained about Miranda's family, developmental, medical, psychological, and educational history through an interview with Miranda's mother, Mrs. Perez, and review of school records."

After including this content, we then identify the source of information by using phrases such as "According to Mrs. Perez," and using a variety of verbs following the informant's name to indicate what was reported. You should (1) vary these verbs, such as by using *said, stated, reported, conveyed, indicated, communicated, described, gave details about, acknowledged, articulated,* or *recounted,* versus using only one (e.g., *reported*) and (2) use past-tense verbs versus "clinical-ese," which employs primarily present-tense verbs (e.g., "Mrs. Perez reports that . . ."). In general, if you are writing about events that happened in the past and that are not happening currently, use the past tense (e.g., "Miranda completed 2 years of tutoring" or "Miranda's mother reported that her pregnancy with Miranda was filled with medical problems."). If the behaviors or conditions of interest still continue, use present tense (e.g., "Miranda currently is in the second grade" and "Miranda reads each night before going to sleep").

Second, include the information in this section only if it has potential impact on the test taker in relation to the referral concern. For example, the existence of a family pet, the family's religious affiliation, and the test taker's favorite movies, books, or video games need not be addressed if they are not relevant. As you consider the relevance of the content in this section, weigh issues related to the test taker's privacy against this relevance. Do not "air dirty laundry"; instead, consider whether the content is too personal or too peripheral to the presenting problem to include. For example, in many cases, information about test taker's parents, such as their mental health history (e.g., prior hospitalizations and addiction treatments) and their relationship history (e.g., prior marriages), will be too personal and too peripheral to the referral concern to include. Although we encourage comprehensive descriptions of the background information, writers should be mindful of their own value judgments and avoid using biased terms (see Table 10.2 and APA, 2019).

Third, summarize prior assessment results in this section. Prior assessments may be formal ones such as the one you are describing in your report—from school districts, community mental health agencies, and the like. Report previous psychological assessment results in summary form (and refer to the dates of prior assessments, the report authors, and the agency through which assessments were completed). In addition, a lot of other assessment information often is available. For example, report card grades, discipline reports, and academic screening results may be available from a teacher or through a review of records. Pepper this section with reference to time markers. You may choose to report the age of the test taker, the grade level, or the year (or some combination of them) when events occurred to support your chronological sequencing of events across this section.

Table 10.2. Recommendations for General Writing Style and Word Selection in Reports

GENERAL WRITING STYLE

- Remember that clear communication is the goal of report writing.
- Do not set a goal to be "creative," "witty," or "lively" in your report writing.
- Choose words with care, and do not vary them when describing the same concept.
- Use simple language and a straightforward writing style. Write in short, simple sentences. Avoid lots of clauses, and use semicolons and dashes sparingly. When you struggle to make a long sentence clear, break it up into shorter sentences.
- Write concisely. Eliminate needless words.
- Avoid jargon and technical terms (including medical terms). Use the most accessible terms, or define the most technical ones (e.g., *trichotillomania* as hair pulling).
- Reduce the frequency of long words. Usually, the more letters a word includes, the more difficult it is for readers to "process" it.
- Either (1) define abbreviations and acronyms initially and then use the abbreviation or acronym, or (2) spell them out each time and avoid them altogether.
- In contrast to the APA (2019) recommendations, avoid writing in the first person (i.e., using *I* and *we*). If you must refer to yourself, write in the third person, calling yourself *the examiner* or the like.
- Emphasize words rather than numbers when describing results.
- Headings are important in reports, and they should be parallel across sections. Although centered headings and left-justified headings seem appropriate for reports, the indented headings followed by periods as, recommended by the APA (2019), are cumbersome and easily can be avoid.

Using the Optimal Terms

- Describe individuals as specifically, sensitively, and humanely as possible.
- Typically, refer to children as *boys* and *girls*, and adults as *men* and *women*. In the case of adolescents, consider *adolescent males* and *adolescent females* or *young man, young woman*, or *young person*. These labels will not apply to persons with nonbinary, gender queer, gender fluid, agender, and other identities outside the gender binary, and the test taker should be described using the term consistent with their identity. When in doubt, ask the test taker about their gender.
- Consider whether reporting gender identity and sexual orientation is relevant to your testing. When referring to gender identity, use *transgender, cisgender, agender, gender fluid*, and *gender nonconforming* as adjectives (e.g., *transgender boy*). When referring to sexual orientation, use *gay, lesbian, bisexual*, and *straight* as adjectives (e.g., *bisexual adolescent female*) and not *homosexual*. Recognize that a variety of terms are currently used and that they are likely to change across time.
- Use a test taker's pronouns, including *ze, hir*, and *hirs; zie, zir, zirs*, as well as *they, them*, and *theirs* as singular, as many gender-inclusive pronouns exist beyond *she, her*, and *hers* and *he, him*, and *his*. In order to be accurate in your reporting, you may need to ask test takers, "What pronouns do you use?" When in doubt about pronouns, repeat the test taker's name (e.g., Andy reported wearing prescription glasses to correct problems with near vision, but Andy could not recall when Andy began doing so).

Table 10.2. *Continued*

- When referring to race or ethnicity, capitalize the designation: *Black* or *African American*; *White* or *European American*; *Asian American*; *Hispanic*; *Latinx*; *Native American*, *Native North American*, or *American Indian*; *Indigenous People*; and *Aboriginal People*. The terms *biracial*, *multiracial*, and *multiethnic* need not be capitalized. Do not use terms such as *Negro*, *Caucasian*, and *Oriental*.
- When it is possible to be more specific by referring to a family's region or country of origin, do so (Latino or Mexican; Asian or Vietnamese, Middle Eastern or Egyptian, Western European or French, and Western African or Nigerian). You may need to inquire to ensure that you use the proper term.
- Capitalize languages (e.g., English, Spanish, and Mandarin Chinese).
- Avoid referring to people solely in terms of their educational, psychiatric, or medical conditions (e.g., "a class for the learning-disabled"). Use person-first language instead (e.g., "a class for students with learning disabilities").
- Spell out disorders in lowercase (e.g., attention-deficit/hyperactivity disorder), but, when necessary, abbreviate in uppercase (e.g., ADHD). However, special education eligibility categories can be capitalized (e.g., Intellectual Disability and Learning Disability).
- Avoid creating false hierarchies by using terms such as *normal* and marginalizing test takers by using terms such as *minority* and *underprivileged*. If necessary, use the most precise term (e.g., *racial minority* or *underfunded schools*).
- Avoid loaded terms or those that might be misunderstood (e.g., *borderline* and *suffering from*).
- Recognize that some test takers and their families may employ an identity-related term (e.g., *deaf* versus *hard of hearing* as well as *blind person* versus *person with a vision impairment*) to describe the test taker. Seeking out self-advocacy groups online and making sensitive inquires with those involved with the assessment will be key.

Punctuation, Numbers, and Abbreviations

- Use a comma
  - Between items in a series (e.g., apples, oranges, and grapes). Put one before the conjunction.
  - To set off a clause that can be removed from the sentence without hurting its message. For example, "The testing session, which lasted 3 hours, was conducted in the school cafeteria." If the "unnecessary" clause can be removed without affecting the meaning or the grammar of the sentence, use commas. An appositive can be included here (e.g., "John's mother, Charlene, stated that he acts like he's driven by a motor").
  - After words that introduce a clause ("For example").
  - To separate two independent clauses (thus, both have subjects and verbs and could stand alone) separated by a conjunction. Thus, "John completed the testing, and his teacher returned him to the classroom" needs a comma. However, do not use a comma when you have only a compound predicate. For example, "John completed the testing and asked for a piece of candy for a reward" does not need a comma because "John" is the subject of both clauses. (The clause beginning with "asked" is dependent on "John" for meaning.)
  - To set off years (e.g., John was hit by a car on January 31, 2019. He was hospitalized until February 9, 2020).
- Typically, you should use double quotation marks. Use single quotation marks only when quoted material, a coined expression, or a title of a publication is inside another quotation.

(continued)

Table 10.2. *Continued*

- When you use quotation marks, know that periods and commas are almost always placed inside of quotation marks and that question marks are tricky in these cases. Put them inside the quotation marks if what has been quoted is a question. If the sentence is a question with a quoted phrase at the end, put the quotation mark on the outside of the quotation marks.
- Typically, use parentheses versus brackets.
- Use numbers for all ages—even if the number is less than 10 (e.g., "Miguel is a 6-year-old boy" and "Ze began taking Ritalin when he was 10 years old").
- In general, use numerals for all numbers unless the number begins a sentence. We see no need to follow the APA PM rule that numbers less than 10 should be spelled out and numbers 10 or greater should be written in numeral form.
- Hyphenate age (e.g., "She has a 3-year-old brother.") when it is an adjective and not when it is a noun (e.g., "He is 6 years old").
- Capitalize the titles of tests, subtests, scales, and factors (e.g., WISC-V Full Scale IQ, the BASC-3 Hyperactivity scale, and Fluid Reasoning). There is no need to italicize them.
- Avoid using Latin abbreviations such as "etc." Spell out "that is" for "i.e." and "for example" for "e.g."

Grammar and Word Selection

- Avoid using the pronouns "this," "these," and "those" as subjects of sentences (e.g., "This is a sign of major depressive disorder."). Instead use them as adjectives preceding nouns to link prior references nouns (e.g., "This sign indicates major depressive disorder.")
- Use "since" to refer to time that has passed. Use "because" to indicate causal relations.
- Use "while" to refer to events in time. Use "whereas," "although," and "but" to point out contrasts.
- Use "which" with commas when a clause can be removed without sacrificing meaning or correct grammar. Use "that" (without commas) when the information is necessary (i.e., in a restrictive or essential clause).
- Place an adjective or an adverb as close as possible to the word it modifies.
- Beware of dangling or misplaced modifiers. When they are used, it is unclear, based often on their placement, what they describe. In particular, beware of participle phrases (those starting with a verb followed by "ing" ["indicating that," "stating that," and "feeling that"]). Make sure that such a phrase directly follows or is very near the word it modifies.
- Strive for parallel construction. Ensure that common elements in a series appear consistently within each element. For example, "He likes to ride his bike, to eat pizza, and to watch TV." When you have items in a series and when you use "not only . . . but also," "both . . . and," "between . . . and," "neither . . . no," and "either . . . or," be conscious of this issue.
- Use lowercase letters (or numbers) enclosed in parentheses to identify elements in a series. For example, "John is involved in several extracurricular activities: (a) baseball, (b) soccer, and (c) hockey." These markers also help ensure parallel construction.
- Capitalize the names of schools, hospitals, clinics, and universities when they refer to specific institutions. Typically, *kindergarten* is not capitalized.

Note. Based on American Psychological Association (2019), except as noted.

BEHAVIORS DURING TESTING SESSION AND VALIDITY OF ASSESSMENT

In the section on test session behaviors and assessment validity, describe in some detail the test taker's reaction to the testing environment. To accomplish this goal, you probably will include several pieces of qualitative idiographic information about the test taker (see Chapter 8 and Box 10.2). First, consider the importance of describing the test taker's appearance and dress. Such data may be relevant to the referral concern or educational outcome (e.g., if the child is extremely overweight or wearing obviously dirty clothes), or they may not be relevant. We do not recommend typically including content related to appearance and dress in this section—at least in part due to fear of making inappropriate value judgments—but it is a matter of professional style and judgment. Second, consider the test taker's behaviors that may have affected performance (for better or worse) during testing (see Chapter 5 for a detailed discussion of these issues). Because testing sessions typically are poor representations of the typical behaviors of children and adolescents, attend to behaviors during testing, such as social skills, attention, and conversational proficiency, but do not place too much trust in them as representing the "real things" in home and school settings. Do consider and place more emphasis on behaviors affecting item-level responding (and, ultimately, test scores). In technical terms, describe the test taker's behavior in the past tense. When you appraise or make judgment about a behavior (e.g., "Gracie appeared nervous during testing"), support this statement with quotes and descriptions of the child's behaviors (e.g., describing trembling hands, foot tapping, and inappropriate laughter).

Perhaps the most important standard of this section is its ending. According to the APA's Ethical Principles of Psychologists and Code of Conduct (APA, 2002, 2010a):

> When interpreting assessment results . . . psychologists take into account the purpose of the assessment as well as the various test factors, test-taking abilities and other characteristics of the person being assessed, such as situational, personal, linguistic and cultural differences, that might affect psychologists' judgments or reduce the accuracy of their interpretations. They indicate any significant limitations of their interpretations. (Standard 9.06)

You must make a judgment about the meaningfulness of the test results—concluding that construct-irrelevant influences did not affect the test scores. For example, for test takers from diverse backgrounds, it is important to rule out cultural and linguistic factors (e.g., opportunity to learn test content and English-language proficiency) before interpreting intelligence test standard scores that are well below average as representing low general intelligence (see Chapter 14). In this section of the report, summarize the results of your direct screening for vision, hearing, fine motor, and articulation problems and color blindness via the Screening Tool for Assessment (see Chapter 5) and describe accommodations made to the standard test administration to address these problems (see Box 10.2). When all has gone well, we typically include a brief validity statement such as, "The results from the testing appear to be valid estimates of Miranda's current cognitive abilities and academic achievement." When construct-

Box 10.2. Examples of Text from the Behaviors during Testing Session and Validity of Assessment Section

EXAMPLE 1

Oliver completed one session with the examiner. He completed the Screening Tool for Assessment Direct Screening Form, and his vision, hearing, and articulation were found to be adequate for testing. However, Oliver had difficulties accurately tracing a straight line, a circle, and a star. In addition, in order to print letters neatly, Oliver wrote very slowly. As a result of these screening tests, the Wechsler Intelligence Scale for Children, Fifth Edition (WISC-V) General Ability Index was interpreted rather than the WISC-V Full Scale IQ. His fine motor skills did not appear to affect Oliver's manipulation of blocks during the WISC-V Block Design subtest. Overall, the results presented in this report are valid estimates of Oliver's general intelligence.

EXAMPLE 2

Zahan completed two sessions during the course of the assessment. His conversational proficiency in English was typical for his age and grade level. Zahan appeared at ease and comfortable during each session. Zahan's vision, hearing, fine motor skills, and the intelligibility of his speech were found to be adequate for testing based on the Screening Tool for Assessment Direct Screening Form. Zahan noticeably increased his level of effort during difficult tasks, but at times, he responded too quickly, which led to errors. During achievement subtests requiring him to write sentences, Zahan sometimes stopped to stretch his hand as if it was hurting him. However, this same behavior was not observed during timed subtests on intelligence tests requiring rapid written responses. The results of testing appear to be valid estimates of Zahan's current cognitive abilities, reading skills, and math skills. However, some question remains about whether the results of the extended writing subtests accurately reflect Zahan's ability to generate short sentences quickly and to write sentences clearly to convey meaning to potential readers.

EXAMPLE 3

Avery completed three sessions during the course of the assessment, following an interview with their parents. During the first testing session, Avery completed the Woodcock-Johnson IV Tests of Cognitive Abilities. They was very tired because they stayed up late to finish an essay. Avery appeared drowsy and was slow in responding, and their performance was far below what was expected based on other information. The results were deemed invalid in representing their day-to-day display of cognitive abilities. As a result, Avery completed the Wechsler Adult Intelligence Scale—Fourth Edition (WAIS-IV). Avery's performance produced scores that were closer to what was expected, and scores were more congruent with those on the Woodcock-Johnson IV Tests of Achievement; therefore, Avery's scores from

> the Woodcock-Johnson IV Tests of Cognitive Abilities are not included in this report. During all other testing, Avery's level of conversational proficiency and cooperation were typical for their age. They was slow and careful in responding and generally persisted with difficult tasks. Overall, results presented in this report are valid estimates of Avery's overall intellectual, academic, and psychosocial functioning.
>
> **EXAMPLE 4**
>
> Rachelle completed three test sessions during the course of assessment. During each session, she was cooperative and maintained attention to the tasks, and she required no breaks in testing. Her conversational proficiency was typical for her age. Rachelle appeared at ease and comfortable throughout the assessment, and she generally persisted with difficult tasks.
>
> After all testing sessions had been completed, Rachelle's mother, Mrs. Freedman, notified the clinic that Rachelle had just been prescribed reading glasses. Her prescription revealed spherical refractive error of +3.50 for the right eye and +3.00 for the left eye, indicating moderate hyperopia or farsightedness. Although Rachelle displayed no notable behaviors during testing that indicated that she had trouble seeing the letters and numbers presented to her, it is possible that her test results may have been affected by her hyperopia. In the absence of additional testing, which was declined, it cannot be concluded that the results of the current assessment are valid estimates of Rachelle's intellectual and academic functioning.
>
> **EXAMPLE 5**
>
> Riley completed one session with the examiner. Zie completed the Screening Tool for Assessment Direct Screening Form, and zir vision, hearing, and articulation were all found to be adequate for testing. However, in order to print letters in a sentence neatly, Riley wrote very slowly and erased several times to ensure that zir letters were properly formed. Based on these results, the tablet-based version of the Wechsler Intelligence Scale for Children, Fifth Edition (called Q-Interactive) was administered to remove the requirement of pencil use on the speeded subtest Coding. Overall, the results presented in this report are valid estimates of Riley's general intelligence.

irrelevant influences did affect the test scores, do not report or interpret those that are invalid. You can address construct-irrelevant influences on test scores and invalid scores in a number of ways; several examples are included in Box 10.2.

ASSESSMENT RESULTS

With knowledge of the measurement properties of your assessment instruments (see Chapters 6 and 7) and interpretive strategies (see Chapter 9), feel empowered to craft text to convey the full meaning of your results. When writing test-based reports as well as other styles of reports, the assessment results section usually highlights nomothetic and quantitative results in the form of standardized scores, score ranges, confidence intervals, and percentile ranks.

Standardized scores and score labels. The norm-referenced standardized scores yielded from testing—be they deviation IQ scores ($M = 100$, $SD = 15$), T scores ($M = 50$, $SD = 10$), or scaled scores ($M = 10$, $SD = 3$)—are the data from which meaning most typically is derived. You should pair these scores with narrative classification labels that enhance their meaning. We agree with Kamphaus (2001) and Woods et al. (2019) that score-labeling terminology should be consistent across tests; using varied terms proposed by test authors and publishers for the same scores can only lead to errors on your part and to confusion on the part of your report's consumers. Table 10.3 includes a summary of narrative classifications of scores for the most commonly produced standardized scores. In Form 10.1, this summary is expanded to address narrative classifications of scores for each score type and to provide narrative descriptions of percentile ranks.

Although we have seen score labels that are not only descriptive of performance but also may be considered somewhat snobby, such as *Superior* and *Exceptional,* we suggest using score classifications that do not have such connotations. Further, we do not condone the use of the classification *Borderline* to label standard scores ranging from 70 to 79. It may be confused with borderline personality disorder (American Psychiatric Association, 2013), and it also indicates that about 10% of the population has either intellectual disability (ID) or borderline ID (see Chapter 11). The term has surplus meaning, and to us, it seems antiquated and misleading. Following A. Kaufman and N. Kaufman (1983), Fish (1990), and Woods et al. (2019), we assert that score labels should focus on statistical deviation from what is considered average (e.g., High Average and Low Average).

We believe that (1) capitalizing score classifications and (2) making frequent and explicit reference to the norm group on which scores are based are wise practices. For example, you can report that "Phillip's Full Scale IQ is in the Low range when compared to others his age," and then follow such statements with brief references to standardized scores and percentile ranks in parentheses. Further, make reference to the high end or low end of a score range and occasionally report dual score ranges (Average to High Average) if the standard score is within 3 points of another score range or the

Table 10.3. Summary of Narrative Classifications Associated with Varying Standardized Scores

Narrative classification	Standard scores	T scores	Scaled scores
Extremely High	≥ 140	≥ 77	18–19
Very High	130–139	70–76	16–17
High	120–129	63–69	14–15
High Average	110–119	57–63	12–13
Average	90–109	43–56	8–11
Low Average	80–89	37–43	6–7
Low	70–79	30–36	4–5
Very Low	60–69	23–29	2–3
Extremely Low	< 60	≤ 23	1

T score is within 2 points of another score range. Examples of text used to describe standard scores and their associated score ranges appear in Box 10.3.

Confidence intervals. We urge you to employ confidence intervals during interpretation and reporting of results. As described in Chapter 4, norm-referenced scores from intelligence tests never are perfectly accurate. To account for this less-than-perfect accuracy, report a band of uncertainty around scores by using confidence intervals.

Confidence intervals are reported in a number of ways, and there appears to be no convention for doing so. As evident in Box 10.3, they may be reported as a range

---

Box 10.3. Text for Standardized Scores, Confidence Intervals, and Percentile Ranks

DEVIATION IQ SCORES

- Ronald's Wechsler Intelligence Scale for Children, Fifth Edition Full Scale IQ, which measures general intelligence, was in the High Average range (SS = 116) when compared to other test takers his age.
- According to age-based norms, Jill's overall cognitive ability is in the Very Low range (Reynolds Intellectual Assessment Scales, Second Edition Composite Intelligence Index = 67).
- Juan's general ability to acquire knowledge, reason, and think abstractly is in the Average range when compared to that of others his age (Universal Nonverbal Intelligence Test, Second Edition Full Scale Battery = 103).

CONFIDENCE INTERVALS

- The chances are 9 out of 10 that Antwan's true Full Scale IQ score falls within the range of 101 to 109 when compared to others his age.
- Parker obtained a Fluid-Crystallized Index score of 122. With 95% confidence, zirs true Fluid-Crystallized Index score falls within the range of 117–125.
- Ivy's Detroit Tests of Learning Abilities, Fifth Edition, General Cognitive Ability score was 91 (±7).
- When considering that general intelligence cannot be measured perfectly, Mallory's Woodcock-Johnson IV Tests of Cognitive Abilities General Intellectual Ability score falls between 95 and 105 with 95% confidence.

PERCENTILE RANKS

- Sarah scored as high as or higher than only approximately 10% of children her age.
- Kay's percentile rank of 99.5 indicates that only 5 in 1,000 test takers her age would have a score higher than hers.
- Peyton scored at the 28th percentile; they scored as high as or higher than only about one-quarter of others their age.
- According to age norms, about 98% of Jack's peers would be expected to have earned a higher score (percentile rank = 2).

of scores following the obtained score or with a plus or minus indicating what number was added to and subtracted from an obtained score. We often include them in another sentence following the initial report of the standardized score (e.g., the IQ) that addresses the confidence interval in a more detailed manner. We believe that either the 90% confidence interval (as recommended by Kamphaus, 2001) or the 95% confidence interval should be applied. We have found that the 90% confidence interval seems to be easier to describe (referring to the probability as 9 out of 10 times) and understand than the 95% confidence interval (referring to the probability as 19 out of 20 times).

Percentile ranks. Remember that percentile ranks represent some of the same information about normative variation as standard scores, and the same score labels can be applied to them (see Form 10.1 and Box 10.3). They seem to be understood more easily by parents and teachers than standardized scores, so their judicious use in reports is wise (Wiener & Constaris, 2011). Typically, these scores are reported to reflect the percentage of test takers the same age (if age-based norms were used) who would have performed the same or lower on a task. Reporting that "Justice's performance on the Wechsler Intelligence Scale for Children, Fifth Edition Full Scale IQ exceeded that of approximately 25% of adolescents the same age" is appropriate. Alternatively, the reflected percentile rank value can be used when scores are very low or very high. For example, a percentile rank of 1 indicates that 99% (100% − 1% = 99%) of test takers would score higher. Conversely, a percentile rank of 99 indicates that only 1% of test takers would score higher. Narrative descriptions used to describe percentile ranks appear in Form 10.1.

Test information. We recommend that you consistently capitalize the names of tests and subtests but not capitalize words such as *subtest, composite, index,* or *cluster,* unless such a word is part of the proper noun (e.g., the Verbal Comprehension Index). (Note that we have used italics here to mark linguistic examples; italics are unnecessary for these terms in reports.) Unlike Kamphaus (2001) and others, we do not believe that there is much utility in describing the structure of and intended use of intelligence tests. For example, many authors will include a full paragraph describing the number of subtests included in an intelligence test, the age range for which it is appropriate, and the range of score types yielded. Just as you probably are not concerned about the calibration of the electronic thermometer used in your primary care physician's office or the method used to determine your cholesterol levels, we believe that most consumers are not interested in the specifics of the test you used. A brief statement introducing the name of the test and what types of constructs it targets is satisfactory.

Score tables. Score tables appearing within the body of or at the end of reports are intended for use primarily by other professionals (see Tallent, 1993). Despite our advocacy of the KISS model, which suggests that interpretation be based primarily on the most reliable and general scores yielded by intelligence tests, we recognize that it is tradition to include several relevant score types (e.g., subtest scores, composite scores, and IQs) in the score tables so that others can access your most basic norm-referenced scores for consideration. However, if you fear that others may misinterpret your results (e.g., emphasize the patterns of subtests strengths and weaknesses), you should omit scores from these tables that may lead to these misinterpretations.

The Informing Session: Presenting the Results of Your Assessment

Whereas report writing can be completed in the quiet of your office or a room in a school, clinic, or hospital, you are on stage and in the spotlight when you are asked to describe your findings to the parents or others involved in the assessment of the text takers themselves. In providing this information, channel your expertise in test selection, score interpretation, and identification of mental disorders and educational conditions to answer the referral concerns and facilitate the implementation of interventions.

The informing session represents a collaborative process by which you convey the most important findings from your assessment and guide your clients toward effective interventions. We have developed scripts for presenting segments of results and have seen many other assessment professionals do the same. We provide our general outline for presenting results in Form 10.2. Below, we offer three broad recommendations when presenting these results: (1) be prepared, (2) communicate clearly, and (3) promote discussion and use proper listening skills.

PREPARATION

Campbell (2006a) stated that preparation can manifest itself in selecting a setting that is private, quiet, and comfortable for all involved. Although most clinics have conference rooms for such meetings, those working in school settings may need to devote more thought to the setting and the timing of the meeting than those working in other settings. You also should make sure you have allowed enough time for a parent who needs consultation, consoling, or a referral. In addition, it is wise to anticipate low-probability events (e.g., a parent's anger or their revealing of information previously withheld) and develop contingency plans for dealing with them.

We suggest scheduling informing sessions for at least an hour and perhaps more, depending on the level of support needed based on the conclusions from the assessment. In addition, it is wise to be prepared for tears—either of joy or of sorrow. Having a box of tissues nearby reflects that wisdom. Preparation also is needed to determine when to convey the most potentially upsetting results—for instance, a diagnosis of intellectual disability, or the presentation of results indicating suboptimal performance when there is striving for entrance to programs. We generally recommend saving potentially distressing content for the last segment of the meeting. In addition, provide parents with resources (such as handouts, website listings, and the titles of books, and the names of those who can provide interventions) at the informing session. We highly recommend resources such as *Helping Handouts: Supporting*

Students at School and Home (Bear & Minke, 2018), which contains forms that can be provided to parents or appended to the report.

COMMUNICATION

Once you are in the session, communicate the assessment results clearly. We agree with Kamphaus (2001) that you should be genuine, honest, and forthcoming with information, while also considering the experiences and expectations of those to whom you are reporting the results. To promote clarity, we suggest that you organize your results into meaning-based clusters, guided, in part, by the referral concerns. This organization is consistent with the hypothesis-oriented reports (Ownby, 1997), referral-based reports (Hass & Carriere, 2014), major findings reports (Kranzler & Floyd, 2013), and question-and-answer format reports (Wiener, 1985, 1987; Wiener & Kohler, 1986) discussed previously. In addition, supplement your verbal statements with concrete visual aids. For example, we encourage you to consider using a drawing of the normal curve (similar to Form 10.3) when presenting results. This figure will allow you to increase the meaningfulness of descriptions of the norm-referenced scores.

When presenting these results, you also may convey messages that you would not necessarily write in your report. For example, we teach students to differentiate standardized scores (especially deviation IQ scores) and percentile ranks from typical scores on school-based exams, which are measured in the *percentage correct* metric. For example, we say,

> Based on your time in school and from reviewing your child's tests and homework, you are probably accustomed to reviewing 100 as the best score. These scores we will be discussing today include two types. For one type, standard scores, 100 is the perfectly average score—with about 50% of test takers obtaining higher scores and about 50% obtaining lower scores. For the other type, percentile ranks, 100 is an unattainable score, because we are roughly considering where scores fall in ranking your child's performance when it is compared to the performance of 100 typical children her age. I will give these percentile ranks to you as percentages ranging from 1% to 99%.

Finally, it is acceptable to share the responses written on protocols and response booklets to convey your message more clearly. Such sharing should be done sparingly to protect test security, however.

DISCUSSION

You must not only communicate your messages clearly, but also promote discussion and listen carefully to parents' questions and concerns. We urge you, early in the informing session, to encourage questions and comments on findings. We also urge you to issue "check-ins" throughout. For example, ask open-ended questions—such as "Can I clarify any point I made?" and our favorite, "Are those the results you expected?"—after you have presented a key point. When the parents respond, use your best listening skills, such as maintaining eye contact, leaning toward them, summarizing their points, and describing the emotions they must be feeling.

Meetings in which assessment results are presented can be challenging, and we strongly urge students in training and emerging professionals to practice their communication skills—especially with parents from a variety of backgrounds—and to seek feedback about them from supervisors and others who may be attending the same meeting (e.g., during a school-based team meeting). Recording these sessions with audio or video devices (with approval from all involved) and reviewing them carefully often will reveal areas to target for improvement.

Staffing a Case with a Supervisor

For students, interns, and those engaging in postdoctoral supervision, we offer some guidelines for sharing your results with your supervisors during staffings. Staffings differ from presentations of assessment results to parents and other caregivers, because you and your supervisors generally have the same knowledge base. As a consequence, you are free to use acronyms and technical terms during your oral presentation, and to move rapidly through your assessment results. We offer the following general recommendations, and an outline is provided in Form 10.4.

BEING ORGANIZED

When entering the supervision session, have all of your assessment results with you and have these materials organized in the order you plan to present the results, so that you can access them easily. In a staffing, you typically are referring to the hard copies of the actual interview forms, protocols, and scoring software output, so striving for completeness and organization of these materials is vital. Further, because a staffing occurs so quickly after the assessment is complete, it is not expected that you will have initiated your report writing or will have summarized test results in a written document; however, you should have begun to conceptualize the case and consider prevailing and rival hypotheses.

PRESENTING RESULTS

As you begin presenting your test results, strive for brevity and focus on the results and your evaluation of them. You also should be prepared to respond to your supervisor's questions and to search for additional information from your notes, test protocols, and scoring software output to answer those questions. We have found that the following sequence of presenting results is common, logical, and consistent with most psychological reports, and we encourage you to adhere to it during initial staffings with your supervisor.

First, present the demographic information about the examinee (such as name, gender, age, race, ethnicity, and grade). Second, describe the referral concern and those involved in it. Third, present background information. Focus on information directly relevant to the referral concern, but consider addressing the family constellation, developmental history, and academic history. Do not forget to label the source of any information that may not be a verifiable fact. Fourth, present your valid assessment results. Typically, begin with intelligence test results and follow with achievement test results. Consistent with the KISS model of interpretation, focus primarily on the most reliable composite scores. Fifth, focus on the results from other forms of assessment. For example, report results of rating scales targeting social–emotional functioning completed by parents and caregivers, teachers, and the test taker. Again, focus on the most reliable composite scores and on scores that are normatively deviant; ignore others if they are irrelevant to the referral concern and not elevated. Finally, integrate the results. Consider "rule-outs," engage in steps to make a differential diagnosis, and consider eligibility or diagnostic criteria. Recommendations typically are not developed until after the results have been summarized, so withhold coverage of them until later.

Summary

Even after you have completed and scored your tests and other assessment instruments, your job is not complete. You must make meaning of the results, integrate them, and consider relevant questions brought to you by referral agents. This chapter has highlighted pathways by which you can address these goals through communicating the results of a psychological assessment in writing and orally. It also included models and other resources for facilitating completion of these activities.

FORM 10.1

Narrative Classifications Associated with Varying Standardized Scores and Percentile Ranks Three Standard Deviations above and below the Mean, and Narrative Descriptions of Percentile Ranks

Narrative Classification	Standard Score	T Score	Scaled Score	Percentile Rank	Narrative Description of Percentile Ranks
Extremely High	160	90		99.99%	Only about 1 in 10,000 would score as high
	159	89		99.99%	
	158	89		99.99%	
	157	88		99.99%	
	156	87		99.99%	
	155	87		99.99%	
	154	86		99.98%	
	153	85		99.98%	
	152	85		99.97%	
	151	84		99.97%	
	150	83		99.96%	
	149	83		99.95%	
	148	82		99.93%	
	147	81		99.91%	Only about 1 in 1,000 would score as high
	146	81		99.89%	
	145	80	19	99.87%	
	144	79		99.83%	
	143	79		99.79%	
	142	78		99.74%	
	141	77		99.69%	
	140	77	18	99.62%	
Very High	139	76		99.53%	
	138	75		99.44%	
	137	75		99.32%	
	136	74		99.18%	Only about 1 in 100 would score as high
	135	73	17	99.02%	
	134	73		98.83%	
	133	72		98.61%	
	132	71		98.36%	
	131	71		98.06%	
	130	70	16	97.72%	

(continued)

FORM 10.1

Continued

Narrative Classification	Standard Score	T Score	Scaled Score	Percentile Rank	Narrative Description of Percentile Ranks
High	129	69		97.34%	
	128	69		96.90%	Obtaining roughly the highest score in a typical class of 25 students
	127	68		96.41%	
	126	67		95.85%	
	125	67	15	95.22%	Obtaining roughly the highest score in a typical class of 20 students
	124	66		94.52%	
	123	65		93.74%	
	122	65		92.88%	
	121	64		91.92%	
High Average	120	63	14	90.88%	Scoring higher than about 9 out of 10 peers; only about 1 out of 10 would score as high
	119	63		89.74%	
	118	62		88.49%	
	117	61		87.15%	
	116	61		85.69%	
	115	60	13	84.13%	
	114	59		82.47%	
	113	59		80.69%	Scoring higher than about 4 out of 5 peers; only about 1 in 5 would score as high
	112	58		78.81%	
	111	57		76.83%	
	110	57	12	74.75%	Scoring higher than about 3 out of 4 peers; only about 1 in 4 would score as high

Narrative Classification	Standard Score	T Score	Scaled Score	Percentile Rank	Narrative Description of Percentile Ranks
Average	109	56		72.57%	
	108	55		70.31%	Scoring higher than about 7 out of 10 peers
	107	55		67.96%	
	106	54		65.54%	
	105	53	11	63.06%	
	104	53		60.51%	Scoring higher than about 3 out of 5 peers
	103	52		57.93%	
	102	51		55.30%	
	101	51		52.66%	
	100	50	10	50.00%	Like most other children; perfectly average
	99	49		47.34%	
	98	49		44.70%	
	97	48		42.07%	
	96	47		39.49%	Scoring lower than about 3 out of 5 peers
	95	47	9	36.94%	
	94	46		34.46%	
	93	45		32.04%	
	92	45		29.69%	Scoring lower than about 7 out of 10 peers
	91	44		27.43%	
	90	43	8	25.25%	Scoring lower than about 3 out of 4 peers; only about 1 in 4 would score as low
	89	43		23.17%	
	88	42		21.19%	
	87	41		19.31%	
	86	41		17.53%	
	85	40	7	15.87%	
	84	39		14.31%	
	83	39		12.85%	

(*continued*)

FORM 10.1

Continued

Narrative Classification	Standard Score	T Score	Scaled Score	Percentile Rank	Narrative Description of Percentile Ranks
Low Average	82	38		11.51%	
	81	37		10.26%	Scoring lower than about 9 out of 10 peers; only about 1 out of 10 would score as low
	80	37	6	9.12%	
Low	79	36		8.08%	
	78	35		7.12%	
	77	35		6.26%	Obtaining roughly the lowest score in a typical class of 20 students
	76	34		5.48%	Obtaining roughly the lowest score in a typical class of 20 students Obtaining roughly the lowest score in a typical class of 25 students
	75	33	5	4.78%	
	74	33		4.15%	Obtaining roughly the lowest score in a typical class of 25 students
	73	32		3.59%	
	72	31		3.10%	
	71	31		2.66%	
	70	30	4	2.28%	
Very Low	69	29		1.94%	
	68	29		1.64%	
	67	28		1.39%	
	66	27		1.17%	Only about 1 in 100 would score as low
	65	27	3	0.98%	Only about 1 in 100 would score as low
	64	26		0.82%	
	63	25		0.68%	
	62	25		0.56%	
	61	24		0.47%	
	60	23	2	0.38%	

Narrative Classification	Standard Score	T Score	Scaled Score	Percentile Rank	Narrative Description of Percentile Ranks
Extremely Low	59	23		0.31%	
	58	22		0.26%	
	57	21		0.21%	
	56	21		0.17%	
	55	20	1	0.13%	
	54	19		0.11%	Only about 1 in 1,000 would score as low
	53	19		0.09%	Only about 1 in 1,000 would score as low
	52	18		0.07%	
	51	17		0.05%	
	50	17		0.04%	
	49	16		0.03%	
	48	15		0.03%	
	47	15		0.02%	
	46	14		0.02%	
	45	13		0.01%	Only about 1 in 10,000 would score as low
	44	13		0.01%	
	43	12		0.01%	Only about 1 in 10,000 would score as low
	42	11		0.01%	
	41	11		0.01%	
	40	10		0.01%	

FORM 10.2

Script for Presentation of Assessment Results to Parents and Other Caregivers

1. Make small talk. Ask for updates about the child or adolescent and family.
2. Explain why you are meeting and mention upcoming goals.

    "I wanted us to come together to discuss the findings from the assessment. One thing I will do today is summarize all that we have learned about _____ during the assessment process. Please know that I will have completed the final written report within 2 weeks, and I will contact you when it is ready for you to pick up."

    "I also wanted to thank you for giving me the opportunity to work with _____."

3. Summarize the assessment process.

    "About ___ months ago, we met to discuss your goals for the assessment. We also discussed _____'s history during that meeting. I gave you some rating scales to complete, and you gave me permission to communicate with _____'s teacher and to ask the teacher to complete a rating scale, too. Afterward, I visited _____'s school to observe him or her with peers and in the classroom. Then _____ came to visit the clinic and completed a number of tests—tests of reading, writing, and math, as well as intellectual abilities. In addition, I chatted some with _____ about home and school life, and and we completed a rating scale. Finally, you and I met again to complete another interview focusing on what behaviors _____ displays in the home setting. Now we can discuss the results of the entire assessment grouped into the most central concerns for _____, and after each one, I will provide some recommendations. As I am discussing them, please do not hesitate to interrupt me and to ask questions. Do you have any questions before we begin?"

4. Summarize the referral concern.

    "When we first met, you said you were concerned about [referral concern]. Is that correct?"

5. Present results in a structured manner—perhaps organized by Major Findings—and address some recommendations after each set of results.

    "I am going to start by discussing . . ."

    "In particular, you were most concerned about _____," or "You particularly wanted to understand better _____. The results of the assessment indicate . . ."

    "Next, I would like to discuss . . ."

6. Ask for a response, and be prepared to listen.

    "Now that we have reviewed the results, do you have any further questions or concerns or issues I can clarify?" or "Were these findings what you were expecting?"

7. Close the meeting.

    "Thank you again for your time and for meeting with me—and for being helpful and patient throughout this process."

FORM 10.3

Understanding Scores from Testing

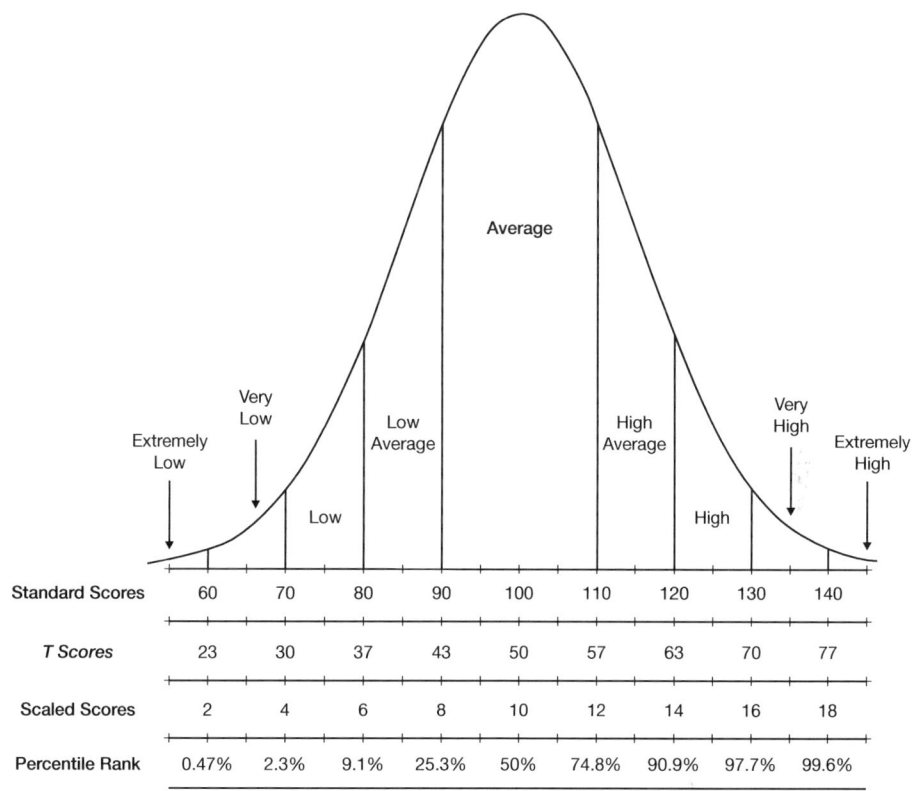

FORM 10.4

Content to Include When Staffing a Case with a Supervisor

1. Child or adolescent's first name (and last name, if requested): _____
   _____

2. Child or adolescent's gender: _____

3. Child or adolescent's age: _____

4. Child or adolescent's race/ethnicity: _____

5. Child or adolescent's grade and school: _____

6. Child or adolescent's referral agent and referral concern: _____
   _____

7. Background information: _____
   _____
   _____

8. Intelligence test results: _____
   _____
   _____

9. Achievement test results: _____
   _____
   _____

10. Behaviors in home and community settings: _____
    _____
    _____

11. Behaviors in school setting: _____
    _____
    _____

12. Child or adolescent's reports: _____
    _____
    _____

13. Summary:_____
    _____
    _____
    _____

CHAPTER 11

Assessment of Intellectual Disability

The purpose of this chapter is to describe the condition known as *intellectual disability* (ID) and to offer practical guidelines for assessing children and adolescents suspected of having this condition. For details about the history of the conception and identification of persons with ID, review Wehmeyer (2013), and for information about the development, course, and treatment of this condition, consult Witwer, Lawton, and Aman (2014). In this chapter, we begin by presenting varying diagnostic and eligibility criteria for ID and end by offering recommendations for best practices in assessment.

Definition, Diagnosis, and Eligibility

Across both diagnostic and special education eligibility criteria, the general characteristics of ID are consistent. According to the *dual-criterion approach* (Schalock et al., 2010), deficits in intellectual functioning and deficits in adaptive behaviors must be identified, and these dual criteria must be evident during infancy, childhood, or adolescence. This following section addresses the specific criteria for ID as outlined by the American Association on Intellectual and Developmental Disabilities (Schalock et al., 2010); the American Psychiatric Association (2013); the Individuals with Disabilities Education Improvement Act of 2004 (IDEA; Public Law 108-446, 2004) and Rosa's Law (Public Law 111-256, 2010). Seek out Farmer and Floyd (2018) for descriptions of classification criteria from other sources.

AMERICAN ASSOCIATION ON INTELLECTUAL AND DEVELOPMENTAL DISABILITIES

Intellectual Disability: Definition, Classification, and Systems of Support (Schalock et al., 2010) is the premier text guiding the assessment and identification of individuals with ID.[1] Published in the 2010s, its 11th edition contained one of the most striking

---

1. The American Association on Intellectual and Developmental Disabilities' *Intellectual Disability: Definition, Classification, and Systems of Support* currently is being revised for publication in 2021.

changes to diagnostic terminology in recent memory: labeling the disorder as *intellectual disability* rather than *mental retardation*. This change is summarized in the following sentence:

> We stipulate . . . that the term ID covers the same population of individuals who were diagnosed previously with mental retardation in number, kind, level, type, and duration of the disability and the need of people with this disability for individualized services and supports; and every individual who is or was eligible for a diagnosis of mental retardation is eligible for a diagnosis of ID. (Schalock et al., 2010, p. xvi)

Consistent with prior definitions of mental retardation offered by the American Association on Intellectual and Developmental Disabilities under its previous title (American Association on Mental Retardation, 2002), ID is a developmental disorder emerging before age 18 and characterized by "significant limitations both in mental functioning and in adaptive behavior as expressed in conceptual, social, and practical adaptive skills" (Schalock et al., 2010, p. 1). In contrast to earlier definitions, Schalock et al. (2010) narrowed the focus on intellectual functioning to general mental ability and its key features: abstract reasoning and thinking, the capacity to acquire knowledge, and problem-solving ability. As described in Chapter 1, general mental ability and these three features are synonymous with the construct of psychometric g, and they are measured by IQs in the practice of psychology. Schalock et al. suggested that a significant limitation in intellectual functioning is evident when an individual produces an IQ of approximately 70 or below. The effects of measurement error must also be considered via use of confidence intervals. Test session behaviors (e.g., display of fatigue or anxiety) and relevant measurement issues (e.g., age of norms)—as discussed in Chapters 5 and 4, respectively—must also be considered.

Adaptive behaviors represent the collection of skills typically performed by people in their everyday lives to demonstrate personal and social responsibility based on the expectations from their culture. Schalock et al. (2010) focused on three classes of adaptive behaviors: *conceptual, social,* and *practical. Conceptual skills* are employed when higher-order thinking and achievement-oriented skills are applied to situations; they include expressive and receptive language skills, reading and writing skills, knowledge of money concepts, and self-direction. These skills are most strongly related to those measured by intelligence tests. *Social skills* are displayed when an individual is interacting with others in school and community settings; they include interpersonal skills, personal responsibility, self-esteem, following rules, and engaging in social problem solving to avoid being victimized by others (due to naiveté or gullibility). Finally, *practical skills* are applied when the individual is engaging independently in activities of daily living, and they include engaging in enriching personal activities and self-care, displaying occupational skills, and maintaining a safe environment.

Schalock et al. (2010) were explicit in recommending formal assessment instruments targeting adaptive behavior skills. They stated that "significant limitations in adaptive behavior should be established through the use of standardized measures normed with general populations, including persons with disabilities and people without disabilities" (Schalock et al. 2010, p. 43). Deficits in adaptive behaviors were operationalized by the following when age-based norms are used: (1) at least one score representing the conceptual domain, social domain, or practical domain that is at least two standard deviations below the mean or (2) an overall score stemming from items representing the conceptual, social, and practical domains that is at least two standard deviations below the mean. As with the criterion requiring a significant limitation in intellectual functioning, consideration must be given to confidence intervals associated with each of these adaptive behavior scores. More generally, Schalock et al. recommended that assessors focus on typical performance of adaptive behaviors (and not maximum performance) across environments in which such behaviors normally are displayed (e.g., home, school, and community) and on identifying skills in which training and accommodations are most needed.

AMERICAN PSYCHIATRIC ASSOCIATION

Like Schalock et al. (2010), the *Diagnostic and Statistical Manual of Mental Disorders, Fifth Edition* (DSM-5; American Psychiatric Association, 2013) presents three criteria for ID. The first refers to "deficits in intellectual functions, such as reasoning, problem solving, planning, abstract thinking, judgment, academic learning, and learning from experience" (American Psychiatric Association, 2013, p. 33) in a manner consistent with Schalock et al.'s focus on psychometric g. Although the DSM-5 diagnostic criteria refer to *intellectual functions* rather than *intellectual functioning*—which may indicate that the focus should be increased on assessment of specific cognitive abilities rather than psychometric g—and IQ is not explicit mentioned in the diagnostic criteria, frequent references to *general mental abilities*, occasional references to *intellectual capacity* (an outdated term), and discussion of IQs in the text supporting its diagnostic criteria indicate that the focus of the assessment should be on psychometric g. To meet this criterion, IQs should be two standard deviations below the mean (i.e., 70), considering error represented in the use of confidence intervals.

The prior edition of the DSM-5 (2013) highlighted adaptive behavior deficits in 11 *skill areas*: communication, use of community resources, functional academics, home living, health, safety, leisure, self-care, self-direction, social and interpersonal skills, and work (American Psychological Association, 2000). For a diagnosis of ID, deficits must have been evident in at least two of the skill areas. Now, the DSM-5 lists adaptive behavior deficits in the conceptual, social, and practical domains that are closely aligned with Schalock et al. (2010). Impairment in at least one of these domains must be evident.

The prior edition of the DSM-5 (2013) also defined subtypes of ID based on IQ levels (American Psychiatric Association, 2000). Those persons with IQs ranging from approximately 55 to approximately 70 could be labeled as having *mild mental retardation,* those with IQs from approximately 40 to approximately 55 could be labeled as having *moderate mental retardation,* those with IQs from approximately 25 to approximately 40 could be labeled as having *severe mental retardation,* and those with IQs below approximately 25 could be labeled as having *profound mental retardation.* Basing these divisions on population estimates, about 85% of those with ID were estimated to have mild mental retardation; 10%, moderate mental retardation; 3%, severe mental retardation; and 2%, profound mental retardation (American Psychiatric Association, 2000). The DSM-5, instead, specified four severity levels of ID (*mild, moderate, severe,* and *profound*) based on the intensity and amount of support needed from others (and not IQs per se).

INDIVIDUALS WITH DISABILITIES EDUCATION IMPROVEMENT ACT AND ROSA'S LAW

In 2004, the federal definition of *mental retardation* characterized the condition as follows: "significantly subaverage general intellectual functioning, existing concurrently with deficits in adaptive behavior and manifested during the developmental period, that adversely affects a child's educational performance" (IDEA, 2004). In October 2010, a bill introduced by U.S. senator Barbara Mikulski in November 2009, Rosa's Law, was signed. Rosa's Law (2010) eliminated the terms *mental retardation* and *mentally retarded* from the federal legal code; it was named after a child with Down syndrome who, with her family, worked to have these terms removed from the Maryland health and education code. Consistent with the recommendations of Schalock et al. (2010), the official term for this condition in the United States became *intellectual disability*.

Although ID is addressed in the federal special education legislation, each individual state has autonomy in labeling this condition as well as determining the specific eligibility criteria. McNicholas et al. (2018) and Polloway, Auguste, Smith, and Peters (2017) extended prior research examining these criteria across states. For example, McNicholas et al. obtained state-level regulations and guidelines for identification of ID from the Departments of Education of the 50 United States and the District of Columbia during 2014. At that time, 32 states (63%) used the term *intellectual disability*, which was a striking change from results from prior studies of state regulations that highlighted the preponderance of the term *mental retardation* (e.g., Bergeron, Floyd, & Shands, 2008). However, McNicholas et al. found that another five states (10%) retained the term *mental retardation*, while others used terms such as *cognitive impairment* and *mental disability*.

McNicholas et al. (2018) reported that five states (California, Maryland, Massachusetts, Pennsylvania, and Washington) did not provide specific guidelines for identification of ID beyond reproducing the federal definition. States that did provide specific guidelines for identification varied somewhat in their markers of significantly subaverage intellectual functioning. Slightly more than half of states recommended an IQ cutoff of at least two standard deviations below the normative mean (or standard scores of 70 or below), whereas only approximately one-fifth required the IQ to be *more than* two standard deviations below the mean (or standard scores *below* 70). One state (Vermont) required an IQ of 1½ standard deviations below the mean (or standard scores below approximately 78). Almost half of states (47%) recommended consideration of measurement error using either an IQ range (e.g., 70–75) or confidence intervals. Based on these findings from McNicholas et al. and Polloway et al. (2017), those involved in assessment of ID should be well informed about the special education eligibility criteria for ID not only in their state but those nearby them because these criteria are likely to differ across states and from the American Association on Intellectual and Developmental Disabilities (Schalock et al., 2010) and American Psychiatric Association (2013) criteria.

Causes of ID

The causes of ID tend to fall into two classes: (a) those stemming primarily from biological influences and (b) those stemming primarily from environmental influences (Floyd, Farmer, Schneider, & McGrew, in press). As we stated in Chapter 2, individuals with mild intellectual disabilities (IQs between 55 and 70) represent the lower tail of normal variability in intelligence. Moderate, severe, and profound intellectual disabilities (IQs below 55), however, tend not to result from normal variability but from single gene defects (e.g., Fragile X syndrome), chromosomal abnormalities (e.g., Down syndrome), or brain damage (e.g., birth complications and extreme nutritional deficiency). Thus, the biological causes of the significantly limited intellectual functioning during the developmental period include genetic conditions as well as environmental agents and infections affecting brain development. Vissers, Gilissen, and Veltman (2016) reported that more than 700 genes have been linked to ID, and up to 20% of cases of ID can now be attributed to genetic disorders (see L. Kaufman, Ayub, & Vincent, 2010). In particular, clinicians are most likely to see these genetic influences in persons with Down syndrome and Fragile X syndrome, as they are the two most prevalent conditions associated with ID.

Other biological influences occurring prior to, during, or after birth also appear to cause ID through their effects on the developing brain. They include teratogens such as alcohol exposure during pregnancy that causes early alterations in embryonic development and lead exposure during any point during development that slows brain growth (Khoury, Milligan, & Girard, 2015; World Health Organization, 2010). Prenatal complications leading to extreme preterm birth as well as perinatal complications, such as anoxia, are associated with development of ID (Marlow, Wolke, Bracewell, Samara, & EPICure Study Group, 2005). In addition, other congenital and degenerative health conditions as well as head injuries stemming from physical accidents may lead to intellectual impairment consistent with ID.

Typically, the more severe symptoms of ID are, the more likely it is that identifiable biological causes have produced them. Environmental influences on ID, sometimes referred to as cultural-familial influences (Weisz, 1990) and psychosocial disadvantage (Grossman, 1983), are more difficult to identify. Examples of such documented influences include lack of complex language usage in the home (i.e., lack of cognitive stimulation), parents who are not prepared for the role (i.e., parental immaturity), and neglect of the child by caregivers. The exact mechanisms through which these influences affect brain development, contribute to deficits in intellectual functioning, and manifest in impairment associated with ID are not well understood. It is likely that multiple interactive environmental and genetic influences are at play in most cases of ID.

Issues in Assessment of Intellectual Disability

Psychologists and others working with children and adolescents who have or are suspected of having ID should engage in best practices by being knowledgeable about the most recent diagnostic criteria and eligibility guidelines affecting their decision making during their assessment and identification process. Sound clinical judgment also is needed, as Schalock et al. (2010) emphasized:

> Clinical judgment is essential, and a higher level of clinical judgment is frequently required in complex diagnostic and classification situations in which the complexity of the person's functioning precludes standardized assessment alone, legal restrictions significantly reduce opportunities to observe and assess the person, historical information is missing and cannot be obtained, or there are serious questions about the validity of the data. Clinical judgment is defined as a special type of judgment rooted in a high level of clinical expertise and experience and judgment that emerges directly from extensive training, experience with the person, and extensive data. (p. 29)

To apply research-based knowledge, professional ethics, and professional standards to clinical judgments, we offer a brief checklist to consult during the process of assessing a child or adolescent suspected of having ID (see Form 11.1), and we elaborate on its components in the section that follows.

INTELLIGENCE TESTING

Test and score selection. Because low IQs have marked (and continue to mark) what is perhaps the key feature of ID, the first three questions in our checklist target the selection of at least one intelligence test and the interpretation of its primary score, the IQ. Consistent with the psychometric standards outlined in Chapter 4, those involved in assessment of ID should select intelligence tests that meet at least four important criteria.

Recent norms. During assessment of ID, only intelligence tests that have been normed recently (preferably during the past 10 years) should be employed. Due to the Flynn effect (see Chapter 4; Flynn, 1984, 1987, 1999), tests with older norming samples tend to inflate IQs. As a consequence, results may yield a false negative—an instance of ID that was not identified based on the inflated IQ. With a 9-year gap between norming and use of an intelligence test, the score may be inflated about 3 points, and with a 15-year gap, that inflation may be 5 points, which can be two times the standard error of measurement of the IQ and as large as half of the confidence interval range.

Ideally, examiners should administer only recently normed intelligence tests, but they may not always have an appropriate one at their disposal or they may be asked to interpret results from testing conducted by others. In these instances (Cunningham & Tassé, 2010; McGrew, 2015), they may need to adjust the IQ to consider the Flynn effect. According to Floyd et al. (in press), McGrew (2015) outlined guidelines for calculating Flynn effect adjustments. When current or historical IQs are impacted by the Flynn effect and those IQs are to be used as part of the possible diagnosis of ID, the impacted scores should be adjusted downward by 3 points per decade (0.3 points per year). The adjustment procedure includes three steps: (1) subtract the mid-year of the norming data collection dates from the year of test administration and multiply the difference times 0.3, (2) subtract the adjustment value (obtained in step 1) from the impacted IQ, and (3) round the adjusted IQ score to the nearest whole integer value. Based on our experience, Flynn effect adjustments are not employed commonly when testing children and adolescents in school, clinic, and hospital settings, but as the research examining the Flynn effect is extensive (e.g., Pietschnig & Voracek, 2015; Trahan et al., 2014), these score adjustments probably should be employed more frequently in the field.

Adequate subtest floors. It is important to pay particular attention to inadequate subtest floors as well as to subtest requirements that may interfere with accurate measurement of psychometric g. Tests with multiple subtests with floor violations will overestimate intellectual functioning and fail to correctly identify true cases of ID, and tests with these problems should not be employed. As noted in Chapter 4, Bracken (1987) and others asserted that an adequate floor for a subtest is indicated when a raw score of 1 produces a standardized score that is at least two standard deviations below the mean. Our review of the intelligence tests described in Chapters 6 and 7 suggests that inadequate floors are not problems for IQs but that inadequate floors sometimes exist at the subtest level for the youngest age groups covered by these tests. Without adequate subtest floors, the truest estimate of psychometric g will be unattainable. Examiners should ensure that every subtest has an adequate floor before initiating testing. In addition, examiners should identify probable floor effects during testing (indicated by a test taker's raw score of 0 or 1).

Highly reliable IQs. Intelligence tests employed during ID assessments should yield IQs that have satisfactory reliability and validity evidence. In particular, these IQs should have demonstrated high internal consistency (values of .95 or higher) and high short-term test–retest reliability (values of .90 or higher). Most IQs meet these standards, and as all intelligence tests we feature in this book base their confidence interval calculations on internal consistency reliability coefficients, the higher this coefficient, the narrower the confidence intervals surrounding the IQ will be. It is rare to see these coefficients presented for only those with ID, but we are confident that internal consistency reliability estimates obtained from this group would be uniformly lower than those produced from the population as a whole (Nicewander, 2018; Raju, Price, Oshima, & Nering, 2007).

Validity evidence supporting IQs. In addition to high reliability, we believe that three types of validity evidence are most important when selecting IQs during ID assessment. First, the item content and subtests employed to generate the IQs should be sufficiently varied. According to Floyd et al. (in press), "IQs should include subtests that sample as many CHC broad abilities as practically possible, and tests that sample broad abilities in a limited manner (e.g., using the same methods of assessment, such as matrix reasoning tasks, repeatedly) should be avoided" (para. 49). Second, the IQ should have demonstrated evidence that they are strong measures of psychometric g, as revealed primarily through analysis of subtest g loadings and evaluation of IQ g loadings (as addressed in Chapter 4). Based on research by Detterman and Daniel (1989), M. Reynolds, Keith, and Beretvas (2010), and M. Reynolds (2013) focused on *ability differentiation* (often called *Spearman's law of diminishing returns*), the IQs of test takers with ID represent the construct of psychometric g better than do IQs of test takers with higher IQs (those who score in the average range or higher). Thus, these findings strengthen the validity of IQs as the key measure reflecting intellectual functioning during the assessment of ID. Finally, it is important that studies exist that employed the intelligence test in question with samples of test takers with ID. In particular, such studies should evaluate the classification accuracy (including *sensitivity* and *specificity*) of IQs in identifying those with ID relative to comparison groups. Far too few intelligence tests provide this information.

Adequate access. Due to the common co-occurrence of sensory and motor impairments (American Psychiatric Association, 2013; Schalock et al., 2010) and speech and language problems (Pinborough-Zimmerman et al., 2007) in children and adolescents with ID, it is important to be particularly selective in choosing intelligence tests that minimize the influence of access skills (as discussed in Chapter 5). Access skills are irrelevant to the targeted construct and might preclude the accurate measurement of psychometric g. For example, a child with cerebral palsy and minor fine motor problems who is suspected of having ID should not be administered subtests that require quick and facile movement of manipulatives or drawing of intricate symbols with a pencil during a speeded administration. As described in Chapter 5, the Screening Tool for Assessment rating scales and the Screening Tool for Assessment direct screening form evaluate vision and hearing acuity; fine motor skills; and color differentiation that might indicate problems with test access. Although the Screening Tool for Assessment direct screening form has not been extensively tested with ID populations and also may need to be adapted for those who cannot identify letters or hold a pencil, administering it prior to intelligence testing may prevent situations in which test results ultimately are deemed invalid.

Intelligence tests also should be selected that will reflect psychometric g without the undermining effects of limited English proficiency (LEP) and lack of acculturation (see Chapter 14). Accommodations may be needed during test administrations to reduce or eliminate the effects of these influences (Braden & Elliott, 2003, and Chapter 5). When any modification to standardized administration (e.g., use of a reinforcement system, inclusion of a caregiver in the room, or use of an interpreter) is made, this modification should be noted in both oral and written reports (see Chapter 10).

SCORE INTERPRETATION

After tests are administered and a determination can be made that the administration led to meaningful, valid results, interpretation can begin. In particular, three considerations most relevant to ID diagnosis and identification must be undertaken.

Confirm a valid administration. When engaged in assessment of ID, the resulting validity of the IQ must be verified. It is important to determine—*before obtaining* *the norm-based scores*—whether all of the subtests contributing to the IQ appear to have yielded reasonably accurate results. As discussed previously and in Chapter 5, the test taker's engagement during the testing and access to the subtests' content should have been ensured. Even in the case of careful planning and after use of accommodations, anomalies during testing should be evaluated, and further accommodations, alternate scores, and administration of additional tests (yielding IQs) should be considered.

Use confidence intervals. To meet the primary criterion for ID, the IQ must be approximately two standard deviations below the mean (i.e., a standard score of 70) or lower, according to age-based norms (see Form 11.1). Wide confidence intervals around the IQs (often equivalent to plus or minus 5 points) should be considered and reported. In our opinion, if any portion of the 95% confidence interval band includes an IQ of 70 or lower, this diagnostic or eligibility criterion for ID has been met. Thus, IQs as high as 75 may produce confidence interval bands that enter this range. As discussed in Chapter 4, it is also important to remember that reliability is typically lower and random error often is much more pervasive at low (and high) levels of the targeted ability than for those at or near the average range. This fact has led some (e.g., McGrew, 2015) to suggest routine use of 95% confidence intervals that span 5 points above and below the obtained score (regardless of the IQ's reliability).

Do not expect a flat profile. It is highly probable that test takers with ID (who obtain IQs of approximately 70 or below) will have subtest scores or composite scores above this criterion and far closer to the mean, except in the most extreme cases of ID (Bergeron & Floyd, 2006, 2013). This pattern is particularly true for low *g*-loading subtests and composites targeting the ability Processing Speed (Floyd et al., in press). This means that it is highly likely that statistically significant and rare discrepancies will occur between these subtest and composites scores in such samples. Consistent with our KISS model described in Chapter 8, we cannot support the practice of disregarding the IQs from wisely selected and validly completed intelligence tests when these scores are substantially varied. This practice is not a prudent one when the goal is to identify children or adolescents with ID. Research has shown that the predictive power of IQ is not undermined when substantial differences across subtests or index scores are contributing to the IQ (e.g., Freberg, Vandiver, Watkins, & Canivez, 2008; Watkins, Glutting, & Lei, 2007), and we have no reason to expect that this finding would be any different with children and adolescents with ID. Thus, we reiterate that the practice of invalidating the IQ because of variability in the subtests or composites contributing to it (when they were obtained under reasonably ideal conditions) appears to be outdated.

Substantial variation across subtest and composites scores and discrepancies between them are due, in part, to two well-known measurement issues: *regression toward the mean* and *combinatorial probabilities*. *Regression toward the mean* is the general statistical phenomenon by which repeated measurements produce scores that are less extreme and closer to average due to chance occurrence alone (Nesselroade, Stigler, & Baltes, 1980). Because of regression toward the mean, we would expect (1) that test takers with very low IQs will exhibit some subtest or composite scores that are closer to the population mean than their IQs and (2) that the subtests and composite scores demonstrating the lowest correlations with the others will be most affected. In addition, when ID cannot be linked to biological causes (i.e., single-gene defects or chromosomal abnormalities), IQs for those falling in this group will rise over time due to regression toward the mean of the general population (Humphreys, 1989). In contrast, when ID is due to biological causes, we expect regression toward the mean of the population with that condition (e.g., Down syndrome).

When test takers obtain scores indicating extreme normative weaknesses across the vast majority of subtests or composite scores—in many ways, going against the expectation of regression toward the mean—the relations between these scores and the IQ can be explained by *combinatorial probabilities*. Just as it is increasingly improbable that a person will roll a 5 on each consecutive roll of a die, it is increasingly improbable that an examinee will score consistently lower than their peers across subtests and composite scores. As a result of combinatorial probabilities, IQs will be more deviant (i.e., farther away from the mean) than the average of the scores that contribute to them, representing this increasing improbability (see the excellent instructional video by Schneider, 2011). Accordingly, for individuals with very low IQs, some subtest scores and composite scores will be higher than expected in comparison to their IQs. The effects of regression toward the mean and combinatorial probabilities on these scores may result in errors in decision making when considering ID.

ADAPTIVE BEHAVIOR ASSESSMENT

It is insufficient to rely only on IQs when determining ID. The presumption is stated explicitly in recent diagnostic and eligibility guidelines (e.g., Schalock et al., 2010) that that low general mental ability will lead to adaptive behavior deficits in cases of ID, but these constructs are somewhat loosely associated. For example, Alexander (2017) revealed that the average correlation (corrected for sampling error) between IQs and total scores from adaptive behavior scales is only .46. Correlations tend to be even lower when results from informant-based rating scales and interviews (such as the Adaptive Behavior Assessment System, Third Edition [ABAS-3; Harrison & Oakland, 2015] and the Vineland Adaptive Behavior Scales, Third Edition [Vineland-3; Sparrow, Cicchetti, & Saulnier, 2016]) were considered. Scores from teacher rating scales produced some of the lowest correlations. Thus, contrary to common expectations during assessment of ID, the probability of convergence of low IQs and low total adaptive behavior scores is quite low.

Consistent with best practices in adaptive behavior assessment (e.g., Schalock et al., 2010), we encourage assessors to consider adaptive behaviors from an ecological perspective. Thus, we support collection of adaptive behavior assessment data from multiple informants who observe the children and adolescents in different settings. At a minimum, these practices prevent the identification of the "6-hour retarded child" (President's Committee on Mental Retardation, 1969)—that is, a child who is perceived as being impaired only in the school setting—and they promote identification of patterns of relative strengths and weaknesses in adaptive behaviors that children and adolescents display across settings.

To identify adaptive behavior deficits, assessors should draw on the most well-developed norm-referenced assessment instruments and interpret those scores that are the most reliable and that are supported by the most validity evidence (Floyd et al., 2015). Consistent with the American Association on Intellectual and Developmental Disabilities's (Schalock et al., 2010) guidelines, we encourage (1) considering adaptive behavior total composite scores (e.g., the Global Adaptive Composite score from the ABAS-3 [Harrison & Oakland, 2015] and the Adaptive Behavior Composite from the Vineland-III [Sparrow et al., 2016]) and (2) following the same guidelines presented previously for interpretation of IQs. In other words, these adaptive behavior total composite scores must be well below the mean, and the confidence intervals around them should be considered. Diagnostic and eligibility criteria also recommend consideration of conceptual, social, and practical domain scores, but these specific domain scores tend to be lower in reliability and to be supported by weaker bodies of validity evidence than total composite scores (see Floyd et al., 2015).

The American Association on Intellectual and Developmental Disabilities' guidelines (Schalock et al., 2010) that require such an extreme deficit in adaptive behavior (as indicated by total or domain scores at least two standard deviations below the mean) appear to be restrictive. Thus, many cases in which individuals with ID who have received intensive interventions from an early age may not be identified (National Research Council, 1992). A more relaxed standard (e.g., adaptive behavior deficits more than 1½ standard deviations below the mean) appears to be more appropriate (Alexander, 2017; National Research Council, 1992). Following the National Research Council (1992), we also see that identifying an adaptive behavior deficit across a range of score options (e.g., a total score or one of three domain scores) increases the likelihood of identifying those persons in need. In particular, it appears that (a) adaptive behavior total scores are most likely to converge with low IQs than (b) domain scores or skill area scores (in part due to combinatorial probabilities, as noted previously). Scores representing conceptual skills also are more likely to converge with IQs, as they are more highly correlated with IQs than are practical and social domain scores (see Harrison & Oakland, 2015). In sum, (a) application of guidelines specifying extreme deficits in adaptive behavior (i.e., very low cut scores) and (b) requiring multiple adaptive behavior deficits (e.g., two very low domain scores) likely interferes with identification of true cases of persons with ID.

We encourage consideration of other more qualitative evidence of deficits in conceptual, practical, and social domains beyond that yielded by norm-referenced adaptive behavior assessment instruments. This evidence may surface from oral reports of parents and teachers, review of records, and observations in the home setting or in preschool or classroom settings. Specific examples include a parent's statement about a child's intellectual development compared to that of their siblings, documentation of language delays and related services during development, and classroom documents indicating low scores during academic benchmarking (e.g., early literacy probes).

OTHER CONSIDERATIONS

When engaging in decision making about diagnosis or eligibility for ID, it is important to consider potential causes of ID. Thus, when conducting an assessment of ID, draw on the knowledge of parents, caregivers, and other professionals to examine the developmental and medical history of the child or adolescent being tested. Thorough interviews should be conducted to explore these issues, and medical tests (e.g., genetic testing and tests for lead poisoning) may be warranted. In addition, other conditions that may lead to the symptoms of ID (to make a differential diagnosis) as well as physical and mental health problems that co-occur with ID should be evaluated. Further, levels of supports (Schalock et al., 2010) should be considered. Questions in the last section in Form 11.1 address differential diagnosis and levels of supports.

Differential diagnosis. A thorough assessment helps to ensure that sensory and motor disorders are eliminated as the primary causes of the symptoms of ID. Despite the fact that persons with sensory and motor disorders would be expected to demonstrate lower scores on most adaptive behavior assessment instruments, considering the test taker's access problems when selecting an intelligence test should allow for these effects to be eliminated as causes of low IQs. Similarly, wisely selected intelligence tests also can eliminate the influence of LEP and lack of acculturation to U.S. mainstream culture on IQs. In many cases, screening for LEP should be conducted before testing, but even after testing, it could be conducted to confirm the hypothesis that LEP did not confound test results.

Other learning or psychiatric disorders also should be eliminated as the primary cause of the ID symptoms. We have seen that severe language problems—such as the DSM-5's *language disorder* (American Psychiatric Association, 2013)—can lead to low IQs and adaptive behavior deficits in communication and social skills, and as such, may indicate ID. When faced with these specific findings, review the American Speech-Language-Hearing Association website, consult a speech–language therapist for advice, and complete additional assessment to make a differential diagnosis. Further, test takers with attention-deficit/hyperactivity disorder, oppositional defiant disorder, or other disruptive behavior disorders may obtain low IQs due to interfering factors and fail to demonstrate adaptive behaviors at the expected level. Under ideal testing conditions, however, test takers with these conditions tend to score in or near the Average range on intelligence tests and to function only slightly below their peers on adaptive behavior measures.

When learning disabilities are considered in the era of multitiered systems of supports, it is likely that a child with ID (especially with a mild form of the condition) would be identified first as being at risk for reading problems, based on performance on early literacy benchmarking assessments. This child might be moved through the multiple levels of support and be determined eligible for special education services as having a learning disability (see Chapter 13). Teachers should look for more general deficits across academic content areas and areas of adaptive functioning among such children. Psychologists and other assessment professionals should consider administering well-validated brief or abbreviated intelligence tests (see Chapter 7) and having teachers complete adaptive behavior rating scales to rule out ID as a cause of the academic problems or to initiate a comprehensive assessment.

Mental health problems. Persons with ID are likely to demonstrate other mental disorders at a rate three or four times greater than in the general population. This high incidence of other disorders may lead to two challenges during completion of a comprehensive assessment. First, it may be difficult to identify mental disorders in children and adolescents with ID, because these other disorders may have "atypical" clinical presentations. For example, you may be asked to make the judgment about whether attention-deficit/hyperactivity disorder symptoms displayed by a child with ID are more severe than would be expected from the child's cognitive developmental level. A test taker's cognitive developmental level traditionally has been synonymous with *mental age* (MA), which has its roots in early intelligence testing metrics (see Chapter 2), but MA often is represented by age equivalent scores from modern developmental screening and intelligence tests (see Chapter 4). A child with an IQ associated with an age equivalent score of 3.4 might be expected to display the same levels of attention problems and impulsive behaviors as an average 3-year-old—which is a rather low expectation for self-control. In light of the challenges posed by atypical clinical presentations of these other disorders, rating scales targeting common behavior problems in the general population of children and adolescents (e.g., C. Reynolds & Kamphaus, 2015a) may not be appropriate for children and adolescents with ID.

Second, other disorders may overshadow the deficits associated with ID to such an extent that ID goes undiagnosed. For example, the qualitative differences in communication and social interactions and behavioral excesses associated with severe autism spectrum disorder and the aggressive and defiant behavior associated with oppositional defiant disorder may be incredibly problematic to parents and teachers seeking services; in such cases, general intellectual functioning may be largely ignored. In light of this challenge, we recommend routine screening for deficits in intellectual functioning and deficits in adaptive behaviors during comprehensive assessments targeting a variety of presenting problems.

Physical health problems. As some medical conditions commonly are associated with ID (e.g., heart conditions and epilepsy; American Academy of Pediatrics, Committee on Bioethics, Committee on Genetics, & American College of Medical Genetics and Genomics, Social, Ethical, and Legal Issues Committee, 2013), greater consideration should be given to the health of children and adolescents suspected of having ID (Schalock et al., 2010). We encourage completion of medical examinations as part of multidisciplinary assessments or routing parents and caregivers to medical professionals who can complete a thorough medical examination. A medical examination may identify possible biological causes for the ID in order to eliminate or treat them. Although the effects of most biological causes cannot be reversed, some may be treatable through medical interventions (e.g., through use of dietary restrictions for a child with phenylketonuria).

Levels of needed support. The final consideration during assessment is to determine how the child or adolescent's independent functioning could be improved with additional supports. Schalock et al. (2010) defined *supports* as "resources and strategies that aim to promote the development, education, interests, and personal well-being of a person and that enhance individual functioning" (p. 18). In considering these supports, examiners should identify not only the current absolute limitations that the child or adolescent may be displaying but also strengths across domains. For example, despite meeting criteria for ID, a child may have strong social skills, display adequate attention to assignments in class, and engage in sporting activities. With a personalized support plan targeting areas of deficits for intervention while also building on existing strengths, a child or adolescent's long-term functioning will be vastly improved across development.

Summary

ID is a developmental disorder characterized by significant limitations in both intellectual functioning and the display of adaptive behavior. Assessing a child or adolescent with ID presents some unique challenges, and extensive preparation is needed. Knowledge of consensus-based definitions of ID, consideration of psychometric standards, awareness of anomalies that may surface from testing, and clinical sensitivity during the assessment all are needed to provide the best services for these children and adolescents and their families.

FORM 11.1

Questions to Consider during Diagnostic and Eligibility Assessment for Intellectual Disability

INTELLIGENCE

1. Was at least one intelligence test administered under conditions that should ensure valid results?
   a. Was it recently normed?
   b. Do the test's subtests have sufficiently low floors?
   c. Does the IQ demonstrate internal consistency reliability of .95 or higher and test–retest reliability of .90 or higher?
   d. Is the IQ supported by sufficient validity evidence—especially heterogeneous sampling of specific abilities, strong g loadings or g saturation, and classification accuracy with samples of persons with ID?
   e. Was the child or adolescent sufficiently motivated to respond, and was there an absence of interfering factors that allowed full access to the test items?
2. Was an IQ obtained that is approximately 70 or below?
3. Was a 95% confidence interval considered when the IQ was interpreted?

ADAPTIVE BEHAVIOR

4. Were adaptive behavior assessment instruments completed by multiple informants who observed the child or adolescent in distinct settings (e.g., teachers in school classrooms and on playgrounds, and parents or other caregivers at home and in the community)?
5. Does an adaptive behavior composite score or domain scores (especially in the areas of conceptual, practical, and social skills) indicate development deviance (e.g., as indicated in scores that are well below the mean)?
6. Were 95% confidence intervals considered when the adaptive behavior composite score or domain scores were interpreted?
7. Is there other evidence that the child or adolescent is developmentally delayed in important conceptual, practical, and social domains?

OTHER ISSUES

8. Have other explanations for the symptoms of ID been eliminated?
   a. Have severe sensory disorders (e.g., visual impairment and hearing impairment) or motor disorders been eliminated as the primary causes of the low IQ and deficits in adaptive behavior evident from the assessment?
   b. Have limited English proficiency and lack of acculturation been eliminated as the primary causes of the low IQ and deficits in adaptive behavior evident from the assessment?
   c. Have other learning or psychiatric disorders (e.g., language disorder and ADHD) been eliminated as the primary causes of the low IQ and deficits in adaptive behavior evident from the assessment?
9. Has a thorough medical evaluation been completed?
   a. Have medical causes for the ID been investigated?
   b. Have comorbid medical conditions associated with ID been investigated?
10. Does the child or adolescent need increased levels of support from teachers and caregivers to function in a general education setting or to be independent as a young adult?

CHAPTER 12

Assessment of Intellectual Giftedness

Francis Galton (1822–1911) is widely regarded as the founder of "differential psychology," the scientific study of the ways in which individuals and groups differ in their psychological traits (Jensen, 2002). Galton (1869) defined "genius" as exceptionally high mental ability that is largely attributable to heredity (p. viii). Because practical tests of intelligence did not yet exist, Galton examined the family trees of individuals who were famous for their intellectual accomplishments. He found that eminence tended to run in families, which is consistent with the genetic basis of genius, but not always in the same field of accomplishment. Galton conceptualized intelligence as a very broad, general ability. As he stated,

> In statesmanship, generalship, literature, science, poetry, art, just the same enormous differences are found between man and man; and numerous instances recorded in this book, will show in how small degree, eminence, either in these or any other class of intellectual powers, can be considered as due to purely special powers. They are rather to be considered in those instances as the result of concentrated efforts, made by men who are widely gifted. People lay too much stress on apparent specialties, thinking over-rashly that, because a man is devoted to some particular pursuit, he could not possibly have succeeded in anything else. They might just as well say that, because a youth had fallen desperately in love with a brunette, he could not possibly have fallen in love with a blonde. He may or may not have more natural liking for the former type of beauty than the latter, but it is more probably as not the affair was mainly or wholly due to a general amorousness of disposition. (p. 64; as cited by Jensen, 2002, pp. 146–147)

Although Galton also recognized the importance of "special abilities" or talents in particular fields (e.g., mathematics, music, art), he believed they were not sufficient for outstanding accomplishment; a high level of general intelligence also was necessary. He did not equate genius with high general ability, however. According to Galton (1865),

> Success of this kind implies the simultaneous inheritance of many points of character, in addition to mere intellectual capacity. A man must inherit good

> health, a love of mental work a strong purpose, and considerable ambition, in order to achieve successes of the high order of which we are speaking. (p. 318)

Nevertheless, with Galton's work the conceptualization of giftedness as hereditary was clearly established (Luciano et al., 2018). His assertion that genius results from some combination of a number of interacting inherited characteristics is quite consistent with the contemporary emergenic models of greatness (e.g., Plomin & Deary, 2015; Simonton, 2018).

In the United States, the scientific study of intellectual giftedness began with the work of Lewis Terman (1877–1956). In 1916, Terman published a revision of the Binet-Simon intelligence test, which he named the Stanford-Binet Scale of Intelligence. He translated the test into English and expanded the number of items administered at each age to facilitate the assessment of children and youth at all levels of intellectual ability. He also standardized test administration and provided norms for score interpretation. Last, he adopted and popularized the concept of the intelligence quotient, or IQ, developed several years earlier by Stern (1912). For the next two decades, the Stanford-Binet was the most widely used individually administered test of intelligence in the United States and a major part of the measurement movement in education (Chapman, 1988).

Terman was greatly influenced by Galton's theory of genius. He conceptualized intellectual giftedness as primarily determined by high IQ and classified those with scores above 135 as "moderately" gifted, those with scores above 150 as "exceptionally" gifted, and those with scores greater than 180 as "profoundly" gifted. Terman (1916) argued for the use of intelligence tests to identify and place intellectually gifted students in special classes in schools. Thus, although Terman believed that intellectual giftedness is largely inherited, he nevertheless advocated for early identification and special services or programs for the intellectually gifted so that they could reach their full potential, thereby recognizing the important roles both nature and nurture played in the development of giftedness.

Prior to the advent of intelligence tests, research on intellectual giftedness consisted largely of retrospective studies. In these studies, researchers first identified adults who were considered geniuses and then looked back at events that took place in their childhood to shed light on the nature and development of giftedness (e.g., Cox, 1926). With the availability of intelligence tests, however, it became possible to conduct prospective studies in which samples of intellectually gifted children and youth could be following over time.

In 1921, Terman initiated the famous *Genetic Studies of Genius*, the first longitudinal study of more than 1,500 intellectually gifted children and youth with IQs of 140 or above. Terman and his colleagues gathered an extensive amount of data on these individuals for more than 50 years. The "twofold purpose of the project was, first of all, to find what traits characterize children of high IQ, and secondly, to follow them for as many years as possible to see what kind of adults they might become" (Terman, 1954, p. 223).

It is noteworthy that he first attempted to identify children and youth who showed exceptional talent in any of the following areas, regardless of level of IQ: music, art, mechanical inventiveness, and ingenuity. However, he quickly became aware that the instruments available for measuring specific talents were lacking in reliability and validity. Further, he found a high degree of overlap between those identified with exceptional talent and those identified with high general intelligence (Zigler & Farber, 1985).

Results of Terman's seminal study indicated that as adults, on average, the intellectually gifted sample was happier, healthier, and more successful than their normal peers (Terman, 1925, 1954; Terman & Ogden, 1947, 1959). Moreover, his results contradicted the then prevailing stereotype that the intellectually gifted tended to have poor social skills and were more prone to emotional maladjustment. Nevertheless, despite the fact that the gifted participants in Terman's study generally were very successful in life, some did not achieve to their full potential, and very few were recognized as adults for eminence in their field. These results, therefore, indicated that high general intelligence is necessary, but not sufficient, for the highest levels of performance and productivity in society. In other words, in addition to a sufficiently high level of general intelligence, other domain-specific or noncognitive factors (e.g., motivation, creativity, task commitment) are required. As Terman (1954) stated:

> The follow-up of these gifted subjects has proved beyond question that tests of "general intelligence," given as early as six, eight, or ten years, tell a great deal about the ability to achieve either presently or 30 years hence. Such tests do not, however, enable us to predict what direction the achievement will take, and least of all do they tell us what personality factors or what accidents of fortune will affect the fruition of exceptional ability. Granting that both interest patterns and special aptitudes play important roles in the making of a gifted scientist, mathematician, mechanic, artist, poet, or musical composer, I am convinced that to achieve greatly in almost any field, the special talents have to be backed up by a lot of Spearman's g, by which is meant the kind of general intelligence that requires ability to form many sharply defined concepts, to manipulate them, and to perceive subtle relationships between them; in other words, the ability to engage in abstract thinking. (pp. 309–310)

Contemporary Theories of Giftedness

Over the past 40 years, many different theories of intellectual giftedness have been proposed, almost all of which expand upon the historical conception of giftedness as an all-purpose, inherited quality of the individual that is identified primarily by an intelligence test (e.g., Pfeiffer, Shaunessy-Dedrick, & Foley-Nicpon, 2018). Contemporary conceptions of giftedness have expanded beyond an emphasis on general intelligence to include domain-specific cognitive and other abilities related to leadership, creativity, and the arts. In the following section we provide examples of a few prominent contemporary theories of intellectual giftedness.

DOMAIN-SPECIFIC MODELS

Domain-specific models of giftedness focus on different areas of aptitude and the development of capacity within those areas. Gardner's (2011) theory of multiple intelligences (MI) is perhaps the most widely recognized domain-specific conceptualizations of giftedness (cf. Brody & Stanley, 2005). In Gardner's theory, intelligence is viewed as a complex system that stems from the interaction of many cognitive and noncognitive variables. Cognitive ability is described by a distinct set of mental abilities, or "intelligences," not as a single thing. These intelligences are held to be independent, yet often interact. Gardner (1999) defined an intelligence as "a biopsychological potential to process information that can be activated in a cultural setting to solve problems or create products that are of value in a culture" (p. 33). According to the MI theory, bona fide intelligences must be universal to humans and rooted in biology; they also must (a) have an identifiable set of core operations and (b) be capable of being represented in a symbol system (Walters & Gardner, 1986). Based upon his results, Gardner (1999) asserted that eight different kinds of intelligence exist: linguistic, logical-mathematical, spatial, musical, bodily-kinesthetic, interpersonal, intrapersonal, and naturalist.

Gardner's MI theory has helped broaden conceptions of giftedness to include other domains in which giftedness can be recognized beyond general intelligence. According to Chen and Gardner (2018), intelligence tests only measure those intelligences that are valued in formal schooling, such as the logical-mathematical and linguistic intelligences. He maintained that all eight intelligences should be assessed in a contextually relevant way and that the focus of assessment should be on the natural products of each kind of intelligence. To date, however, Gardner and his colleagues have not developed reliable and valid measures of these intelligences. Although they have developed an assessment instrument called the Spectrum battery, which consists of a set of 15 activities in seven domains of knowledge (language, math, music, art, social understanding, sciences, and movement) to provide a narrative description of a child's diverse intellectual strengths and weaknesses, psychometric support for it currently is lacking. Moreover, so much empirical evidence has been gathered in support of a general factor of cognitive ability (see Chapters 1 and 2) that the notion of separate logical-mathematical and linguistic intelligences, at least, is untenable. Gardner (2006) himself conceded that the general factor underlying individual differences on all tests of cognitive ability, psychometric g, may account for some but not all of his proposed intelligences.

SYSTEMS MODELS

In systems models, giftedness is conceptualized as an integrated system in which "the total operation is dependent on a confluence of psychological processes operating together" (Kaufman & Sternberg, 2008, p. 76). One of the initial and most influential systems models is Renzulli's (1978, 1986) three-ring model of giftedness. As shown in Figure 12.1, in his model, giftedness is viewed as resulting from an interaction of three characteristics: above-average cognitive ability, exceptional creativity, and a very high level of task commitment. According to the three-ring model, "individuals capable of developing gifted behavior are those possessing, or capable of developing, this composite set of traits and applying them to any potentially valuable area of human performance" (Renzulli & Reis, 2018, p. 190). Renzulli distinguished between the so-called *schoolhouse* gifted, which refers to those who only excel in school (e.g., test

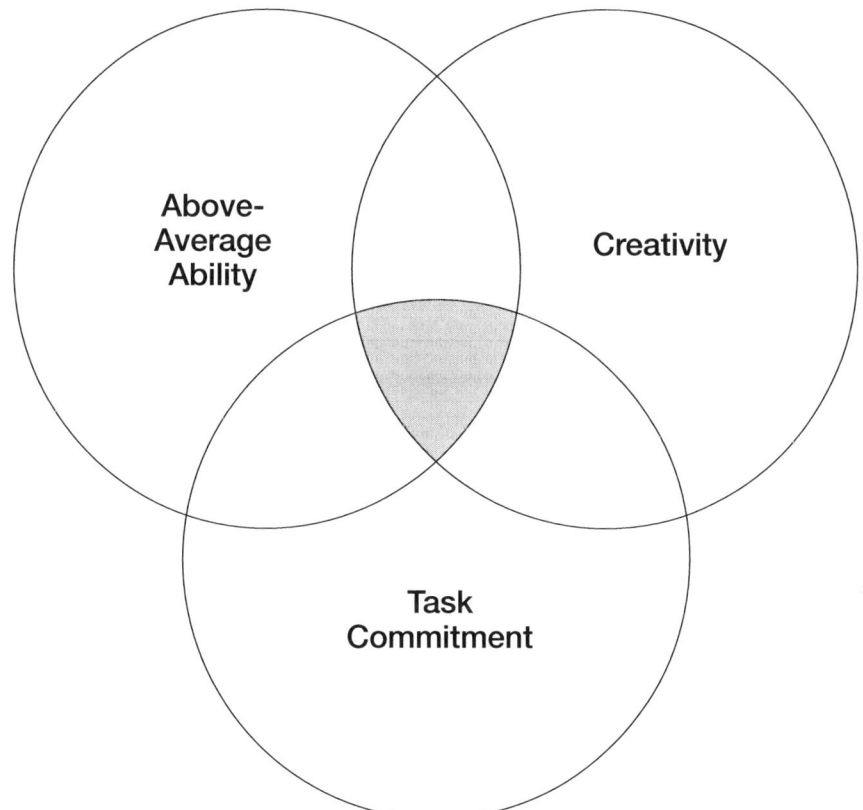

Figure 12.1. Renzulli's three-ring model of giftedness. Renzulli and Reis (2018, p. 187).

taking and academic assignments) and are identified as gifted but do not distinguish themselves during their professional careers; and the *creative-productive* gifted, which refers to those who make creative contributions to society as adults. The former group is considered to have high ability but is lacking in either creativity, task commitment, or both, whereas the latter group possesses all three important characteristics.

In the three-ring model, above-average ability is defined as either general or domain-specific. In this model, general ability appears to consist not only of psychometric g but also of the broad abilities at stratum II of Carroll's (1993) three-stratum (see Chapter 1). According to Renzulli, general ability primarily reflects abstract thinking that is mostly applicable in academic contexts and in novel situations and is measured well by intelligence and aptitude tests. Domain-specific abilities, in contrast, are reflected in the ways in which individuals perform in specialized real-world situations, such as mathematics, musical performance, dance, and art (e.g., sculpture and photography). According to him, domain-specific abilities that are closely related to academic achievement (e.g., mathematics and creative writing) can be measured adequately with achievement tests and tests of specific aptitudes, but others require the use of performance-based or portfolio assessments (e.g., dance and art).

In the three-ring model, general ability is viewed as a "threshold variable" below which socially significant accomplishment is highly unlikely. Renzulli estimated this minimum level of requisite IQ to be approximately 120, which is more than one standard deviation above the mean and consists of approximately the top 15% of the population on intelligence. This percentage is considerably more than the 3–5% typically identified by intelligence tests using a score of 130 or above (McClain & Pfeiffer, 2012). In addition, research suggests that this threshold may be different across various fields and subject matter (e.g., Barron, 1968). Thus, after one's IQ surpasses this threshold, other factors become more important in the prediction of real-world success, such as creativity and task commitment.

Recent research, however, has questioned the cognitive ability threshold component of the model (e.g., Lubinski, 2016; Makel, Kell, Lubinski, Putallaz, & Benbow, 2016). Results of Makel et al. (2016), for example, indicated that individual differences in general cognitive ability among a large sample of profoundly gifted (IQs > 160) adolescents were significantly related to educational, occupational, and creative outcomes many years later. As they stated, "Just as there is not an ability threshold for intellectually demanding performances, neither is there a threshold beyond which more height does not matter for competing at the most elite level in basketball (i.e., the National Basketball Association, or NBA)" (p. 1014). They also found that, beyond extremely high general ability, patterns of mathematical, spatial, and verbal reasoning abilities—as well as educational and occupational interests—were importantly related to development in particular domains.

Other criticisms of the three-ring model include the lack of measures with psychometric support for the assessment of creativity and a number of domain-specific abilities (e.g., Zigler & Farber, 1985; Worrell, 2009). Others have argued that creativity may be better used as an outcome variable than as a predictor of giftedness, as outstanding creative products usually result from the persistent pursuit of goals in a specific talent domain (e.g., Winner, 1996). Thus, although the three-ring model broadens the definition of giftedness and criteria for identification, it is not without its detractors (e.g., see Delisle, 2003; VanTassel-Baska, 2005).

DEVELOPMENTAL MODELS

In developmental models of giftedness, emphasis is placed on "the constantly changing nature of these so-called 'gifts,' and broaden[s] the net even wider than the systems model by including various *external* factors that might interact with the *internal* factors of the individual to produce gifted behavior" (Kaufman & Sternberg, 2008, p. 77). In other words, these models attempt to identify the underlying factors that lead to the manifestation of gifted potential. Tannenbaum's (2003) talent development model was one of the first attempts to explain the development of natural abilities into specific expert skills or talents. Tannenbaum (1986) defined giftedness as follows:

> Keeping in mind that developed talent exists only in adults, a proposed definition of giftedness in children is that it denotes their potential for

becoming critically acclaimed performers or exemplary producers of ideas in spheres of activity that enhance the moral, physical, emotional, social, intellectual, or aesthetic life of humanity. (p. 33)

In Tannenbaum's theory, the environment plays a central role in the manifestation and development of giftedness. As shown in Figure 12.2, according to him, five factors must be present: (a) superior general ability, (b) special or domain-specific aptitude, (c) psychosocial abilities (e.g., motivation, perseverance), (d) external support, and (e) chance. Tannenbaum asserted that the amount of general ability required for high performance varies by domain. In addition to sufficiently general intelligence, the gifted individual also possesses other domain-specific aptitudes or psychosocial abilities associated with that domain (Worrell, Subotnik, & Olszewski-Kubilius, 2018).

One component of developmental models such as Tannenbaum's is that intellectual giftedness requires a special environment to develop fully (Worrell et al., 2018). This environment includes the presence of significant others who are interested in and supportive of the developing gifted child. It is also important to note the important role that chance can play in the development of giftedness. Children do not select the environments into which they are born. Environments that are favorable or unfavorable to the development of particular traits often are imposed upon them—for example, when a child with superior musical ability is born to and raised by parents who provide a musically stimulating environment. Environments can be selected or created by others in reaction to an individual's predisposition, such as when teachers nominate children based on demonstrated academic promise for special programs for the intellectually gifted. Of course, gifted individuals often select or create environments that

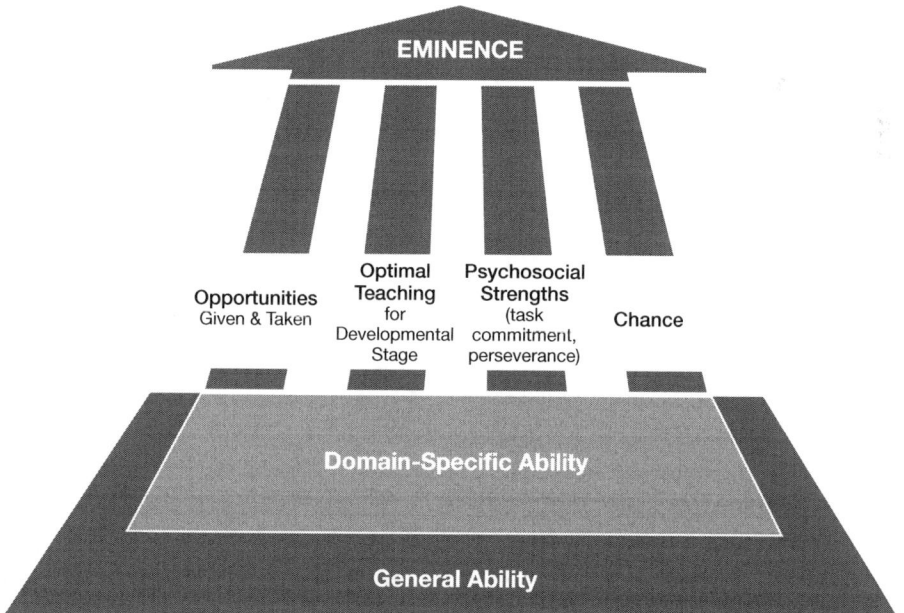

Figure 12.2. The path to eminence. Worrel, Subotnik, and Olszewski-Kubilius (2018, p. 248).

are correlated with their natural abilities. For example, children with superior musical ability may spend more time listening to, thinking about, and practicing music than other children, regardless of whether anyone wants them to.

Another important implication of developmental models is the emphasis on "giftedness" as an outcome reflecting advanced performance in a specific domain that is attained over time through a combination of cognitive and noncognitive factors. In other words, according to this model, giftedness is not as an enduring characteristic of an individual that someone either is or is not. Research within talent development models also emphasizes that different domains have different developmental trajectories and that exceptional talents may not be stable over time (e.g., Simonton, 2018). In fact, Simonton (2009) estimated that the correlation between general intelligence and achieved eminence in most domains of achievement is only about .25. Thus, as Simonton (2018) stated, some early bloomers may demonstrate relative declines over time and so-called late bloomers may overtake them. According to Worrell and Erwin (2011), the field gradually is moving toward a conceptualization that "(a) giftedness involves more than just ability or potential in a domain and (b) the classification of giftedness may shift across developmental periods" (pp. 319–320). The developmental models also underscore the fact that giftedness is a culture-bound conceptualization, which means that what is considered gifted in one culture may not be in another (e.g., Pfeiffer et al., 2018).

Summary

As this brief review hopefully makes clear, at the present time, a rather large number of diverse conceptions of giftedness can be found in the literature. Nonetheless, as Kaufman and Sternberg (2008) asserted, "No serious giftedness researcher today believes that general intelligence is the whole picture, or believes that gifted abilities are solely the result of innate, genetic endowment" (p. 79). As Reis and Renzulli (2011) stated, "Despite decades of attempts to study and identify a standard pattern of intellectual giftedness among high-potential children and individuals, no clear pathway has been identified and no specific formula exists regarding the 'right' combination of genes, personality, and environment needed to produce intellectual giftedness" (p. 237). Despite the progress made over the past century, none of these contemporary models is considered the predominant model of giftedness—and all have had minimal impact on the process of identifying giftedness in the schools. In the next section, we examine current definitions of giftedness in the schools.

Gifted Identification

FEDERAL AND STATE DEFINITIONS OF GIFTEDNESS

In 1972, the commissioner of education, Sydney Marland, presented the first national report on gifted education to the Congress of the United States. The purpose of the

Marland Report was to examine the degree to which intellectually gifted students were being served in schools across the nation. This report is widely viewed as groundbreaking insofar as it recognized six different types of giftedness: general intellectual ability, specific academic aptitude, creative or productive thinking, leadership ability, visual and performing arts, and psychomotor ability. The Marland Report also encouraged states to identify a minimum of 3–5% of the school population as gifted and provide them with appropriate educational programs.

In 1978, the federal definition of gifted and talented was revised to include "children and, whenever applicable, youth who are identified at the pre-school, elementary, or secondary level as possessing demonstrated or potential abilities that give evidence of high performance capability in areas such as intellectual, creative, specific academic, or leadership ability or in the performing and visual arts, and who by reason thereof require services or activities not ordinarily provided by the school." The main difference between the 1972 and 1978 definitions was the elimination of psychomotor ability as a domain of giftedness.

The Marland Report also led to the enactment of subsequent legislation, such as the Jacob Javits Gifted and Talented Students Education Act (1988), which was passed as part of the Elementary and Secondary Education Act and reauthorized in 1994. For many years, the Javits Act was the only federal legislation that specifically supported the development of gifted and talented students in the United States. Unfortunately, in 2011 Congress eliminated all funding for the Javits Act. Moreover, in contrast with the Individuals with Disabilities in Education Act (IDEA, 2004), the Javits Act does not afford any federal protections for the gifted and talented (such as due process and equal protection rights; Stephens, 2011).

Given the absence of a federal mandate related to gifted education identification and services, states and/or school districts are left to their own devices. According to the most recent report from the National Association for Gifted Children (NAGC), in 2014–2015, out of 42 states reporting, only 32 states indicated that they had mandates related to gifted and talented identification, education, or both. Eight states had no mandate. Of those states with mandates, only 4 states reported full funding, 20 reported partial funding, and 8 reported no funding. Perhaps needless to say, insufficient funding continues to be a primary area for gifted and talented education (NAGC, 2014–2015).

Historically, most states' definitions of giftedness were based on the 1978 federal definition of giftedness (McClain & Pfeiffer, 2012). Nevertheless, until only recently the majority of states have identified giftedness predominantly in terms of high general intelligence. More than 20 years ago, most state definitions were closely aligned with the 1978 definition and defined giftedness according to a single criterion (i.e., IQ; Cassidy & Hossler, 1992). Since then, substantial changes have been made in both the definition and categories of giftedness in many states across the nation (cf. McClain & Pfeiffer, 2012; Stephens & Karnes, 2000). In a national survey of coordinators of state gifted programs, McClain and Pfeiffer (2012) found that all but two states (South Dakota and Massachusetts) have established definitions of giftedness. Half of the states with definitions of giftedness have revised their definition during the past 10 years. All but three states use *gifted and talented*, or simply *gifted*, as the terminology for this category of exceptional students. The other three states (Indiana, Nebraska, and Washington) use the term *high-ability* student in their definition. Thus, as McClain and Pfeiffer's results showed, educators continue to lack consensus on how to define giftedness.

With regard to the categories of giftedness recognized in state definitions, intelligence is the most widely recognized category of giftedness, followed by academic achievement. Changes in these categories over the past decade suggest an increasing emphasis on intelligence and achievement in state definitions. According to Worrell, Subotnik, Olszewski-Kubilius, and Dixson (2019), the sustained focus on general intelligence and academic domains likely results from (a) the fact that educational programming predominantly is focused on core academic subjects (i.e., reading, writing, arithmetic, and science) and (b) the lack of resources available to provide educational services in other areas of talent. S. Kaufman and Sternberg (2008) stated that intelligence tests most likely are widely used because they are relatively cheap and have demonstrated construct validity and because they are known to be predictive of general achievement outcomes, which is the primary emphasis of many gifted education programs.

McClain and Pfeiffer (2012) also examined the decision-making models used by states for determining gifted eligibility. These five modes were

1. *single cutoff*—wherein a single cut score on an intelligence test (e.g., IQ score > 130) is used to determine eligibility;
2. *single cutoff, flexible criterion*—wherein only one test score is used, but flexibility is allowed in selecting the type of test (e.g., intelligence test or test of creativity) and the specific cut score used;
3. *multiple cutoff*—wherein cut scores on more than one measure are used (e.g., IQ and achievement tests);
4. *averaging*—wherein scores on multiple measures are averaged across domains (e.g., IQ, achievement, and creativity); and
5. *dynamic*—wherein one or more measures are used to measure the amount of growth over time.

McClain and Pfeiffer found that 27 states reported using a multiple-cutoff or averaging decision-making model. None of the states used the single-cutoff model, but seven used the single-cutoff, flexible-criterion model. A total of 16 states reported that they do not require a specific decision-making model for gifted eligibility determination. Table 12.1 shows the states that do and do not use specific cut scores. As can be seen here, when cut scores are used for gifted identification, they correspond to selection of 3–5% of all students.

Issues in Gifted Identification

Intelligence tests and achievement tests are the two most widely required assessments for the identification of giftedness, followed by teacher and parent nominations (McLain & Pfeiffer, 2012). It is beyond the scope of this chapter to describe each of

Table 12.1. States Using Specific Models for the Selection and Identification of Gifted Students

State	Single cutoff	Single cutoff, flexible criterion	Multiple cutoff or averaging	Dynamic	No model
Alabama		×			
Alaska					×
Arizona		×			
Arkansas			×		
California			×		
Colorado		×			
Connecticut			×		
Delaware					×
Florida			×		
Georgia			×		
Hawaii			×		
Idaho			×		
Illinois					×
Indiana					×
Iowa					×
Kansas			×		
Kentucky			×		
Louisiana		×			
Maine					×
Maryland					×
Massachusetts					×
Michigan					×
Minnesota					×
Mississippi			×		
Missouri			×		
Montana			×		
Nebraska			×		
Nevada			×		
New Hampshire					×
New Jersey			×		
New Mexico			×		
North Dakota					×
Ohio		×			
Oklahoma		×			
Oregon			×		
Pennsylvania		×			
Rhode Island					×
South Carolina			×		
South Dakota					×
Tennessee			×		
Texas			×		
Utah			×		
Vermont					×
Virginia			×		
Washington			×		
West Virginia			×		
Wisconsin			×		
Total	0	7	27	0	16
%	0%	14%	54%	0%	32%

Note: Adapted from McClain and Pfeiffer (2012).

these methods and their advantages and limitations (for reviews, see Pfeiffer, 2015; McIntosh, Dixon, & Pierson, 2018). Rather, here we discuss several important issues pertaining to the use of intelligence tests for determining eligibility for giftedness.

WHO IS INTELLECTUALLY GIFTED?

If we agree with Humphreys (1989), who stated that "the fundamental basis for intellectual giftedness is a high level of general intelligence" (p. 332), then what level of intelligence constitutes giftedness? Should one use an IQ score of 120, 130, 140, or above? Wherever one draws the line, it is completely arbitrary. As mentioned in Chapter 2, the distribution of intelligence in the population is approximately normal. Above the mean, the distribution of intelligence is continuous and not discrete. Qualitative differences do not exist between those at the high end of the intelligence distribution, as they do at the extreme low end (e.g., below IQs of 55), where intellectual disability tends to result from single gene defects or chromosomal abnormalities and not normal variability. Given that the differences among those at the high end of the intelligence distribution are quantitative and not qualitative, the label of *giftedness* is nothing more than a social construction indicating high aptitude in one or more domains (Pfeiffer, 2003).

As one moves from the mean toward the extremely high end of the distribution, however, the number of cases becomes increasingly rare. If a cut score of 130 is used, then about 20 out of every 1,000 students would be eligible. If a cut score of 140 is used, then only about 4 out of every 1,000 could meet the criterion. The belief that 3–5% of the school-age population is gifted is a longstanding myth, most likely resulting from Marland's recommendations in 1972 (Borland, 2009). The percentage of students identified for gifted and talented programs, therefore, depends wholly on aims of educators for some desired social purpose and the availability of funding for special programs and services for the gifted.

GIFTEDNESS AS A DEVELOPMENTAL CONSTRUCT

Historically, children and youth were identified early in the primary grades on the basis of a high score on an intelligence test and placed in a program for the gifted for their entire educational careers, regardless of their future performance in school. As Foley-Nicpon and Pfeiffer (2011) observed, however:

> Many students identified as gifted in kindergarten, for any number of reasons, do not distinguish themselves academically in the later years. And many students who are not identified as high IQ, intellectually precocious, or academically advanced in the early years are late bloomers and prove to have extraordinary potential and excel in their later years. (p. 296)

The categorical approach wherein children are either determined to be eligible for gifted programs and services and others ineligible—once and forever—presumably is based on the incorrect notion that intelligence tests measure something that is innate and therefore fixed. The presumed constancy of IQs has resulted in policies and practices that are based on long-term predictions of students' cognitive abilities that are not justified.

Scores on intelligence test reflect the repertoire of knowledge and skills that an individual has developed at a particular point in time. They do not reflect something "bred in the bone." Indeed, the size of an individual's repertoire is a function of both their genetic endowment and the environments to which they have been exposed. Although scores on intelligence tests are highly reliable after children reach school age, an individual's IQ can change considerably over time (e.g., Neisser et al., 1996).

The stability of IQs is related to the interval between test occasions—the longer the interval, the lower the stability. Assuming a stability coefficient of .70 over a 10-year period, "gifted" students with an IQ of 140 will obtain, on the average, a score of 125 on retesting a decade later. This change in scores is simply the result of the ubiquitous measurement phenomenon of regression toward the mean—not that schools have failed to develop the cognitive abilities of these children.

The instability of IQ scores over development implies that the "educational system should be forgiving of early performance that is less than illustrious and should not give undue weight to early illustrious performance" (Humphreys, 1989, p. 203). It further implies that determining eligibility for gifted programs and services should be an ongoing process. Students classified for gifted on the basis of high potential (i.e., IQ > some cut score) should be held to high standards of domain-based performance to retain the gifted label (Worrell et al., 2018). This perspective is consistent with developmental models of giftedness (e.g., Subotnik, Olszewski-Kubilius, & Worrell, 2011), as well as Response to Intervention (RtI) service delivery models (e.g., Kovaleski, VanDerHeyden, & Shapiro, 2013).

FAIRNESS IN GIFTED ASSESSMENT

Most experts agree that a sufficiently high level of general intelligence is a necessary but not sufficient condition for giftedness (e.g., see Pfeiffer et al., 2018). Although intelligence tests are better predictors of outcomes in educational settings than any other measurable human characteristic (e.g., Gottfredson, 2018), the prediction of real-world criteria by intelligence tests is not perfect. Nonetheless, in schools, at most, *half* of the variance in school grades and on achievement tests is explained by intelligence tests, thereby indicating that other cognitive and noncognitive variables are also important. This means that the identification of giftedness should never rely upon the result of one test, including intelligence tests.

In addition, research clearly indicates that the most widely used intelligence tests are not significantly biased against English-speaking children born and raised in the United States (see Chapter 14). These findings, however, do not generalize to children and youth who are not native born or who are limited English proficient. The results of verbally loaded tests with this population should be interpreted carefully, if at all, and should be supplemented by nonverbal tests. A number of nonverbal intelligence tests with adequate psychometric properties and norms are available for use with children and youth from diverse linguistic and cultural backgrounds (for reviews, see McCallum, 2017). Recent research has found that nonverbal tests are an important component of eligibility determination for gifted and talented programs with diverse populations (e.g., Lohman & Gambrell, 2012).

According to the Code of Ethics of the American Psychological Association (2002):

> When interpreting assessment results, including automated interpretations, psychologists take into account the purpose of the assessment as well as the various test factors, test taking abilities, and other characteristics of the person being assessed, such as situational, personal, linguistic, and cultural differences, that might affect psychologists' judgments or reduce the accuracy of their interpretations. They indicate any significant limitations of their interpretations. (Standard 9.06)

When interpreting assessment results, therefore, it is important always to consider the potential impact of cultural and linguistic background on test performance.

TWICE-EXCEPTIONALITY

Twice-exceptional refers to students who are simultaneously gifted and have a diagnosed disability. These children and youth, in other words, have above average general intelligence but experience learning difficulties as a result of a disability, such as specific learning disability (SLD), obsessive-compulsive disorder, autism spectrum disorder, and attention-deficit/hyperactivity disorder. Estimates of the prevalence of twice-exceptional students range from 2–5% of the gifted population, although it is possible that this is a conservative estimate (Foley-Nicpon & Candler, 2018). Given the number of potential concomitant disabilities, no consistent profile of these students is possible.

In a recent longitudinal study 13,176 students with disabilities, 330 (3%) participants obtained scores above the 90th percentile on a test of academic achievement, yet only 11% of those students were identified for gifted and talented programs (Barnard-Brak, Johnsen, Hannig, & Wei, 2015). According to Assouline and Whiteman (2011), gifted students with SLD are among the most underserved in the schools today. Gifted children who are twice-exceptional tend to exhibit a marked pattern of talents or strengths on the one hand and areas of weaknesses on the other. These students generally fall into three groups: (1) identified gifted students with learning difficulties in specific domains, (2) students with identified SLD who are also gifted, and (3) students who are intellectually gifted and have a disability but are not identified because their academic achievement falls in the average range.

Controversy currently surrounds the identification of this latter group given that an IQ-achievement discrepancy no longer is required for the identification of SLD in IDEA. As Pfeiffer (2015) noted, in an RtI service delivery model, the focus is on the identification of students who do not meet minimum expectations in comparison to age or grade peers. In an RtI model, gifted students with SLD may not be identified unless their academic performance falls below expected benchmarks. Without the administration of intelligence tests, it is unclear how these students can be identified when their performance falls within normal expectations. Assouline and Whiteman (2011), therefore, recommended the administration of a comprehensive evaluation, including an individually administered intelligence test, to identify achievement discrepancies and areas of strengths and disability.

SELECTING INTELLIGENCE TESTS

As we did in Chapter 11, we offer a brief checklist to guide the process of assessing a child or adolescent suspected of having intellectual giftedness (see form 12.1), and in this section we elaborate on some of its components related to intelligence tests. Because normatively high IQs often are required in determining eligibility for intellectual giftedness, only intelligence tests that meet at least four important criteria should be employed.

Recent norms. As noted in other chapters, tests with older norming samples tend to inflate IQs (see Chapter 4; Flynn, 1984, 1987, 1999). Although the Flynn effect has been discussed far less in the gifted literature than in that focused on ID, the fact remains that scores yielded from outdated tests are likely to produce false positives—instances of intellectual giftedness identified based on inflated IQs. For example, a 15-year gap between norming and use of an intelligence test may inflate scores about 5 points, which may be enough to move some test takers' scores above the critical threshold for identification. Ideally, you should administer only recently normed intelligence tests. We have not identified any discussion in the professional literature of using Flynn-effect adjustments (see Cunningham & Tassé, 2010; McGrew, 2015) during assessment of giftedness; this most likely is because of a positive bias toward obtaining higher IQs. In most cases, Flynn-effect adjustments would lower IQs in this population.

Adequate subtest ceilings. It is important to pay particular attention to inadequate subtest ceiling, as tests with multiple subtests with ceiling violations will underestimate intellectual functioning and fail to correctly identify true cases. As noted in Chapter 4, an adequate ceiling for a subtest is indicated when the highest subtest raw score produces a standardized score that is at least two standard deviations above the mean. Our review of the intelligence tests described in Chapters 6 and 7 suggests that inadequate ceilings are not problematic for IQs; however, inadequate ceilings sometimes exist at the subtest level for the oldest age groups covered by tests. Examiners should ensure that every subtest has an adequate ceiling before initiating testing. They also should monitor ceiling effects if they cannot be avoided in selection. Thus, if a test taker earns a perfect raw score during completion of a subtest, ceiling effects might be at play and the true general intelligence of the test taker may be underestimated.

Highly reliable IQs. As described in previous chapters, IQs should have demonstrated high internal consistency (values of .95 or higher) and high short-term test–retest reliability (values of .90 or higher). As most IQs meet these standards, and as all intelligence tests we feature in this book base their confidence interval calculations on internal consistency reliability coefficients, the higher this coefficient, the narrower the confidence intervals surrounding the IQ will be. It is rare to see these coefficients presented for only gifted test takers, but we are confident that internal consistency reliability estimates would be uniformly lower than those produced for the population as a whole (Nicewander, 2018; Raju, Price, Oshima, & Nering, 2007).

Validity evidence supporting IQs. Three types of validity evidence are particularly important when selecting IQs during assessment of intellectual giftedness. First, studies should exist that employed the intelligence test in question with a sample of test takers with intellectual giftedness. These studies should evaluate the classification accuracy (including sensitivity and specificity) of IQs in identifying those with intellectual giftedness.

Second, the IQs in question should have demonstrated evidence that they are strong measures of psychometric g, as revealed primarily through analysis of subtest g loadings and evaluation of IQ g loadings. The item content and subtests employed to generate the IQs should be sufficiently varied, so as not to focus on only a subset of cognitive abilities that may reflect the test taker's specific interests and highly practiced skills. Research focused on *ability differentiation* (i.e., *Spearman's law of diminishing returns*; Detterman & Daniel, 1989; M. Reynolds, 2013; M. Reynolds, Keith, & Beretvas, 2010) further informs these recommendations. In particular, this research has revealed that IQs and most all other scores from intelligence tests represent psychometric g with far less fidelity for those with intellectual giftedness than those with ID. Basically, these scores tend to be more independent of psychometric g in the gifted population. This is evident in the diminished g loadings of IQs, composite scores, and subtest scores at high levels of IQ versus at low levels of IQ. Further, some findings (e.g., M. Reynolds, 2013) indicate that composites measuring Processing Speed are nearly completely independent of psychometric g at high levels of IQ—a finding that suggests that measures of this construct be omitted from tests designed to identify giftedness based on psychometric g. In contrast, measures of Fluid Reasoning appeared to be immune to this effect producing diminished g loadings. In fact, M. Reynolds (2013) found that a Fluid Reasoning composite was more highly g saturated than the IQ itself at high levels of ability. This finding suggests that tests designed to identify giftedness based on psychometric g should include multiple measures of Fluid Reasoning.

Adequate access. As applied to all test takers, intelligence tests should be selected that will reflect psychometric g without undermining effects from a test taker's linguistic background or ethnic/cultural differences (see Chapter 14). Accommodations also may be needed during test administrations to reduce or eliminate the effects of these and other influences (see Chapter 5). When any modification to standardized administration is made, this modification should be noted in both oral and written reports (see Chapter 10).

SCORE INTERPRETATION

Confirm a valid administration. As discussed earlier, it is important to determine—*before obtaining the norm-based scores from the testing*—whether all of the subtests contributing to the IQ appear to have yielded reasonably accurate results. When test takers are likely gifted, examiners must be aware of potential unique features of this population. In particular, it is possible that perfectionism and anxiety (Guignard, Jacquet, & Lubart, 2012) may undermine performance during testing. For example, a test taker might feel the need to form each shape perfectly on a speeded symbol reproduction task or to mark responses with perfect circles; both strategies would lead to lower scores and would underestimate intelligence. Other test takers may become flustered after recognizing that they answered an item incorrectly and then lose focus while worrying about that incorrect answer across the remainder of the related items.

Use confidence intervals. As reported earlier, McClain and Pfeiffer (2012) reported that almost all states reference measurement of intelligence, more than one-third require intelligence testing, and seven states employed the single-cutoff, flexible-criterion model involving IQs. Wide confidence intervals around the IQs should be considered and reported. In our opinion, if any portion of an IQ's 95% confidence interval band includes the cut score, this criterion for eligibility has been met. As discussed in Chapter 4, it is also important to remember that reliability typically is lower, and random error often is much more pervasive at high (and low) levels of the targeted ability than for those at or near the average range.

Do not expect a flat profile. It is highly probable that children and adolescents with giftedness who obtain IQs of approximately 130 or higher will have subtest scores or composite scores below this criterion and far closer to the mean (Margulies & Floyd, 2009; McIntosh, Dixon, & Pierson, 2018; Wechsler, 2014c). As for test takers with ID who have obtained higher scores (that are closer to the mean) on measures of Processing Speed than their IQs would indicate (as noted in Chapter 11), subtests and composites measuring Processing Speed are likely to be far lower (and closer to the mean) than the IQs of test takers who are gifted. The same pattern may be evident with other subtests and scores—even if they are highly g loaded—partially due to regression toward the mean (Nesselroade, Stigler, & Baltes, 1980) and ability differentiation (M. Reynolds, 2013), described earlier. This means that statistically significant and rare discrepancies between these subtest and composites scores in such samples are highly likely.

Consistent with our interpretive model described in Chapter 8, we cannot support the routine practice of disregarding the IQs from wisely selected and validly completed intelligence tests when these scores are substantially varied. However, we are open to the idea that those who are gifted also may have highly elevated scores on specific ability composites that reflect areas of intense interest and study. Although their IQs still may be valid predictors of general outcomes, highly elevated composite scores (representing stratum II abilities) supported by high levels of reliability and validity evidence may be better predictors of specific outcomes than the IQ and also serve as aptitudes for specific courses of study (Lubinski, 2010; M. Reynolds, 2013). These considerations are consistent with some models of giftedness described previously and would lead to more differentiated interventions than models based primarily on measures of psychometric g. Consistent with this perspective, Warne (2015) stated,

> A child with higher than average ability in one or more Stratum II areas—but whose general ability is not high enough to warrant a global intervention—still needs differentiation. However, this differentiation will still likely be geared to the child's strengths, even though they are less general than the strengths of a child with high global intelligence. . . . An appropriate intervention for this child might be a subject-specific honors course, an Advanced Placement course, single-subject acceleration, an intensive independent study program, or an academic competition in their area of strength (such as a science fair). (pp. 7–8)

We see this option as most viable in this population of persons who are gifted, and we await further study of classification systems that consider both IQs and relevant stratum II composite scores.

CONCLUSION

Over the past 20 years, much has changed in the field of gifted education. New theories have been proposed that expand the conception of giftedness beyond the traditional definition of high general intelligence and attempt to explain the factors related to the development of outstanding accomplishments. This chapter reviewed a number of contemporary theories and current assessment practices. Although the assessment of intelligence currently plays an important role in determining eligibility for gifted and talented programs in many states, intelligence tests are rarely the sole determinant of eligibility; if the present trend continues, even less emphasis may be placed on their results in the future.

FORM 12.1

Questions to Consider during Eligibility Assessment for Intellectual Giftedness

PRE-ASSESSMENT CONSIDERATIONS

1. Is the goal of the gifted program (a) to allow students to examine concepts in greater depth or in an earlier grade than they might in a typical classroom (acceleration) or (b) to allow students to move through the curriculum at a faster pace than peers (acceleration)?
2. What academic and other domains (e.g., mathematics, language arts, and science) is the gifted program planning to target?
3. What domain-specific skills are important to measure alongside general intelligence?
4. Are the individuals being identified likely to have well-developed skills in the domain, or do pre-skills need to be assessed?
5. Is the level of exposure to the domain likely to vary widely among individuals being assessed on the basis of background variables, such as socioeconomic status or first language? If yes, how are these concerns addressed in your identification protocol?

INTELLIGENCE

6. Was at least one intelligence test administered under conditions that should ensure valid results?
   a. Was it recently normed?
   b. Does the IQ demonstrate internal consistency reliability of .95 or higher and test–retest reliability of .90 or higher?
   c. Is the IQ supported by sufficient validity evidence (ideally, studies of children with intellectual giftedness)?
   d. Do the test's subtests have sufficiently high ceilings?
   e. Was the child sufficiently motivated to respond, and was there an absence of interfering factors?
7. Was an IQ obtained that indicates a high level of general intelligence?
8. Were 90% or 95% confidence intervals considered when the IQ was interpreted?
9. If measures targeting more specific cognitive abilities are targeted in the assessment, do they meet psychometric standards for assessment of students with giftedness?
   a. Does the measure demonstrate internal consistency reliability of .90 or higher and test–retest reliability of .90 or higher?
   b. Is the measure supported by sufficient validity evidence (ideally, studies of children with intellectual giftedness)?
   c. Do the test's subtests contributing to the measures (and the measure itself) have sufficiently high ceilings?

OTHER ASSESSMENT CONSIDERATIONS

10. Has a comprehensive achievement test been administered, and does it meet psychometric standards for assessment of students with giftedness?
11. Has screening for mental health disorders (e.g., obsessive-compulsive disorder or ADHD) been conducted?

Note: Adapted from Worrell and Erwin (2011).

CHAPTER 13

Assessment of Specific Learning Disabilities

In 2017–18, more than 2.3 million children and youth in the United States, or more than 5% of the entire school-age population, were classified as having a specific learning disability (SLD; National Center for Education Statistics [NCES], 2019). SLD is by far the largest disability category in special education. Approximately 34% of all students receiving special education and related services under the Individuals with Disabilities Education Improvement Act of 2004 (IDEA, 2004) have SLD as their primary disability category; this exceeds the percentages of children with the second and third most prevalent disability categories (viz., Speech or Language Impairment and Other Health Impairment) *combined*. Moreover, the number of children and youth identified as having SLD has increased more than 100% since passage of the Education for All Handicapped Children Act of 1975 (i.e., Public Law 94-142, the original version of IDEA). According to results of a recent national survey by Benson et al. (2019a), school psychologists spend about 25% of their time conducting comprehensive assessments for suspected SLD. Given its prevalence in the schools, it is imperative that school psychologists and other school-based professionals employ identification methods and diagnostic criteria that result in the reliable grouping of children and adolescents with and without SLD.

In this chapter, we first review the definition of SLD in IDEA and the methods allowed for its identification. Although the IDEA definition applies only to schools, it is particularly important, because virtually all individuals are diagnosed with SLD while in school. After this, we discuss research on the nature of SLD. Next, we examine strengths and weakness of the three main methods for identifying SLD and the role intelligence tests played within each. We conclude with a discussion of best practices for the identification of SLD.

What Is a Learning Disability?

The term *learning disability* can be conceptualized in either a broad or narrow sense. In the broad sense, it refers to a general difficulty in learning that does not meet the criteria for intellectual disability (ID; see Chapter 11). Individuals with learning disabilities in this sense often are referred to as *slow learners*, because they have difficulty grasping concepts at the same rate and depth of understanding as their same-age peers do. These students tend to have their greatest difficulty grasping new concepts that are abstract or complex and require higher-order reasoning. As the name implies, slow learners do indeed learn. However, they tend to benefit from very explicit, hands-on instruction, and they often need more time and repetition than their peers to be successful in school. Although the term *slow learner* is not a diagnostic category, because it represents the low end of the normal range in intelligence, it typically refers to individuals with IQs between 70 and 85 (e.g., Shaw, 2010). Given the approximately normal distribution of intelligence, this means that about 14% of the school-age population—or one in every seven students—are slow learners. Because these children and youth tend to learn at a rate that is commensurate with their below average general cognitive ability, they are learning *disabled* in general, and their underachievement is expected.

In contrast to the broad-sense conceptualization, learning disability in the narrow sense refers to *unexpected underachievement*. These are individuals who experience difficulty learning in some, but not all, areas of academic achievement (e.g., reading, writing, or mathematics), despite adequate educational opportunity, motivation, and general cognitive ability. These learning difficulties typically are specific to particular achievement domains, hence use of the disability category of SLD in IDEA. The narrow-sense conceptualization of learning disability is the traditional definition of SLD and is what most people mean when they refer to SLD (Grigorenko et al., 2019). At the heart of this conceptualization is the concept of *discrepancy* from expected academic achievement.

IDEA AND SLD

The term *learning disability* first was introduced in 1962 in a textbook by Samuel Kirk titled *Educating Exceptional Children*. According to Kirk,

> A learning disability refers to a retardation, disorder, or delayed development in one or more of the processes of speech, language, reading, spelling, writing, or arithmetic resulting from a possible cerebral dysfunction and/or emotional or behavioral disturbance and not from mental retardation, sensory deprivation, or cultural or instructional factors. (p. 263)

Kirk later stated that a learning disability refers to "a discrepancy between a child's achievement and his apparent capacity to learn as indicated by aptitude tests, verbal understanding, and arithmetic computation" (S. Kirk & W. Kirk, 1983, p. 20). He operationalized scholastic aptitude as the overall score on intelligence tests. Therefore, in the *IQ-achievement discrepancy approach*, SLD is identified when an individual's level of performance or rate of skill acquisition in a particular academic domain falls substantially below what one would predict based on his or her intelligence. Although multiple exclusionary criteria exist in this definition (i.e., ID, sensory deprivation, and cultural or instructional factors), a discrepancy between IQ and achievement is the primary inclusionary criterion for SLD diagnosis.

The definition of SLD in IDEA has remained unchanged since 1975. In IDEA (2004), SLD is defined as follows:

> *Specific learning disability* means a disorder in one or more of the basic psychological processes involved in understanding or in using language, spoken or written, which may manifest itself in the imperfect ability to listen, think, speak, read, write, spell, or do mathematical calculations. Such term includes such conditions as perceptual disabilities, brain injury, minimal brain dysfunction, dyslexia, and developmental aphasia. Such term does not include a learning problem that is primarily the result of visual, hearing, or motor disabilities, of mental retardation, of emotional disturbance, or of environmental, cultural, or economic disadvantage.

When IDEA was first passed in 1975, the federal definition of SLD *required* the identification of a "severe discrepancy" between IQ and achievement for eligibility for special education and related services. Over the next three decades, virtually every state used this approach for identifying SLD (C. Mercer, Jordan, Allsop, & A. Mercer, 1996). With the reauthorization of IDEA in 2004—although there was no change in the definition of SLD—a provision was added allowing the use of response to intervention (RtI) to encourage the use of SLD identification procedures that are more relevant to classroom instruction.

RtI refers to "a process that determines if the child responds to scientific, research-based intervention as a part of the evaluation procedures" (IDEA, 2004; see section 614[b][6]). In this approach, children and youth in the general education classroom are screened several times a year for achievement deficits. Additional and more intensive intervention is delivered in multitiered systems of support (MTSS) to students not meeting expectations for achievement based on local or national norms (e.g., Kovaleski, VanDerHeyden, & Shapiro, 2013). Achievement in the targeted domain is measured frequently, and growth over time is monitored.

In RtI, the determination of SLD is based on an academic performance discrepancy, inadequate rate of progress, or both, after ruling out exclusionary criteria. Thus, in an RtI model, SLD is identified when an individual's level of performance or rate of skill acquisition in a particular academic area falls substantially below what one would predict based on his or her age or grade peer group, rather than general cognitive ability. Intelligence tests typically are not used in the RtI method of SLD identification, but they may be included as part of a comprehensive assessment completed at the end of this process to determine eligibility for special education and related services by ruling out ID as a cause of underachievement (Wodrich, Spencer, & Daley, 2006).

In addition to allowing the use of the IQ-achievement discrepancy and RtI approaches for the identification of SLD, IDEA also permits states to use "other alternative research-based procedures" (34 CFR § 300.307.a.3). These alternative procedures were included, and purposefully left undefined, to give states the flexibility to allow research-based methods that could not be categorized as one of the other two approaches for SLD identification. The most prominent of these alternative procedures is based on analysis of the pattern of strengths and weaknesses (PSW) in an individual's cognitive abilities and academic achievement. At the current time, three PSW methods have received the most attention in the literature:

1. the Discrepancy-Consistency method (Naglieri, 2011),
2. the Concordance-Discordance method (Fiorello, Hale, & Wycoff, 2012), and
3. the Dual Discrepancy-Consistency method (Flanagan & Alfonso, 2017).

Although these PSW methods differ in important ways, all three define SLD as unexpected underachievement and corresponding weakness in one or more specific cognitive abilities.

In sum, the IQ-achievement discrepancy, RtI, and PSW methods for identifying SLD in IDEA are similar in at least three ways. They all agree that (1) individuals with SLD share a difficulty with school learning, (2) certain exclusionary factors must be ruled out before SLD can be identified (e.g., inadequate educational or language background, sensory impairment, and ID), and (3) discrepancy in achievement is a fundamental aspect of identification. The biggest point of disagreement concerns the need for the administration of intelligence tests to assess general cognitive ability, specific cognitive abilities, or both, for the identification of SLD (see Fletcher-Janzen & Reynolds, 2009). As Grigorenko et al. (2019) stated:

> It has been difficult to agree on the best way to identify SLDs, although there is consensus that their core is unexpected underachievement. A source of active research and controversy is whether "unexpectedness" is best identified by applying solely exclusionary criteria (i.e., simple low achievement), inclusionary criteria based on uneven cognitive development (e.g., academic skills lower than IQ or another aptitude measure, such as listening comprehension), or evidence of persisting difficulties . . . despite effective instruction. (p. 3)

Despite their differences, all three methods for identifying SLD are used to a considerable extent in the schools today. Results of a recent survey by Benson et al. (2019b) found that school psychologists vary greatly with respect to the frameworks they use to identify SLD, and many reported using more than one framework. According to their results, 53% of school psychologists reported using the PSW framework, 51% the RtI framework, and 37% the IAD framework. Maki and Adams (2019) also found that school psychologists reported using the PSW and RtI frameworks more frequently than the IAD framework (cf. Cottrell & Barrett, 2016). In addition, they found that state SLD identification rules and regulations had a moderate effect on the SLD framework used, whereas age, educational level, and years of experience had small effects. This pattern of results highlights the importance of state regulations on district-level and individual school psychologists' practices.

The Nature of SLD

According to the most recent position statement on SLD by the National Association of School Psychologists (NASP, 2010b), researchers widely agree on the following:

- Specific learning disabilities are endogenous in nature and are characterized by neurologically based deficits in cognitive processes.

- These deficits are specific; that is, they impact particular cognitive processes that interfere with the acquisition of academic skills.
- Specific learning disabilities are heterogeneous—there are various types of learning disabilities, and no single defining academic or cognitive deficit or characteristic is common to all types of specific learning disabilities.
- Specific learning disabilities may coexist with other disabling conditions (e.g., sensory deficits, language impairment, behavior problems) but are not primarily due to these conditions.
- Of children identified as having specific learning disabilities, the great majority (more than 80%) have a disability in the area of reading.
- The manifestation of an SLD is contingent to some extent upon the type of instruction, supports, and accommodations provided and the demands of the learning situation.
- Early intervention can reduce the impact of many specific learning disabilities.
- Specific learning disabilities vary in their degree of severity, and moderate to severe learning disabilities can be expected to impact performance throughout the life span.
- Multitiered systems of student support have been effective as part of comprehensive approaches to meet students' academic needs. (p. 1)

In a review of research on the etiology of SLD, Brown, Daly, and Stafanatos (2009) concluded that "while no single biological marker has been implicated among individuals with learning disabilities, there is evidence from genetics, neuroimaging studies, and studies of the neurotransmitters to suggest that this disorder is firmly rooted in the brain" (p. 166). Results of quantitative behavior genetic research strongly indicate that SLD has a substantial heritable component and therefore is related to brain functioning (e.g., Fletcher & Grigorenko, 2017). In a meta-analysis of 95 studies with 21 independent data sets, for example, Snowling and Melby-Lervåg (2016) found that children and youth in families with a history of reading disability (RD) are four times more likely to have a reading disability than offspring in control families with no history of RD. The prevalence rate for RD among children and youth in at-risk families ranged from 29% to 66%, with a mean of 45%. Differences in the criteria used to define RD are one likely cause of at least some of the variability in the results of these studies. Results of twin studies also have found substantially higher concordance rates for RD for monozygotic twins than for dizygotic twins (e.g., Erbeli, Hart, & Taylor, 2019). Although less is known about the heritability of SLD in other academic areas (e.g., mathematics, spelling, and written expression), behavior genetic research clearly shows that SLD has a sizable genetic component.

In addition, multivariate quantitative genetic research enables examination of the degree to which the genetic and environmental factors that influence one trait (e.g., intelligence) are the same as those that influence another (e.g., academic achievement) through the calculation of *genetic correlations*. Genetic correlations are calculated to estimate the overlap between the genetic effects on two traits independent of their respective heritabilities. They are interpreted as the probability that the genes associated with one trait are the same as those related to another trait (e.g., Haworth et al., 2009). In a review of multivariate studies of learning disabilities and abilities, Plomin and Kovas (2005) found that the genetic correlation among the academic domains of reading, mathematics, and language performance was approximately .70. Results also revealed a substantial genetic correlation of .68 between reading and mathematics and general cognitive ability. Haworth et al. (2009) found similar results in a sample of 8,000 12-year-old twins. Results such as these led to the postulation of the *generalist genes hypothesis*, which states that it is highly likely that a single set of genes affects different learning abilities and disabilities.

As Plomin, Haworth, and Davis (2010) asserted, "These results suggest that learning disabilities are the quantitative extreme of the *same* genetic and environmental influences that operate throughout the normal distribution of learning disabilities" (p. 300). In other words, SLD is a not a distinct diagnostic category from a genetic perspective. Nevertheless, despite the substantial amount of evidence substantiating the generalist genes hypothesis, molecular genetic research has been unable to identify the specific genes affecting common disorders such as SLD. In other words, there is no gene for SLD. Indeed, it appears that SLD results from many genes of very small effect size (Grigorenko et al., 2019). At the present time, rather than investigating the few candidate genes that have been tentatively identified, research is now investigating genome-wide association. Genome-wide association, which examines association across the entire genome, has shown that most genome-wide association effects explain less than 1% of the variance in the traits that have been studied, including SLD (e.g., Selzam et al., 2017).

Currently, the majority of behavior genetic and neurocognitive research that has been conducted has focused on RD. A number of neurological and biological theories of RD have been postulated, including those related to biochemical and electrophysiological functioning of the brain, as well as its neurological structure (e.g., Fletcher-Janzen & Reynolds, 2009). Although it is difficult to summarize the results of this research, evidence suggests that disruption of the language-processing system in specific brain regions results in difficulty with phonological processing for many individuals with RD (e.g., Grigorenko et al., 2019). *Phonological processing* involves the ability to associate the letters of words with discrete sounds. Phonological processing includes three components that are important for reading: (1) phonological awareness (i.e., knowledge that letters represent certain sounds), (2) rapid naming/word retrieval, and (3) working memory. Most individuals with RD experience difficulty with phonological awareness.

Despite the considerable progress neuroscience has made in clarifying the biological basis of SLD, translation of the results of this research to effective educational interventions has been limited (e.g., Therrien, Zaman, & Banda, 2011). As Swanson (2009) stated, "although brain studies linking neurological underpinnings to behavioral function are necessary to provide a theoretical context to understanding LD, altering instruction as a function of this knowledge base has not been clearly formulated" (p. 30). Indeed, some have summarized what is known about SLD as "a rather arbitrarily defined class of unclearly differentiated deficits in cognitive functions broadly conceived, but less behaviorally pervasive than would be implied by mental retardation" (Jensen, 1987, p. 68).

One potential explanation for the unsuccessful identification of the processing deficits hypothesized to underlie SLD concerns the use of traditional psychometric tests. In Chapter 8 and elsewhere (Floyd & Kranzler, 2012), we have argued that these instruments are far too complex for the assessment of underlying processing disorders. Not only do individual differences on these tests reflect various factors of human cognitive ability, but the test scores involve many distinct lower-order cognitive processes and reflect only the results of mental activity, not the cognitive processes themselves. Given the complexity of psychometric tests, advances in the assessment of SLD are likely to depend on the development of new assessment instruments that are closer to the interface between brain and behavior.

Methods for Determining Achievement Discrepancy

Despite the fact that no consensus definition of SLD exists, at the core of each of these definitions is the concept of discrepancy in academic functioning. Figure 13.1 presents a scatterplot of the correlation between an IQ and a broad reading achievement score for 1,485 children and youth who completed both a multidimensional intelligence test and an achievement test that were co-normed (Woodcock, McGrew, & Mather, 2001). As shown here, general intelligence and reading achievement have a strong positive correlation of +.68. This correlation means that, on average, the higher one's general intelligence, the better one is at reading, and vice versa. If we exclude those with ID (i.e., IQ < 75), who has SLD? The child with an

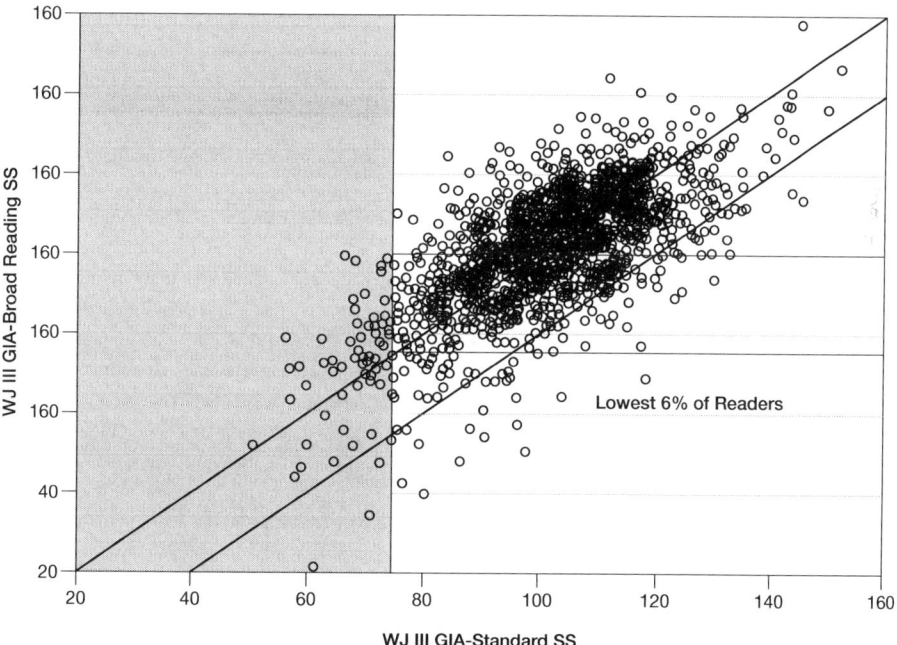

Figure 13.1. Correlation between reading and intelligence (r = +0.68; N = 1,485). Data obtained from the Woodcock Munoz Foundation.

above-average IQ who is reading in the average range? Or the child who is reading in the lowest quartile, regardless of IQ?

In this section, we address this question by briefly reviewing the three alternative approaches in IDEA for identifying an achievement discrepancy and, therefore, determining whether an individual has SLD: (1) the traditional IQ-achievement discrepancy approach, (2) the RtI approach, and (3) the PSW approach. As we will see, the use of the different methods of SLD eligibility determination in IDEA likely results in the identification of somewhat different groups of children and youth.

IQ-ACHIEVEMENT DISCREPANCY METHODS

In the IQ-achievement discrepancy approach, SLD is identified when an individual's level of performance or rate of skill acquisition in a particular academic area falls substantially below what one would predict from his or her general intelligence. In this approach, IQ is used as a benchmark against which to compare achievement, and students' achievement is assumed to be commensurate with their IQ.

The simplest, most straightforward way to determine the presence of IQ-achievement discrepancy is to determine whether a large difference (D) exists between scores on IQ and achievement tests, when scores are expressed in the same metric, such as standard-score (z-score) units, as in this formula:

$$D = Z_{IQ} - Z_{ach}$$

A significant discrepancy exists if

$$D > Z_{critical}$$

where $Z_{critical}$ is some predetermined cutoff score, such as a z score of 1.0 or 1.5.

Figure 13.1 shows the individuals who would qualify for a diagnosis of SLD when this simple discrepancy approach is used. The diagonal line in the middle of the scatterplot is the expected level of achievement across levels of general intelligence. Achievement scores below the diagonal line that is parallel to but lower than the line in the middle of the scatterplot are significantly lower than the level of performance expected on the basis of general intelligence. These are the students who potentially are eligible for a diagnosis of SLD in the IQ-achievement discrepancy approach. As can be seen here, within this approach, the group with SLD consists of individuals with IQs largely in the average to above-average range. Children and youth with IQs in the below-average range who do not have ID generally are not eligible for special education services, despite the fact that their reading achievement is among the lowest in mainstream classes. Because their IQ and reading achievement scores are comparably low, the discrepancy between them is not of a significant magnitude to qualify for special education.

One criticism of the use of the IQ-achievement discrepancy approach is that it precludes the identification of low-performing students (without ID) who have serious educational needs for special education and related services. Because it is often difficult to determine a severe discrepancy until as late as the third grade, the IQ-achievement discrepancy model often is referred to as a "wait-to-fail" model (e.g., Vaughn & D. Fuchs, 2003). The simple discrepancy model, however, also has been criticized on psychometric grounds, because it does not account for regression toward the mean and measurement error. Regression models, therefore, generally are seen as an improvement over the simple discrepancy model for determining significant IQ-achievement discrepancies, because they take into account the phenomenon of regression toward the mean.

As noted in earlier chapters, *regression toward the mean* refers to the fact that when two variables are correlated (imperfectly), as general intelligence and achievement are, an individual's score on the predicted variable tends to be not as extreme as his or her score on the predictor. Also, the more extreme the score on the predictor is, the more that score is subject to regression. Campbell and Stanley (1963) stated 50 years ago:

> The more deviant the score, the larger the error of measurement it probably contains. Thus, in a sense, the typical extremely high scorer has had unusually good "luck" (large positive error) and the extremely low scorer bad luck (large negative error). Luck is capricious, however, so on a posttest we expect the high scorers to decline somewhat on the other average, the low scorers to improve their average. . . . Regression toward the mean is a ubiquitous phenomenon, not confined to pre-testing and post-testing with the same test or comparable forms of a test. (p. 11)

In other words, some degree of academic "underachievement" is predictable for students with high IQs. The opposite is true for individuals scoring near the bottom of the IQ distribution. When regression to the mean is *not* taken into account in the identification of SLD, this results in the *overidentification* of children with above-average IQs and the *under-identification* of children with below-average IQs.

Simple regression models, therefore, compare the difference between the *obtained* achievement score and the *predicted* achievement score, which is determined by the regression of IQ on achievement. In this way, "real" underachievement is compared with "expected" underachievement. If the obtained achievement score is significantly below what one would predict from that child's level of general intelligence, then a discrepancy is said to exist. Thus, this model is actually an expected-actual achievement discrepancy model and not an IQ-achievement discrepancy model. Although the simple regression model adequately takes regression toward the mean into account, it does not control for errors of measurement that creep into assessment as a function of unreliability.

To correct for measurement error, the full regression model was developed to "evaluate the difference between regressed achievement and aptitude scores (but regressed as a function of the unreliability of the scores)" (C. Reynolds, 1984–1985, p. 462). In other words, the full regression model examines the difference between the *obtained* IQ and achievement scores that have been regressed independently to their respective means on the basis of measurement error, as estimated by the internal consistency reliability of each instrument. Unlike the simple regression model, this model takes into account errors of measurement. Unfortunately, this model does not actually correct for the problem of regression. Therefore, it can be criticized on the same grounds as the z-score discrepancy model.

C. Reynolds (1984–1985) and Shepard (1989) argued that the full regression model is not only "mathematically unacceptable," but "conceptually flawed" as well. Reynolds stated that the full regression model is appropriate for use only when measures of low reliability are available. Of course, virtually every IQ and academic achievement composite score in use today has more than adequate reliability, so there is little or no need for the full regression formula. Shepard (1989) concurred, pointing out that the full regression model does not consider the well-established empirical relationship between measures of IQ and achievement. According to Shepard, this model is inappropriate because it treats intelligence tests and achievement tests "as if they were estimators of the same underlying ability" (p. 560). This is problematic, she added, because it "contradicts our understanding of SLD as specific learning deficits that are distinct from general intellectual functioning" (p. 560). Neither Reynolds nor Shepard, therefore, recommended the use of the full regression model.

In addition to these concerns, critics have argued that intelligence tests are irrelevant to the identification of SLD (e.g., Siegel, 1989, 1992; Stanovich & Siegel, 1994). As Francis et al. (2005) stated, "These arguments are supported by studies demonstrating that IQ-discrepant and low achieving groups overlap and are difficult to differentiate on cognitive and behavioral characteristics, response to intervention, prognosis, and other areas" (p. 98). Consequently, they have argued for the identification of SLD simply on the basis of significant low achievement (e.g., see Shinn, 2005). At the current time, the IQ-achievement discrepancy approach has few proponents among researchers, despite the fact that it continues to be widely used in the schools (Maki & Adams, 2019).

RTI METHODS

L. Fuchs (1995) proposed an RTI problem-solving model within which the assessment of disabilities occurs in three phases:

1. Tier 1 involves tracking the academic performance of all students in general education classes to determine whether instruction is adequate. Progress in RtI models typically is tracked in elementary schools with curriculum-based measurement (CBM) of basic academic skills. Most CBM approaches involve administering a set of short-duration fluency measures to assess basic skills in such academic areas as reading, spelling, written expression, and mathematics computation (e.g., Shinn & Bamonto, 1998).
2. In Tier 2, students who are performing well below grade-level expectations are identified and given more intensive instruction. The academic progress of students identified at Tier 2 is then monitored.
3. Special education and related services at Tier 3 are considered only when these educational adaptations fail to improve student academic performance.

Thus, in the RtI approach, the identification of SLD is based on an achievement discrepancy from that expected based on same-age or same-grade peers.

Differentiating among those students who do not respond to academic interventions is the key question in determining eligibility for special education services. In the RtI model, "CBM-guided decision making relies primarily on a norm-referenced approach" (Shinn & Habedank, 1992, p. 12). Academic progress is monitored during instructional intervention by examining change in CBM performance within students (i.e., rate of growth on CBM). In contrast, screening and determination of eligibility for special education and related services depend upon norm-referenced interpretation (i.e., comparison of a student's CBM performance with that of same-age or -grade peers).

At the current time, RTI literature describe three main ways to categorize responders and nonresponders (see D. Fuchs & Deshler, 2007):

1. examination of academic growth rate, as measured by the slope of CBM scores over time;
2. comparison of academic achievement to a final benchmark, as measured either by a standardized achievement test or CBM; or
3. a dual-discrepancy approach, as measured by both the slope of CBM scores over time and a comparison of final performance on fluency CBM to a benchmark at the end of instruction.

In each of these methods, nonresponders are defined by performance that falls below a predetermined cutoff point, in comparison to either school, district, or national norms. For example, nonresponders have been defined alternatively as having a CBM slope that is below the median in comparison with same-grade peers (Christ, Zopluoglu, Long, & Monaghen, 2012; Vellutino et al., 1996); a standardized achievement test score that is below the 25th percentile (Torgesen et al., 2001); or a CBM slope and final CBM score that are one standard deviation below those of classroom peers (L. Fuchs & D. Fuchs, 1998). In Figure 13.1, the two horizontal lines show the average level of achievement for all students and the cutoff for those whose level of achievement is in the lowest 6% of all readers. In RtI achievement discrepancy approach, those falling below the lower of the two horizontal lines would be considered to have SLD.

According to Shinn (2007), "Using a[n] RTI model, it is not expected that different students will be identified as SLD than those identified historically" (p. 601). In actuality, however, very little is known about whether the different RtI methods will identify students with profiles of disability similar to those produced via the IQ-achievement discrepancy method (D. Fuchs & Deshler, 2007). C. Reynolds (2009) asserted that, given the strong positive correlation between intelligence and achievement, use of the RtI achievement discrepancy approach inevitably will lead to the overrepresentation of children and youth with IQs < 85. As shown in Figure 13.1, regardless of where one sets the cutoff point for a significant achievement discrepancy, it seems highly likely that slow learners will be overrepresented among those identified as having SLD. In fact, the results of recent research by Kranzler, Yaraghchi, Matthews, and Otero-Valles (2019) provide some support for Reynolds's contention. Statistically significant differences in their study were observed between the SLD and general education groups, with considerably lower mean scores for the SLD group. Almost 75% of those in the SLD group had IQs below the mean of the normative sample and almost half had IQs below 90.

If Reynolds (2009) is correct, then the RtI achievement discrepancy approach to identification represents a fundamental shift in the concept of SLD from the narrow-sense definition of unexpected underachievement to the broad-sense definition of being a slow learner. As he argued, individuals with above-average IQs and academic achievement in the average range will not receive individualized or special education services because their performance compares favorably to the mean performance of their peers. We agree with Reynolds (2009) that although one might argue that this pattern is consistent with the principles of social justice, it is in the best interests of society to promote the optimal academic achievement of all children and not only the lowest-performing ones.

Moreover, the RTI achievement discrepancy approach has been found to be susceptible to psychometric criticisms similar to those leveled at the IQ-achievement discrepancy approach. For example, Francis et al. (2005) examined the stability of diagnoses of SLD based on the IQ-achievement and RTI achievement discrepancy (e.g., Shinn, 2007) approaches. Results of their study, using both simulated and actual longitudinal data, revealed that both methods were relatively unstable in terms of diagnosis over time (see Brown Waesche et al., 2011). Thus, a major criticism of the IQ-achievement discrepancy method of identification—that is, the unreliability of SLD diagnosis—also applies to the RtI achievement discrepancy method. Francis et al. (2005) concluded that neither approach is viable by itself, because both essentially use a single indicator (viz., IQ-achievement discrepancy or low achievement) as the inclusionary criterion to identify SLD. They concluded that this criticism does not invalidate the concept of SLD in the narrow sense (i.e., unexpected underachievement); it only means that other factors need to be considered, such as exclusionary criteria and responsiveness to intervention, in making a diagnosis of SLD.

Figure 13.1 shows the proportions of children and youth who will be identified with SLD under the different diagnostic approaches. As can be seen, the groups of students identified with SLD will differ in largely predictable ways according to identification method. The IQ-achievement discrepancy method will tend to identify a greater number of students with above-average IQs, depending on the method of discrepancy used (e.g., simple or regression), whereas the RtI achievement discrepancy approach will tend to result in more students with below-average IQs, many of whom will fall in the slow-learner range of general intelligence.

PSW METHODS

In response to criticisms of the IQ-achievement and RtI achievement discrepancy approaches, a number of alternative research-based procedures for SLD identification have been proposed, the most prominent of which is the PSW approach (e.g., Fiorello et al., 2012; Flanagan et al., 2018; Naglieri, 2011). Proponents of the PSW approach assert that comprehensive psychoeducational assessments must include tests of cognitive ability to measure basic psychological processes in order to be consistent with the federal definition of SLD. They maintain that contemporary intelligence test batteries can be used to identify specific cognitive abilities that can serve as "early screening markers or collectively as pattern indicators of a potential SLD process disorder" (e.g., McGrew & Wendling, 2010, p. 652). In contrast to the IQ-achievement and RtI discrepancy approaches, the PSW methods define SLD as unexpected academic underachievement (i.e., general intelligence in the average range or above and academic weakness in one or more areas) and corresponding weakness in one or more specific cognitive abilities. Thus, in the PSW methods, SLD results from deficits in cognitive processing that are importantly related to different academic areas.

In their survey, Maki and Adams (2019) found that, of the school psychologists who reported using of the PSW framework, approximately 48% used the Dual Discrepancy-Consistency method; 9%, the Discrepancy-Consistency method; and 7%, the Concordance-Discordance method. Interestingly, about 22% of those using PSW methods reported that they did not use a specific model, and 5% reported using a lesser known PSW model than those listed above. Given that the Dual Discrepancy-Consistency Method is the predominant PSW method, we briefly describe the steps involved in SLD identification for this approach.

Dual Discrepancy-Consistency PSW Method. The Dual Discrepancy-Consistency Method of SLD identification consists of five levels of evaluation (Flanagan, Ortiz, & Alfonso, 2013). *Level I* involves the assessment of academic achievement to determine the presence of a normative (or population relative) weakness or deficit. This typically involves the administration of standardized, norm-referenced tests of achievement ($M = 100$, $SD = 15$). A "weakness" is defined by a standard score that falls between 85 and 89, and a "deficit" by a score that falls below 85. As Flanagan et al. (2013) stated, "The presence of a weakness or deficit . . . is a necessary (but insufficient) condition for SLD determination" (pp. 244–245). If a normative weakness or deficit in academic performance is not found, then the student does not meet SLD classification criteria, and the Dual Discrepancy-Consistency method evaluation process stops.

After one or more academic weaknesses or deficits are identified, *Level II* involves the examination of exclusionary factors. Exclusionary factors are alternative explanations for underachievement other than a cognitive processing disorder, such as intellectual disability, psychiatric disorders, lack of motivation, limited English proficiency, environmental or economic disadvantage, and medical conditions (e.g., hearing or vision disorder), among others. Flanagan et al. (2013) stated that "careful examination of exclusionary factors is intended to rule out other possible explanations for deficient academic performance" (p. 251). In other words, examination of exclusionary factors is intended to preclude a diagnosis of SLD for students who otherwise meet the Dual Discrepancy-Consistency eligibility criteria.

Level III involves the assessment of broad and narrow cognitive abilities of the Cattell-Horn-Carroll (CHC) theory (e.g., Schneider & McGrew, 2018) that are deemed to be important for the diagnosis of learning difficulties. According to Flanagan et al. (2013),

> A particularly salient aspect of the [Dual Discrepancy-Consistency] operational definition of SLD is that a weakness or deficit in one or more cognitive abilities or processes underlies difficulties in academic performance and skill development. Because research demonstrates that the relationship between the cognitive dysfunction and the manifest learning problems are causal in nature . . . data analysis at this level should seek to ensure that identified weaknesses or deficits on cognitive and neuropsychology tests bear an empirical relationship to those weaknesses or deficits on achievement tests identified previously. (pp. 252–253)

Moreover, "this consistency is a necessary marker for SLD because SLD is *presumably* caused by cognitive processing weaknesses or deficits" (Flanagan & Alfonso, 2017, p. 436, emphasis in the original). These data typically are gathered through the administration of one or more intelligence tests.

Level IV involves analysis of the achievement and cognitive data gathered at Levels I and III to determine whether the individual displays a PSW characterized by dual discrepancy-consistency within an otherwise normal cognitive ability profile. These analyses are conducted using software developed by Flanagan and colleagues called the Cross-Battery Assessment Software System (X-BASS 2.0; Flanagan, Ortiz, & Alfonso, 2017). After ruling out exclusionary factors, the diagnosis of SLD is made when five criteria are met:

1. general intelligence in the average range or higher (standard score of ≥ 90);
2. a weakness is found for at least one broad cognitive ability (standard score < 90);
3. a statistically significant difference is observed between general ability and one or more cognitive weaknesses;
4. a weakness is found for at least one academic achievement area (standard score < 90); and
5. a statistically significant difference is observed between general intelligence and one or more academic weaknesses.

Last, *Level V* involves the meeting of a multidisciplinary team to determine whether special education and related services are necessary for children and youth meeting the Dual Discrepancy-Consistency eligibility criteria for SLD.

Evidence for the PSW Methods. According to Fletcher and Miciak (2017), five arguments have been presented in support of the use of comprehensive cognitive assessment and the PSW methods of SLD identification:

1. The statutes defining LD in federal legislation mandate cognitive assessments.
2. Cognitive assessments are correlated with achievement domains that do not develop adequately in LD.
3. Patterns of cognitive strengths and weaknesses discriminate LD from non-LD "slow learners."
4. Cognitive tests permit better treatment planning and intervention outcomes.
5. Clinicians using cognitive tests make more informed decisions. (p. 3)

Although Fletcher and Miciak effectively debunked four of these arguments, empirical evidence does exist for one—research demonstrating that a number of broad and narrow cognitive abilities of the Cattell-Horn-Carroll theory (e.g., Schneider & McGrew, 2018) are positively correlated with different domains of academic achievement. Nonetheless, results of a recent meta-analysis of the relations between CHC cognitive abilities and academic achievement by Zaboski, Kranzler, and Gage (2018) found that only one CHC broad ability, Crystallized Intelligence, had a medium-to-large effect for each achievement domain, with the largest effects for reading with older students. For the other broad abilities, effect sizes tended to be small and explained less than 10% of the variance in achievement. In contrast, general intelligence had by far the strongest relations with achievement, with ubiquitous large effect sizes. The variance explained by general intelligence was typically more than that accounted for by all broad abilities combined.

Moreover, as Fletcher and Miciak (2017) asserted, "Demonstrating that cognitive measures and achievement are correlated does not establish that such measures are related to intervention outcomes or provide value-added information to identification" (p. 3). Before practices based on the PSW methods are widely adopted and implemented in the schools, empirical research must substantiate their utility for differential diagnosis, treatment planning, or both. A number of studies have been conducted to address the question of whether the PSW methods are capable of reliably grouping children and adolescents with and without characteristics of SLD (Kranzler, Floyd, Benson, Zaboski, & Thibodaux, 2016a; Miciak, Fletcher, Stuebing, Vaughn, & Tolar, 2014; Miciak, Taylor, Denton, & Fletcher, 2015; Miciak, Taylor, Stuebing, & Fletcher, 2018; Stuebing, Fletcher, Brahum-Martin, & Francis, 2012; Taylor, Miciak, Fletcher, & Francis, 2017). Results of these studies have found that the PSW methods do not reliably classify children and youth with and without SLD. In sum, results of the extant empirical research suggest that school psychologists using the PSW methods will spend a great deal of time conducting assessments that have a very low probability of accurately identifying true SLD (e.g., Kranzler et al., 2016b).

CONCLUSION

Given such widespread variability in the field, which SLD identification model should be used? As our review hopefully made clear, each SLD identification framework has been subject to criticism, and each likely identifies a somewhat different group of children and youth as SLD. Nevertheless, results of a comprehensive evaluation must be used to determine whether a student meets the eligibility criteria for a disability under IDEA. When determining eligibility, multidisciplinary teams must make a dichotomous decision (eligible versus not eligible) using continuous variables that are measured imperfectly at one point in time. Use of cut scores will result in poor decision accuracy largely due to measurement error. This is the primary reason that the IAD and PSW frameworks do not reliably classify children and youth with and without SLD. As Francis et al. (2005) asserted, "A single assessment at a single point of time is not psychometrically adequate for determinations that have a significant long-term impact on a child's development" (p. 104). Instead, the identification of SLD should be based on more than one assessment at more than one point in time.

Fletcher and Miciak (2017) contended that the construct of SLD is best conceptualized as inadequate response to intervention within an RTI/MTSS framework. At the current time, the hybrid model for SLD identification has the most psychometric support. As they stated:

> We believe evidence supports a hybrid method based on a comprehensive assessment that includes assessment of instructional response, low achievement based on well-validated, standardized academic assessments, and contextual factors that interfere with achievement, such as the presence of other disabilities or environmental circumstances (Bradley, Danielson & Hallahan, 2002). These assessments should be brief, directly assess the behaviors of interest, and focused on hypotheses about why the child's learning is not adequate. If other disabilities or comorbid disorders are suspected, the comprehensive assessment process should include assessments to evaluate this possibility (e.g., assessment for ADHD). Any assessment should lead to intervention. (p. 6)

According to the results of Kranzler et al. (2020b), however, the main shortcoming of the hybrid model is that the inclusionary criteria for identification of SLD are based primarily on the RtI model, which leads to the overidentification of children and youth with weaknesses in general cognitive ability. They argued that the traditional conceptualization of SLD as unexpected underachievement is correct, and that "a disability is recognized as a psychopathological condition primarily associated with the individual" (Reynolds, 2009, p. 16). Thus, unexpected underachievement should not be based on discrepancy from the average academic performance of same-age or -grade peers, but on discrepancy from expected achievement for students at different levels of learning aptitude, or intelligence.

To address this shortcoming in the hybrid model, they proposed a Modified Hybrid Model (MHM) in which unexpected underachievement is defined as when an individual's level of performance or rate of skill acquisition in a particular academic area falls substantially below the level one would predict based on their general cognitive ability, after ruling out exclusionary criteria. The primary inclusionary criterion for the identification of SLD in their model is the same as in the hybrid model—that is, inadequate response to intervention within an RTI/MTSS framework—while enabling the identification of children and youth displaying unexpected underachievement at all levels of cognitive ability. Further research on the MHM is needed, however, before it can be considered viable for implementation.

Best Practices in SLD Diagnosis

GENERAL RECOMMENDATIONS

The position statement on the identification of NASP, which is based on the research and the requirements in federal regulations (IDEA, 2004), supports the following:

- Identification of and instruction for children suspected of having SLD should be implemented within the context of an evidence-based multitiered service delivery system. Such systems provide high quality and timely educational strategies and a continuum of data-based academic/behavioral instruction within general education for children with learning problems.
- A multitiered model in which instructional strategies are more focused or intensively delivered, providing quality instruction in the general education classroom in addition to timely interventions before a special education referral is considered.
- Universal screening of academic and behavior skills should be conducted during all elementary school years and selectively, as needed, in the middle and high school years.
- When an SLD is suspected, and appropriate instruction and intervention within general education fail to meet a child's educational needs, a comprehensive evaluation by qualified professionals is an essential step in determining SLD eligibility and individualized educational needs.
- It is best practice to look at multiple sources of data, including how students respond to scientifically based instruction, including environmental and instructional conditions. Relying upon an ability-achievement discrepancy as the sole means of identifying children with specific learning disabilities is at odds with scientific research and with best practice. (p. 2)

The diagnosis of SLD is made by multidisciplinary teams in schools. In schools, IDEA (2004) provides a definition of SLD and the legal underpinnings for the identification process. Rules and regulations at the state and district levels, however, define the required steps in the assessment process within individual schools. Because federal law defines SLD primarily in terms of exclusionary criteria—that is, by what SLD is not, not by what it is—conceptual definitions of SLD and their accompanying classification criteria generally are consistent with federal law but tend to vary from state to state (e.g., Maki, Floyd, & Roberson, 2015). The implication of this variability is that eligibility determination for SLD for special education and related services in schools depends to some degree upon an individual's state of residence. Outside schools, private practitioners may adopt the definition of SLD and identification criteria of the state educational agency or use another classification approach, such as that of the American Psychiatric Association (2013).

Regardless of the regulations used to diagnose SLD, it important to follow best-practice recommendations, such as those by the NASP (2010b) and the National Joint Committee on Learning Disabilities (NJCLD, 2010). Because the identification of SLD occurs primarily in schools, we focus on best-practice guidelines within the educational context. Moreover, given the variability in conceptual definitions of SLD and their classification criteria, we provide general best-practice guidelines for SLD diagnosis. The rules and regulations of every state education agency specify the requirements for a comprehensive assessment of SLD, according to IDEA (2004).

Table 13.1 provides recommendations by the NJCLD (2010) for conducting a comprehensive assessment for the identification of SLD by multidisciplinary teams for IDEA purposes. As indicated here, the identification of SLD cannot be based only on

Table 13.1. Procedures for Comprehensive Assessment and Evaluation of Specific Learning Disabilities under IDEA

A comprehensive assessment and evaluation should:

1. Use a valid and the most current version of any standardized assessment.
2. Use multiple measures, including both standardized and nonstandardized assessments, and other data sources, such as

   - case history and interviews with parents, educators, related professionals, and the student (if appropriate);
   - evaluations and information provided by parents;
   - direct observations that yield informal (e.g., anecdotal reports) or data-based information (e.g., frequency recordings) in multiple settings and on more than one occasion;
   - standardized tests that are reliable and valid, as well as culturally, linguistically, developmentally, and age appropriate;
   - curriculum-based assessments, task and error pattern analysis (e.g., miscue analysis), portfolios, diagnostic teaching, and other nonstandardized approaches;
   - continuous progress monitoring repeated during instruction and over time.

3. Consider all components of the definition of specific learning disabilities in IDEA 2004 and/or its regulations, including

   - exclusionary factors;
   - inclusionary factors;
   - the eight areas of specific learning disabilities (i.e., oral expression, listening comprehension, written expression, basic reading skill, reading comprehension, reading fluency, mathematics calculation, mathematics problem solving);
   - the intra-individual differences in a student, as demonstrated by "a pattern of strengths and weaknesses in performance, achievement, or both relative to age, State-approved grade level standards or intellectual development" 34 CFR 300.309(a)(2)(ii).

4. Examine functioning and/or ability levels across domains of motor, sensory, cognitive, communication, and behavior, including specific areas of cognitive and integrative difficulties in perception; memory; attention; sequencing; motor planning and coordination; and thinking, reasoning, and organization.
5. Adhere to the accepted and recommended procedures for administration, scoring, and reporting of standardized measures. Express results that maximize comparability across measures (i.e., standard scores). Age or grade equivalents are not appropriate to report.
6. Provide confidence interval and standard error of measure, if available.
7. Integrate the standardized and informal data collected.
8. Balance and discuss the information gathered from both standardized and nonstandardized data, which describes the student's current level of academic performance and functional skills and informs decisions about identification, eligibility, services, and instructional planning.

Source: NJCLD (2010).

any single assessment method or measure. In other words, SLD diagnosis cannot be based solely on the identification of a significant IQ-achievement discrepancy, the level and rate of achievement data in an RtI service delivery model, or a particular PSW of cognitive abilities and achievement. Data from RtI can be an important component of SLD identification, however. In fact, RtI can be seen as a primary means of eliminating the instructional context as a viable explanation of academic failure and thereby suggesting that the cause is a disabling condition within the individual (Fuchs, Fuchs, & Compton, 2004). Also important is the consideration of information gathered from both formal methods (e.g., norm-referenced tests) and informal methods (e.g., interviews and observations).

Each state's eligibility criteria must guide the multidisciplinary team. The team must carefully consider all components of the definition of SLD, including inclusionary criteria (e.g., the RtI achievement discrepancy) and exclusionary criteria. As stated by the NJCLD (2010), "underachievement is common among students with learning disabilities, but it is not synonymous with learning disabilities" (p. 7). Underachievement is a necessary but not sufficient condition for SLD identification. In addition to determining that achievement deficits are evident, competing explanations of underachievement must be eliminated before an individual can be diagnosed with SLD. Factors that must be ruled out before a diagnosis of SLD can be made include ID, sensory impairments, problems in social–emotional functioning, cultural and linguistic background (e.g., limited English proficiency), and inadequate educational opportunity.

The NJCLD guidelines also call for comprehensive assessment across multiple domains of behavior, including motor, sensory, cognitive, communication, and behavioral functioning. This breadth is important for two reasons. First, SLD is often comorbid with other disabilities (e.g., attention-deficit/hyperactivity disorder). Although these disabilities may not cause SLD, their identification is important for appropriate intervention planning. Second, as stated by the NJCLD (2010), "learning disabilities can occur in students who are also gifted and/or talented. These 'twice exceptional' students often [demonstrate] achievement at age and grade expectations and are thus not considered to be struggling in school" (p. 9). Examination of intra-individual differences in skills and performance across domains can suggest SLD.

Table 13.2 presents critical decision points in the determination of SLD within an RtI model. It can be seen that important decisions about diagnosis of SLD occur at all stages, from pre-referral to eligibility determination. The administration of intelligence tests is an important component of the comprehensive assessment process, usually occurring at Tier 3 in an RtI model.

Table 13.2. Critical Decision Points in Determination of Specific Learning Disability

Stage	Methods	Critical Decision Points
Prereferral	Student may be designated as at-risk during screening and progress monitoring, student may be identified through child study teams, parent may note concern for a student's progress	Current performance identifies student as "at risk"; Data collected does not indicate positive response to interventions
Referral	Failure to progress even with Tier 2 level intervention in an RtI model, failure to progress given substantial, research-based accommodations and modifications	Data collected does not indicate positive response to interventions
Evaluation	List your components in order of evaluation of SLD Components to Assess, for example: 1. Inter-individual academic ability analysis 2. Evaluation of exclusionary factors 3. Inter-individual cognitive ability analysis 4. Reevaluation of exclusionary factors 5. Integrated ability analysis—evaluation of underachievement—in what areas does the underachievement occur? 6. Evaluation of interference with functioning—why is it occurring? 7. Related considerations—limitations in social skills, motor, vision, hearing 8. Other	Patterns or level of evidence, criteria for evidence of a component
Eligibility	Individualized, comprehensive evaluation	Criteria and patterns indicate presence of SLD

Source: Adapted from National Special Education Association Conference on SLD determination (April 2006).

A FINAL WORD ON INTELLIGENCE TESTS AND SLD DIAGNOSIS

At the current time, there is a great deal of disagreement about the usefulness of intelligence tests in the SLD identification process (e.g., Fletcher & Miciak, 2017). In the IQ-achievement and PSW approaches, the primary rule-in criteria are based on the results of intelligence tests. Nonetheless, given that the results of intelligence tests and the design of effective instructional interventions have little connection, some argue that there is little use in administering intelligence tests in the SLD identification process (e.g., Shinn, 2005). Although at present evidence does not support the treatment utility of intelligence test results for children with SLD, they are necessary for differentiating between SLD and ID in any identification model. As Wodrich et al.

(2006) noted, not only are SLD and ID different disability categories in IDEA, but they have different etiologies and prognoses in schools. In addition, Fuchs and Young (2006) found IQ to be significantly related to educational outcomes for individuals with reading difficulties. Thus, inclusion of intelligence tests is an important component of any comprehensive assessment for SLD. Caution must be used in selecting and interpreting intelligence tests during a comprehensive assessment for SLD, however. On heavily English-language-loaded tests, for example, the results for individuals with language impairment or limited English proficiency may not be valid. In these cases, it is advisable to select an appropriate intelligence test that will yield an estimate of psychometric g while avoiding the assessment of such construct-irrelevant variance (see Chapters 5 and 13).

Summary

Controversy long has surrounded the definition and diagnosis of SLD. At present, no consensus definition of SLD exists. SLD can either be viewed as a disability in learning in general (i.e., slow learner) or as unexpected underachievement in some, but not all, areas of academic achievement (e.g., reading or mathematics). Nonetheless, contemporary definitions of SLD are similar insofar as they refer to individuals who share a common difficulty with school learning. In addition, ruling out certain exclusionary criteria (e.g., inadequate educational or language background and intellectual disability) and determining a significant discrepancy in achievement are important components of SLD identification regardless of definition. Although the use of intelligence tests may not be required for determining a discrepancy in achievement in every state, they are necessary for ruling out intellectual disabilities.

CHAPTER 14

Assessment of Children and Adolescents from Diverse Cultural and Linguistic Backgrounds

The racial and ethnic diversity of students enrolled in public elementary and secondary schools in the United States is changing dramatically. According to the National Center for Education Statistics (NCES, 2019), the percentage of students in the public schools who were white decreased from 61% to 49% between 2000 and 2015. While the percentage of black students also decreased somewhat during this period (from 17% to 15%), the percentage of Hispanic students increased from 16% to 26% and Asian and Pacific Islander students from 4% to 5%, respectively. These trends were observed in all regions of the country and are projected to continue to increase between 2015 and 2027.

The increasing diversity in the public schools is further reflected in the number of students identified as English language learners (ELL). These are students who are in the process of learning English as a second language. ELL students are a heterogeneous group that varies greatly in terms of race, ethnicity, country of birth, home language spoken, and English proficiency in different domains (i.e., listening, speaking, reading, and writing). Between 2000 and 2016, the percentage of public school students who were ELL increased from 8% (or 3.8 million students) to 19% (or 4.9 million students), with Kansas reporting the highest percentage point increase. In 2016, the percentage of students who were ELL was 10% or more in nine or more states. The states with the highest percentage of ELL students were California (20%), Texas (17%), and Nevada (16%). A higher percentage of public school students were identified as ELL in lower grades (e.g., 16% of kindergartners) than in upper grades (e.g., 9% of sixth graders), which reflects the fact that most students are identified as ELL when they enter elementary school but obtain English language proficiency while in school. In 2016, the most prevalent home language reported among ELL students in 2016 was Spanish, which was spoken by 77% of all ELL students (or 3.8 million students) and 8% of all public school students. The next most prevalent home languages spoken were Arabic, Chinese, and Vietnamese. In addition, a higher percentage of Hispanic students (30%), Asian students (21%), and Pacific Islander students (16%) were identified as ELL than students overall (10%).

Given the trend toward increasing diversity in public schools, the validity of cognitive assessment of children and youth from diverse backgrounds is an important concern. Intelligence tests are administered routinely in schools as part of the process of identification for special education and related services, despite the fact that some view them as biased against children and youth from diverse backgrounds (e.g., see Vazquez-Nuttall et al., 2007). Critics argue that the overrepresentation of certain racial and ethnic groups in programs for students with intellectual disability (ID) and specific learning disability (SLD), and their underrepresentation in programs for the gifted and talented, are related to the inappropriate interpretation and use of intelligence tests (e.g., Sullivan, Artiles, & Hernandez-Saca, 2017). The fact that many students from racial and ethnic minority groups do not have the same experiential backgrounds as the white majority group is seen as one probable cause of test bias. Attempts to reduce the cultural loading of intelligence tests, most often by using abstract figural material as a basis for relation eduction (e.g., Cattell, 1971), however, have not eliminated mean group differences in intelligence test performance (see Reynolds & Suzuki, 2013).

Despite disagreement on the interpretation and use of intelligence tests in the schools with students from diverse linguistic and cultural backgrounds, it may come as a surprise to know that no one today seriously questions whether socioeconomic and racial and ethnic groups differ, on average, in the scores obtained on standardized intelligence tests. The empirical evidence is simply too great for anyone to argue convincingly otherwise, although mean group differences do appear to be declining somewhat over time (e.g., see Nisbett et al., 2012). Nevertheless, a prolonged and heated debate has raged on the *meaning* of these differences. Do they reflect real differences in intelligence? Or do they result from test bias or possibly invalid tests? What, then, are best practices for school psychologists and other professionals assessing the intelligence of children and youth from diverse backgrounds? Before reviewing the recommended best practices, in this chapter we briefly discuss fundamental issues and research on test bias.

Conceptualizations of Test Bias

What is *test bias?* Unfortunately, "discussions" of test bias are often conducted in a metaphorical Tower of Babel, where productive discourse, unfortunately, is rare. Due to the conflicting assumptions and theoretical orientations of researchers on opposing sides of the debate, a consensus-based definition of test bias does not exist. Moreover, the various conceptualizations of test bias that have been articulated in the literature vary considerably, especially in terms of their scientific merit. In the following section, we review the most common definitions of test bias (cf. Jensen, 1980, 1981).

THE EGALITARIAN DEFINITION

The "American dream" is based on the assumption that all people are created equal. Many Americans see success in life as resulting primarily from ambition, hard work, and good character, regardless of the circumstances into which one was born (e.g., gender, race, ethnicity, and socioeconomic status). This commitment to the concept of equality underlies much of the controversy related to test bias and intelligence testing. Perhaps the simplest definition of test bias, the egalitarian definition, is based on the widespread belief that no differences exist between groups in the population. Underlying this notion of bias is the postulate that the genotypic intelligence of all socioeconomic and racial and ethnic groups is the same. According to the egalitarian definition, an unbiased test reveals differences among individuals in intelligence but not among groups. Any test on which group differences are found, therefore, must be a biased test. However, if this definition of bias is accepted, then weight scales are biased, because men are heavier, on average, than women.

The main reason that the egalitarian definition of test bias is fallacious is not that it leads to clearly untenable conclusions such as this. The main reason is that it is based on the a priori assumption of group equality. The fallacy of this definition is that it assumes the answer to the question in point. It is based on the unwarranted assumption of group equality. There simply is no way empirically to prove or disprove the postulate of group equality in intelligence; by definition, any observed difference in mean test scores between groups is taken as evidence of bias. Because the egalitarian definition of bias is unfalsifiable, it is a pseudoscientific definition of bias and should be rejected. Moreover, the presence or absence of group differences says nothing about test bias. A biased test also can result in the performance of two groups that differ significantly being the same, just because the test is biased against the higher scoring group or biased in favor of the lower scoring group.

It is important to note that, just as we have no valid a priori reason to believe that there are no mean racial and ethnic group differences on tests of intelligence, we have no valid a priori reason to be believe that there are. "More important," as Reynolds and Suzuki (2013) stated, "a mean difference provides no information on *why* two groups differ" (p. 94). Mean group differences on intelligence tests might result from test bias, but they might not. Understanding the cause of group differences after test bias has been ruled out is a matter for further scientific research.

THE CULTURE BOUND DEFINITION

Another common definition of test bias concerns the fact that most standardized intelligence tests include a significant number of *culture-loaded* items. Culture loading is defined as the

> specificity or generality of the informational content of a test item, as contrasted with the item's demands for educing relationships, reasoning, and mental manipulations of its elements. Test items can be ordered along a continuum of culture loading in terms of the range of cultural backgrounds in which the item's informational content could be acquired. The answer to an item may depend on knowledge that could only be acquired within a particular culture, or locality, or time period. The opportunity for acquiring the requisite bit of knowledge might be greatly less in some cultures, localities, or time periods than in others. (Jensen, 1981, p. 130)

According to this definition, intelligence tests with items that are culturally loaded are biased against racial and ethnic minority groups, because their backgrounds are presumed to be significantly different from the majority.

Table 14.1 shows example items with differing degrees of culture loading. Item 1 is an item with a high degree of culture loading, because the correct answer (David) is only known to the family members and close friends of one of us (JHK). Carolyn is JHK's mother and Jerry is his father, whereas Koko is his mother-in-law and David is his father-in-law. Because this item involves the simple relation eduction of husband to wife, this is a very easy item for members of his family, but a difficult one for others, because they do not have the relevant background information to answer the item correctly. Item 2 is an example of the kind of item commonly thought to be biased, because it possibly requires information that may be more prevalent or easily accessible in some cultures than in others. Items 3 and 4 have decreasing degrees of culture loading. One involves knowledge of basic mathematics, whereas the other involves only abstract symbols. As can be seen in these examples, culture loading is not related to item difficulty per se but to the opportunity to acquire the necessary information to respond correctly. Culture loading and complexity of processing are entirely different things.

It is also important not to equate culture loading with test bias. Test items can be arranged on a continuum, with *culture-reduced* (one cannot have a *culture-free* test, because testing itself is a cultural activity) at one end of the continuum and *culture-saturated* at the other. Items typically thought to be biased are those near the culture-saturated end of the continuum. These items typically involve esoteric kinds of knowledge (e.g., the fine arts, literature, and history of science). Although panels of racial and ethnic majority and minority psychologists tend to agree on the degree of culture loading of specific items, research has shown that they are unable reliably to identify items that are biased (e.g., Frisby & Braden, 1999; Jensen, 1980; Reynolds & Kaiser, 1992). Hence, test bias cannot be identified by subjective judgments of an item's culture loading (e.g., Cormier, McGrew, & Evans, 2011; Kranzler, Flores, & Coady, 2010). The only way to identify test bias related to culture loading is to analyze actual data with objective statistical methods. The fallacy in this definition is the argument that a test is biased against certain groups simply because it contains items that are culture loaded.

THE STANDARDIZATION DEFINITION

According to the standardization definition of bias, intelligence tests that are standardized using certain groups (e.g., age, gender, race, and ethnicity) are ipso facto biased

Table 14.1. Test Items Reflecting Different Degrees of Culture Loading

1. Carolyn is to Jerry as Koko is to: (a) Steve, (b) David, (c) Bill, or (d) Fred.
2. Romeo is to Juliet as Tristan is to: (a) Carmen, (b) Elizabeth, (c) Isolde, or (d) Marguerite.
3. 60 is to 30 is to 15, as 20 is to 10 is to ___.
4. Continue the series: X OOOO XX OOO XXX OO ___.

Source: Adapted from Jensen (1981).

against all groups that are omitted from the standardization sample. This definition is based on the a priori assumption that these groups are inherently different, which is exactly the opposite of that assumed by the egalitarian definition of bias. (Interestingly, critics of intelligence tests sometimes use both of these fallacious definitions simultaneously as evidence of bias, despite the fact that they are based on contradictory assumptions.) Although also based on an a priori assumption, standardization bias on tests can be proven or disproven.

Test standardization involves two main steps: the selection of items and the norming of scores. Test items are selected on the basis of difficulty level and ability to discriminate between high and low test scores. Norming involves the development of standard scores. Intelligence test developers go to great lengths to include in the norming sample important characteristics of the population (e.g., age, gender, race, ethnicity, geographic region, and parental education). Standardization bias exists when the test items that meet rigorous criteria for selection for the groups included in the test norming sample differ from those items selected for those groups not included. Norming itself does not lead to bias, because it involves the linear transformation of raw scores into standardized scores and does not affect item selection or change the shape of the distribution.

Contemporary intelligence test developers, however, routinely analyze items for evidence of standardization bias by applying state-of-the-art item selection procedures (e.g., item response theory) to groups included in the standardization sample separately and retaining only those items meeting similar standards of item selection across them (see Reynolds & Suzuki, 2013). The important thing to remember here is that a test is not ipso facto biased against groups that are omitted from the standardization sample (e.g., bilinguals). Such a test might very well be biased against those groups, but it might not be. The only way to identify standardization bias is to analyze empirical data with objective statistical methods. The fallacy in this definition is the argument that a test is biased against certain groups simply because they are not represented in the standardization sample.

THE STATISTICAL DEFINITION

Psychometricians widely agree that test bias is best defined in a strictly mathematical sense (e.g., Frisby & Braden, 1999; Jensen, 1980; Reynolds & Carson, 2005; Reynolds & Kaiser, 1992; Reynolds & Suzuki, 2013). According to this definition, test bias is *systematic* (i.e., nonrandom) *measurement error* (Reynolds, Lowe, & Saenz, 1999). According to Jensen (1980), "in psychometrics, bias refers to systematic errors in the predictive validity or the construct validity of tests scores of individuals that are associated with the individual's group membership" (p. 375). Bias does not refer to *random* error, of which there are two kinds: *measurement* error and *sampling* error.

No measurement for any group of individuals is perfect—it always includes some degree of error—and the different kinds of measurement error on psychological tests can be estimated by reliability coefficients (r_{xx}; e.g., internal consistency and stability), where $1 - r_{xx}$ = error. Sampling error refers to variability in the values of a statistic that is observed whenever one selects a portion of the population (i.e., a sample) for study. In contrast to these two types of error, systematic measurement error occurs when an intelligence test either (a) measures one thing for one group and another thing for another group or (b) better predicts performance on some external criterion (e.g., academic achievement or performance on the job) for one group than for another. For example, if a verbally loaded intelligence test is administered to ELL students, their test scores likely would be affected by their limited proficiency in the English language, not their intelligence. When the test performance of children and youth from diverse backgrounds primarily reflects English-language proficiency rather than the cognitive ability constructs the test was intended to measure, the interpretation of test scores is biased.

Statistical indicators of test bias fall into two main categories: *internal* and *predictive*. Internal criteria of bias concern statistical properties of the test and its items (e.g., reliability, rank order of item difficulty, and factor structure). Bias is detected by comparing these and other *internal* indicators across socioeconomic, racial, ethnic, or other groups. If any of these indicators differs significantly across groups, then bias is objectively determined to exist.

Bias in *predictive* validity involves the comparison of regression parameters (slopes, intercepts, and standard errors) across groups. For instance, predictive bias is present when persons with the same test score from different groups perform differently, on average, on relevant external criteria, such as academic performance or job success. Tests that are biased against certain groups tend to under-predict performance on the criterion. Test bias can also be biased in favor of certain groups, however, resulting in the over-prediction of those groups' performance on the external criterion (i.e., their performance is better in the "real world" than predicted by test scores). The term *systematic measurement error* in the context of test bias, therefore, does not reflect a "reliability-based view of test bias" (e.g., see Ortiz, Piazza, Ochoa, & Dynda, 2018, p. 685). Rather, the focus of the statistical definition of test bias is clearly on the validity of intelligence test score interpretation (i.e., inferences and actions based on test scores) across different groups.

RESEARCH ON TEST BIAS

Numerous reviews of the empirical research have been conducted on test bias over the years, all of them reaching essentially the same conclusion (for reviews, see Brown, Reynolds, & Whitaker, 1999; Frisby & Braden, 1999; Gordon, 1987; Jensen, 1980; Neisser et al., 1996; Reynolds & Carson, 2005; Reynolds et al., 1999; Reynolds & Suzuki, 2013; Wigdor & Garner, 1982). The research literature on test bias is robust and clear: For native-born, English-speaking children in the United States, regardless of socioeconomic status or racial and ethnic group, standardized tests of intelligence are not substantially biased. As Reynolds and Suzuki (2013) concluded in a recent review, "Test bias exists but is small, which raises questions about its importance" (p. 107). Further, when bias is detected, it is usually on predictive criteria and in favor of—not against—racial and ethnic groups that tend to obtain the lowest average scores on intelligence tests (e.g., Berry, 2015). Last, but perhaps most important, often overlooked in discussions of test bias is the fact that the highest-scoring racial and ethnic group on intelligence tests, on average, is not whites but Asians and Pacific Islanders (e.g., Suzuki, Short, & Lee, 2011). This simple fact alone demonstrates that standardized intelligence tests are not biased against all racial and ethnic minority groups. The relatively high performance of Asians and Pacific Islanders tends to be overlooked by critics of the use of intelligence tests with diverse populations (e.g., see Ortiz et al., 2018; Rhodes, Ochoa, & Ortiz, 2005).

In sum, the robust research literature on test bias shows that, for native-born, English-speaking children in the United States, regardless of socioeconomic status or racial and ethnic group, the major tests of intelligence are *not* significantly biased. It is, however, extremely important to note that these results are not clearly generalizable to children and youth who do not speak English well, recently have immigrated to the United States, or both. As Jensen (1981) stated, "The fact that all these groups obtain lower scores on verbal than nonverbal tests, and on reading tests than on arithmetic tests, strongly suggests that their different language background may handicap their performance on verbal or language-loaded tests" (pp. 138–139).

FAIRNESS AND TEST BIAS

Before discussing best practices for the assessment of children and youth from diverse cultural and linguistic backgrounds, it is important to differentiate between test bias and the notion of fairness. As noted above, critics of intelligence testing argue that it is *unfair* to use intelligence tests for determining eligibility for special education and related services, mainly because it leads to the disproportionate representation of racial and ethnic groups in certain disability categories (e.g., Sullivan et al., 2017). Disproportionate representation is related to a phenomenon known as *adverse impact*. Given that the distribution of IQ scores within each racial and ethnic group is roughly normal, adverse impact occurs because small mean differences between groups result in disparities in the proportion of each respective group falling below an extreme low threshold or cut-score for determining eligibility for ID (e.g., IQ < 75) and above an extreme high score for intellectual giftedness (e.g., IQ > 130).

The concept of adverse impact underlies the tension that surrounds debates about the fair use of tests of intelligence. Central to these debates are the principles of individual and group rights. Arguments for group rights are based on the moral-political premises of collectivism and egalitarianism (Locke, 1995). According to Locke, "Collectivism . . . asserts that the group, not the individual, is the unit of significance and value, and that therefore members of a collective are interchangeable" (p. 179). He defines egalitarianism as "the doctrine that everyone or every group must be equal in outcomes, regardless of attributes or actions" (p. 180). Individual rights, in contrast, are based on the meritocratic ideal that individuals should be judged on the basis of their merits, without consideration of group membership (Locke, 1995). The fair use of tests is an important issue, but it "is a moral, philosophical, or legal issue on which reasonable people can legitimately disagree" (Reynolds & Suzuki, 2013, p. 87). Test bias, in contrast, is a matter for psychometrics and the statistical properties of tests with two or more groups. In any case, the completely overlapping distributions of test scores for all racial, ethnic, and socioeconomic groups contradict any public policy or use of tests that supports the differential treatment of groups on the basis of mean group differences in IQ test scores alone.

Best Practices in Assessment of Diverse Children and Youth

Reschly and Grimes (1990) stated that "best practices considerations require careful judgments about *when* intellectual assessments are used, *how* they are used, the selection, administration, and interpretation of tests, and efforts to protect children and youth from misuses and misconceptions" (p. 436; emphasis in the original). Although written almost three decades ago, the following recommendations for best practices still apply to all assessment situations, including the assessment of children from culturally and linguistically diverse backgrounds:

1. Appropriate use requires a context that emphasizes prevention and early intervention rather than eligibility determination as the initial phase in services to students with learning and behavior problems.
2. Intellectual assessment should be used when the results are directly relevant to well-defined referral questions, and other available information does not address those questions.
3. Mandatory use of intellectual measures for all referrals, multifactored evaluations, or reevaluations is not consistent with best practices.
4. Intellectual assessment must be part of a multifactored approach, individualized to a child's characteristics and the referral problems.
5. Intellectual assessment procedures must be matched carefully to characteristics of children and youth.
6. Score reporting and interpretations must reflect the known limitations of tests, including technical adequacy, inherent error in measurement, and general categories of performance.
7. Interpretation of performance and decisions concerning classification must reflect consideration of overall strengths and weaknesses in intellectual performance, performance on other relevant dimensions of behavior, age, family characteristics, and cultural background.
8. Users should implement assertive procedures to protect students from misconceptions and misuses of intellectual test results. (Reschly & Grimes, 1990, pp. 436–438)

These are excellent recommendations for practice that should not be compromised. We emphasize several of these points within the context of assessment with children from culturally and linguistically diverse backgrounds before discussing the pros and cons of the main assessment alternatives with these populations.

CULTURAL AND LINGUISTIC BACKGROUND

When assessing diverse children and youth, it is important to consider their *cultural background* (e.g., Elizalde-Utnick & Romero, 2017; Ortiz et al., 2018; Pham, Castro-Olivo, Chun, & Goforth, 2017; Ryan-Arredondo & Sandoval, 2005). Valencia and Lopez (1992) defined culture as "the particular traditions, values, norms, and practices of any people who share a common ancestry" (p. 400). As they stated,

> it is widely acknowledged that tests and other assessment tools measure samples of behavior. Furthermore, it is well known that culture influences behavior. Thus, in the context of psychoeducational assessment, the connection between measurement instruments and culture is clear: Assessment information, especially test data, gathered by school psychologists and other practitioners is—[to] varying degrees—culturally shaped. (p. 400)

Indeed, as we noted in Chapter 1, the behavior measured on intelligence tests is not only related to biological functioning, but also to one's experiences during development, which includes the cultural environment in which one is raised.

According to Ortiz et al. (2018), school psychologists must familiarize themselves with the diverse cultural backgrounds of their local student population and understand that such diversity could influence all phases of assessment—from the collection of data to the interpretation and use of results. They further recommended caution when generalizing from cultural groups as a whole to individuals within cultures, because individual differences within cultural groups are generally greater than the differences between groups. In assessment, therefore, a nomothetic perspective is best complemented by an idiographic one. Pham et al. (2017) also recommended that (a) information about cultural background should be gathered from as many sources as possible, particularly parents and teachers, and (b) the focus of assessment should be on the demonstrated skills and actual school and home experiences of children and youth.

In addition, *level of acculturation* is important to consider when assessing children and youth from diverse backgrounds. Acculturation is defined as "those phenomena, which result when groups of individuals having different cultures come into continuous first-hand contact, with subsequent changes in the original cultural patterns of either or both groups" (Redfield, Linton, & Herskovitz, 1936, p. 149, as cited in Ryan-Arredondo & Sandoval, 2005, pp. 861–862). According to Marín (1992), acculturation involves "changes in individuals that are produced by contact with one or more cultural groups" (p. 237), and it is best viewed "as a fluid process (probably a lifelong event) that involves many dimensions of an individual's life (e.g., behaviors, attitudes, norms, and values) and that does not typically follow a deficit model, but rather implies growth across a variety of continua" (p. 242).

Assessment of acculturation is not a simple task, however. As Ryan-Arredondo and Sandoval (2005) stated, "There is little agreement among researchers as to which cultural aspects, behaviors, and constructs accurately comprise acculturation" (p. 865). Moreover, given that the vast majority of research in this area has been conducted with college students and adults, little is known about the process of acculturation among school-age children and youth. Finally, at present, the acculturation scales that have been developed are limited in their psychometric support and the quality of their norms. According to Celenk and Van de Vijver (2014), the majority of the available measures of acculturation consist of short, single-scale instruments that measure behavioral acculturation outcomes (e.g., sociocultural competence) rather than acculturation conditions (e.g., personal characteristics) and orientations (i.e., adopting the mainstream culture or maintaining heritage and ethnic culture). These measures also do not include children and youth of all age ranges in their standardization samples and are limited to one or two ethnic groups (for more details, see Ryan-Arredondo & Sandoval, 2005). Perhaps for these reasons, the most widely used method for gathering information on level of acculturation by school psychologists is interviews (O'Bryon & Rogers, 2010).

Linguistic background is another important consideration in the psychological assessment of children and youth from diverse backgrounds. For children with academic problems who are ELL, assessment of the home language and development in English is essential. Unfortunately, the availability of formal language assessments of Spanish-speaking and other children and youth who are ELL is rather limited. Moreover, according to Elizalde-Utnick and Romero (2017), standardized tests of languages other than English often yield equivocal results—or they simply do not exist at all—for many students who are ELL in the United States. Therefore, determining whether an individual's academic problems result from LEP or from a language disorder is difficult. According to Elizalde-Utnick and Romero, "The consensus of researchers is that language use is an integrated process, rather than a composite of discrete skills; therefore, best practices in language proficiency assessment entail examining language use within more integrated, contextualized, and meaning tasks, rather than relying solely on discrete language measures" (p. 203). Qualitative measures can be useful, but they only can be counted on to provide a rough estimate of a child's level of native-language functioning. The best practice, therefore, is to use multiple sources of information gathered from a variety of sources, including qualitative measures, interviews, observations, and standardized tests (see Pham et al., 2017, for a list of available standardized tests of language proficiency). Results of a recent survey of bilingual school psychologists found that informal assessment was the method most frequently used to assess language proficiency (O'Bryon & Rogers, 2010).

In addition to gathering information on the primary language proficiency of children who are ELL, evaluators also should assess their English-language development. This is done most effectively with a single-subject (time-series) research design (see Kazdin, 2016). According to Cummins (1984), one of the most common errors in evaluating children who are ELL is to equate basic communication skills in English with competence in using English in decontextualized academic settings. He stated that it takes about 1–2 years for most children to learn to communicate effectively in English, but that it may take 5 years on average for them to learn to use English in academic contexts as effectively as do native speakers.

In sum, informal approaches to gathering information about the cultural and linguistic background of diverse children and youth arguably are best (e.g., Elizalde-Utnick & Romero, 2017). This information can be gathered easily during an interview or via rating forms prior to testing. To assist in this process, the Screening Tool for

Assessment rating forms for parents and teachers presented in Chapter 5 include items designed to identify cultural and linguistic differences that may undermine the validity of intelligence tests. In addition, the Screening Tool for Assessment Direct Screening Form includes an item that assesses linguistic differences.

SELECTING ACCEPTABLE TESTS

When evaluating the appropriateness of a test for *any* assessment situation, one *always* should consider the nature and purpose of the test, the quality of its norms, the available reliability and validity data, and the examinee's particular capabilities and limitations, among other criteria. Because of the wide cultural and linguistic backgrounds of children in the schools, we next discuss the characteristics of acceptable tests in general terms.

Quality of Test Norms

As we have mentioned above, tests that have been standardized in certain racial and ethnic groups are *not* ipso facto biased against all groups omitted from the standardization sample. The best-case scenario is when the racial and ethnic group of the child being assessed is included in the standardization sample, but the absence or disproportionately low representation of that child's group does not necessarily imply that the test is biased against him or her. It may be biased, but it may not be. Valencia (1988), for example, found that the average performance of English-speaking Hispanic American children was at the mean of 100 on the McCarthy Scales, despite their virtual absence from the standardization sample. Tests that do not include a particular child's racial and ethnic group should, therefore, be considered, but additional information about the norms and how they were developed always should be examined, too. Such information usually can be found in the test manual, but one should be sure to consult the published scholarly literature to get a balanced opinion of the test's advantages and limitations.

Reliability and Validity

Valencia and Lopez (1992) stated that "racial and ethnic minority populations, given their cultural and linguistic diversity, present challenges to test measurement specialists in the establishment of adequate reliability and validity of tests" (p. 409). This is an understatement. Unfortunately, for many minority groups this information simply is nonexistent. Validity, of course, refers to the soundness with which test scores can be interpreted for a particular purpose. Therefore, tests are *not* unconditionally valid (or invalid) for every socioeconomic or racial and ethnic group and for all psychoeducational purposes. For tests to be used with confidence, information on a test's reliability and validity should be available.

Alternative Assessment Practices for the Assessment of Children and Youth from Diverse Backgrounds

Four main alternatives are available for assessing the intelligence of children from diverse backgrounds: native-language assessment, modified or adapted assessment, assessment using a clinical tool called the Culture-Linguistic Interpretative Matrices (C-LIM), and nonverbal assessment.

NATIVE-LANGUAGE ASSESSMENT

Native-language assessment consists of the administration of standardized tests of intelligence that have been developed and validated in the ELL student's native language by an assessor who is fluent in the language of the test. The main limitation of this approach is that few tests of intelligence are available for the assessment of children and youth in languages other than English. In addition, according to the results of a recent survey of members of the National Association of School Psychologists, 87% of all school psychologists are white and speak only English (Walcott, McNamara, Hyson, & Charvat, 2018). Despite the fact that the proportion of practitioners who are fluent in languages other than English has increased somewhat in recent years, only 8% reported that they provide multilingual psychological services in the schools. Thus, although the administration of an intelligence test in a child's native language might be best practice in some cases, the limited number of bilingual school psychologists suggests that most practitioners must use other assessment alternatives for the assessment of diverse children and youth other than native-language assessment.

Despite the paucity of native-language tests of intelligence tests overall, several tests have been developed or adapted for the native-language assessment of ELL students who speak Spanish (see Pham et al., 2017). At the current time, according to results of the Benson et al. (2019) survey of school psychology practitioners, the most widely used native-language test of intelligence for Spanish-speaking students is the Batería-III Woodcock-Muñoz Normative Update (Batería III, Woodcock, Muñoz-Sandoval, McGrew, & Mather, 2007). The Batería III is the parallel Spanish version of the Woodcock-Johnson Tests of Cognitive Ability—Third Edition (WJ-III; Woodcock, McGrew, & Mather, 2001), which was developed to measure general cognitive ability and seven broad abilities in the Cattell-Horn-Carroll (CHC) theory of the structure of intelligence (e.g., Schneider & McGrew, 2018). Spanish versions of all the WJ-III tests are available in the Batería III. Batería III consists of 20 subtests, some of which can be administered to children as young as 2 years of age, but all of the subtests can be used with individuals between 5 to 95 years of age. The Batería III was normed on 1,413 native Spanish-speaking individuals between 2 and 90 years of age from different regions of the world, including Argentina, Mexico, Central America, Spain, and the United States. Administrators of the test must be fluent in Spanish.

Benson et al. (2019) found that the Batería III is administered 0.13 times per month (*SD* = 0.70) by approximately 10% of all respondents.

Woodcock et al. (2019) recently published the Batería IV, the most recent Spanish version of the WJ. Like its predecessor, this instrument was developed to measure psychometric *g* and seven CHC broad abilities. In contrast to the Batería III, the Batería IV consists of 14 selected subtests from the WJ IV that were translated or adapted for use. Only the item instructions were translated for use. The Batería IV consists of four new subtests that were included in the Batería III. Some of Batería IV subtests can be administered to children as young as 2 years of age, but the majority of subtests are more appropriate for individuals between 5 to 95 years of age. Both the Batería IV and the WJ IV rely on the same norming sample. Calibration and equating of test norms using Rasch modeling for the Batería IV was based on a sample of 601 native Spanish speakers between the ages of 2 and 81 years. In contrast to the Batería III, participants in the calibration study were from different regions of the United States, and their Hispanic origin primarily was from Mexico (70%). Through equating, the Batería IV is intended for the assessment of children and youth in Spanish and for their results to be compared to the normative sample of the WJ-IV.

Although the Batería III is the native-language test of intelligence most widely used by school psychologists, Ortiz et al. (2018) questioned the appropriateness of the norms for the Batería III for Spanish-speaking ELL students in the United States, given that it was based on monolingual speakers from other countries. Thus, "caution should be used when interpreting results of ELLs in the U.S., since differences in levels of Spanish language proficiency, regional dialects, and educational backgrounds can contribute to linguistic bias" (Pham et al., 2017, p. 275). The *Technical Manual* for the Batería IV does not specify whether the calibration study examines were monolingual Spanish speakers or bilingual English-Spanish speakers (LaForte, Wendling, Mather, Schrank, & McGrew, 2019).

Another potential limitation related to the use of the Batería III concerns the Flynn effect (see Kranzler, 1997). The Flynn effect refers to the increase in intelligence test scores observed in the United States and elsewhere over the past century. Flynn (1987) estimated that IQ scores in this country increase an average of 3 points per decade, or 0.3 points per year. The secular increase in IQ implies that scores on older tests, such as the Batería III, which was published in 2005, may be inflated in comparison tests with contemporary norms by as much as 4 points. Although this limitation to the Batería III does not apply to the Batería IV, the representativeness of the calibration study group in terms of Spanish and English language proficiency currently is unknown. It is also important to note that, due to its recency of publication, no independent research has been published on the psychometric properties of the Batería IV with ELL children and youth in the United States.

As noted in Chapter 6, another option for native-language assessment with Spanish speakers is the Wechsler Intelligence Scale for Children—Fifth Edition (WISC-V) Spanish version (Wechsler, 2017). The WISC-V Spanish is a translation and adaptation of the WISC-V for use with Spanish-speaking children and adolescents 6 through 16 years of age. The WISC-V Spanish is intended to assess the cognitive ability of Spanish-speaking bilingual children and youth in the United States.

It can only be administered by bilingual school psychologists in Spanish in either the traditional or digital format via Q-global. The WISC-V Spanish was developed to parallel the content, structure, and theoretical foundations of the WISC-V. The amount of adaptation of test content from the WISC-V to the WISC-V Spanish varied across subtests, as noted in Chapter 6.

The WISC-V Spanish version was developed to produce scores that are equivalent to the WISC-V norms. Similar to the Batería IV, the WISC-V Spanish version does not have separate norms. The WISC-V Spanish version was equated to the WISC-V with a sample of Spanish speakers (n = 290) and a matched sample of Spanish-English speakers (n = 220). Through equating, the WISC-V Spanish is intended for the assessment of children and youth in Spanish and for their results to be compared to the normative sample of the WISC-V. The matched sample also is used to derive adjusted scores for the Verbal Comprehension Index score and its subtests to correct for differences in personal (e.g., language use and preferences) and environmental (e.g., home, neighborhood, and school) background variables on test performance.

Nonetheless, these norm samples, even when combined, fall below the minimum overall sample size of 600 recommended by the International Test Commission (2016) for adapted tests. Moreover, in contrast to the use of one-year intervals and a minimum of 100 test takers per age group for norms on widely used English-language intelligence tests, the equating sample of the WISC-V Spanish version consists of five age groups with two-year intervals and less than 60 test takers per group. In addition to use of an equating sample of questionable size, its representativeness also raises concerns. Although the manual states that "effort was made to ensure that each region was represented in the sample" (p. 87), the equating sample significantly over-sampled Hispanics in the South region of the United States and significantly under-sampled those in the West, which is where the highest proportions of Spanish-speaking ELL students are located (NCES, 2019).

According to the International Test Commission's (2016) *Guidelines for Translating and Adapting Tests*,

> The norms, validity evidence, and reliability evidence of a test in its source language version do not automatically apply to other possible adaptations of the test into different cultures and languages. Therefore, empirical validity and relatability evidence of any new versions developed must also be presented. (p. 22)

For the WISC-V Spanish, scant information on its reliability and validity is presented in the manual. For example, the manual only reports split-half reliability coefficients for non-speeded subtests and does not report any coefficients for speeded subtests and the index scores. No information is presented in the manual on the construct validity of the WISC-V Spanish. Instead users are referred to the WISC-V, stating that, "because the WISC-V Spanish has been subjected to equating procedures, the same evidence supports WISC-V Spanish validity" (Wechsler, 2017, p. 91). No evidence is presented to support the equivalence of test scores for the matched bilingual sample, however. In addition, none of the research that has been conducted on the WISC-V can be generalized to validate the use of adjusted scores on the WISC-V

Spanish. Currently, we are not aware of any independent research that has been published on the validity of the WISC-V Spanish version or the equivalence of the two administration formats. Until further research has been conducted substantiating the validity and utility of the WISC-V Spanish, we cannot recommend its use for the assessment of Spanish-speaking children and youth.

USE OF A TRANSLATED TEST OR A TRANSLATOR

One logical solution to the issue of assessing the intelligence of a student with limited English proficiency (ELP) is to translate a test with a moderate to high degree of linguistic demand in English into the student's dominant language. Translation of a verbal test is problematic, however, because some English words do not have exact equivalents in other languages. In addition, common words in English may be unusual in another language, and vice versa. As a result, the difficulty level for a translated word could be quite different than the difficulty level for its English counterpart. Advances have been made in research on the translation and adaptation of educational and psychological tests in recent years, however, involving both judgmental and statistical means of establishing item equivalence (for a review, see Krach, McCreery, & Guerard, 2017).

Administration of verbal tests with the assistance of a translator also is problematic, even though translators may have received training. The literature offers no real guidelines based on empirical research on how to train and use an interpreter (Vazquez-Nuttall et al., 2007). Moreover, little, if anything, is known about the validity of measuring a bilingual child's intelligence when an interpreter is used (Ortiz et al., 2018). As Rhodes et al. (2005) stated, "Very little information is available . . . regarding how to best incorporate interpreters into daily practice" (p. 91). If interpreters are used, it is recommended that they be well prepared; this preparation should include instructions on the patterns of communication (viz., who talks to whom and when), seating arrangements, and the like. Care should be taken in instructing translators on whether to employ a literal, word-for-word translation without regard for context, or a free translation in which an interpreter attempts to communicate the exact meaning of the original communication (Hambleton & Li, 2005). According to O'Bryon and Rogers (2010), the most common problems related to the use of interpreters by school psychologists was the failure to perform translations verbatim and the lack of knowledge of professional terms. Review Rhodes et al. (2005) for further guidelines for the selection and use of translators in intellectual assessment.

MODIFIED OR ADAPTED ASSESSMENT

In modified or adapted assessment, also referred to as *testing the limits*, tests of intelligence primarily are administered to ELL students in English but with alterations made to the standardized administration format to account for cultural and linguistic differences (Ortiz et al., 2018). "Testing the limits" involves a deliberate departure from standardized assessment procedure and is a way to obtain further clinical information on a child's cognitive abilities. These modifications may include altering the administration format or language (e.g., from English to native language), eliminating or rephrasing items or subtests that are culturally or linguistically loaded, providing additional cues or prompts, modeling responses, altering the stimulus or response modality, eliminating time limits, and asking probing questions. Modified or adapted assessment contains what commonly is referred to as "bilingual assessment." This occurs whenever a qualified school psychologist who is fluent in the native language of the ELL student conducts the assessment. In this situation, both the examiner and the examinee may use English and the ELL student's native languages to alter the standardized administration to facilitate testing.

One example of this approach is the "test-teach-test" paradigm derived from Vygotsky's notions of the *zones of proximal and distal development*. Such assessment often is called *dynamic assessment*. Some have viewed Feuerstein's Learning Potential Assessment Device (LPAD; see Feuerstein, Rand, & Hoffman, 1979), for example, as a promising alternative for the assessment of children from culturally and linguistically diverse backgrounds (e.g., Oades-Ses, Esquivel, & Añon, 2007). Although Kirschenbaum (1998) argued that dynamic assessment may be a promising approach for assessing the intelligence of children and youth with LEP for gifted and talented programs, little is known about the use of the LPAD for children and youth with LEP. Frisby and Braden (1992), however, asserted that dynamic assessment amounts to "little more than ideological philosophy in search of empirical support" (p. 283). As Vazquez-Nuttall (2007) stated, "What advantages such approaches might hold [with linguistically and culturally diverse individuals] are not entirely clear and yet to be demonstrated" (p. 280).

Regardless of the specific modifications or adaptions used for assessment, the important thing to keep in mind is that all approaches should be based on sound theory *and* should be supported by the results of empirical research. At present, many of these assessment approaches simply do not have sufficient empirical support. Although testing limits may provide qualitative clinical information that is valuable for the interpretation and use of intelligence tests, it is important to note that any departure from standardized procedures during test administration may change the meaning of test scores, because the normative sample was not administered the test under those conditions. Therefore, it is best practice for modifications or adaptions to the standard intelligence test administration format to be done after the entire test is completed and should not be counted toward the scores obtained on the test.

CULTURE-LANGUAGE INTERPRETIVE MATRICES

A relatively new direction for the assessment of diverse populations involves the interpretation of standardized intelligence tests within *culture-language interpretive matrices* (C-LIMs). Flanagan, Ortiz, and Alfonso (2007) created a C-LIM for each of the most widely used standardized intelligence tests. Each C-LIM consists of a 3 x 3 table in which the test's subtests are categorized according to whether they are judged to have a Low, Medium, or High degree of linguistic demand and cultural loading. According to this approach, analysis of the pattern of test scores in the C-LIM can facilitate identification of students whose academic difficulties stem from language or cultural differences and those whose difficulties are attributable to other causes (e.g., SLD). Figure 14.1 shows the general pattern of expected results in a generic C-LIM for individuals from diverse cultural and linguistic backgrounds. When test scores are lowest on subtests with the highest degree of cultural loading and linguistic demand, and highest on subtests with the lowest degree of cultural loading and linguistic demand, this is interpreted as evidence that LEP and acculturation have invalidated the test results. In contrast, when subtest scores do not follow this pattern in the C-LIM, then it is believed that LEP and acculturation can be ruled out as the cause of a student's learning difficulties.

Flanagan, Ortiz, and Alfonso's (2013) asserted that the "use of the C-LIM appears to provide a solid, evidence-based method for systematically examining and firmly establishing test score validity" (p. 324). At the current time, however, empirical support for this approach is rather limited and consists solely of unpublished doctoral dissertations (e.g., Aziz, 2010; Dhaniram-Beharry, 2008; Lella, 2010; Nieves-Brull, 2006; Tychanska, 2009; Verderosa, 2007). In addition, results of independent research have raised issues about the validity of this interpretive approach and the need to refine it (Calderón, Styck, Vega, & Kranzler, 2019; Cormier et al., 2011; Kranzler et al., 2010; Styck & Watkins, 2013, 2014). For example, Kranzler et al. (2010) examined the utility of the C-LIM for the Woodcock-Johnson Tests of Cognitive Ability—Third Edition (WJ III; Woodcock, McGrew, & Mather, 2001) with a sample of 46 ELL students ages 5 to 18 years old. They investigated the predicted effects of cultural loading and linguistic demand on test performance. Although they found a statistically significant (decreasing) trend for the effect of linguistic demand and cultural loading combined, post hoc analyses revealed that this result was attributable to a significantly higher score on one subtest and did not reflect significant

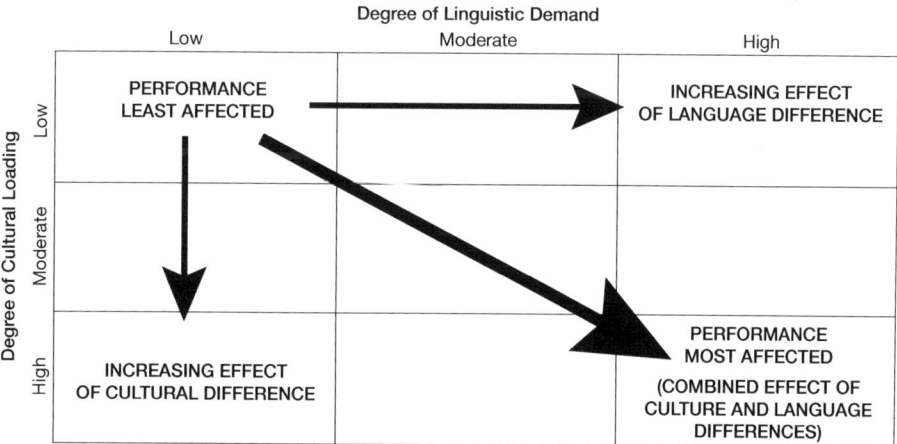

Figure 14.1. Predicted test performance for individuals from culturally and linguistically diverse backgrounds within a generic culture-language interpretive matrix (C-LIM). Flanagan, Ortiz, and Alfonso (2013).

differences among all of the subtests contrasted in the C-LIM. In addition, only 13% of the sample had a pattern of test scores that was consistent with Flanagan et al.'s C-LIM predictions for linguistic demand and acculturation combined, and less than half (41%) had scores that followed *any of the three predicted patterns* on the C-LIM for the WJ III. As Kranzler et al. (2010) concluded,

> Despite the fact that our results do not substantiate the use of C-LIMs, our findings should *not* be interpreted to suggest that cultural and linguistic background do not have an impact on cognitive ability test performance. Nothing could be further from the truth—language and cultural background matter on tests—especially for English language learners who were not born and raised in the USA. Nonetheless, our results do suggest that revision of the theory underlying the use of the C-LIMs, the test-specific matrices (at least for the WJ-III), or perhaps both, is needed. (p. 443)

Thus, until further research has been conducted substantiating their utility, we cannot recommend use of the C-LIMs for the assessment of children and youth from diverse backgrounds (cf. Ortiz et al., 2018).

NONVERBAL ASSESSMENT

The best option, in our opinion, for assessing the intelligence of children and youth from diverse backgrounds is to administer a nonverbal test. Level of acculturation and limited English-language proficiency can be important construct-irrelevant sources of variance in the assessment of intelligence. When test performance primarily reflects these two factors and not cognitive ability, then the interpretation of test scores is invalid. The language of the test is important, especially for those who speak a foreign language or are bilingual (with English as their second language). Interpretation of the results of verbally loaded tests for children with LEP, therefore, should be supplemented with non-language-based tests and other assessment data. When using nonverbal intelligence tests, assessors should take care to ensure that the examinees completely understand the instructions, because the administration of all tests requires communication of some kind between examiner and examinee, and some nonverbal tests do in fact have English instructions. Results of a recent survey found that 89% of school psychologists who assess students from culturally and linguistically diverse backgrounds administer a nonverbal test of intelligence' (Sotelo-Dynega & Dixon, 2014).

Reviews of nonverbal measures of intelligence by DeThorne and Schaefer (2004) and by Braden and Athanasiou (2005) concluded that a number of these instruments are appropriate for use with diverse populations. Many of the contemporary nonverbal tests used today—such as the Universal Nonverbal Intelligence Test—Second Edition (UNIT2; Bracken & McCallum, 2016) and the Leiter International Performance Scale—Third Edition (Leiter-3; Roid, Miller, Pomplun, & Koch, 2013)—have strong psychometric properties, are based upon articulated theoretical frameworks, and are excellent measures of psychometric g (see Chapter 7 for full reviews of these tests). Moreover, a number of studies support the validity of the use of nonverbal intelligence tests with children and youth from diverse backgrounds in practical settings (e.g., Lohman, Korb, & Lakin, 2008; Lohman & Lakin, 2008; Naglieri, Booth, & Winsler, 2004).

When using nonverbal intelligence tests, examiners must note that, as a whole, they tend not to predict academic achievement as well as verbal tests—for all groups. This is because the content of verbal tests overlaps to a greater extent with past academic achievement. Although the predictive validity of these instruments generally is acceptable, recommendations and interventions based on the results of nonverbal tests for children with LEP *always* should be tentative and short-term (no longer than 1 year at most). In addition, as Flanagan et al. (2007) have noted, "Nonverbal tasks may actually carry as much if not more cultural content than that found in verbal tests" (p. 165). Given that testing is itself a cultural activity, all tests have some degree of cultural loading.

Although all nonverbal tests of intelligence have in common a reduction in language loading during test administration, one of the most important ways in which they differ is in the number of cognitive abilities that they purport to measure (e.g., McCallum, 2013). Unidimensional nonverbal tests are designed to measure general intelligence, or psychometric g, and thus scoring and interpretation focus on the direct effect that psychometric g has on performance. Examples of current unidimensional tests include the Comprehensive Test of Nonverbal Intelligence, Second Edition (Hammill, Pearson, & Wiederholt, 2009); the Naglieri Nonverbal Ability Test, Third Edition (Naglieri, 2016) and the Test of Nonverbal Intelligence, Fourth Edition (Brown, Sherbenou, & Johnsen, 2010). Multidimensional nonverbal tests, in contrast, assume a higher-order structure in which psychometric g has indirect effects on performance that are mediated through multiple cognitive abilities (e.g., short-term memory, fluid intelligence, and processing speed). These cognitive abilities are reflected by group factors—that is, subsets of measured variables that differ with respect to stimuli and response format (e.g., arranging cubes, finger pointing, and drawing with a pencil). Examples of published multidimensional tests are the UNIT2 (Bracken & McCallum, 2016) and Leiter-3 (Roid et al., 2013).

Unidimensional nonverbal tests of intelligence tend to be good measures of general intelligence and often are more cost effective than multidimensional tests, as they require less administration time and effort. McCallum (2013), however, asserted that, given their narrow focus, unidimensional tests are best used as screening measures. Because multidimensional tests purportedly measure multiple cognitive abilities, he argued that they are more appropriate for high-stakes decision making, such as determining eligibility for special education and related services.

UNIT2. Of the currently available multidimensional nonverbal tests of intelligence, none has attracted as much attention in the literature as the Universal Nonverbal Intelligence Test (UNIT; Bracken & McCallum, 2001) and its successor, the UNIT2. The UNIT2 is an individually administered, norm-referenced test of intelligence for children and youth ages 5 to 21 years. It is the only multidimensional nonverbal test that is administered entirely nonverbally (i.e., via pantomime). Receptive language is not required as part of the input demands for completing items, and expressive language is not required as part of the output demands, as the examinee responds by manipulating chips or blocks or by pointing rather than by providing verbal responses. As described in Chapter 7, the UNIT2 consists of six subtests intended to assess general intelligence as well as three facets of intelligence (Reasoning, Memory, and Quantitative Reasoning) with two organizational strategies (Symbolic and Non-symbolic).

In an attempt to substantiate the purported advantages of multidimensional nonverbal tests, Benson, Kranzler, and Floyd (2018) examined the dimensionality of the UNIT2 and the interpretability of its factors. They also examined the invariance of constructs measured by the UNIT2 across age groups, gender, race, and ethnicity. Structural analyses were conducted using data from the norming of the UNIT2. Results indicate that the UNIT2 primarily is a measure of psychometric g. Benson et al. found that 81% of the variance in the Full Scale Battery can be attributable to general intelligence. However, their results also indicated that unique, reliable variance is insufficient for the interpretation of the index scores reflecting Quantitative and Reasoning, and Memory is marginal. Last, they found that the abilities the UNIT2 measured are calibrated differently across age, gender, racial, and ethnic groups, thereby indicating that the instrument may not be "universal." Results of their study, therefore, question whether the administration of multidimensional tests of nonverbal intelligence—or at least the UNIT2—is worth the time and effort when unidimensional tests also tend to be good measures of general intelligence and therefore provide the same information.

Nonverbal composite scores. As we discussed in Chapters 6 and 7, a number of tests for the assessment of intelligence in children and youth that are administered in English include nonverbal composite scores that are derived from subtests with reduced language loading and culture loading, such as the Nonverbal Index on the WISC-V and the Kaufman Assessment Battery for Children, Second Edition (Normative Update; A. Kaufman & N. Kaufman, 2018). Nonverbal Index scores can be very helpful when deciding upon a "best" estimate of general intelligence, particularly when concerns surface related to performance on language-loaded subtests when assessing diverse students. On the WISC-V, for example, the Nonverbal Index is derived from six subtests that minimize the expressive language demands of examinees. Despite being based on fewer tests than the WISC-V's Full Scale (FSIQ), the Nonverbal Index has high overall internal consistency (.95 across all ages) and is highly correlated with the FSIQ (i.e., .93 across all ages). Nonetheless, caution should be used when interpreting any nonverbal composites score for children and youth from diverse backgrounds, because the subtests from which these scores are derived typically are administered in English and therefore still may be affected to some extent by construct-irrelevant sources of variance in the assessment of intelligence.

Summary

Test bias is best defined in the statistical sense as *systematic* measurement error or estimation. Research on test bias has shown that the major standardized tests of intelligence are not substantially biased for English-speaking children born and raised in the

United States. When assessing the cognitive ability of children who are not proficient in English, fully acculturated in mainstream American society, or both, information should be gathered from multiple sources, including qualitative measures, interviews, observations, and standardized tests, to determine whether culture or language background invalidate the results of intelligence test scores. The longstanding best practice recommendation for assessing diverse children and youth is to use a nonverbal test of intelligence. The most widely used nonverbal tests are excellent measures of psychometric g. Recent research, however, questions whether the additional time and resources required for the administration of multidimensional tests of nonverbal intelligence is worth the time and effort, when the same information might be obtained from the administration of a unidimensional test.

References

Achenbach, T. M., McConaughy, S. H., & Howell, C. T. (1987). Child/adolescent behavioral and emotional problems: Implications of cross-informant correlations for situational specificity. *Psychological Bulletin, 101*, 213–232.

Ackerman, P. L. (2018). Intelligence-as-process, personality, interests, and intelligence-as-knowledge: A framework for adult intellectual development. In D. P. Flanagan & E. M. McDonough (Eds.), *Contemporary intellectual assessment: Theories, tests, and issues* (p. 225–241). New York, NY: Guilford Press.

Adams Costa, E. B., Day, L. A., & Raiford, S. E. (2016). *WISC-V technical report 4: Children with hearing differences who utilize spoken language and have assistive technology.* Bloomington, MN: Pearson.

Alexander, R. M. (2017). *The relation between intelligence and adaptive behavior: A meta-analysis.* ProQuest Dissertations & Theses Full Text: The Humanities and Social Sciences Collection. Retrieved from https://search.proquest.com/docview/1937953949

Allport, G. W. (1937). *Personality: A psychological interpretation.* New York, NY: Wiley.

Alter, P., & Haydon, T. (2017). Characteristics of effective classroom rules: A review of the literature. *Teacher Education and Special Education, 40*, 114–127.

American Academy of Pediatrics, Committee on Bioethics, Committee on Genetics, & American College of Medical Genetics and Genomics, Social, Ethical, and Legal Issues Committee. (2013). Ethical and policy issues in genetic testing and screening of children. *Pediatrics, 131*, 620–622.

American Association on Intellectual and Developmental Disabilities (AAIDD). (2010). *Intellectual disability: Definition, classification, and systems of support (11th ed.).*

American Educational Research Association, American Psychological Association, & National Council on Measurement in Education. (2014). *Standards for educational and psychological testing.* Washington, DC: American Educational Research Association.

American Psychiatric Association. (2000). *Diagnostic and statistical manual of mental disorders* (4th ed., text rev.). Washington, DC: Author.

American Psychiatric Association. (2013). *Diagnostic and statistical manual of mental disorders* (5th ed.). Arlington, VA: Author.

American Psychological Association. (2002). Ethical principles of psychologists and code of conduct. *American Psychologist, 57*, 1060–1073.

American Psychological Association. (2007). Record keeping guidelines. *American Psychologist, 62*, 993–1004. http://dx.doi.org/10.1037/0003-066X.62.9.993

American Psychological Association. (2010). Amendments to the 2002 ethical principles of psychologists and code of conduct. *American Psychologist, 65*, 493.

American Psychological Association. (2016). Revision of ethical standard 3.04 of the "Ethical Principles of Psychologists and Code of Conduct" (2002, as amended 2010). *American Psychologist, 71*, 900.

American Psychological Association. (2019). *Publication manual of the American Psychological Association* (7th ed.). Washington, DC: Author.

American Psychological Association Presidential Task Force on Evidence-Based Practice. (2006). Evidence-based practice in psychology. *American Psychologist, 61*, 271–285.

American Speech-Language-Hearing Association. (n.d.). *Self-test for hearing loss.* Retrieved from www.asha.org/public/hearing/Self-Test-for-Hearing-Loss

American Speech-Language-Hearing Association. (2018c, June 4). Intellectual disability. Retrieved from https://www.asha.org/PRPSpecificTopic.aspx?folderid=8589942540&section=Assessment.

American Speech-Language-Hearing Association. (2019, July 24). *Collaborating with interpreters.* Retrieved from https://www.asha.org/Practice-Portal/Professional-Issues/Collaborating-With-Interpreters/

American Speech-Language-Hearing Association. (2019a, July 24). *Augmentative and alternative communication.* Retrieved from https://www.asha.org/PRPSpecificTopic.aspx?folderid=8589942773&section=Key_Issues

Armistead, L., Bole Williams, B., & Jacob, S. (2011). *Professional ethics for school psychologists* (2nd ed.). Bethesda, MD: National Association of School Psychologists.

Assouline, S. G., & Whiteman, C. S. (2011). Twice-exceptionality: Implications for school psychologists in the post-IDEA 2004 era. *Journal of Applied School Psychology, 27*, 380–402.

Aziz, N. (2010). *English language learners with global cognitive impairment: Evaluation of patterns within the Culture-Language Interpretive Matrix* (Unpublished doctoral dissertation). St. John's University, Jamaica, NY.

Bain, S. K., & Allin, J. D. (2005). Test review. [Review of the test *Stanford-Binet Intelligence Scales, Fifth Edition*]. *Journal of Psychoeducational Assessment, 23*, 87–95.

Bain, S. K., & Gray, R. (2008). Test review. [Review of the test *Kaufman Assessment Battery for Children—Second Edition*]. *Journal of Psychoeducational Assessment, 26*, 92–101.

Bain, S. K., & Jaspers, K. E. (2010). Test review. [Review of the test *Kaufman Brief Intelligence Test, Second Edition*]. *Journal of Psychoeducational Assessment, 28*, 167–174.

Bandura, A. (1978). The self system in reciprocal determinism. *American Psychologist, 33*, 344–358.

Barnard-Brak, L., Johnsen, S. K., Pond Hannig, A., & Wei, T. (2014). The incidence of potentially gifted students within a special education population. *Roeper Review, 37*, 74–83.

Barnard-Brak, L., Johnsen, S. K., Pond Hannig, A., & Wei, T. (2015). The incidence of potentially gifted students within a special education population. *Roeper Review, 37*, 74–83.

Barron, F. (1968). *Creativity and personal freedom.* New York, NY: Van Nostrand.

Bear, G. G., & Minke, K. M. (2018). *Helping handouts: Supporting students at school and home.* Bethesda, MD: National Association of School Psychologists.

Beaujean, A. A. (2015a). Adopting a new test edition: Psychometric and practical considerations. *Research and Practice in the Schools, 3*, 51–57.

Beaujean, A. A. (2015b). John Carroll's views on intelligence: Bi-Factor vs. higher-order models. *Journal of Intelligence, 3*, 121–136. doi:10.3390/jintelligence3040121

Beaujean, A. A., & Benson, N. F. (2019a). The one and the many: Enduring legacies of Spearman and Thurstone on intelligence test score interpretation. *Applied Measurement in Education, 32*, 198–215.

Beaujean, A. A., & Benson, N. F. (2019b). Theoretically-consistent cognitive ability test development and score interpretation. *Contemporary School Psychology, 23*, 126–137.

Beaujean, A. A., Parkin, J., & Parker, S. (2014). Comparing Cattell-Horn-Carroll factor models: Differences between bifactor and higher order factor models in predicting language achievement. *Psychological Assessment, 26*, 789–805.

Belitz, J. (2018). Ethics in assessing and treating children and adolescents. In J. N. Butcher & P. C. Kendall (Eds.), *APA handbooks in psychology series. APA handbook of psychopathology: Child and adolescent psychopathology* (pp. 589–606). Washington, DC: American Psychological Association.

Benson, N. F., Beaujean, A. A., McGill, R. J., & Dombrowski, S. C. (2018). Revisiting Carroll's survey of factor-analytic studies: Implications for the clinical assessment of intelligence. *Psychological Assessment, 30*, 1028–1038.

Benson, N. F., Floyd, R. G., Kranzler, J. H., Eckert, T. L., Fefer, S. A., & Morgan, G. B. (2019). Test use and assessment practices of school psychologists in the United States: Findings from the 2017 National Survey. *Journal of School Psychology, 72*, 29–48.

Benson, N., Hulac, D., & Kranzler, J. (2010). Independent examination of the Wechsler Adult Intelligence Scale—Fourth Edition (WAIS-IV): What does the WAIS-IV measure? *Psychological Assessment, 22*, 121–130.

Benson, N., Kranzler, J. H., & Floyd, R. G. (2016). Examining the integrity of measurement of cognitive abilities in the prediction of achievement: Comparisons and contrasts across variables from higher-order and bifactor models. *Journal of School Psychology, 58*, 1–19.

Benson, N., Kranzler, J. H., & Floyd, R. G. (2018). Exploratory and confirmatory factor analysis of the Universal Nonverbal Intelligence Test-Second Edition: Testing dimensionality and invariance across age, gender, race, and ethnicity. *Assessment*. doi:10.1177/1073191118786584

Beran, T. N. (2007). Test review. [Review of the test *Differential Ability Scales, Second Edition*]. *Canadian Journal of School Psychology, 22*, 128–132.

Berg, C. A., & Sternberg, R. J. (1992). Adults' conceptions of intelligence across the adult life span. *Psychology and Aging, 7*, 221–231.

Bergeron, R., & Floyd, R. G. (2006). Broad cognitive abilities of children with mental retardation: An analysis of group and individual profiles. *American Journal of Mental Retardation, 111*, 417–432.

Bergeron, R., & Floyd, R. G. (2013). Individual part score profiles of children with intellectual disability: A descriptive analysis across three intelligence tests. *School Psychology Review, 42*, 22–38.

Bergeron, R., Floyd, R. G., & Shands, E. I. (2008). States' eligibility guidelines for mental retardation: An update and consideration of part scores and unreliability of IQs. *Education and Training in Developmental Disabilities, 41*, 123–131.

Berry, C. M. (2015). Differential validity and differential prediction of cognitive ability tests: Understanding test bias in the employment context. *Annual Review of Organizational Psychology and Organizational Behavior, 2*, 435–463.

Beukelman, D. R., & Mirenda, P. (2013). *Augmentative and alternative communication: Supporting children and adults with complex communication needs.* Baltimore, MD: Brooke.

Borland, J. (2009). The gifted constitute 3% to 5% of the population. Moreover, giftedness equals high IQ, which is a stable measure of aptitude: Spinal tap psychometrics in gifted education. *Gifted Child Quarterly, 53*, 236–238.

Borsuk, E. R., Watkins, M. W., & Canivez, G. L. (2006). Long-term stability of membership in a Wechsler Intelligence Scale for Children—Third Edition (WISC-III) subtest core profile taxonomy. *Journal of Psychoeducational Assessment, 24*, 52–68. doi:10.1177/0734282905285225

Bouchard, T. J., Jr., & McGue, M. (1981). Familial studies of intelligence: A review. *Science, 250*, 223–238.

Bowen, C. (1998). *Developmental phonological disorders: A practical guide for families and teachers*. Melbourne: Australian Council for Educational Research.

Bracken, B. A. (1987). Limitations of preschool instruments and standards for minimal levels of technical adequacy. *Journal of Psychoeducational Assessment, 5*, 313–326.

Bracken, B. A. (2000). Maximizing construct relevant assessment: The optimal preschool testing situation. In B. A. Bracken (Ed.), *The psychoeducational assessment of preschool children* (pp. 33–44). Boston, MA: Allyn & Bacon.

Bracken, B. A., Keith, L. K., & Walker, K. C. (1998). Assessment of preschool behavior and social-emotional functioning: A review of thirteen third-party instruments. *Journal of Psychoeducational Assessment, 16*, 153–169.

Bracken, B. A., & McCallum, R. S. (2001). *Universal nonverbal intelligence test*. Austin, TX: PRO-ED.

Bracken, B. A., & McCallum, R. S. (2016). *Universal Nonverbal Intelligence Test—Second Edition*. Austin, TX: PRO-ED.

Braden, J. P., & Athanasiou, M. S. (2005). A comparative review of nonverbal measures of intelligence. In D. P. Flanagan & P. L. Harrison (Eds.), *Contemporary intellectual assessment: Theories, tests, and issues* (pp. 557–577). New York, NY: Guilford Press.

Braden, J. P., & Elliott, S. N. (2003). *Accommodations on the Stanford-Binet Intelligence Scales, Fifth Edition* (Stanford-Binet Intelligence Scales, Fifth Edition, Assessment Service Bulletin No. 2). Itasca, IL: Riverside Publishing.

Braden, J. P., & Kratochwill, T. R. (1997). Treatment utility of assessment: Myths and realities. *School Psychology Review, 26*, 467–474.

Braden, J. P., & Shaw, S. R. (2009). Intervention validity of cognitive assessment: Knowns, unknowables, and unknowns. *Assessment for Effective Intervention, 34*, 106–115.

Bradley-Johnson, S., & Durmusoglu, G. (2005). Evaluation of floors and item gradients for reading and math tests for young children. *Journal of Psychoeducational Assessment, 23*, 262–278.

Briesch, A. M., Volpe, R. J., & Floyd, R. G. (2018). *School-based observation: A practical guide to assessing student behavior*. New York, NY: Guilford Press.

Brody, L. E., & Stanley, J. C. (2005). Youths who reason exceptionally well mathematically and/or verbally: Using the MVT:D4 model to develop their talents. In R. J. Sternberg & J. E. Davidson (Eds.), *Conceptions of giftedness* (2nd ed., pp. 20–37). New York, NY: Cambridge University Press.

Brody, N. (1994). Cognitive abilities. *Psychological Science, 5*, 63–68.

Brooks, B. L., Fay-McClymont, T. B., MacAllister, W. S., Vasserman, M., & Sherman, E. M. (2019). A new kid on the block: The Memory Validity Profile (MVP) in children with neurological conditions. *Child Neuropsychology, 25*(4), 561–572.

Brophy, J. (1981). Teacher praise: A functional analysis. *Review of Educational Research, 51*, 5–132.

Brown, L., Sherbenou, R. J., & Johnsen, S. K. (2010). *Tests of nonverbal intelligence—fourth edition*. Los Angeles, CA: Western Psychological Services.

Brown, R. T., Daly, B. P., & Stefanatos, G. A. (2009). Learning disabilities: Complementary views from neuroscience, neuropsychology, and public health. In E. Fletcher-Janzen & C. R. Reynolds (Eds.), *Neuropsychological perspectives on learning disabilities in the era of RTI: Recommendations for diagnosis and intervention* (pp. 159–178). Hoboken, NJ: Wiley.

Brown, R. T., Reynolds, C. R., & Whitaker, J. W. (1999). Bias in mental testing since "Bias in mental testing." *School Psychology Quarterly, 14*, 208–238.

Brown, W. (1910). Some experimental results in the correlation of mental abilities. *British Journal of Psychology, 3,* 296–322.

Brown Waesche, J. S., Schatschneider, C., Maner, J. K., Ahmed, Y., & Wagner, R. K. (2011). Examining agreement and longitudinal stability among traditional and RTI-based definitions of reading disability using the affected-status agreement statistic. *Journal of Learning Disabilities, 44,* 296–307.

Brunnert, K. A., Naglieri, J. A., & Hardy-Braz, S. T. (2008). *Essentials of WNV assessment.* Hoboken, NJ: Wiley.

Buckingham, B. R. (1921). Intelligence and its measurement: A symposium—XIV. *Journal of Educational Psychology, 12,* 271–275.

Burns, M. K., Peterson-Brown, S., Haegele, K., Rodriguez, M., Schmitt, B., Cooper, M., . . . VanDerHeyden, A. M. (2016). Meta-analysis of academic interventions derived from neuropsychological data. *School Psychology Quarterly, 31,* 28–42.

Burns, M. K., VanDerHeyden, A. M., & Zaslofsky, A. F. (2014). Best practices in delivery intensive academic interventions with a skill-by-treatment interaction. In A. Thomas & J. Grimes (Eds.), *Best practices in school psychology* (6th ed.): Student level services (pp. 129–142). Bethesda, MD: National Association of School Psychologists.

Calamia, M., Markon, K., & Tranel, D. (2012). Scoring higher the second time around: Meta-analyses of practice effects in neuropsychological assessment. *Clinical Neuropsychologist, 26,* 543–570.

Calderón, C. O., Styck, K. M., Vega, D., & Kranzler, J. H. (submitted). Evaluating the cultural and linguistic load of IQ scores for English language learners. *International Journal of School and Educational Psychology.*

Campbell, D. T., & Stanley, J. C. (1963). *Experimental and quasi-experimental designs for research.* Boston, MA: Houghton Mifflin.

Campbell, J. M. (2006a). Autism spectrum disorders. In R. W. Kamphaus & J. M. Campbell (Eds.), *Psychodiagnostic assessment of children: Dimensional and categorical approaches* (pp. 119–168). Hoboken, NJ: Wiley.

Canivez, G. L. (2008). Orthogonal higher-order factor structure of the Stanford-Binet Intelligence Scales for children and adolescents. *School Psychology Quarterly, 23,* 533–541.

Canivez, G. L. (2011). Hierarchical factor structure of the Cognitive Assessment System: Variance partitions from the Schmid–Leiman (1957) procedure. *School Psychology Quarterly, 26,* 305–317.

Canivez, G. L. (2013). Incremental criterion validity of WAIS-IV factor index scores: Relationships with WIAT-II and WIAT-III subtest and composite scores. *Psychological Assessment, 25,* 484–495.

Canivez, G. L. (2019). Evidence-based assessment for school psychology: Research, training, and clinical practice. *Contemporary School Psychology, 23,* 194–200.

Canivez, G. L., Dombrowski, S. C., & Watkins, M. W. (2018). Factor structure of the WISC-V for four standardization age groups: Exploratory and hierarchical factor analyses with the 16 primary and secondary subtests. Psychology in the Schools, 55, 741–769. http://dx.doi.org/10.1002/pits.22138

Canivez, G. L., & McGill, R. J. (2016). Factor structure of the Differential Ability Scales—Second Edition: Exploratory and hierarchical factor analyses with the core subtests. *Psychological Assessment, 28,* 1475–1488.

Canivez, G. L., McGill, R. J., Dombrowski, S. C., Watkins, M. W., Pritchard, A. E., & Jacobson, L. A. (2018). Construct validity of the WISC-V in clinical cases: Exploratory and confirmatory factor analyses of the 10 primary subtests. Assessment. https://doi.org/10.1177/1073191118811609

Canivez, G. L., & Watkins, M. W. (2010a). Exploratory and higher-order factor analyses of the Wechsler Adult Intelligence Scale—Fourth Edition (WAIS-IV) adolescent subsample. *School Psychology Quarterly, 25*, 223–235.

Canivez, G. L., & Watkins, M. W. (2010b). Investigation of the factor structure of the Wechsler Adult Intelligence Scale—Fourth Edition (WAIS-IV): Exploratory and higher-order factor analyses. *Psychological Assessment, 22*, 827–836.

Canivez, G. L., & Watkins, M. W. (2016). Review of the Wechsler Intelligence Scale for Children-Fifth Edition: Critique, commentary, and independent analyses. In A. S. Kaufman, S. E. Raiford, & D. L. Coalson (Eds.), *Intelligence testing with the WISC-V* (pp. 683–702). Hoboken, NJ: Wiley.

Canivez, G. L., Watkins, M. W., & Dombrowski, S. C. (2016). Factor structure of the Wechsler Intelligence Scale for Children—Fifth Edition: Exploratory factor analyses with the 16 primary and secondary subtests. *Psychological Assessment, 28*, 975–986. http://dx.doi.org/10.1037/pas0000238

Canivez, G. L., Watkins, M. W., & Dombrowski, S. C. (2017). Structural validity of the Wechsler Intelligence Scale for Children—Fifth Edition: Confirmatory factor analyses with the 16 primary and secondary subtests. *Psychological Assessment, 29*, 458–472. http://dx.doi.org/10.1037/pas0000358.

Canivez, G. L., & Youngstrom, E. A. (2019). Challenges to the Cattell-Horn-Carroll Theory: Empirical, clinical, and policy implications. *Applied Measurement in Education, 32*, 232–248. https://doi.org/10.1080/08957347.2019.1619562

Carpenter, P. A., Just, M. A., & Shell, P. (1990). What one intelligence test measures: A theoretical account of the processing in the Raven Progressive Matrices Test. *Psychological Review, 97*, 404–431.

Carroll, J. B. (1982). The measurement of intelligence. In R. J. Sternberg (Ed.), *Handbook of human intelligence* (pp. 29–122). Cambridge, UK: Cambridge University Press.

Carroll, J. B. (1993). *Human cognitive abilities: A survey of factor-analytic studies.* New York, NY: Cambridge University Press.

Cassidy, J., & Hossler, A. (1992). State and federal definitions of the gifted: An update. *Gifted Child Quarterly, 15*, 46–53.

Cattell, R. B. (1971). *Abilities: Their structure, growth, and action.* Boston, MA: Houghton Mifflin.

Ceci, S. J. (1990). *On intelligence . . . more or less: A bio-ecological treatise on intellectual development.* Englewood Cliffs, NJ: Prentice-Hall.

Celenk, O., & van de Vijver, F. J. R. (2014). Assessment of psychological acculturation and multiculturalism: An overview of measures in the public domain. In V. Benet-Martínez & Y.-Y. Hong (Eds.), *The Oxford handbook of multicultural identity* (pp. 205–226). New York, NY: Oxford University Press.

Centers for Disease Control and Prevention. (n.d.). *Vision loss fact sheet.* Retrieved from www.cdc.gov/ncbddd/actearly/pdf/parents_pdfs/VisionLossFactSheet.pdf

Chalk, K., & Bizo, L. A. (2004). Specific praise improves on-task behaviour and numeracy enjoyment: A study of year four pupils engaged in the numeracy hour. *Educational Psychology in Practice, 20*, 335–351. doi:1O.10801· 02667360420003 14277

Chapman, P. D. (1988). *Schools as sorters: Lewis M. Terman, applied psychology, and the intelligence testing movement, 1890–1930.* New York, NY: New York University Press.

Charity, A. H., Scarborough, H. S., & Griffin, D. M. (2004). Familiarity with school English in African American children and its relation to early reading achievement. *Child Development, 75*, 1340-1356.

Chase, W. G., & Ericsson, K. A. (1982). Skill and working memory. In G. H. Bower (Ed.), *Psychology of learning and motivation* (Vol. 16, pp. 1–58). San Diego, CA: Academic Press.

Chen, H., Zhang, O., Raiford, S. E., Zhu, J., & Weiss, L. G. (2015). Factor invariance between genders on the Wechsler Intelligence Scale for Children—Fifth Edition. *Personality and Individual Differences, 86*, 1–5. http://dx.doi.org/10.1016/j.paid.2015.05.020

Chen, J., & Gardner, H. (2018). Assessment from the perspective of multiple-intelligences theory: Principles, practices, and values. In D. P. Flanagan & E. M. McDonough (Eds.), *Contemporary intellectual assessment: Theories, tests, and issues* (4th ed., pp. 164–173). New York, NY: Guilford.

Chipeur, H. M., Rovine, M., & Plomin, R. (1990). LISREL modeling: Genetic and environmental influences on IQ revisited. *Intelligence, 14*, 11–29.

Christ, T. J., Zopluoglu, C., Long, J. D., & Monaghen, B. D. (2012). Curriculum-based measurement of oral reading: Quality of progress monitoring outcomes. *Council for Exceptional Children, 78*, 356–373.

Cizek, G. J., Bowen, D., & Church, K. (2010). Sources of validity evidence for educational and psychological tests: A follow up. *Educational and Psychological Measurement, 70*, 732–743.

Clark, S. W., Gulin, S. L., Heller, M. B., & Vrana, S. R. (2017). Graduate training implications of the Q-interactive platform for administering Wechsler intelligence tests. *Training and Education in Professional Psychology, 11*(3), 148–155. http://dx.doi.org/10.1037/tep0000155

Clarke, A. M., & Clarke, A. D. B. (1989). The later cognitive effects of early intervention. *Intelligence, 13*, 289–297.

Climie, E. A., & Rostad, K. (2011). Test review. [Review of the test *Wechsler Adult Intelligence Scale, Fourth Edition*]. *Journal of Psychoeducational Assessment, 29*, 581–586.

Colom, R., Karama, S., Jung, R. E., & Jaier, R. J. (2010). Human intelligence and brain networks. *Dialogues in Clinical Neuroscience, 12*, 489–501.

Colour Blind Awareness. (n.d.). *Early symptoms*. Retrieved from www.colourblindawareness.org/parents/early-symptoms

Cooper, J. O., Heron, T. E., & Heward, W. L. (2020). *Applied behavior analysis* (3rd edition). Hoboken, NJ: Pearson.

Cormier, D. C., McGrew, K. S., & Evans, J. J. (2011). Quantifying the "degree of linguistic demand" in spoken intelligence test directions. *Journal of Psychoeducational Assessment, 29*, 1–19.

Cormier, D. C., Van Norman, E. R., Cheong, C., Kennedy, K. E., Bulut, O., & Mrazik, M. (2019). Developing proficiency in standardized cognitive assessment scoring: How much is enough? *Canadian Journal of School Psychology, 34*, 215–233.

Cottrell, J. M., & Barrett, C. A. (2017). Examining school psychologists' perspectives about specific learning disabilities: Implications for practice. *Psychology in the Schools, 54*, 294–308.

Cox, C. M. (1926). *Genetic studies of genius: Vol. 2. The early mental traits of three hundred geniuses*. Stanford, CA: Stanford University Press.

Cronbach, L. J. (1957). The two disciplines of scientific psychology. *American Psychologist, 12*, 671–684.

Cronbach, L. (1989). Construct validation after thirty years. In R. Linn (Ed.), *Intelligence: Measurement, theory, and public policy* (pp. 147–167). Urbana, IL: University of Illinois Press.

Cronbach, L. J. (1990). *Essentials of psychological testing* (5th ed.). New York, NY: Harper & Row.

Cronbach, L. J., & Meehl, P. (1955). Construct validity of psychological tests. *Psychological Bulletin, 52*, 281–302.

Cronbach, L. J., & Snow, R. E. (1977). *Aptitudes and instructional methods: A handbook for research on interactions*. Oxford, UK: Irvington.

Cummins, J. (1984). *Bilingual and special education: Issues in assessment and pedagogy*. San Diego, CA: College-Hill Press.

Cunningham, M. D., & Tassé, M. J. (2010). Looking to science rather than convention in adjusting IQ scores when death is at issue. *Professional Psychology: Research and Practice, 41*, 413–419.

Daniel, M. H. (2007). "Scatter" and the construct validity of the FSIQ: Comment on Fiorello et al. (2007). *Applied Neuropsychology, 14*, 291–295.

Daniel, M. H., Wahlstrom, D., & Zhang, O. (2014). *Q-interactive technical report 8: Equivalence of Q-interactive and paper administrations of cognitive tasks: WISC-V*. San Antonio, TX: Pearson. http://www.helloq.com/research.html

Das, J. P. (1999). *PASS Reading Enhancement Program (PREP)*. Edmonton: Developmental Disabilities Centre, University of Alberta.

Das, J. P. (2004). *The Cognitive Enhancement Training program (COGENT)*. New York, NY: Springer.

Davis, O. S. P., Haworth, C. M. A., & Plomin, R. (2009). Learning abilities and disabilities: Generalist genes in early adolescence. *Cognitive Neuropsychiatry, 14*, 312–331.

Day, L. A., Adams Costa, E. B., & Raiford, S. E. (2015). *WISC-V technical report 2: Testing children who are deaf or hard of hearing*. Bloomington, MN: Pearson.

Deary, I. J. (2001). *Intelligence: A very short introduction*. Oxford, UK: Oxford University Press.

Deary, I. J. (2012a). Intelligence. *Annual Review of Psychology, 63*, 453–482.

Deary, I. J. (2012b). 125 years of intelligence in the American Journal of Psychology. *American Journal of Psychology, 125*, 145–154.

De Jong, T. (2010). Cognitive load theory, educational research, and instructional design: Some food for thought. *Instructional Science, 38*(2), 105–134.

Delisle, J. R. (2003). To be or to do: Is a gifted child born or developed? *Roeper Review, 26*, 12–13.

DeThorne, L. S., & Schaefer, B. A. (2004). A guide to child nonverbal IQ measures. *American Journal of Speech—Language Pathology, 13*, 275–290.

Detterman, D. K., & Daniel, M. H. (1989). Correlations of mental tests with each other and with cognitive variables are highest for low-IQ groups. *Intelligence, 13*, 349–359.

Detterman, D. K., & Sternberg, R. J. (Eds.). (1993). *Transfer on trial: Intelligence, cognition, and instruction*. Norwood, NJ: Ablex.

Devereaux, R. L., & Gottlieb, M. C. (2012). Record keeping in the cloud: Ethical considerations. *Professional Psychology: Research and Practice, 43*, 627–632. http://dx.doi.org/10.1037/a0028268

Dhaniram-Beharry, E. (2008). *Cultural and linguistic influences on test performance: Evaluation of alternate variables* (Doctoral dissertation). Retrieved from ProQuest (Accession No. 3336081).

DiStefano, C., & Dombrowski, S. C. (2006). Investigating the theoretical structure of the Stanford-Binet, Fifth Edition. *Journal of Psychoeducational Assessment, 24*, 123–136.

Dombrowski, S. C., Canivez, G. L., & Watkins, M. W. (2018). Factor structure of the 10 WISC-V primary subtests across four standardization age groups. *Contemporary School Psychology, 22*, 90–104.

Dombrowski, S. C., Canivez, G. L., Watkins, M. W., & Beaujean, A. (2015). Exploratory bifactor analysis of the Wechsler Intelligence Scale for Children—Fifth Edition with the 16 primary and secondary subtests. *Intelligence, 53*, 194–201. http://dx.doi.org/10.1016/j.intell.2015.10.009

Dombrowski, S. C., McGill, R. J., & Canivez, G. L. (2017). Exploratory and hierarchical factor analysis of the WJ-IV Cognitive at school age. *Psychological Assessment, 29*, 394–407.

Dombrowski, S. C., McGill, R. J., & Canivez, G. L. (2018a). An alternative conceptualization of the theoretical structure of the Woodcock-Johnson IV Tests of Cognitive Abilities at school age: A confirmatory factor analytic investigation. *Archives of Scientific Psychology, 6*, 1–13.

Dombrowski, S. C., McGill, R. J., & Canivez, G. L. (2018b). Hierarchical exploratory factor analyses of the Woodcock-Johnson IV Full Test Battery: Implications for CHC application in school psychology. *School Psychology Quarterly, 33*, 235–250.

Dumont, R., Willis, J. O., & Elliott, C. D. (2008). *Essentials of DAS-II assessment.* Hoboken, NJ: Wiley.

Dries, C., Dumont, R., & Viezel, K. D. (2017). WISC-V and Q-Interactive. In D. P. Flanagan & V. C. Alfonso (Eds.), *Essentials of WISC-V Assessment,* (pp. 591–615). Hoboken, NJ: Wiley.

Drozdick, L. W., Raiford, S. E., Wahlstrom, D., & Weiss, L. G. (2018). The Wechsler Adult Intelligence Scale—Fourth Edition and the Wechsler Memory Scale—Fourth Edition. In D. P. Flanagan & E. M. McDonough (Eds.), *Contemporary intellectual assessment: Theories, tests, and issues* (4th ed., pp. 486–511). New York, NY: Guilford Press.

Drozdick, L. W., Singer, J. K., Lichtenberger, E. O., Kaufman, J. C., Kaufman, A. S., & Kaufman, N. L. (2018). The Kaufman Assessment Battery for Children—Second Edition and KABC-II Normative Update. In D. P. Flanagan & E. M. McDonough (Eds.), *Contemporary intellectual assessment: Theories, tests, and issues* (4th ed., pp. 333–359). New York, NY: Guilford Press.

Education for All Handicapped Children Act of 1975, Pub. L. No. 94-142 (1975).

Elizalde-Utnick, G., & Romero, P. A. (2017). Assessment of English language learners. In E. C. Lopez, S. G. Nahari, & S. L. Proctor (Eds.), *Handbook of multicultural school psychology: An interdisciplinary perspective* (pp. 193–217). New York, NY: Routledge.

Elliott, C. D. (2007). *Differential Ability Scales—Second Edition.* San Antonio, TX: Harcourt Assessment.

Elliott, C. D., Salerno, J. D., Dumont, R., & Willis, J. O. (2018). The Differential Ability Scales—Second Edition. In D. P. Flanagan & E. M. McDonough (Eds.), *Contemporary intellectual assessment: Theories, tests, and issues* (4th ed., pp. 360–382). New York, NY: Guilford Press.

Elliott, J. G., & Resing, W. C. (2015). Can intelligence testing inform educational intervention for children with reading disability? *Journal of Intelligence, 3*, 137–157.

Embretson, S. E., & Reise, S. P. (2000). *Item response theory for psychologists.* Mahwah, NJ: Erlbaum.

Emhoff, S. M., Lynch, J. K., & McCaffrey, R. J. (2018). Performance and symptom validity testing in pediatric assessment: A review of the literature. *Developmental Neuropsychology, 43*, 671–707.

Emmons, M. R., & Alfonso, V. (2005). Critical review of the technical characteristics of current preschool screening batteries. *Journal of Psychoeducational Assessment, 23*, 111–127.

Erbeli, F., Hart, S. A., & Taylor, J. (2019). Genetic and environmental influences on achievement outcomes based on family history of learning disabilities status. *Journal of Learning Disabilities, 52*, 135–145.

Ericsson, K. A., & Simon, H. A. (1993). *Protocol analysis: Verbal reports as data* (rev. ed.). Cambridge, MA: MIT Press.

Eysenck, H. J. (1973). *The measurement of intelligence.* Baltimore, MD: Williams & Wilkins.

Eysenck, H. J. (1979). *The structure and measurement of intelligence.* New York, NY: Springer-Verlag.

Eysenck, H. J. (1994). Review of *human cognitive abilities: A survey of factor-analytic studies. Personality and Individual Differences, 16*, 199.

Eysenck, H. J. (1998). *Intelligence: A new look*. New Brunswick, NJ: Transaction.

Farmer, R. L., Floyd, R. G., Reynolds, M. R., & Berlin, K. S. (2019). How can general intelligence composites most accurately index psychometric g and what might be good enough? *Contemporary School Psychology*. doi:10.1007/s40688-019-00244-1

Farmer, R. L., Floyd, R. G., Reynolds, M. R., & Kranzler, J. H. (2014). IQs are very strong but imperfect indicators of psychometric g: Results from joint confirmatory factor analysis. *Psychology in the Schools, 51*, 801–813.

Feuerstein, R., Rand, Y., & Hoffman, M. B. (1979). *The dynamic assessment of retarded performers: The Learning Potential Assessment Device theory, instruments, and techniques*. Baltimore, MD: University Park Press.

Fiorello, C. A., Hale, J. B., & Wycoff, K. L. (2012). Cognitive hypothesis testing: Linking test results to the real world. In D. P. Flanagan & P. L. Harrison (Eds.), *Contemporary intellectual assessment: Theories, tests, and issues* (pp. 484–496). New York, NY: Guilford Press.

Fish, J. M. (1988). Reinforcement in testing: Research with children and adolescents. *Professional School Psychology, 3*, 203–218.

Fish, J. M. (1990). IQ terminology: Modification of current schemes. *Journal of Psychoeducational Assessment, 8*, 527–530.

Flanagan, D. P., & Alfonso, A. C. (1995). A critical review of the technical characteristics of new and recently revised intelligence tests for preschool children. *Journal of Psychoeducational Assessment, 13*, 66–90.

Flanagan, D. P., & Alfonso, V. C. (Eds.). (2016). *WJ IV clinical use and interpretation: Scientist-practitioner perspectives*. New York, NY: Academic Press.

Flanagan, D. P., & Alfonso, V. C. (2017). *Essentials of WISC-V assessment*. New York, NY: Wiley.

Flanagan, D. P., Costa, M., Palma, K., Leahy, M. A., Alfonso, V. C., & Ortiz, S. O. (2018). Cross-battery assessment, the cross-battery assessment software system, and the assessment-intervention connection. In D. P. Flanagan & E. M. McDonough (Eds.), *Contemporary intellectual assessment: Theories, tests, and issues* (4th ed., pp. 731–776). New York, NY: Guilford.

Flanagan, D. P., Ortiz, S. O., & Alfonso, V. C. (2007). *Essentials of cross-battery assessment* (2nd ed.). New York: Wiley.

Flanagan, D., P., Ortiz, S. O., & Alfonso, V. C. (2013). *Essentials of cross-battery assessment* (3rd ed.). New York, NY: Wiley.

Flanagan, D. P., Ortiz, S. O., & Alfonso, V. C. (2017). *Cross-battery assessment software system 2.0* (X-BASS 2.0). New York, NY: Wiley.

Flanagan, D. P., Ortiz, S. O., Alfonso, V. C., & Mascolo, J. (2006). *Achievement test desk reference: A guide to learning disability identification* (2nd ed.). New York, NY: Wiley.

Flesch, R. (1948). A new readability yardstick. *Journal of Applied Psychology, 32*, 221–233.

Flesch, R. (1949). *The art of readable writing*. New York, NY: Harper.

Fletcher, J. M., & Grigorenko, E. L. (2017). The neurology of learning disabilities: The past and the future. *Journal of the International Neuropsychological Society, 23*, 930–940.

Fletcher, J. M., & Miciak, J. (2017). Comprehensive cognitive assessments are not necessary for the identification and treatment of learning disabilities. *Archives of Clinical Neuropsychology, 32*, 2–7. doi:10.1093/arclin/acw103

Fletcher-Janzen, E., & Reynolds, C. R. (Eds.). (2009). *Neuropsychological perspectives on learning disabilities in the era of RTI: Recommendations for diagnosis and intervention*. Hoboken, NJ: Wiley.

Flipsen, P., Jr. (2006). Measuring the intelligibility of conversational speech in children. *Clinical Linguistics and Phonetics, 20*, 202–312.

Floyd, R. G., & Bose, J. E. (2003). Behavior rating scales for assessment of emotional disturbance: A critical review of measurement characteristics. *Journal of Psychoeducational Assessment, 21*, 43–78.

Floyd, R. G., Farmer, R. L., Schneider, W. J., & McGrew, K. S. (in press). Theories and measurement of intelligence. In L. M. Glidden (Ed.), *APA handbook of intellectual and developmental disabilities*. Washington, DC: American Psychological Association.

Floyd, R. G., & Kranzler, J. H. (2012). Processing approaches to interpretation of information from cognitive ability tests: A critical review. In D. P. Flanagan & P. L. Harrison (Eds.), *Contemporary intellectual assessment: Theories, tests, and issues* (3rd ed., pp. 497–523). New York, NY: Guilford Press.

Floyd, R. G., & Kranzler, J. H. (2019). Remediating student learning problems: Aptitude-by-treatment interaction vs. skill-by-treatment interaction. In M. K. Burns (Ed.), *Introduction to school psychology: Controversies and current practice* (pp. 413–434). New York, NY: Oxford University Press.

Floyd, R. G., McGrew, K. S., Barry, A., Rafael, F. A., & Rogers, J. (2009). General and specific effects on Cattell-Horn-Carroll broad ability composites: Analysis of the Woodcock-Johnson III Normative Update CHC factor clusters across development. *School Psychology Review, 38*, 249–265.

Floyd, R. G., Reynolds, M. R., Farmer, R. L., & Kranzler, J. H. (2013). Are the general factors from different child and adolescent intelligence tests the same? Results from a five-sample, six-test analysis. *School Psychology Review, 42*, 383–401.

Floyd, R. G., Shands, E. I., Phillips, J., Autry, B., Mosteller, J., Alfonso, V., Skinner, M., & Irby, S. M. (2015). A systematic review and evaluation of the technical characteristics of adaptive behavior scales. *Journal of Applied School Psychology, 31*, 83–113.

Floyd, R. G., Shaver, R. B., & McGrew, K. S. (2003). Interpretation of the Woodcock-Johnson III Tests of Cognitive Abilities: Acting on evidence. In F. A. Schrank & D. P. Flanagan (Eds.), *WJ III clinical use and interpretation* (pp. 1–46, 403–408). Boston, MA: Academic Press.

Floyd, R. G., Woods, I. L., Singh, L. J., & Hawkins, H. K. (2016). Use of the Woodcock-Johnson IV in the diagnosis of intellectual disability. In D. P. Flanagan & V. C. Alfonso (Eds.), *WJ IV clinical use and interpretation: Scientist-practitioner perspectives* (pp. 272–290). New York, NY: Academic Press.

Flynn, J. R. (1984). The mean IQ of Americans: Massive gains 1932 to 1978. *Psychological Bulletin, 95*, 29–51.

Flynn, J. R. (1987). Massive IQ gains in 14 nations: What IQ tests really measure. *Psychological Bulletin, 101*, 171–191.

Flynn, J. R. (1999). Searching for justice: The discovery of IQ gains over time. *American Psychologist, 54*, 5–20.

Flynn, J. R. (2007). *What is intelligence?* New York, NY: Cambridge University Press.

Foley-Nicpon, M., & Candler, M. (2018). Psychological interventions for twice-exceptional youth. In S. I. Pfeiffer, E. Shaunessy-Dedrick, & M. Foley-Nicpon (Eds.), *APA handbook of giftedness and talent* (pp. 545–558). Washington, DC: American Psychological Association.

Foley-Nicpon, M., & Pfeiffer, S. (2011). High-ability students: New ways to conceptualize giftedness and provide psychological services in the schools. *Journal of Applied School Psychology, 27*, 293–305.

Francis, D. J., Fletcher, J. M., Stuebing, K. K., Lyon, R. L., Shaywitz, B. A., & Shaywitz, S. E. (2005). Psychometric approaches to the identification of LD: IQ and achievement scores are not sufficient. *Journal of Learning Disabilities, 38*, 98–108.

Frazier, T. W., & Youngstrom, E. A. (2007). Historical increase in the number of factors measured by commercial tests of cognitive ability: Are we overfactoring? *Intelligence, 35*, 169–182.

Freberg, M. E., Vandiver, B. J., Watkins, M. W., & Canivez, G. L. (2008). Significant factor score variability and the validity of the WISC-III Full Scale IQ in predicting later academic achievement. *Applied Neuropsychology, 15*, 131–139.

Frisby, C. L., & Braden, J. P. (1992). Feuerstein's dynamic assessment approach: A semantic, logical, and empirical critique. *Journal of Special Education, 26*, 281–301.

Frisby, C. L., & Braden, J. P. (Eds.). (1999). Bias in mental testing [Special issue]. *School Psychology Quarterly, 14*(4).

Fuchs, D., & Deshler, D. D. (2007). What we need to know about responsiveness to intervention (and shouldn't be afraid to ask). *Learning Disabilities Research and Practice, 22*, 129–136.

Fuchs, D., Fuchs, L. S., & Compton, D. L. (2004). Identifying reading disabilities by responsiveness-to-instruction: Specifying measures and criteria. *Learning Disability Quarterly, 27*, 216–227.

Fuchs, D., & Young, C. L. (2006). On the irrelevance of intelligence in predicting responsiveness to reading instruction. *Exceptional Children, 73*, 8–30.

Fuchs, L. S. (1995). Best practices in defining student goals and outcomes. In A. Thomas & J. Grimes (Eds.), *Best practices in school psychology III* (pp. 539–546). Washington, DC: National Association of School Psychologists.

Fuchs, L. S., & Fuchs, D. (1998). Treatment validity: A unifying concept for reconceptualizing the identification of learning disabilities. *Learning Disabilities Research and Practice, 13*, 204–219.

Gable, R. A., Hester, P.H., Rock, M. L., & Hughes, K. G. (2009). Back to basics: Rules, praise, ignoring, and reprimands revisited. *Intervention in School and Clinic, 44*, 195–205.

Galanter, C. A., & Patel, V. L. (2005). Medical decision making: A selective review for child psychiatrists and psychologists. *Journal of Child Psychology and Psychiatry, 46*, 675–689. http://dx.doi.org/10.1111/j.1469-7610.2005.01452.x

Galton, F. (1865). Hereditary talent and character. *Macmillan's Magazine, 12*, 318–327.

Galton, F. (1869). *Hereditary genius: An inquiry into its laws and consequences.* London: Macmillan.

Garber, H. L. (1988). *The Milwaukee project.* Washington, DC: American Association on Mental Retardation.

Gardner, H. (1999). *Intelligences reframed: Multiple intelligences for the 21st century.* New York, NY: Basic Books.

Gardner, H. (2006). *Multiple intelligences: New horizons.* New York, NY: Basic Books.

Gardner, H. (2011). *Frames of mind: The theory of multiple intelligences* (30th-year ed.). New York, NY: Basic Books.

Gignac, G. E. (2008). Higher-order models versus bifactor models: g as a superordinate or breadth factor? *Psychology Science, 50*, 21–43.

Gignac, G. E., & Watkins, M. W. (2013). Bifactor modeling and the estimation of model-based reliability in the WAIS-IV. *Multivariate Behavioral Research, 48*, 639–662.

Gilmore, L., & Campbell, M. (2019). "It's a lot trickier than I expected": Assessment issues and dilemmas for intern psychologists. *Educational and Developmental Psychologist, 36*(1), 3–7. doi:10.1017/edp.2019.3

Glutting, J. J., McDermott, P. A., & Stanley, J. C. (1987). Resolving differences among methods of establishing confidence limits for test scores. *Educational and Psychological Measurement, 47*, 607–614.

Glutting, J. J., & Oakland, T. (1993). *Manual for the guide to the assessment of test session behavior*. San Antonio, TX: Psychological Corporation.

Glutting, J. J., Watkins, M. W., Konold, T. R., & McDermott, P. A. (2006). Distinctions without a difference: The utility of observed versus latent factors from the WISC-IV in estimating reading and math achievement on the WIAT-II. *Journal of Special Education, 40*, 103–114.

Gordon, R. A. (1987). Jensen's contributions concerning test bias: A contextual view. In S. Modgil & C. Modgil (Eds.), *Arthur Jensen: Consensus and controversy* (pp. 77–154). Philadelphia, PA: Falmer.

Gordon-Brannan, M. (1994). Assessing intelligibility: Children's expressive phonologies. *Topics in Language Disorders, 14*, 17–25.

Gottfredson, L. S. (1997). Why g matters: The complexity of everyday life. *Intelligence, 24*, 79–132.

Gottfredson, L. S. (2008). Of what value is intelligence? In A. Prifitera, D. Saklofske, & L. G. Weiss, (Eds.), *WISC-IV applications for clinical assessment and intervention* (2nd ed.; pp. 545–563). Amsterdam, the Netherlands: Elsevier.

Gottfredson, L. S. (2011). Intelligence and social inequality: Why the biological link? In T. Chamorro-Preuzic, S. von Stumm, & A. Furnham (Eds.), *The Wiley–Blackwell handbook of individual differences* (pp. 538–575). Malden, MA: Wiley-Blackwell.

Gottfredson, L. S. (2016). A g theorist on why Kovacs and Conway's process overlap theory amplifies, not opposes, g theory. *Psychological Inquiry, 27*(3), 210–217.

Gottfredson, L. S. (2018). g theory: How recurring variation in human intelligence and the complexity of everyday tasks create social structure and the democratic dilemma. In R. J. Sternberg (Ed.), *The nature of human intelligence* (pp. 130–151). New York: Cambridge University Press.

Gottfredson, L., & Saklofske, D. H. (2009). Intelligence: Foundations and issues in assessment. *Canadian Psychology, 50*, 183–195.

Graesser, A. C., McNamara, D. S., Louwerse, M. M., & Cai, Z. (2004). Coh-Metrix: Analysis of text on cohesion and language. *Behavior Research Methods, Instruments, and Computers, 36*, 193–202.

Gresham, F. M., & Witt, J. C. (1997). Utility of intelligence tests for treatment planning, classification, and placement decisions: Recent empirical findings and future directions. *School Psychology Quarterly, 12*, 249–267.

Grigorenko, E. L, Compton, D. L., Fuchs, L. S., Wagner, R. K., Willcutt, E. G., & Fletcher, J. M. (2019). Understanding, educating, and supporting children with specific learning disabilities: 50 years of science and practice. *American Psychologist.* http://dx.doi.org/10.1037/amp0000452

Grossman, H. (Ed.). (1983). *Manual on terminology and classification in mental retardation*. Washington, DC: American Association on Mental Deficiency.

Guignard, J. H., Jacquet, A. Y., & Lubart, T. I. (2012). Perfectionism and anxiety: A paradox in intellectual giftedness. *PLoS ONE, 7*(7), e41043.

Gustafsson, J. (1984). A unifying model for the structure of intellectual abilities. *Intelligence, 8*, 179–203.

Gustafsson, J.-E. (2002). Measurement from a hierarchical point of view. In H. I. Braun, D. N. Jackson, & D. E. Wiley (Eds.), *The role of constructs in psychological and educational measurement* (pp. 73–96). Mahwah, NJ: Erlbaum.

Hagopian, L. P., Long, E. S., & Rush, K. S. (2004). Preference assessment procedures for individuals with developmental disabilities. *Behavior Modification, 28*, 668–677. doi:10.1177/0145445503259836

Haier, R. J. (2017). *The neuroscience of intelligence*. New York, NY: Cambridge University Press.

Haier, R. J. (2018). The parieto-frontal integration theory: Assessing intelligence from brain images. In D. P. Flanagan & E. M. McDonough (Eds.), *Contemporary intellectual assessment: Theories, tests, and issues* (4th ed., pp. 219–224). New York, NY: Guilford.

Hale, J. B., & Fiorello, C. A. (2001). Beyond the academic rhetoric of "*g*": Intelligence testing guidelines for practitioners. *School Psychologist, 55*, 113–139.

Hambleton, R. K., & Li, S. (2005). Translaterion and adaptation issues and methods for educational and psychological tests. In C. L. Frisby & C. R. Reynolds (Eds.), *Comprehensive handbook of multicultural school psychology* (pp. 882–903). Hoboken, NJ: Wiley.

Hammill, D. D., Brown, L., & Bryant, B. R. (1992). *A consumer's guide to test in print* (2nd ed.). Austin, TX: PRO-ED.

Hammill, D. D., McGhee, R. L., & Ehrler, D. J. (2018). *Detroit Tests of Learning Abilities—Fifth Edition: Examiner's manual.* Austin, TX: PRO-ED.

Hammill, D. D., Pearson, N. A., & Wiederholt, J. L. (2009). *Comprehensive Test of Nonverbal Intelligence, Second Edition.* Austin, TX: PRO-ED.

Harrison, P. L., & Oakland, T. (2015). *Adaptive Behavior Assessment System* (3rd ed.). New York, NY: Pearson.

Hartman, D. E. (2009). Test review. [Review of the test *Wechsler Adult Intelligence Scale, Fourth Edition*]. Return of the gold standard. *Applied Neuropsychology, 16*, 85–87.

Harvey, V. S. (1997). Improving readability of psychological reports. *Professional Psychology: Research and Practice, 28*, 271–274.

Hass, M., & Carriere, J. A. (2014). *Writing useful, accessible, and legally defensible psychoeducational reports.* Hoboken, NJ: Wiley.

Hattie, J. (2008). *Visible learning: A synthesis of over 800 meta-analyses relating to achievement.* New York, NY: Routledge.

Hawkins, H. (2016). *Experimental evaluation of the Screening Tool for Assessment: Direct Screening Test (STA: DST) in upper elementary school-age children* (Unpublished doctoral dissertation). University of Memphis, Memphis, TN.

Hawkins, H. K., Farmer, R. L., & Floyd, R. G. (2014, February). *Development and Evaluation of the Screening Tool for Assessment (STA): A pre-assessment measure for vision, hearing, and articulation difficulties of preschool students in a Head Start setting.* Poster presented at the National Association of School Psychologists, Washington, DC.

Haworth, C. M. A., Kovas, Y., Harlaar, N., Hayiou-Thomas, M. E., Petrill, S. A., Dale, P. S., & Plomin, R. (2009). Generalist genes and learning disabilities: A multivariate genetic analysis of low performance in reading, mathematics, language and general cognitive ability in a sample of 8000 12-year-old twins. *Journal of Child Psychology and Psychiatry, 50*, 1318–1325.

Hayes, S. C., Nelson, R. O., & Jarrett, R. B. (1987). The treatment utility of assessment: A functional approach to evaluating assessment quality. *American Psychologist, 42*, 963–503.

Haynes, S. N., Smith, G. T., & Hunsley, J. D. (2018). *Scientific foundations of clinical assessment* (2nd ed.). New York, NY: Routledge.

Herrnstein, R. J., & Murray, C. (1994). *The bell curve: Intelligence and class structure in American life.* New York, NY: Free Press.

Herschell, A. D., Greco, L. A., Filcheck, H. A., & McNeil, C. B. (2002). Who is testing whom? Ten suggestions for managing the disruptive behavior of young children during testing. *Intervention in School and Clinic, 47*, 140–148.

Holdnack, J. A., Dozdick, L. W., Weiss, L. G., & Iverson, G. (2013). *WAIS-IV/WMS-IV advanced clinical solutions.* San Diego, CA: Academic Press.

Homack, S. R., & Reynolds, C. R. (2007). *Essentials of assessment with brief intelligence tests.* Hoboken, NJ: Wiley.

Horn, J. L. (1994). Theory of fluid and crystallized intelligence. In R. J. Sternberg (Ed.), *Encyclopedia of intelligence* (pp. 443–451). New York, NY: Macmillan.

Horn, J. L., & Noll, J. (1997). Human cognitive capabilities: Gf-Gc theory. In D. P. Flanagan, J. L. Genshaft, & P. L. Harrison (Eds.), *Contemporary intellectual assessment: Theories, tests, and issues* (pp. 53–91). New York, NY: Guilford Press.

Howard, D. (1992). Knowing who may have a hearing loss: A simple speech reception game for use by teachers and parents. *Aboriginal Child at School, 19*, 33–51.

Humphreys, L. G. (1989). Intelligence: Three kinds of instability and their consequences for policy. In R. L. Linn (Ed.), *Intelligence: Measurement, theory, and public policy* (pp. 193–216). Urbana, IL: University of Illinois Press.

Hunsley, J., & Mash, E. J. (2018). *A guide to assessments that work* (2nd ed.). New York, NY: Oxford University Press.

Hutton, J. B., Dubes, R., & Muir, S. (1992). Assessment practices of school psychologists: Ten years later. *School Psychology Review, 21*, 271–284.

Hyvarinen, L. H., Nasanen, R. & Laurinen, P. (1980). New visual acuity test for preschool children. *Acta Ophthalmologica Copenhagen, 58*, 507–511.

Individuals with Disabilities Education Improvement Act of 2004, Pub. L. No. 108-446 (2004).

Institute of Education Sciences (2009). *Practice Guide for Assisting Students Struggling with Reading: Response to Intervention (RtI) and Multi-Tier Intervention in the Primary Grades.* https://ies.ed.gov/ncee/wwc/PracticeGuide/3

International Test Commission (2016). *The ITC guidelines for translating and adapting tests* (2nd ed.). http://www.InTestCom.org

Irby, S. M., & Floyd, R. G. (2013). Test review. [Review of the test *Wechsler Abbreviated Scales of Intelligence, Second Edition*]. *Canadian Journal of School Psychology, 28*, 295–299.

Irby, S. M., & Floyd, R. G. (2017). Exchangeability of brief intelligence tests: Illuminating error variance components' influence on IQs for children with intellectual giftedness. *Psychology in the Schools, 54*, 1064–1078.

Iseman, J. S., & Naglieri, J. A. (2011). A cognitive strategy instruction to improve math calculation for children with ADHD and LD: A randomized controlled study. *Journal of Learning Disabilities, 44*(2), 184–195.

Jacob, S., Decker, D. M., & Timmerman Lugg, E. (2016). *Ethics and law for school psychologists* (7th ed.). Hoboken, NJ: Wiley.

Jacob K. Javits Gifted and Talented Students Education Act of 1988, 20 U.S.C. 3061 *et seq.* (1988).

Janzen, H. L., Obrzut, J. E., & Marusiak, C. W. (2004). Test review. [Review of the test *Stanford–Binet Intelligence Scales, Fifth Edition*]. *Canadian Journal of School Psychology, 19*, 235–244.

Jaquett, C. M., & Kirkpatrick, B. A. (2017). Wechsler Nonverbal Scale of Ability. In R. A. McCallum (Ed.), *Handbook of nonverbal assessment* (2nd ed., pp. 151–166). New York, NY: Springer.

Jensen, A. R. (1980). *Bias in mental testing.* New York, NY: Free Press.

Jensen, A. R. (1981). *Straight talk about mental tests.* New York, NY: Free Press.

Jensen, A. R. (1987). Mental chronometry in the study of learning disabilities. *Mental Retardation & Learning Disability Bulletin, 15*, 67–88.

Jensen, A. R. (1989). Raising IQ without raising *g*?: A review of "The Milwaukee Project: Preventing mental retardation in children at risk." *Developmental Review, 9*, 234–258.

Jensen, A. R. (1998a). *The g factor: The science of mental ability.* Westport, CT: Preager.

Jensen, A. R. (1998b). The *g* factor and the design of education. In R. J. Sternberg and W. M. Williams (Eds.), *Intelligence, instruction, and assessment* (pp. 111–131). Hillsdale, NJ: Erlbaum.

Jensen, A. R. (2002). Galton's legacy to research on intelligence. *Journal of Biosocial Sciences, 34*, 145–172.

Johnson, te Nijenhuis, H., & Bouchard, T. J., Jr. (2008). Still one *g*: Consistent results from five test batteries. *Intelligence, 36*, 81–95.

Jung, R. E., & Haier, R. J. (2007). The parieto-frontal integration theory (P-FIT) of intelligence: Converging neuroimaging evidence. *Behavioral and Brain Sciences, 30*, 135–154.

Kalb, L. M., & Loeber, R. (2003). Child disobedience and noncompliance: A review. *Pediatrics, 111*, 641–652.

Kamphaus, R. W. (2001). *Clinical assessment of child and adolescent intelligence* (2nd ed.). Boston, MA: Allyn & Bacon.

Kamphaus, R. W., Winsor, A. P., Rowe, E. W., & Kim, S. (2018). A history of intelligence test interpretation. In D. P. Flanagan & E. M. McDonough (Eds.), *Contemporary intellectual assessment* (4th ed., pp. 56–70). New York, NY: Guilford Press.

Kaplan, E. (1998). A process approach to neuropsychological assessment. In T. Boll & B. K. Bryant (Eds.), *Clinical neuropsychology and brain function: Research, measurement, and practice* (pp. 125–167). Washington, DC: American Psychological Association.

Kaplan, E., Fein, D., Kramer, J., Delis, D., & Morris, R. (1999). *WISC-III as a Process Instrument*. San Antonio, TX: Psychological Corporation.

Kassai, R., Futo, J., Demetrovics, Z., & Takacs, Z. K. (2019). A meta-analysis of the experimental evidence on the near- and far-transfer effects among children's executive function skills. *Psychological Bulletin, 145*, 165–188.

Kaufman, A. S. (1979). *Intelligent testing with the WISC-R*. New York, NY: Wiley.

Kaufman, A. S. (1994). *Intelligent testing with the WISC-III*. New York, NY: Wiley.

Kaufman, A. S., & Kaufman, N. L. (1983). *Kaufman Assessment Battery for Children*. Circle Pines, MN: American Guidance Service.

Kaufman, A. S., & Kaufman, N. L. (2004). *Kaufman Assessment Battery for Children—Second Edition: Technical manual*. Circle Pines, MN: American Guidance Service.

Kaufman, A. S., & Kaufman, N. L. (2004a). *Kaufman Assessment Battery for Children, Second Edition*. Circle Pines, MN: American Guidance Service.

Kaufman, A. S., & Kaufman, N. L. (2004b). *Kaufman Brief Intelligence Test, Second Edition*. Circle Pines, MN: American Guidance Service.

Kaufman, A. S., & Kaufman, N. L. (2018). *Kaufman Assessment Battery for Children, Second Edition Normative Update*. San Antonio, TX: Pearson.

Kaufman, A. S., Lichtenberger, E. O., Fletcher-Janzen, E., & Kaufman, N. L. (2005). *Essentials of KABC-II assessment*. Hoboken, NJ: Wiley.

Kaufman, A. S., Raiford, S. E., & Coalson, D. L. (2016). *Intelligent testing with the WISC-V*. Hoboken, NJ: Wiley.

Kaufman, L., Ayub, M., & Vincent, J. B. (2010). The genetic basis of non-syndromic intellectual disability: a review. *Journal of Neurodevelopmental Disorders, 2*, 182–209.

Kaufman, S. B., Reynolds, M. R., Liu, X., Kaufman, A. S., & McGrew, K. S. (2012). Are cognitive *g* and academic achievement *g* one and the same *g*?: An exploration on the Woodcock–Johnson and Kaufman tests. *Intelligence, 40*, 123–138.

Kaufman, S. B., & Sternberg, R. J. (2008). Conceptions of giftedness. In S. I. Pfeiffer (Ed.), *Handbook of giftedness in children: Psychoeducational theory, research, and best practices* (pp. 71–91). New York, NY: Springer.

Kazdin, A. E. (2016). Experimental and observational designs: An overview. In A. E. Kazdin (Ed.), *Methodological issues and strategies in clinical research* (pp. 155–180). Washington, DC: American Psychological Association.

Kearns, D. M., & Fuchs, D. (2013). Does cognitively-focused instruction improve the academic performance of low-achieving students? *Exceptional Children, 79*, 263–290.

Keith, T. Z., & Kranzler, J. H. (1999b). The absence of structural fidelity precludes construct validity: Rejoinder to Naglieri on what the Cognitive Assessment System does and does not measure. *School Psychology Review, 28*, 303–321.

Keith, T. Z., Kranzler, J. H., & Flanagan, D. P. (2001). What does the Cognitive Assessment System (CAS) measure?: Conjoint confirmatory factor analysis of the CAS and the Woodcock-Johnson Tests of Cognitive Ability (3rd ed.). *School Psychology Review, 30*, 89–117.

Keith, T. Z., Low, J. A., Reynolds, M. R., Patel, P. G., & Ridley, K. P. (2010). Higher-order factor structure of the Differential Ability Scales—II: Consistency across ages 4 to 17. *Psychology in the Schools, 47*, 676–697.

Keith, T. Z., & Reynolds, M. R. (2010). Cattell-Horn-Carroll theory and cognitive abilities: What we've learned from 20 years of research. *Psychology in the Schools, 47*, 635–650.

Keith, T. Z., & Reynolds, M. R. (2012). Using confirmatory factor analysis to aid in understanding the constructs measured by intelligence tests. In D. P. Flanagan & P. L. Harrison (Eds.), *Contemporary intellectual assessment: Theories, tests, and issues* (3rd ed., pp. 758–799). New York, NY: Guilford Press.

Kelley, T. E. (1927). *Interpretation of educational measurements*. Yonkers-on-Hudson, NY: World Book.

Kettler, R. J. (2019). *Research methodologies of school psychology: Critical skills*. New York, NY: Routledge.

Khoury, J. E, Milligan, K., & Girard, T. A. (2015). Executive functioning in children and adolescents prenatally exposed to alcohol: A meta-analytic review. *Neuropsychology Review, 25*(2), 149–170.

Kirby, F. D., & Shields, F. (1972). Modification of arithmetic response rate and attending behavior in a seventh-grade student. *Journal of Applied Behavior Analysis, 5*, 79–84. doi:1O.1901/jaba.1972.S–79

Kirk, S. A. (1962). *Educating exceptional children*. Boston, MA: Houghton Mifflin.

Kirk, S. A., & Kirk, W. D. (1983). On defining learning disabilities. *Journal of Learning Disabilities, 16*, 20–21.

Kirschenbaum, R. J. (1998). Dynamic assessment and its use with underserved gifted and talented populations. *Gifted Child Quarterly, 42*, 140–147.

Koocher, G. P., & Keith-Spiegel, P. (2016). *Ethics in psychology and the mental health professions: Standards and cases*. Oxford, UK: Oxford University Press.

Kotz, K. M., Watkins, M. W., & McDermott, P. A. (2008). Validity of the general conceptual ability score from the Differential Ability Scales as a function of significant and rare interfactor variability. *School Psychology Review, 37*, 261–278.

Kovaleski, J. F., VanDerHeyden, A. M., & Shapiro, E. S. (2013). *The RTI approach to evaluating learning disabilities*. New York, NY: Guilford Press.

Krach, S. K., McCreery, M. P., & Guerard, J. (2017). Cultural-linguistic test adaptations: Guidelines for selection, alteration, use, and review. *School Psychology International, 38*, 3–21.

Kraemer, H. C., Wilson, G. T., Fairburn, C. G., & Agras, W. S. (2002). Mediators and moderators of treatment effects in randomized clinical trials. *Archives of General Psychiatry, 59*, 877–883.

Kranzler, J. H. (1997). Educational and policy issues related to the use and interpretation of intelligence tests in the schools. *School Psychology Review, 26*, 150–162.

Kranzler, J. H., Benson, N., & Floyd, R. G. (2015). Using estimated factor scores from a bifactor analysis to examine the unique effects of the latent variables measured by the WAIS-IV on academic achievement. *Psychological Assessment, 27*, 1402–1416.

Kranzler, J. H., Flores, C. G., & Coady, M. (2010). Examination of the cross-battery approach for the cognitive assessment of children and youth from diverse linguistic and cultural backgrounds. *School Psychology Review, 39*, 431–446.

Kranzler, J. H., & Floyd, R. G. (2013). *Assessing intelligence in children and adolescents: A practical guide.* New York, NY: Guilford Press.

Kranzler, J. H., Floyd, R. G., Benson, N., Zaboski, B., & Thibodaux, L. (2016a). Classification agreement analysis of cross-battery assessment in the identification of specific learning disorders in children and youth. *International Journal of School and Educational Psychology, 3*, 124–136. doi:10.1080/21683603.2016.1155515

Kranzler, J. H., Floyd, R. G., Benson, N., Zaboski, B., & Thibodaux, L. (2016b). Cross-battery assessment pattern of strengths and weaknesses approach to the identification of specific learning disorders: Evidence-based practice or pseudoscience? *International Journal of School and Educational Psychology, 3*, 146–157. doi:10.1080/21683603.2016.1192855

Kranzler, J. H., & Keith, T. Z. (1999). Independent confirmatory factor analysis of the Cognitive Assessment System (CAS): What does the CAS measure? *School Psychology Review, 28*, 117–144.

Kranzler, J. H., Maki, K. E., Eckert, T. L., Benson, N. F., Floyd, R. G., & Fefer, S. A. (2020a). How do school psychologists interpret intelligence tests for the identification of specific learning disabilities? *Contemporary School Psychology.* doi: 10.1007/s40688-020-00274-0.

Kranzler, J. H., Yaraghchi, M., Matthews, K., & Otero-Valles, L. (2020b). Does the response-to-intervention model fundamentally alter the traditional conceptualization of specific learning disability? *Contemporary School Psychology 24*, 80–88.

Krasa, N. (2007). Is the Woodcock-Johnson III a test for all seasons?: Ceiling and item gradient considerations in its use with older students. *Journal of Psychoeducational Assessment, 25*, 3–16.

Kratochwill, T. (2007). Preparing psychologists for evidence-based school practice: Lessons learned and challenges ahead. *American Psychologist, 62*, 829–843.

Kroesbergen, E. H., Van Luit, J. E., & Naglieri, J. A. (2003). Mathematical learning difficulties and PASS cognitive processes. *Journal of Learning Disabilities, 36*, 574–582.

LaForte, E. M., Wendling, B. J., Mather, N., Schrank, F. A., & McGrew, K. S. (2019). *Batería IV assessment service bulletin number 1.* Itasca, IL: Riverside Insights.

Lella, S. (2010). *Evaluating speech-language and cognitive impairment patterns via the Culture-Language Interpretive Matrix* (Unpublished doctoral dissertation). St. John's University, Jamaica, NY.

Lenhard, A., Lenhard, W., Suggate, S., & Segerer, R. (2018). A continuous solution to the norming problem. *Assessment, 25*, 112–125.

Lerman, D. C., & Vorndran, C. M. (2002). On the status of knowledge for using punishment: Implications for treating behavior disorders. *Journal of Applied Behavior Analysis, 35*, 431–464.

Lichtenberger, E. O., & Kaufman, A. S. (2012). *Essentials of WAIS-IV assessment* (2nd ed.). Hoboken, NJ: Wiley.

Lichtenstein, R. (2010, June). How soon must you switch to the new version of a test? *Communiqué, 38*(8), 1, 12, 14–15.

Lichtenstein, R., & Ecker, B. (2019). *High-impact assessment reports for children and adolescents: A consumer-responsive approach.* New York, NY: Guilford.

Lilienfeld, S. O., Ammirati, R., & David, M. (2012). Distinguishing science from pseudoscience in school psychology: Science and scientific thinking as safeguard against human error. *Journal of School Psychology, 50,* 7–36.

Locke, E. A. (1995). Review of the book *The Bell Curve: Intelligence and Class Structure in American Life. Personnel Psychology, 48,* 177–182.

Locurto, C. (1990). The malleability of IQ as judged from adoption studies. *Intelligence, 14,* 275–292.

Locurto, C. (1991). *Sense and nonsense about IQ: The case for uniqueness.* New York, NY: Praeger.

Loehlin, J. C. (2007). The strange case of $c2 = 0$: What does it imply for views of human development? *Research in Human Development, 4,* 151–162.

Lohman, D. F. (2000). Complex information processing and intelligence. In R. J. Sternberg (Ed.), *Handbook of intelligence* (pp. 285–340). Cambridge, UK: Cambridge University Press.

Lohman, D. F., & Gambrell, J. L. (2012). Using nonverbal tests to help identify academically talented children. *Journal of Psychoeducational Assessment, 30,* 25–44.

Lohman, D. F., Korb, K., & Lakin, J. (2008). Identifying academically gifted English language learners using nonverbal tests: A comparison of the Raven, NNAT, and CogAT. *Gifted Child Quarterly, 52,* 275–296.

Lubinski, D. (2010). Spatial ability and STEM: A sleeping giant for talent identification and development. *Personality and Individual Differences, 49,* 344–351.

Lubinski, D. (2016). From Terman to today: A century of findings on intellectual precocity. *Review of Educational Research, 86,* 900–944.

Luciano, M., Weiss, A., Gale, C. R., & Deary, I. J. (2018). Personality, intelligence and genes. In M. Kivimäki, G. Batty, G. David, A. Steptoe, & I. Kawachi (Eds.), *The Routledge international handbook of psychosocial epidemiology* (pp. 170–187). New York: Routledge/Taylor & Francis Group.

Lugo, A. M., King, M. L., Lamphere, J. C., & McArdle, P. E. (2017). Developing procedures to improve therapist-child rapport in early intervention. *Behavior Analysis in Practice, 10,* 395–401. doi:10.1007/s40617-016-0165-5

Luria, A. R. (1973). *The working brain: An introduction to neuropsychology.* New York, NY: Basic Books.

Lustgarten, S. D. (2015). Emerging ethical threats to client privacy in cloud communication and data storage. *Professional Psychology: Research and Practice, 46,* 154–160. http://dx.doi.org/10.1037/pro0000018

Lohman, D. F., & Lakin, J. (2008). Nonverbal test scores as one component of an identification system: Integrating ability, achievement, and teacher ratings. In J. L. VanTassel-Baska (Ed.), *Alternative assessments of identifying gifted and talented students* (pp. 41–66). Austin, TX: Prufrock Press.

Makel, M. C., Kell, H. J., Lubinski, D., Putallaz, M., & Benbow, C. P. (2016). When lightning strikes twice: Profoundly gifted, profoundly accomplished. *Psychological Science, 27,* 1004–1018.

Maki, K. E., & Adams, S. R. (2019). A current landscape of specific learning disability identification: Training, practices, and implications. current landscape of specific learning disability identification: Training, practices, and implications. *Psychology in the Schools, 56,* 18–31. https://doi.org/10.1002/pits.22179

Maki, K. E., Floyd, R. G., & Roberson, T. (2015). State learning disability eligibility criteria: A comprehensive review. *School Psychology Quarterly, 30,* 457–469. doi:10.1037/spq0000109

Margulies, A. S., & Floyd, R. G. (2009). *A preliminary examination of the CHC cognitive ability profiles of children with high IQ and high academic achievement enrolled in services for intellectual giftedness.* Nashville, TN: Woodcock–Muñoz Foundation Press.

Marín, G. (1992). Issues in the measurement of acculturation among Hispanics. In K. F. Geisinger (Ed.), *Psychological testing of Hispanics* (pp. 235–251). Washington, DC: American Psychological Association.

Marland, S. P., Jr. (1972). *Education of the gifted and talented: Report to the Congress of the United States by the U.S. Commissioner of Education.* Washington, DC: U.S. Government Printing Office.

Marlow, N., Wolke, D., Bracewell, M. A, Samara, M., & EPICure Study Group. (2005). Neurologic and developmental disability at six years of age after extremely preterm birth. *New England Journal of Medicine, 352*(1), 9–19.

Marshal, S. M., McGoey, K. E., & Moschos, S. (2011). Test review. [Review of the test *Differential Ability Scales—Second Edition*]. *Journal of Psychoeducational Assessment, 29,* 89–93.

Mash, E. J., & Barkley, R. A. (Eds.). (2014). *Assessment of childhood disorders* (3rd ed.). New York, NY: Guilford Press.

Massa, I., & Rivera, V. (2009). Test review. [Review of the test *Wechsler Nonverbal Scale of Ability*]. *Journal of Psychoeducational Assessment, 27,* 426–432.

Matarazzo, J., Carmody, T. P., & Jacobs, L. D. (1980). Test-retest reliability and stability of the WAIS: A literature review with implications for clinical practice. *Journal of Clinical Neuropsychology, 2,* 89–105.

Mather, N., & Jaffe, L. E. (2016). *Woodcock-Johnson IV: Reports, recommendations, and strategies.* Hoboken, NJ: Wiley.

Mathers, M., Keyes, M., & Wright, M. (2010). A review of the evidence on the effectiveness of children's vision screening. *Child: Care, Health and Development, 36,* 756–780.

Maynard, J. L., Floyd, R. G., Acklie, T. J., & Houston, L. (2011). General factor loadings and specific effects of the Differential Ability Scales, Second Edition composites. *School Psychology Quarterly, 26,* 108–118.

Mazur-Mosiewicz, A., Ford, A. I., Chapman, W. D., Crawford, J. H., & Farabough, M. C. (2018). Why children fail the test of memory malingering: Review of false positive performance in pediatric studies. *Journal of Pediatric Neuropsychology, 4,* 113–126.

McCallum, R. S. (2013). Assessing intelligence nonverbally. In K. F. Geisinger, B. A. Bracken, J. F. Carlson, J.-I. C. Hansen, N. R. Kuncel, S. P. Reise, & M. C. Rodriguez (Eds.), *APA handbooks in psychology. APA handbook of testing and assessment in psychology, Vol. 3. Testing and assessment in school psychology and education* (pp. 71–99). Washington, DC: American Psychological Association.

McCallum, R. S. (Ed.). (2017). *Handbook of nonverbal assessment* (2nd ed.). Cham, Switzerland: Springer International Publishing.

McCallum, R. S., & Bracken, B. A. (2018). The Universal Nonverbal Intelligence Test—Second Edition: A multidimensional nonverbal alternative for cognitive assessment. In D. P. Flanagan & E. M. McDonough (Eds.), *Contemporary intellectual assessment: Theories, tests, and issues* (4th ed., pp. 567–586). New York, NY: Guilford Press.

McCallum, R. S., Bracken, B. A., & Wasserman, J. (2001). *Essentials of nonverbal assessment.* New York, NY: Wiley.

McClain, M., & Pfeiffer, S. (2012). Identification of gifted students in the United States today: A look at state definitions, policies, and practices. *Journal of Applied School Psychology, 28,* 59–88.

McConaughy, S. H. (2005). Direct observational assessment during test sessions and child clinical interviews. *School Psychology Review, 34,* 490–506.

McConaughy, S. H., & Achenbach, T. M. (2004). *Manual for the Test Observation Form for Ages 2–18*. Burlington, VT: University of Vermont, Research Center for Children, Youth, & Families.

McCrimmon, A. W., & Smith, A. D. (2013). Review of the Wechsler Abbreviated Scale of Intelligence, Second Edition (WASI-II). *Journal of Psychoeducational Assessment, 31*, 337–341.

McDaniel, M. A. (2005). Big-brained people are smarter: A meta-analysis of the relationship between in vivo brain volume and intelligence. *Intelligence, 37*, 422–427.

McDermott, P. A., Fantuzzo, J. W., & Glutting, J. J. (1990). Just say no to subtest analysis: A critique on Wechsler theory and practice. *Journal of Psychoeducational Assessment, 8*, 290–302.

McDermott, P. A., & Glutting, J. J. (1997). Informing stylistic learning behavior, disposition, and achievement through ability subtests: Or more illusions of meaning? *School Psychology Review, 26*, 163–175.

McGill, R. J. (2015). Test review. [Review of the test *Cognitive Assessment System—Second Edition*]. *Journal of Psychoeducational Assessment, 33*, 375–380.

McGill, R. J. (2016). Invalidating the full scale IQ score in the presence of significant factor score variability: Clinical acumen or clinical illusion? *Archives of Assessment Psychology, 6*(1), 49–79.

McGill, R. J. (2018). Confronting the base rate problem: More ups and downs for cognitive scatter analysis. *Contemporary School Psychology, 22*, 384–393.

McGill, R. J. (2019). An instrument in search of a theory: Structural validity of the Kaufman Assessment Battery for Children—Second Edition Normative Update at school-age. *Psychology in the Schools*. doi:10.1002/pits.22304

McGill, R. J., & Dombrowski, S. C. (2018). Factor structure of the CHC model for the KABC-II: Exploratory factor analyses with the 16 core and supplementary subtests. *Contemporary School Psychology, 22*, 279–293.

McGill, R. J., & Dombrowski, S. C. (2019). Critically reflecting on the origins, evolution, and impact of the Cattell-Horn-Carroll (CHC) model. *Applied Measurement in Education, 32*, 216–231.

McGill, R. J., Dombrowski, S. C., & Canivez, G. L. (2018). Cognitive profile analysis in school psychology: History, issues, and continued concerns. *Journal of School Psychology, 71*, 108–121. http://dx.doi.org/10.1016/j.jsp.2018.10.00

McGill, R. J., Styck, K. M., Palomares, R. S., & Hass, M. R. (2016). Critical issues in specific learning disability identification: What we need to know about the PSW model. *Learning Disability Quarterly, 39*, 159–170.

McGrew, K. S. (2015). Norm obsolescence: The Flynn Effect. In E. Polloway (Ed.), *The death penalty and intellectual disability* (pp. 155–172). Washington, DC: American Association on Intellectual and Developmental Disabilities.

McGrew, K. S., & Flanagan, D. P. (1998). *The intelligence test desk reference (ITDR): Gf-Gc cross-battery assessment*. Boston, MA: Allyn & Bacon.

McGrew, K. S., LaForte, E. M., & Schrank, F. A. (2014). *Technical manual: Woodcock-Johnson IV*. Rolling Meadows, IL: Riverside Publishing.

McGrew, K. S., & Wendling, B. J. (2010). Cattell-Horn-Carroll cognitive-ability achievement relations: What we have learned from the past 20 years of research. *Psychology in the Schools, 47*, 651–675.

McGue, M., Bouchard, T. J., Jr., Iacono, W. G., & Lykken, D. T. (1993). Behavioral genetics of cognitive ability: A life-span perspective. In R. Plomin & G. E. McClearn (Eds.), *Nature, nurture, and psychology* (pp. 59–76). Washington, DC: American Psychological Association.

McIntosh, D., E., Dixon, F. A., & Pierson, E. E. (2018). Use of intelligence tests in the identification of giftedness. In D. P. Flanagan, & E. M. McDonough (Eds.), *Contemporary intellectual assessment: Theories, tests, and issues* (4th ed.) (pp. 587–607). New York: Guilford Press.

McNicholas, P. J., & Floyd, R. G. (2017). Test review. [Review of the test *Reynolds Intellectual Assessment Scales, Second Edition and Reynolds Intellectual Screening Test, Second Edition*]. *Canadian Journal of School Psychology, 32*, 176–180.

McNicholas, P. J., Floyd, R. G., Woods, I. L., Singh, L. J., Manguno, M. S., & Maki, K. E. (2018). State special education criteria for identifying intellectual disability: A review following revised diagnostic criteria and Rosa's Law. *School Psychology Quarterly, 33*, 75–82.

McNulty, R. J. & Floyd, R. G. (2019, August). *Exploratory factor analysis of the DTLA-5*. Poster Presentation for the 2019 annual meeting of the American Psychological Association (APA), Chicago, IL.

Meehl, P. E. (1990). Appraising and amending theories: The strategy of Lakatosian defense and two principles that warrant it. *Psychological Inquiry, 1*(2), 108–141, 173–180.

Melby-Lervåg, M., & Hulme, C. (2013). Is working memory training effective? A meta-analytic review. *Developmental Psychology, 49*, 270–291.

Melby-Lervåg, M., Redick, T. S., & Hulme, C. (2016). Working memory training does not improve performance on measures of intelligence or other measures of "far transfer": Evidence from a meta-analytic review. *Perspectives on Psychological Science, 11*(4), 512–534. https://doi.org/10.1177/1745691616635612

Mercer, C. D., Jordan, L., Allsopp, D. H., & Mercer, A. R. (1996). Learning disabilities definitions and criteria used by state education departments. *Learning Disability Quarterly, 19*, 217–232. doi:10.2307/1511208

Merrell, K. W. (2008). *Behavioral, social, and emotional assessment of children and adolescents* (3rd ed.). Mahwah, NJ: Erlbaum.

Messick, S. (1995). Validity of psychological assessment: Validity of inferences from persons' responses and performances as scientific inquiry into score meaning. *American Psychologist, 50*, 741–749.

Miciak, J., Fletcher, J. M., Stuebing, K. K., Vaughn, S., & Tolar, T. D. (2014). Patterns of cognitive strengths and weaknesses: Identification rates, agreement, and validity for learning disabilities identification. *School Psychology Quarterly, 29*, 21–37. doi:10.1037/spq0000037

Miciak, J., Taylor, W. P., Denton, C. A., & Fletcher, J. M. (2015). The effect of achievement test selection on identification of learning disabilities within a patterns of strengths and weaknesses framework. *School Psychology Quarterly, 30*, 321–334. doi:10.1037/spq0000091

Miciak, J., Taylor, W. P., Stuebing, K. K., & Fletcher, J. M. (2018). Simulation of LD identification accuracy using a pattern of processing strengths and weaknesses method with multiple measures. *Journal of Psychoeducational Assessment, 36*, 21–33. doi:10.1177/0734282916683287

Moore, A. F., McCallum, R. S., & Bracken, B. A. (2017). The Universal Nonverbal Intelligence Test: Second Edition. In R. A. McCallum (Ed.), *Handbook of nonverbal assessment* (2nd ed., pp. 105–126). New York, NY: Springer.

Mrazik, M., Janzen, T. M., Dombrowski, S. C., Barford, S. W., & Krawchuk, L. L. (2012). Administration and scoring errors of graduate students learning the WISC-IV: Issues and controversies. *Canadian Journal of School Psychology, 27*, 279–290.

Naglieri, J. A. (2011). The discrepancy/consistency approach to SLD identification using the PASS theory. In D. P. Flanagan & V. C. Alfonso (Eds.), *Essentials of specific learning disability identification* (pp. 145–172). Hoboken, NJ: Wiley & Sons.

Naglieri, J. A. (2016). *Naglieri Nonverbal Ability Test, Third Edition*. New York, NY: Pearson.

Naglieri, J. A. (2017). *Essentials of CAS2 assessment*. New York, NY: Wiley.

Naglieri, J. A., Booth, A. L., & Winsler, A. (2004). Comparison of Hispanic children with and without limited English proficiency on the Naglieri Nonverbal Ability Test. *Psychological Assessment, 16*, 81–84.

Naglieri, J. A., & Das, J. P. (1997). *Cognitive Assessment System*. Itasca, IL: Riverside Publishing.

Naglieri, J. A., Das, J. P., & Goldstein, S. (2014a). *Cognitive Assessment System, Second Edition*. Austin, TX: PRO-ED.

Naglieri, J. A., Das, J. P., & Goldstein, S. (2014b). *Cognitive Assessment System, Second Edition: Brief*. Austin, TX: PRO-ED.

Naglieri, J. A., Das, J. P., & Goldstein, S. (2014c). *Cognitive Assessment System, Second Edition: Rating Scale*. Austin, TX: PRO-ED.

Naglieri, J. A., Moreno, M. A., & Otero, T. (2017). *Cognitive Assessment System, Second Edition: Spanish*. Austin, TX: PRO-ED.

Naglieri, J. A., & Otero, T. M. (2018a). Redefining intelligence with the planning, attention, simultaneous, and successive theory of neurocognitive processes. In D. P. Flanagan & E. M. McDonough (Eds.), *Contemporary intellectual assessment: Theories, tests, and issues* (4th ed., pp. 195–218). New York, NY: Guilford.

Naglieri, J. A., & Otero, T. M. (2018b). The Wechsler Nonverbal Scale of Ability: Assessment of culturally and linguistically diverse populations. In D. P. Flanagan & E. M. McDonough (Eds.), *Contemporary intellectual assessment: Theories, tests, and issues* (4th ed., pp. 512–532). New York, NY: Guilford Press.

National Association for Gifted Children (2014–2015). *State of the states in gifted education: Policy and practice*. Washington, DC: National Association for Gifted Children.

National Association of School Psychologists. (2010a). *Principles for professional ethics*. Bethesda, MD: Author. Retrieved from www.nasponline.org/standards/2010standards.aspx

National Association of School Psychologists. (2010b). *Position statement on identification of students with specific learning disabilities*. Bethesda, MD: Author. Retrieved from www.nasponline.org/profdevel/online-learning.aspx

National Center for Education Statistics. (2019). *Digest of education statistics: 2019*. Washington, DC: U.S. Department of Education. https://nces.ed.gov/.

National Joint Committee on Learning Disabilities. (2010, June). Comprehensive assessment and evaluation of students with learning disabilities. Retrieved from www.ldanatl.org/pdf/NJCLD%2520Comp%2520Assess%2520Paper%2520

National Research Council. (2002). *Mental retardation: Determining eligibility for Social Security benefits*. Washington, DC: National Academy Press.

Neisser, U., Boodoo, G., Bouchard, T. J., Jr., Boykin, A. W., Brody, N., Ceci, S. J., et al. (1996). Intelligence: Knowns and unknowns. *American Psychologist, 51*, 77–101.

Nelson, J. M., & Canivez, G. L. (2012). Examination of the structural, convergent, and incremental validity of the Reynolds Intellectual Assessment Scales (RIAS) with a clinical sample. *Psychological Assessment, 24*, 129–140.

Nelson, J. M., Canivez, G. L., Lindstrom, W., & Hatt, C. V. (2007). Higher-order exploratory factor analysis of the Reynolds Intellectual Assessment Scales with a referred sample. *Journal of School Psychology, 45*, 439–456.

Nelson, J. M., Canivez, G. L., & Watkins, M. W. (2013). Structural and incremental validity of the Wechsler Adult Intelligence Scale—Fourth Edition (WAIS–IV) with a clinical sample. *Psychological Assessment, 25*, 618–630.

Nelson-Gray, R. O. (2003). Treatment utility of psychological assessment. *Psychological Assessment, 15*, 521–531.

Nese, J. F. T., Biancarosa, G., Anderson, D., Lai, C.-F., Alonzo, J., & Tindal, G. (2012). Within-year oral reading fluency with CBM: A comparison of models. *Reading and Writing, 25*, 887–915.

Nesselroade, J. R, Stigler, S. M., & Baltes, P. B. (1980). Regression toward the mean and the study of change. *Psychological Bulletin, 88*, 622–637.

Nicewander, W. A. (2018). Conditional reliability coefficients for test scores. *Psychological Methods, 23*(2), 351–362.

Nieves-Brull, A. I. (2006). *Evaluation of the culture–language matrix: A validation study of test performance in monolingual English speaking and bilingual English/Spanish speaking populations* (Doctoral dissertation). Retrieved from ProQuest (Accession No. 3286026).

Nisbett, R. E., Aronson, J., Blari, C., Dickens, W., Flynn, J., Halpern, D. F., & Turkheimer, E. (2012). Intelligence: News findings and theoretical developments. *American Psychologist, 67*, 130–159.

Nisbett, R. E., Zukier, H., & Lemley, R. E. (1981). The dilution effect: Nondiagnostic information weakens the implications of diagnostic information. *Cognitive Psychology, 12*, 248–277.

Noland, R. M. (2017). Intelligence testing using a tablet computer: Experiences with using Q-Interactive. *Training and Education in Professional Psychology, 11*(3), 156–163.

Norcross, J. C. (2010). The therapeutic relationship. In B. L. Duncan, S. D. Miller, B. E. Wampold, & M. A. Hubble (Eds.), *The heart and soul of change: Delivering what works in therapy* (pp. 113–141). Washington, DC: American Psychological Association. http://dx.doi.org/10.1037/12075-004

Norcross, J. C., Hogan, T. P., Koocher, G. P., & Maggio, L. A. (2017). *Clinician's guide to evidence-based practices: Behavioral health and addictions* (2nd ed.). New York, NY: Oxford University Press.

Norfolk, P. A., Farmer, R. L., Floyd, R. G., Woods, I. L., Hawkins, H. K., & Irby, S. M. (2015). Norm block sample sizes: A review of 17 individually administered intelligence tests. *Journal of Psychoeducational Assessment, 33*, 544–555.

Nunnally, J. C., & Bernstein, I. H. (1994). *Psychometric theory* (3rd ed.). New York, NY: McGraw-Hill.

Oades-Sese, G. V., Esquivel, G. B., & Añon, C. (2007). Identifying gifted and talented culturally and linguistically diverse children and adolescents. In G. B. Esquivel & E. C. Lopez (Eds.), *Handbook of multicultural school psychology: An interdisciplinary perspective* (pp. 453–478). Mahwah, NJ: Erlbaum.

O'Bryon, E. C., & Rogers, M. R. (2010). Bilingual school psychologists' assessment practices with English language learners. *Psychology in the Schools, 47*, 1018–1034.

Ortiz, S. O., Piazza, N., Ochoa, S. H., & Dynda, A. M. (2018). Testing with culturally and linguistically diverse populations: New directions in fairness and validity. In D. P. Flanagan & E. M. McDonough (Eds.), *Contemporary intellectual assessment: Theories, tests, and issues* (pp. 684–712). New York, NY: Guilford Press.

Ownby, R. L. (1997). *Psychological reports: A guide to report writing in professional psychology* (3rd ed.). New York, NY: Wiley.

Pagel, L. G. (2011). *Proofreading and editing precision*. Mason, OH: South-Western Cengage Learning.

Parrila, R. K., Das, J. P., Kendrick, M. E., Papadopoulos, T. C., & Kirby, J. R. (1999). Efficacy of a cognitive reading remediation program for at-risk children in grade 1. *Developmental Disabilities Bulletin, 27*, 1–31.

Payton, A. (2009). The impact of genetic research on our understanding of normal cognitive aging: 1995 to 2009. *Neuropsychological Review, 19*, 451–477.

Percy, M. (2007). Factors that cause or contribute to intellectual and developmental disabilities. In I. Brown & M. Percy (Eds.), *A comprehensive guide to intellectual and developmental disabilities* (pp. 125–148). Baltimore, MD: Brookes.

Pfeiffer, S. I. (2003). Challenges and opportunities for students who are gifted: What the experts say. *Gifted Child Quarterly, 47*, 161–169.

Pfeiffer, S. I. (2015). Gifted students with a coexisting disability: The twice exceptional. *Estudos de Psicologia, 32*, 717–727.

Pfeiffer, S. I., & Foley-Nicpon, M. (2018). Knowns and unknowns about students with disabilities who also happen to be intellectually gifted. In S. B. Kaufman (Ed.), *Twice exceptional: Supporting and educating bright and creative students with learning difficulties* (pp. 104–119). New York, NY: Oxford University Press.

Pfeiffer, S. I., Reddy, L. A., Kletzel, J. E., Schmelzer, E. R., & Boyer, L. M. (2000). The practitioner's view of IQ testing and profile analysis. *School Psychology Quarterly, 15*, 376–385.

Pfeiffer, S. I., Shaunessy-Dedrick, E., & Foley-Nicpon, M. (Eds.). (2018). *APA handbook of giftedness and talent*. Washington, DC: American Psychological Association.

Pham A. V., Castro-Olivo, S., Chun, H., & Goforth, A. N. (2017). Cognitive abilities in bilinguals in L1 and L2. In A. Ardila, A. Cieślicka, R. Heredia, & M. Rosselli (Eds.), *Psychology of bilingualism. The bilingual mind and brain book series* (pp. 269–291). Cham, Switzerland: Springer International Publishing.

Phillips, S. E. (1994). High stakes testing accommodations: Validity versus disabled rights. *Applied Measurement in Education, 7*, 93–120.

Pietschnig, J., & Voracek, M. (2015). One century of global IQ gains: A formal meta-analysis of the Flynn effect (1909–2013). *Perspectives on Psychological Science, 10*, 282–306.

Pinborough–Zimmerman, J., Satterfield, R., Miller, J., Bilder, D., Hossain, S., & McMahon, W. (2007). Communication disorders: Prevalence and comorbid intellectual disability, autism, and emotional/behavioral disorders. *American Journal of Speech–Language Pathology, 16*, 359–367.

Piovesana, A. M. Harrison, J. L., & Ducat, J. J. (2019). The development of a motor-free short-form of the Wechsler Intelligence Scale for Children—Fifth Edition. *Assessment, 26*, 1564–1572.

Platt, S. A., & Sanislow, C. A. (1988). Norm-of-reaction: Definition and misinterpretation of animal research. *Journal of Comparative Psychology, 102*, 254–261.

Ploetz, D. M., Mazur-Mosiewicz, A., Kirkwood, M. W., Sherman, E. M., & Brooks, B. L. (2016). Performance on the Test of Memory Malingering in children with neurological conditions. *Child Neuropsychology, 22*, 133–142.

Plomin, R., & Deary, I. J. (2015). Genetics and intelligence differences: Five special findings. *Molecular Psychiatry, 20*, 98–108.

Plomin, R., Haworth, C. M. A., & Davis, O. S. P. (2010). Genetics of learning abilities and disabilities: Recent developments from the UK and possible directions for research in China. *Behavior Genetics, 40*, 297–305.

Plomin, R., & Kovas, Y. (2005). Generalist genes and learning disabilities. *Psychological Bulletin, 131*, 592–617.

Polloway, E. A., Auguste, M., Smith, J. D., & Peters, D. (2017). An analysis of state guidelines for intellectual disability. *Education and Training in Autism and Developmental Disabilities, 52*, 332–339.

Popper, K. (1968). *Conjectures and refutations: The growth of scientific knowledge*. New York, NY: Harper.

Preacher, K. J., & Sterba, S. K. (2019). Aptitude-by-treatment interactions in research on educational interventions. *Exceptional Children, 85*, 248–264.

President's Committee on Mental Retardation. (1969). *The six-hour retarded child*. Washington, DC: U.S. Government Printing Office.

Prinstein, M. J., Youngstrom, E. A., Mash, E. J., & Barkley, R. A. (Eds.). (2019). *Treatment of disorders in childhood and adolescence* (4th ed.). New York, NY: Guilford Press.

Protzko, J. (2017). Raising IQ among school-aged children: Five meta-analyses and a review of randomized controlled trials. *Developmental Review, 46*, 81–101.

Raiford, S. E. (2017). *Essentials of WISC-V integrated assessment.* Hoboken, NJ: Wiley.

Raiford, S. E. (2018). The Wechsler Intelligence Scale for Children—Fifth Edition Integrated. In D. P. Flanagan & E. M. McDonough (Eds.), *Contemporary intellectual assessment: Theories, tests, and issues* (4th ed., pp. 302–332). New York, NY: Guilford Press.

Raiford, S. E., & Coalson, D. L. (2014). *Essentials of WPPSI-IV assessment.* Hoboken, NJ: Wiley.

Raiford, S. E., Drozdick, L., Zhang, O., & Zhou, X. (2015). *WISC-V technical report 1: Expanded index scores.* Bloomington, MN: Pearson.

Raiford, S. E., Zhang, O., Drozdick, L. W., Getz, K., Wahlstrom, D., Gabel, A., Holdnack, J. A., & Daniel, M. (2016). *Q-interactive technical report 12: WISC-V coding and symbol search in digital format: Reliability, validity, special group studies, and interpretation.* San Antonio, TX: Pearson.

Raines, T. C., Reynolds, C. R., & Kamphaus, R. W. (2018). The Reynolds Intellectual Screening Test, Second Edition, and the Reynolds Intellectual Screening Test, Second Edition. In D. P. Flanagan & E. M. McDonough (Eds.), *Contemporary intellectual assessment: Theories, tests, and issues* (4th ed., pp. 533–552). New York, NY: Guilford Press.

Raju, N. S., Price, L. R., Oshima, T. C., & Nering, M. L. (2007). Standardized conditional SEM: A case for conditional reliability. *Applied Psychological Measurement, 31*(3), 169–180.

Rambo, P. L., Callahan, J. L., Hogan, L. R., Hullmann, S., & Wrape, E. (2015). Effort testing in children: Can cognitive and symptom validity measures differentiate malingered performances? *Applied Neuropsychology: Child, 4*, 1–8.

Rasch, G. (1960). *Probabilistic models for some intelligence and attainment tests.* Copenhagen: Danmarks Paedagogiske Institut.

Reddy, L. A., Forman, S. G., Stoiber, K. C., & Gonzalez, J. E. (2017). A national investigation of school psychology trainers' attitudes and beliefs about evidence-based practices. *Psychology in the Schools, 54*, 261–278.

Redfield, R., Linton, R., & Herskovitz, M. J. (1936). Memorandum for the study of acculturation. *American Anthropologist, 38*, 149–152.

Reis, S. M., & Renzulli, J. S. (2011). Intellectual giftedness. In R. J. Sternberg & S. B. Kaufman (Eds.), *The Cambridge handbook of intelligence* (pp. 235–252). Cambridge, UK: Cambridge University Press.

Reise, S. P. (2012). The rediscovery of bifactor measurement models. *Multivariate Behavioral Research, 47*, 777–696.

Renzulli, J. S. (1978). What makes giftedness?: Reexamining a definition. *Phi Delta Kappan, 60*, 180–184, 261.

Renzulli, J. S. (1986). The three ring conceptualization of giftedness: A developmental model for creative productivity. In R. J. Sternberg & J. E. Davidson (Eds.), *Conceptions of giftedness* (pp. 246–279). New York, NY: Cambridge University Press.

Renzulli, J. S., & Reis, S. M. (2018). The three-ring conception of giftedness: A developmental approach for promoting creative productivity in young people. In S. I. Pfeiffer, E. Shaunessy-Dedrick, & M. Foley-Nicpon (Eds.), *APA handbook of giftedness and talent* (pp. 185–199). Washington, DC: American Psychological Association.

Reschly, D. J., & Grimes, J. P. (1990). Intellectual assessment. In A. Thomas & J. Grimes (Eds.), *Best practices in school psychology II* (pp. 425–439). Washington, DC: National Association of School Psychologists.

Revelle, W., Wilt, J., & Condon, D. M. (2011). Individual differences and differential psychology: A brief history and prospect. In T. Chamorro-Premuzic, S. von Stumm, & A. Furnham

(Eds.), *The Wiley-Blackwell handbook of personality and individual differences* (pp. 3–38). Malden, MA: Wiley-Blackwell.

Reynolds, C. R. (1984–1985). Critical measurement issues in learning disabilities. *Journal of Special Education, 18*, 451–476.

Reynolds, C. R. (2009). RTI, neuroscience, and sense: Chaos in the diagnosis and treatment of learning disabilities. In E. Fletcher-Janzen & C. R. Reynolds (Eds.), *Neuropsychological perspectives on learning disabilities in the era of RTI: Recommendations for diagnosis and intervention* (pp. 14–27). Hoboken, NJ: Wiley.

Reynolds, C. R., & Carson, A. D. (2005). Methods for assessing cultural bias in tests. In C. L. Frisby & C. R. Reynolds (Eds.), *Comprehensive handbook of multicultural school psychology* (pp. 795–823). Hoboken, NJ: Wiley.

Reynolds, C. R., & Kaiser, S. (1992). Test bias in psychological assessment. In T. B. Gutkin & C. R. Reynolds (Eds.), *The handbook of school psychology* (2nd ed., pp. 487–525). New York, NY: Wiley.

Reynolds, C. R., & Kamphaus, R. W. (2015a). *Behavioral Assessment System for Children, Third Edition*. New York, NY: Pearson.

Reynolds, C. R., & Kamphaus, R. W. (2015b). *Reynolds Intellectual Assessment Scales, Second Edition*. Lutz, FL: Psychological Assessment Resources.

Reynolds, C. R., Lowe, P. A., & Saenz, A. (1999). The problem of bias in psychological assessment. In C. R. Reynolds & T. B. Gutkin (Eds.), *The handbook of school psychology* (3rd ed., pp. 549–595). New York, NY: Wiley.

Reynolds, C. R., & Shaywitz, S. E. (2009). Response to intervention: Ready or not? Or, from wait-to-fail to watch-them-fail. *School Psychology Quarterly, 24*, 130–145.

Reynolds, C. R., & Suzuki, L. A. (2013). Bias in psychological assessment: An empirical review and recommendations. In J. R. Graham, J. A. Naglieri, & I. B. Weiner (Eds.), *Handbook of psychology: Assessment psychology* (pp. 82–113). Hoboken, NJ: Wiley.

Reynolds, M. R. (2013). Interpreting intelligence test composite scores in light of Spearman's law of diminishing returns. *School Psychology Quarterly, 28*, 63–76.

Reynolds, M. R., Floyd, R. G., & Niileksela, C. R. (2013). How well is psychometric g indexed by global composites? Evidence from three popular intelligence tests. *Psychological Assessment, 25*, 1314–1321.

Reynolds, M. R., & Keith, T. Z. (2017). Multi-group and hierarchical confirmatory factor analysis of the Wechsler Intelligence Scale for Children—Fifth Edition: What does it measure? *Intelligence, 62*, 31–47.

Reynolds, M. R., Keith, T. Z., & Beretvas, S. N. (2010). Use of factor mixture modeling to capture Spearman's law of diminishing returns. *Intelligence, 38*, 231–241.

Reynolds, M. R., Keith, T. Z., Fine, J. G., Fisher, M. E., & Low, J. (2007). Confirmatory factor structure of the Kaufman Assessment Battery for Children—Second Edition: Consistency with Cattell-Horn-Carroll theory. *School Psychology Quarterly, 22*, 511–539.

Reynolds, M. R., & Niileksela, C. R. (2015). Test review. [Review of the test *Woodcock-Johnson IV Tests of Cognitive Abilities*]. *Journal of Psychoeducational Assessment, 33*, 299–311.

Rhodes, R. L., Ochoa, S. H., & Ortiz, S. O. (2005). *Assessing culturally and linguistically diverse students: A practical guide*. New York, NY: Guilford Press.

Rigney, A. M. (2018). Test review. [Review of the test *Detroit Tests of Learning Abilities—Fifth Edition*]. *Journal of Psychoeducational Assessment*, 1–5. https://doi.org/10.1177/0734282918793291

Roid, G. H. (2003). *Stanford-Binet Intelligence Scales, Fifth Edition*. Itasca, IL: Riverside Publishing.

Roid, G. H., & Barram, A. (2004). *Essentials of Stanford-Binet Intelligence Scales (SB5) assessment*. Hoboken, NJ: Wiley.

Roid, G. H., & Koch, C. (2017). Leiter-3: Nonverbal cognitive and neuropsychological assessment. In R. A. McCallum (Ed.), *Handbook of nonverbal assessment* (2nd ed., pp. 127–150). New York, NY: Springer.

Roid, G. H., Miller, L. J., Pomplun, M., & Koch, C. (2013). *Leiter International Performance Scale, Third Edition*. Wood Dale, IL: Stoelting.

Rosa's law, Pub. L. No. 111-256 (2010).

Roth, B., Becker, N., Romeyke, S. Shaefer, S., Domnick, F., & Spinath, F. (2015). Intelligence and school grades: A meta-analysis. *Intelligence, 53*, 118–137.

Rowe, D. C. (1994). *The limits of family influence: Genes, experience, and behavior*. New York, NY: Guilford Press.

Rushton, P. J. (1995). *Race, evolution and behavior: A life history perspective*. New Brunswick, NJ: Transaction.

Rushton, J. P., & Ankney, C. D. (2009). Whole brain size and general mental ability: A review. *International Journal of Neuroscience, 119*, 692–732.

Ryan-Arredondo, K., & Sandoval, J. (2005). Psychometric issues in the measurement of acculturation. In C. L. Frisby & C. R. Reynolds (Eds.), *Comprehensive handbook of multicultural school psychology* (pp. 861–880). Hoboken, NJ: Wiley.

Sala, G., & Gobet, F. (2016). Do the benefits of chess instruction transfer to academic and cognitive skills? A meta-analysis. *Educational Research Review, 18*, 46–57.

Sala, G., & Gobet, F. (2017). Does far transfer exist? Negative evidence from chess, music, and working memory training. *Current Directions in Psychological Science, 26*(6), 515–520.

Sala, G., & Gobet, F. (2019). Cognitive training does not enhance general cognition. *Trends in Cognitive Sciences, 23*, 10–20.

Salthouse, T. A. (2010). *Major issues in cognitive aging*. New York, NY: Oxford University Press.

Salthouse, T. A. (2019). Trajectories of normal cognitive aging. *Psychology and Aging, 34*, 17–24.

Sattler, J. M. (2008). *Assessment of children: Cognitive foundations* (5th ed.). San Diego, CA: Author.

Sattler, J. M. (2018). *Assessment of children: Cognitive foundations and applications* (6th ed.). La Mesa, CA: Author.

Schalock, R. L., Luckasson, R. A., Bradley, V., Buntinx, W. H. E., Lachapelle, Y., Shogren, K. A., . . . Wehmeyer, M. L. (2012). *Intellectual disability: Definition, classification, and system of supports (11th edition) user's guide*. Washington, DC: American Association on Intellectual and Developmental Disabilities.

Schneider, W. J. (2011, March 29). A geometric representation of composite scores [Video file]. Retrieved from http://assessingpsyche.wordpress.com/2011/03/29/a-geometric-representation-of-composite-scores

Schneider, W. J. (2013). What if we took our models seriously? Estimating latent scores in individuals. *Journal of Psychoeducational Assessment, 31*, 186–201.

Schneider, W. J. (2016). Why are WJ IV cluster scores more extreme than the average of their parts? A gentle explanation of the composite score extremity effect. *Woodcock-Johnson IV Assessment Service Bulletin* (No. 7). Itasca, IL: Houghton Mifflin Harcourt.

Schneider, W. J., Lichtenberger, E. O., Mather, N., & Kaufman, N. L. (2018). *Essentials of assessment report writing*. Hoboken, NJ: Wiley.

Schneider, W. J., & McGrew, K. S. (2018). The Cattell-Horn-Carroll theory of cognitive abilities. In D. P. Flanagan & E. M. McDonough (Eds.), *Contemporary intellectual assessment: Theories, tests, and issues* (4th ed., pp. 73–162). New York, NY: Guilford.

Schneider, W. J., & Roman, Z. (2018). Fine-tuning cross-battery assessment procedures: After follow-up testing, use all valid scores, cohesive or not. *Journal of Psychoeducational Assessment, 36*, 34–54.

Schrank, F. A., Decker, S. L., & Garruto, J. M. (2016). *Essentials of WJ IV Cognitive Abilities assessment*. Hoboken, NJ: Wiley.

Schrank, F. A., Mather, N., & McGrew, K. S. (2014a). *Woodcock-Johnson IV Tests of Achievement*. Rolling Meadows, IL: Riverside Publishing.

Schrank, F. A., Mather, N., & McGrew, K. S. (2014c). *Woodcock-Johnson IV Tests of Oral Language*. Rolling Meadows, IL: Riverside Publishing.

Schrank, F. A., McGrew, K. S., & Mather, N. (2014b). *Woodcock-Johnson IV Tests of Cognitive Abilities*. Rolling Meadows, IL: Riverside Publishing.

Schrank, F. A., & Wendling, B. J. (2018). The Woodcock-Johnson IV: Tests of Cognitive Abilities, Tests of Oral Language, and Tests of Achievement. In D. P. Flanagan & E. M. McDonough (Eds.), *Contemporary intellectual assessment: Theories, tests, and issues* (4th ed., pp. 383–451). New York, NY: Guilford Press.

Selzam, S., Dale, P. S., Wagner, R. K., DeFries, J. C., Cederlöf, O'Reilly, P. F., Drapohl, E., & Plomin, R. (2017). Genome-polygenic scores predict reading performance throughout the school years. *Scientific Studies of Reading, 21*, 334–349.

Semrud-Clikeman, M., Wilkinson, A., & Wellington, T. M. (2005). Evaluating and using qualitative approaches to neuropsychological assessment. In R. C. D'Amato, E. Fletcher-Janzen, & C. R. Reynolds (Eds.), *Handbook of school neuropsychology* (pp. 287–302). Hoboken, NJ: Wiley.

Shaw, S. R. (2010, February). Rescuing students from the slow learner trap. *Principal Leadership, 10*(6), 12–16.

Shepard, L. A. (1989). Identification of mild handicaps. In R. L. Linn (Ed.), *Educational measurement* (3rd ed., pp. 545–572). New York, NY: American Council on Education/Macmillan.

Sherman, E. M. S., & Brooks, B. L. (2015). *Memory validity profile*. Lutz, FL: Psychological Assessment Resources, Inc.

Shinn, M. R. (2005). Identifying and validating academic problems in a problem-solving model. In R. Brown-Chidsey (Ed.), *Assessment for intervention: A problem-solving approach* (pp. 219–246). New York, NY: Guilford Press.

Shinn, M. R. (2007). Identifying students at risk, monitoring performance, and determining eligibility within response to intervention: Research on educational need and benefit from academic intervention. *School Psychology Review, 36*, 601–617.

Shinn, M. R., & Bamonto, S. (1998). Advanced applications of curriculum-based measurement: "Big ideas" and avoiding confusion. In M. R. Shinn (Ed.), *Advanced applications of curriculum-based measurement* (pp. 1–31). New York, NY: Guilford Press.

Shinn, M. R., & Habedank, L. (1992). Curriculum-based measurement in special education problem identification and certification decisions. *Preventing School Failure, 36*, 11–15.

Shriberg, L. D. (1993). Four new speech and prosody voice measures for genetics research and other studies in developmental phonological disorders. *Journal of Speech and Hearing Research, 36*, 105–140.

Siegel, L. S. (1989). I.Q. is irrelevant to the definition of learning disabilities. *Journal of Learning Disabilities, 22*, 469–478.

Siegel, L. S. (1992). An evaluation of the discrepancy definition of dyslexia. *Journal of Learning Disabilities, 25*, 618–629.

Simonton, D. K. (2009). The "other IQ": Historiometric assessments of intelligence and related constructs. *Review of General Psychology, 13*, 315–326.

Simonton, D. K. (2018). From giftedness to eminence: Developmental landmarks across the lifespan. In S. L., Pfeiffer, E. Shaunessy-Dedrick, & M. Foley-Nicpon (Eds.), *APA handbook of giftedness and talent* (pp. 273–285). Washington, DC: American Psychological Association.

Skibbe, L. E., Grimm, K. J., Bowles, R. P., & Morrison, F. J. (2012). Literacy growth in the academic year versus summer from preschool through second grade: Differential effects of schooling across four skills. *Scientific Studies of Reading, 16*, 141–165.

Streiner, D. L. (2003). Starting at the beginning: An introduction to coefficient alpha and internal consistency. *Journal of Personality Assessment, 80*, 99–103.

Snow, R. E. (1998). Abilities as aptitudes and achievements in learning situations. In J. J. McArdle & R. W. Woodcock (Eds.), *Human cognitive abilities in theory and practice* (pp. 93–112). Mahwah, NJ: Erlbaum.

Snow, R. E., & Lohman, D. F. (1984). Toward a theory of cognitive aptitude for learning from instruction. *Journal of Educational Psychology, 76*, 347–376.

Snow, R. E., & Yalow, E. (1984). Education and intelligence. In R. J. Sternberg (Ed.), *Handbook of intelligence* (pp. 493–585). New York, NY: Cambridge.

Snowling, M. J., & Melby-Lervåg, M. (2016). Oral language deficits in familial dyslexia: A meta-analysis and review. *Psychological Bulletin, 142*, 498–545.

Snyderman, M., & Rothman, S. (1987). Survey of expert opinion on intelligence and aptitude testing. *American Psychologist, 42*, 137–144.

Sotelo-Dynega, M., & Dixon, S. G. (2014). Cognitive assessment practices: A survey of school psychologists. *Psychology in the Schools, 51*, 1031–1045.

Sparrow, S. S., Cicchetti, D. V., & Saulnier, C. A. (2016). *Vineland Adaptive Behavior Scales* (3rd ed.). New York, NY: Pearson.

Spearman, C. E. (1904). "General intelligence" objectively determined and measured. *American Journal of Psychology, 15*, 201–293.

Spearman, C. E. (1927). *The abilities of man.* London: Macmillan.

Spearman, C. E., & Jones, L. (1950). *Human ability.* London: Macmillan.

Spitz, H. H. (1986). *The raising of intelligence: A selected history of attempts to raise retarded intelligence.* Hillsdale, NJ: Erlbaum.

Spitz, H. H. (1999). *Attempts to raise intelligence.* Hove, UK: Psychology Press/Taylor & Francis.

Stanovich, K. E., & Siegel, L. S. (1994). Phenotypic performance profile of children with reading disabilities: A regression-based test of the phonological-core variable-difference model. *Journal of Educational Psychology, 86*, 24–53.

Steege, M. W., Pratt, J. L., Wickerd, G., Guare, R., & Watson, T. S. (2019). *Conducting school-based functional behavioral assessments: A practitioner's guide* (3rd ed.). New York, NY: Guilford Press.

Stephens, K. R. (2011). Federal and state response to the gifted and talented. *Journal of Applied School Psychology, 27*, 306–318.

Stephens, K. R., & Karnes, F. A. (2000). State definitions for the gifted and talented revisited. *Exceptional Children, 66*, 219–238.

Stern, W. (1912). *The psychological methods of intelligence testing.* Baltimore, MD: Warwick & York.

Sternberg, R. J. (1994). 468 factor-analyzed data sets: What they tell us and don't tell us about human intelligence. *Psychological Science, 5*, 63–65.

Sternberg, R. J. (1996). Myths, countermyths, and truths about intelligence. *Educational Researcher, 25*, 11–16.

Sternberg, R. J. (2018). The triarchic theory of successful intelligence. In D. P. Flanagan & E. M. McDonough (Eds.), *Contemporary intellectual assessment: Theories, tests, and issues* (4th ed., pp. 174–194). New York, NY: Guilford.

Sternberg, R. J., & Detterman, D. K. (1986). *What is intelligence?: Contemporary viewpoints on its nature and definition.* Norwood, NJ: Ablex.

Sternberg, R. J., & Kaufman, S. B. (Eds.). (2011). *The Cambridge handbook of intelligence.* New York, NY: Cambridge.

Stojanoski, B., Lyons, K. M., Pearce, A. A. A., & Owen, A. M. (2018). Targeted training: Converging evidence against the transferable benefits of online brain training on cognitive function. *Neuropsychologia, 117*, 541–550.

Styck, K. M., Beaujean, A. A., & Watkins, M. W. (2019). Profile reliability of cognitive ability subscores in a referred sample. *Archives of Scientific Psychology, 7*, 119–128.

Styck, K. M., & Walsh, S. M. (2016). Evaluating the prevalence and impact of examiner errors on the Wechsler scales of intelligence: A meta-analysis. *Psychological Assessment, 28*(1), 3–17.

Styck, K. M., & Watkins, M. W. (2013). Diagnostic utility of the Culture-Language Interpretive Matrix for the Wechsler Intelligence Scales for Children—Fourth Edition among referred students. *School Psychology Review, 42*, 367–382.

Styck, K. M., & Watkins, M. W. (2014). Discriminant validity of the WISC-IV Culture-Language Interpretive Matrix. *Contemporary School Psychology, 18*, 168–177.

Subotnik, R. F., Olszewski-Kubilius, P., & Worrell, F. C. (2011). Rethinking giftedness and gifted education: A proposed direction forward based on psychological science. *Psychological Science in the Public Interest, 12*, 3–54.

Sullivan, A. L., Artiles, A. J., & Hernandez-Saca, D. (2017). Systemic approaches to addressing disproportionality of culturally and linguistically diverse students in special education. In E. C. Lopez, S. G. Nahari, & S. L. Proctor (Eds.), *Handbook of multicultural school psychology: An interdisciplinary perspective* (pp. 306–322). New York, NY: Routledge/Taylor & Francis Group.

Suttle, C. M. (2001). Visual acuity assessment in infants and young children. *Clinical and Experimental Optometry, 84*, 337–345.

Suzuki, L. A., Short, E. L., & Lee, C. S. (2011). Racial and ethnic group differences in intelligence in the United States. In R. J. Sternberg & S. B. Kaufman (Eds.), *The Cambridge handbook of intelligence* (pp. 273–292). Cambridge, UK: Cambridge University Press.

Swanson, H. L. (2009). Neuroscience and RTI: A complementary role. In E. Fletcher-Janzen & C. R. Reynolds (Eds.), *Neuropsychological perspectives on learning disabilities in the era of RTI: Recommendations for diagnosis and intervention* (pp. 28–53). Hoboken, NJ: Wiley.

Sweller, J. (1994). Cognitive load theory, learning difficulty, and instructional design. *Learning and instruction, 4*, 295–312.

Sweller, J. (2010). Element interactivity and intrinsic, extraneous, and germane cognitive load. *Educational psychology review, 22*(2), 123–138.

Syeda, M. M., & Climie, E. A. (2014). Test review. [Review of the test *Wechsler Preschool and Primary Scale of Intelligence, Fourth Edition*]. *Journal of Psychoeducational Assessment, 32*, 265–272.

Tallent, N. (1993). *Psychological report writing* (4th ed.). Englewood Cliffs, NJ: Prentice-Hall.

Tannenbaum, A. J. (1986). Giftedness: A psychosocial approach. In R. J. Sternberg & J. E. Davidson (Eds.), *Conceptions of giftedness* (pp. 21–52). New York, NY: Cambridge University Press.

Tannenbaum, A. J. (2003). Nature and nurture of giftedness. In N. Colangelo & G. A. Davis (Eds.), *Handbook of gifted education* (pp. 45–59). Boston, MA: Allyn & Bacon.

Taylor, W. P., Miciak, J., Fletcher, J. M., & Francis, D. J. (2017). Cognitive discrepancy models for specific learning disabilities identification: Simulations of psychometric limitations. *Psychological Assessment, 29*, 446–457. doi:10.1037/pas0000356

Teller, D. Y., McDonald, M. A., Preston, K., Sebris, S. L., & Dobson, V. (2008). Assessment of visual acuity in infants and children: The acuity card procedure. *Developmental Medicine and Child Neurology, 28*, 779–789.

Terman, L. M. (1916). *The measurement of intelligence*. Boston, MA: Houghton Mifflin.

Terman, L. M. (Ed.). (1925). *Genetic studies of genius: Vol. 1. Mental and physical traits of a thousand gifted children*. Stanford, CA: Stanford University Press.

Terman, L. M. (1954). The discovery and encouragement of exceptional talent. *American Psychologist, 9*, 221–230.

Terman, L. M., & Oden, M. H. (1947). *Genetic studies of genius: Vol. 4. The gifted child grows up: Twenty-five years' follow up of a superior group*. Stanford, CA: Stanford University Press.

Terman, L. M., & Oden, M. H. (1959). *Genetic studies of genius: Vol. 5. The gifted group at midlife: Thirty-five years' follow up of the superior child*. Stanford. CA: Stanford University Press.

Therrien, W. J., Zaman, M., & Banda, D. (2011). How can meta-analyses guide practice?: A review of the learning disability research base. *Remedial and Special Education, 32*, 206–218.

Thompson, B. (2004). *Exploratory and confirmatory factor analysis: Understanding concepts and applications*. Washington, DC: American Psychological Association.

Thompson, T., Coleman, J. M., Riley, K., Snider, L. A., Howard, L. J., Sansone, S. M., & Hessl, D. (2018). Standardized assessment accommodations for individuals with intellectual disability. *Contemporary School Psychology, 22*, 443–457.

Thorndike, R. L. (1985). The central role of general ability in prediction. *Multivariate Behavioral Research, 20*, 241–254.

Thorndike, R. L. (1994). g. [Editorial]. *Intelligence, 19*, 145–155.

Thurstone, L. L. (1938). *Primary mental abilities*. Chicago, IL: University of Chicago Press.

Thurstone, L. L. (1954). An analytical method for simple structure. *Psychometrika, 19*, 173–194.

Tombaugh, T. N. (1996). *Test of Memory Malingering*. North Tonawanda, NY: Multi-Health Systems.

Tonks, J., Whitfield, C. K., Williams, W. H., Slater, A. M., & Frampton, I. J. (2018). "Must try harder." Is effort and performance validity testing a necessary part of pediatric neuropsychological assessment? *Applied Neuropsychology: Child*. doi:10.1080/21622965.2018.1524766

Torgesen, J. K., Alexander, A., Wagner, R., Rashotte, C., Voeller, K., & Conway, T. (2001). Intensive remedial instruction for children with severe reading disabilities: Immediate and long-term outcomes from two instructional approaches. *Journal of Learning Disabilities, 34*, 33–58.

Trahan, L., Stuebing, K. K., Hiscock, M. K., & Fletcher, J. M. (2014). The Flynn effect: A meta-analysis. *Psychological Bulletin, 140*, 1332–1360.

Tychanska, J. (2009). *Evaluation of speech and language impairment using the culture–language test classifications and interpretive matrix* (Doctoral dissertation). Retrieved from ProQuest (Accession No. 3365687).

United States Census Bureau. (2019, December 16). *Language use in the United States: 2011*. Retrieved from https://www.census.gov/library/publications/2013/acs/acs-22.html

Valencia, R. R. (1988). The McCarthy scales and Hispanic children: A review of psychometric research. *Hispanic Journal of Behavioral Sciences, 10*, 81–104.

Valencia, R. R., & Lopez, R. (1992). Assessment of racial and ethnic minority students: Problems and prospects. In M. Zeidner & R. Most (Eds.), *Psychological testing: An inside view* (pp. 399–439). Palo Alto, CA: Consulting Psychologists Press.

VanTassel-Baska, J. (2005). Domain-specific giftedness: Applications in school and life. In R. J. Sternberg & J. E. Davidson (Eds.), *Conceptions of giftedness* (pp. 358–376). New York, NY: Cambridge University Press.

Vaughn, S., & Fuchs, L. S. (2003). Redefining learning disabilities as inadequate response to instruction: The promise and potential problems. *Learning Disabilities Research and Practice, 18*, 137–146.

Vazquez-Nuttall, E., Li, C., Dynda, A. M., Ortiz, S. O., Armengol, C. G., Walton, J. W., & Phonenix, K. (2007). Cognitive assessment of culturally and linguistically diverse students. In G. B. Esquivel & E. C. Lopez (Eds.), *Handbook of multicultural school psychology: An interdisciplinary perspective* (pp. 265–288). Mahwah, NJ: Erlbaum.

Vellutino, F. R., Scanlon, D. M., Sipay, E. R., Small, S. G., Pratt, A., & Chen, R., et al. (1996). Cognitive profiles of difficult-to-remediate and readily remediated poor readers: Early intervention as a vehicle for distinguishing between cognitive and experiential deficits as basic causes of specific reading disability. *Journal of Educational Psychology, 88*, 601–638.

Verderosa, F. A. (2007). *Examining the effects of language and culture on the differential ability scales with bilingual preschoolers* (Doctoral dissertation). Retrieved from ProQuest (Accession No. 3286027).

Vissers, L. E. L. M., Gilissen, C., & Veltman, J. A. (2016). Genetic studies in intellectual disability and related disorders. *Nature Reviews Genetics, 17*, 9–18.

Wahlstrom, D., Raiford, S. E., Breaux, K. C., Zhu, J., & Weiss, L. G. (2018). The Wechsler Preschool and Primary Scale of Intelligence—Fourth Edition, Wechsler Intelligence Scale for Children—Fifth Edition, and Wechsler Individual Achievement Test—Third Edition. In D. P. Flanagan & E. M. McDonough (Eds.), *Contemporary intellectual assessment: Theories, tests, and issues* (4th ed., pp. 245–282). New York, NY: Guilford Press.

Walcott, C. M., McNamara, K., Hyson, D., & Charvat, J. L. (2018). *The NASP 2015 membership survey, part one: Demographics and employment conditions.* Washington, DC: National Association of School Psychologists.

Walters, J., & Gardner, H. (1986). The crystallizing experience: Discovery of an intellectual gift. In R. Sternberg & J. E. Davidson (Eds.), *Conceptions of giftedness* (pp. 163–182). New York, NY: Cambridge University Press.

Warne, R. T. (2016). Five Reasons to put the g back into giftedness: An argument for applying the Cattell-Horn-Carroll theory of intelligence to gifted education research and practice. *Gifted Child Quarterly, 60*, 3–15.

Wasserman, J. D. (2019) Deconstructing CHC. *Applied Measurement in Education, 32*, 249–268. doi:10.1080/08957347.2019.1619563

Watkins, M. W. (2009). Errors in diagnostic decision making and clinical judgment. In T. B. Gutkin & C. R. Reynolds (Eds.), *The handbook of school psychology* (4th ed., pp. 210–229). Hoboken, NJ: Wiley.

Watkins, M. W. (2017). The reliability of multidimensional neuropsychological measures: From alpha to omega. *Clinical Neuropsychologist, 31*, 1113–1126.

Watkins, M. W., & Beaujean, A. A. (2014). Bifactor structure of the Wechsler preschool and primary scale of intelligence—fourth edition. *School Psychology Quarterly, 29*, 52–63.

Watkins, M. W., & Canivez, G. L. (2004). Temporal stability of WISC-III subtest composite: Strengths and weaknesses. *Psychological Assessment, 16*, 133–138.

Watkins, M. W., Glutting, J. J., & Lei, P. (2007). Validity of the Full-Scale IQ when there is significant variability among WISC-III and WISC-IV factor scores. *Applied Neuropsychology, 14*, 13–20.

Watkins, M. W., & Smith, L. (2013). Long-term stability of the Wechsler Intelligence Scale for Children—Fourth Edition. *Psychological Assessment, 25*, 477–483.

Wechsler, D. (1939). *The measurement of adult intelligence.* Baltimore, MD: Williams & Wilkins.

Wechsler, D. (1949). *Wechsler Intelligence Scale for Children.* San Antonio, TX: Psychological Corporation.

Wechsler, D. (1974). *Wechsler Intelligence Scale for Children, Revised.* San Antonio, TX: Psychological Corporation.

Wechsler, D. (1991). *Wechsler Intelligence Scale for Children* (3rd ed.). San Antonio, TX:

Wechsler, D. (2003). *Wechsler Intelligence Scale for Children* (4th ed.). San Antonio, TX: Psychological Corporation.

Wechsler, D. (2008). *Wechsler Adult Intelligence Scale* (4th ed.). San Antonio, TX: Pearson Assessments.

Wechsler, D. (2011). *Wechsler Abbreviated Scale of Intelligence* (2nd ed.). San Antonio, TX: Pearson Assessments.

Wechsler, D. (2012). *Wechsler Preschool and Primary Scale of Intelligence* (4th ed.). San Antonio, TX: Pearson Assessments.

Wechsler, D. (2014a). *Wechsler Intelligence Scale for Children* (5th ed.). San Antonio, TX: Pearson Assessment.

Wechsler, D. (2014b). *Wechsler Intelligence Scale for Children, Canadian Edition* (5th ed.). Toronto, Ontario: Pearson Canada Assessment.

Wechsler, D. (2014c). *Wechsler Intelligence Scale for Children technical and interpretive manual* (5th ed.). San Antonio, TX: Pearson Assessment.

Wechsler, D. (2017). *Wechsler Intelligence Scale for Children, Spanish* (5th ed.). San Antonio, TX: Pearson Assessment.

Wechsler, D., & Kaplan, E. (2014). *Wechsler Intelligence Scale for Children Integrated* (5th ed.). Bloomington, MN: Pearson.

Wechsler, D., & Naglieri, J. A. (2006). *Wechsler Nonverbal Scale of Ability.* New York, NY: Pearson.

Wharton-Michael, P. (2008). Print vs. computer screen: Effects of medium on proofreading accuracy. *Journalism and Mass Communication Educator, 63*, 28–41.

Wehmeyer, M. L. (Ed.). (2013). *The story of intellectual disability: An evolution of meaning, understanding, & public perception.* Baltimore, MD: Brookes.

Weiss, L. G., Saklofske, D. H., Coalson, D., & Raiford, S. E. (2010). *WAIS-IV clinical use and interpretation: Scientist-practitioner perspectives.* London: Academic Press.

Weisz, J. R. (1990). Cultural-familial mental retardation: A developmental perspective on cognitive performance and "helpless" behavior. In R. M. Hodapp, J. A. Burack, & E. Zigler (Eds.), *Issues in the developmental approach to mental retardation* (pp. 137–168). New York, NY: Cambridge University Press.

Whitcomb, S. A. (2017). *Behavioral, social, and emotional assessment of children and adolescents* (5th ed.). New York, NY: Routledge.

Whitehurst, G. J. (2003). *Identifying and implementing educational practices supported by rigorous evidence: A user friendly guide.* Washington, DC: U.S. Department of Education, Institute of Education Sciences, National Center for Education Evaluation. Retrieved from http://www2.ed.gov/rschstat/research/pubs/rigorousevid/rigorousevid.pdf

Wiener, J. (1985). Teachers' comprehension of psychological reports. *Psychology in the Schools, 22*, 60–64.

Wiener, J. (1987). Factors affecting educators' comprehension of psychological reports. *Psychology in the Schools, 24*, 116–126.

Wiener, J., & Costaris, L. (2012). Teaching psychological report writing: Content and process. *Canadian Journal of School Psychology, 27*, 119–135.

Wiener, J., & Kohler, S. (1986). Parents' comprehension of psychological reports. *Psychology in the Schools, 23*, 265–270.

Wigdor, A. K., & Garner, W. R. (Eds.). (1982). *Ability testing: Uses, consequences, and controversies.* Committee on Ability Testing, Assembly of Behavioral and Social Sciences. Washington, DC: National Academy Press.

Wilson, M. S., & Reschly, D. J. (1996). Assessment in school psychology training and practice. *School Psychology Review, 25*, 9–23.

Winner, E. (1996). *Gifted children: Myths and realities.* New York, NY: Basic Books.

Witwer, A. N., Lawton, K., & Aman, M. G. (2014). Intellectual disability. In E. J. Mash and R. A. Barkley (Eds.), *Intellectual disability* (3rd ed., pp. 593–624). New York, NY: Guilford.

Wodrich, D. L., Spencer, M. L. S., & Daley, K. B. (2006). Combining RTI and psychoeducational assessment: what we must assume to do otherwise. *Psychology in the Schools, 43*, 797–806.

Woodcock, R. W., Alvarado, C. G., Schrank, F. A., McGrew, K. S., Mather, N., & Muñoz-Sandoval, A. F. (2019). *Batería IV Woodcock-Muñoz*. Itasca, IL: Riverside Insights.

Woodcock, R. W., McGrew, K. S., & Mather, N. (2001). *Woodcock-Johnson III*. Itasca, IL: Riverside Publishing.

Woodcock, R. W., Muñoz-Sandoval, A. G., McGrew, K. S., & Mather, N. (2007). *Batería-III Woodcock-Muñoz normative update*. Itasca, IL: Riverside Publishing.

Woods, I. L., Floyd, R. G., Singh, L. J., Hawkins, H. K., Norfolk, P. A., & Farmer, R. L. (2019). What's in a name? A historical review of intelligence test score labels. *Journal of Psychoeducational Assessment, 37*, 692–705.

World Health Organization. (2010). *mhGAP intervention guide for mental, neurological and substance use disorders in non-specialized health settings: Mental health Gap Action Programme (mhGAP)*. Geneva, Switzerland: Author.

Worrell, F. C. (2009). What does gifted mean?: Personal and social identity perspectives on giftedness in adolescence. In F. D. Horowitz, R. F. Subotnik, & D. J. Matthews (Eds.), *The development of giftedness and talent across the lifespan* (pp. 131–152). Washington, DC: American Psychological Association.

Worrell, F. C., & Erwin, J. O. (2011). Best practices in identifying students for gifted and talented education programs. *Journal of Applied School Psychology, 27*, 319–340.

Worrell, F. C., Subotnik, R. F., & Olszewski-Kubilius, P. (2018). Talent development: A path toward eminence. In S. I. Pfeiffer, E. Shaunessy-Dedrick, & M. Foley-Nicpon (Eds.), *APA handbook of giftedness and talent* (pp. 247–258). Washington, DC: American Psychological Association.

Worrell, F. C., Subotnik, R. F., Olszewski-Kubilius, P., & Dixson, D. D. (2019). Gifted students. *Annual Review of Psychology, 70*, 551–576.

Yin Foo, R., Guppy, M., & Johnston, L. M. (2013). Intelligence assessments for children with cerebral palsy: A systematic review. *Developmental Medicine & Child Neurology, 55*, 911–918.

Youngstrom, E. A., Choukas-Bradley, S., Calhoun, C. D., & Jensen-Doss, A. (2015). Clinical guide to the evidence-based assessment approach to diagnosis and treatment. *Cognitive and Behavioral Practice, 22*, 20–35.

Zaboski II, B. A., Kranzler, J. H., & Gage, N. A. (2018). Meta-analysis of the relationship between academic achievement and broad abilities of the Cattell-Horn-Carroll theory. *Journal of School Psychology, 71*, 42–56.

Zachary, R. A., & Gorsuch, R. L. (1985). Continuous norming: Implications for the WAIS-R. *Journal of Clinical Psychology, 41*, 86–94.

Zhu, J., & Chen, H.-Y. (2011). Utility of inferential norming with smaller sample sizes. *Journal of Psychoeducational Assessment, 29*, 570–580.

Zigler, E., & Farber, E. A. (1985). Commonalities between the intellectual extremes: Giftedness and mental retardation. In F. D. Horowitz & M. O'Brien (Eds.), *The gifted and talented: Developmental perspectives* (pp. 387–408). Washington, DC: American Psychological Association.

Index

Abbreviated Battery, 182–84
Abbreviated IQ, 168, 172
ability differentiation, 274
ability factor scores, 209
ability scores, 58
abstractness, 7
academic achievement domains, *219*
academic performance, 1–2
access: to intelligence tests, 298; skills, 90–95; subtest problems of, *149*
acculturation, level of, 334
Achenbach System for Empirically Based Assessment Test Observation Form (TOF), 116–17
achievement discrepancies, 309–17
achievement scores, 311
Ackerman, P. L., 13
Adams, S. R., 306, 315
Adams Costa, E. B., 150
Adaptive Behavior Composite from the Vineland-III, 277
adaptive behaviors, 268, 276–77
adaptive functioning, 1–2
administration flexibility, of WISC-V, 149–50
adolescence: gifted, 299; picture vocabulary item for, 108; successive-level approach for, 197–98; WISC-V test used in, 154
adoption studies, 24
adulthood, 21, 25–26
AEP. *See* averaged evoked potentials
AERA. *See* American Educational Research Association

age equivalents, 49–50
age-related start point, 105
Alfonso, V. C., 107, 341
alternative scores, 96
Aman, M. G., 267
American Association on Intellectual and Developmental Disabilities, 267–69, 277
American Educational Research Association (AERA), 33
American Psychological Association (APA), 58, 223, 269–70, 319; competence from, 37–38; *Diagnostic and Statistical Manual of Mental Disorders* from, 87–88; ethical principles of, 33–38, *34–36*; *Ethical Principles of Psychologists and Code of Conduct* from, 249; high-quality assessments by, 34–35; *Publication Manual of the American Psychological Association, Seventh Edition* from, 243; results interpretation from, 37
American Sign Language, 96, 151
American Speech-Language-Hearing Association (ASHA), 91, 96, 278
ancillary indexes, 143
Ankney, C. D., 27
APA. *See* American Psychological Association
aptitude-by-treatment interactions (ATIs), 217, 223–29
aptitude tests, 304
Arithmetic, 136–37, 138, 143
arithmetic computation, 304
articulation screening, *127–28*

ASHA. *See* American Speech-Language-Hearing Association
Assessment for Effective Intervention, 85
assessment process, *235*; access skills in, 90–95; background information in, 89; caregivers in, 88; components in, 88; computer-assistance in, 98; direct screening in, 92–95; eligibility for giftedness in, *301*; follow-up in, 119; giftedness from fair, 295–96; high-quality, 34–35; intelligence tests in, 89; Kamphaus on purpose of, 102–3; psychoeducational, 90; of psychological assessment reports, 237; purpose, 102–3; rating forms in, 91–92; reasons for, 87–88; screening tools in, 91–95
assessment results: case supervisor presentation of, 257–58; of cognitive abilities, *235*; to parents and caregivers, *263*; in psychological assessment report, 238, 251–54; WISC-V and, 254
Assouline, S. G., 296–97
Athanasiou, M. S., 342
ATIs. *See* aptitude-by-treatment interactions
audience, of psychological assessment report, 242–43
audio files, 98
audio presentations, 103–4
auditory acuity, 93
Auditory Working Memory, 146
Auguste, M., 270
averaged evoked potentials (AEP), 4
averaging, 292

BA. *See* Brodmann area
background information: in assessment process, 89; caregivers and, 237; children and, 245, 332–36; cultural, 333–35; of psychological assessment reports, 237, 244–48
Bandura, A., 227
Barkley, R. A., 89
basal sets, *106*
BASC-3. *See* Behavior Assessment System for Children-Third Edition
Batería-III Woodcock-Muñoz Normative Update, 337–38
Batería IV Woodcock-Muñoz, 180
Bear, G. G., 255

Behavior Assessment System for Children-Third Edition (BASC-3), 89
behaviors: adaptive, 268; adaptive assessment of, 276–77; challenging, 113; of children, 112–15; excesses and deficits in, 112–15; genetics, 22–24; observation recording of, 117; in psychological assessment reports, 237–38, 249, *250–51*; reactive strategies, 114–15; reinforcement of, 114; testing observance of, 115–17, 249, *250–51*; of test takers, 108–9, 111–12
behavior-specific praise (BSP), 114–15
Benson, N. F., 238, 306, 337, 344; intelligence test survey by, 40; WISC-V survey by, 131
Beretvas, S. N., 274
Berlin, K. S., 156
best practices: in adaptive behavior assessment, 276; children's background diversity and, 332–36; SLD diagnosis, 318–21
bifactor model, of intelligence, 14–15
bilingual assessment, 340
Binet, Alfred, 1, 19
Binet-Simon intelligence test, 284
biological basis, of SLD, 308
biological intelligence, 3–4, *4*
blind test takers, 152
Block Design, 8, 133–34, 138
borderline label, 252
Boston Process Approach, 195
Bouchard, T. J., Jr., 24
Bowen, C., 94
Bracken, B. A., 60, 90, 155, 273
Braden, J. P., 97, 340, 342
brain: biochemical functioning of, 4–5; intelligence and role of, 27–28; networks, 28; neural plasticity of, 30; regions of, *28*
Brief Intellectual Ability, 179
brief intelligence test, 155–56
Briesch, A. M., 89
Brodmann area (BA), *28*
Brooks, B. L., 111–12
Brown, R. T., 307
BSP. *See* behavior-specific praise
Buros Center for Testing, 85

CA. *See* chronological age
Callahan, J. L., 111

Campbell, D. T., 311
Campbell, J. M., 255
Canadian Journal of School Psychology, 85
Cancellation, 136, 140, 143
Canivez, G. L., 173, 205; CHC-based scores and, 206–7; dilution effect from, 213; omega hierarchical value from, 162; psychometric *g* findings of, 12, 148; WISC-V subtests findings of, 145n3
caregivers: assessment components and, 88; assessment results to, 238, 242, *263*; background information and, 237; face-to-face contact with, 233; ID symptoms and, 271; physical health problems and, 279; screening forms for, 91–92, *120*, 214; STA for, *120–21*
Carriere, J. A., 233, 239
Carroll, J. B.: fourth wave and, 212; Schmid-Leiman transformation used by, 80; three-stratum theory from, 10–11, *11*, 15, 26, 287
CAS. *See* Cognitive Assessment System
CAS-2. *See* Cognitive Assessment System, Second Edition
case supervisor, 257–58, *265*
Cattell, R. B., 10
Cattell-Horn-Carroll (CHC) theory, 133, 157, 317; Canive and scores from, 206–7; of cognitive abilities, 11–12; Horn-Cattell theory and, 10; IQ testing and, 11–12; levels of, 315–16; native-language assessment and, 337. *See also* Carroll, J. B.; Horn, J. L.
CBM. *See* curriculum-based measurement
CD players, 98
Ceci, S. J., 13, 22
ceiling violations, 65, 105–6
Celenk, O., 334
cell phones, 97, 102
central nerve conduction velocity (CNV), 4
CFA. *See* confirmatory factor analysis
change-sensitive scores, 58
Chapman, W. D., 112
Chase, W. G., 221
CHC. *See* Cattell-Horn-Carroll theory
Chen, H., 140, 146, 286
children: background information and, 245, 332–36; behavior challenges of, 112–15; education failure of, 1; as ELL, 335; English-speaking, 331; general intelligence of, 25–26; gifted, 299; intelligibility of, 94; IQ scores of, 20–21; over and under identification of, 311; performance validity measures for, 111–12; successive-level approach for, 197–98; TOMM scores of, 111–12; WISC-V test used by, 154; WPPSI-IV for, 177
chronological age (CA), 19
classification agreement, *83*
C-LIM. *See* Culture-Linguistic Interpretative Matrices
clinical interpretations, 213
clinical neuropsychologists, 195
CNV. *See* central nerve conduction velocity
Code of Ethics of the American Psychological Association (2002), 296
coefficients, 67–69
cognitive abilities, *11*, 286; in adulthood, 21; assessment results of, *235*; in bifactor model, 15; brain size and, 27; CHC theory of, 11–12; evidence-based practices for, 221–23; intelligence tests measuring, 10–12, 15, 88; neural plasticity and, 30; norm-based scores of, 51; psychometric paradigm and, 13–14, 20; tests measuring, 84–85; in three-stratum model, 26; working memory training for, 31
Cognitive Assessment System (CAS), 226n1
Cognitive Assessment System, Second Edition (CAS-2): psychometric evaluation of, *158*; stratum III composites from, 157; test construction of, 159
cognitive complexity, 73–75
cognitive growth, 20
cognitive interventions, 221–23
cognitive load, 227
cognitive-training programs, 30
Colom, R., 27
color-blindness, 92; screening, *125*; of test takers, 152
combinatorial probabilities, 275–76
communalities, in one-factor model, *78*
communications, in informing sessions, 256
comparability, 41
competence, 37–40
complementary indexes, 143

Composite Intelligence Index, 168, 170
composite scores, 168; composition, *147*; interpretive infrastructure of, 192; of nonverbal assessment, 344; pairwise comparisons of, *193*; profile analysis of, *194*; reliability of, 208; variance influencing, *207*
Comprehension subtests, 136–38
Comprehensive Test of Nonverbal Intelligence-Second Edition, 343
computer-assisted assessments, 98
conceptual skills, 268
concurrent validity, 81
confidence intervals: of intelligence tests, 54–58, 299; in psychological assessment reports, *253*, 253–54; in SEM, 56–57; test scores and, 275
confidentiality, 102
confirmatory factor analysis (CFA), 10, 78
construct-irrelevant variance, 72–73, 90, 113, 119
construct underrepresentation, 72–73
construct validity, 71–72, 88
contingency tables, *83*
continuous norming, 61
continuous variable, 61
conventional teaching, 224
convergent relations, 81
conversations, with test takers, 101
copyright law, 40
correlates, eduction of, 75
correlations, 25
Costaris, L., 239
creative-productive gifted, 287
criterion-related validity, 81
Cronbach, L. J., 68, 85, 223, 226
Cross-Battery Assessment Software System (X-BASS), 316
Crystallized Ability composite, 210
Crystallized Intelligence, 75, 79, 203, 218
cultural background, 333–35
cultural-familial influences, 271
Culture-Linguistic Interpretative Matrices (C-LIM), *328*, 336, 341–42
culture-loaded bias, 327–29, *328*
culture-saturation, 329
Cummins, J., 335
curriculum-based measurement (CBM), 312–13

Daly, B. P., 307
Daniel, M. H., 138, 274
DAS-II. *See* Differential Ability Scales-Second Edition
Davis, O. S. P., 26, 308
Day, L. A., 150–51
deaf test takers, 150–51
Deary, I. J., 26
debriefing, 117
decision-making models, 292
Decker, D. M., 33
Demetrovics, Z., 223
dependent variables, 219
DeThorne, L. S., 342
Detroit Test of Learning Abilities-Fifth Edition (DTLA-5), 160–62, *161*, 199
Detterman, D. K., 3, 274
developmental construct, of giftedness, 294–95
developmental models, of giftedness, 288–90
developmental sensitivity, of norms, 60–61
diagnosed disability, 296–97
diagnosis: of differential ID, 278; disability with giftedness, 296–97; ID and, *281*; of SLD, 316; SLD best practices for, 318–21
diagnostic accuracy studies, 81
Diagnostic and Statistical Manual of Mental Disorders (APA), 87–88
Diagnostic and Statistical Manual of Mental Disorders-Fifth Edition (DSM-5), 269
Differential Ability Scales-Second Edition (DAS-II), 58, 162–65
differential diagnosis, 278
differential model, 23–24
differential psychology, 17
digital administration, 137–38
Digit Span subtest, 7–8, 134–35, 138, 146, 221–22
dilution effect, 213
Direct Screening Response Form, *129–30*; articulation screening, *127–28*; color-blind screening, *125*; fine motor screening, *126*; hearing screening, *126–27*; intelligibility, *128*; vision screening, *125*
discontinue rules, 104–6
Discrepancy-Consistency method, 315
discrepancy model, 311

discriminant relations, 81
discriminative validity, 81
discussions, in informing sessions, 256–57
disordinal interaction, 225
disrupting indicators, 116
diversity: children's background and, 332–36; language and, *328*; U.S. language, 152–53
Dixon, S. G., 198
Dixson, D. D., 292
dizygotic (DZ), 23
domain-based reports, 239
domain-general interventions, 222
domain-specific abilities, 287
domain-specific models, 285–86
domains scores, 160
Dombrowski, S. C., 145
Down syndrome, 270–71
dressing comfortably, 97
DSM-5. *See* Diagnostic and Statistical Manual of Mental Disorders-Fifth Edition
DTLA-5. *See* Detroit Test of Learning Abilities-Fifth Edition
dual-criterion approach, 267
Dual Discrepancy-Consistency Method, 315–16
Ducat, J. J., 151
DZ. *See* dizygotic

Early Cognitive and Academic Development (ECAD), 180
Ecker, B., 233, 242
Educating Exceptional Children (Kirk), 303
education: children's failure of, 1; records of, 37; system of, 295
Education for All Children Act (1975), 217
eduction: of correlates, 7, 75; of relations, 7, 75
EEG. *See* electroencephalograph
EFA. *See* exploratory factor analysis
effect size estimate, 220
egalitarian definition, 326–27
electroencephalograph (EEG), 4
Elementary and Secondary Education Act (1994), 291
eligibility assessment, *301*
eligibility determination, 87
Elizalde-Utnick, G., 334

ELL. *See* English language learners
Elliott, S. N., 97
Emhoff, S. M., 112
eminence, *289*
encouragement, in testing process, 108–9
English language learners (ELL), 91, 152, 325, 335
English-speaking children, 331
enhancing indicators, 116
environment: gene interplay and, 23; h^2 and role of, 25–26; of intellectual giftedness, 289–90; in testing process, 99, 113–14
environmentality, 23, 25
equivalence, 41
Ericsson, K. A., 221
error bands, 55
errors, influence of, 67–71
Erwin, J. O., 290
estimated true scores, 57
ethical principles, of APA, 33–38, *34–36*
Ethical Principles of Psychologists and Code of Conduct (APA), 38, 41–42, 249
evidence, validity evaluated by, 72–84
evidence-based practice, 218–21
examiners, 214–15, 224
experimental psychology, 17
exploratory factor analysis (EFA), 78
external relations, 81–82
extraneous cognitive load, 227
extrapolated norms, 60
Eysenck, H. J., 8

factor-analysis methods, 80, 208
factor loadings, 80; in one-factor model, *78*; from Schmid-Leiman transformation, *80*
fairness, test bias and, 331–32
false alarms, 82
family members, IQ of, *25*
Farabough, M. C., 112
Farmer, R. L., 93, 110, 156
far-transfer effects, 31, 222–23
Fay-McClymont, T. B., 112
feedback, test takers getting, 109
fifth wave, 212–13
Figure Weights, 135
Filcheck, H. A., 113
fine motor screening, *126*
Fish, J., 252
Flanagan, D. P., 107, 315, 341, 343

Flesch–Kincaid Grade Level formula, 242–43
Fletcher, J. M., 316–18
Flipsen, P., Jr., 94
floor violations, 63–64, 273
Floyd, R. G., 89, 272, 273, 344; challenging behaviors and, 113; General Conceptual Ability and, 162; performance validity and, 110; STA Direct Screening Form and, 93; stratum III composites and, 156
Fluid-Crystallized Index, 165, 167, 201
Fluid Reasoning Index, 146, 148, 176, 207
Flynn, J. R., 59, 338
Flynn effect, 59, 272, 338
fMRI. *See* functional magnetic imagining
Foley-Nicpon, M., 294
follow-up assessment, 119
Ford, A. I., 112
foreign editions, of WISC-V, 153–54
forms, assessment rating, 91–92
Fragile X syndrome, 271
Francis, D. J., 312, 317
French Ministry of Education, 19
frequency distribution, 19
Frisby, C. L., 340
frontal lobes, 27
FSIQ. *See* Full Scale IQ
Fuchs, L., 312
full length multidimensional intelligence tests, 157–80
Full Scale Battery, 344
Full Scale Core Battery, 157
Full Scale Extended Battery, 157
Full Scale IQ (FSIQ), 132, 145, 150, 170, 176; nonverbal composite scores and, 344; subtest score substitute and, 150n4; of WAIS-IV, 172–74
functional magnetic imagining (fMRI), 4
Futo, J., 223

Gage, N. A., 12, 317
GAI. *See* General Ability Index
Galton, Francis, 18, 283–84
galvanic skin response (GSR), 4
Gardner, H., 285–86
gene-environment interplay, 23
General Ability Index (GAI), 96, 145, 173, 176
General Cognitive Ability, 160, 199

General Conceptual Ability, 162
general factor, 6, 15
General Intellectual Ability, 179–80
generalist genes, 26
generality, 10–11, 203
general mental abilities, 269
genetic correlations, 307
Genetic Studies of Genius (study), 284
genius, 283–84
genotype-environment correlation, 26
genotypes, *29*
Gf-Gc composite, 179
gifted and talented, 291
giftedness: adolescence and children with, 299; creative-productive, 287; decision-making models for, 292; developmental construct of, 294–95; developmental models of, 288–90; diagnosed disability with, 296–97; domain-specific models of, 285–86; eligibility assessment for, *301*; environment for intellectual, 289–90; fair assessment of, 295–96; federal and state definitions of, 290–92; identification issues of, 292–94, *293*; intellectual, 284–86, 289; label of, 294; schoolhouse, 286; systems models of, 286–88; three-ring model, 286, *287*, 288
Gilissen, C., 271
Glutting, J. J., 116
Gobet, F., 31, 222
Gottfredson, L. S., 1, 4–5, 13, 27, 75
grade equivalents, 50–51
grammar, *248*
Greco, L. A., 113
Grigorenko, E. L., 306
Grimes, J. P., 332
group-based tests, 104
group factors, 8–10
GSR. *See* galvanic skin response
Guare, R., 89
Guidelines for Translating and Adapting Tests (International Test Commission), 338–39
Guide to Assessment of Test Session Behavior (Glutting and Oakland), 116

h^2. *See* heritability
Haier, R. J., 27
Hammill, D. D., 160, 199–200

hard-of-hearing test takers, 150–51
Harrison, J. L., 151
Harvey, V. S., 242
Hass, M., 233, 239
Hawkins, H., 92–94
Haworth, C. M. A., 26, 308
heading, of psychological assessment reports, 237
hearing screening, *126–27*
Helping Handouts (Bear & Minke), 255
heritability (h^2), 23; environment role in, 25–26; genotype-environment correlation and, 26; of intelligence, 24–27
Herschell, A. D., 113
high-ability student, 292
higher-order factor analysis, 9
high-order models, *14*, 15
high-quality assessments, 34–35
Hogan, L. R., 111
Hogan, T. P., 220
Horn, J. L., 212
Horn-Cattell theory, 10
Hullmann, S., 111
Hulme, C., 31, 220, 222
Humphreys, L. G., 294
hypothesis-oriented report, 239

ID. *See* intellectual disability
IDEA. *See* Individuals with Disabilities Education Improvement Act
identification: of children, 311; giftedness and issues of, 292–94, *293*; SLD process of, 322–23
Identifying and Implementing Educational Practices Supported By Rigorous Evidence (Whitehurst), 220
idiographic interpretations, 191–92
IES. *See* Institute of Education Sciences
IES Practice Guide for Assisting Students Struggling with Reading (WWC), 228
imperfectly malleable, 31
incremental validity, 204–5
independent variables, 219
indifference of the indicator, 8
indirect interventions, 88
Individuals with Disabilities Education Improvement Act (IDEA), 1, 217, 303–6, *320*
inferential norming, 61

information: background, 89, 237, 244–48, 332–36; control of, 36–37; sources of, 245; test, 254
informing sessions, 233, 255–57
innovative practices, 116–17
Institute of Education Sciences (IES), 228
instructional strategies, 229, *229–31*
instructional treatments, *225*
intellectual capacity, 269
intellectual disability (ID), 19; adaptive functioning with, 1–2; assessment norms of, 272–73; associations for, 267–70; causes of, 271; cultural-familial influences in, 271; deficits and, 269; diagnosis and, *281*; differential diagnosis of, 278; eligibility assessment for, *281*; identifying, 82; intelligence testing and, 272–74; mental health problems and, 278–79; physical health problems and, 279; support needed for, 279
Intellectual Disability (Schalock), 267–69
intellectual functions, 269
intellectual giftedness, 284–86, 289
intellectual property, 40
intelligence: bifactor model of, 14–15; biological, 3–4, *4*; brain's role in, 27–28; conceptions of, 3–5; definition of, 2–3; development differences in, 19–22; distribution of, 18–19; existence of, 2; Galton's conceptualized, 283; group factors in, 8–10; h^2 of, 24–27; individual differences in, 22; intellectual giftedness in, 284–86, 289; levels of, 212; malleability of, 28–31; nonverbal assessment of, 342–44; psychometric, *4*; psychometric *g* theory on, 6–8; psychometric paradigm theory on, 5–6; quantitative behavioral genetics of, 22–24; reading correlation with, *309*; social, *4*; structures of, 10–11
Intelligence (report), 29
intelligence-as-process, personality, interests, and intelligence-as-knowledge (PPIK), 13
intelligence quotient (IQ), 1; achievement discrepancy methods and, 310–12; CHC testing of, 11–12; children's scores of, 20–21; educational system and, 295; among family members, 25; imperfectly malleable of, 31; psychometric *g* theory

and, 20, 228; ranges of, 66–67; reliability on, 273, 297–98; students with high, *231*; students with low, *230*; validity evidence of, 273–75, 298; WISC-V tests of, 11–12. *See also* Full Scale IQ
intelligence tests: abbreviated, 155–56; access to, 298; age equivalents in, 49–50; age-related start point in, 105; alternative scores from, 96; in assessment process, 89; ATIs and, 223–29; Binet-Simon, 284; brief, 155–56; CHC theory and, 11–12; cognitive abilities measured by, 10–12, 15, 88; confidence intervals of, 54–58, 299; construct-irrelevant components of, 73; digital administration of, 137–38; full length multidimensional, 157–80; grade equivalents in, 50–51; ID and, 272–74; intellectual disability and, 272–74; item sets in, 45–48; nonverbal, 295–96; nonverbal full length, 181–86; norm-based scores in, 51–54; norm group of, 196; norms of, 297; percentage correct of, 48; potential confounds of, 214; presentation of, 76; psychometric *g* and, 12; purpose of, 213–14; raw scores of, 48–49, *49*; reading comprehension in, 13; retesting, 68–69, 118, 202; reviews of, 85; scaled scores of, *49*; scores on, 295; selection of, 84–85, 297–98; standardization of, 59; stratum II composites from, 208; technology's influence on, 40–42; WISC-V used as, 11–12, 154
intelligence test scores: comparisons of, 210–11; interpretation in isolation of, 205–10; interpretation of, 202–5; interpretation waves of, 211–12; predictive and incremental validity of, 204–5; reliability of, 202–3; stratum II composites and, 206–9; stratum III composites and, 205–6
intelligibility, 94, *128*
interaction effects, 223
internal consistency, 67–68
internal structure, 77–81
International Phonetic Alphabet, 93
International Test Commission, 338–39
interpretation: APA results, 37; of assessment instruments, 251–52; clinical, 213; of composite scores, 192; idiographic and nomothetic, 191–92; of intelligence test scores, 202–5; intelligence test scores in isolation, 205–10; of item-level responses, 209–10; quantitative idiographic methods in, 192–95; results, 37; of subtests, 209; of test scores, 274–75, 298–300; test-specific approaches to, 199–202; waves of test, 211–12
interrater agreement indexes, 69–71, *70*
interrater reliability coefficients, 69–71, *70*
intervention limits, 195
intrinsic cognitive load, 227
iPads, 98
ipsative analysis, 192
IQ. *See* intelligence quotient
IQ-achievement discrepancy approach, 304
IQ Composite, 186
item gradients, 65–66
item-level responses, 209–10
item scaling techniques, 62–63
item scoring, *70*

Jacob, S., 33
Jacob Javits Gifted and Talented Students Education Act (1988), 291
Jaffe, L. E., 233
jangle fallacy, 72
Jensen, A. R., 13, 29, 73, 156, 331; nonverbal tests from, 77; vocabulary tests from, 75
jingle fallacy, 72
Journal of Educational Psychology, 2
Journal of Psychoeducational Assessment, 85
Jung, R. E., 27

KABC-II NU. *See* Kaufman Assessment Battery for Children, Second Edition Normative Update
Kamphaus, R. W., 252, 254; assessment's purpose, 102–3; informing sessions and, 256; interpretation and, 211–12; parents during testing from, 99–100; test scores and, 243; test taker rapport and, 117; timing and, 104
Kaplan, E., 196, 210
Karama, S., 27
Kassai, R., 223
Kaufman, A. S., 116, 201, 252

Kaufman, N. L., 116, 201, 233, 252
Kaufman, S. B., 290, 292
Kaufman Assessment Battery for Children, Second Edition Normative Update (KABC-II NU), 344; psychometric evaluation of, *166*; stratum II composites from, 167; stratum III composites from, 165, 200
Kaufman Brief Intelligence Test, Second Edition (KBIT-2), 186, *187*
Keith, T. Z., 11, 145–46, 145n3, 274
Keith-Spiegel, P., 33
Kelley, T. E., 72
Kettler, R. J., 220
Kim, S., 211
Kirk, Samuel, 303
Kirkwood, M. W., 111
Kirschenbaum, R. J., 340
KISS Model, 212–15, 254, 258, 275
Koocher, G. P., 33, 220
Kovas, Y., 308
Kranzler, J. H., 317–18, 341–42, 344; IQ scores and, 198; psychometric *g* analysis from, 12; SLD and, 313
Krasa, N., 65

language: American Sign Language, 96, 151; assessment of native, 336–39; culture and, 333–35; disorder, 278; diversity and, *328*; ELL and, 91, 152, 325, 335; learners of English, 91; nonverbal tests and, 77; U.S. diversity of, 152–53
language-reduced composites, 95
Lawton, K., 267
learner aptitudes, 91, 224, 304
learning disability: definition of, 303–4; multivariate studies of, 307–8; unexpected underachievement and, 304
Learning Potential Assessment Device (LPAD), 340
LEA symbols test, 94
Leiter International Performance Scale-Third Edition (Leiter-3), *181*, 181–82
LEP. *See* limited English proficiency
Letter-Number Sequencing, 136, 146
level of acculturation, 334
Lichtenberger, E. O., 233
Lichtenstein, R., 233, 242

limited English proficiency (LEP), 274
Locke, E. A., 332
Lohman, D. F., 226, 228
Long-Term Retrieval composite, 210
Lopez, R., 333, 335–36
LPAD. *See* Learning Potential Assessment Device
Luria, A. R., 195
Luria neuropsychological model, 165
Lustgarten, S. D., 42

MA. *See* mental age
MacAllister, W. S., 112
Maggio, L. A., 220
main effects, 223
major findings report, 239
Makel, M. C., 288
Maki, K. E., 306, 315
malingering, 111
malleability: imperfect, 31; of intelligence, 28–31; research on, 30–31
Marland Report, 291, 294
Mash, E. J., 89
mask cognitive problems, 199
material organization, 257, *265*
Mather, N., 233
Matrix Reasoning, 134–35
Matthews, K., 313
Mazur-Mosiewicz, A., 111–12
McCallum, R. S., 155, 343
McCarthy scales, 335–36
McClain, M., 291–92, 299
McDaniel, M. A., 27
McGill, R. J., 162
McGrew, K. S., 110, 179, 272
McGue, M., 24
McNeil, C. B., 113
McNicholas, P. J., 270
mean, regression toward, 275, 311
measurements: error of, 67, 330; issues in, 275–76; of psychometric *g* theory, 168–70; of stratum III composites, 156
medical examination, 279
Melby-Lervåg, M., 31, 220, 222, 307
Memory Validity Profile (MVP), 112
mental age (MA), 19, 50, 279
mental disorder, 87
mental energy, 8
mental health problems, 278–79

Mental Measurement Yearbooks (Buros Center for Testing), 85
Mental Processing Composite, 167, 201
mental quotient, 20
mental retardation, 268–70
Messick, S., 77
meta-analysis, 220–22
MFIQ. *See* Motor-Free Intelligence Quotient
MHM. *See* Modified Hybrid Model
MI. *See* multiple intelligences
Miciak, J., 316–18
Microsoft Word, 244
Mikulski, Barbara, 270
Milwaukee Project, 30
Minke, K. M., 255
mistakes, avoiding, 243–44
moderators, 221
Modified Hybrid Model (MHM), 318
monozygotic (MZ), 23
motivation, in testing process, 108–9
Motor-Free Intelligence Quotient (MFIQ), 151
motor impairments, test takers with, 151
MTSS. *See* multitiered systems of support
multiple cutoff, 292
multiple factor analysis, 8
multiple intelligences (MI), 285
multitiered systems of support (MTSS), 305
multivariate studies, of learning disability, 307–8
MVP. *See* Memory Validity Profile
MZ. *See* monozygotic

NAGC. *See* National Association for Gifted Children
Naglieri, J. A., 159
narrative classifications, of standardized scores, *252, 259–62*
NASP. *See* National Association of School Psychologists
National Association for Gifted Children (NAGC), 291
National Association of School Psychologists (NASP), 33, 58, 306, 336; assessment competence from, 39–40; Principles for Professional Ethics from, 41–42; principles of, 38–39
National Center for Education Statistics (NCES), 303, 325

National Council on Measurement in Education (NCME), 58
National Joint Committee on Learning Disabilities (NJCLD), 319
native-language assessment, 336–39
NCES. *See* National Center for Education Statistics
NCME. *See* National Council on Measurement in Education
near-transfer effects, 31, 222–23
Nelson, J. M., 173
neural plasticity, 30
neuropsychologists, 165, 195
Niileksela, C. R., 162
NJCLD. *See* National Joint Committee on Learning Disabilities
nomothetic interpretations, 191–92
nonverbal assessment, 155; composite scores of, 344; of intelligence, 342–44; intelligence tests, 181–86; multidimensional, 343
Nonverbal composite, 186
Nonverbal Index, 96, 151, 201
nonverbal intelligence tests, 295–96
Nonverbal IQ composites, 170
nonverbal tests, 77, 95
Norcross, J. C., 220
Norfolk, P. A., 61–62, 143, 165
normal distribution, 18, *18*
Normative Update, 165
norm-based scores, 274–75; of cognitive abilities, 51; in intelligence tests, 51–54; percentile ranks in, 54; standardized scores and, 52–54
norm group, 196
norm-referenced scores: item gradient adequacy in, 65–66; item scaling techniques of, 62–63; scale ceilings adequacy in, 64–65; scale floor adequacy in, 63–64, 273; stratum II composites, 214–15; from subtests, 212
norms: blocks, 61–62; continuous, 61; developmental sensitivity of, 60–61; evaluation of, 58–62; extrapolated, 60; ID assessment, 272–73; inferential, 61; of intelligence tests, 297; quality of test, 335–36; recency of, 59; representativeness of, 59–60; sample size of, 61–62; tables, 65; of WISC-V, 143

Oakland, T., 116
oblique rotation, 79, *79*
O'Bryon, E. C., 340
observation recording, 117
Olszewski-Kubilius, P., 292
omega hierarchical subscale, 81
omega hierarchical value, 162, 167
one-factor model, *78*, 80
one-on-one administration, 100–101
open-ended questions, 101
Open Science Framework, 94
optimal terms, *246–47*
ordinal interaction, 224
Ortiz, S. O., 333, 337, 341
Otero-Valles, L., 313
outcome averages, *225*
outcome-on-aptitude regressions, *225*

pairwise comparisons, *193*, 199
parents, 99–100, *120–21*, *263*
PAR iConnect, 40
parieto-frontal integration theory (P-FIT), 27, *28*
PASS. *See* Planning, Attention, Simultaneous, and Successive processes theory
PASS processes, 159, 165
pattern coefficients, *79*
pattern of strengths and weaknesses (PSW), 305–6, 322; Dual Discrepancy-Consistency Method in, 315–16; evidence for, 316–17; for SLD, 314–17
Pearson correlations, 78
Pearson product-moment correlation, 68–69
Pearson's Q-Interactive, 40
pencils, 98–99
percentage agreement, 69
percentage correct, 48, 256
percentile rank, 18, 54, *253*, 254, *259–62*
Perceptual Organization and Freedom from Distractibility, 132
Perceptual Reasoning Index, 174
performance validity, 110–12
person variable, 227
Peters, D., 270
Pfeiffer, S., 291–92, 294, 296, 299
P-FIT. *See* parieto-frontal integration theory
Pham, A. V., 333
phenotypic variance, 25, 28–29

phonological processing, 308
physical-energetic model, 31
physical health problems, 279
Picture Concepts, 136
Picture Span, 135–36, 210
picture vocabulary item, 108
Piovesana, A. M., 151
Planning, Attention, Simultaneous, and Successive (PASS) processes theory, 14
Planning and Attention composites, 157
Platt, S. A., *29*
pleiotropy, 26
Ploetz, D. M., 111
Plomin, R., 26, 307–8
PMAs. *See* primary mental abilities
Polloway, E. A., 270
Popper, Karl, 5
positive manifold, 6
PPIK. *See* intelligence-as-process, personality, interests, and intelligence-as-knowledge
practical skills, 268
Pratt, J. L., 89
Preacher, K. J., 226
predictive validity, 81, 204–5, 330
preparation, for informing sessions, 255
presentation: audio, 103–4; of intelligence tests, 76; in test accommodations, 96–97
primary indexes, 143
primary mental abilities (PMAs), 8–9
Principles for Professional Ethics, 41–42, 58
Prinstein, M. J., 89
probabilities, combinatorial, 275–76
problem solving, 88, 312–14
Processing Ability composite, 160
Processing Speed Index, 138, 148, 159, 174, 207
profile analysis, 192, 200; of composite scores, *194*; of subtests, 210–11
Project Head Start, 30
pseudoscientific theories, 5
PSW. *See* pattern of strengths and weaknesses
psychoeducational assessment process, 90
psychological assessment report: assessment process of, 237; assessment results in, 238, 251–54; audience for, 242–43; background information in, 237, 244–48; behavior observance in, 237–38, 249, *250–51*; confidence intervals in, *253*,

253–54; mistakes avoided in, 243–44; sample, *234–36*; standardized scores in, 252–54, *253*; structure of, 233–38, 254; style of, *240–41*; templates for, 238–39; writing rules for, 243; writing style of, 246–48
psychologists, 36–40, 198
psychometric evaluation: of CAS2, *158*; of DAS-II, *163–64*; of DTLA-5, *161*; of KABC-II NU, *166*; of KBIT-2, *187*; of Leiter-3, *181*; of RIAS-2, *169*; of SB5, *171*; of UNIT2, *183*; of WAIS-IV, *173*; of WASI-II, *188*; of WJ IV COG, *178*; of WNV, 185; of WPPSI-IV, *175–76*
psychometric *g* theory: Canivez findings on, 12, 148; growth curve of, *21*; instructional strategies of, 229, *229*; on intelligence, 6–8; intelligence tests and, 12; IQ scores and, 20, 228; person variable of, 227; RIAS-2 measurement of, 168–70; subtests measuring, 140; three-stratum theory and, 10–11; validity in, 80–81; WISC-V evaluation of, *144*; WISC-V variance of, *141–42*
psychometric paradigm, 5–6, 13–14, 20
psychometrics, *4*, 58
psychomotor ability, 291
psychosocial functioning, 34
Publication Manual of the American Psychological Association, Seventh Edition (APA), 243
public schools, 325–26
punctuation, *247–48*

Q-Interactive, 40, 105–6, 133–36
Q-Interactive Central, 98
qualitative data, 191
qualitative idiographic approaches, 195–96, 209–10
qualitative indicators, 116
qualitative nomothetic approaches, 196–97
quantitative behavioral genetics, 22–24
quantitative data, 191
quantitative idiographic methods, 192–95
quantitative interpretive methods, 197–98
quantitative nomothetic approach, 196
Quantitative Reasoning Index, 146
question-and-answer format report, 239
Quetelet, Adolphe, 18

Raiford, S. E., 138, 150
Rambo, P. L., 111
random errors, 67
randomized controlled trials, 220
rapport building, 100–101
Rasch modeling, 63
raw scores, 48–49, *49*, 58, *64*
RD. *See* reading disability
reaction range (RR), 28, *29*
reaction time (RT), 4
reactive strategies, 114–15
reading, 13, *309*
reading disability (RD), 307
Reasoning Ability composite, 160
recency, of norms, 59
Redick, T. S., 220
referral-based report, 239
referral reasons, of psychological assessment reports, 237
regressed true scores, 57
regression toward the mean, 275, 311
reinforcement, of behaviors, 114
Reis, S. M., 290
relations, eduction of, 75
relative strength, 192
relative weakness, 192
reliability: coefficient, 55; of composite scores, 208; definition of, 66–67; errors influencing, 67–71; of intelligence test scores, 202–3; internal consistency in, 68; interrater coefficients for, 69–71, *70*; on IQ, 273, 297–98; scorer consistency in, 69–71; split-half method of, 139; standard deviation in, 56; from stratum III composites, 202–3; of subtest scores, 138–40; test–retest, 67–69; validity and, 336; WISC-V coefficients for, *139*; WISC-V retest, 156
Renzulli, J. S., 286–88, *287*, 290
representativeness, of norms, 59–60
Reschly, D. J., 332
residual reliable variance, 80
response clarification, 106–7, 136
response processes, 76–77
response scoring, 107
response to intervention (RtI), 296, 305–6, 318, 321
results interpretation, 37
retesting, 67–69, 118, 156, 202

reversal rules, 104–6
Reynolds, C. R., 312–14, 327, 331
Reynolds, M. R.: ability differentiation focus of, 274; omega hierarchical value reported by, 162, 167; stratum III composites and, 156; WISC-V studies by, 11, 145–46, 145n3
Reynolds Intellectual Assessment Scales (RIAS-2), *236*; psychometric evaluation of, *169*; psychometric *g* measurement of, 168–70; stratum III composites, 168
Rhodes, R. L., 340
RIAS-2. *See* Reynolds Intellectual Assessment Scales
risks, subtests, 156–57
Rogers, M. R., 340
Romero, P. A., 334
Rosa's Law, 270
Roth, B., 12
Rowe, E. W., 211
RR. *See* reaction range
R-squared (ΔR2), 204
RT. *See* reaction time
RtI. *See* response to intervention
RTI problem-solving model, 312–14
Rushton, J. P., 27
Rushton, P. J., 24
Ryan-Arredondo, K., 334

Saklofske, D. H., 75
Sala, G., 31, 222
Salthouse, T. A., 21–22
sample size, of norms, 61–62
sampling bias, 219
sampling errors, 330
Sandoval, J., 334
Sanislow, C. A., *29*
Sattler, J. M., 100, 102–3, 117, 197
SB5. *See* Stanford-Binet Intelligence Scales, Fifth Edition
scaled scores, 54; ceilings of, 64–65; floors of, 63–64, 273; of intelligence tests, *49*; subtest, *64*
scatter analysis, 192
Schaefer, B. A., 342
Schalock, R. L., 267–69
Schmid-Leiman transformation, 80, *80*
Schneider, W. J., 110, 207, 233, 242
schoolhouse gifted, 286

school psychologists, 38–40, 198
score tables, in psychological assessment report, 238, 254
scoring guides, 108
screening purposes, 87
Screening Tool for Assessment (STA), 214, 249; Direct Screening Response Form for, *125–30*; direct screening test record for, *124*; forms for, 91–93; for parent and caregiver, *120–21*; teacher screening form in, *122–23*
screening tools, 91–95
seating patterns, 99
SEE. *See* standard error of estimated true score
SEM. *See* standard error of measurement
sensitivity, 82
severe discrepancy, 305
SGDs. *See* speech-generating devices
Shepard, L. A., 312
Sherman, E. M., 111–12
Shinn, M R., 313
Short-Term Memory, 157
Shriberg, L. D., 93
Simon, Théophile, 1, 19
Simonton, D. K., 290
simple structure, 9, *9*, 79
single cutoff, flexible criterion, 292
SLD. *See* specific learning disability
slow learners, 304
Smith, J. D., 270
Snow, R. E., 226, 228
Snowling, M. J., 307
social intelligence, *4*
social skills, 268
soft time limits, 104
Sotelo-Dynega, M., 198
Spanish versions, 338–39
Spearman, C. E., 75; indifference of indicator from, 8; mental energy from, 8; two-factor theory from, 6, *7*, 79
Spearman-Brown formula, 68, 139
Spearman's law of diminishing returns, 274
special abilities, 283
Special Nonverbal Composite, 164
specificity, 82
specific learning disability (SLD), 296, 303; academic performance with, 1–2; achievement discrepancies and, 309–17;

assessment and evaluation of, *320*; biological basis of, 308; characteristics of, 306–9; definition of, 305; determination of, *322*; diagnosis best practices for, 318–21; diagnosis criteria of, 316; Dual Discrepancy-Consistency Method for, 315–16; identification process of, 322–23; Kranzler and, 313; PSW for, 314–17; RTI problem-solving model for, 312–14
speech-generating devices (SGDs), 96
spell check, 244
split-half reliability method, 139
STA. *See* Screening Tool for Assessment
stability coefficient, 295
STA Direct Screening Form, 92–93
staffings, 233
Standard Battery with Memory, 182–84
Standard Battery without Memory, 182–84
standard deviation, 52, 55–56, *259–62*, *264*
standard error of estimated true score (*SEE*), 57
standard error of measurement (SEM), 55, 56–57
Standard II.4.1, of Principles for Professional Ethics, 41–42
standardization definition, 329–30
standardization sample, 51–52
standardized scores: narrative classifications of, *252*, *259–62*; norm-based scores and, 52–54; percentile ranks and, *259–62*; in psychological assessment report, 252–54, *253*; from test sessions, *264*; text for, *253*
Standards for Educational and Psychological Testing (AERA), 33, 58, 67, 71–73
Stanford-Binet Intelligence Scales, Fifth Edition (SB5), 58, 170–72, *171*
Stanley, J. C., 311
STA Parent and Caregiver Screening Form, 91
statistical definition, 330–31
statistical indicators, 330
Steege, M. W., 89
Stefanatos, G. A., 307
Sterba, S. K., 226
Stern, W., 20, 284
Sternberg, R. J., 3, 13, 290, 292
strategic breaks, 115
stratum II composites: from intelligence tests, 208; from intelligence test scores, 206–9; from KABC-II NU, 167; norm-referenced, 214–15; test takers and, 201; validity of, 146–48; in WISC-V, 145–46; of WPPSI-IV, 177
stratum III composites, 145; from CAS2, 157; from DAS-II, 162; intelligence test scores and, 205–6; from KABC-II NU, 165, 200; of KBIT-2, 186; of Leiter-3, 181–82; lower-order scores of, 213; measurements of, 156; reliability from, 202–3; from RIAS-2, 168; from SB5, 170–72; successive-level approach and, 205–6; of UNIT2, 182–84, 202; of WAIS-IV, 172–74; of WASI-II, 187–88; in WISC-V, 145, 210; of WJ IV COG, 179; of WNV, 185; of WPPSI-IV, 176–77
structural fidelity, 77–78
students: high-ability, 292; high IQ, *231*; low IQ, *230*; low-performing, 310–11
Subotnik, R. F., 292
subtests: Canivez's WISC-V findings of, 145n3; ceilings, 297; Comprehension, 136–38; Digit Span, 7–8, 134–35, 138, 146, 221–22; of DTLA-5, 160, 199; floors, 63–64, 273; interpretation of, 209; memory and retrieval in, 137; norm-referenced scores from, 212; profile analysis of, 210–11; psychometric *g* measured in, 140; risks associated with, 156–57; scores from, 203; simple structure in, 79; split-half reliability method in, 139; stratum II composites in, 145–46; stratum III composites in, 145; in WISC-V, 133–37; WISC-V access problems of, *149*; WISC-V substitutions of, 150
subtest scores, 63, 137; of DAS-II, 164–65; FSIQ and substitute of, 150n4; raw and scaled, *64*; reliability of, 138–40; validity evidence in, 140–43
successive-level approach, 197–98, 205–6, 209
Suzuki, L. A., 327, 331
Symbol Search, 136
systematic measurement errors, 330
systems models, of giftedness, 286–88

T2. *See* Treatment 2
T3. *See* Treatment 3

Takacs, Z. K., 223
Tannenbaum, A. J., 288–89
target skills, 90
teachers, *122–23*
technology, 40–42
Terman, Lewis, 284–85
test accommodations, 96–97
test-based report, 239
test bias: culture-loaded definition of, 327–29; egalitarian definition of, 326–27; fairness and, 331–32; research on, 331; standardization definition of, 329–30; statistical definition of, 330–31; statistical indicators in, 330
test content, 73–77
test information, in psychological assessment report, 254
testing of limits, 119
testing process: assessment purpose in, 102–3; audio presentations in, 103–4; cognitive abilities measured in, 84–85; environment in, 99, 113–14; introduction to, 103; materials in, 100; motivation and encouragement in, 108–9; parents in, 99–100; preparation for, 97–100; question response in, 110; rapport building in, 100–101; response clarification in, 106–7; response scoring in, 107; retesting in, 67–69, 118, 156, 202; reversal and discontinue rules in, 104–6; scoring guides for, 108; test taker interactions in, 103–10; timing in, 104
testing sessions, 249, *250–51*
test items, *328*
test norms, quality of, 335–36
Test of Memory Malingering (TOMM), 111–12
test–retest reliability, 67–69
tests, translation for, 339–40
test scores, 43; confidence intervals and, 275; consistency, 67, 69–71; on intelligence test, 295; interpretation of, 274–75, 298–300; labels, 252–54; selection of, 272
test security, 37
test sessions: behaviors observed in, 115–17, 249, *250–51*; common practices in, 116; debriefing after, 117; follow-up assessment of, 119; innovative practices in, 116–17; results validity of, 117–18; standardized scores from, *264*
test-specific interpretive approaches, 199–202
test takers: behavior excesses and deficits of, 112–15; behaviors of, 108–9, 111–12; combinatorial probabilities and, 276; conversations with, 101; Crystallized Intelligence scores of, 218; deaf or hard-of-hearing, 150–51; Digit Span subtest and, 134–35; ELL, 152–53; feedback given to, 109; goals for, 102; with motor impairments, 151; open-ended questions for, 101; query and response for, 107–8; question response to, 110; rapport with, 117; response clarification for, 106–7, 136; strategic breaks for, 115; stratum II composites and, 201; testing process interactions with, 103–10; visual impairment of, 152
test-teach-test paradigm, 340
Thompson, T., 97
Thorndike, E. L., 2
three-factor model, *79*
three-ring model, 286, *287*, 288
three-stratum theory, 10–11, *11*, 26, 157
Thurstone, L. L., 8–9
timing, in testing process, 104
Timmerman Lugg, E., 33
TOF. *See* Achenbach System for Empirically Based Assessment Test Observation Form
TOMM. *See* Test of Memory Malingering
translation, for tests, 339–40
Treatment 2 (T2), 224
Treatment 3 (T3), 224
true scores, 56–57
twice-exceptional, 296–97
"The Two Disciplines of Scientific Psychology" (Cronbach), 223
two-factor theory, 6, *7*, 79

uncommon sense, 203
unexpected underachievement, 304
UNIT2. *See* Universal Nonverbal Intelligence Test-Second Edition
United States (U.S.): English-speaking children in, 331; intellectual giftedness in, 284; language diversity in, 152–53

INDEX

Universal Nonverbal Intelligence Test-Second Edition (UNIT2), 182–84, 202, 343–44
U.S. *See* United States

Valencia, R. R., 333, 335–36
validity: concurrent, 81; construct, 71–72; criterion-related, 81; definition of, 71–72; discriminative, 81; incremental and predictive, 81, 204–5, 330; IQ evidence of, 273–75, 298; performance, 110–12; predictive, 81, 330; in psychometric *g*, 80–81; reliability and, 336; response processes in, 76; of stratum II composites, 146–48; subtest scores, 140–43; test results, 117–18
validity evidence: consequences in, 82–84; evaluating, 72–84; external relations in, 81–82; internal structure of, 77–81; of IQ, 273–75, 298; methods in, *74*; response processes in, 77; in subtest scores, 140–43; in test content, 73–77; understanding, 84
Van de Vijver, F. J. R., 334
variance, 22, *207*
Vasserman, M., 112
Veltman, J. A., 271
Verbal composite, 186
Verbal Comprehension Index, 146, 173–74, 176
Verbal IQ, 170
verbal reasoning, 21
verbal tests, 339–40
vision screening, *125*
Vissers, L. E. L. M., 271
visual acuity, 92
visual impairment, of test takers, 152
Visual Processing, 159, 218
Visual Puzzles, 135
Visual Spatial Index, 177
vocabulary, 22, 75, 206
Vocabulary, 8, 135, 143
vocalized self-derision, 195
Volpe, R. J., 89

WAIS-IV. *See* Wechsler Adult Intelligence Scales-Fourth Edition
WAIS-V. *See* Wechsler Adult Intelligence Scales-Fifth Edition

wait-to-fail model, 311
WASI-II. *See* Wechsler Abbreviated Scale of Intelligence-Second Edition
Wasserman, J., 155, 205, 208
Watkins, M. W., 12, 145, 148, 173
Watson, T. S., 89
Wechsler Abbreviated Scale of Intelligence-Second Edition (WASI-II), 187–88, *188*
Wechsler Adult Intelligence Scales-Fifth Edition (WAIS-V), 131–32, 195; adaption of, 148–53; administration flexibility of, 149–50; used in adolescence, 154; Canivez's findings of, 145n3; composite score composition of, *147*; composites of, 143–46; evolution of, 132–33; foreign editions of, 153–54; intelligence test use of, 11–12, 154; as IQ test, 11–12; norming of, 143; psychometric *g* evaluation of, *144*; psychometric *g* variance in, *141–42*; reliability coefficients for, *139*; retest reliability of, 156; Reynolds, M., studies of, 11, 145–46, 145n3; stratum II composites in, 145–46; stratum III composites in, 145; subtest access problems of, *149*; subtest scores reliability of, 138–40; subtest scores validity of, 140–43; subtests in, 133–37; subtest substitutions of, 150
Wechsler Adult Intelligence Scales-Fourth Edition (WAIS-IV), 21, 132–33, 172–74, 205
Wechsler Intelligence Scale for Children (Wechsler), 132
Wechsler Intelligence Scale for Children-Fifth Edition (WISC-V), 7, 96; assessment results and, 254; bifactor models and high-order for, *14*; Digit Span subtest of, 221–22; IQ tests from, 11–12; native-language assessment and, 338; stratum III composite in, 210
Wechsler Intelligence Scale for Children-Fifth Edition Integrated (WISC-V Integrated), 153–54, 195
Wechsler Intelligence Scale for Children-Third Edition (WISC-III), 132
Wechsler Nonverbal Scale of Ability (WNV), 184–86, *185*

Wechsler Preschool and Primary Scale of Intelligence-Fourth Edition (WPPSI-IV), 174; for children, 177; psychometric evaluation of, *175–76*; stratum II composites of, 177; stratum III composites of, 176–77
Wehmeyer, M. L., 267
What Is Intelligence? (Sternberg and Detterman), 3
What Works Clearinghouse (WWC), 228
Whitcomb, S. A., 89
Whitehurst, G. J., 220
Whiteman, C. S., 296–97
Wickerd, G., 89
Wiener, J., 239
Winsor, A. P., 211
WISC-III. *See* Wechsler Intelligence Scale for Children-Third Edition
WISC-V. *See* Wechsler Intelligence Scale for Children-Fifth Edition
WISC-V Integrated. *See* Wechsler Intelligence Scale for Children-Fifth Edition Integrated
Witwer, A. N., 267
WJ III. *See* Woodcock-Johnson Tests of Cognitive Ability-Third Edition
WJ IV COG. *See* Woodcock-Johnson IV Tests of Cognitive Abilities
WNV. *See* Wechsler Nonverbal Scale of Ability

Wodrich, D. L., 322
Woodcock, R. W., 337
Woodcock-Johnson IV Tests of Cognitive Abilities (WJ IV COG), 58, 177, *178*, 179–80
Woodcock-Johnson Tests of Cognitive Ability-Third Edition (WJ III), 341
Woods, I. L., 252
word meanings, 75
word selection, *248*
working memory, 30–31, 222, 227
Working Memory Index, 146, 174, 176–77
Worrell, F. C., 290, 292
WPPSI-IV. *See* Wechsler Preschool and Primary Scale of Intelligence-Fourth Edition
Wrape, E., 111
writing rules, 243
writing style, *246–48*
W scores, 58
WWC. *See* What Works Clearinghouse

X-BASS. *See* Cross-Battery Assessment Software System

Yaraghchi, M., 313
Youngstrom, E. A., 89, 206, 208

Zaboski, B. A., 12, 205, 317

About the Authors

Dr. John H. Kranzler is professor and director of the school psychology program in the School of Special Education, School Psychology, and Early Childhood Studies and affiliate professor of pediatrics at the University of Florida. Dr. Kranzler's major area of scholarly interest concerns the nature, development, and assessment of human cognitive abilities. He has received a number of awards for his teaching and research, including the University of Florida Teaching Incentive Program award for undergraduate teaching, the Mensa Education and Research Foundation Award for Excellence in Research, and Article of the Year awards from *School Psychology Review* and *School Psychology Quarterly*. In 1997 and 2017, Dr. Kranzler received the University of Florida Research Foundation Professorship award for distinguished scholarship and was recently named a University of Florida Term Professor in 2019. Dr. Kranzler has served as associate editor of *School Psychology Quarterly* and the *International Journal of School and Educational Psychology* and currently serves on the editorial board of the *Journal of School Psychology*. He is a Fellow of the American Psychological Association and an elected member of the Society for the study of School Psychology.

Randy G. Floyd, Ph.D., is a professor of psychology and chair in the Department of Psychology at the University of Memphis. His research focuses on understanding the measurement properties of psychological assessment techniques, including intelligence tests. Dr. Floyd has authored or coauthored more than 100 professional publications. He is the former editor of the *Journal of School Psychology*, and he serves on the editorial boards of the *Journal of Psychoeducational Assessment, Journal of School Psychology, School Psychology International*, and *School Psychology Review*. He is a Fellow of the American Psychological Association Division 16 (school psychology) and an elected member of the Society for the Study of School Psychology.